LOCAL MEANINGS OF PROPORTIONALITY

This book offers one of the rare empirical studies on the different meanings of proportionality as part of a global constitutional discourse. It develops and applies a theoretically informed comparative methodology for the study of differences in the use of legal transfers. Beyond the transplant versus culture controversy, it enriches our understanding of the relationship between law and its social context. Beyond the common law and civil law cleavage, it provides an in-depth comparison of French, English and Greek judicial review, rendering some core features of these systems accessible to non-initiated readers. The last part of the book provides insights as to the different visions of Europe underlying different phases of European integration and thus enriches our understanding of the process of integration through law.

Afroditi Marketou is a postdoctoral researcher in Law at the University of Luxembourg. She studied Law at the University of Athens, the University Paris 1 Panthéon-Sorbonne (Master's), and the European University Institute (PhD). She has taught Public Law in several French universities and regularly publishes in peer-reviewed academic journals in English and in French. Her research interests lie in public and European law and include the interplay between domestic and European legal systems, the reception of legal transfers, the local meanings of Europeanisation and globalisation, as well as the study of legal cultures from an anthropological perspective.

CAMBRIDGE STUDIES IN CONSTITUTIONAL LAW

The aim of this series is to produce leading monographs in constitutional law. All areas of constitutional law and public law fall within the ambit of the series, including human rights and civil liberties law, administrative law, as well as constitutional theory and the history of constitutional law. A wide variety of scholarly approaches is encouraged, with the governing criterion being simply that the work is of interest to an international audience. Thus, works concerned with only one jurisdiction will be included in the series as appropriate, while, at the same time, the series will include works that are explicitly comparative or theoretical – or both. The series editor likewise welcomes proposals that work at the intersection of constitutional and international law, or that seek to bridge the gaps between civil law systems, the USA, and the common law jurisdictions of the Commonwealth.

Books in the series

Local Meanings of Proportionality
Afroditi Marketou

Property Rights and Social Justice: Progressive Property in Action
Rachael Walsh

Carl Schmitt's Early Legal-Theoretical Writings: Statute and Judgment and the Value of the State and the Significance of the Individual
Lars Vinx and Samuel Garrett Zeitlin

Remedies for Human Rights Violations: A Two-Track Approach to Supranational and National Law
Kent Roach

A.W. Dicey and the Common Law Constitutional Tradition
Mark D. Walters

Europe's Second Constitution: Crisis, Courts and Community
Markus W. Gehring

A.V. Dicey and the Common Law Constitutional Tradition: A Legal Turn of Mind
Mark D. Walters

Administrative Competence: Reimagining Administrative Law
Elizabeth Fisher and Sidney A. Shapiro

Legal Sabotage: Ernst Fraenkel in Hitler's Germany
Douglas Morris

Proportionality in Action: Comparative and Empirical Perspectives on the Judicial Practice
Edited by Mordechai Kremnitzer, Tayla Steiner and Andrej Lang

Constitutional Dialogue: Democracy, Rights, Institutions
Edited by Geoffrey Sigalet, Grégoire Webber and Rosalind Dixon

The Veiled Sceptre: Reserve Powers of Heads of State in Westminster Systems
Anne Twomey

Vigilance and Restraint in the Common Law of Judicial Review
Dean Knight

The Alchemists: Questioning Our Faith in Courts as Democracy-Builders
Tom Gerald Daly

Australia's Constitution after Whitlam
Brendan Lim

Building the Constitution: The Practice of Constitutional Interpretation in Post-Apartheid South Africa
James Fowkes

Dimensions of Dignity: The Theory and Practice of Modern Constitutional Law
Jacob Weinrib

Reason of State: Law, Prerogative, Empire
Thomas Poole

Bills of Rights in the Common Law
Robert Leckey

The Guardian of the Constitution: Hans Kelsen and Carl Schmitt on the Limits of Constitutional Law
Translated by Lars Vinx, with an introduction and notes by Lars Vinx

Parliamentary Bills of Rights: The Experiences of New Zealand and the United Kingdom
Janet L. Hiebert and James B. Kelly

Lawyering for the Rule of Law: Government Lawyers and the Rise of Judicial Power in Israel
Yoav Dotan

Balancing Constitutional Rights: The Origins and Meanings of Postwar Legal Discourse
Jacco Bomhoff

Judges on Trial: The Independence and Accountability of the English Judiciary
Shimon Shetreet and Sophie Turenne

Proportionality and Constitutional Culture
Moshe Cohen-Eliya and Iddo Porat

The Politics of Principle: The First South African Constitutional Court, 1995–2005
Theunis Roux

The New Commonwealth Model of Constitutionalism: Theory and Practice
Stephen Gardbaum

Searching for the State in British Legal Thought: Competing Conceptions of the Public Sphere
Janet McLean

Judging Social Rights
Jeff King

Proportionality: Constitutional Rights and Their Limitations
Aharon Barak

Parliamentary Sovereignty: Contemporary Debates
Jeffrey Goldsworthy

LOCAL MEANINGS OF PROPORTIONALITY

AFRODITI MARKETOU
University of Luxembourg

CAMBRIDGE
UNIVERSITY PRESS

CAMBRIDGE
UNIVERSITY PRESS

University Printing House, Cambridge CB2 8BS, United Kingdom

One Liberty Plaza, 20th Floor, New York, NY 10006, USA

477 Williamstown Road, Port Melbourne, VIC 3207, Australia

314–321, 3rd Floor, Plot 3, Splendor Forum, Jasola District Centre, New Delhi – 110025, India

79 Anson Road, #06–04/06, Singapore 079906

Cambridge University Press is part of the University of Cambridge.

It furthers the University's mission by disseminating knowledge in the pursuit of education, learning, and research at the highest international levels of excellence.

www.cambridge.org
Information on this title: www.cambridge.org/9781108834483
DOI: 10.1017/9781108993364

First published 2021

A catalogue record for this publication is available from the British Library.

Library of Congress Cataloging-in-Publication Data
Names: Marketou, Afroditi, 1986– author.
Title: Local meanings of proportionality / Afroditi Marketou, University of Luxembourg.
Description: Cambridge, United Kingdom ; New York, NY : Cambridge University Press, 2021. | Series: Cambridge studies in constitutional law | Based on author's thesis (doctoral - European University Institute, 2018) issued under title: Local meanings of proportionality : judicial review in France, England and Greece. | Includes bibliographical references and index.
Identifiers: LCCN 2020058393 (print) | LCCN 2020058394 (ebook) | ISBN 9781108834483 (hardback) | ISBN 9781108995108 (paperback) | ISBN 9781108993364 (ebook)
Subjects: LCSH: Proportionality in law – Europe. | Proportionality in law – Great Britain. | Proportionality in law – France. | Proportionality in law – Greece.
Classification: LCC KJC390 .M37 2021 (print) | LCC KJC390 (ebook) | DDC 340/.11–dc23
LC record available at https://lccn.loc.gov/2020058393
LC ebook record available at https://lccn.loc.gov/2020058394

ISBN 978-1-108-83448-3 Hardback

CONTENTS

Acknowledgements *page* viii

1 Proportionality as a Cultural Practice 1

PART I **Questioning the Success of Proportionality** 37

2 Proportionality in French Public Law 45

3 Proportionality in English Public Law 75

4 Proportionality in Greek Public Law 105

PART II **Great Expectations** 135

5 Searching for a Legal Science 143

6 Searching for an English Public Law 187

7 Searching for a 'Species of Sympathetic Magic' 223

PART III **European Integrations** 263

8 A Common European Culture of Rights 271

9 A Common Market 299

10 Disintegration 329

Conclusion 360

Bibliography 370

Index 407

ACKNOWLEDGEMENTS

This work would have never been accomplished without the support, advice and valuable comments of Bruno De Witte, to whom I am particularly grateful. Mattias Kumm provided precious guidance during the early stages of this project. I thank Rián Derrig, Conor Gearty, Claire Kilpatrick, Toni Marzal, Kai Möller, Giorgio Monti, Thomas Poole, Vincent Réveillère, Giovanni Sartor, Antonin Sopena, Mathieu Touzeil-Divina, Stavros Tsakyrakis, Sebastiaan Van Ouwerkerk and Constantinos Yannakopoulos for valuable discussions and critical readings of parts of this work. I am particularly grateful to Loïc Azoulai, Jacco Bomhoff and Guillaume Tusseau for commenting on the doctoral manuscript on which this book is based. My family and friends have influenced this work much more than they know. Special thanks to Agni, Maria and Kostakis for making life in London so merry. Loutraki and its sporadic inhabitants also merit my sincerest gratitude. The colleagues and friends who contributed to this work bear no responsibility for errors and omissions in the pages that follow. This book would have not even been imagined without the support and comments of Vincent. He merits my deepest appreciation for being a source of inspiration and thought over all these years. This book is dedicated to him.

1

Proportionality as a Cultural Practice

Popular imagination has connected proportion to justice since antiquity. In legal thought, the notion of proportion was present in the philosophy of Aristotle and was developed by legendary figures such as Aquinas and Grotius. Beccaria used it to express a requirement of fairness in retribution. And yet the image of proportion has probably never been as pervasive in the minds of lawyers as in post-war constitutionalism. The principle of proportionality was first applied in German constitutional case law. During the second half of the twentieth century, courts in liberal constitutional democracies all over the world have progressively interpreted their own constitution as imposing a requirement of proportionality on rights limitations. Today, proportionality is much more than a metaphor that represents justice in the minds of constitutional lawyers. It is increasingly perceived as a model of legal reasoning, a theory and even an emerging global paradigm of constitutional adjudication. It is understood as an advanced tool of liberal constitutional science and its rise appears to be an irresistible natural development. Since the beginnings of the twenty-first century, proportionality has been at the core of a prescriptive human rights theory first developed in the work of Alexy and claiming universal application. In comparative law, proportionality is a commonly used example of a legal transplant that attests to the convergence between legal systems, if not globally, at least within Europe.

This research was inspired by the intuition that even though courts and lawyers around the world increasingly reason in proportionality terms, they do not necessarily apply the proportionality model, neither do they subscribe to the Alexyan theory. In fact, proportionality can have very different meanings in different contexts, even within the same legal system. The relevant literature, both in legal theory and comparative law, has paid little attention to differences in the use of proportionality. This is due to the widespread assumption that when legal actors around the world use proportionality terminology, they refer to the principle of proportionality as applied in Germany or to the model theorised by Alexy and his followers. Taking a different tack, I argue that identifying the different local meanings of proportionality is crucial to making sense of its spread, to assessing the success of the Alexyan model and to appraising the possibility of convergence between legal systems. Following theoretical and methodological developments in comparative law, intellectual history and cultural anthropology, I propose to see proportionality as an instance of legal discourse, as a *way of speaking* that legal actors around the world have found convenient for formulating legal arguments. This entails a shift in the focus of research, from proportionality as a principle or a model of reasoning to proportionality as *language*. Through an in-depth study and comparison of the use of proportionality by legal actors in France, England and Greece, my purpose is to show that the different local meanings of proportionality reflect the legal cultures in which they evolve, local paths of cultural change and local patterns of Europeanisation.

In the paragraphs that follow, I present the mainstream literature on proportionality (Sections 1.1–1.3), and connect it to the transplant v. culture debate in comparative law (Sections 1.4 and 1.5). Then, I introduce the questions that have guided this research and the approach adopted in this book (Sections 1.6 and 1.7).

1.1 The Success of Proportionality

Born in Prussian administrative scholarship at the end of eighteenth century, proportionality was established as a method of judicial review with the creation of administrative courts in the second half of the nineteenth century. It migrated to constitutional law after the Second World War, in parallel with the progressive 'constitutionalisation' of the legal order and the increasing 'juridicisation' of politics. By the end of the 1960s, proportionality was announced and applied as a constitutional principle in the jurisprudence of the German Federal Constitutional Court (GFCC). The German constitutional judges conceived of it as a framework, a pronged structure for balancing conflicting constitutional rights. In the following decades, courts in liberal constitutional democracies all over the world interpreted their constitution as guaranteeing the principle of proportionality. Proportionality, together with its surrounding fundamental rights discourse, spread all over Europe and far beyond.

Among the jurisdictions that have adopted it we find Canada, Turkey, South Africa, Israel and New Zealand. Apart from the area of domestic public law, it is also applied in international and international humanitarian law. During the 1970s, the European Court of Human Rights (ECtHR) and the European Court of Justice (ECJ) pronounced proportionality a necessary condition for the validity of rights limitations.[1]

Hence, we have entered the 'age of balancing' in constitutional law.[2] Proportionality is said to be 'a universal criterion of constitutionality',[3] 'a foundational element of global constitutionalism'[4] and 'a suitable candidate for construing a global grammar of constitutionality'.[5] According to Möller, it is '*the* central concept in contemporary constitutional rights law'.[6] Although US exceptionalism still resists local pressure for its adoption as a general principle, the idea shared by most constitutional lawyers is that contemporary democracies are converging on a common constitutional model, in which proportionality has a central role. Beatty has gone so far as to see in proportionality the ultimate rule on which judicial reasoning is based. He considers proportionality to be 'a constitutive, immutable part of every constitution'.[7] Proportionality has become somewhat of a constitutional '*grande idée*', a conceptual centre point for a global constitutional discourse.[8] The relevant studies and collective volumes abound.[9] Kumm suggests that proportionality's utility could transcend the limits of legal analysis to provide a model for political decision-making and practical reasoning.[10]

Alexy's *Theorie der Grundrechte* is a reference for studying and debating proportionality. Published in 1985, the book offered a comprehensive systematisation of proportionality doctrine and anchored it to a solid

[1] On the spread of proportionality, Stone Sweet and Mathews (2008), pp. 97–111 and Barak (2012), pp. 175–210.

[2] Aleinikoff (1987).

[3] Beatty (2004), p. 162.

[4] Stone Sweet and Mathews (2008), p. 160.

[5] Klatt and Meister (2012a), p. 3.

[6] Möller (2007), p. 13 (emphasis in original).

[7] Beatty (2004), p. 176.

[8] Geertz (2000), p. 3, citing Susanne Langer.

[9] Huscroft, Miller and Webber, eds. (2014); Ranchordás and de Waard, eds. (2015); Jackson and Tushnet, eds. (2017); Petersen (2017); Urbina (2017); Kremnitzer, Steiner, and Lang, eds. (2020).

[10] Kumm (2009a), p. 10. See also Kumm (2017), p. 30. The belief that proportionality is a useful framework for decision-makers more generally is recurrent among proportionality scholars; for another example, Jackson (2017). On the actual use of proportionality by constitutional-political actors, see Michelman (2017), p. 13.

theoretical background.[11] Alexy's theory met with considerable success and was translated into English in the early 2000s.[12] It has found many defenders all over the world, who have refined and developed it in many ways.[13] Inspired by Dworkin's interpretative theory, Alexy and his followers purport to offer a reconstruction of the practice of constitutional courts, that is, an account that 'fits' it while it coherently 'justifies' it. Under this account, whenever a sub-constitutional norm restricts a constitutional right, its validity depends on the test of proportionality, comprising a check as to the legitimacy of its goal, the suitability of the means chosen, the necessity of the restrictions and their *stricto sensu* proportionality. The last stage of proportionality consists in a balancing enterprise, where the constitutional values adversely affected by the measure are weighed against the constitutional values that it advances. The mainstream literature thus describes a 'proportionality structure' that is objective and neutral as to the particular substantive political moral theory that one adopts.[14]

Because of its claim to substantive neutrality, proportionality analysis seeks general application as a model that is compatible with different types of reasonable political moral theory.[15] Hence, while Alexy's initial purpose was to provide a theory for German basic rights, the aspiration of proportionality scholarship progressively became that of offering 'a prescriptive theory applicable to constitutional democracies generally'.[16] Proportionality's function is to liberate courts from the constraints of classical legalistic analysis and to allow judges to engage in public and structured reasoning based on rights. In this way, according to its promoters, proportionality emphasises the need for justification of legislative action and increases transparency in judicial decisions. It involves individuals in the policy-making process, while it does not compromise the protection of rights.[17] Beatty goes further to argue that proportionality, by focusing on facts, 'can claim an objectivity and integrity no other model of judicial review can match'.[18] Thus, it enables judges to mitigate

[11] Alexy (1985).
[12] Alexy (2002).
[13] For some examples, Beatty (2004); Rivers (2006); Pulido (2007); Möller (2012); Klatt and Meister (2012a); Contiades and Fotiadou (2012a).
[14] For a more detailed analysis of the proportionality structure, see Part I, Introduction.
[15] On the structural character of the proportionality analysis, see Alexy (2003b); Kumm (2006a).
[16] Kumm (2004), p. 575.
[17] Kumm (2006a), p. 131; Kumm (2007); Kumm (2009a); Kumm (2010), p. 141.
[18] Beatty (2004), p. 171.

conflicts between majorities and minorities on socially sensitive matters, while showing equal respect to both. In Beatty's view, proportionality 'serves as an optimizing principle that makes each constitution the best it can possibly be'.[19]

Comparative research plays an important role in proportionality theory, since it offers an empirical basis for its claims. The relevant comparative studies include the examination of cases from a variety of legal contexts, ranging from the USA and Canada, to Israel, India and Japan, passing from South Africa to Europe, the UK and international courts.[20] However, scholars do not adopt a particular comparative law approach, since their purpose is not to compare different decisions, rules or institutions in the jurisdictions they study. Rather, it is to attest to the spread of proportionality or to substantiate the analytical model they propose with concrete examples. The proportionality literature is isolated from debates on the theory and method of comparative law. To the eyes of a legal comparatist, the methodology of mainstream studies would seem poor. Scholars usually limit themselves to a frantic search for similarities, only selecting examples that confirm their hypotheses in a 'cherry-picking' way,[21] even distorting the meaning of local practice in their attempt to cram it into the pre-constructed categories of their theory. Appeal to proportionality by courts in different jurisdictions works as a confirmation of proportionality's success, no matter how different its application and its outcomes. In some cases, even in the absence of such an appeal and in cases of explicit rejection, local concepts and methods are presented as synonymous or equivalent to different prongs of proportionality analysis.[22]

It is generally accepted that proportionality is 'one of the most successful legal transplants in the second half of the twentieth century'.[23] Its success is usually explained by reference to its function in an emerging global paradigm of constitutional rights. The defenders of proportionality combine it with a vision of rights as values interpreted expansively to comprise trivial or even illegal activities, as well as the protection of social

[19] Ibid, p. 163.

[20] Beatty (2004); Barak (2012); Möller (2012); Schlink (2012), p. 718.

[21] Hirschl (2005), p. 153.

[22] Scholars often use examples taken from the US Supreme Court case law, while this court rejects proportionality as a generally applicable doctrine. See Beatty (2004); Barak (2012); Jackson (2015).

[23] Kumm (2004), p. 595. See also Möller (2017, p. 103), who talks about the 'global success' of proportionality.

rights. Under this approach, rights are not only negative requirements of abstention, as the liberal tradition has long professed. They also impose positive obligations on state authorities and 'radiate' in the regulation of private relations. In the view of proportionality scholars, 'there is no area of policy-making which remains unaffected by constitutional rights'.[24] In Alexy's theory, balancing and proportionality necessarily result from the structure of constitutional rights. The idea is that the ever-expanding nature of rights entails compromise as to the special priority that they traditionally enjoyed over public policy considerations; their application necessarily implies limitations to their scope. Following the Alexyan legacy then, and contrary to the liberal intuition, rights are not categorically defined rules, but principles. As such, they require optimal realisation according to the normative and factual possibilities of each case. Balancing under the proportionality framework is the method for accomplishing this task.[25]

Even scholars who contest the conceptual necessity of proportionality analysis in rights-based judicial review, argue for its desirability. According to Stone Sweet and Mathews, for example, proportionality is 'the best available procedure' for balancing constitutional rights.[26] These authors mobilise strategic elements to account for the spread of proportionality in modern constitutional democracies and claim that its function is to mitigate legitimacy problems in politically salient cases that often arise in rights-based judicial review.[27] Möller offers a substantive moral theory of rights based on the concept of autonomy that justifies and promotes the global spread of proportionality.[28] Perju, focusing on the justification of judicial decisions, contends that proportionality's normative appeal lies in its 'integrative ethos', that is, the fact that it aims to integrate sensitivity to fact and context within a formal structure that enhances the predictability of judicial solutions.[29] In a study with a more practical focus, Barak claims that, 'while proportionality is not the

[24] Möller (2012), p. 110.

[25] Alexy (2002), pp. 66 f.; Alexy (2003a). See also Klatt and Meister (2012a), chap. 8. On proportionality scholars' vision of rights, see Part II, Introduction.

The necessary connection between principles and proportionality balancing has been criticised by Möller (2007), p. 458. Barak (2012, pp. 240–1) also rejects the necessity of the connection between balancing and principles.

[26] Stone Sweet and Mathews (2008), p. 76; Mathews and Sweet (2011).

[27] Stone Sweet and Mathews (2008).

[28] Möller (2012).

[29] Perju (2012), p. 350.

only way to realize constitutional rights, it is by far the best way available'.[30]

1.2 A Lingua Franca?

Efforts to identify a common core of rules in European contract law have met with vigorous criticism from comparative lawyers. The harmonisers' instrumental vision of law was impugned for inaccurately describing legal practice, for lacking attention to difference and for neglecting law's connection to local sentiments and traditions.[31] However, such criticism has not yet touched on proportionality. Scepticism in this field is usually formulated in abstract philosophical or political moral terms. Typically, proportionality is criticised for being incompatible with liberal philosophical conceptions of rights and for favouring judicial prerogatives to the detriment of democratic decision-making.[32] In a recent paper, Tushnet contested the merits of proportionality as compared to categorical methods of reasoning from an American Legal Realist perspective. According to the author, proportionality 'lacks the resources for preventing skilled advocates from turning seemingly easy cases into hard ones'.[33]

Criticism has pushed proportionality scholars to refine the model that they propose, so as to allow judges to take into account the special nature of certain rights or to accord broader discretion to public authorities in certain contexts. Thus, Kumm and Walen stress the influence of deontological constraints, especially connected to human dignity, in the application of proportionality.[34] Scholars sometimes argue that the proportionality model is not appropriate for the adjudication of positive rights[35] or that primary decision-makers should enjoy a greater degree of discretion in this field.[36] In their book on the structure of proportionality, Klatt and Meister analyse different kinds and degrees of discretion according to the uncertainty of the moral and factual issues that proportionality raises and to the reliability of the primary decision-maker's

[30] Barak (2012), p. 226.

[31] See, most notably, Legrand (1996).

[32] Tsakyrakis (2008); Webber (2017); Urbina (2017). On the critique of proportionality, see Part II, Introduction.

[33] Tushnet (2017), p. 309.

[34] Kumm and Walen (2014), p. 67.

[35] Klatt and Meister (2012a), pp. 89 f.; Möller (2012), pp. 165 f.; Gardbaum (2017), albeit for different reasons.

[36] Kumm (2004), p. 586; Klatt and Meister (2012a), chap. 5.

assessments on these issues.[37] Rivers and Brady propose institutionally sensitive approaches to proportionality, including theories of deference and restraint, to sufficiently reflect considerations of relative institutional competence and legitimacy.[38] The above studies account for contextual factors that influence the application of proportionality and propose ways to systematise and channel this influence. Thus, it is a commonly shared idea that the subject matter, the legal tradition and the institutional context surrounding each case will affect the choice of the proportionality prongs that the judge will apply or the intensity of judicial review in concrete cases.

Due to its flexibility, proportionality acquires the characteristics of a lingua franca and its spread revives the 'liberal aspiration for a global order of law'.[39] It appears broad enough to accommodate local divergence and abstract enough to transcend institutional conflicts, both within state borders and across them.[40] The courts that speak it are given access to a 'global community of judges', engaging in transnational communication and dialogue on universally shared values.[41] Its rejection, on the contrary, is attributed to a kind of misunderstanding of a court's own practice or role in a liberal constitutional democracy. The spread of proportionality and of fundamental rights announces 'an a-historical society based on universal standards'.[42] Möller, for instance, proposes a 'global model' of constitutional rights, based on the reconstruction of judicial practice around the world.[43] Kumm defends the universal character of human rights as the Alexyan legacy describes them.[44] And Schlink affirms that '[t]here is nothing inherently German about the roots of the principle of proportionality, nor is the introduction of the principle into other constitutional contexts a transfer of a German principle. It is a response to a universal legal problem'.[45] Moreover, this author considers proportionality to be 'part of a deep structure of

[37] Klatt and Meister (2012a), chap. 6.

[38] Rivers (2006); Brady (2012). For an institutionally sensitive account of proportionality in international law, see Pirker (2013).

[39] Kahn (2004), p. 2679.

[40] Cohen-Eliya and Porat (2013), pp. 103 f. Lasser (2009, p. 3) makes the same remark on human rights.

[41] Cohen-Eliya and Porat (2013), pp. 134 f., citing Anne-Marie Slaughter.

[42] Muir-Watt (2006), p. 729.

[43] Möller (2012).

[44] Kumm (2017).

[45] Schlink (2012), p. 729.

constitutional grammar that forms the basis of all different constitutional languages and cultures'.[46]

Legal actors in different contexts increasingly argue in proportionality terms and pressure for the adoption of the proportionality framework by courts and law-makers.[47] While, initially, Alexy's structure was purported to reconstruct judicial practice, today it is increasingly perceived as the correct method of legal decision-making and it increasingly constrains legal reasoning. The metaphor of law-as-proportionality is slowly 'literalised'; proportionality *becomes law* and constitutes legal knowledge.[48] Much of the relevant debates focus on whether it should be embraced in the USA.[49] Scholars often proceed to the schematisation of models of constitutional rights and judicial review practices. Typically, the German model, also presented as European or even global, is confronted with the exceptional American one and usually found to be more appealing[50] or better in terms of coherence, transparency or morality.[51] US hesitations to embrace proportionality and the global paradigm of human rights are seen as peculiar resistances to what appears to be an irresistible evolution. Explanations for this phenomenon range from the traditional insularity and archaism of US constitutional law, to its historical origins and the political context that has framed its evolution.[52]

Nonetheless, at least until quite recently, most jurisdictions did not frame questions raised through judicial review as fundamental rights conflicts, neither did they present judicial solutions as instances of proportionality balancing. This is the case in Europe too, where the global model of rights and proportionality is said to find its origins. In fact, Kennedy has shown the important influence that US private law doctrines of balancing have had on the development of proportionality rhetoric.[53] What proportionality theorists often neglect is the particularity and contingency of proportionality as they describe it. This book is not about the moral desirability of proportionality or about its merits as a method of judicial review. Simply, it is 'a plea for a hint of empiricism'

46 Ibid, p. 736.

47 On the USA, for instance, Sullivan and Frase (2009); Breyer (2010), pp. 163–71; Jackson (2015).

48 On the literalisation of metaphors used for making sense of legal knowledge and legal reasoning, see Riles (2005), pp. 1008 f.

49 See 'Proportionality and the United States', in Jackson and Tushnet, eds. (2017).

50 Cohen-Eliya and Porat (2013), conclusion.

51 Mathews and Sweet (2011); Möller (2012), pp. 15 f.; Jackson (2017).

52 On this, see Ignatieff (2005); Cohen-Eliya and Porat (2017), p. 75.

53 Kennedy (2011).

in the relevant debates.[54] Claims as to proportionality's global success or failure should take into account its actual use by courts and other legal actors in different contexts. Proportionality theorists also agree on the necessity for research on judicial practice.[55] Schauer describes it as 'an empirical agenda that must wait for another day – and a cohort of empirically trained researchers – to investigate'.[56] I am certainly not such a cohort and my purpose is not to offer a comprehensive and exhaustive empirical account of the application of proportionality around the world. More modestly, this work aims at showing through an in-depth study of three systems, that developments in the field of comparative law can offer valuable insights into the meaning of proportionality and the reasons of its spread.

1.3 Proportionality and Difference

No one denies that differences exist in the application of proportionality in judicial practice. However, differences are not taken seriously when reconstructing proportionality's meaning.[57] Judges using the concept are typically thought to refer to the global proportionality model. Variance is often attributed to the flexibility of proportionality's structure, whose application can be limited to only some of its prongs.[58] Another factor of variance is the fact that proportionality theory purports solely to provide an analytical structure that is neutral as to substantive outcomes. Judicial solutions in concrete cases largely depend on the substantive moral theory that complements proportionality's application and on the local perception of rights.[59] In consequence, the failures of proportionality are

[54] Paraphrasing Tusseau (2013).

[55] See, for example, Gardbaum (2017), pp. 221 f.; Perju (2017), p. 201.

[56] Schauer (2014), p. 185.

[57] Barak (2012, p. 181), for example, points out that '[m]any legal systems use proportionality today, while filling it with their own content'. This does not discourage the author from asserting as in the following that 'the systems are very similar'. His book thus describes what the author perceives as the 'universal understanding of the concept of proportionality in constitutional democracies', mainly drawing on the Alexyan model (p. 4). In a similar vein, while Stone Sweet and Mathews (2008) stress that 'judges shape PA [meaning: proportionality analysis] to their own purposes, with use', they still consider the model of proportionality and its function in judicial review to be generally similar across jurisdictions (p. 162).

[58] Stone Sweet and Mathews (2008, p. 75), for example, observe that, 'in its fully developed form, the analysis involves four steps', while they observe in a footnote that some important courts normally use a three-part test.

[59] See, for example, different kinds of variance and their explanation by Kumm (2017).

often attributed to excessive judicial deference, to subjective bias on the part of the judge who applied it or to 'poor judging' more generally.[60] The defenders of proportionality are cautious enough to reserve evangelical claims about its function only to *correct* applications of the model. 'When correctly applied', 'when properly deployed' and other similar phrases are recurrent in proportionality studies. Good institutional design and strong legitimacy of the judiciary are thus important conditions for the felicity of the theory of proportionality.[61] Möller, for instance, stresses that judicial review and proportionality achieve their purpose only when they are exercised by 'well-designed courts working under well designed procedural rules'.[62]

Analyses that are more sensitive to judicial practice account for divergence in the application of proportionality, even by courts that are deemed to be pioneers in the field. Grimm contrasts the German model of proportionality with its application in Canada. He observes that the Canadian Supreme Court does not apply the balancing stage and proceeds to a more intrusive examination of the legitimate aim requirement.[63] Rivers goes further, schematising two different conceptions of proportionality. The first, which he terms the 'state-limiting' conception, does not involve balancing of competing interests. Instead, rights are categorically defined and are either absolute or require the protection of a minimum core. In Rivers' view, this conception, usually applied by British courts, considerably contrasts with the 'optimising' conception of proportionality that one finds in the case law of European courts. The author takes as an example the ECtHR jurisprudence, where he considers balancing to be 'endemic'.[64] While accounting for a difference in the practice of proportionality, both Rivers and Grimm agree on their preference for the German proportionality model. Grimm concludes that 'the disciplining and rationalizing effect, which is a significant advantage of the proportionality test' is reduced when its four prongs are not orderly applied.[65] In the same vein, Rivers considers the British *Wednesbury* test to be 'a rough cut version of

60 Khosla (2010), p. 308; Klatt and Meister (2012b), section 7.

61 The term 'felicity' is used to accentuate the performative nature of the theory of proportionality. On the felicity conditions for speech acts, see Austin (1975).

62 Möller (2012), p. 128.

63 Grimm (2007).

64 Rivers (2006), p. 187.

65 Grimm (2007), p. 397.

proportionality'.[66] Put briefly, in the proportionality literature, difference observed in judicial practice is invariably demoted to 'a *modus deficiens* of sameness'.[67]

Consensus on the desirability of the German proportionality model is connected to the pervasiveness of the balancing metaphor and to the instrumental view of law that underpins it.[68] Because legal decision-making is increasingly seen as involving balancing constitutional rights, proportionality is preferred to other reasoning models. Its analytical structure is believed to rationalise and theoretically inform legal reasoning. Stone Sweet and Mathews conclude their analysis of the spread of proportionality by briefly considering alternative models for rights-based adjudication. They observe that the US Supreme Court in particular has developed a 'complicated, variegated approach to rights'. However, in their view, the various components of the Supreme Court's doctrine are outcomes of 'seminal acts of balancing that then congeal as precedent'.[69] The authors express their preference for proportionality as a method of adjudication, since it renders balancing explicit and open to negotiation between the parties. In a similar vein, Rivers notes that the '[t]he inevitability of balancing rights with the public interest means that in practice it creeps unnoticed' into the prongs of the 'state-limiting' version of proportionality. 'Since it is unnoticed', the author continues, 'it is uncontrolled'.[70] In contrast, the 'optimising' version of proportionality increases transparency in judicial reasoning and exposes balancing to criticism.

However, to see legal reasoning as balancing and to choose proportionality as a method for this process is *in itself* not neutral or natural. It constrains legal argumentation in a particular way, as it also creates new possibilities for it. When inserted into different legal contexts, proportionality implies a change in pre-existing rules, concepts, distinctions and patterns of reasoning that local legal actors sometimes deem fundamental.[71] Whether this change is wanted or not is not only

66 Rivers (2006), p. 187.

67 Legrand (2003), p. 245.

68 On the connection between balancing and instrumentalism, see Bomhoff (2013a), pp. 17–18.

69 Stone Sweet and Mathews (2008), p. 164.

70 Rivers (2006), p. 187.

71 The term 'local legal actors' is used here instead of 'national' or 'domestic legal actors', in order to accentuate the contingent nature of the boundaries of legal discourses and legal systems. Indeed, the boundaries of a legal system might not coincide with national boundaries and might change over time.

a moral or philosophical matter, but it also depends on the meaning of what proportionality replaces and on the meaning of proportionality itself. This meaning is not universal or a-temporal. In fact, a survey of the use of proportionality by legal actors shows that the instances of proportionality reasoning that *actually correspond* to the pronged framework described by mainstream scholars are rare. So rare that it appears as '*un grand hasard*', if proportionality is ever correctly applied.[72] In the different contexts in which proportionality has spread, it is not necessarily understood as a pronged structure for balancing constitutional rights. In most cases, it does not imply balancing or reasoning in prongs. In some cases, it is not employed in judicial review but is only used by scholars. And in yet others, proportionality is not even connected to rights at all. In a recent contribution, Bomhoff shows that 'proportionality', but also connected terms such as 'US exceptionalism', can have very different meanings even in comparative law studies, according to the branches of law compared.[73] Therefore, the tendency to perceive proportionality as the European or even global way of 'doing balancing' is misleading.

My approach differs from that of mainstream proportionality scholarship, in the sense that I do not purport to improve the proportionality model that already exists or to identify variables that affect its application in practice. Instead, I propose to consider differences in the application of proportionality as an object worthy of study in and of themselves. Cotterrell observes that 'differences between laws and legal systems may not be just matters of contingency; they may express profound characteristics of the cultures that produce them'.[74] Law is not only instrumental to the maximisation of rights as principles neither is it only there to make democracy work. It also expresses local beliefs, values and sentiments, local ways of thinking and local expectations and aspirations. Hence, legal rules are not scientific or technical means to achieve ends imposed by a universal reason. Rather, they express particularly local representations of society, of its problems and of possible solutions, they are

[72] Montesquieu (1979), chap. 3, cited by Kahn-Freund (1974), p. 6. Montesquieu used this phrase to say that it would be very rare, a great hazard, if the laws of a nation were found to suit another one.

[73] Bomhoff (2017). The author examines the understanding of proportionality in comparative scholarship in the fields of criminal law and rights-based judicial review.

[74] Cotterrell (2007), p. 135.

'part of a distinctive manner of imagining the real'.[75] I propose an inquiry into law's expressive function as a 'species of social imagination'.[76] My purpose is to render less enigmatic local perceptions of proportionality that mainstream scholarship would perceive as deviant or incorrect, without reducing the differences that exist between them. This kind of inquiry shares with ethnographic studies the fact that it attempts to make sense of law and of proportionality as they are *locally* perceived and not to explain them causally according to a preconceived theory or model. 'Meaning, in short, not machinery', as Geertz puts it.[77]

The study of difference is crucial to understanding the spread of proportionality. While the coherence of local discourses is largely neglected in the relevant studies, it plays a major role in the version of proportionality that local legal actors have adopted and in the expectations that they have attached to it. Context shapes the meaning and function of proportionality every time. Comparative research should not sacrifice the infinite local meanings of proportionality for the sake of the integrity and coherence of a global model. A-temporal and universal staples are the product of legal theory and jurisprudence.[78] However, comparative lawyers are increasingly aware of the ethnocentrism, the 'subjugation of the other to the self', that underlies any theory with pretensions to universality.[79] The merits of the study of difference lie in its pluralistic and non-hierarchical approach to alternative ways of legal thinking, in the respect that it shows for legal alterity. Therefore, it is not my purpose to make conclusions about which version of proportionality is preferable or more adapted to each of the contexts studied. Neither do I generally argue for diversity against a rising global model of proportionality and constitutionalism. Without embracing any normative approach on proportionality, rights or constitutional law, I simply suggest that things are more complex than the mainstream proportionality literature would assume. This study consists in an investigation of the 'infinitely rich varieties of human experience and their specifically legal expressions' in the different local versions of proportionality.[80]

[75] Geertz (1983), p. 173.
[76] Ibid, p. 232.
[77] Ibid.
[78] Krygier (1986), p. 237.
[79] Legrand (2003), p. 310.
[80] Cotterrell (2007), p. 152.

1.4 Proportionality as a Legal Transfer

Perju has shed light on the impact that local legal context can have on proportionality. This author does not consider proportionality to be inherent to the notion of constitution or necessary for the adjudication of rights, but proposes to see it as a legal transfer. He argues that as proportionality crosses borders, its form should not be taken for granted. In his view, 'proportionality's distinctiveness and merits do not depend on the preservation of its current formal structure, but rather on the existence of *a* formal structure'.[81] It is precisely the versatility of proportionality that has favoured its spectacular spread around the world. Perju considers that the successful transplant of the proportionality model to environments such as the USA requires its adaptation so as to sufficiently respond to local standards for the justification of judicial decisions. He considers the main obstacles to the success of proportionality in the USA to be the particularly strong local demands for doctrinal stability. Thus, he proposes an 'experimentation' with proportionality's structure by adding a final prong to the analysis.[82] This prong would require judges to compare the outcome of the previous steps against precedent and assess the disruption that such an outcome would cause to the *stare decisis* doctrine. This would allow proportionality to accomplish its function of justification and transparency in US constitutional case law, while it would not compromise the rationality of proportionality reasoning.[83]

Perju's analysis shows that the literature on legal transplants can offer a framework for understanding how legal rules, institutions, concepts and ideas change as they travel across systems. During the 1970s, Watson pointed out that, contrary to traditional perceptions of the law as embedded in history and society, the transplantation of legal rules and institutions from one system to another is the most recurrent form of legal change since antiquity. Watson attributed this to the 'socially easy' character of the transplantation of legal rules, connected to legal elites' insulation from society.[84] In his view, 'usually legal rules are not peculiarly devised for the particular society in which they now operate and [. . .] this is not a matter for great concern'.[85] By accentuating the impact of

[81] Perju (2017), p. 203.
[82] Ibid.
[83] Ibid, pp. 214 f.
[84] Watson (1974), p. 95.
[85] Ibid, p. 96.

foreign influence on legal change and legal reform, Watson also provided a project for comparative legal studies: the study of others' laws could be a source of inspiration, since other systems could provide better legal solutions to problems that also exist in one's own system. The study of legal transplants is part of a broader functionalist trend in comparative law. Following this trend, similar problems arise in different legal contexts and allow for a focused comparison of the solutions given every time. The aim of comparative law is to enhance communication between national legal systems and to eventually promote their unification or harmonisation.[86]

The legal transplants literature has long been limited to the field of private law, since the embeddedness of public and especially constitutional law in local socio-political contexts was believed to hinder the transplantation of rules and institutions.[87] Yet the emergence of a global paradigm of constitutionalism has increasingly pushed comparative constitutional lawyers to think about cross-border influence. It is accepted nowadays that while transfers among constitutional jurisdictions are possible, this process is less mechanical than in private law. Comparatists have thus employed new metaphors, like borrowing, migration or cross-fertilisation to express this.[88] Drawing on these analyses, Perju proposes to see proportionality as a transplant that must adapt to the needs of the host environment. While he does not take for granted the structure of proportionality, he does take for granted a lot: first of all, proportionality's meaning as a prong-structured reasoning framework, and, second, proportionality's function, which, in his view, is to enhance judicial responsiveness. The US legal culture, or rather environment, in the author's terms, is seen as a *variable* that can be accommodated within the model of proportionality.

However, as Cotterrell observed, 'in different legal systems, local values, traditions or sentiments may differently colour the definition of [legal rules, institutions or concepts'] functions, the importance attached to them and the tests of their successful fulfilment'.[89] Concerning US constitutional law in particular, Bomhoff explains that balancing has been perceived as a dangerous, anti-formalist doctrine in US

[86] The most well-known and influential functionalist comparative study is that by Zweigert and Kötz (1977). For an interesting account and evaluation of functionalist approaches, see Graziadei (2003).
[87] See, most notably, Kahn-Freund (1974).
[88] See, for example, Choudhry, ed. (2006).
[89] Cotterrell (2007), p. 136.

constitutional thought.[90] Suspicion towards balancing would be at odds with its inclusion in a rational prong-structured reasoning framework, like the one proposed by proportionality scholars. Kahn also explains that US lawyers view proportionality with suspicion, as a doctrine concealing political decisions.[91] This author compares US constitutionalism to a religion and explains how the will of the sovereign people, expressed in the constitutional text, is foundational in US legal thought. The mission of the Supreme Court is to speak in the name of the people, much in the same way that a priest speaks in the name of God. This makes sense of the importance of constitutional text and precedent in American constitutional thought, sometimes to the detriment of substantive justification and considerations of justice. Perju's functionalist approach neglects the particular local meaning of proportionality and balancing in the USA. Local lawyers' suspicion towards proportionality is not placed within a larger context in which it makes sense. By attributing US resistance to a general concept of proportionality to special local demands for doctrinal stability, Perju misses a lot of the 'local knowledge' that this resistance embodies.[92]

Cohen-Eliya and Porat are more sensitive to local perceptions of law and to the coherence of local legal discourses. In their book *Proportionality and Constitutional Culture*, they contrast the USA with jurisdictions in which proportionality enjoys the status of a general constitutional principle. To do so, they draw on the distinction between two ideal types of constitutional culture, the 'culture of authority' and the 'culture of justification'. The authors argue that in a culture of authority legitimacy of public action results from the authorisation of a public authority to exercise power, whereas in a culture of justification, it results from the rationality and reasonableness of public action. Cohen-Eliya and Porat consider proportionality to be 'an indispensable – inherent – part of the culture of justification'.[93] In their view, such a culture is characterised by a vision of rights very akin to Alexy's optimisation requirements. Rights as substantive values are largely detached from the constitutional text. They expand to comprise all domains of power and provide guidance to judicial review and public action. In contrast, following the authors, the US Supreme Court's refusal to embrace proportionality is explained by the culture of authority that underpins its

90 Bomhoff (2013a).
91 Kahn (2004), pp. 2698 f.
92 Geertz (1983), p. 231.
93 Cohen-Eliya and Porat (2013), p. 126.

decisions. Such a culture is hostile towards balancing. Public law consists in the delimitation of state actors' spheres of competence and the constitutional text remains important in judicial review. Rights are categorically defined requirements of abstention and entire fields of public action escape judicial review.

Proportionality and Constitutional Culture is animated by the same enthusiasm about proportionality that underpins the mainstream literature. While the authors stress the particularity of proportionality and locate its historical origins in formalist Prussian doctrine, they claim that it evolved in German law to acquire a universal character. Indeed, in their view, proportionality, once again understood as a prong-structured framework for balancing rights, can be easily adapted to different contexts, since it expresses universally shared ideals, like coherency, systematisation and logical structure. The authors compare proportionality to a species of bird that, despite having evolved in a particular environment, has developed certain features 'that make it adaptable to all types of environments'.[94] While they do not use the transplant metaphor, this analogy is not so different from the way Watson has described his perception of legal transfers: 'Just as very few people have thought of the wheel yet once invented its advantages can be seen and the wheel used by many, so important legal rules are invented by a few people or nations, and once invented their value can readily be appreciated, and the rules themselves adopted for the needs of many nations.'[95] Whether the analogy is taken from biology or technology, proportionality seems to be part of a 'hidden science of constitutionalism that should unite all liberal constitutions as variations on a common theme'.[96]

1.5 Proportionality, Culture and European Integration

Still, Cohen-Eliya and Porat add a key element to the discussion of proportionality's spread: the importance of culture.[97] In their analysis, law and proportionality are embedded in local perceptions of society, democracy and reason. In their view, the culture of authority is animated by scepticism regarding human rationality and by a pluralist vision of society and of the democratic process as a field of constant power struggles

[94] Ibid, p. 156.
[95] Watson (1974), p. 100.
[96] Kahn (2004), p. 2684.
[97] The concept of culture is hardly explained in their analysis, though. For a critical review of Cohen-Eliya and Porat's book, see Schneiderman (2015).

between interest groups. On the contrary, the perception of democracy that underpins the culture of justification is substantive, in the sense that it imposes basic requirements of rationality or morality on the expression of political claims. In this context, constitutional adjudication is animated by a rationalist perception of law and legal knowledge as a quasi-scientific enterprise. The authors suggest that the trauma of the Second World War led the turn towards a culture of justification in Europe.[98] In a recent paper, they refine this argument by observing that the development of constitutional law in post-war Europe built on already developed administrative law doctrine and practice. Cohen-Eliya and Porat suggest that the administrative origins of European constitutional law might explain the success of proportionality in this context in contrast to the USA, where constitutional law was well-established as a discipline much before the emergence of administrative law.[99]

The embeddedness of law in culture is a core problem for the theory and method of comparative law. Most famously, Legrand criticises the legal transplant metaphor, which, in his view, is based on a positivist misconception of law as rules, that is, as bare propositional statements, disconnected from social ideas and values. Indeed, it is typical for comparatists in this field to consider that rules travel from one society to another and are 'equally at home everywhere'.[100] On the contrary, Legrand perceives legal rules as 'incorporative cultural forms' whose transplantation is simply impossible.[101] In this author's view, even when a rule does cross borders, its culturally specific meaning does not. This would require the transportation of the whole language and culture. In Legrand's terms:

> as the words cross boundaries there intervenes a different rationality and morality to underwrite and effectuate the borrowed words: the host culture continues to articulate its moral inquiry according to traditional standards of justification. Thus, the imported form of words is inevitably ascribed a different, local meaning which makes it ipso facto a different rule.[102]

For Legrand, any legal transfer leads to an idiosyncratic *métissage* that results from the domestication of the initial concept, rule, institution or

[98] Cohen-Eliya and Porat (2013), pp. 122 f.
[99] Cohen-Eliya and Porat (2017).
[100] Legrand (1997), p. 113.
[101] Ibid, p. 116.
[102] Ibid, p. 115.

idea. The transplant metaphor is nothing but 'a convenient variance reducer'.[103]

The perception of law as a cultural construction leads Legrand to deny the possibility and desirability of effective convergence between legal systems, even in the context of European integration.[104] In his view, 'any attempt at globalisation ultimately resolves itself as an original experience of "glocalisation"'.[105] This is due to the incommensurability of the epistemological approaches underpinning different legal cultures. Concerning the common law and the civil law in particular, Legrand suggests that they are separated by an irreducible '*primordial* cleavage – a *summa differentia*', which lies in the completely different ways in which they answer the question of what constitutes legal knowledge.[106] This prevents mutual understanding between civil and common lawyers.[107] Legrand argues that there is no common framework for measuring and evaluating the epistemological premises that separate the civil law from the common law. These cultures are thus 'irrevocably irreconcilable'.[108] The denial of epistemological commensurability between different legal cultures leads Legrand to deny the possibility of legal comparison as a scientific enterprise.[109] In his view, the comparatist simply cannot understand the meaning of foreign law as local lawyers do, since immersion in a fully internal perspective is impossible to achieve in practice. Every comparative enterprise is bound to conclude in the alterity of foreign law.[110]

Legrand's approach has been criticised as too radical, animated by a 'naïve epistemological pessimism'.[111] Comparatists have seen in such an approach the danger of essentialising culture, of perceiving it as an over-bounded and homogeneous unity that can be opposed to any effort of social change.[112] Legrand, by accentuating the nation-state as a privileged site for the formation of cultural identity, silences the asymmetries of power and knowledge that national legal cultures maintain

[103] Ibid, p. 122.
[104] Legrand (1996), p. 62.
[105] Legrand (2002), p. 251.
[106] Legrand (1996), p. 63.
[107] Ibid, p. 76.
[108] Legrand (2003), p. 245.
[109] Ibid, p. 254.
[110] Ibid, pp. 282 f.
[111] Van Hoecke (2004), p. 8, cited by Cotterrell (2006), fn. 70.
[112] Nelken (1995), pp. 443 f.; Nelken (2003), p. 446; Cotterrell (2006), p. 729; Glenn (2004), pp. 14 f.

and reproduce. Legrand's approach encloses the danger of using culture as a 'discussion-stopper' and even as a 'thought-stopper'.[113] Including something within the realm of legal culture would endow it with some kind of traditional nobility and exclude the possibility of contesting or reforming it, without providing further insights as to how this feature is connected to law's wider socio-political context. Further, Legrand is criticised for underestimating the importance of transnational or supranational movements and networks in shaping collective identities. Most notably, he does not seem to take seriously the EU legal order as constituting *its own, legal* culture, in which domestic actors find new resources for contesting dominant mentalities and patterns in their own legal sphere.[114] Instead, Legrand seems to assume that Europeanisation, like other instances of globalisation, 'operates in a deracinating world of markets'.[115]

How can comparative law account for difference and the embeddedness of law in culture without eliminating the possibility for integration through law? This is particularly relevant in the study of proportionality. Not only because proportionality's function is precisely the integration of minorities into the policy-making process, but also due to the crucial role of proportionality in the process of European integration. Proportionality is a core principle both in the ECHR and in the EU legal orders. Applied by supranational courts, it is one of the most important legal mechanisms for ensuring the realisation of supranational interests and values. Hence, European courts encourage domestic actors to reason in proportionality terms and sometimes even impose the application of proportionality as a supranational legal obligation. Once received as a European principle, proportionality often deconstructs domestic categories, blurs traditional distinctions and transforms well-established ways of thinking. To deny the integrative and transformative dynamic of proportionality would be to neglect one important aspect of its spread. It would also lead us to discard an important element of domestic legal cultures themselves, that is, local legal actors' vision of Europe and European integration.

Still, the fact that the adoption of proportionality in certain contexts might not be voluntary but imposed by supranational institutions does not tell us much about the way proportionality is *locally* understood and

[113] Putnam (2002), p. 44, referring to the fact/value dichotomy.
[114] Walker (2002), pp. 262 f.
[115] Legrand (2002), p. 254.

applied. Even when imposed, legal transfers do not lead to harmonisation. In different contexts, they deploy their integration dynamic according to local patterns of legal change and local visions of European integration. For instance, even within the scope of supranational treaties, proportionality will be applied differently according to whether the host culture adopts a dualist or a monist perception of the relationship between domestic law and European legal orders. Categorisations and typologies of legal transfer based on their form of adoption, while relevant when seeking to causally explain the spread of proportionality as a rule or technique, are of little help in the search for proportionality's local meanings.[116]

Teubner's autopoietic theory is an attempt to bridge the divide between legal autonomy and cultural embeddedness and to account for legal change, albeit in a particularly local way. Following Luhmann's social systems theory, Teubner sees law as a discursive system that meets society as 'a fragmented multiplicity of discourses'.[117] In modern societies, law's professionalization and technicity are sources of operational closure in relation to the social subsystems that it purports to regulate. Law's autonomy is expressed in the 'normative self-reference and recursivity' on which the legal discourse builds.[118] Lawyers prefer arguments from legal authority and precedent to arguments on the social consequences of a certain solution. In this context, the fact that proportionality is sometimes imposed as a *legal* obligation by supranational courts acquires a particular importance. Indeed, it is precisely law's autonomy that makes convergence between national legal systems possible: as Teubner remarks, 'social subsystems define their borders in terms of their own logic and tradition, independent of the political definition of local, regional, or national boundaries'.[119] Still, law's autonomy is only relative, since law, as every operationally closed system, is 'structurally coupled to its niche' and uses influence from social, political or other context to build or to change its internal structures.[120] Law is closely tied to other fragments of society and its social ties are manifested in relatively fixed 'binding arrangements' with social power structures.[121]

[116] For such a typology, Cohn (2010), pp. 591–2.

[117] Teubner (1998), p. 21. On the utility of Teubner's theory in the study of legal transfers, see Nelken (2003), pp. 459 f.

[118] Teubner (1998), p. 16.

[119] Friedman and Teubner (1986), p. 363.

[120] Teubner (1991/1992), p. 1446.

[121] Teubner (1998), p. 17.

Teubner's approach offers tools that can be useful to the cultural study of law in apprehending the complex relationship between law and its surrounding social context. Most importantly, it offers conceptual tools that allow accounting for legal change and convergence within the context of European integration, without neglecting the distinctive logic of the legal systems studied. Indeed, while Teubner accepts the possibility of legal transfers, he rejects the transplant metaphor as too simplistic. In his view, legal transfers are better described as legal irritants, 'an outside noise which creates wild perturbations in the interplay of discourses'.[122] As external influences, they provoke discursive change and irritate law's binding arrangements. Still, law's social ties 'reappear in new disguises in which they are barely discernible'.[123] Change remains internal to the legal system and reconstructs 'from scratch' the transferred rule, institution or concept itself.[124] The concept of legal irritant can thus be a useful tool in describing how a legal transfer changes local legal culture, while it is itself transformed when it meets this culture's deep structures.

1.6 Comparing the Local Meanings of Proportionality

Legal transfers offer an ideal opportunity to study the embeddedness of law in its local context, since they express the internal logic of the systems involved. As Teubner observes, transfers more generally 'do not create a new unity of the separate discourses involved, they only link them transcending the boundaries but respecting, even reaffirming them. In spite of their identical *nom propre* they are purely internal constructs of each discourse involved.'[125] Transfers can thus provide what Legrand calls a 'semantic commonality or dialogical interface', which allows for comparison and translation between different legal cultures.[126] Interestingly, this author actually uses reasonableness and proportionality as an example of such commonality, which, in his view, demonstrates the irreducible difference of common law and civil law representations of judicial review. The study of legal transfers is probably the field in which comparative law can best deploy its '*fonction subversive*' in the face of

[122] Ibid, p. 12.
[123] Ibid, p. 18.
[124] Ibid, p. 12.
[125] Teubner (1991/1992), p. 1458.
[126] Legrand (2003), p. 283.

well-established legal dogmas, mentalities and taboos.[127] And proportionality offers a unique chance to undertake this task, precisely due to its spectacular spread and its importance in global constitutionalism rhetoric. Differences in the use of proportionality reveal important aspects of the worldviews shared not only by national legal actors or public lawyers in particular, but also by transnational and supranational actors that use proportionality, such as the ECJ, the ECtHR or proportionality theorists themselves.

Bomhoff has neatly shown how comparative research can indeed proceed through the creation of 'comparable local meanings' of legal arguments.[128] The author takes the example of balancing in the USA and Germany and shows that despite the commonality of the balancing metaphor, the ways in which local legal actors use it are very different. The difference mainly lies in the extent to which legal actors perceive balancing argumentation to have a political nature.[129] Taking a cue from Bomhoff's analysis, the study of the use of proportionality as a *particular* balancing argument allows for a sharpening of the focus of the comparison and for the identification of other sources of difference between legal systems. Indeed, in the application of proportionality divergence might not (or not only) result from local perceptions of balancing, but also from local legal taboos concerning the identification and criticism of policy aims, the evaluation of policy-making means or the consideration of facts. Proportionality, by clearly separating the stages of the balancing process, renders the identification of sources of diversity across legal systems easier. Further, due to its theoretical perception as an analytical structure, the application of proportionality expresses the relative importance that local legal actors attach to structure in legal argumentation. Divergence in the practice of proportionality reveals clashes in styles of reasoning between transnational, supranational and domestic legal actors. Finally, in the scope of European law in particular, formal pressure for the application of proportionality unravels certain instances of local practice as cases of resistance, which would be difficult to identify otherwise.

Legrand compares the process of legal transfer to an author who finds it convenient to quote from foreign authors. In his view, transfers are only 'a rhetorical strategy involving the ordinary act of repetition as an

[127] Muir-Watt (2000).
[128] Bomhoff (2012b), pp. 74 f.
[129] Bomhoff (2010).

enabling discursive method'.[130] Thus, the study of legal actors' reactions to this strategy and, more generally, the debates that legal transfers provoke unveil local perceptions of what constitutes a successful legal argument and local expectations of law. Bomhoff's study shows that legal discourses have their proper criteria for evaluating legal arguments and their proper alternatives for legal argumentation.[131] Therefore, the success or failure of legal transfers is relative; it depends on the point of view.[132] This is particularly relevant for the comparative study of proportionality. Due to its focus on US exceptionalism, comparative scholars tend to assume that, wherever adopted, proportionality's transplant is successful. The use of proportionality by European supranational courts has certainly nourished this belief, which is also enhanced by the fact that local legal actors themselves are often enthusiastic about proportionality and increasingly refer to the European and to the Alexyan proportionality models. Put briefly, not only *is* proportionality a legal transfer, but it is often *perceived* as such both by national and by transnational actors. This feature distinguishes proportionality from generic balancing arguments and provides it with an impressive capacity to express local imagination.

Legal actors in domestic systems often privilege this or that context as the source of proportionality, thus expressing more general local patterns of legal change. Proportionality can be presented as a transfer from Germany, from Europe, but also from France, Canada, New Zealand, or even from other disciplines such as philosophy, mathematics or finance. The choice of the source context will often depend on the traditional sources of influence in the legal system. It might also indicate that different characteristics of proportionality are accentuated: its analytical structure, its substantive content or the type of review that it implies. Furthermore, the version of proportionality that local legal actors choose to adopt expresses their vision as to how the local legal discourse *can* change, as well as their expectations of this transformation. Divergence observed in the use of proportionality indicates that local expectations differ both from the objectives of European integration endorsed by European legal actors, and from the aims that transnational proportionality scholarship advances. Often asymmetries in the use of proportionality exist not only across legal systems, but also within the same legal system, across branches of law and groups of legal actors

130 Legrand (1997), p. 121.
131 Bomhoff (2012b), pp. 84 f.
132 See also Nelken (2003), pp. 452 f.

(academics, judges, lawyers or law-makers). The observation of such asymmetries is insightful as to the role that different actors might play in local processes of legal change.

This work consists in a focused case study of the use of proportionality in France, England and Greece. Contrary to the mainstream focus on the US and European models of judicial review, it investigates jurisdictions that have already embraced proportionality and in which proportionality is sometimes a core issue of debate or even a hegemonic method of reasoning. Comparative study thus allows the identification of similarities and differences in local processes of receiving of proportionality, in its local perceptions of, and the place that it occupies in the contexts studied. Further, France, England and Greece are all subject to the jurisdiction of the ECJ and the ECtHR. Comparison of the application of proportionality in the scope of European law thus reveals similarities and differences in the ways that the dynamics of European integration are locally deployed and perceived. Finally, the systems chosen undergo more or less impressive socio-political shocks that are expressed in the legal sphere. The recent, two-year long state of emergency in France is testimony to a crisis in French constitutional politics. Brexit crystallises Eurosceptic tendencies that have long been rising in the UK. The Eurozone crisis provokes social and political instability in Greece and entails a huge delegation of powers to the executive. It is interesting to investigate how these evolutions colour the local meaning of proportionality.

The cases chosen, sufficiently similar to be comparable, are sufficiently different to make the comparison fruitful. While France, the archetype civil law jurisdiction, and England, the oldest common law jurisdiction, are both known for their insular legal traditions and their long and often glorious past, and frequently attract the attention of comparative lawyers, Greece is a relatively new legal order, which is rarely studied by non-local lawyers. This is probably due to language difficulties, but also to the limited influence of the Greek model of administration and judicial review. Greece belongs to the civil law family, but domestic lawyers have built on eclectic influences coming from all over the world, with France, the USA, the UK and Germany being the most common sources of legal inspiration. These differences are also connected to the different roles that the countries studied have played in the European integration process. France and the UK were among the founding states of the Council of Europe and have exercised important influences on the architecture and political orientation of European supranational organisations. For Greece, in contrast, the process of European integration decisively started in the mid-1970s and the country has always been part of the European periphery. The legal relationships between these jurisdictions and Europe also display differences, the UK's being a dualist state, while France and Greece are monist, at least at the level of legal texts. The choice of the three countries thus allows for an investigation of how different legal cultures and European trajectories, across the common law/civil law cleavage, affect the local meaning of proportionality and shape the process of legal convergence within Europe.

What do French, English and Greek lawyers do when they 'speak' proportionality and what are the expectations that they have attached to the use of this particular language? What do different local meanings of proportionality tell us about the legal cultures in which they have evolved and how has proportionality affected local patterns of cultural evolution? Finally, what does the application of proportionality in the field of EU law and the ECHR tell us about local visions of Europe and European integration?

1.7 A Cultural Study of Law

Proportionality proliferates in comparative constitutional law but it is not always clear what it means. The relevant literature tends to describe it as a method, a framework, a principle, an ideal or even the ultimate rule of law. Recently, Jackson distinguished the substantive aspect of proportionality as an ideal or a principle from the structured proportionality doctrine.[133] This second meaning seems to be more important in proportionality theory, since most scholars connect the merits of proportionality to the particular reasoning process that it implies. In spite of scholarly concern with the substance or the analytical structure of proportionality, however, the unanimous affirmation of proportionality's success is commonly based on the observation of the pervasiveness of proportionality language.[134] Indeed, it is because courts around the world explicitly refer to proportionality as a general constitutional principle and in some cases engage in proportionality analysis that scholars consider proportionality to be a successful transplant. But while scholarship usually does not take the spread of proportionality for granted, it

[133] Jackson (2015), p. 3098.

[134] Bomhoff (2010, p. 112) makes the same observation about balancing and proportionality. Gardbaum (2017, p. 223) observes that if scholars assumed proportionality in the absence of the relevant terminology, it would mean that 'the dominance of proportionality is significantly achieved by stipulation'.

does generally take proportionality's meaning, form and function for granted. In other words, the relevant studies often assimilate the spread of a particular *form of language* into the spread of a particular *process of reasoning*[135] and, in some cases, into the spread of a more general human rights paradigm and of a culture of justification.

Quite differently, I propose to start from Legrand's sole concession to the legal transplants' literature: 'At best, what can be displaced from one jurisdiction to another is, literally, a *meaningless* form of words.'[136] This is a good starting point because comparative lawyers, like linguists and historians, are aware that the same words might have very different meanings across jurisdictions and across time. In this minimalist view of legal transfers, then, proportionality is only a particular form of language, a way of speaking, and its identification is primarily based on the use of a particular vocabulary: the term *proportion* or *proportionality* and its translations *proportion* or *proportionnalité*, *αναλογία* or *αναλογικότητα*. In the absence of these terms, other structural features might indicate the use of proportionality language, such as prong-structured reasoning, containing formulae such as *necessary and appropriate*, *nécessaire et approprié*, *αναγκαίο και κατάλληλο* or their synonyms in each context. Reference to *balancing*, *balance* or *weighing*, *conciliation* or *pesée*, and *στάθμιση* might also indicate the use of proportionality language when combined with other features, such as reference to German or European case law or reasoning in prongs. Understood in this way, the comparative study of the use of proportionality in different jurisdictions is not very different from practising intellectual history. Its goal is, through the reconstruction of ways of speaking, to 'unravel mental worlds'.[137] Only, instead of reconstructing past uses of language, comparative law reconstructs foreign ones.

The purpose of this book is not to argue that similar ideas and reasoning to those that proportionality designates have not existed before the emergence of proportionality language in French, English and Greek public law. Taking my cue from intellectual history and linguistics, I simply argue that *the way* in which ideas are expressed is important. Language itself is important, since it is constitutive of thought. As Brett put it: 'To use words in a particular way within a particular linguistic horizon just *is* to "think".'[138] Ideas do not exist independently of the text

[135] Bomhoff (2010) calls this the 'discourse/process assimilation'.
[136] Legrand (1997), p. 120.
[137] Brett (2002), p. 128.
[138] Ibid, p. 117.

in which they are expressed; they are not 'contingent to the book'.[139] Even though ideas, methods or concepts similar or comparable to proportionality have existed before its emergence in the legal systems studied, my inquiry concerns the *particular* expression of such ideas, methods or concepts *in proportionality terms*. While the linguistic turn is quite recent in comparative legal studies, intellectual historians have long been concerned with the relationship between language, meaning and context. Hence, intellectual history provides us with precious conceptual and methodological tools for studying the transfer and evolution of proportionality in different settings.

Words make sense only when inserted into a discourse, in the case of law, a legal discourse. As proportionality spreads in different legal spheres, it is connected to already existing categories, concepts and reasoning techniques. It is perceived as quasi-synonymous with legal terms and formulae, such as the *contrôle de nécessité* in France and the *αρχή του ήττονος επαχθούς μέτρου* in Greece, or as antithetical to others, such as, at times, the *Wednesbury* unreasonableness standard in England. Only within a legal discourse does proportionality terminology acquire its function in legal argumentation, it becomes a *head of review*, a *standard* or an *αρχή*. In other words, it is the insertion of proportionality into a broader legal language, a 'structure of content', in the words of Thomas[140] or 'a system of signification', in Balkin's terms,[141] that fills it with legal content. Any inquiry into the local meaning of proportionality should thus start from its relationship with pre-existing concepts and categories in the legal discourses where it is received.[142] Such relationships are established through the study of constitutional or legislative texts, academic writings, as well as judicial opinions, deliberations and decisions.

This study shares with ethnographic approaches to law the fact that it takes local reasoning practices and local worldviews seriously. However, it is not based on the results of field research and it does not necessarily involve immersion in a particular legal community. This is related to the purpose of this book, which is not to make conclusions about French, English and Greek legal culture more generally, but about *the culturally specific logic of proportionality* in French, English and Greek public law.

[139] Ibid.

[140] Thomas (1973), p. 111.

[141] Balkin (1990b), p. 1121.

[142] On this method of legal semiotics, see Balkin (1990b, 1991). For one of the rare applications in comparative legal studies, see Bomhoff (2010).

Hence, the legal discourse that is relevant to this inquiry is limited to the use (or non-use) of proportionality arguments and is mainly found in traditional legal material. Legal discourse is principally used by legal actors, who often correspond to Watson's legal elites. In this sense, the comparative analysis of law undertaken here is also 'a cratology, that is, a study of power' and is different from works in legal anthropology and legal sociology, concerned with the use of legal discourse in other settings.[143] Drawing on the work of Pottage, I argue that reflective research based on traditional legal material can offer a legal 'counterpart' to ethnographic approaches.[144]

That being said, *national* legal actors do not monopolise legal discourse and meaning. The boundaries of legal communities might be broader or narrower than state borders. I consider uses of proportionality by European courts or by transnational actors as equally *legal* and not (or not solely) as dictated by a certain economic rationality. In different settings, proportionality is appropriated by different groups of legal actors. The relevance of the different types of research material in making sense of its content varies accordingly. Thus, while in France, the most sophisticated analyses on proportionality are found in academic writings, in England, judges have had a more important role in developing proportionality's semantic content and only recently have scholars taken the lead in this respect. The use of proportionality language in official legal texts such as the constitution, parliamentary statutes and administrative decisions also offers information about its content and indicates its importance for legal actors. Such use is much more current in Greece, where proportionality enjoys explicit constitutional status, than in the other cases. While in practice proportionality language is often employed in the field of fundamental rights, connection to rights is not necessary. The scope of the research is not limited in this respect. All uses of proportionality as a legal language are relevant to my analysis, insofar as they can serve to make sense of its content.

Legal concepts, categories and distinctions used in a particular jurisdiction reflect and constitute local lawyers' peculiar '*decoupage du monde*',[145] their way of imagining the real and of characterising social situations. Different legal worldviews are themselves based on local narratives, collectively shared representations of the past. Like myths,

[143] Legrand (2002), p. 237.
[144] Pottage (2014), p. 147. I thank Vincent Réveillère for illuminating discussions on this point.
[145] Expression used by Thomas (1973), p. 113.

these narratives are used by legal actors to explain the present and to aspire to the future.[146] They shape local representations, taboos and rituals, local ways of thinking about law and producing legal knowledge, legal actors' 'collective mental programmes' when interpreting legal texts and when producing legal arguments.[147] In other words, law reflects and constitutes a particular legal culture. Legal culture defines 'a realm of possibility' for legal argumentation and meaning, it defines 'the ultimate horizons for what can plausibly be considered rhetorically convincing and morally acceptable'.[148] Proportionality, when received in different legal discourses, affects the way legal actors think about law and its relation to society. At the same time, it is itself affected by culture. It remodels local narratives and is itself reinvented within them. In different settings, proportionality is understood as a ground of review, a method or a principle, depending on what is locally perceived as important by legal actors, on local sources of law and on local ways of producing legal knowledge, what Sacco calls 'legal formants'.[149] Proportionality's success or failure ultimately depends on local legal actors' expectations of its use and on locally prevalent criteria for evaluating legal arguments.[150] In different legal contexts, proportionality is ascribed different meanings. Apart from a principle of rights optimisation, it can also be a vector of modernisation, rationalisation or Europeanisation. What is more, these terms themselves might be understood very differently across jurisdictions and across time.

The use of the term 'culture' does not presuppose the internal coherence of local legal worldviews. As Nelken insists, legal culture is a product of historical contingencies and its internal contradictions leave place for interpretation and manipulation by legal actors, for struggle and disagreement.[151] Or, in Geertz's terms, 'the elements of a culture's own negation are, with greater or lesser force, included within it'.[152] The practice of proportionality reflects the internal incoherency of local legal cultures. A survey of its evolution in each context shows that proportionality's meaning is constantly being negotiated and changing. At different times, proportionality is appropriated by different groups of

[146] Lévi-Strauss (1955), p. 430.
[147] Legrand (1996), p. 56.
[148] Legrand (2002), p. 241.
[149] Sacco (1991).
[150] Bomhoff (2012b), pp. 84 f.
[151] Nelken (2007), p. 114.
[152] Geertz (2000), pp. 404 f., esp. p. 406.

legal actors (lawyers, judges, scholars or law-makers) and is inserted into local debates about formality, rights, European law, public prerogatives or judicial power. Asymmetries or incoherencies in its use, locally specific critiques and typically proposed alternative arguments might reverberate with more fundamental disagreements between legal ideologies within the same culture.[153] Taking the example of proportionality and reasonableness in the UK, Cohn has shown that the historical survey of the evolution of legal transfers can offer a better understanding of tensions that traditionally exist in their host culture.[154] My purpose is to push the analysis further and show that locally specific stories of proportionality reflect its locally specific meaning and what local legal actors expect of its use. The comparison of different local meanings of proportionality reveals a lot about the legal cultures in which these meanings evolved and about the possibilities of legal convergence.

The use of the term 'culture' purports to connect comparative law to developments in cultural anthropology. It purports to accentuate the fact that law is a symbolic system that, like science, politics, economics or religion, offers a complete vision of the world. Kahn explains that: '[F]rom within law, we can look out on science and politics – law offers an understanding of both. But it does so without collapsing into either.'[155] Thus, comparative law is an exercise in cultural interpretation and translation, concerned with law's own structures.[156] It does not purport to reconstruct moral theories hidden behind judicial decisions using proportionality, or the political or other ideologies that underpin scholarly proportionality doctrines. Its aim is to understand legal cases and doctrines in their own context, to represent them in an intelligible way by displaying their culturally specific logic. Legal culture is neither universal nor individual; it is connected to the identity of a particular legal community and constitutes this community's self-understanding. Of course, legal communities are situated in a certain society and at a certain moment of history. Legal culture itself is influenced by social, economic, political and other circumstances. Still, the cultural study of law does not collapse into social or political science. While science aims at

[153] On the importance of past debates for reconstructing the meaning of legal arguments and legal actors' expectations, see Bomhoff (2012b), pp. 81 f. The author refers to the contextualist approach in intellectual history. On the 'crystallisation' of legal debates, see Balkin (1986).

[154] Cohn (2010).

[155] Kahn (2004), pp. 2686 f., esp. p. 2692.

[156] Geertz (1983), p. 218.

explaining and predicting causes and effects, the study of legal culture aims at 'making sense' of legal concepts, rules and techniques.[157] From this point of view, the study of local meanings of proportionality is very different from sociological or political analyses of its spread and of the spread of global constitutionalism more generally.[158]

This does not mean that the interpretation of legal cultures is simply interpretation of legal norms or doctrinal analysis, like the one performed by local legal actors. The purpose of the research is not to conclude on three general proportionality theories or doctrines, one for each national context, and to list similarities and differences between them. Instead, it is to expose the unstated and taken for granted elements of local legal thought, the aspects of legal reasoning that are fundamental for local lawyers but remain unnoticed, because they are deemed to be common-sensical.[159] The reflective attitude adopted here involves a symmetrical study of different instances of legal discourse, regardless of their relative importance for local legal actors. Hence, the material of the research is not limited to what are perceived as 'great texts' or important decisions concerning proportionality in different contexts. Proportionality's local meaning is also sought in features that domestic lawyers perceive as mundane. Failed proportionality arguments or theories, neglected cases and unmethodical *obiter* expressed in proportionality terms, forgotten structural transformations that proportionality has been subject to or has itself produced and commonly shared misinterpretations of proportionality decisions are just as important as the solemn pronouncement of the principle in the constitution. As Geertz points out, common-sense wisdom 'is shamelessly and unapologetically ad hoc. It comes in epigrams, proverbs, *obiter dicta*, jokes, anecdotes, *contes morales* – a clatter of gnomic utterances-not in formal doctrines, axiomized theories, or architectonic dogmas.'[160] Proportionality has an impressive capacity to express local lawyers' taken for granted assumptions, because it presents itself as common-sensical and inherent into legal reasoning. Indeed, proverbs such as 'You should never use a cannon to kill a sparrow' are often mobilised in its use.

Albeit ever-changing and difficult to grasp, the meaning of proportionality is public. It does not always coincide with what legal actors have in mind when 'speaking' proportionality, or with what their addressees

[157] Geertz (2000), p. 13.
[158] For an example of such a study, see Hirschl (2004).
[159] On this aspect of culture, see Cotterrell (2006), p. 722.
[160] Geertz (1983), p. 90.

finally understand. In Brett's words: '[T]he publicity of language defies its complete appropriation to the purposes of any individual agent.'[161] My purpose is not to *speculate* on legal actors' personal sources of inspiration and intellectual references when using proportionality, when such influences are not explicit or recoverable from the discursive context. Further, it is not because a judge or a scholar referred to proportionality as a principle of rights optimisation that she *actually used* it as such. Even when employing a transnational idiom and even when referring to foreign authors and doctrines, local legal actors understand and use proportionality in their particular way, according to the constraints that the discursive context imposes on them. In order to identify and make sense of the local meanings of proportionality we need to get rid of our a priori ideas and beliefs concerning legal actors, but also of our perception of proportionality itself as a transplant.

This is not to say that cross-border influences do not exist. Lawyers do travel and read foreign legal writings. They translate them into their own legal language, often with the purpose of provoking legal change. The spread of proportionality itself is the perfect evidence of legal promiscuity. The cultural study of law does not exclude the possibility of observing such influences or the possibility of legal convergence. The plural contexts in which proportionality is used inscribe their peculiar logic into it and charge it with different semantic baggage.[162] As proportionality spreads, its semantic baggage, too, might cross borders. In some cases, proportionality is indeed very akin to the prong-structured framework described by the mainstream proportionality literature and assumes a function of rights protection that is not very different from the one it has in the global human rights paradigm. In the case law of European supranational courts in particular, proportionality acquires its proper dynamic and postulates the adaptation of national legal discourses accordingly. However, legal actors respond differently to European or other pressures, following particular local patterns of legal change and local understandings of Europeanisation. My purpose is not to deny the European or other integration dynamics of proportionality. Rather, it is to show that they operate in much more complex ways than the dominant rhetoric of convergence assumes.

The analysis that follows is divided into three parts. The purpose of Part I is to question the dominant narrative of the spread of

[161] Brett (2002), p. 123.
[162] Ibid.

proportionality as a successful transplant. It starts with a presentation of the global model of proportionality, which is subsequently contrasted with the peculiar versions of proportionality observed in France, England and Greece. Through a historical account of proportionality's emergence and evolution in these contexts, Part I shows that, even though proportionality has provoked discursive change, it has rarely corresponded to a pronged structure for rights-based adjudication. In some cases, it is not even used by the judge, but rather serves scholars in their reconstruction of judicial discourse. In other cases, while it is employed in judicial reasoning, it does not involve judicial balancing. And in yet others, proportionality is not connected to rights at all.

Part II purports to make sense of the three different proportionality stories described in Part I, by reconstructing the cultural contexts in which they unfold. It provides three culturally specific meanings of proportionality that render differences in its local forms and functions less enigmatic. It shows that legal actors' expectations of proportionality's transfer have been very different to the optimisation of rights advanced by the mainstream literature. Even though, under the impulsion of proportionality, local cultures have been subject to change in the directions of modernisation, rationalisation and Europeanisation, the local understandings of these terms and the reactions that proportionality has provoked are very different, even opposed.

Part III focuses on the role of proportionality in the process of European integration. It shows that in the ECJ and the ECtHR case law, proportionality acquires a particular function connected to the realisation of the supranational goals that these courts promote. While this creates formal pressure for the consistent application of proportionality in domestic contexts, it does not always lead to convergence or harmonisation, not even in the scope of European law. Proportionality deploys its Europeanisation dynamics differently, according to local patterns of influence and change, to local narratives of European integration, and to local visions of Europe, which themselves, of course, change over time.

PART I

Questioning the Success of Proportionality

The Global Model of Proportionality. Alexy and his followers describe proportionality as a method for the optimal realisation of constitutional principles. They conceive of it as a model of legal reasoning and argumentation used when a statute or a lower ranking norm restricts the realisation of a constitutional right.[1] As such, proportionality is primarily purported to serve judges. In theory, it is part of a twofold reasoning: first, the decision-maker identifies the restriction to the right in question; then, she proceeds to a concrete examination of its constitutionality according to the proportionality test. Proportionality invites the decision-maker to take into account certain types of consideration, which differ according to the stage of analysis in which she engages. It is an argumentative framework that 'aims at clarifying constitutional rights concepts, thereby presenting a way to structure one's argument when reasoning about constitutional rights'.[2] Proportionality claims to be neutral with regard to substantive outcomes. It merely represents a structure within which substantive moral arguments can be mobilised. It provides 'little more than a check-list of individually necessary and collectively sufficient criteria that need to be met for the assessment' of the relevant arguments.[3]

Scholars generally identify a four-pronged structure as representative of the correct application of the model. Proportionality is analysed in a check as to the legitimacy of the reviewed measures' end, the suitability of the means chosen, the necessity of the restrictions and their *stricto sensu* proportionality. The legitimate end and the *stricto sensu* proportionality requirements aim to optimise rights within the scope of what is *normatively* possible in the legal system. The suitability and the necessity requirements aim to optimise rights to the extent that it is *factually*

[1] Barak (2012), p. 151.
[2] Möller (2007), p. 458.
[3] Kumm (2009a), p. 6.

possible.[4] Proportionality theorists hold that the clear distinction of the various subtests is important, since each one performs a special function. Only after the decision-maker has verified the fulfilment of the conditions imposed by the first stage, can she move to the second one, and so on. Questions of institutional legitimacy and competence are accommodated through the variation of the intensity of scrutiny under the different prongs. On this point, the Alexyan theory considerably benefited from development by scholars with a more institutionally sensitive approach.[5]

The first two stages of proportionality are concerned with the reviewed authority's intents. They are threshold requirements, which do not entail balancing between competing principles. Stone Sweet and Mathews observe that they are often used by courts 'to pay [their] respects, first, to the importance of the policy consideration generally, and, second, to the legislator's own deliberations on the proportionality of the law'.[6] The legitimate aim requirement implies that the law-maker can limit a constitutional right only for certain reasons connected to the preservation of foundational social values. Legitimate aims are generously defined to leave broad discretion to the reviewed authorities.[7] The suitability requirement is conceived of as a merely factual test, which purports to guarantee that the means chosen by the primary decision-maker are rationally connected to the goal of the reviewed act. For it to be fulfilled, it is sufficient that the measure in question promotes to a certain extent or is likely to promote in the future, the goal of the primary decision-maker. The suitability test is comparable to the 'rational basis review' in American constitutional law. The appropriateness of means is assessed through a prognosis of factual and social probabilities. The burden of proof lies with the reviewed authority, which must provide the relevant information.[8]

The next step of proportionality analysis involves necessity review. Under this prong, the judge must check for the existence of less restrictive alternatives to the reviewed act. In order to lead to the invalidation of the reviewed act, the alternative measure must provide equal advancement of the public goal pursued by the reviewed act 'quantitatively, qualitatively,

4 Alexy (2003a), pp. 135 f.

5 See, among others, Rivers (2006), p. 174; Klatt and Meister (2012a), chaps 4 and 6.

6 Stone Sweet and Mathews (2008), pp. 163–4.

7 Klatt and Meister (2012a), pp. 48 f.

8 See Barak (2012), pp. 303 f. On issues of reliability, see Rivers (2007), p. 167; Klatt and Meister (2012a), pp. 109 f.

and probability-wise'.[9] Furthermore, that alternative restriction of the right in question must be less harmful, considering 'the scope of the limitation, its effect, its duration, and the likelihood of its occurrence'.[10] These elements are assessed objectively and do not concern the state of mind of the reviewed authority. Less restrictive alternatives must not affect other parameters, such as the cost of the pursuit of the goal, the realisation of other constitutional values or the burdens imposed on third parties.[11] The necessity test shares a lot with the 'narrowly tailored' requirement in American constitutional doctrine, even though it remains broader.[12] Proportionality scholars attribute particular importance to this stage and observe that in some jurisdictions it is the core requirement, since judges de facto engage in practical reasoning under the necessity prong.[13]

Whereas the three previous subtests serve to ascertain the existence of *genuine* conflicts between constitutional principles, the requirement of proportionality in the narrow sense involves the resolution of such conflicts.[14] Under this prong, the decision-maker examines whether the limitation imposed on the constitutional right is of proportionate importance to the gain in relation to its legitimate goal. In other words, this stage of proportionality analysis consists in a balancing exercise, based on the evaluation of how severely the various alternative measures affect the constitutional right at stake.[15] The reasoning that it implies has been schematised by Alexy in the famous Law of Balancing: 'The greater the degree of non-satisfaction of, or detriment to, one principle, the greater must be the importance of satisfying the other'.[16] The Law of Balancing is also illustrated by a mathematical formula, called weight formula. The balancing enterprise professed by the proportionality theory does not presuppose Benthamite quantifications or cost-benefit analysis, but the

[9] Barak (2012), p. 324.
[10] Ibid, p. 326.
[11] Ibid, p. 317. On the suitability and necessity tests, see also Möller (2012), pp. 193 f.
[12] See Kumm (2004), p. 580; Barak (2012), p. 333.
[13] This is the case of the ECJ and the ECtHR, for example. See Stone Sweet and Mathews (2008), pp. 163 f.
[14] See Möller (2012), p. 181.
[15] Alexy (2002), p. 401.
[16] Alexy (2002), p. 102. The Law of Balancing has been reformulated and refined by many scholars, purporting to clarify the nature of the various factors taken into account. See, for example, Klatt and Meister (2012a); Barak (2012), pp. 340 f.

confrontation of practical and moral arguments.[17] At the balancing stage, the decision-maker unavoidably engages in practical reasoning. Proportionality requires judges to render explicit the substantive moral theory that they apply when deciding cases.[18]

Proportionality theorists generally describe two types of balancing: 'definitional' and ad hoc. The former leads to the establishment of a norm that is then applied to other cases without further balancing; the latter is applied from case to case, taking into account the particular circumstances.[19] It is this second type of balancing that Alexy and his followers advance.[20] Indeed, proportionality excludes a pre-established hierarchy between constitutional norms, 'freezing in place a prior act of balancing',[21] in the form of categories or precedents. Its application does not involve legal analysis of the conventional kind, based on categorical reasoning and working from authoritative legal pronouncements. This follows from proportionality theorists' particular vision of legal reasoning as a 'special case' of practical reasoning, which obeys special formal and institutional constraints.[22] Proportionality aims to liberate judges from such constraints and to focus on the substantive justification of legal solutions. The importance of formal sources in legal argumentation varies between the different authors. Beatty, for example, rejects arguments resulting from the strict interpretation of legal texts or from precedent and proposes to focus on the facts of each case.[23] In contrast, most scholars accept the importance of legal texts, precedent and legal certainty.[24]

Three Different Stories on Proportionality. The proportionality theory is underpinned by the idea that proportionality has roughly the same content in the systems where it is received. Thus, Barak's book aims to provide a 'universal understanding of the concept of proportionality in constitutional democracies'.[25] Perju argues that, despite differences in its

17 Alexy (2002), pp. 13, 99, 409; Klatt and Meister (2012a), p. 57 and fn. 74. On the distinction of different types of balancing, see Möller (2012), pp. 137 f.
18 Alexy (2002), p. 105; Kumm (2006a), pp. 21 f.; Klatt and Meister (2012a), pp. 22 f.
19 Aleinikoff (1987), p. 948, citing Melville Nimmer.
20 Alexy (2003b), p. 433. For a concise presentation of Alexy's theory of law, see Alexy (2008).
21 Stone Sweet and Mathews (2008), pp. 87–8. See also Waldron (1994), pp. 819–20.
22 Kumm (2006a), pp. 3 f. and 12 f.; Alexy (2010), pp. 212 f.; Klatt and Meister (2012a), pp. 51 f.
23 Beatty (2004), pp. 72 f.
24 See, for example, Alexy (2002), p. 376.
25 Barak (2012), p. 4.

application, the formal structure of proportionality analysis has remained unchanged. In his words: 'Virtually everywhere, at least at the level of national courts, judges structure their analysis using the formal four-step structure.'[26] Focusing on the method of the review, Beatty also contends that no matter the subject matter or the nature of the right invoked, 'the test is always the same'.[27] And Schlink suggests that application of proportionality has had a 'standardizing effect' on different constitutional cultures.[28] Interestingly, Cohen-Eliya and Porat point out that due to its compelling appeal as 'a logical, coherent and systematic doctrine' proportionality might displace local doctrines that have long been shaped and reshaped to adapt to their environment.[29] The authors call this characteristic of proportionality 'doctrinal imperialism' and once again give the example of a universally adaptable species of bird 'that migrates beyond its natural environment and drives out the local species in its new environment'.[30]

A survey of the emergence and evolution of proportionality in France, England and Greece shows that proportionality is indeed an imperialist doctrine. As it spreads in different systems, it tends to replace pre-existing methods of reasoning, or at least to reframe them. In some cases, proportionality becomes hegemonic. The pervasiveness of proportionality gives the observer the impression of success. Since legal actors, and particularly judges, refer to proportionality, they *must* mean the global model and they *must* be applying the proportionality framework. Nonetheless, following Bomhoff, one should note that when judges use proportionality language, it does not necessarily mean that they *think* within the proportionality framework. Just as when they do not use any argument, it does not mean that they do not think at all.[31] Once we see proportionality as a form of language and we focus on the way it is inserted into local discursive structures, the impression of proportionality's success is qualified. Attention to practice reveals that the use of proportionality by local legal actors has been very different to the structure that the proportionality theory professes. In fact, the doctrinal imperialism of

[26] Perju (2017), section 1.
[27] Beatty (2004), p. 160.
[28] Schlink (2012), p. 736.
[29] Cohen-Eliya and Porat (2013), p. 150.
[30] Ibid.
[31] Bomhoff (2010), pp. 114 f.

proportionality does not imply that it is applied in a logical, coherent or systematic way.

The purpose of this part is to establish an *état de lieux* of the different forms and functions of proportionality language across jurisdictions and across time. The analysis consists of three different stories about the emergence and spread of proportionality as a form of legal language, that is, as a legal way of speaking. Legal actors in France, England and Greece did not always reason in proportionality terms. While in some cases homonym or quasi-homonym concepts existed in legal writings, they were not part of the domestic legal webs of significance neither did they convey a particular dynamic. Since the 1970s, under the influence of fundamental rights rhetoric and the case law of European courts, proportionality acquired its own legal content in domestic contexts. But, even after its emergence, the use of the language of proportionality has not been uniform in the different systems or stable across time. It has been determined by the discursive contexts into which proportionality was inserted and evolves.

Part I provides information about proportionality's connection with pre-existing concepts, and the discursive change that it has provoked. The study of the semantic content of proportionality is complemented by a more contextual account of the role of proportionality in the domestic legal discourse, and of the reactions of public lawyers to its emergence and spread. From the point of view of comparative law, the purpose of this part is relatively modest. Across the various chapters, I observe similarities or differences between the domestic versions of proportionality and the transnational proportionality model described in the Alexyan legacy, which at this point serves as a *tertium comparationis*.

The spread of proportionality in France is characterised by domestic actors' search for continuity with pre-existing concepts and methods of review. The use of proportionality language has not brought about radical changes to existing legal structures but has rather been accommodated within them (Chapter 2). Continuity with existing concepts and structures has also been decisive for the use of proportionality in English public law. In this context, proportionality has always been defined against the background of *Wednesbury* reasonableness, as either a departure from it, or a confirmation of it (Chapter 3). In contrast, existing language structures have hardly controlled the spread of proportionality in Greece. The emergence of proportionality in the Council of State case law met with the enthusiasm of domestic lawyers and soon proportionality spread in domestic legal discourse. Since 2001, proportionality is explicitly entrenched in the constitution, and in its Alexyan version, it is a hegemonic method of reasoning in Greek legal thought. However, the use of proportionality in judicial practice is more nuanced (Chapter 4).

2

Proportionality in French Public Law: *Plus Ça Change, Plus C'est la Même Chose*[32]

If a French public lawyer were to read this work, she might be surprised, perhaps even frustrated, by the story that follows. It is a commonplace in France that limiting the study of a method to the instances where the judge *explicitly* applies it is a methodological error. This is especially the case for proportionality. Thus, starting his contribution on proportionality, Kalflèche tells us that, while the judge sometimes employs the term 'proportionate', 'it would be a methodological error' to limit the instances of proportionality review to the decisions that explicitly refer to this term.[33] Similarly, Duclerq affirms that: '[I]t is hardly doubted that, to study the "origin" of proportionality, properly speaking, by focusing on the entrenchment of a term, is a trap. The idea does not need to be named in order to have been thought of and to find application in reality.'[34]

In the minds of French public lawyers, proportionality represents much more than a discourse used in judicial justifications and in legal practice. It is a value, an ideal that finds its source in Aristotelian thought and underpins the legal mottos used by Roman jurists.[35] It cannot be reduced to the formulas and expressions used in judicial decisions, since it exists independently of them. In order to grasp its essence, one has to search for its origins in previous case law, in other legal orders, in other historic periods or even in other disciplines. Put briefly, there is a very strong and commonly shared belief among French public lawyers that proportionality pre-existed its emergence as a discourse, it has long been present in case law and legislation, and continues to exist in positive law and practice, even when no explicit reference is made to it. Its contemporary proliferation is accepted as a natural necessity, the result of an

[32] This expression is used by Graziadei (2006), p. 462. The expression is inspired by Karr (1871).
[33] Kalflèche (2009), p. 46, before fn. 3.
[34] Duclerq (2015), pp. 1–2. Similarly, Philippe (1990), pp. 7 f.
[35] See, for example, Muzny (2008).

'irresistible rise',[36] connected to the human rights turn of modern legal systems.

My approach departs from the French common sense on proportionality in that it pays particular attention to the way thoughts are expressed, to the *language* used by lawyers in particular contexts, and to the way this language has evolved. While ideas, methods or concepts similar or comparable to proportionality have existed before its emergence in French public law, my inquiry concerns the *particular* expression of such ideas, methods or concepts *in proportionality terms.* It is only since the 1970s that French public lawyers have found it opportune or convincing to express their thoughts by using the language proportionality. Why has this been so? What has this language added to already existing linguistic structures? Has it been used more in the legal literature than in judicial practice, and if so why? How has this language evolved since? Does the use of proportionality in this context fit the global model of proportionality?

France is among the *mauvais élèves* of proportionality, namely, among the systems that for long resisted its pervasive dynamic. Proportionality emerged in expropriation case law during the early 1970s, in a context of dissatisfaction with the Council of State's methods (Section 2.1). Soon, the concept of proportionality in the legal literature was detached from the actual application of proportionality as a norm or principle and started being used in the systematisation of case law (Section 2.2). In the context of constitutionalisation of the legal order, the Constitutional Council affirmed the constitutional status of proportionality (Section 2.3). Since the mid 1990s, constitutional scholars started reconstructing the constitutional case law as instances of three-pronged proportionality analysis. Proportionality analysis was soon applied as a method for the adjudication of constitutional rights (Section 2.4). However, a survey of the relevant case law reveals that proportionality has brought about no radical changes in judicial reasoning. It is inconsistently applied and rarely involves a value-laden balancing (Section 2.5).

2.1 The Emergence of Proportionality in Administrative Law

The Absence of Proportionality Until the 1970s. Even though *Benjamin* is known as the most emblematic application of proportionality in the French context, the Council of State did not employ

[36] Martens (1992).

proportionality terminology in this case. Neither did contemporary commentators.[37] In the first edition of the *Grands arrêts de la jurisprudence administrative* (*GAJA*) in 1956, the term 'proportionality' was not mentioned in the comment on *Benjamin* and probably not anywhere else in the book either.[38] This is because it was not until the 1970s that proportionality emerged as a particular language in French public law. It was first employed in the field of expropriation.

The Emergence of Judicial Balancing. Until 1971, the Council of State affirmed *in abstracto* the public utility of expropriation, checking only whether, according to the reviewed authority, the public project in question served a public interest goal. However, this deferent stance was criticised in the *doctrine*, as French lawyers call the extra-judicial analysis of positive law. This solution was perceived as too formalist and not adapted to the reality of administrative action. In *Ville Nouvelle Est*, the *Commissaire de gouvernement* Braibant proposed to his colleagues to abandon this traditional case law.[39] According to him, the concrete circumstances of the case, such as the choice of the expropriated lands, should no longer be seen as a matter of *opportunité* but of legality, which could be reviewed by the court. The public utility appraisal should involve 'balancing the advantages [of an operation] against its disadvantages, its cost against its benefit, or as the economists would say, its disutility against its utility'.[40] Braibant defined the cost of an expropriation as not only financial but also social.

The Council of State Plenum followed Braibant's opinion. In what was to become a *considérant de principe*, the judges declared that:

> an operation cannot be legally declared of public utility, unless the harm to private property, the financial cost and the social disadvantages that it entails are not excessive with regard to the interest that it presents.[41]

Judicial balancing in the form of cost-benefit analysis (*bilan coût-avantages*) was explicitly announced as a method for the scrutiny

[37] CE, 19 May 1933, *Benjamin*, nos. 17413 and 17520, ECLI:FR:CEORD:1933:17413.19330519; Mestre (1934).

[38] See Prélot (2013), making the same remark. The *GAJA* (Cassin et al., 1956) is one of the most important books in French public law, containing comments on milestone administrative law decisions. It is written by members of the Council in State and academics.

[39] Braibant, 'Conclusions sur CE Ass., 28 mai 1971, *Ville Nouvelle Est*', *Rev. Adm*, no. 142 (1971), p. 422.

[40] Ibid, pp. 425–6.

[41] CE (Pl.), 28 May 1971, *Ville Nouvelle Est*, *Rev. Adm*, p. 427, no. 78825, ECLI:FR:CEASS:1971:78825.19710528.

concerning public utility declarations. The court used the same reasoning in other decisions during the same year, always to declare that the disadvantages of the reviewed projects were not serious enough to deprive them of their public utility character.[42] Some saw the recognition of a new general principle in the Council of State case law.[43]

Although the *bilan* did not lead to an intensive scrutiny of administrative decisions, scholars at first reacted with enthusiasm to this outburst of judicial balancing. In the instrumentalist rhetoric dominant in the French *doctrine*, the abandonment of traditional formalism for more pragmatist and efficient judicial review methods was generally seen as progress, even though judges were usually prudent in their first applications.[44] Interestingly, in the beginning, it was not proportionality language that was used to describe the balancing operation to which the council proceeded. The connection of the *bilan* to proportionality took place only one year later, in the observations of another *Commissaire du gouvernement*.

The Connection of Proportionality to Judicial Balancing. Examining the public utility of a highway near Nice, Morisot proposed an *in concreto* review to his colleagues.[45] Even though he observed that the preliminary procedure followed by the administration was not legally flawed, he argued for a judicial evaluation of the public utility of the project, which would include an appreciation of its social cost. In Morisot's words, 'the notion of public utility is relative' and cannot be appreciated and scrutinised without balancing the advantages and the disadvantages of a project. In his view:

> the legality of the exercise of prerogatives requires that the damage caused to public and private rights and interests remains proportionate to the advancement of the public interest that one can expect of the imposed restriction.[46]

Proportionality language was thus officially connected to judicial balancing. Morisot went on to appreciate in detail the advantages and disadvantages of the plan in question. Despite its uncontested utility for its future users and for the residents of Nice, the highway would cause

[42] CE (Pl.), 20 October 1972, *Societe civile Sainte-Marie-de-l'Assomption*, no. 78829, ECLI: FR:CEASS:1972:78829.19721020.
[43] Lemasurier (1974).
[44] Waline (1974), p. 812.
[45] Morisot, 'Conclusions sur CE Ass., 20 octobre 1972, *Société Sainte-Marie-de-l'Assomption*', *RDP*, 1973, p. 843.
[46] Ibid, p. 848.

very serious disturbance to a psychiatric hospital in proximity. Morisot thus concluded that, 'failing to ensure the necessary reconciliation between public interests, [. . .] the administration had exceeded its power'.[47] In the case *Société civile Sainte-Marie-de-l'Assomption*, the Council of State Plenum partially followed Morisot's *conclusions*. It found that the construction of the highway undermined the general interest and annulled the declaration of its public utility.[48] However, the court made no reference to proportionality or proportion whatsoever.

One must wait another year to see an explicit reference to proportionality in the official justification of judicial balancing. In *Grassin*, the Council of State concluded that the construction of an airport in Peyratte was not an operation of public utility. The court found that the advantages of this project would be unimportant, whereas its cost would be 'out of proportion with the financial resources of the municipality'.[49] Similarly, in 1974, the Council of State annulled the declaration of public utility of a town road plan in Corsica, since the damages it would cause to neighbouring properties were 'out of proportion' with the advantages that it entailed.[50]

Proportionality as a General Principle in the French *Doctrine*. In 1974, two influential extra-judicial contributions argued for the explicit recognition of the 'principle of proportionality' in domestic judicial review of administrative discretionary powers.[51] The first was written by Dreyfus, at the time *Maîtresse de conférences* in Paris. The second was the work of the *Commissaire du gouvernement* Braibant, who reconstructed his own reasoning in *Ville Nouvelle Est* as an application of the principle of proportionality. In these writings, proportionality required a relation of 'fair proportion' between three elements: the factual situation, the administrative decision, and its goal.[52] It designated a legal requirement of adequacy of administrative action, which was to be appreciated according to the particular factual circumstances on which the decision was grounded, the *motifs de fait*. Braibant connected proportionality to equity and to the protection of individuals, using Jellinek's well-known

[47] Ibid, p. 853.

[48] CE (Pl.), 20 October 1972, *Société civile Sainte-Marie-de-l'Assomption*, no. 78829, ECLI:FR:CEASS:1972:78829.19721020.

[49] CE, 26 October 1973, *Sieur Grassin*, no. 83261, ECLI:FR:CEASS:1973:83261.19731026.

[50] CE, 4 October 1974, no. 86978, ECLI:FR:CESJS:1974:86978.19741004.

[51] Dreyfus (1974); Braibant (1974).

[52] Dreyfus (1974), pp. 695–6; Braibant (1974), p. 298.

image of killing a sparrow with a canon.[53] In the same vein, Dreyfus perceived proportionality review as a method for eliminating administrative abuses and for 'distinguishing between the just and the unjust'.[54] A similar idea can be found in Dubouis' study of the abuse of power.[55]

Both Dreyfus and Braibant 'read' the development of the Council of State's methods of judicial review since the 1930s, most notably the necessity and the manifest error review, as expressing the idea of proportionality. In the words of Braibant, French administrative judges were applying the principle 'without knowing it, or more precisely, without saying it'.[56] However, for both authors, the explicit recognition of a general principle of proportionality as an autonomous legal norm would be a fortunate evolution.

In this regard, they encouraged the supreme administrative court to follow the example of foreign courts. Dreyfus referred to three decisions by the ILO administrative tribunal, where proportionality had been applied in the field of disciplinary sanctions. She held that even though traditionally the Council of State was perceived as a source of inspiration for foreign and international legal systems, principles developed in these systems could be 'imported' and applied in domestic law without disturbing its fundamental traits.[57] Braibant also underscored that proportionality had been applied by the ILO administrative tribunal (although he did not fail to point out that the *Conseiller d'Etat* Letourneur presided over the tribunal), and that it was recognised as a general principle of constitutional status in Germany and Switzerland. Both authors emphasised that this would not be the first time that the French Council of State was inspired by foreign jurisdictions. Only some years before, the manifest error of appreciation had been imported from Geneva to serve the judicial review of the factual grounds of administrative acts.[58]

The 1974 contributions consolidated the linking of proportionality to necessity and judicial balancing in domestic public law. Proportionality was inscribed in the rhetoric that surrounded the practice of judicial review. Thereafter, it became part of the reflection on the limits of administrative discretion. Braibant's opinion in the *Ville Nouvelle Est* case became a point of reference concerning the study of the concept in

53 Braibant (1974), p. 298.
54 Dreyfus (1974), p. 703.
55 Dubouis (1962), p. 402.
56 Braibant (1974), p. 299.
57 Dreyfus (1974), pp. 691–2.
58 Ibid, p. 692; Braibant (1974), p. 306.

French public law. It has been cited in virtually every analysis on the matter ever since. In this way, proportionality was instituted as an autonomous administrative law concept and started being the object of technical scholarly systematisations.[59] Scholars identified several degrees or intensities of proportionality review, what Bienvenu called 'proportionality scale [*échelle de proportionnalité*]',[60] a term still used by French public lawyers. By the late 1970s proportionality had acquired its first enthusiasts. Yet it was much more important in the writings of the *doctrine* than in the actual reasoning of public law courts. The asymmetry between the perception of proportionality in the literature and its use in practice persisted at least for a decade.

2.2 Conspicuous in Spite of Its Absence

The Failure of Proportionality in Practice. In spite of expectations and pressure to the contrary, proportionality long remained unannounced as a general principle in the Council of State case law. Proportionality terminology was often used in town planning and expropriation decisions, as well as in cases concerning taxation or the remuneration of public employees. Rather than a general principle concerning administrative restrictions, however, it usually represented a mathematic equation. At most, it expressed a general requirement of financial prudence. Proportionality was not announced as a general principle in legislation either. In certain contexts, it had acquired a particular autonomy that made some scholars speak of 'a particular principle'.[61] This was especially the case for the *proportionnalité de l'impôt*, where the concept preserved its arithmetic nature. Only some rare legal texts announced a legal requirement of proportionality. Even when applying these texts, however, courts did not use the vocabulary of proportionality. Instead, they preferred more classical methods of reasoning like the manifest error standard or necessity review.[62] Clearly, although proportionality was a term commonly used by French public lawyers, it did not correspond to a particular reasoning structure or method of review in case law.

The same goes for the Constitutional Council. The rising fundamental rights language in the council's decisions seemed apt to the employment

[59] Guibal (1978).

[60] Bienvenu (1979), p. 116.

[61] Philippe (1990), p. 88.

[62] See, for example, CE, 28 January 1987, no. 37945, ECLI:FR:CESSR:1987:37945.19870128; 12 June 1987, no. 75276, ECLI:FR:CESSR:1987:75276.19870612.

of proportionality terminology. Some scholars saw proportionality as a method for the reconciliation of constitutional rights. Thus, proportionality was deemed to be the principle applied behind the manifest error review exercised by the constitutional judge since the early 1980s.[63] Yet the Constitutional Council never expressed its review in proportionality terms. Proportionality was sometimes employed as a mathematic assessment of representation.[64] However, it did not designate a constitutional principle, rule or structure of reasoning. Judges explicitly refused to acknowledge the existence of a strict proportionality requirement imposed on the legislator. The council sometimes invoked 'the arithmetic difficulties that the strict respect of proportionality would entail'.[65] In the words of Vedel, 'the legislator in the republican tradition has never respected a millimetred notion of equality'.[66]

Proportionality in Administrative Law *Doctrine* During the 1980s. Lacking anchorage in positive law, proportionality did not attract much interest from French academics, at least during the 1980s. Although its application through other judicial methods was a commonplace among French public lawyers, its structure or content was not specified, contrary to the meticulous and technical analyses of legal concepts that generally pervade in the French *doctrine*. Writing in 1990, Philippe was surprised by academics' lack of interest in a notion which was deemed as given and understood.[67]

Significantly, the two major studies on proportionality during the 1980s were framed in a transnational context. The first, written by Teitgen, an eminent lawyer in Paris, was presented at a conference in 1982 on 'the general principle of proportionality in the European legal order' and was included in a collective volume, in which most chapters were written in German.[68] The second, written by Costa, a member of the Council of State, later member and President of the ECtHR, was initially a speech presented during a meeting between the Council of State, the Constitutional Council and the ECtHR.[69]

63 Drago (1991), p. 265, citing Dominique Turpin. See also Bienvenu (1985).

64 Decision no. 83–162 DC, 20 July 1983, *Loi relative à la démocratisation du secteur public*, ECLI:FR:CC:1983:83.162.DC; Decision no. 86–218 DC, 18 November 1986, *Loi relative à la délimitation des circonscriptions pour l'élection des députés*, ECLI:FR:CC:1986:86.218.DC.

65 Decision no. 83–162, cons. 63.

66 Deliberation, 7 July 1987, p. 39, available at www.conseil-constitutionnel.fr.

67 Philippe (1990), p. 7.

68 Teitgen (1985).

69 Costa (1988).

Strangely, both studies affirmed the existence of a principle of proportionality in French positive law: '*mais le principe existe bien*'.[70] In these writings proportionality represented an 'unwritten rule for which [judges] use[d] periphrases'.[71] Broadly perceived as some kind of relation between the 'trilogy' of the concrete factual situation, the contested decision and the goal of public action, proportionality was deemed to be among those 'transversal concepts that imprint, implicitly, the whole of administrative action and largely overlap with the review exercised on it by the administrative judge'.[72] The notion was presented as conspicuous, in spite of the absence of its explicit recognition as a legal concept, rule or method. Proportionality was perceived as synonymous with methods used for the substantive review of administrative discretion, most notably the necessity and the manifest error tests. Appealing to some kind of moral-legal ideal or quality, it established consistency between the different judicial methods and justified their evolution.

Philippe's Thesis on Proportionality. Contiguous to the above contributions, an influential thesis was published in 1990. Its author is Philippe, a member of the *École d'Aix*, who situated himself in the progressive, anti-formalist camp of French public law research to which this *École* belonged. Philippe did not follow the traditional *deux parties, deux sous-parties* model and dedicated fifteen pages to the study of 'social sciences' and another thirty to the study of foreign and supranational legal systems. He defined proportionality broadly, as 'a requirement of a rational and consistent relation between two or more elements'.[73] Proportionality was inherent in concepts such as necessity, normal, harmony, balance and excess. Hence, it was omnipresent, 'likely to slide into the most recurrent legal rules'.[74] The concept expressed nothing more and nothing less than the relativity of legal norms; the fact that, in their announcement or in their application, every public authority (and especially the judge) should be guided by extra-legal considerations.

One of Philippe's major contributions was the distinction between two facets of proportionality. On the one hand, the *principle* of proportionality represented a value pursued through public action. It corresponded to a standard of consistency, rationality or efficiency, a 'non-written rule'

[70] Ibid, p. 434.
[71] Ibid.
[72] Ibid.
[73] Philippe (1990), p. 8.
[74] Ibid, p. 7.

imposed on every norm-producing authority.[75] On the other hand, the *scrutiny* of proportionality (*contrôle de proportionnalité*) designated something even vaster. While it comprised the instances where the judge monitored the proportionality of the reviewed decision to its ends, it further included all the cases in which proportionality was itself a means, an instrument used by the judge to increase the efficiency of judicial review. Proportionality scrutiny was thus an element of judicial reasoning, part of the *méthodes* of the administrative judge, even though this was not expressed in the reasoning structures of administrative case law.[76]

The distinction between *principe* and *contrôle* consolidated the shift between the perception of proportionality in the public law literature and the use of the term in practice. According to Philippe, proportionality was mainly monitored through methods of substantive review, including the scrutiny of the material exactness of facts, the manifest error, the *bilan* or the necessity test.[77] Its malleable character rendered it 'an ultimate weapon' against abuses on the part of public authorities.[78] What mainly characterised proportionality review was the quest for equilibrium, be it at an institutional level, between the powers of the judge and those of the reviewed authority, or at a substantive level, between antagonistic norms of the same scope.[79] Hence, proportionality established continuity between different methods of review and supported the scholarly systematisation of case law, so dear to the *École d'Aix* at the time.

Another major contribution of Philippe's thesis was the introduction of reflection on proportionality in constitutional law. Situating himself in a narrative typical of the *École d'Aix* (which has now become mainstream in French public law), Philippe stressed that the constitutional judge was inspired by the Council of State in the exercise of judicial review and in the application of proportionality in particular.[80] In this way, proportionality was perceived as a common-sense requirement imposed both on the administration and on the legislator. Although the legislator enjoyed a larger 'discretionary power',[81] this power was circumscribed by constitutional rules and by the proportionality scrutiny of the

[75] Ibid, pp. 9; 24 f.
[76] Ibid, pp. 9–10.
[77] Ibid, pp. 159 f.
[78] Ibid, p. 420.
[79] Ibid, pp. 109–10; 113–15; 198 f.
[80] Ibid, pp. 436 f.
[81] Ibid, p. 147.

Constitutional Council. In other words, just like the administration, the legislator should be consistent, rational and efficient. It is indicative that Philippe talks about a principle of 'good legislation' in the model of 'good administration'.[82] In this way, proportionality performed a 'function of unification' of all the branches of public law.[83]

Taking his cue from administrative law analyses on the matter, Philippe stressed the importance of the circumstances surrounding the application of proportionality. In his view, proportionality scrutiny should not be automatised, since the concept of proportionality itself 'rejects any spirit of systematisation'.[84] The intensity of the review should vary as a function of requirements of institutional expertise, which are more present in particular subject matters such as economic intervention.[85] In constitutional law, proportionality had a more significant role in the area of fundamental rights and freedoms, where the substantive aspect of the constitution was more pronounced.[86] Inherent in the notion of fundamental rights and freedoms, proportionality assumed a crucial function of intermediary (*relais*) between the perception of a right and the reconciliation of its exercise with countervailing values.[87] The analysis on this point is reminiscent of the transnational proportionality literature.

Philippe's work connected the administrative law concept of proportionality to fundamental rights discourse rising at the time in French constitutional law. Since 1990, proportionality has been commonly perceived as a technique for the reconciliation of competing constitutional values.[88] The Constitutional Council's reference to 'excessive interferences' with or to 'excessive hindrances' to constitutional rights and imperatives, or to 'the equilibrium that the respect of the constitution imposes to ensure' began to be perceived as implicit and variable instances of judicial balancing.[89] In parallel with these evolutions, the Constitutional Council explicitly affirmed proportionality as a constitutional principle, albeit with a more limited scope and function.

82 Ibid, p. 412.
83 Ibid, p. 427.
84 Ibid, p. 416.
85 Ibid, p. 395.
86 Ibid, pp. 342 f.
87 Ibid, pp. 83; 105 f.
88 Drago (1991).
89 See, for example, Goesel-Le Bihan (1997); Rousseau (2001), p. 137.

2.3 Affirming the Constitutional Basis of Proportionality

Proportionality and Necessity of Penalties in Constitutional Case Law. While, until the 1970s, proportionality did not constitute a public law concept, it was not unknown to French public lawyers. During the 1960s, Vedel had mentioned proportionality as a principle guaranteed by Article 8 of the Declaration of the Rights of Man and of the Citizen (*DDHC*).[90] This indicates that, before its application as a technique in the field of judicial balancing, proportionality had another content, which was much more morally charged. It corresponded to a requirement of moderation concerning criminal punishment, expressed in the work of modern philosophers and connected to the French Revolutionary texts. However, the Council of State had consistently refused to apply proportionality in this sense in the scrutiny of administrative sanctions.[91] This aspect of proportionality long remained a political moral ideal, rejected by judges and forsaken by public law scholars. It is thus not surprising that, until the mid 1980s, the connection of proportionality to the *DDHC* was not explicit in the case law of the Constitutional Council. Indeed, though Article 8 *DDHC* had already been invoked before the constitutional judges, it was usually the principle of legality of penalties and not proportionality that was at stake, even when it was the severity of a sentence that was contested.[92]

The first reference to proportionality in constitutional case law is found in decision *Loi relative à la lutte contre la criminalité et la délinquance*.[93] The bill brought before the Constitutional Council was purported to 'fight criminality and delinquency' and, among other repressive provisions, it defined a safety period (*période de sûreté*) during which convicted individuals could not obtain adjustment of their sentence. Opposition senators contested the compatibility of the legislation with the principle of necessity of punishment. According to the *Rapporteur* of the decision Jozeau-Marigné, the main constitutional problem was whether the principles of the 1789 Declaration were applicable in the execution of sentences or whether they only concerned their pronouncement. In his view, the principle at stake in this case was

[90] Vedel (1960).

[91] CE, 13 October 1967, no. 71629, ECLI:FR:CEORD:1967:71629.19671013; 12 July 1969, no. 72648, ECLI:FR:CEORD:1969:72648.19690712.

[92] See Decision no. 84–176 DC, 25 July 1984, *Loi modifiant la loi du 29 juillet 1982 sur la communication audiovisuelle et relative à certaines dispositions applicables aux services de communication audiovisuelle soumis à autorisation*, ECLI:FR:CC:1984:84.176.DC.

[93] Decision no. 86–215 DC, 3 September 1986, ECLI:FR:CC:1986:86.215.DC.

proportionality of punishment. He thus proposed a *considérant de principe*, in which the council would announce the extension of the application of proportionality to the execution of the penalties.[94]

Interestingly, the *Rapporteur* held the application of proportionality in the *pronouncement* of penalties as given, despite the absence of any explicit reference to the principle in constitutional case law. This did not escape the attention of Vedel, prominent professor of public law and, at the time, member of the council. While he agreed in substance with the *Rapporteur*'s arguments, he objected to the formulation of the decision in the way Jozeau-Marigné had proposed. He stressed that proportionality was not entrenched in the constitutional text and that, until then, relevant decisions were pronounced under the principle of necessity, which comprised proportionality in certain of its aspects. In Vedel's view, in the area of criminal law the relevant appreciations are delicate and touch the evolution of public morality. Thus, 'the Council should not appear to give lessons to the legislator'.[95] In the absence of a manifest error in appreciation, the court should not exercise an intrusive review of legislation. Although Vedel observed that during the 1960s he himself had argued for the connection of proportionality to the *DDHC*, he considered proportionality of punishment to be a moral value and not an enforceable constitutional norm. He thus argued against what he saw as an audacious invocation of proportionality.[96]

Vedel's proposition was finally adopted in the official justification of the decision. Proportionality was not mentioned as a general principle, but for the first time in constitutional case law it was connected to the manifest error test. Thus, it explicitly acquired legal-constitutional content in the council's reasoning:

> [I]n the absence of manifest disproportionality between the offence and the incurred penalty, it is not within the competence of the Constitutional Council to substitute its proper appreciation for that of the legislator concerning the necessity of the penalties attached to the offences defined by law. [. . .] no provision of the first title of the law is manifestly contrary to the principle entrenched in article 8 of the Declaration of 1789.[97]

[94] See the deliberation of the Constitutional Council, 3 September 1986, p. 19. I am grateful to Vincent Réveillère for giving me a copy of this deliberation, which is not accessible online.

[95] Ibid, p. 20.

[96] Ibid, p. 21.

[97] Decision no. 86–215, cons. 7.

The application of the manifest disproportionality standard more than a year later, in decision *Loi de finances pour 1988*, was perceived by scholars as the first explicit application of the principle of proportionality in French constitutional law.[98] The bill brought before the council prohibited the publication of individuals' revenues or tax contributions in the press. In an effort to dissuade potential offenders, the bill specified that violation of the prohibitions would be punished with an administrative fine equal to the amount of the disclosed revenues or tax contributions. The council had expanded the application of the principle of necessity to administrative sanctions in previous case law.[99] In continuity with these cases, it stated that the scope of Article 8 *DDHC* did not only comprise criminal law but 'every sanction having a punitive character', even when Parliament had delegated the competence to pronounce it to a non-judicial authority.[100] The judges went on to state that:

> [B]y prescribing that the fiscal fine [. . .] will be, in every case, equal to the amount of the disclosed revenues, article 92 of the law edicts a sanction that could be, in certain cases, manifestly disproportionate.[101]

The Announcement of Proportionality as a Constitutional Principle. The announcement of proportionality as a constitutional principle in subsequent case law came as natural and was not celebrated or even debated by French public lawyers. In decision *Conseil supérieur de l'audiovisuel*, the judges accepted, in principle at least, the power of an independent administrative authority to impose sanctions, while setting conditions on its exercise. Among these conditions, they included a requirement of proportionality, even though no reference to the principle can be found in the claimant MPs' argumentation. In the words of the council:

> [T]he power to impose the sanctions enumerated in article 42–1 is conferred on the Conseil supérieur de l'audiovisuel which is an independent authority; [. . .] from the terms of the law it follows that no sanction is automatically imposed; [. . .] as article 42–6 requires, every decision imposing a sanction must be justified; [. . .]the principle of proportionality applies to all the sanctions enumerated in article 42–1; [. . .] the same fault cannot ground but one administrative sanction, be it imposed by law or

[98] Decision no. 87–237 DC, 30 December 1987, *Loi de finances pour 1988*, ECLI:FR:CC:1987:87.237.DC.

[99] Decision no. 82–155 DC, 30 December 1982, *Loi de finances rectificative pour 1982*, ECLI:FR:CC:1982:82.155.DC, cons. 33. See Genevois (1988), pp. 353–4.

[100] Decision no. 87–237 DC, cons. 14–15.

[101] Ibid, cons. 16.

contract; [. . .] it results from the title of article 42–1 (3°) that a pecuniary sanction cannot be cumulated with a criminal sanction.[102]

Proportionality was thus solemnly recognised by the constitutional judges as a requirement of constitutional legality imposed on administrative sanctions. Commenting on the decision, Genevois, a well-known judge and at the time Secretary General of the Constitutional Council, perceived the above *considérants* to lay down an 'overall theory of administrative sanctions'.[103] This theory followed on the application of the constitutional guarantees until then specific to criminal law, 'mainly resulting from article 8 *DDHC*', to the whole of public sanctions.[104] Proportionality, as part of this theory, demanded the administration to choose a sanction that corresponded to the seriousness of the impugned fault. Ever since, constitutional judges have applied this version of proportionality both in criminal and in administrative sanctions, while in certain decisions the content of the principle was further specified.[105] Clearly, the version of *proportionnalité des peines et des sanctions* applied by the Constitutional Council was very different from the Alexyan proportionality model, despite them sharing a quasi-identical *nom propre*. The French constitutional court's version of the principle did not imply reasoning in prongs and was only indirectly connected to the realisation of constitutional rights.

Proportionality as a Principle for the Protection of Public Freedoms. Six years after its *Conseil supérieur de l'audiovisuel* decision, the council recognised the constitutional basis of the principle of proportionality in the field of police measures as well. In *Loi d'orientation et de programmation relative à la sécurité*, the contested bill empowered the

[102] Decision no. 88–248 DC, 17 January 1989, *Loi modifiant la loi no 86–1067 du 30 septembre 1986 relative à la liberté de communication*, ECLI:FR:CC:1989:88.248.DC, cons. 30.

[103] Genevois (1989), p. 222.

[104] Ibid, p. 223.

[105] See Decision no. 89–260 DC, 28 July 1989, *Loi relative à la sécurité et à la transparence du marché financier*, ECLI:FR:CC:1989:89.260.DC, cons. 22; Decision no. 93–325 DC, 13 August 1993, *Loi relative à la maîtrise de l'immigration et aux conditions d'entrée, d'accueil et de séjour des étrangers en France*, ECLI:FR:CC:1993:93.325.DC, cons. 37 f.; Decision no. 94–345 DC, 29 July 1994, *Loi relative à l'emploi de la langue française*, ECLI:FR:CC:1994:94.345.DC, cons. 26 f.; Decision no. 99–411 DC, 16 June 1999, *Loi portant diverses mesures relatives à la sécurité routière et aux infractions sur les agents des exploitants de réseau de transport public de voyageurs*, ECLI:FR:CC:1999:99.411.DC; Decision no. 97–395 DC, 30 December 1997, *Loi de finances pour 1998*, ECLI:FR:CC:1997:97.395.DC, cons. 39.

administration to enact measures for maintaining public order.[106] The bill authorised video surveillance, as well as the seizure of objects that could serve as weapons, especially during protests. The application of proportionality as a requirement of necessity, invoked by the plaintiff MPs, was not contested by the government.[107] The council started by declaring that the maintenance of public order and the search for criminals were objectives enjoying constitutional status, since they were necessary for the protection of other constitutional rights and principles. Parliament could thus empower the administration to enact restrictive police measures in order to pursue them. However, administrative discretion should be accompanied by guarantees for individuals.

It is among these guarantees that we find proportionality. According to the council, the administrative police measures must be strictly limited in space and time and 'must remain proportionate to the necessities of the circumstances'.[108] Proportionality was thus explicitly recognised as a 'narrowly tailored' requirement imposed by the constitution on restrictive administrative action. This requirement led the council to announce a *réserve d'interprétation*: according to the judges, 'the legislator must be understood' as having limited the scope of the relevant provisions in light of proportionality. However, the council still held that the law was unconstitutional. Even though the legislator had the power to prohibit the carrying of objects that could possibly serve as weapons during protests, the extension of this prohibition to 'all objects that can be used as projectiles' was 'by nature by its general and imprecise formulation likely to lead to excessive interferences with individual freedom', and was contrary to the constitution.[109]

Thus, proportionality was announced as a principle for the protection of constitutional freedoms. While its function was akin to the Alexyan proportionality model, its structure and application was not: proportionality was a standard of necessity primarily addressed to the *administration*. Therefore, it was to be applied by the ordinary judge, and most notably the Council of State. Indeed, the constitutional entrenchment of proportionality led to a more recurrent use of proportionality language by ordinary courts in the field of sanctions and in the review of the

[106] Decision no. 94–352 DC, 18 January 1995, *Loi d'orientation et de programmation relative à la sécurité*, ECLI:FR:CC:1995:94.352.DC, cons. 17.

[107] See the *saisine* and the observations by the government, available at www.conseil-constitutionnel.fr.

[108] Decision no. 94–352 DC, cons. 17.

[109] Ibid, cons. 18.

necessity of police action.[110] This evolution was combined with the reception of proportionality in convention-compatibility review.[111] It seems that the decisive impulse for the spread of proportionality in constitutional case law came from abroad.

2.4 The Transfer of Proportionality Analysis

The Use of the German Proportionality Doctrine in the Constitutional Law Literature. During the 1990s, one observes French constitutionalists' increasing interest in comparative law. This is also apparent in the literature on proportionality. More and more, scholars looked abroad for the correct content and application of proportionality. Since the mid-1990s they started invoking the three-pronged structure applied in German law in the systematisation of domestic constitutional case law. The first to do so was Xynopoulos in his comparative study of the application of proportionality in German, French and English public law.[112] Although the author adopted a French-centred analysis based on the concept of discretionary powers, he understood proportionality as a technique for the balancing of competing values or interests. Thus, Xynopoulos regrouped different methods of review employed by domestic public law judges, such as necessity or the *bilan*, under the label of proportionality. In this context, proportionality was taken as naturally connected to the new role of the judiciary as the protector of fundamental rights. Its function was that of a method for imposing the realisation of fundamental rights on the legislator and on other public authorities.

Since 1997, Goesel-Le Bihan also started using the three-pronged test to reconstruct constitutional case law. Following her allegedly 'iconoclastic' hypothesis, the intensity of proportionality scrutiny and the prong applied varied according to the importance of the right at stake, but also according to other factors, such as the status of the goal pursued by the legislator. The different intensities of proportionality scrutiny led to the employment of different methods of constitutional review, such as manifest error, manifest inappropriateness, necessity or appropriateness review. Goesel-Le Bihan thus argued that proportionality analysis

[110] CE, 13 October 1989, no. 84133, ECLI:FR:CESJS:1989:84133.19891013; 21 January 1994, no. 120043, ECLI:FR:CESSR:1994:120043.19940121; 20 October 1995, no. 154868, ECLI:FR:CESSR:1995:154868.19951020; 28 July 1999, nos. 202606, 203438, 203487, 203541, and 203589, ECLI:FR:CESSR:1999:202606.19990728.

[111] On this point, see Part III, Chapter 8.1.

[112] Xynopoulos (1995).

provided a new framework through which the theory of fundamental rights that presumably underpinned Constitutional Council decisions could be revisited.[113]

While these authors had different objectives, they both used proportionality to reconstruct judicial reasoning in line with the representation of the constitutional judge as a protector of fundamental rights. This attributed a new prestige to the council's decisions and to the council as an institution itself. Soon, scholarly interest in proportionality led to its actual application as a fundamental rights principle in constitutional case law.

The Application of Proportionality as a Fundamental Rights Principle. In 2000, Parliament had imposed restrictions on the concentration of TV channels. The measures were contested by the opposition as 'disproportionate with respect to the constitutional objective of pluralism'.[114] Criticism of the disproportionate character of legislation had been a recurrent phenomenon in French constitutional law since the 1990s. However, it did not usually lead the council to express its scrutiny in proportionality terms. Instead, the court preferred categorical methods of justification, for example by referring to the 'substance' of the rights at stake.[115] Particularly in freedom of enterprise case law, after announcing that this freedom is not general or absolute, the council typically checked whether the contested legislation had 'perverted its scope'.[116]

In decision *Loi modifiant la loi n° 86-1067 du 30 septembre 1986 relative à la liberté de communication*, the constitutional judges followed a different reasoning. After affirming the constitutional status of the freedom of enterprise, guaranteed by Article 4 *DDHC*, they announced that Parliament may impose restrictions when they are 'justified by the general interest or connected to constitutional requirements'. The council held that Parliament has the power to reconcile the competing rules and principles, having taken into account 'the specific technical constraints and economic necessities related to the general interest in the

[113] Goesel-Le Bihan (1997).

[114] Decision no. 2000–433 DC, 27 July 2000, *Loi modifiant la loi no 86–1067 du 30 septembre 1986 relative à la liberté de communication*, ECLI:FR:CC:2000:2000.433.DC, cons. 38.

[115] See Decision no. 90–284 DC, 16 January 1991, *Loi relative au conseiller du salarié*, ECLI:FR:CC:1991:90.284.DC, cons. 2–3.

[116] Decision no. 89–254 DC, 4 July 1989, *Loi modifiant la loi no 86–912 du 6 août 1986 relative aux modalités d'application des privatisations*, ECLI:FR:CC:1989:89.254.DC, cons. 5.

field of audio-visual communication'.[117] Nonetheless, legislative power in this field is not limitless. The legislator, when fixing the applicable rules in the field of media, 'should ensure that their application does not limit the freedom of enterprise in excessive proportions with regard to the constitutional objective of pluralism'.[118]

Proportionality was thus announced as a limit to Parliament's power to reconcile competing constitutional values. While its form remained that of a threshold requirement, its function was one of fundamental rights protection, and was thus akin to the function described by the Alexyan theory. While proportionality was not a principle for the optimisation of fundamental rights, it imposed rights as decision-making standards on Parliament. In their comparative study on proportionality and balancing, Cohen-Eliya and Porat identify this kind of intermediate type of review as 'indifference' review: its function is to ensure that domestic authorities are not indifferent to rights infringements.[119]

Moreover, again following the Alexyan model, the language used by the council indicates that the intensity of proportionality review varied according to institutional and other circumstances. The judges held that, not having Parliament's general power of appreciation and decision, they could not seek for alternative, less restrictive measures that could advance the legislative objectives. Hence, they contented themselves with ascertaining that the measures in question were not 'manifestly inappropriate' for preserving media pluralism.[120] The manifestly inappropriate standard, until then applied independently of proportionality, was thus employed as one of the proportionality prongs, implying a minimal review of the appropriateness of the contested measures. In the exercise of this review, the council deferred to the legislative choices, in view of the 'new technical data' brought about by digital TV.[121]

A few months later, the constitutional judges applied proportionality to censure the choices of Parliament. A bill authorised local authorities in Paris, Lyon and Marseille to impose an administrative license requirement on central shops for changes in the nature of their commercial activity. The council declared that, while 'the preserving of the commercial diversity of neighbourhoods' corresponded to a general interest goal, the legislator had infringed on the right to property and on the freedom

[117] Decision no. 2000–433 DC, cons. 40.
[118] Ibid.
[119] Cohen-Eliya and Porat (2013), pp. 73 f.
[120] Decision no. 2000–433 DC, cons. 41 f.
[121] Ibid, cons. 42.

of enterprise to an extent 'that was disproportionate to the objective pursued'.[122] Proportionality was progressively established as a method for constitutional rights adjudication.[123] The council's reasoning was increasingly akin to a prong-structured proportionality analysis. For example, the council typically required that derogations from the principle of equality pursue a general interest, follow objective and rational criteria connected to the legislative goal and are not disproportionate with respect to their expected result.[124] Influence from abroad became increasingly explicit in the documents taken into account by the council in its various decisions. The transfer of the three-pronged structure of proportionality in French constitutional law was not long to come.

The Reception of Proportionality as a Three-Pronged Test. The *Rétention de sûreté* case concerned contentious measures of post-sentence preventive surveillance and detention, instituted in 2008.[125] The restrictive measures were applicable to individuals convicted for particularly serious crimes and considered dangerous due to a severe personality disorder. Among other arguments, the opposition deputies claimed that the measures constituted an unnecessary restriction to individual rights. The council accepted that 'post-sentence preventive detention and surveillance must comply with the principle, deriving from Article 9 of the Declaration of 1789 and Article 66 of the Constitution, whereby the freedom of the individual should not be restricted with undue harshness'.[126] The council stressed that it is within the competence of the legislator to reconcile 'the necessary maintenance of law and order to ensure the safeguarding of rights and principles of constitutional value and the exercising of constitutionally guaranteed freedoms'.[127] The

[122] Decision no. 2000–436 DC, 7 December 2000, *Loi relative à la solidarité et au renouvellement urbain*, ECLI:FR:CC:2000:2000.436.DC, cons. 20.

[123] Decision no. 2000–439 DC, 16 January 2001, *Loi relative à l'archéologie préventive*, ECLI:FR:CC:2001:2000.439.DC, cons. 14 (concerning the freedom of enterprise); Decision no. 2001–452 DC, 6 December, 2001, *Loi portant mesures urgentes de réformes à caractère économique et financier*, ECLI:FR:CC:2001:2001.452.DC, cons. 7 (concerning the principle of equality).

[124] Decision no. 2007–555 DC, 16 August 2007, *Loi en faveur du travail, de l'emploi et du pouvoir d'achat*, ECLI:FR:CC:2007:2007.555.DC, cons. 3; see also Decision no. 2005–528 DC, 15 December 2005, *Loi de financement de la sécurité sociale pour 2006*, ECLI:FR:CC:2005:2005.528.DC, cons. 15.

[125] Decision no. 2008–562 DC, 21 February 2008, *Loi relative à la rétention de sûreté et à la déclaration d'irresponsabilité pénale pour cause de trouble mental*, ECLI:FR:CC:2008:2008.562.DC.

[126] Ibid, cons. 13 (English translation).

[127] Ibid.

judges went on to state the criteria that the legislative reconciliation should fulfil: 'Any infringement of the exercising of these freedoms should be tailored, necessary and proportionate to the aims of preventing the commission of offences it is sought to attain.'[128]

Proportionality analysis was thus announced as a judicial review method in the field of individual freedom. More surprising than the announcement of the proportionality prongs was the actual structuring of the council's reasoning. The judges divided the remaining ten *considérants* of their decision in a successive analysis of the adequacy, the necessity and the proportionality of the legislative measures at stake, which was notably long and detailed by its reasoning standards. The influence of foreign constitutional courts, and especially Karlsruhe, was even explicit in the official comment on the decision published in the council's website.[129] Moreover, the file of the legal documents taken into account in the deliberations reveals how the text of the ECHR and the Strasbourg case law were taken into consideration by the constitutional judges.[130]

The Proliferation of Proportionality. Since 2008, proportionality proliferates in French public law. The Constitutional Council has applied the proportionality prongs in more than twenty decisions, most of them issued in the context of the *question prioritaire de constitutionnalité* procedure (*QPC*), which, since 2010, allows claimants to invoke the incompatibility of legislation with constitutional rights and freedoms, after its promulgation. Proportionality sometimes leads to a detailed scrutiny of legislation, since it is applied distinctly to every legislative provision contested by the plaintiffs. Apart from constitutional rights cases, the proportionality structure has been applied in other fields, such as in the review of electoral ineligibilities or of derogations to the principle of equality.[131] The Council of State also adopted the three-pronged structure of proportionality, both in the convention-compatibility review and in the application of domestic law.[132] As for the *Cour de cassation*, while it does

[128] Ibid.

[129] See the official comment on the decision, 'Commentaire de la décision no 2008-562 DC du 21 février 2008', *Cahiers du Conseil constitutionnel*, no. 24 (2008), p. 5.

[130] *Dossier documentaire*, Décision no. 2008-562 DC, available at www.conseil-constitution nel.fr.

[131] Decision no. 2008-24 ELEC, 28 May 2008, *Observations du Conseil constitutionnel relatives aux élections législatives des 10 et 17 juin 2007*, ECLI:FR:CC:2008:2008.24. ELEC; Decision no. 2016-620 QPC, 30 March 2017, *Société EDI-TV [Taxe sur la publicité diffusée par les chaînes de télévision]*, ECLI:FR:CC:2017:2016.620.QPC.

[132] CE (Pl.), 16 October 2011, *Association pour la promotion de l'image et autres*, no. 317827, ECLI:FR:CEASS:2011:317827.20111026, in the review of compatibility with the ECHR.

not use proportionality language in its review, it often requires searching and structured proportionality scrutiny from lower courts.[133]

The importance of proportionality is rising in judicial practice, and an explosion of academic interest in the principle can be observed during the last decade.[134] Scholars often criticise the domestic application of proportionality in contradistinction to foreign and European jurisprudence and urge French courts to apply it in a more consistent and transparent way.[135] Although proportionality long remained a concept mainly used by public lawyers,[136] its pronged structure has now become common knowledge among *privatistes* and *publicistes*. Particularly in private law, proportionality acquires a pervasive dynamic. Some consider it a major instrument for the radical institutional transformation that the *Cour de cassation* is undergoing, following the model of other continental and common law courts.[137] Proportionality is at the centre of current debates concerning the reform of the supreme civil court.[138] It seems that, after a long period of resistance, the French legal order has entered the era of proportionality . . . but in its own special way.

2.5 *Proportionnalité* 'à la Française', *Especially in a State of Emergency*

The Expulsion of Facts from Proportionality Analysis. How did the transfer of the proportionality structure affect French judicial review? The first element that strikes the reader of *Rétention de sûreté* is the absence of facts. Adequacy review was confined to a survey of the norms in question. The Constitutional Council contented itself with verifying that 'the scope of post-sentence preventive detention appears to be

CE (Pl.), 21 December 2012, *Société Groupe Canal Plus et autres*, no. 362347, ECLI:FR:CEASS:2012:362347.20121221, concerning proportionality as a domestic principle. On the adoption of the proportionality structure, see Sauvé (2017).

133 See, for example, Cass. soc., 11 May 2010, no. 08–45307, Bull. 2010, no. 105; 17 March 2015, no. 13–27142, Bull. 2015, no. 53; Cass. civ. 1, 14 April 2016, no. 14–29981, Bull. 2016. See also Jeuland (2016).

134 See Goesel-Le Bihan (2007b); Bousta (2007); Koumpli (2010); Goesel-Le Bihan (2012); Prélot (2013); Duclerq (2015); Jamin (2015); de Béchillon (2016); Jeuland (2016); Vigneau (2017). See also the special issue dedicated to proportionality, *Les Petites Affiches*, no. 46 (2009).

135 Goesel-Le Bihan (2007a); Bousta (2011); Jamin (2015); Jeuland (2016).

136 Seube (2009).

137 Zenati-Castaing (2016); see also Jamin (2015).

138 On this, see *La Semaine Juridique*, Regards d'universitaires sur la réforme de la Cour de cassation – conférence débat 24 novembre 2015, supplément au no 1–2 (2016).

appropriate for the purpose it is sought to achieve'.[139] Procedure also played a role in the council's conclusion. Without any recourse to statistical or other data that show the contested measures' actual effectiveness, the council affirmed their appropriateness, since, in its view, the law provided for 'suitable guarantees that post-sentence preventive detention will be reserved solely for persons who are particularly dangerous because they suffer from serious personality disorders'.[140]

Similarly, the necessity review remained at the level of scope and guarantees. The council underscored that post-sentence preventive detention will only be imposed exceptionally, in cases of very serious crimes when recidivism is highly probable. It also took into account the fact that the law requires that already existing measures be insufficient to prevent the convicted persons from committing serious crimes. On this point, the council announced a *réserve d'interprétation*:

> It will thus be left to the regional court competent to order post-sentence preventive detention to check whether the person who is the subject of such an order has been able, during his sentence, to have the benefit of care and treatment suitable for the personality disorders from which he suffers.[141]

Proportionality as a 'Narrowly Tailored' Test. The judges thus contented themselves with demanding the strict necessity of the application of the post-sentence detention. Contrary to the impact-based reasoning professed by the defenders of the proportionality model, judicial review in *Rétention de sûreté* consisted in an examination of the narrowly tailored character of the contested provisions.[142] In reality, it was not the impact of the contested measures on individual rights that was examined, or the effectiveness of the measures in the advancement of their aim (an examination that, especially in the context of *a priori* constitutional review, is difficult). The reasoning that the different proportionality prongs implied is difficult to distinguish, leading the court to wearisome repetitions in its judgment. This is a more general characteristic of the Constitutional Council proportionality case law. Scholars talk about a French 'specificity' in the application of proportionality and see a formal interpretation or a 'proceduralisation' of the principle in this field.[143]

139 Decision no. 2008–562 DC, cons. 15 (English translation).
140 Ibid, cons. 16.
141 Ibid, cons. 21. Similarly, particularly concerning the duration of the measures, cons. 23.
142 In the same vein, see Bousta (2011).
143 Bousta (2007), p. 875.

Nonetheless, 'narrowly tailored' scrutiny and procedural guarantees are anything but new in the council's reasoning. They have been among the constitutional judges' methods long before the use of proportionality language.[144] Most importantly, these methods fit perfectly the traditional image of judicial review as a syllogism only concerned with norms. They also fit the image of the Constitutional Council as a 'watchdog' of Parliament. While announcing a new method of review, the constitutional judges were constrained in their traditional role of distribution of competences between the various state authorities. In conformity with its traditional perception in French public law, proportionality was analysed in a factual requirement of adaptation to the circumstances. Thus, its application was entrusted to the authorities who are closer to the facts of each case.[145]

The Expulsion of Values from Proportionality Analysis. As for the *stricto sensu* proportionality prong, the reasoning of the Constitutional Council in *Rétention de sûreté* consisted, again, in a survey of the guarantees provided for by the law. In the words of the judges:

> Parliament has therefore accompanied the placing of persons under post-sentence preventive detention orders by guarantees such as to ensure the conciliation between freedom of the individual [. . .] and the aim of preventing persons from re-offending.[146]

The council's application of proportionality involves no balancing of competing constitutional values as it does in Karlsruhe or in the global model. It is the legislator and not the judge that should proceed to the reconciliation of various constitutional rules and principles. The long and detailed proportionality review to which the judges proceeded in *Rétention de sûreté* did not lead to any significant criticism of Parliament's choices. This, in spite of the fact that preventive detention challenges the punitive character of criminal measures, which is deemed a fundamental feature of French criminal law. *Rétention de sûreté* is among the decisions that have provoked the quasi-unanimous criticism of constitutional scholars, and this, despite its inclusion in the *Grandes décisions* collection.

[144] For a well-known example on the right to strike, see Decision no. 79–105 DC, 25 July 1979, *Loi modifiant les dispositions de la loi no 74–696 du 7 août 1974 relatives à la continuité du service public de la radio et de la télévision en cas de cessation concertée du travail*, ECLI:FR:CC:1979:79.105.DC.

[145] See also Bousta (2007), pp. 866–7.

[146] Decision no. 2008–562 DC, cons 22 (English translation).

More generally, what is specifically French in the application of proportionality is that it does not entail any principled contestation of the legislative choices. The legitimate aim test is not part of the proportionality prongs. Usually, the legitimacy of the objectives pursued by Parliament is affirmed by the council in an abstract way, through indeterminate notions such as public order, the objectives of constitutional value or the general interest.[147] The constitutional court, which does not possess 'any general power of appraisal and decision-making similar to that vested in Parliament', does not contest the legitimacy of the legislative goal, or the rationality and the necessity of the measures adopted for its achievement.[148] Deference to important value choices of Parliament is combined with the formalist and fragmented examination of the scope of certain provisions, which usually does not involve any global appreciation of their significance. All this gives the impression of a constitutional review 'filtering out mosquitos to open the way to camels'.[149]

Proportionality Under the State of Emergency. Formalism and judicial restraint are accentuated in the series of cases concerning the broad police powers provided to the administration under the state of emergency declared after the 2015 terrorist attacks. Restrictive measures, such as administrative searches and seizures or house arrests, have been contested through the *QPC* procedure by individuals subjected to them. The council recognises that these measures generally interfere with the plaintiffs' constitutional rights. However, the judges never contest the legislative choices in principle. According to consistent case law:

> [T]he Constitution does not exclude the possibility that the legislator may establish a regime to govern the state of emergency; that within this context, it falls to [the legislator] to ensure that a balance is struck between, on the one hand, the prevention of public order offences and, on the other hand, the respect for the rights and freedoms granted to all persons resident in the Republic.[150]

[147] Bousta (2007); Bousta (2011).

[148] Decision no. 2008-564 DC, 19 June 2008, *OGM*, ECLI:FR:CC:2008:2008.564.DC, cons. 34; Decision no. 2010-2 QPC, 11 June 2010, *Loi dite 'anti-Perruche'*, ECLI:FR:CC:2010:2010.2.QPC, cons. 4; Decision no. 2012-249 QPC, 16 May 2012, *Société Cryo-Save France [Prélèvement de cellules du sang de cordon ou placentaire ou de cellules du cordon ou du placenta]*, ECLI:FR:CC:2012:2012.249.QPC, cons. 7–8.

[149] Rivero (1981), p. 275; Wachsmann (2007), p. 279; Champeil-Desplats (2012).

[150] Decision no. 2015-527 QPC, 22 December 2015 *M. Cédric D. [Assignations à résidence dans le cadre de l'état d'urgence]*, ECLI:FR:CC:2015:2015.527.QPC, cons. 8. Similarly, Decision no. 2016-536 QPC, 19 February 2016, *Ligue des droits de l'homme*

In certain cases, the council has appeared to set limits on Parliament by repeating that the state of emergency is 'a regime of exceptional powers the effects of which must be limited in time and space and which contribute to preventing the imminent danger or consequences with the character of a public disaster to which the country is exposed'.[151] However, this statement never involved detailed scrutiny of the necessity of the state of emergency, which lasted for almost two years in France. Arguably, the council's attitude is quite different from what one would expect of a constitutional court in a culture of justification.

Since the balancing or reconciliation of competing constitutional values is a competence of Parliament, the council's proportionality scrutiny has been limited to a review of the procedural guarantees offered by legislation.[152] The court has sometimes pronounced *réserves d'interprétation* concerning the scope of the contested measures.[153] The formal review exercised by the council has sometimes led to the censure of certain provisions.[154] This notwithstanding, more often the enforcement of the principle of proportionality has been delegated to ordinary courts. The council has typically required that the restrictive measures 'be justified by and proportionate with the reasons that [ground them under] the particular circumstances'.[155] It holds that 'the administrative courts are charged with ensuring that [the contested] measure is suitable, necessary and proportionate with the goal pursued'.[156] Following this reasoning, the council usually holds that the broad police powers grounded on the state of emergency do not violate fundamental rights.

The introduction of proportionality language to the council's case law did not radically affect the traditional formalism and judicial restraint

[Perquisitions et saisies administratives dans le cadre de l'état d'urgence], ECLI:FR:CC:2016:2016.536.QPC, cons. 5; Decision no. 2016-600 QPC, 2 December 2016, *M. Raïme A. [Perquisitions administratives dans le cadre de l'état d'urgence III]*, ECLI:FR:CC:2016:2016.600.QPC, cons. 6; Decision no. 2017-624 QPC, 16 March 2017, *M. Sofiyan I. [Durée maximale de l'assignation à résidence dans le cadre de l'état d'urgence]*, ECLI:FR:CC:2017:2017.624.QPC, cons. 13 (English translations).

151 Decision no. 2016-536 QPC, cons. 12 (English translation).

152 Ibid, cons. 9–11.

153 Decision no. 2017-624 QPC, cons. 17.

154 See Decision no. 2016-536 QPC, cons. 14; Decision no. 2016-600 QPC, cons. 16; Decision no. 2016-611 QPC, 10 February 2017, *M. David P. [Délit de consultation habituelle de sites internet terroristes]*.

155 Decision no. 2016-536 QPC, cons. 10 (English translation).

156 Decision no. 2015-527 QPC, cons. 12; Decision no. 2016-536 QPC, cons. 10; Decision no. 2017-624 QPC, cons. 17. See also CE (Pl.), 6 July 2016, no. 398234, ECLI:FR:CEASS:2016:398234.20160706.

that characterises this court's decisions. Values and facts are external to proportionality analysis. Attentive commentators thus observe that its announcement as a method of review in 2008 corresponded to a 'tricky appearance of innovation'.[157] Besides, the fact that proportionality was first announced in the context of a priori review indicates precisely this: proportionality entails an abstract and objective reasoning, and brings about no revolutionary changes to already existing judicial methods. It seems that the only change that *Rétention de sûreté* brought about is the establishment of the proportionality structure, without involving value-laden balancing. However, in subsequent case law, the proportionality structure has not been consistently applied.

The Inconsistent Application of Proportionality. Deprived of its main function as a framework for the balancing of competing values, proportionality lacks any structural integrity in French constitutional case law. Rarely does the announcement of different proportionality prongs lead the Constitutional Council to structure its reasoning around them.[158] In most cases, proportionality is limited to a review under the disproportionate or the manifest disproportionate standard, whose fulfilment is deemed to be self-evident and does not involve any justification.[159] Apart from its fundamental rights function, proportionality preserves its traditional form as a rule in the field of taxation or sanctions.[160] In the *Loi de finances pour 2003* decision, the council even applied proportionality as a financial prudence principle, in what looks like an echo of the *bilan* case law in constitutional law.[161] Since 2005, the *Charte de l'environnement* was inscribed in the Preamble of the Constitution. Article 5 imposes on public authorities to adopt temporary and proportionate measures, in order to prevent serious and irreversible environmental damages. Thus, another version of proportionality was added in domestic constitutional discourse.[162]

[157] Bousta (2011), p. 14.

[158] Decision no. 2008–571 DC, 11 December 2008, *Loi de financement de la sécurité sociale pour 2009*, ECLI:FR:CC:2008:2008.571.DC, cons. 14.

[159] See, for example, Decision no. 2010–71 QPC, 26 November 2010, *Mlle Danielle S. [Hospitalisation sans consentement]*, ECLI:FR:CC:2010:2010.71.QPC, cons. 32; Decision no. 2013–318 QPC, 7 June 2013, *M. Mohamed T. [Activité de transport public de personnes à motocyclette ou tricycle à moteur]*, ECLI:FR:CC:2013:2013.318.QPC, cons. 14.

[160] Decision no. 2008–564 DC, cons. 34.

[161] Decision no. 2002–464 DC, 22 December 2001, *Loi de finances pour 2003*, ECLI:FR:CC:2002:2002.464.DC, cons. 34.

[162] Decision no. 2008–564 DC, cons. 18.

Even though proportionality proliferates in French constitutional law, its form and function result from the circumstances of each case rather than from a commonly shared meaning of the term among French lawyers. The spread of proportionality in constitutional case law was not combined with a more general constitutional rights theory. Everything seems to depend on the way the judge will choose to formulate the constitutional problem at stake. Even scholars that were the most faithful in seeing consistency in constitutional case law doubt the actual rationality of the council's choices.[163] As for sceptics, most notably 'normativists' and 'legal realists', if they are interested in proportionality at all, they perceive it as nothing but an argumentative weapon for legitimising the norm-making power of the constitutional judges.[164] Just like the fundamental rights discourse surrounding it, proportionality in the Constitutional Council's decisions leaves its readers with an 'impressionist' depiction of the concept and of its function in judicial reasoning: it is casuistically constructed by the judge and imposed as self-evident on the addressees of constitutional justice.[165]

The general confusion surrounding proportionality is aggravated by its diffusion in the case law of ordinary courts. In administrative law, the inconsistent application of proportionality gives the impression of a method that is '*protéiforme et en mutation*'.[166] Public lawyers' thirst for consistency results in highly technical and complex systematisations that provoke 'vertigo' and 'headaches' among their audience.[167] The adoption of the three-pronged proportionality structure did not correspond to any substantial change in the Council of State's reasoning.[168] In private law, the application of the principle is characterised by '*tâtonnements, approximations et hésitations*', both concerning its form and its scope

[163] Goesel-Le Bihan (2007b), p. 277: '*La complexité du tableau que dessine la jurisprudence récente n'en est pas moins réelle, au point que l'existence d'une rationalité – consciente ou non – de détail de la jurisprudence constitutionnelle peut parfois être mise en doute.*'

[164] Koumpli (2010), for the normativists; Brunet (2005a), for the realists. Brunet does not refer to proportionality but to balancing more generally.

The terms 'normativist' and 'realist' are used in the sense that French public lawyers give to them: normativists are the adepts of the Kelsenian pure theory of law; French realists can be described as a 'heretic' branch of Kelsenian theory, developed by Troper and Nanterre University, which exposes judicial interpretation as a norm-producing activity, limited by legal and extra-legal constraints (*contraintes*).

[165] Champeil-Desplats (2012), esp. section I.

[166] Kalflèche (2009).

[167] Seube (2009), p. 86.

[168] Sauvé (2017).

of application.[169] Besides, the *Cour de cassation* does not apply proportionality at all, a practice that provokes Strasbourg criticism.[170] While private lawyers call for a proportionality test '*propre à la Cour de cassation*', such a test has not been yet invented.[171] Proportionality is often perceived as an equity method that raises problems for legal certainty.[172] Both in administrative law and in private law, its application remains a matter of facts and circumstance left to the appreciation of lower courts or of the reviewed authorities.[173]

Proportionality in French public law did not acquire the form and function that the Alexyan model attributes to it. Instead of increasing transparency in judicial reasoning, its varying application provokes confusion. Instead of leading to a value-laden balancing of competing constitutional values, it leads judges to a formalist reasoning akin to the one they performed before the emergence of proportionality language. The deferent stance of French courts vis-à-vis public authorities provokes doubt as to whether the introduction of proportionality discourse in French public law has enhanced the protection of fundamental rights.

***

Plus ça change, plus c'est la même chose. The most important advances in French judicial review have occurred without recourse to proportionality terminology. And where this terminology finally spread in the language used by courts, it has not brought about important changes to pre-existing judicial methods. Even the introduction of the three-pronged proportionality structure did not lead French courts to engage in value-laden reasoning, neither has it entailed a more fact-sensitive approach to judicial review. The proliferation of proportionality has not radically changed the formal style of judicial reasoning, neither has it enhanced the transparency of judicial value-judgments, even though it has affected the length and detail of official justifications. Besides, proportionality has no precise function in judicial reasoning and its application is not necessarily connected to fundamental rights. The use of proportionality language in France is very different from that instantiated in the Alexyan model. Scholars even talk about a French specificity in this field.

169 Seube (2009), p. 86.
170 ECtHR, *Henrioud* v. *France*, 5 November 2015, no. 21444/11.
171 Jeuland (2016), p. 20.
172 For some examples, see Cadiet (2016), p. 13; Louvel (2016). *Contra* de Béchillon (2016).
173 Cass. civ. 1, 5 July 2017, no. 16–22183, Bull. 2017; CE, 9 November 2015, *Le Mur (Dieudonné)*, no. 376107, ECLI:FR:CESSR:2015:376107.20151109, cons. 6.

This has not impeded French public lawyers from perceiving proportionality to be an omnipresent notion and a key feature in the evolution of judicial review, both at an administrative and at a constitutional level. While for decades it did not attract much academic interest, since its emergence in the 1970s proportionality has been widely accepted and cherished by the *doctrine*. In reality, it has been much more useful in the analysis and the reconstruction of case law than in the justification of judicial decisions. Proportionality, understood as a judicial method, has designated the pragmatist application of the law in the search for equilibrium or balance. This is why, in this context, the concept of *contrôle de proportionnalité* has been at least as important as the concept of *principe de proportionnalité*.

It seems that in French public law, rather than a judicial tool, proportionality represents some kind of legal knowledge or legal common sense. Proportionality is one among the conceptual tools by which French lawyers make sense of the practice of courts, reconstruct or even guide it. Its main function has been to establish the continuity of judicial methods and the consistency of case law, through an appeal to some kind of moral-legal ideal. This is quite different from what is observed in the English context, where proportionality is a concrete concept with its own well-defined function in judicial reasoning.

3

Proportionality in English Public Law: *Continuity and Change*[1]

The story of proportionality in English public law is a story of constant transformation. Transformation of the meaning, form and function of proportionality in the domestic legal discourse; but, in addition, of the culture in which proportionality operates. Initially, proportionality was a marginal element to which domestic lawyers rarely turned their attention. Today, however, it is a core feature of legal debates and an engine of cultural change. This chapter attempts to present the story of how proportionality became a core concept in English public law.

The analysis presented here focuses on judicial discourse and generally corresponds to what was until recently the dominant narrative on proportionality in English public law. In contrast to their French colleagues, who perceive proportionality as some kind of value or ideal pursued by legal decision-making, English public lawyers have long perceived proportionality as a concrete judicial tool. Thus, they have paid a good deal of attention to the structural changes that it brings about in judicial reasoning, especially in judicial review cases.[2] In studies concerning the domestic application of proportionality, English lawyers have generally looked for similarities or differences between proportionality and existing patterns of reasoning, standards and concepts, most notably *Wednesbury* unreasonableness. The form and function of proportionality in judicial practice have always been part of the domestic conceptual content of proportionality. Scholarly analyses have long been loyal to the practice of courts, to the detriment of the construction of a coherent theory on proportionality and its application in judicial review.

[1] This expression is often used by domestic lawyers to describe the evolution of the common law constitution. See Allison (2007), p. 205; Qvortrup, ed. (2013).

[2] It is indicative that, in a study on the French system of judicial review in 1986, Bell distinguished the manifest error from proportionality review. In this way, he departed from the French common sense at the time. See Bell (1986).

Hence, English lawyers will encounter no surprises in reading this chapter. Perhaps the main difference from a mainstream English study on proportionality is the absence of an explicit position in the 'proportionality v. *Wednesbury*' debate.[3] The question of the spill-over of proportionality in common law judicial review, as well as some important recent cases in this respect, such as *Kennedy* or *Pham*, will be discussed in Parts 2 and 3.

This chapter describes the emergence and evolution of proportionality as language in English public law. As in the study of the French case, it is not my purpose to argue that ideas similar to proportionality did not exist before the emergence of proportionality language in this context. In a recent contribution, Craig traces the use of terms such as 'proportionability', 'proportionable' and 'disproportionate' in legal texts back to the late sixteenth century and argues that the UK had a concept akin to proportionality.[4] While the author admits that the old, domestic version of proportionality was different from the modern one, he suggests that the two concepts share a common substantive content: '[T]he proscription of excessive regulatory burdens and the need to ensure that the burden was objectively justified.'[5] Quite differently, such occurrences of proportionality terminology are not relevant to the kind of study that I propose. Indeed, the scope of this study is limited to the use of proportionality *as a particular way of speaking*. Even though the terms 'proportion' and 'proportionability' might appear in statutes and case law since the sixteenth century (mostly as a mathematic equation, as Craig himself acknowledges), it was not until the 1970s that English lawyers started expressing their arguments in proportionality terms and that proportionality acquired a particular dynamic as language in English public law. This chapter seeks to shed light on what it is that this new vocabulary added to domestic legal argumentation.

During the 1970s, proportionality language is mainly found in private law. Very soon, however, debates on proportionality acquired particular importance in the context of judicial review. Proportionality started being perceived by English lawyers as a public law concept, even when used in private law cases. Today, it is in public, even constitutional law that proportionality exerts its transformative dynamic. Following the advice of Lord Wilberforce, however, the term 'public law' is used with

[3] See, for example, Davies and Williams (2015), p. 73.
[4] Craig (2017).
[5] Ibid.

caution. It does not designate a separate category of norms and procedures such as the one found in continental systems. The reader should keep in mind that, 'typically, English law fastens not on principles but on remedies'.[6] Certain authors attentive to the common law tradition even deem the public/private law divide to be an 'ill-considered transplantation' of a distinction with foreign roots in the English context.[7]

The reader might have noticed that this analysis focuses on *English* law. While similar observations might often apply to Wales, Northern Ireland or even Scotland, their consideration would necessarily bring into play institutional, doctrinal and cultural particularities of these countries. This would certainly render the analysis more complete, but also more complicated, while it would add little in clarifying its main points and arguments. Therefore, the choice to exclude the devolved territories from the scope of this research is connected to its purposes and implies no claim whatsoever as to the interest that their study might present.

English lawyers' interest in proportionality is characterised by an impressive crescendo. During the 1970s, there are no relevant writings, but only some sparse judicial uses of the term. At the time, proportionality was nothing but a shade of reasonableness, accommodated by the traditional judicial review structures. It is only with its connection to European law during the 1980s that proportionality acquired conceptual autonomy (Section 3.1). The House of Lords rejected the application of proportionality in domestic judicial review during the 1990s. The promoters of proportionality thus sought continuity between the convention and common law standards (Section 3.2). Since the incorporation of the ECHR in the domestic sphere in 2000, proportionality acquired its proper dynamic and became a major issue of concern in English law. Its application as a different head of review from the *Wednesbury* test implies an important constitutional shift (Section 3.3). Proportionality under the HRA is a prong-structured test very akin to the one described by Alexy and his followers (Section 3.4). While it involves a significant extension of judicial powers, English lawyers insist that the role of courts remains different from the one ascribed to the reviewed authorities. This distinction is ensured through the doctrine of deference (Section 3.5).

[6] *Davy* v. *Spelthorne Borough Council* [1983] 3 All ER 278 (HL, 13 October 1983), p. 285, cited by Allison (1996), p. 12.

[7] Allison (1996), p. 108.

3.1 From a Shade of Reasonableness to an Independent Head of Review

Proportionality as Reasonableness. The first use of proportionality language in English judicial writings is the *Hook* case, decided in 1976.[8] Mr Hook, a trader in a local market in Barnsley, urinated on the side street after the market lavatories were closed. A security officer rebuked him and they exchanged insults. The next day, the market manager terminated Mr Hook's licence to trade. The case was brought before the High Court, which refused to quash the decision. The Court of Appeal reversed the lower court's decision. To reach this conclusion, Denning and Pennycuick LJJ took into account procedural considerations of natural justice, but also the asymmetry between the triviality of Mr Hook's offence and the severe punishment that it received. According to Denning LJ: '[T]he court can interfere by certiorari if a punishment is altogether excessive and out of proportion to the occasion.'[9] Similarly, Pennycuick LJ argued that: '[T]he isolated and trivial incident at the end of a working day is manifestly not a good cause justifying the disproportionately drastic step of depriving Mr Hook of his licence, and indirectly of his livelihood.'[10]

In the following years, proportionality language infiltrated private law cases involving balancing of competing interests.[11] Usually, it was employed as synonymous with reasonableness. Indeed, as Hickman observes, reasonableness has been a requirement for the lawful exercise not only of administrative discretion, but in certain cases of private rights as well.[12] In judicial review, however, proportionality was forgotten for almost a decade. It was not until the mid-1980s that English judges rediscovered *Hook* and started using proportionality in this field. Proportionality cases had in common the existence of some kind of punishment or sanction for previous misconduct or failure. In *Benwell*, a prison officer challenged his dismissal as a disguised sanction of his trade union activities.[13] *Assegai* concerned a local authority's decision to

8 *R* v. *Barnsley MBC, ex parte Hook* [1976] 1 WLR 1052 (CA, Civil Division, 20 February 1976).
9 Ibid, p. 1057.
10 Ibid, p. 1063.
11 See, for instance, *International Drilling Fluids Ltd* v. *Louisville Investments (Uxbridge) Ltd* [1986] 1 Ch. 513 (CA, Civil Division, 20 November 1985).
12 Hickman (2010), pp. 194 f., chap. 7.
13 *R* v. *Secretary of State for the Home Department, ex parte Benwell* [1985] 1 QB 554 (HC, Queen's Bench Division, 24 May 1984).

exclude an individual from its premises.[14] Finally, *Nolan* concerned the decision of the Board of Examiners of Manchester Metropolitan University to fail a student for cheating.[15] During the late 1980s, this version of proportionality also appeared in some administrative law textbooks.[16]

Proportionality of penalties then, as in *proportionnalité des peines et des sanctions* ? Maybe so, since Denning LJ had expressed admiration for French law in his extrajudicial writings.[17] Besides, the term 'proportion' was already used in this sense in clause 20 of the Magna Carta, recently rediscovered by English scholars studying proportionality.[18] In any case, what is important is that proportionality was perceived as synonymous with pre-existing domestic standards of review. In *Hook*, the leading case, Denning LJ equated 'out of proportion' to what in older decisions had been referred to as 'excessive' and 'unreasonable'.[19] In *Benwell*, Hodgson J applied a very high threshold test requiring a disciplinary sanction 'so disproportionate to the offence as to be perverse'.[20] According to Woolf LJ's dicta in *Assegai*, '[w]here the response is out of proportion with the cause to this extent, this provides a very clear indication of unreasonableness in a *Wednesbury* sense'.[21] Finally, in *Nolan*, Sedley J used the terms 'rational' and 'proportionate' as synonymous.[22]

Initially, then, proportionality lacked conceptual autonomy. It was absorbed by the domestic concept of reasonableness and applied interchangeably with it. In judicial review in particular, disproportionality was synonymous with unreasonableness.[23] It corresponded to an exception, a negative standard, a threshold and not a prong-structured test. Disproportionality needed to be so apparent as to be self-evident, without

[14] *R* v. *London Borough of Brent, ex parte Assegai, The Times*, 18 June 1987 (CA, Civil Division, 11 June 1987).

[15] *R* v. *Manchester Metropolitan University, ex parte Nolan* (HC, Queen's Bench Division, 15 July 1993), unreported. Generally, see Craig (1999a), pp. 91 f.

[16] Craig (1989, p. 287) only talks about proportionality of punishment.

[17] Denning (1949), pp. 115 f., 122 f., cited by Allison (1996), p. 178.

[18] Jowell (2018), p. 2.

[19] The judge referred to *R* v. *Northumberland Compensation Appeal Tribunal, ex parte Shaw* [1952] 1 K.B. 338 (CA, Civil Division, 19 December 1951), p. 350. See *Hook*, p. 1057.

[20] *Benwell*, p. 569.

[21] *Assegai*.

[22] *Nolan*.

[23] This content of proportionality is mentioned in 'Proportionality', *Halsbury's Laws of England* (1989).

the need for further explanations from the judge.[24] Like other domestic standards of judicial review, its function was one of 'mistake avoidance'.[25] It was used to confine administrative authorities in the 'four corners' of their powers and thus to ensure the respect of the *ultra vires* principle, which, according to the Diceyan orthodoxy, provides the justification for judicial review. Hence, proportionality fitted well the supervisory role of courts and the traditional image of the judge as a referee. Constrained by existing concepts and doctrines, it had quite limited application and did not attract scholarly attention. It was not even mentioned as a category of unreasonableness in the long catalogue of such categories included in Wade and Forsyth's *Administrative Law* handbook.[26] It is through its connection to European law that proportionality acquired an autonomous content in judicial reasoning.

The Connection of Proportionality to European Law. The timid spread of proportionality in judicial review roughly coincides with the first applications of proportionality through the 'gateway' of the European Communities Act 1972 (ECA).[27] In early studies, the EC principle of proportionality was translated into a reasonableness requirement.[28] As time passed, however, the European version of proportionality was progressively perceived as distinct from domestic standards of judicial review, and especially *Wednesbury* unreasonableness.

In *Bell Line*, national regulations had banned the importation of milk from two ports that were the most convenient to Irish importers. The government had justified the measures on grounds of public health, and had designated some 'meat' ports instead, with experience in performing health controls. The High Court quashed the secretary of state's decision as a disguised restriction to trade: the exclusion of the two ports was unnecessary, especially in view of the fact that the government had already imposed licence requirements ensuring the protection of public health. Forbes J

24 For some examples, see *R* v. *Warwick Crown Court, ex parte Smalley* [1987] 1 WLR 237 (HC, Queen's Bench Division, 10 June 1986); *R* v. *International Stock Exchange of the UK and the Republic of Ireland Ltd, ex parte Else* [1993] BCC 11 (HC, Queen's Bench Division, 20 July 1992).

25 Craig (2016), chap. 1.

26 Wade and Forsyth (1988), pp. 416 f.

27 *Regina* v. *Goldstein* [1982] 1 WLR 804 (CA, Criminal Division, 2 April 1982); [1983] 1 WLR 151 (HL, 20 January 1983).

28 Brown (1978). This was sometimes expressed in the ECJ case law. In *Henn and Darby*, for example, Advocate General Warner stated that, in certain contexts, 'reasonableness' and 'proportionality' are the same concept (Opinion C-34/79, 14 December 1979, *Henn and Darby*, ECLI:EU:C:1979:295, 3830).

admitted that he 'would find it perhaps difficult if this were purely a question of the ordinary *Wednesbury* principles to say that the Minister had gone wrong in such a way that his decision should be interfered with'.[29] But he did not consider it necessary to deal with this question, since a different, more intrusive standard of review applied in this decision.

Bell Line was followed in subsequent case law. Even when a margin of appreciation was due to national public authorities, proportionality was deemed to impose a more intensive standard of review than irrationality.[30] The distinction between EC law and common law concepts and heads of review became increasingly solid during the following years. The European test of proportionality was less concerned with the intent of the reviewed authorities and instead focused on the impacts of domestic measures on economic freedoms.[31]

The distinctiveness of proportionality was progressively established in domestic cases too, due to its connection to a concept emerging in English law at the time: the concept of fundamental human rights. Since no bill of rights existed in the English constitution, proportionality was connected to another growing supranational legal order, the rights order of the ECHR. With the number of Strasbourg decisions condemning the UK for human rights violations increasing, it was progressively felt as 'wrong and embarrassing' that the convention protected rights better than the common law.[32] In the absence of incorporation, convention standards were taken into account in private law cases and in the judicial evolution of the common law.[33]

Calling for Change. By the late 1980s, proportionality had acquired its first enthusiasts, mainly certain well-known barristers and judges. In two articles published in 1988, Lester and Jowell called for the adoption of a doctrine proportionality to sanction the unjustifiable limitation of fundamental rights.[34] The same connection of proportionality to

[29] *R* v. *Minister of Agriculture, Fisheries and Food, ex parte Bell Line* [1984] 2 CMLR 502 (HC, Queen's Bench Division, 9 April 1984), para. 17.

[30] See, for example, *R* v. *Secretary of State for the Environment, ex parte NALGO* [1992] 5 AdminLR 785 (HC, Queen's Bench Division, 20 December 1991), pp. 800–1. See Green (1999), p. 150, citing relevant case law.

[31] *WH Smith Do-It-All Ltd* v. *Peterborough City Council* [1991] 4 All ER 193 (HC, Queen's Bench Division, 4 June 1990); *R* v. *Minister of Agriculture, Fisheries and Food, ex parte Roberts* [1991] 1 CMLR 555 (HC, Queen's Bench Division, 11 November 1990).

[32] Craig (2016), para. 18–003. See ECtHR, *Handyside* v. *The UK*, 7 December 1976, no. 5493/72; *The Sunday Times* v. *The UK*, 26 April 1979, no. 6538/74.

[33] See, for example, the *Spycatcher* litigation, analysed in Part III, Chapter 8.2.

[34] Jowell and Lester (1988a, 1988b).

fundamental rights language is seen in the extra-judicial writings of Laws.[35] Clearly, the application of proportionality as an aspect of *Wednesbury* unreasonableness in judicial review compromised its function considerably. This was noticed by the promoters of proportionality, who claimed that, though a decision may not meet the *Wednesbury* standard of perversity, it could still constitute an abuse of power. In their writings, proportionality was defined by opposition to the *Wednesbury* standard, as a standard that goes 'beyond' it.[36]

Proportionality as an autonomous principle could only be applied through an additional head of review. This had already been envisaged in the famous *GCHQ* case. In the words of Lord Diplock:

> Judicial review has I think developed to a stage today when [. . .] one can conveniently classify under three heads the grounds on which administrative action is subject to control by judicial review. The first ground I would call 'illegality', the second 'irrationality' and the third 'procedural impropriety'. That is not to say that further development on a case by case basis may not in course of time add further grounds. I have in mind particularly the possible adoption in the future of the principle of 'proportionality' which is recognised in the administrative law of several of our fellow members of the European Economic Community.[37]

The *GCHQ* decision provoked confusion as to whether proportionality constituted a ground separate from irrationality. While, in some cases, it was applied as an aspect of the *Wednesbury* test, in others its application was simply rejected since no authority existed for it.[38] In *Brind*, the House of Lords gave clear guidance on the matter.

3.2 The Rejection of Proportionality as a Domestic Head of Review

The Brind Affair. *Brind* concerned directives issued by the home secretary refraining the British Broadcasting Corporation (BBC) and the Independent Broadcasting Authority (IBA) from broadcasting speeches

35 Laws (1992).

36 Jowell and Lester (1988a), p. 860.

37 *Council of Civil Service Unions* v. *Minister for the Civil Service* [1984] 3 All ER 935 (HL, 22 November 1984), p. 950. This case is also known as *GCHQ*, and this name will be used here.

38 See, for example, *R* v. *Secretary of State for Transport, ex parte Pegasus Holidays (London) Ltd and Another* [1989] 2 All ER 481 (HC, Queen's Bench Division, 7 August 1987); *R* v. *Bournemouth Crown Court, ex parte Jobson and Another* (HC, Queen's Bench) CO/1917/89; *R* v. *General Medical Council, ex parte Colman* [1990] 1 All ER 489 (CA, Civil Division, 6 December 1989).

by members of Northern Ireland organisations deemed terrorist. The public interest invoked in justification of the restrictions was public safety, the prevention of crime and the protection of the rights of others. According to an affidavit provided by a member of the secretary of state, the broadcasting of direct speeches of suspected terrorists was likely to offend its listeners or even to encourage crime and lead to disorder. The applicants, represented by Lester QC and Pannick, claimed that this decision was contrary to the ECHR as it was out of proportion with the mischief that it sought to avoid.

In the Queen's Bench Division, even though Watkins LJ accepted that the minister should have regard to article 10 ECHR in the exercise of statutory powers, he declined to apply proportionality as an independent ground of review. In his view, proportionality would lead the court to substitute its view for that of the minister and thus to exceed its supervisory role. Still, Strasbourg case law did play a role in the judicial evaluation of the legality of public action. The judge examined whether the minister had invoked a pressing social need for limiting the freedom of speech, and if he had adduced prima facie evidence for its existence. Otherwise, Watkins LJ contented himself with sanctioning only manifest disproportionality, as an indicator of unreasonableness in the *Wednesbury* sense. He held that such disproportionality did not exist in the case at hand and approved the minister's decision.[39]

In the Court of Appeal, Lord Donaldson MoR was even more reluctant to follow the precepts of Strasbourg. He stated that even though treaty obligations may be taken into account in case of ambiguous statutory provisions, they cannot be deemed to supplement the intent of Parliament when it has conferred a power to another public authority. Consequently, the judge concluded that 'the doctrine of proportionality had no place in English law as a separate ground for the judicial review of administrative action since it was but one aspect of the test of reasonableness'.[40]

Proportionality v. Parliamentary Sovereignty. The House of Lords confirmed this decision.[41] For the Lords of Appeal, the matter mainly

[39] *R* v. *Secretary of State for the Home Department, ex parte Brind and Another, The Times*, 30 May 1989 (HC, Queen's Bench Division).

[40] *R* v. *Secretary of State for the Home Department, ex parte Brind* [1990] 1 All ER 469 (CA, Civil Division, 6 December 1989).

[41] *R* v. *Secretary of State for the Home Department, ex parte Brind* [1991] 1 AC 696 (HL, 7 February 1991).

concerned the incorporation of international treaties in the domestic sphere. According to the decision:

> Unless and until Parliament incorporates the Convention into domestic law, a course which it is well-known has a strong body of support, there appears [. . .] to be at present no basis upon which the proportionality doctrine applied by the European Court can be followed by the courts of this country.[42]

At the heart of the judicial rejection of proportionality, then, one finds traditional common law dualism and the doctrine of parliamentary sovereignty. The judges held that if they imposed on the minister the obligation to have regard to the convention they would be incorporating it 'by the back door', against Parliament's will.[43]

Parliamentary sovereignty also impeded the application of proportionality as a separate domestic ground of review. This is because such application would confer to the court an appellate jurisdiction, without statutory empowerment in this respect. Indeed, proportionality would lead the court to substitute its own view on the merits of the decision to that of primary decision-makers, who were 'very often elected'.[44] This was at odds with the traditionally supervisory role of courts and the *ultra vires* justification of judicial review. As Lord Ackner put it:

> [I]n order to invest the proportionality test with a higher status than the *Wednesbury* test, an inquiry into and a decision upon the merits cannot be avoided. Mr. Pannick's (Mr. Lester's junior) formulation – could the Minister reasonably conclude that his direction was necessary – must involve balancing the reasons, pro and con, for his decision, albeit allowing him 'a margin of appreciation' to use the European concept of the tolerance accorded to the decision-maker in whom a discretion has been vested.[45]

The adoption of proportionality would thus allow judicial scrutiny of the merits of public action and would upset the distribution of competences long effectuated by the English constitution.[46] Contrary to the will of Parliament, it would blur a distinction that is fundamental in this context: that of review and appeal. Indeed, as far as the outcomes of a decision were concerned, *Wednesbury* remained the 'touchstone of

42 Ibid.
43 Ibid, p. 762. On this point, see Hunt (1997), pp. 7 f.
44 *Brind* (HL), p. 762 (per Lord Ackner).
45 Ibid.
46 See also Elliott (2001).

legitimate judicial intervention'.[47] Put briefly, following constitutional orthodoxy in English law at the time, merits review was taboo, no matter how severely an act infringed fundamental rights.

Conceptual Fragmentation. The *Brind* decision was followed by lower courts.[48] The rejection of proportionality as an autonomous domestic ground led to its conceptual fragmentation in case law. Where it enjoyed statutory basis, as it did whenever the ECA was in play, proportionality was applied as an independent European ground of review. Whenever the common law principles applied, however, the independent application of proportionality was rejected and, at most, proportionality was applied as an aspect of reasonableness. The dichotomy between European and domestic proportionality is obvious in *International Stock Exchange*, where Popplewell J applied both versions of the principle separately.[49] Proportionality could invest different forms and accomplish different functions, according to the circumstances of the case. In private law, for example, where courts were charged with the balancing of competing interests, proportionality was applied as a principle for the protection of fundamental rights developed in Strasbourg case law. The same applied whenever there was an ambiguity in the common law and thus recourse could be made to the convention.[50]

The fragmentation of proportionality held back its spread as a fundamental rights principle and this was reflected in scholarship. In administrative law manuals, proportionality was mainly analysed as an EC law principle.[51] In the minds of English public lawyers it remained a concept of limited application, 'a foreign will-o'-the wisp'.[52] Apart from analyses by its promoters, English scholarship was not much preoccupied with the 'Euro-speak' of proportionality.[53] Even more, the rejection of proportionality as an autonomous domestic ground menaced its conceptual autonomy. In a 1992 article, Boyron considered proportionality as equivalent to the French *erreur manifeste*

[47] Craig (2016), para. 21–004.

[48] *R* v. *Chief Constable of Kent and Another, ex parte Absalom* (HC, Queen's Bench Division, 6 May 1993), unreported; *NALGO*.

[49] *International Stock Exchange*. See also *R* v. *Secretary of State for Health, ex parte Eastside Cheese Company (a firm)* [1999] 3 CMLR 123 (CA, Civil Division, 1 July 1999).

[50] *Derbyshire County Council* v. *Times Newspapers Ltd. and Others* [1992] QB 770 (CA, Civil Division, 19 February 1992), p. 813. On the limited instances where courts could rely on the ECHR before the HRA, see Hunt (1997).

[51] See Craig (1994), pp. 411 f.; de Smith et al. (1995), paras. 13–070 f.

[52] Taggart (2008), p. 424.

[53] Hoffmann (1999), p. 109.

d'appréciation. She suggested that the transfer of the principle into English administrative law would be a 'faulty translation', since she located its origins in the Anglo-Saxon notion of reasonableness.[54] Similarly, in an extra-judicial contribution in 1999, Hoffmann suggests that the classification of proportionality as an additional ground to irrationality is an 'analytical error' and that proportionality is only a method to explain how a certain decision is irrational.[55]

Seeking for Continuity. The 1990s was thus a 'frustrating time' for English judges, who could not apply proportionality in domestic law but knew that their decisions would be held as wrong in Strasbourg.[56] Indeed, in many cases, the ECtHR reproached the lack of proportionality of English measures.[57] English courts tried to align the domestic case law to the ECHR without explicitly engaging in proportionality analysis. Since it was impossible to comply with Strasbourg case law at the level of judicial reasoning structures, continuity was sought at the level of judicial methods. In *Bugdaycay*, the House of Lords declared that, in presence of fundamental rights, it would exercise intrusive scrutiny of public action, what came to be commonly called 'anxious scrutiny'.[58] Domestic judicial review standards started being interpreted as imposing 'important competing public interest' reasons for the justification of rights' infringement.[59] In *ITF*, Lord Cooke proposed a loosened formula of the *Wednesbury* test: 'Whatever the rubric under which the case is placed, the question here reduces, as I see it, to whether the Chief Constable has struck a balance fairly and reasonably open to him.'[60] Similarly, in *Chesterfield Properties*, Laws J stressed that the *Wednesbury* principle requires the primary decision-maker to balance the competing rights and public interests at stake.[61] Scholars have described the 'heightened'

[54] Boyron (1992).

[55] Hoffmann (1999), p. 109.

[56] Neuberger (2014), para. 4.

[57] ECtHR, *Observer and Guardian* v. *The UK*, 26 November 1991, no. 13585/88; *Campbell* v. *The UK*, 25 March 1992, no. 13590/88; *McLeod* v. *The UK*, 23 September 1998, no. 24755/94.

[58] *Bugdaycay* v. *Secretary of State for the Home Department* [1986] UKHL 3 (HL, 19 February 1986).

[59] See *Brind* (HL), pp. 748–9, per Lord Bridge. Similarly, per Lord Templeman.

[60] *R* v. *Chief Constable of Sussex, ex parte International Trader's Ferry Ltd (ITF)* [1998] UKHL 40 (HL, 11 November 1998).

[61] *Chesterfield Properties Plc* v. *Secretary of State for the Environment* [1998] 76 P & CR 117 (HC, Queen's Bench Division, 24 July 1997), p. 132.

application of traditional judicial review standards as proportionality 'in all but name'.[62]

Continuity between proportionality and domestic judicial review standards was not only established with the ECHR but also with EC law. Indeed, despite their perception as distinct grounds of review, proportionality under the ECA and *Wednesbury* unreasonableness were perceived to imply the same kind of judicial enquiry when EC law left a margin of appreciation to the reviewed public authority. In *ITF*, for example, Lord Slynn referred to the distinction between proportionality and irrationality as standards of review that the House of Lords had established in *Brind*. However, according to the judge, due to the margin of appreciation that the ECJ usually accords to national authorities, 'whichever test is adopted, and even allowing for a difference in onus, the result is the same'.[63] This marks an important difference with the first applications of the EC principle of proportionality, where despite the existence of a margin of appreciation, proportionality was explicitly applied as a more stringent test than *Wednesbury*.

The rejection of proportionality as an independent ground of review led to its diffusion and dilution in domestic judicial review standards. Proportionality was perceived as a doctrine that was applied through domestic concepts. This deprived the concept of its clarity and integrity in judicial practice. It is only with its reception as an autonomous head of rights-based review that proportionality acquired its proper dynamic in English public law.

3.3 The Reception of Proportionality in Human Rights Cases

A Commonwealth Transfer. The first time that proportionality was applied by a domestic court in the field of human rights was in *de Freitas*, a case that did not concern English law.[64] The Civil Servants Act of Antigua and Barbuda prohibited any expression of opinion by civil servants on politically controversial matters. Mr de Freitas, an individual affected by this provision, claimed that the restriction was disproportionately infringing his freedom of expression and of peaceful assembly and association guaranteed by the Antigua and Barbuda Constitution. In

[62] Hunt (1997), p. 216; Kavanagh (2009), p. 268; Craig (2016), pp. 624 f. See Part II, Chapter 6.3.

[63] *ITF*.

[64] *Elloy de Freitas* v. *Permanent Secretary of Ministry of Agriculture, Fisheries, Lands and Housing and Others* [1999] 1 AC 69 (Privy Council (Antigua and Barbuda), 30 June 1998).

response, the government contended that the constitution itself allowed for restrictions to civil servants' rights when they are 'reasonably required for the proper performance of their functions' and when they are 'reasonably justifiable in a democratic society'. The case was brought before the Privy Council, in its function as a supreme court of appeal.

The judges recalled the special position of civil servants in a democratic society. In their view, a 'proper balance' had to be struck between the public interest in well-functioning public services, and public servants' constitutional rights.[65] Examining the justification of the restrictions to civil servants' freedom of expression, the judges adopted a three-pronged proportionality test: the restriction should pursue a sufficiently important objective; it should be rationally connected to this objective; and the measures adopted should not be more than necessary for its achievement. Even though the judges held the restriction to satisfy the first two criteria, its blanket character 'raised a question of proportionality'.[66] More precisely, the lack of regard to the special circumstances surrounding each case could not, according to the court, be justified in a democratic society.

Interestingly, as Cohn has observed, proportionality was first applied by English judges as a Commonwealth transfer.[67] Connection to continental Europe was only indirect and informal. Indeed, the Privy Council cited case law from many jurisdictions, including the ECHR, English, or Canadian courts. Concerning the proportionality test in particular, the judges referred to the way other Commonwealth courts had interpreted clauses similar to the 'reasonably justifiable in a democratic society' clause of the Antigua and Barbuda Constitution. The court first cited a South African case where the Supreme Court had adopted a similar test, drawing on Canadian case law. However, the South African and Canadian tests contained an additional prong: apart from legitimate, adequate and necessary, the restriction of the right in question should have 'no disproportionately severe effect on those to whom [it] applies'.[68] This criterion was absorbed by the necessity prong in two subsequent

[65] Ibid, p. 76.

[66] Ibid, p. 80.

[67] See Cohn (2010), p. 621. However, one should bear in mind that *de Freitas* concerned the application of the Antigua and Barbuda Constitution, which possesses an extensive bill of rights and a special clause governing restrictions to these rights. Moreover, although reference to a 'democratic society' echoes the ECHR, Antigua and Barbuda are not signatory parties to the convention and have received this clause via Commonwealth influence.

[68] *De Freitas*, 80.

Zimbabwean cases, on which the Privy Council finally based its own application of proportionality in *de Freitas*.[69]

European Proportionality and Common Law Standards: A Continuum? With the entry into force of the Human Rights Act (HRA) in 2000 proportionality was received as a *European* human rights principle. The Act incorporated most of the rights protected by the ECHR in English law and provided a statutory 'gateway' to the application of proportionality in judicial review. Indeed, section 2 requires that domestic courts and tribunals 'take into account' Strasbourg case law in the application of the convention.

Daly has attracted scholarly attention as the first application of proportionality under the HRA. However, the principle was actually applied before, in *Mahmood*. In this case, Mr Mahmood was refused asylum by the British authorities and would be removed from the UK. He contested the decision as a disproportionate infringement of his right to family life, as he was married to a British citizen and had two children in the UK. The High Court held that the restriction of the applicant's right to family life served the public interest of immigration control and dismissed Mr Mahmood's application. The Court of Appeal confirmed this decision.[70] The facts of the case took place before the entry into force of the HRA. That is why Laws and May LJJ did not apply the proportionality test but resolved the dispute according to the traditional *Wednesbury* principles, adjusted to the human rights context. They found that the secretary of state's decision was reasonable. In response to the applicants' claims based on the convention, Laws LJ stated that, even under the HRA, judicial decisions would 'form part of a continuum with what the common law ha[d] already said'.[71] Thus, he concluded that, even if the convention were applied in the case before him, no violation of Article 8 would be found and the secretary of state would be entitled to reach the conclusions that he did.

The idea of a continuum between the ECHR and common law principles underlies Lord Phillips MoR's opinion too. In contrast to his colleagues in the Court of Appeal, he considered that since the secretary of state claimed to have taken into account Article 8 of the convention, the court should review the application of the ECHR. Hence, the court

[69] See also *Thomas* v. *Baptiste* [2000] 2 AC 1 (Privy Council (Trinidad and Tobago), 17 March 1999).

[70] *R* v. *Secretary of State for the Home Department, ex parte Mahmood* [2001] 1 WLR 840 (CA, Civil Division, 8 December 2000).

[71] Ibid, para. 30.

should not only confine itself to requiring a 'substantial justification' in order to approve the decision, as it did in domestic fundamental rights cases. It should further impose an objective necessity requirement on the primary decision-maker. In Lord Phillips's words:

> When anxiously scrutinising an executive decision that interferes with human rights, the court will ask the question, applying an objective test, whether the decision-maker could reasonably have concluded that the interference was necessary to achieve one or more of the legitimate aims recognised by the Convention. When considering the test of necessity in the relevant context, the court must take into account the European jurisprudence.[72]

That being, Lord Phillips' opinion did not lead to a different result from the one reached by his colleagues, the appeals were dismissed. In fact, Lord Phillips observed that, just like when common law rights were at stake, under the HRA the role of the court would remain supervisory and would only concern the reasonableness of the decision. After a long survey of Strasbourg case law on the matter, the judge concluded that the removal of the applicant was necessary in the interest of immigration control was one that a reasonable secretary of state was entitled to take.[73]

From *Wednesbury* to Proportionality: A Constitutional Shift. The issue of continuity between proportionality and *Wednesbury* was explored in more detail in *Daly*.[74] The case concerned the compatibility with the HRA of a government policy requiring prisoners to be absent when their cell and their legal correspondence were searched. Lord Steyn disagreed with the Court of Appeal judges in *Mahmood*. He observed that there is 'a material difference' between the traditional common law conceptual tools and the proportionality test.[75] Referring to the three proportionality criteria articulated in *de Freitas*, he stressed that they are 'more precise and more sophisticated than the traditional grounds of review'.[76] Then he went on to compare the two approaches, based on academic works on the subject. He observed that, even though in many

[72] Ibid, para. 40.

[73] Lord Philip's dicta were followed in *R* v. *Secretary of State for Home Department, ex parte Isiko and Another* [2000] EWCA Civ 346 (CA, Civil Division, 20 December 2000) and in *R* v. *Secretary of State for the Home Department, ex parte Samaroo* [2000] EWHC Admin 435 (HC, Queen's Bench Division, 20 December 2000).

[74] *R* v. *Secretary of State for the Home Department, ex parte Daly* [2001] UKHL 26 (HL, 23 May 2001).

[75] Ibid, para. 26.

[76] Ibid, para. 27.

cases, proportionality and rationality may overlap and lead to the same results, in certain cases, they do not. Under proportionality, the intensity of review is 'somewhat greater'. Indeed, according to Lord Steyn, even the 'anxious scrutiny' effectuated until then in fundamental rights cases did not entail such a thorough examination as 'the twin requirements [. . .] of meeting a pressing social need, and the question whether the interference was really proportionate to the legitimate aim being pursued'.[77]

Differences between the two approaches did not only concern the intensity of review but also its quality. In Lord Steyn's words, contrary to the traditional irrationality review, proportionality may require the court to 'assess the balance' struck by the reviewed authority. It may also require 'attention to be directed to the relative weight accorded to interests and considerations'.[78] What *Daly* made clear then, is that the principle of proportionality does not confine judgment to whether the decision was reasonable; rather it might lead the court to substitute its own judgment concerning the substance of the case for that of the primary decision-maker. Thus, it entails an important constitutional shift. Under the HRA, apart from the interpretation of convention terms and the scope of convention rights, the courts also decide for themselves the question of proportionality.[79] As a consequence, under the HRA, it is the responsibility of the judiciary to determine 'the essentially constitutional question, namely, whether the measure fulfils the constitutive requirements of a modern democracy'.[80]

In *Daly*, the House of Lords accepted proportionality as an autonomous head of review in English public law.[81] This decision remains the leading authority in HRA cases. It defined proportionality as the correct test for the assessment of rights limitations.[82] This is even more important, if one considers that human rights standards and proportionality also apply in the review of legislation. In this context, proportionality plays a crucial role in the convention-compatible interpretation of domestic law. Indeed, according to section 3 HRA: 'So far as it is possible to do so, primary legislation and subordinate legislation must be read and

[77] Ibid.

[78] Ibid.

[79] Kavanagh (2009), pp. 239 f.; Craig (2016), paras. 18–041 f. See also *R* v. *Headteacher and Governors of Denbigh High School, ex parte Begum* [2006] UKHL 15 (HL, 22 March 2006), p. 30, per Lord Bingham.

[80] Jowell (2000), p. 680.

[81] Hickman (2010), p. 173.

[82] *Regina* v. *Shayler* [2003] 1 AC 247 (HL, 21 March 2002), para. 33.

given effect in a way which is compatible with the Convention rights.' Ever since, proportionality has proliferated in case law under the HRA and has inspired elaborate analyses and debates in scholarship. Mainstream scholars have used constitutional language to describe its operation in domestic law.[83] Proportionality is considered a crucial feature in the transformation of English public law into a fundamental rights order. The consistent and coherent way that judges apply the principle has contributed significantly to this shift.

3.4 The Structure of Proportionality Analysis

A Prong-Structured Test for Fundamental Rights Restrictions. Contrary to its first applications in administrative law, it is now generally accepted among English lawyers that proportionality consists of a prong-structured test for assessing the justification of fundamental rights limitations. Since the voting through of the HRA scholars have urged the courts to apply proportionality consistently.[84] Proportionality has fitted well with the 'grid aesthetic' of common law legal reasoning.[85] Just like in Strasbourg case law or in the global proportionality model, typically judicial reasoning under the HRA is twofold. Courts engage in proportionality analysis only after ascertaining that a public authority has interfered with human rights. If such interference has taken place, the judge will examine whether interference is justified under the framework of proportionality. The local conception of proportionality is thus much akin to the Alexyan theory. Argumentation under its prongs in the separate personal opinions of English judges acquires a level of analytical clarity impossible to find in French judgments, where compromise among the members of the judiciary impedes detailed judicial argumentation. The analysis of some landmark cases illustrates the way proportionality is applied in judicial review.

The Legitimate Aim and Rationality Requirements. Influenced by Strasbourg, the typical English approach to the legitimate aim criterion requires a 'pressing' necessity, aim or social need. When judges defer to the choices of the primary decision-makers, the objective of the reviewed

[83] Dyzenhaus, Hunt and Taggart (2001); Jowell (2003a), p. 68; Kavanagh (2009), pp. 271 f.; Craig (2016), paras. 18–004 f.

[84] Pannick (1998), p. 549; Laws (1998), pp. 262, 265; Craig (1999a); Wong (2000); Elliott (2001); Fordham and de la Mare (2001), p. 27. More recently, Rivers (2014); Ramshaw (2019).

[85] Schlag (2002), p. 1051.

measures is defined in general terms.[86] On the contrary, when the necessity of the measures is doubted, their objective can be very concretely defined in order to assess less restrictive alternatives. The judge will form her own view on the legitimacy of the justification provided by the primary decision-maker. In *Lambert*, for example, Lord Steyn described in a detailed way the mischief that the law sought to face:

> [S]ophisticated drug smugglers, dealers and couriers typically secrete drugs in some container, thereby enabling the person in possession of the container to say that he was unaware of the contents. Such defences are commonplace and they pose real difficulties for the police and prosecuting authorities.[87]

Since the legitimacy of the justification provided by the reviewed authorities is objectively established, the relation between the legitimate aim and the suitability test is not always clear. This is very well exemplified in the famous *Belmarsh Prison* case.[88] After the terrorist attacks of September 2001, the British Parliament enacted the Anti-Terrorism, Crime and Security Act 2001. Derogating from Article 5 ECHR, the act provided for the indefinite detention without trial or deportation of non-British nationals suspected of being a threat to national security. The derogation was based on Article 15 ECHR and justified by a terrorist threat to the UK. The British Parliament's Joint Committee on Human Rights and other human rights institutions had expressed doubts as to the necessity of the derogation under the terms of the convention. Their statements were invoked by the appellants who contested the proportionality of the measures. In response, the attorney general submitted that the international terrorists of Al Qaeda constituted 'a public emergency threatening the life of the nation' as Article 15 requires. He founded his submission on evidence that was partly secret.

Concerning the legitimacy of the aim pursued by the derogation, namely, the existence of a threat to the life of the nation, Lord Bingham observed that the appellants had not succeeded in showing an error in law in the reviewed authorities' decision. He observed that national governments enjoyed a wide margin of appreciation in determining whether there existed a public emergency that justified derogations

86 *R* v. *Attorney General and Another, ex parte Countryside Alliance and Others* [2007] UKHL 52 (HL, 28 November 2007).

87 *Regina* v. *Lambert* [2002] 2 AC 545 (HL, 5 July 2001), para. 36.

88 *A and Others* v. *Secretary of State for the Home Department; X and Another* v. *Secretary of State for the Home Department* [2004] UKHL 56 (HL, 16 December 2004). On this point, see Wade (2004), p. 366.

from the ECHR. For him, the question was 'a pre-eminently political judgment', requiring predictions about human behaviour, on which reasonable disagreement can exist.[89] A political resolution of the question would be more appropriate than the court substituting its own view for that of the home secretary. Lord Bingham thus accepted that the objective invoked by the attorney general was sufficiently important to justify derogation from Article 5.

The judge then proceeded to the proportionality test. He observed that the measures did not address the threat constituted by UK nationals, which, even though quantitatively less important, was not qualitatively different from the one posed by foreign nationals. Moreover, the executive did not explain 'why a terrorist, if a serious threat to the UK, ceases to be so on the French side of the English Channel or elsewhere'.[90] On the contrary, the impugned provisions were understandable if the measures were designed for immigration control. Lord Bingham therefore concluded that a declaration of incompatibility for breach of proportionality would be appropriate: '[T]he choice of an immigration measure to address a security problem had the inevitable result of failing adequately to address that problem.'[91] The majority of the Lords of Appeal agreed with Lord Bingham's opinion.

Lord Hoffmann also agreed with his colleagues that the measures were disproportionate. However, he dissented as to the exact prong of proportionality that was applicable in this case. In his opinion, even if the existence of a terrorist threat was accepted, without regard to the secret evidence invoked by the attorney general, this threat would not be serious enough to constitute a threat to the life of the nation:

> Of course the government has a duty to protect the lives and property of its citizens. But that is a duty which it owes all the time and which it must discharge without destroying our constitutional freedoms. There may be some nations too fragile or fissiparous to withstand a serious act of violence. But that is not the case in the United Kingdom. [...] Terrorist violence, serious as it is, does not threaten our institutions of government or our existence as a civil community. [...] This is a nation which has been tested in adversity, which has survived physical destruction and catastrophic loss of life. I do not underestimate the ability of fanatical groups of terrorists to kill and destroy, but they do not threaten the life of the nation. Whether we would survive Hitler

[89] *A and Others*, paras. 28–9.
[90] Ibid, paras. 30 f.
[91] Ibid, para. 43.

hung in the balance, but there is no doubt that we shall survive Al-Qaeda.[92]

In Lord Hoffmann's view then, derogation from Article 5 did not serve a sufficiently important legitimate aim and, in judging that it did, the lower courts and tribunals had erred in law. There was no need for the court to examine the rationality of the measures, since their compatibility with the convention was already excluded from the first prong of the proportionality analysis.

The Necessity and Balancing Stages. Until recently, in the dominant version of proportionality in English case law, the last prong of proportionality was the necessity test. Under this prong, the court sanctions over-inclusive means such as blanket prohibitions, when a partial one would succeed in achieving the aim. In *Regina* v. *A* for example, the defendant was accused of rape. As a defence, he claimed that he had the consent of the alleged victim and he wanted to adduce evidence that he had had sexual intercourse with the victim some days before the incident. For the protection of victims of sexual crimes, a legislative provision totally excluded such evidence.[93] In examining the compatibility of the provision with the right to fair trial, Lord Slynn observed that: 'Whilst the statute pursued desirable goals, the methods adopted amounted to legislative overkill.'[94] Even though this could not be remedied through the common law rules of statutory construction, section 3 of the HRA imposed a strong interpretative presumption. Thus, the provision should be construed in compatibility with the convention and the principle of proportionality and it should be read as allowing ad hoc relevant evidence.[95]

The English structure of proportionality has been long characterised by an ambiguity as to the balancing exercise, which was usually deemed to be engaged at the necessity stage.[96] In *Huang*, counsel for the claimant said that the *de Freitas* formulation of the test was wrong in ignoring this last prong of proportionality.[97] Considering this claim, Lord Bingham cited with approval his own dicta in *Razgar* and stated that proportionality 'must always involve the striking of a fair balance between the rights

92 Ibid, paras. 95–6.
93 *Regina* v. *A (No. 2)* [2002] 1 AC 45 (HL, 17 May 2001).
94 Ibid, p. 67.
95 Ibid, p. 68.
96 Kavanagh (2009), pp. 235–6.
97 *Huang* v. *Secretary of State for the Home Department; Kashmiri* v. *Same* [2007] 2 AC 167 (HL, 21 March 2007).

of the individual and the interests of the community which is inherent in the whole of the Convention'.[98] In his view, 'the severity and consequences of the interference will call for careful assessment at [the necessity] stage'.[99] Lord Bingham went on to state that whenever the individual is completely deprived of her right, the impact of the impugned measures will be disproportionate in any case. In this way, he detached disproportionality from the necessity stage.

In subsequent case law, the balancing was announced under a fourth stage of proportionality analysis. In *Bank Mellat*, referring to the Canadian Supreme Court decision in *Oakes*, Lord Reed stated that:

> [T]here is a meaningful distinction to be drawn [. . .] between the question whether a particular objective is in principle sufficiently important to justify limiting a particular right (step one), and the question whether, having determined that no less drastic means of achieving the objective are available, the impact of the rights infringement is disproportionate to the likely benefits of the impugned measure (step four).[100]

Hence, the reasoning that the balancing test implies was further refined. While it concerns the value scale of the primary decision-maker, it is distinguished from the legitimate aim requirement, due to its ad hoc nature. While it entails consideration of the circumstances of the case, it is distinguished from the necessity stage, which is only concerned with outcomes, without questioning the aim of the reviewed decision. Resemblance to the Alexyan proportionality model is striking.

Nonetheless, neither in *Huang* nor in *Bank Mellat* did the judges engage in an explicit balancing exercise.[101] In reality, the fourth stage was reduced to a prohibition to interfere with the 'substance' of the right at stake, similar to that existing in the ECHR context. Other decisions invoke 'an irreducible minimum of Convention rights'.[102] Such references imply categorical reasoning. Indeed, during the first decade of the application of proportionality under the HRA, English judges did not engage in balancing, in the sense of the global proportionality model: the

[98] *R* v. *Secretary of State for the Home Department ex parte Razgar* [2004] UKHL 27 (HL, 17 June 2004), para. 20.

[99] *Huang*, para. 19.

[100] *Bank Mellat* v. *Her Majesty's Treasury (No. 2)* [2013] UKSC 39 (SC, 19 June 2013), para. 74.

[101] In *Bank Mellat*, the Supreme Court assessed the fair balance struck by the reviewed authority in view of the requirements of rationality: see per Lord Sumption, esp. para. 20.

[102] *International Transport Roth GmbH and Others* v. *Secretary of State for the Home Department* [2003] QB 728 (CA Civil Division, 22 February 2002), paras. 28–9.

intensity of interference with the right was not compared to the degree of advancement of the legitimate aim according to a certain scale of values.[103] The orthodox scholarly perception of proportionality analysis initially did not involve such balancing either.[104]

The Supreme Court's decision in *Nicklinson* brought about an important change in this respect.[105] Mr Nicklinson, completely paralysed after a stroke, wanted to end his life but could not do so without assistance. Assisted suicide is unlawful under English law and Mr Nicklinson sought a declaration of the current state of the law as incompatible with Article 8 ECHR. Examining the proportionality of the domestic legislation, Lord Mance clearly distinguished the necessity from the balancing stage of proportionality analysis. Lord Neuberger produced extensive practical moral argumentation on the advantages and disadvantages of the reviewed legislation. He stressed that, while the ban interfered with the applicants' right to die, it aimed at the protection of weak and vulnerable persons. The judge considered that the ban could not be justified by arguments based on the value or sanctity of human life. Suicide is legal in the UK and, as evidence shows, people with a progressive degenerative disease are often forced to kill themselves before they would wish to do so, by fear that they will be incapable of committing suicide later. Still, Lord Neuberger accepted that it could be morally corrupting for a person to assist another to commit suicide. In this respect, he considered that there was an important distinction to be drawn, both in moral and legal terms, between euthanasia and assisted suicide, on the basis of the autonomy of the person who wishes to put an end to her life.[106] Proportionality in English public law increasingly resembles the argumentative framework described by Alexy and his followers.

3.5 Culling 'Sacred Cows'

Proportionality and Legislative Reasons. Clearly, the application of proportionality as a distinctive head of judicial review has brought about an important extension of judicial powers in the English context. At first glance however, the first two stages of proportionality seem to

[103] For a survey of judicial practice on the matter, see Rivers (2006).

[104] See, among others, Jowell (2000).

[105] *R* v. *Ministry of Justice, ex parte Nicklinson and Another*; *R* v. *The Director of Public Prosecutions, ex parte AM*; *R* v. *The Director of Public Prosecutions, ex parte AM* [2014] UKSC 38 (SC, 25 June 2014).

[106] Ibid, paras. 92 f.

provide a more sophisticated and intrusive version of already existing methods in English judicial review. Indeed, in many cases, the legitimate aim test will correspond to the exclusion of illicit purposes, traditionally sanctioned by courts under the head of illegality. Similarly, the rationality test in many cases overlaps with the improper purposes or the relevancy test.[107]

Yet, important differences exist between the traditional common law methods and these two proportionality stages. First of all, the scope of proportionality review is much broader, since it generally applies to public actions justiciable under the ECHR. Most notably in this respect, proportionality is not addressed only to the administration but also to Parliament. Moreover, while previously the purposes were concretely determined by the relevant statute through construction or interpretation, now they consist in general and indeterminate values, such as 'national security', 'the protection of morals' or 'the protection of the rights of others'. Therefore, proportionality, through the legitimate aim requirement, in fact imposes a procedural and substantial duty to provide (legitimate) reasons for public action and even for legislation. Such a duty did not exist before in English judicial review.[108] When no legitimate aim at all is advanced by the government, the measure fails without need to evaluate its objective.[109]

In order to understand the mischief that a contested legislative provision is purported to address, courts may be led to consider matters stated in Parliament.[110] There goes a 'sacred cow' of the English legal culture.[111] Long since the Magna Carta, judges have been prohibited from referring to *Hansard*. Such reference was deemed to violate the principle of parliamentary sovereignty, since it entails the danger of the courts scrutinising the seriousness of parliamentary debates and of attributing to the whole legislature the will of a single MP or minister. This long excluded purposive interpretation from the methods of English judicial review. In Lord Scarman's words: 'We are to be governed not by Parliament's

[107] On the common law constraints on administrative discretion, see Craig (2016), paras. 17–009 f.

[108] *R* v. *Secretary of State for the Home Department, ex parte Doody* [1994] 1 AC 531 (HL, 24 June 1993), p. 564. On this point, see Kavanagh (2009), pp. 241 f.

[109] *Ghaidan* v. *Mendoza* [2004] 3 WLR 113 (HL, 21 June 2004), para. 18.

[110] Kavanagh (2014).

[111] Reference to Lord Slynn's dicta in *Lambert*, para. 6. According to this judge, the application of the HRA would require important constitutional changes in English law, 'sacred cows culled'.

intentions but by Parliament's enactments.'[112] In the context of proportionality analysis, judges often have regard to Parliament's decision-making process, but only insofar as it serves the court's understanding of the measures at stake. This does not mean that MPs should themselves reason in proportionality terms. As Lord Nicholls put it in *Wilson*: '[T]he proportionality of legislation is not to be judged by the quality of the reasons advanced in support of it in the course of parliamentary debate, or by the subjective state of mind of individual ministers or other members.'[113]

An Outcome-Based Test. Proportionality is an outcome-based test. Contrary to the traditional judicial review principles, it is the current effect of the legislation that is considered and not the factual situation that existed when the decision was taken.[114] In this sense, proportionality is an objective test.[115] Through the evaluation of the merits of the measures at stake, the judge substitutes her own view as to the justification provided by the reviewed authorities. As Lord Bingham made clear in *Begum*: '[W]hat matters in any case is the practical outcome, not the quality of the decision-making process that led to it.'[116] There goes another 'sacred cow' of English judicial review, traditionally concerned with questions of competence and procedure. In some cases, the court has gone so far as to consider alternative measures advancing the purpose and to require evidence as to the ineffectiveness of such measures.[117] In contrast to the common French perception of proportionality as a 'narrowly tailored' test, in English public law proportionality not only concerns the scope of the contested measures, but also their real impacts. The difference between review and appeal is considerably reduced.[118]

[112] *Duport Steels LTD* v. *Sirs* [1980] 1 All ER 529 (HL, 3 January 1980). See, however, *Pepper (Inspector of Taxes)* v. *Hart* [1992] UKHL 3, where the House of Lords accepted that the court can refer to *Hansard* in certain cases.

[113] *Wilson* v. *First County Trust Ltd* [2003] UKHL 40 (HL, 10 July 2003), para. 67.

[114] Ibid, para. 62.

[115] See *Begum*, per Lord Bingham, para. 30. See also *Belfast City Council* v. *Miss Behavin' Ltd* [2007] 1 WLR 1420 (HL, 25 April 2007), per Lord Hoffmann, para. 13; per Lord Mance, para. 44; per Lord Neuberger, para. 88.

[116] *Begum*, para. 31.

[117] *R* v. *Chief Constable of Gloucestershire Constabulary, ex parte Laporte* [2007] 2 AC 105 (HL, 13 November 2006); in the review of legislation, see *Lambert*, paras. 37 f. On the judicial consideration of alternative measures more generally, see Jowell (2000), pp. 679–80.

[118] On the role of the appellate court in the assessment of proportionality, see *R* v. *Chief Constable of Greater Manchester Police and Another, ex parte AR* [2018] UKSC 47 (SC, 30 July 2018), paras. 53 f.

Judicial enquiry under proportionality is concerned with the concrete facts of the case. *Shayler* concerned the disclosure of information by a former member of the security service.[119] Such a disclosure was banned by an Act of Parliament. The House of Lords found that, *in abstracto*, the impugned act was compatible with the convention, since procedures were available to individuals for exemption from the duty of confidentiality in case a public interest required so. However, the House of Lords stressed the importance of the fact-sensitive application of proportionality. The above legally established procedures satisfied the requirements of the convention, 'if properly applied', that is, given that 'the power to withhold authorisation was not abused and that proper disclosures were not stifled'.[120] In other words, while in the abstract the ban and the possibility to authorise disclosure did not violate Article 10 ECHR, the concrete proportionality of the relevant provisions would depend on their application by the competent authorities in each case.[121] In the case at hand, no disproportionate administrative conduct was at stake, since Mr Shayler had not requested any authorisation in the first place.

While courts evaluate the impact of legislation, proportionality is not understood as an optimisation principle. Instead, what proportionality sanctions is domestic authorities' indifference towards convention rights. Courts defer to Parliament's appreciations concerning the appropriateness or the necessity of the contested measures. *Wilson*, for example, concerned a provision in the Consumer Credit Act that precluded the enforcement of an obligation resulting from an improperly executed consumer credit agreement. The House of Lords accepted that, in some cases, the sanction imposed on the creditor for not fulfilling the formalities of the act would be too harsh. However, the dissuasive goal of the legislation in question rendered the measure proportionate. Lord Nicholls underscored that the Consumer Credit Act pursued the protection of consumers. In his view, imposing the sanction only in cases where it would be proportionate would not achieve the goal of the legislation. As he put it: 'Something more drastic was needed in order to focus attention on the need for lenders to comply strictly with these particular

[119] *Regina* v. *Shayler*.
[120] Ibid.
[121] See also *R* v. *Director of Public Prosecutions, ex parte Kebeline and Others* [2000] 2 AC 326 (HL, 28 October 1999), per Lord Hope.

obligations.'[122] Thus, the preventive goal of the measures justified the government's assessment as to their appropriateness and necessity.[123]

Proportionality and Deference. Despite the outcome-based scrutiny that proportionality entails, English lawyers insist that the roles of the judiciary and the reviewed authority remain distinct. In *Daly*, Lord Steyn stressed that proportionality did not involve a shift to merits review. Monitoring the necessity of a right's restriction in a democratic society differs from expressing an opinion on the general desirability of the measure in socio-political terms.[124] This difference is fundamental for English scholars.[125] The judicial role under proportionality thus remains supervisory and courts are not entitled to take the decision according to what they think appropriate in the abstract. The definition of the public interest belongs to Parliament and to authorities accountable to the people. As Lord Hoffmann neatly put it in *Alconbury*: 'The Human Rights Act 1998 was no doubt intended to strengthen the rule of law but not to inaugurate the rule of lawyers.'[126] Judicial opinions are expressed in legal terms and are based exclusively on legal standards. Proportionality does not impose a general 'correctness' requirement.[127]

The difference between the role of the judiciary and that of the reviewed branches of government is ensured by the doctrine of deference. Following this doctrine, the intensity of the proportionality scrutiny varies as a function of the weight accorded to the opinions of the reviewed authority. Influenced by the European concept of the margin of appreciation, this idea first appeared in one of the earliest HRA cases, *Kebeline*. Lord Hope stated that, when striking a balance among the convention principles, sometimes 'it will be appropriate for the courts to recognise that there is an area of judgment within which the judiciary will defer, on democratic grounds, to the considered opinion of the elected body or person' who issued the contested act.[128] Other terms have also been used to express this cautious approach: 'margin of discretion', 'discretionary area of judgment'.

[122] *Wilson*, para. 71.
[123] Ibid, para. 169.
[124] *Daly*, para. 28.
[125] Hickman (2010), p. 177.
[126] *R* v. *Secretary of State for the Environment, Transport and the Regions, ex parte Alconbury Developments Ltd and Others* [2001] UKHL 23 (HL, 9 May 2001), para. 121.
[127] Craig (1999a), pp. 100 f.; Kavanagh (2009), pp. 239 f.
[128] *Kebeline*, p. 380.

When searching for the appropriate intensity of review, courts take into account various factors. In *Roth*, Laws LJ identified four rationales for deferring to the reviewed authority: democratic legitimacy, definition of the right as qualified in the convention, constitutional responsibility and institutional expertise.[129] Scholars have since produced extended analyses of these rationales, have added more, and often attempt to categorise the various cases under which matters of deference might arise.[130] Once again, the English developments on this point are much akin to the transnational proportionality literature.

There is general consensus that deference does not imply abdication of judgment or injusticiability. Even when significant weight is accorded to the primary decision, judges should still sanction disproportionate violations of fundamental rights. In certain cases of social policy, deference will lead courts to apply a vague and unstructured proportionality test.[131] Generally, however, a categorical subject matter-based approach to deference has been rejected.[132] Even in areas traditionally left to Parliament, deference is taken into account within the proportionality framework.[133] The weight accorded to the reviewed decision may differ according to the various issues arising under the various prongs.[134] The court's access to facts will also be an important factor affecting the intensity of proportionality scrutiny.[135] When faced with sensible subject matter, such as the fight against terrorism, or with matters where the decision-making authority has special expertise, the courts will tend to avoid complex value

129 *Roth*, pp. 765 f.

130 Hunt (2003); Rivers (2006); Kavanagh (2009), pp. 181 f., 211 f.; Hickman (2010), pp. 128 f.; Brady (2012); Craig (2016), paras. 18–033 f.

131 *Poplar Housing and Regeneration Community Association Ltd* v. *Donoghue* [2002] QB 48 (CA, Civil Division, 27 April 2001); *Countryside Alliance*, per Lord Hope; more recently, *Hounslow LBC* v. *Powell; Leeds CC* v. *Hall; Birmingham CC* v. *Frisby* [2011] UKSC 8 (SC, 23 February 2011), para. 41, per Lord Hope. See also *Manchester CC* v. *Pinnock* [2010] UKSC 45 (SC, 3 November 2010). Contra, *Akerman-Livingstone* v. *Aster Communities Ltd* [2015] UKSC 15 (SC, 11 March 2015).

132 Craig (2016), para. 18–044. In case law, *Ghaidan* v. *Mendoza.*

133 Hunt (2003), pp. 349 f. In case law, see, for example, *Begum*; *R* v. *Secretary of State for Health, ex parte Sinclair Collis* [2012] QB 394 (CA, Civil Division, 17 June 2011).

134 *Countryside Alliance*, per Lord Hope, paras. 84 f. See Hunt (2003), pp. 368 f.; Craig (2016), para. 18–036.

135 *R* v. *Secretary of State for the Home Department, ex parte Lord Carlile of Berriew QC, and Others* [2014] UKSC 60 (SC, 12 November 2014).

judgments and will often emphasise procedural requirements of reasoned justification and substantial evidence.[136]

***

After a long period of rejection, proportionality is now flourishing in English public law discourse and has led to an impressive evolution of domestic judicial review. Contrary to the traditional concern only with the irrationality of the primary decision-maker, proportionality is a test for assessing the balance struck by the reviewed authorities. Far from being self-evident, it leads the courts to extensive argumentation concerning the legitimacy of rights restrictions and the intensity of judicial review. While it has not always involved a value-laden balancing of competing rights or principles, it does involve the consideration of the outcomes of legislation by reference to convention rights and it obliges public authorities to justify restrictions to those rights. The content of proportionality in English law is akin to the one described in the proportionality theory. Contrary to their French colleagues, English judges proceed to an intrusive review of the aims of the primary decision-maker, even when this is Parliament. Once more in contrast with the other side of the English Channel, the English application of proportionality has led the courts to review the facts of the case before them assiduously and to consider less restrictive alternative measures.

Proportionality has provoked extensive debates in English public law, both in scholarship and in the courtroom. The question of whether its application is in continuity with or represents a change of the conceptual apparatus of domestic judicial review has always been at the core of discussion. The clear conceptual distinction of proportionality from irrationality long constrained its function in judicial review, since its application presupposed the recognition of an additional ground of review, contrary to the principle of parliamentary sovereignty. Therefore, whenever proportionality was rejected in judicial review, English public lawyers have sought its continuity with existing domestic concepts and distinctions, sometimes at a cost for its conceptual neatness. However, it is through its establishment as different from pre-existing heads that proportionality has flourished in English public law. It is precisely this distinction that liberated its application from the structural constraints that traditionally marked the application of the *Wednesbury* test. This is very different from the thirst for continuity observed in the

[136] See Clayton (2002), p. 124; Hunt (2003), pp. 349 f.; Craig (2016), para. 18–049. In case law, see *Sinclair Collis*, per Lord Neuberger.

French perception of proportionality and is connected to the analytical English public law tradition.

The evolution of proportionality in English public law has primarily been the work of judges, incited to adopt this direction by lawyers. Scholars have followed rather than guided evolution in the courtroom. Compared to the French *doctrine*, the English perception of proportionality has been much more loyal to the actual reasoning patterns of courts. This is because rather than some kind of idea, knowledge or common sense shared by lawyers, proportionality represents a tool, a head of review, a new ground for lawyerly and judicial argumentation. Even though the analysis that follows will show that English public law is undergoing radical transformation that nuances the conclusions just examined, this instrumental, pragmatic perception of proportionality has underpinned its spread in this context. Interestingly, this perception stands in stark contrast with the one underlying the spread of proportionality in the Greek context, where proportionality is perceived as a value in itself.

4

Proportionality in Greek Public Law:

η θριαμβευτική πορεία[1]

The spread of proportionality in Greece would please any proportionality enthusiast. Proportionality emerged in Greek legal discourse earlier than in France or England and has been applied by courts for more than forty years. Greece is one of the rare legal systems in which, since 2001, proportionality explicitly enjoys constitutional status. The generous formulation of Article 25(1) of the Constitution states:

> The rights of the human being as an individual and as a member of society and the principle of the welfare state rule of law are guaranteed by the State. All agents of the State shall be obliged to ensure the unhindered and effective exercise thereof. These rights also apply to the relations between individuals to which they are appropriate. Restrictions of any kind which, according to the Constitution, may be imposed upon these rights, should be provided either directly by the Constitution or by statute, should a reservation exist in the latter's favour, and should respect the principle of proportionality.

Research on the use of proportionality in Greece meets difficulties similar to those observed in the French and English cases. Greek public lawyers believe proportionality to designate much more than its explicit use in judicial decisions or in official legal sources. Proportionality is understood as a universal idea, a value akin to justice, which is inherent in judicial review, despite it being systematised as a concrete method of review abroad. Greek public lawyers generally agree on the conceptual content of proportionality, which eclectically recovers doctrinal developments in other jurisdictions and at home. However, when it comes to judicial practice, local judicial review structures seem to constrain the use of proportionality language, whose content hardly corresponds to the idea described outside courtroom. The above features are neatly expressed in Gerapetritis' thesis on proportionality, which, albeit written

[1] This phrase is used by Gogos (2005), p. 299. It means 'the triumphant march'.

in English, has been very influential in the Greek context.[2] The study consists of an erudite comparative analysis of the application of proportionality in French, English, Greek and European administrative law. In this work, proportionality is perceived as a method of review or an ideal that is rarely applied as such by domestic courts, but rather finds expression through other heads of review, techniques and concepts.

Here, as in the other case studies, legal discourse is studied only insofar as proportionality language is used. My purpose is not to show that the ideas designated by proportionality did not exist before its emergence as a particular discourse or to expose as inexact or incorrect doctrinal analyses on the ideal of proportionality. More modestly, I study how Greek lawyers started to speak in proportionality terms and what content they attached to this particular way of speaking. When did proportionality emerge in Greek public law? What has its function been in the discourse of legal actors? How has proportionality interacted with existing categories, concepts and distinctions? Who uses proportionality and why? In the Greek context, additional difficulties exist. Since Aristotle, 'proportion' (*αναλογία*) has been used as a legal concept and involves moral-legal evaluations. It means simultaneously 'analogy' and 'proportion'. Proportionality corresponds to a different term (*αναλογικότητα*), which did not exist in Greek before. However, in the early uses of proportionality language, Greek lawyers were using the term 'proportion' instead. In order to identify these exceptional uses of proportionality language and to distinguish them from the homonymous language of analogy, other indices were taken into account: reasoning in prongs, reference to Germany, to European case law or to fundamental rights. Further, a major challenge for this study has been access to Greek legal sources, which is much more difficult than in the other systems studied. Only few academic writings are accessible online and Greek legal databases are much less reliable and manageable than French or English ones.

Like in France, proportionality emerged as a Greek public law concept in the field of expropriation. Since the mid-1970s proportionality was sparsely used in scholarly writings and judicial decisions (Section 4.1). In 1984, the Council of State enunciated proportionality as a general constitutional principle in the field of professional freedom, but its application was soon limited to a manifest error test (Section 4.2). Until the late 1990s, the function of proportionality in judicial review was mainly the intensification of formal and procedural requirements in administrative

[2] Gerapetritis (1997).

law. Proportionality was more important in substantive case law, where it had a content close to equity (Section 4.3). It is since its constitutional entrenchment in 2001 that proportionality has become a hegemonic method of reasoning in Greek law (Section 4.4). However, scholarly consensus as to the content of proportionality has not led to its consistent application in case law. In spite of its commonly shared perception as a fundamental rights principle, proportionality in judicial review at most corresponds to a test of efficiency and rationalisation (Section 4.5).

4.1 The Neglected Cases of the 1970s

The Emergence of Proportionality as a Public Law Concept. According to the dominant narrative in Greek public law, proportionality was 'born' in the Council of State case law during the 1980s.[3] However, some sparse uses of proportionality language are to be found already during the 1970s. First it was criminal law scholars who, since the beginning of the decade, used the metaphor of proportion. Procedural requirements and standards taken into account during criminal prosecution and trial were deemed to express more general principles and ideals, such as 'the principle of necessary proportion'.[4] In 1975, Androulakis talked about the requirements of appropriateness, necessity and 'necessary balance' resulting from certain provisions of the code of criminal procedure.[5] These principles were generally connected to the requirement of moderation and non-excess of public officials in this context. However, these ideas did not find concrete expression in case law for some considerable time.

As far as general public law is concerned, proportionality emerged during the year that followed the enactment of the 1975 Constitution, at first in expropriation law. During the 1970s, as today, the administrative procedure of expropriation was replete with technicalities. First, at the stage of urban planning, the administration committed a specific site to public use in service of a public utility purpose. This entailed the prohibition of some kinds of the land use, most notably construction. At a second stage, the administration acquired the land, usually through expropriation. While the urban plan, as a general administrative act, was generally subject to the principle of legality, expropriation in particular should be provided for by law and was subject to stricter legal constraints, like the requirement of a just compensation or the obligation

3 Kontogiorga (1989a), p. 9; Orfanoudakis (2003), p. 79.
4 Androulakis (1972).
5 Androulakis (1975), p. 1.

for the administration to examine less onerous solutions for the affected individuals.[6]

In a decision in 1975, monitoring the act of expropriation for the construction of a cultural centre in Xanthi, the Council of State applied a strict separation between the two procedures. In doing so, it reversed its previous case law, in which the legality of the administrative action was considered as a whole. According to this new decision, at the stage of urban planning, the administration should be guided only by public interest considerations. Individual property rights and other particular legal requirements were to be considered only after the urban plan was concluded, during the expropriation procedure.[7] The clarity of this solution came at the cost of the coherence of administrative action and sometimes had absurd consequences. For example, a town plan could constrain the use of private lands, while, at the same time, the expropriation of these lands could be legally prohibited.

Beginning his career at the Council of State, Pararas pointed out the 'legal absurdum' to which the new case law led.[8] He argued that a way out of this deadlock was to take as a starting point the cohesiveness of administrative action, which in his view underpinned the council's previous case law. The administrative procedure for erecting public buildings was '*substantively* one and only', involving two preliminary stages.[9] At both of these stages, administrative authorities should examine, on the one hand, the legitimate urban planning reasons connected to the public interest and, on the other hand, the legal conditions of expropriation, guaranteeing the property rights of individuals. Yet the young judge's reasoning was more far-reaching. He went on to state that the individual derives from his right to property:

> [A] claim against the administration not to deprive him from his land, unless in application of the *principle of proportionality (Prinzip der Verhältnismäßigkeit)*, and more generally of *Übermaßverbot*, which prohibits the administration from taking a measure if the general harm that it causes overshoots the expected advantages.[10]

Pararas argued that if in a concrete situation the urban-planning criteria were in conflict with the legality requirements of expropriation

[6] StE (Pl.) 300/36 *ΤΝΠΔΣΑ*.
[7] StE (Pl.) 2952/1975 *ΤοΣ* 1976, p. 345.
[8] Pararas (1976), p. 350.
[9] Ibid (emphasis in the original).
[10] Ibid (emphasis in the original, citing contemporaneous German scholarship).

among which was the principle of proportionality, the administration was in principle obliged to favour the protection of the right to property. In support of this argument, the judge stressed the status of proportionality as a general constitutional principle and the individualist ideals that underpinned the liberal Constitution of 1975. Pararas contended that the interpretation that he proposed was 'more successful'.[11]

The Progressively Open Recognition of Proportionality in Case Law. Less than a year later, the principle of proportionality was explicitly mentioned in a judicial opinion.[12] Two foreign joint-stock companies contested the legality of an act of expropriation on the basis of Article 107 of the Constitution. In combination with a law dating from 1953, this provision prohibits the expropriation of foreign properties. The Council of State held that, despite the absolute terms in which this prohibition was expressed, it should nevertheless be interpreted within the limits set out by competing constitutional provisions. More specifically, Article 17 introduces a social conception of property, prohibiting its exercise to the detriment of the public interest. Furthermore, Article 106 provides for the possibility of nationalisation of enterprises that have the character of a monopoly and are of vital importance for the nation. According to the judges, the combined interpretation of these provisions excludes certain expropriations from the prohibition of Article 107. This is the case when the related public works 'have, from their nature, a more general importance for society or are connected to compelling national interests'.[13] In the view of the majority of the judges, the expropriations in question entered this exception, since they served the construction of a highway connecting Athens and Thessaloniki, the two biggest cities of the country.

In this decision, then, the Council of State operated a reconciliation of competing constitutional provisions which was akin to judicial balancing. Yet, it did not refer to proportionality. Instead, it was in a dissenting opinion of one judge that the principle was invoked. The judge argued for a more contextual solution from the one to which the majority had concluded. In his view, even in cases of important public works, expropriation should only be possible if it was the only way to serve a

[11] Ibid.

[12] StE (Pl.) 58/1977 *EEN* 1977, p. 580. The Greek system of judicial review is mixed and displays influences both from civil law and from common law systems. Dissenting opinions are public. The publication of the names of dissenting members of courts started only later, with Law No. 2172/1993.

[13] StE (Pl.) 58/1977.

compelling public interest. If alternative solutions were available the administration should weigh *in concreto* the economic loss incurred by individuals and the public in the various alternative situations. The competent authorities should proceed to this weighing, 'in application of the principle of relativity and the principle of proportion of the means for the achievement of state aims, principles resulting from the notion of the contemporary democratic and social state'.[14] In the instance at hand, the judge concluded as to the illegality of the administrative decision, because the administration had not proceeded to such reasoning.[15]

The importance of the dissenting opinion did not escape the attention of contemporary commentators of the decision. Kassimatis saw in the reasoning of the dissenting judge the invocation of a general constitutional principle, 'the principle of relativity or proportionality (*Verhältnismäßigkeits-prinzip*)'.[16] According to this author, the principle was composed of three more specific ones: the principle of relativity; the principle of proportion of the means; and the principle of the choice of the less restrictive means. Inherent in the ideal of a 'state ruled by law', relativity was founded on the fundamental principles of equality and freedom and had always functioned as a means for the protection of individual rights against state intervention.[17] However, Kassimatis pointed out that it would be 'a dangerous error' to expand the scope of the principle so as to concern the exercise of constitutional rights and not only of public power.[18] Only Parliament could transpose the principle to situations other than public intervention, as it had already done through certain civil code provisions. Kassimatis gave the example of legitimate defence, or of the state of emergency, which exclude the strict application of tort law rules, as manifestations of the principle.

Kassimatis' fears were realised when proportionality found its first judicial application in an interim measures procedure before a private law court. Assessing the legality of a strike organised by bank employees, the judge Chrysikos, President of the Athens Court of First Instance, referred to Article 23 of the Constitution, which explicitly guarantees collective labour rights, among which the right to strike. The judge interpreted this constitutional provision to protect strike only as an *ultimum refugium* for claiming better working conditions. Generally,

[14] Ibid.
[15] Ibid.
[16] Kassimatis (1977), p. 628.
[17] Ibid.
[18] Ibid.

added the judge, labour rights, like all rights, are subject to limitations and should not lead to abuse. Chrysikos concluded that the employees' right to strike was 'manifestly relative and the legality of its exercise [was] subject to judicial review'.[19] In the case at hand, he concluded that there was a manifest disproportionality between the means used by the employees and their ends. He held the strikes to be abusive, in application of 'the constitutional principle of proportion between means and ends'. Proportionality was thus applied against a group of individuals exercising their collective rights. The illegal character of the employees' strike founded the order for interim measures. More importantly, it also founded the banks' claim for due compensation and for abstention from illegal strikes in the future, as well as their right to terminate the individual working contracts of the employees involved.

A timid but progressively open recognition of proportionality was also taking place in the Council of State case law. In decision 1303/1977, the minister of public works had annulled a prefectural decision on land regularisation. While stressing the broad discretion of the prefect on the matter, the minister had specified that it should be 'prudently exercised', so as not to excessively favour one of the properties to the detriment of another.[20] The Council of State confirmed this decision. While recognising the broad discretionary powers enjoyed by the administration in the land regularisation procedure, the court affirmed its power to intervene whenever the administration had exceeded 'the extreme limits of its discretion' (*υπέρβαση άκρων ορίων της διακριτικής ευχέρειας*). According to the council, these limits are trespassed whenever the administration acts 'in violation of the principle of proportion of the means to the legitimate aim pursued by the administrative authority (see Council of State 58/1977)'.[21] Proportionality thus corresponded to a legality requirement limiting the exercise of administrative discretion. By using it, the Council of State translated in legal terms the ministerial decision, which was based on prudence instead. The influence of Pararas, *Rapporteur* (*εισηγητής*) in this decision, is obvious.

Conceptual Confusion. Principle of relativity, proportionality or proportion? On what occasions was proportionality applicable and under what form? Confusion was dominant not only as far as terms were concerned, but also as to the structure and function of this new concept.

[19] MPrAth 10517/1979 *NOMOS* (Athens Court of First Instance, interlocutory injunction).
[20] StE (Pl.) 1303/1977 *ΤΝΠΔΣΑ*.
[21] Ibid.

In some cases, proportionality was used as a threshold prohibiting excess, in others as a reasoning method for balancing costs and benefits. In some cases, it was addressed to public authorities, in others to individuals in the exercise of their rights. Sometimes proportionality was referred to as an individual claim resulting from the legal protection of property rights, other times as an objective standard of legality of administrative action. Sometimes it acquired the meaning of a pronged reasoning process effectuated by the primary decision maker, other times its prongs were deemed to compose 'substantively one principle'.[22]

At first, not many features seemed to unite the various instances of proportionality language. Still, Pararas' and Kassimatis' reference to the same German doctrinal construction shows that they were actually referring to the same thing. Decision 1303/1977 even cited the previous 58/1977 as an application of the same principle. Soon, from this conceptual noise a more concrete perception of proportionality emerged as dominant.

4.2 One Transfer for Another

The Transfer of Proportionality as a German Doctrine: The *Hagiographers* Case. In the 1978 edition of his handbook, Manessis, prominent public law professor, pointed out the relativity of the protection of individual rights and mentioned the limitations imposed by case law on their legislative restrictions. According to him, restrictions on the exercise of rights should have an objective and impersonal character and should be justified by a compelling public interest; they should be necessary and appropriate to achieve their objective, which should not be achievable by less onerous means; they should be proportionate to the legislative goals and should not infringe the substance of the rights at stake.[23] Although Manessis did not use the term 'proportionality', the influence of the German proportionality doctrine on his writings is obvious. A few years later, in an article published in 1983, Gerontas presented elaborate research on the German proportionality doctrine, especially in constitutional rights and professional freedom cases. He stressed that proportionality involved an *in concreto* balancing that enhanced convincing judicial argumentation. Thus, he called for the application of the principle in domestic constitutional law

[22] Kassimatis (1977), p. 628.
[23] Manessis (1978), pp. 37 f.; Manessis (1982), pp. 77 f.

as well.[24] Manessis and Gerontas did not refer at all to the application of proportionality in domestic case law. Instead, Greek public lawyers' fine understanding of the German doctrine is striking.

The transfer of proportionality as a German principle in constitutional case law soon arrived.[25] In decision 2112/1984, a statute dating from 1981 deprived painters who did not possess a degree in arts from the right to receive public commissions. This was an important restriction on the exercise of their profession, particularly because the Orthodox Church, which is a public person in Greece, is the most important client of painters specialising in hagiography. In order to acquire the right to receive public commissions anew, painters had to become members of the Chamber of Artists, which involved a long and complicated procedure with an uncertain outcome. The union of hagiographers, together with individual artists, introduced an action for the annulment of the implementing administrative act before the Council of State.

The fourth section of the council unanimously declared the statute unconstitutional.[26] In doing so, it followed the observations of its *Rapporteur* Pararas. The council located the constitutional basis for the protection of professional freedom in Article 5(1) of the Constitution, concerning the right to freely develop one's personality and to participate in the social, economic and political life of the country. The scope of this protection was defined broadly to comprise the freedom to choose and to exercise any profession. However, the judges declared that Parliament had the power to place limitations on this freedom by imposing positive obligations, restrictions or prohibitions on its holders. Article 5(1) itself declares that the right in question should not be exercised to the detriment of the rights of others, in violation of the constitution or in violation of good morals.

[24] Gerontas (1983).

[25] The Greek system of judicial review comprises no special constitutional court. It comprises three supreme courts (*Areios Pagos*, the supreme court of the private and criminal law jurisdictional orders, *Symvoulio tis Epikrateias*, the equivalent of the French Council of State, and *Elegktiko Synedrio*, the Court of Audit). The Supreme Special Court (*Anotato Eidiko Dikastirio*) is an ad hoc court, whose jurisdiction is strictly defined by the constitution. Judicial review of legislation is a secular practice and is diffused: it can be exercised by every judge and it is part of the judicial office. The Council of State is 'the constitutional court *par excellence*', since its constitutionally relevant case law is richer than that of the other supreme courts. See Venizelos (1983); see, more generally, Kaidatzis (2013).

[26] StE (Pl.) 2112/1984 *ToΣ* 1985, p. 63.

Departing from its traditional laconic style of justification, the Council of State stated that restrictions on professional freedom are constitutional only insofar as they are generally and objectively defined, and justified by sufficiently important reasons of general or public interest. The legislative criteria would be considered to be objective only insofar as the content of the law complied with 'the constitutional principle of proportionality [*αρχήν της αναλογικότητος*], resulting from the ideal of a State ruled by Law'.[27] The judges went on to specify the content of the principle:

> Restrictions imposed by the legislator and the Administration on the exercise of individual rights should only be those necessary and relevant to the aim pursued by the law. More specifically, they should be directly related to this aim, to the candidates' already acquired qualifications for the exercise of a certain profession [...], as well as to the object and the nature of the profession itself.[28]

Proportionality was thus announced as a requirement of necessity and relevance imposed on legislative interference with individual freedoms. As such, it was not an independent standard but was applied in combination with the individual right invoked. In this case, the proportionality scrutiny entailed a close examination of the impacts of the impugned legislation on the professional freedom of the plaintiffs, taking into account the concrete facts of the case. The council observed that the aggrieved individuals were obliged to stop exercising their profession and that no transitional measures were provided for by the law. Further, the procedure they would have to follow in order to qualify as hagiographers was particularly burdensome and long, and the law did not define any objective criteria for attributing this qualification.

While the council did not structure its reasoning according to the proportionality prongs, the function of proportionality was akin to the one it accomplishes in the global model. Proportionality was not directly concerned with the outcomes of the reviewed legislation. Neither was proportionality solely concerned with the public interest grounding the contested provisions. What the Council of State criticised was Parliament's indifference to the constitutional rights involved. In other words, proportionality corresponded to an instance of indifference review.[29] The judges held that the 'strict provisions' in question were unconstitutional, as they 'were not dictated by reasons of general public

[27] Ibid.
[28] Ibid.
[29] On this kind of review, see Chapter 2.4.

interest'.[30] By introducing an impact-based evaluation of the legislative purpose, proportionality blurred the traditional structures of Greek judicial review, most notably the distinction between the 'whether' (*εάν*) and the 'how' (*πώς*) of public discretion. According to this distinction, while the judges can check 'whether' the reviewed authority had the power to issue the decision at stake they have no say as to 'how' this power has been exercised. This is a question of expediency (*σκοπιμότητα*) that exceeds the competence of the judge of legality (*νομιμότητα*).

The Perception of Proportionality in Theory. Voutsakis noticed the important implications that the application of proportionality had for traditional judicial reasoning structures.[31] This did not seem to trouble mainstream scholars, who celebrated the 1984 decision as the consecration of proportionality as a general principle in Greek public law. The solemn announcement of proportionality provoked an explosion of scholarly interest in the matter.[32] Proportionality became part of mainstream public law handbooks,[33] while it was also incorporated in legislative and administrative texts.[34]

As to the concrete form of review that it implied, scholars unanimously saw in the Council of State's dicta the introduction of a prong-structured test similar to the one applied by foreign (especially German) courts. As such, proportionality was to serve the reconciliation of conflicting constitutional values, in particular of individual rights with the public interest. Its application was general and not limited to the field of professional freedom. Proportionality implied a scrutiny of public decisions from the point of view of their appropriateness, necessity and *stricto sensu* proportionality (or rather disproportionality). It ensured the reasonableness of public decisions as means to the ends of public action, what Greek scholars called their 'relevance' (*συνάφεια*).[35] Scholars pointed out that the principle was subject to variable application.[36] The perception of proportionality was akin to the Alexyan model. Similarity can be observed not only at the level of the proportionality structure, but also at a substantive level. Scholars expected the transfer of proportionality to

[30] StE (Pl.) 2112/1984.
[31] Voutsakis (1990).
[32] Tachos (1984); Skouris (1987); Kontogiorga (1989a, 1989b).
[33] Dagtoglou (1985), pp. 160 f.; Tsatsos (1988), pp. 245 f.
[34] See, for example, Article 3(5) Law No. 1867/1989 on imprisonment for debt.
[35] Manitakis (1990a), p. 61; Voutsakis (1990), p. 215.
[36] Kontogiorga (1989a), p. 51.

lead to more intrusive judicial review and to enhance constitutional rights protection.

During the 1980s and 1990s proportionality terminology progressively spread in public law case law.[37] However, its perception in the minds of Greek public lawyers was considerably detached from the way it was actually applied in practice.

Proportionality as Manifest Error: The Medical Centres Case. Four years later, the Council of State Plenum defined more clearly the function of proportionality in judicial review.[38] A statute dating from 1985 prohibited the use of the terms 'medical centre' or 'health centre' in the naming of private clinics. The goal was to avoid the confusion that these terms could provoke, due to the fact that similar denominations were used by public centres providing health services. In application of the law, the prefect of East Attica ordered a private clinic to remove such terms from its name. The order was to be executed within a short deadline or else the clinic would be faced with licence withdrawal. The clinic contested the prefect's decision by arguing that both the decision and its legislative basis were contrary to the principle of proportionality and to Article 5 of the Constitution.

The Council of State rejected these claims, stating that Article 5 allowed for restrictions of economic freedom for public interest purposes. It held that the contested measures did not violate proportionality either. In its view, proportionality can lead to a declaration of unconstitutionality, 'only if it is manifest that the measure is by nature inappropriate [to obtain] the purpose pursued by the law, or that it overshoots this purpose, and not when it is only the expediency of the measure that is contestable'.[39]

The Council thus considerably restricted the scope and function of proportionality. The difference from the reasoning in decision 2112/1984 is obvious. Proportionality no longer concerned the constitutional protection of economic freedom but applied as a self-standing manifest error test, as an exception to the omnipotence of Parliament when it unreasonably exercised its powers. Once the legitimacy of the legislative aim was ascertained in principle, proportionality was almost a given. While it still concerned the content of legislation, it did not imply scrutiny of its

[37] StE 2261/1984 *ΘΕ ΣΤΕ* 110/1984, paras. 107, 179–80; 3682/1986 *ΘΕ ΣΤΕ* 1986, paras. 292 f.; 1426/1989 *ΑΡΜ* 1989, p. 810; 4050–1/1990 *ΔΔΙΚΗ* 1991, p. 566; 1540/1994 *ΤΝΠΔΣΑ*. See also ES (Pl.) 737/1989 *ΔΔΙΚΗ* 1990, p. 1458.

[38] StE 1149/1988 *ΤοΣ* 1988, p. 324.

[39] Ibid.

impact on constitutional rights. In this sense, the Greek version of proportionality, like the French manifest error test, was not very different from *Wednesbury* unreasonableness. The Council of State refused to examine claims concerning the availability of less restrictive measures for obtaining the same legislative purpose.[40] The appraisal of the necessity of legislative restrictions, as well as the balancing of competing constitutional values, remained an exclusively political project. Through a minimal review of the content of legislation (what Greek lawyers call 'marginal review' – *οριακός έλεγχος*), proportionality actually served in the scrutiny of the 'whether' of public action, of its grounds. In this way, it was contained by the traditional distinctions of Greek judicial review.[41]

Still, proportionality did bring about a major structural change in Greek judicial practice: the introduction of the manifest error as a test concerning the legislative means-ends. Indeed, before 1988 the term manifest (*πρόδηλο, κατάδηλο*) had rarely been used in the judicial review of Parliament. It had mostly been invoked in the construction of the normative content of constitutional provisions. After the spread of proportionality in domestic legal discourse, however, its use became frequent in the evaluation of the content of legislation. In other words, what Greek public lawyers have interpreted as the transfer of the proportionality test is (in terms of discursive structures) the transfer of the manifest error test. The structural change that proportionality engineered in judicial review has largely been neglected by Greek scholars. This is probably because the manifest error test fit well the traditional perception of the role of the judge in the 'marginal' scrutiny of the legislator. Indeed, according to the doctrine of the 'presumption of constitutionality' (*τεκμήριο συνταγματικότητας*), legal statutes are only exceptionally declared unconstitutional and the judge intervenes only to sanction cases of manifest incompatibility of domestic legislation with constitutional precepts.

The Deferent Application of Proportionality in Constitutional Law. Decision 1149/1988 became a reference point for the application of proportionality in the judicial review of legislation and was often cited together with decision 2112/1984. Before proceeding to the proportionality test, the Council of State typically examined the legitimacy of the

[40] Ibid.

[41] Venizelos (1990, pp. 220 f.) talks about proportionality as a method for 'marginal' constitutional review.

legislative aim. In this respect, it required 'general, objective and appropriate criteria'.[42] Further, usually it required that restrictions be defined in a general and impersonal way. Review of the legislative criteria sometimes led to an intrusive scrutiny of legislative provisions. However, once the legitimacy of legislative intent was ascertained in principle, disproportionality constituted an exception to the constitutionality of legislation. Sometimes courts required a 'reasonable relationship' between state intervention and its objective, but they subsequently sanctioned manifest errors in this respect.[43]

Judicial restraint considerably limited the function of proportionality in constitutional law. This did not impede scholarly theories on proportionality from following their own brilliant trajectories. While, in theory, proportionality was understood as a guarantee of constitutional rights, in practice it was a free-standing principle, sometimes applied independently from rights. Whereas in theory it was perceived as a three-pronged requirement of necessity, appropriateness and relevance, in practice, it long corresponded to a standard of manifest inappropriateness and manifest overshooting. For a long time, the principle was rarely used in the scrutiny of legislation. Writing in 1997, Gerapetritis observed that at the time only one statute had been declared unconstitutional under proportionality (referring to the 2112/1984 decision). The implications of proportionality were much more important in administrative law, where the concept inspired scholarly analyses with a more concrete, technical content. In this field, proportionality had a completely different form and function to the one it had in the judicial review of legislation.

4.3 Proportionality and Institutional Competence in Administrative Law

The Formal Application of Proportionality. In the Council of State case law, proportionality long designated a principle mainly addressed to the administration rather than to Parliament. It represented a value of equity, reasonableness or non-abuse, which was to be applied *in concreto*, after consideration of the particular circumstances of each case.[44] Its application thus raised questions of institutional competence and balance. Indeed, given that concrete factual considerations were primarily the competence of expert authorities, the council typically deferred to the

[42] See, for example, ES 737/1989 and StE (Pl.) 413/1993 *Δ/NH* 1993, p. 443.
[43] StE 2153/1989 *APM* 1990, p. 382; 392/1993 *ToΣ* 1994, p. 150, para. 14.
[44] See, for example, StE 3682/1986.

substantive appreciations of the administration in judicial review. In this context, proportionality reasoning acquired a particularly formal tone. It mainly implied an intrusive scrutiny of the justification of public decisions, so as to ensure that the administration had taken into account all the relevant circumstances of the case.[45] Even in the field of individual rights, where proportionality was analysed as a requirement of reasonableness and necessity, it was only the justification of the primary decision that was examined. As a 'less onerous means' requirement, proportionality obligated the competent authority to consider individual claims as to the existence of less restrictive alternatives.[46] In this way, it enhanced the participation of citizens in the administrative decision-making process.[47]

Hence, there was no place for the application of proportionality when no justification was required for the reviewed act whatsoever. Insofar as individual acts were concerned, this was generally the case in the presence of 'bound competence' (*δεσμία αρμοδιότητα*, the equivalent of the French *competence liée*, that is, when the conditions for the exercise of administrative competence are clearly defined by law).[48] The same applied for general administrative acts and decrees, which traditionally were not subject to any justification requirement. In these cases, proportionality functioned only as a check that the public authority did not exceed the limits of the competence delegated by Parliament.

Decision 1821/1995 (the *Zante* case) is illustrative in this respect.[49] Zante is an Ionian island on which the *caretta caretta* sea turtle breeds. This is a rare species, the protection of which is mandated by national and international texts. Following legislative delegation, a presidential decree enacted important restrictions on the use of property on part of the island, aiming to preserve the *caretta caretta* birthplaces. This impeded the plaintiff company from constructing a hotel complex. The company claimed that the decree did not respect the limits set by its legislative basis or by the principle of proportionality. The Council of State held these claims unfounded. In the absence of justification requirement concerning general administrative acts, substantive review was confined to a

[45] StE 257/1987 *ΘΕ ΣΤΕ* 16/1987, paras. 10 f.; 1129/2003 *ΕλλΔνη* 2004, p. 1202. On this decision, see Gerapetritis (1997), pp. 113 f.

[46] StE 2173/1988 *ΘΕ ΣΤΕ* 11/1988, paras. 3–4, and 16 f.; 1540/1994 *ΤΝΠΔΣΑ*.

[47] Gerapetritis (2005), p. 198.

[48] StE 3705/1992 *ΤΝΠΔΣΑ*; 4335/1996 *ΤΝΠΔΣΑ*, para. 9, concerning a disciplinary sanction imposed by the prefect on a mayor.

[49] StE (Pl.) 1821/1995 *ΤοΣ* 1996, p. 263.

check of whether the administration had exceeded the limits of the legislative delegation.[50] As for the claims based on the principle of proportionality, the council stated that the contested measures 'aim[ed] to protect the *caretta caretta* sea turtle [. . .] but also to upgrade and develop the region [. . .], and were considered appropriate and necessary for obtaining these purposes, after consideration of all the relevant factual and scientific data'.[51]

Hence, once the legal basis and the public interest aim of the reviewed act were established, no place was left for proportionality review. The council did not even apply the manifest error test concerning the means-ends of the reviewed decision, as it did in the review of legislation. Its scrutiny ended in the affirmation that the competent authorities had proceeded to the proportionality assessments themselves. Judicial review in such cases was very weak, since the council usually constructed the public interest purpose of the reviewed decisions itself and it did so in broad and indeterminate terms.[52] In the review of general administrative acts, then, the principle of proportionality was traditionally reduced to a requirement of 'proportion, or at least plausibility'.[53] It corresponded to a minimal substantive review of unreasonableness akin to the English *Wednesbury* test. Its function was to eliminate abuses of public power. It was often invoked together with the principle of good administration or with the prohibition of abuse of power.

Proportionality as Equity in Substantive Adjudication. Proportionality was much more important in substantive administrative law, where institutional concerns were not so significant. In certain cases involving personal freedom restrictions, the Council of State affirmed the power of lower courts to review *de novo* the facts of the relevant administrative decisions.[54] Imprisonment for debt became the most glorious field of application for proportionality. In this field, proportionality progressively developed from a prohibition of unreasonableness and abuse, to a requirement of proof of the appropriateness and necessity of imprisonment from administrative authorities.[55] Judicial policy on the matter was

50 Ibid.

51 Ibid. For another example, see StE (Pl.) 4027/1998 *ΔΦΟΡΝΟΜΟΘ* 1999, p. 931, para. 9.

52 Yannakopoulos (2013, pp. 173 f.) talks about a presumption that laws and administrative regulations pursue the public interest.

53 Manolakoglou (2011). See also Gogos (2005).

54 StE 2775/1989 *ΑΡΧΝ* 1990, p. 281.

55 DPrAth 6056/1987 *ΕΔΚΑ* 1988, p. 58; 5/1993 *ΔΔΙΚΗ* 1993, p. 447 (Athens Administrative Court of First Instance); DEfAth 3057/1988 *ΕΔΚΑ* 1988, p. 728; 2313/1989 *ΔΦΟΡΝΟΜΟΘ* 1989, p. 914; 1/2000 *ΔΦΟΡΝΟΜΟΘ* 2000, p. 707 (Athens

followed by a legislative reform that imposed a proportionality requirement on the application of the measure.[56]

Proportionality terminology also spread in private law.[57] In its sense of relativity or equity, it guided the interpretation of 'indeterminate legal notions' (*αόριστες νομικές έννοιες*) contained in civil code provisions, like the prohibition of abuse in Article 281. In labour law, proportionality preserved its function as a criterion for identifying abusive strikes.[58] In some rare cases, it had a protective function for labour rights. Its application imposed limits on the employer's right to dismiss an employee, when less restrictive measures were available.[59] In its version as *proportionnalité des peines*, proportionality spread in criminal case law, too.[60] While during the late 1990s *Areios Pagos* (the supreme court of the private and criminal law jurisdictional order) accepted that proportionality applied in private law, the court usually refused to review lower courts case law in this respect, since it understood proportionality to imply appreciations of a factual nature.[61]

Instead of being the object of study in constitutional law, proportionality attracted more scholarly attention as an administrative, criminal or private law principle.[62] While Greek lawyers never forgot to mention its foreign origins, its theoretical content and its protective function for rights, proportionality was re-contextualised in the various technical fields of the Greek legal discourse in which it was inserted. Its concrete implications for the interpretation and application of substantive and procedural rules were studied fragmentally. This did not affect the unitary perception of proportionality in theory. The principle began to

Administrative Court of Appeal); DPrThes 18/1989 *ΕΔΚΑ* 2000, p. 44 (Thessaloniki Administrative Court of First Instance).

56 Law No. 1867/1989. The statute was soon abrogated due to the difficulties of establishing evidence. However, in its decision DPrAth 5/1992 *ΔΔΙΚΗ* 1993, p. 194, the Athens Administrative Court of First Instance declared the abrogation of the statute unconstitutional, contrary to the constitutional principle of proportionality.

57 EfAth 5025/1990 *Δ/ΝΗ* 1992, p. 193; 5846/1998 *Δ/ΝΗ* 1999, p. 1372; 7029/1998, *ΔΕΕ* 1999, p. 75 (Athens Court of Appeal). See also DEfAth 1440/1990 *ΔΔΙΚΗ* 1990, p. 1352 (Athens Administrative Court of Appeal).

58 EfAth 1/92 *ΕΕΔ* 1992, p. 840 (Athens Court of Appeal).

59 MPrAth 458/1991 *ΕλλΔνη* 1991, p. 628; 3308/1992 *ΔΕΝ* 1993, p. 594; 3646/1992 *ΑΡΜ* 1994, p. 561 (Athens Court of First Instance).

60 DStrThess 772/1989 *ΑΡΜ* 1989, p. 1254 (Administrative Military Court of Thessaloniki); Anakr Tripoli 12/1991 *ΠΟΙΝΧΡ* 1991, p. 932 (Tripoli instruction judge); SymbPlim Mesolongi 2/1992 *ΥΠΕΡΑΣΠΙΣΗ* 1992, p. 140 (Mesolongi Correctional Court in Council).

61 AP 451/1999 *NOMOS*; 445/1999 *EEN* 2000, p. 534. See Giakoumis (2005).

62 Triantafyllou (1990); Simantiras (1990), para. 472; Dalakouras (1993).

be described as having two aspects. As a substantive value, it represented a requirement of equity, reasonableness or moderation. From a technical point of view, it served as a tool for the judge in the interpretation and application of legal rules and its content was concretised according to the circumstances of each case.[63]

4.4 All Things in Proportion

The Proliferation of Proportionality and the 2001 Constitutional Amendment. In the years preceding the 2001 reform, one observes an explosion of proportionality language in the decisions of Greek supreme courts. During the period 1990–4 reference to proportionality was found almost exclusively in the Council of State case law.[64] The supreme administrative court used the term less than twice per year on average. Between 1995 and 1998 it used proportionality in an average of five decisions a year, while *Areios Pagos* referred to the principle twice in total, albeit without applying it. In 1999, *Areios Pagos* explicitly referred to proportionality in five cases, as many as the Council of State. In 2000, proportionality terminology was employed in twenty-two cases by all three supreme courts.[65] The spread of proportionality in the supreme courts' language was due to the wider recognition of the scope and function of the principle. After a period of resistance, for the first time in 2000, *Areios Pagos* explicitly recognised the application of proportionality as a matter of law that could be raised by the claimants during cassation and, in some cases, even proceeded itself to the examination of the proportionality requirements.[66]

This evolution paralleled a renewal of scholarly interest in the principle. During the late 1990s one finds elaborate theoretical studies of proportionality in Greek scholarship. These studies share the perception of proportionality as a method for constitutional value-balancing that is very akin to the global model. In 1998, Xynopoulos talked about a 'more comprehensive model of proportionality' that did not simply oppose public interests to individual rights, but also involved a 'weighing of

[63] Manitakis (1990b), pp. 5 f.; Manitakis (1994), pp. 209–10.

[64] These data are based on the results of the research by keywords in the legal database *NOMOS* on the 26 November 2015. Apart from the Council of State case law, one decision by the Supreme Special Court was found and two by the Court of Audit.

[65] The decisions where proportionality was applied were issued by *Areios Pagos* (3), the Council of State (17) and the Court of Audit (2).

[66] AP (Pl.) 17/1999 *Δ/NH* 1999, p. 1288; AP 1597/2000 *Δ/NH* 2001, p. 130; 254/2000 *ΕΕΜΠΔ* 2000, p. 712; 1215/2000 *ΕΕΜΠΔ* 2002, p. 369.

values' for the resolution of constitutional conflicts.[67] One year later, in an influential contribution, Beis adapted the Alexyan constitutional rights theory in the domestic context.[68] This author contended that proportionality was a method for fundamental rights adjudication that involved balancing competing constitutional values. Echoing German constitutional theory, Beis described the Constitution as an 'objective value-order' that could provide rational criteria for balancing.[69] Proportionality thus, as opposed to 'subsumptive automatism', was promoted as a method for constitutional reasoning that would open up the constitutional order to practical reasoning.[70] This aspect of proportionality balancing was extensively analysed by Stratilatis, who reconstructed a famous *Areios Pagos* freedom of speech decision as an instance of proportionality analysis.[71]

The explicit entrenchment of proportionality as a fundamental rights principle seemed in continuity with its increasing use and importance in the discourse of domestic actors. It thus met with consensus among scholars. Almost everyone agreed on the validity, or rather correctness, of proportionality in constitutional law. Voutsakis even argued that proportionality was not entrenched but 'discovered'.[72] Critiques remained quite marginal and did not concern the validity of the principle itself but rather structural features of its application, most notably its status as an autonomous ground of judicial review.[73]

Scholars have stressed the symbolic function of the new Article 25.[74] Symbols should be taken seriously, however, especially when contained in the hierarchically superior text of a legal order. The constitutionalisation of proportionality not only met consensus among mainstream constitutional scholars, but it also *established* consensus on its validity among legal actors more generally.[75] It therefore gave a new impetus to the use of proportionality in practice. It is only after 2001 that *Areios Pagos* engaged itself in an explicit proportionality review of legislation and it did so by referring to the amended Article 25(1) of the

67 Xynopoulos (1998). The author refers to a '*modèle plus large de proportionnalité*' (p. 523), and a '*pondération normative*' (p. 535).

68 Beis (1999).

69 Ibid, pp. 488 f.

70 Ibid, p. 481.

71 Stratilatis (2001).

72 Voutsakis (2002), p. 11.

73 For some examples, see Chryssogonos (2001b); Mitsopoulos (2002).

74 Chryssogonos (2000).

75 In this sense, it had a 'stabilising effect'; see Skouris (2001), p. 462.

Constitution.[76] Since the entry into force of the new constitutional text, all Greek courts abandoned their previously reticent stance and proportionality language became a recurrent mode of judicial argumentation. The constitutional establishment of proportionality as a correct judicial method provoked reactions from certain scholars, who interpreted it as usurpation by the constitutional legislator of an interpretative power that belongs to scholarship or to judges.[77]

The Hegemony of Proportionality. More than an administrative or criminal law principle, more than a substantive requirement of necessity in imprisonment for debt litigation, more than a method for constitutional adjudication, proportionality is an 'overarching principle' in Greek law.[78] The fragmented technical studies on its implications in various legal fields have been replaced by general studies on its content and structure. Proportionality is considered to bind all state authorities in the exercise of legislative, administrative and judicial power. As a norm of constitutional rank, it is deemed 'diffused' in the legal system, influencing norm production and adjudication in all the fields of law.[79]

Scholars saw in the constitutional reform the entrenchment of the fundamental rights paradigm and the advent of the Alexyan proportionality model, which, in the words of Contiades, is 'inherent in the texture of fundamental rights as principles (*Prinzipien*)'.[80] Indeed, the explicit reference to the 'welfare state ruled by law' (*κοινωνικό κράτος δικαίου*) enhances the perception of constitutional rights as socially bound values. In this context, proportionality becomes the ultimate criterion of the constitutionality of rights infringement.[81] Scholars insist on the ad hoc character of the constitutional value scale and reject an a priori hierarchy of constitutional norms.[82] This renders the application of the three prongs of proportionality very important: according to the new dominant scholarly trend, correct application of proportionality as a method leads to correct adjudication of constitutional rights and to transparent judicial reasoning. Proportionality is deemed to 'insert the balancing of

76 AP (Pl.) 14/2001 *ΠΟΙΝΔ/ΝΗ* 2001, p. 832; AP (Pl.) 15/2001 *ΠΟΙΝΧΡ* 2001, p. 798; AP (Pl.) 16/2001 *ΝΟΒ* 2002, p. 411, on Article 20(1) of the Constitution, concerning the right to judicial protection.

77 See, most notably, Mitsopoulos (2002).

78 Gerontas (2006), p. 470.

79 Doris (2004); Giakoumis (2005).

80 Contiades (2002), p. 235. See also Voutsakis (2002), pp. 10 f.; Raikos (2008), pp. 242 f.; Akrivopoulou (2012), p. 29.

81 Orfanoudakis (2003), pp. 21 f.; esp. pp. 24–5.

82 See Beis (1999); Stratilatis (2001).

constitutional values into a systematic and rational argumentative framework'.[83]

The perception of proportionality as a fundamental rights principle is also pervasive in the supreme courts' case law. In this respect, *Areios Pagos* has assumed a pioneer role. According to its case law, 'the principle of proportionality, as a general principle of law, has been consistently recognised by case law [. . .] even before its explicit entrenchment as a constitutional concept'. It 'transpires the whole of public action and binds the legislator, the judge and the administration'.[84] After some initial hesitation, *Areios Pagos* considerably altered its reasoning style to adapt it to proportionality and its fundamental rights baggage. The court often engages in structured proportionality analysis, which, in its view 'tends to rationalise State interferences with the individual and social rights of the human and of the citizen'.[85]

Proportionality analysis typically follows extensive normative considerations concerning the scope of the constitutional rights at stake and the intensity of the court's scrutiny. According to well-established case law, restrictions of individual rights should be objectively defined and justified by reasons of public interest. Proportionality requires that these restrictions be 'restricted on the basis of the conceptual elements of the appropriateness and necessity of the measure and of its proportion to the goal pursued'.[86] The three-pronged structure of proportionality has also been applied by the Council of State and the Court of Audit, albeit not with the same consistency and rigour that one finds in the *Areios Pagos* case law.[87]

In the context of the economic crisis in particular, proportionality seems to offer the *only* possible method for applying constitutional provisions. Courts have used proportionality language in virtually all the decisions that concerned the constitutionality of austerity measures under the economic adjustment programmes.[88] In an article published in *ICON*, Contiades and Fotiadou argue that:

[83] Anthopoulos (2001), p. 174.

[84] AP (Pl.) 43/2005 *NoB* 2005, p. 1587.

[85] AP (Pl.) 5/2013 *ΤΝΠΔΣΑ*.

[86] AP (Pl.) 10/2003 *ΕλλΔνη* 2003, p. 406, para. III.

[87] StE (Pl.) 3177/2007 *ΔΦΟΡΝΟΜΟΘ* 2008, p. 1214; StE 1249/2010 *NoB* 2010, p. 390. See also ES 1376/2002 *ΑΡΧΝ* 2003, p. 593.

[88] See StE (Pl.) 668/2012 *NoB* 2012, p. 384; 2192/2014 *ΤΝΠΔΣΑ*; 2287/2015 *ΑΡΜ* 2015, p. 1371; 4741/2014 *ΕΔΔΔ* 2015, p. 170. See also ES (Pl.) 4327/2014 *ΑΡΜ* 2015, p. 1194. For a more thorough analysis of the Euro-crisis litigation, see Part III, Chapters 9.4 and 10.3.

> Insisting on defining a minimum core content as a prerequisite for the justiciability of social rights is an updated aspiration, which risks the very enforceability of these rights amidst global economic crisis, at the very hour when they are needed the most. Proportionality not only creates the context for litigation, enhancing the justiciability of social rights, but also renders their content concrete by promoting a dialogue between the judge and the lawmaker which enhances their content and upgrades them to a shared narrative with civil and political rights, that of the proportionality idiolect.[89]

While the local perception of proportionality in Greece seems to fit the transnational proportionality theory, judicial practice is much more nuanced.

4.5 'Faces and Guises' of Proportionality

The Inconsistent Application of Proportionality. While the constitutional entrenchment of proportionality has led to the hegemony of proportionality in Greek law and to scholarly consensus as to its validity, it has not led to a consistent application of the three-pronged proportionality structure. Traditional versions of proportionality as a manifest error test have persisted in domestic case law.[90] In many landmark cases involving constitutional rights, proportionality has not been applied at all.[91] In administrative law, proportionality still applies as a standard of equity or reasonableness.[92] To this, one should add the application of proportionality in conformity with the European case law.[93] The various 'faces' and 'guises' of proportionality provoke distrust among Greek public lawyers.[94]

Proportionality as an Efficiency Test in Judicial Review. Most importantly, while proportionality in Greek constitutional law is generally perceived as a fundamental rights principle, it usually corresponds to an efficiency test in judicial review. The constitutional entrenchment of proportionality has transformed judicial review considerably. While traditionally, through a 'marginal' scrutiny of the impacts of public

89 Contiades and Fotiadou (2012a). The quoted part is taken from the abstract.

90 See, for example, StE 4182/2005 *ΔΔΙΚΗ* 2005, p. 970, para. 7; 956/2009 *ΤΝΠΔΣΑ*, para. 6.

91 StE (Pl.) 2281/2001 *ΔΔΙΚΗ* 2001, p. 959, concerning the inscription of religion on ID cards. StE (Pl.) 1685/2013 *ΕΔΔΔ* 2013, p. 391, concerning an exceptional levy imposed on certain properties.

92 See Manolakoglou (2011), citing relevant case law.

93 AP (Pl.) 26/2003 *ΕλλΔνη* 2003, p. 1263, in which the supreme civil court follows closely the ECtHR reasoning in the field of property rights.

94 Gerapetritis (2006).

decisions, proportionality actually served to criticise the grounds of public action, the new version of proportionality is an outcome-based test. Anthopoulos explains that: '[T]he principle of proportionality refers to "how" a restriction has been imposed. "Whether" a restriction is legally permitted or not is determined by the principle of the general interest, which defines which goal is constitutionally justified or, at least, tolerable.'[95]

However, contrary to Greek public lawyers' perception of proportionality as a fundamental rights principle, the outcome-based scrutiny that proportionality entails has come at a cost for its value-laden content in the Council of State case law. The legitimate interest stage is commonly perceived as external to proportionality analysis.[96] Far from being a balancing structure for the adjudication of constitutional rights, the application of proportionality often entails an expulsion of values from constitutional adjudication. Hence, the proportionality test only concerns the efficiency of the reviewed decision. This is observed even in fields where the traditional version of proportionality had found glorious application, most notably in imprisonment for debt cases.[97]

Proportionality and Justification Requirements. As an efficiency test, proportionality has sometimes set considerable justification requirements for public authorities, and especially Parliament. Traditionally, Greek constitutionalists accepted that no justification requirement applied for legal statutes. The litigation concerning pharmacy licenses before the Council of State is an illustrative example of the change that proportionality has brought about in this respect. A legal statute dating from 1991 had imposed strict population criteria for providing a pharmacy license, according to which, one pharmacy should correspond to 3,000 residents in each municipality or community. The introductory report to the law stated that the population quotas were justified by the need to promote public health and more precisely the need to ensure the sustainability of pharmacies. In 1998, aggrieved individuals contested the constitutionality of the measures.

The Council of State declared the relevant legislation as unconstitutional.[98] The court followed its consistent case law in the field of professional freedom: legislative restrictions of the choice and exercise of a

[95] Anthopoulos (2001), p. 173.
[96] Ibid, p. 172; Voutsakis (2002), p. 24; Gerontas (2006), pp. 472 f.
[97] StE (Pl.) 250/2008 *ΕΔΔΔ* 2008, p. 407, para. 5. Contrast decision StE 1624/2002 *ΕΔΚΑ* 2002, p. 343.
[98] StE 2110/2003 *ΕΔΔΔ* 2004, p. 89; StE (Pl.) 3665/2005 *ΕΔΚΑ* 2006, p. 59, para. 4.

certain profession should be generally and objectively defined and justified by sufficient reasons of public or social interest; they should be related to the object of the law and to the character of the profession under consideration; and they should not be aimed solely at the protection of certain persons already exercising a profession.[99] The court then announced the principle of proportionality as a three-pronged requirement. The restrictions should be 'suitable and necessary for obtaining the public or social interest aim pursued by the legislator and should not be disproportionate to this aim'.[100]

The judges went on to specify the way these normative considerations were to be applied in the case at hand. When the restriction concerns not only the exercise but also the access to a profession, the principle of proportionality requires that the necessity of 'such an exceptional restriction' in pursuit of the legislative aim be 'apparent and clearly identifiable'.[101] Like the ECtHR, the supreme administrative court thus applied a variable standard of proportionality review, as a function of the seriousness of the legislative interference with the right at stake. In the case at hand, it concluded that the measures were 'equivalent to the establishment of a closed number of pharmacies, thus depriving the entrants in the profession from the possibility to open a pharmacy'.[102] Hence, it applied a more intensive proportionality standard and found the contested statute to be disproportionate.

Proportionality, Facts and Rationalisation. The judges were divided as to the concrete arguments of unconstitutionality. The first majority opinion argued that the law promoted the goal of public health in a quite irrational and indirect manner, since the measures enacted were 'not apparently connected' to this goal.[103] In these judges' view, the legislative goal would be more rationally promoted if the legislator provided for guarantees and requirements for the exercise of professions related to public health and not by preserving the sustainability of existing pharmacies. The justification of the second majority opinion was quite similar. While the judges accepted the sustainability of pharmacies as an objective for the promotion of public health, they held that access to the profession of pharmacist should be restricted according to criteria connected to public health and not according to whether a pharmacy

[99] StE (Pl.) 3665/2005, para. 4.
[100] Ibid.
[101] Ibid.
[102] Ibid.
[103] Ibid.

already exists or not.[104] A few members of the majority went even further and argued that increase in the number of pharmacies 'has in principle as a consequence the reduction, albeit significant, of the revenue and profits of pharmacies, but does not necessarily result in putting at stake their sustainability'. The judges thus concluded that, even if the appropriateness of the measures for obtaining their goal was accepted, their necessity was 'not evidenced'.[105]

All the concrete opinions of the majority reveal the judges' effort to rationalise the legislative means-ends. The majority was not convinced as to the efficiency of the measures in achieving their goal. Even more, the third opinion went so far as to contest the *concrete factual appreciations* of the law-makers concerning the mischief that Parliament aimed to confront. This is despite the complex character of these assessments, containing economic and statistical data and prognoses. The judges required facts, 'data' and 'evidence' as to the causal relationships established by the legislator when choosing the concrete measures at stake. This is also observed in other Council of State decisions concerned with restrictions to professional freedom.[106] In such cases, the application of proportionality is fact oriented and imposes strict evidence requirements on public authorities.

The rationalising, fact-oriented application of proportionality has sometimes led to a more efficient division of labour between Parliament and the administration in the process of fact-finding. This is exemplified by decision 1910/2001.[107] In this case, legislation dating from 1994 had annulled the extension of leasing contracts for public premises when this extension had been concluded during the last months of 1993. The introductory report to the law justified this measure by arguing that the concerned extension contracts had been agreed on during electoral campaign and served micro-political interests to the detriment of the public financial interest. This resulted in the closure of the nightclub Neraida (meaning 'fairy' in Greek), which contested the constitutionality of the 1994 law, in particular its compatibility with economic freedom.

The Council of State accepted the arguments advanced by the owners of the nightclub. They were of the opinion that the criterion set by the legislator for the application of the law, related to the time of conclusion

[104] Ibid.
[105] Ibid. See also StE 2110/2003.
[106] StE (Pl.) 1621/2012 *ΕΔΔΔ* 2012, p. 2143, para. 7.
[107] StE (Pl.) 1910/2001 *ΑΡΧΝ*/2001, p. 690.

of the relevant agreements, was not 'appropriate and sufficient' to justify the automatic annulment of the concerned contracts. According to the judges, whether the individual contracts were contrary to the public interest, among other reasons because the agreed rent was disproportionate to what is generally agreed in similar contracts, was a matter that required 'investigation of the factual circumstances in each concrete case' and, as such, it entered into the competence of the administration. The council thus declared that the 'automatic' annulment of public contracts was contrary to Article 5(1) of the Constitution.[108]

***

The spread of proportionality in Greek public law has been impressive. The principle has been employed in judicial review since the 1970s and was announced as a constitutional principle in 1984. For nearly forty years, proportionality has been used in the judicial review of both Parliament and the administration. In contrast to English and French public law, proportionality met with no major resistance in Greek public law. However, the 'triumphant march' of proportionality in Greek public law seems detached from the role that the principle has had in judicial practice. Its use by Greek courts is characterised by constant conceptual ambiguity and tension. While it was announced as a requirement of necessity and relevance imposed on legislative restrictions of rights, in subsequent decisions, it was reduced to a manifest error review of the legislative means-ends. At the same time, in administrative law, proportionality preserved its ambiguous content of equity or relativity that it had since the first uses of the term during the 1970s.

The fragmented content of proportionality in positive law has stood in contrast to its unitary and relatively stable perception in Greek legal theory. Indeed, since 1984 and even before, scholars saw in proportionality a three-pronged requirement of appropriateness, necessity and *stricto sensu* proportionality, applied in German law. Similar to the French *doctrine*, Greek academic writings on proportionality have been detached from the structures of judicial reasoning. However, in contrast to France, proportionality in Greece has not so much served the analysis or systematisation of domestic case law either. At best, it has led to a reinterpretation of concrete rules in administrative, criminal and private law. Greek proportionality scholars have rather been concerned with affirming the theoretical content of the principle, sometimes without even defining its relationship with pre-existing concepts and distinctions

[108] Ibid, para. 10.

in domestic judicial review. It seems that, despite its fragmented and incoherent application in practice, the use of proportionality language has a value in itself for Greek public lawyers.

Unsurprisingly, the most solemn affirmation that can be, that is, the constitutional entrenchment of proportionality, met consensus in Greek public law and established proportionality analysis as a correct method of legal reasoning. Proportionality's hegemony in the Greek legal order is not comparable to its limited role in French constitutional law. Still, when it comes to judicial practice, the application of proportionality is inconsistent. Traditional versions have persisted and compete with a new, fact-oriented and rationalising version of proportionality as a test of efficiency. The application of proportionality in Greece differs from the practice of French courts, due to its intrusiveness and fact-oriented nature in some cases. However, it lacks the clarity, the consistency and the attention to values that characterises its application by English judges.

Conclusion of Part I

A survey of the use of proportionality language by French, English and Greek lawyers confirms the 'doctrinal imperialism' of proportionality. Since its emergence in France, proportionality has been perceived as conspicuous, and especially since the 2000s, it proliferates in case law. In England, proportionality spreads as a human rights head of review and culls the 'sacred cows' of common law review. In Greece, it is a hegemonic method of legal reasoning and it replaces pre-existing categories and standards. However, what seems to be an irresistible spread of proportionality is not so much connected to its systematic application in practice. In fact, proportionality's content has been very different across space and time. Contrary to the claims of certain proportionality enthusiasts, proportionality has not always functioned as a pronged test for the optimal realisation of fundamental rights. Very often, structural features of the Alexyan proportionality model, like balancing or reasoning in prongs, are absent from judicial reasoning. In certain cases, it is even more fundamental features of proportionality that are missing, like its connection to rights, and in yet others proportionality is not even a judicial test at all. Proportionality is reconstructed 'from scratch' by its host environments, which inscribe their proper rationality in its use. Convergence at the level of legal language is only superficial. Proportionality as a transnational idiom reaffirms the boundaries of the discourses that have embraced it.

That said, in the following, I will attempt to schematise certain common features in the use of proportionality that transcend national borders and provide what Legrand calls a 'dialogical interface' for pushing the comparison further. These features may seem common-sensical to the reader, since they are part of European lawyers' common understanding of the term. However, they are worth mentioning, since they have guided my search for the expressive function of proportionality and they structure the rest of the presentation of this book.

First, in all the contexts studied, proportionality has been promoted as a transfer from abroad. In 1974, Dreyfus argued for the explicit recognition of the principle of proportionality in French law, which would be imported from other European countries or international jurisdictions. In *GCHQ*, Lord Diplock talked about the transfer of the principle of proportionality, recognised in the administrative law of continental European states, in English judicial review. In his study of the German principle of proportionality in 1983, Gerontas called for its application in Greek constitutional law. The perception of proportionality as a transfer is connected to the fact that certain personalities made a significant contribution to its spread in each domestic context. Braibant, Jowell and Pararas are only some of these personalities, who often, in addition to being influential in scholarship, have an active role in legal and judicial practice. The perception of proportionality as a transfer has persisted in all the systems studied: today, in the minds of French, English and Greek public lawyers, proportionality represents a pronged structure for legal reasoning coming from German law.

Second, the spread or promotion of proportionality has been at some point connected to fundamental rights and has taken a form quite similar to the one described by the Alexyan legacy. In France, the transfer of the prong-structured proportionality test in constitutional law has been explicitly connected to the German version of the principle. Despite its inconsistent application by courts, proportionality is now perceived as a fundamental rights principle, both in scholarship and in case law. In England, fundamental rights language has rapidly expanded under the HRA and proportionality is deemed a crucial feature of this shift. Both the application and the scholarly perception of proportionality roughly correspond to its description in the proportionality theory. In Greece, since its emergence proportionality has been connected to the German three-pronged structure for judicial reasoning, defying its deferent and formalist application in judicial practice. Since 2001, the mainstream perception of proportionality in Greek scholarship is very akin to the Alexyan model. However, this perception contrasts with the inconsistent application of proportionality in judicial practice and the exclusion of value-laden reasoning from its scope.

Third, the perception of proportionality and of its evolution in all domestic contexts has not always depended on the conceptual content assigned to proportionality by courts. Indeed, sometimes domestic public lawyers' perception even defies important structural features of its use in judicial reasoning, such as its form and function. The perception of proportionality in each discursive context thus seems to express more general tendencies in the way domestic public lawyers perceive law and legal knowledge itself. Defying the absence of its recognition in domestic practice, French public lawyers have perceived proportionality as an idea that is omnipresent in domestic law and guides its evolution. Appeal to proportionality has served scholars in establishing coherence between the fragmented concepts and methods of French judicial review. In this way, the use of proportionality in French public law expresses the more general perception of this field as a coherent knowledge system. In contrast, English lawyers have been more attentive to judicial reasoning patterns and to the structural features of proportionality in practice. Proportionality in English public law is perceived as an additional ground for contesting a public act and thus for lawyerly argumentation, which is different from the traditional heads of review. As such it expresses the instrumentalist perception of legal structures that is typical of the common law. Differently to both England and France, the spread of proportionality in Greece has not been connected to its function in judicial practice and has been of little service to the analysis or systematisation of domestic case law or legislation. Expressing the formalism of Greek legal language, in the sense of its disinterest in social practices, even when they are shared by the members of the legal profession, proportionality is perceived as correct, no matter its application in practice.

It is not my purpose at this point to make general conclusions about the perception and characteristics of law as a social practice or cultural system in the different domestic contexts. These observations are too abstract and subject to the 'culture as a thought-stopper' critique. Besides, culture is not static and, in every system, different tendencies and different perceptions of law coexist and compete. So too does the *legal* culture and even the *public law* culture that defines the semantic horizons of the concepts among which proportionality operates. Any similarities and differences observed at this stage can only be but a transitional state of knowledge. The expressive function of proportionality should be sought in its more concrete manifestations. The common features observed above offer a starting point, since they constitute a minimum content in the use of proportionality language by legal actors across the different systems studied. The concretisations of this content each time express local perceptions of the law, rights, the state and society. They also express the way these perceptions may change over time.

PART II

Great Expectations

The Performative Effect of Proportionality Theory. The analysis in Part I has shown that, in spite of divergence in the use of proportionality across legal systems, the narrative of the success of proportionality is not completely lacking a factual basis. Proportionality has, indeed, spread in domestic legal discourses and, even though its judicial application seldom follows *exactly* the proportionality model described by Alexy and his followers, it is sometimes very like it. In the various contexts studied, proportionality has eventually been connected to rights and is increasingly used by judges as a pronged structure. In this sense, Alexy and his followers are right. Besides, one should not neglect the influence that the Alexyan theory itself has had on the spread of proportionality in various settings. Local legal actors increasingly perceive the Alexyan proportionality model as the correct way to 'speak' proportionality and press for its adoption by other actors, especially judges. The proportionality model thus becomes performative. Not only does it *describe* local forms of legal reasoning, it also *constitutes* them. Performativity means success for the proportionality theory, which, like every interpretative theory, offers a self-consciously normative account of legal reasoning.

The Rational Human Rights Paradigm. Scholars usually attribute proportionality's success to its inherent qualities as a reasoning structure. This is connected to the particular perception of rights that underpins the relevant studies, which Kumm has called the 'Rational Human Rights Paradigm'.[1] Based on a reconstruction of judicial practice in modern liberal constitutional democracies, proportionality theorists contend that rights are not rules but principles, that is, abstract 'ideal-ought' statements.[2] Principles are only prima facie commands; they become definite only after they are balanced against other competing principles, in the set

[1] Kumm (2009a).

[2] Alexy (2002), pp. 86 f.; Kumm (2004), p. 578. The distinction between rules and principles was first introduced by Dworkin (1967), no. 3.

of facts of each case.[3] Thus, they empower the applying authority to realise them to a lesser degree, when their realisation is not possible. In the rational paradigm, rights consist in optimisation requirements, they command the decision-maker to realise them to the greatest extent possible, according to the factual and legal possibilities of each case. Proportionality serves as a methodological framework for accomplishing this task.

The advocates of proportionality opt for a wide definition of the prima facie scope of rights. 'Definitional generosity' includes trivial and even illegal actions in the scope of constitutional protection.[4] The consequence of the broad conception of constitutional rights is that almost every action or omission of public authorities can be submitted to a process of justification, according to which its legal validity is assessed. That is because almost every action or omission of public authorities will affect the realisation of a constitutional right. Thus, the domain of constitutional justice becomes 'prima facie coextensive with the domain of political justice generally'.[5] Rights serve as guidance for virtually every act of the legislative and administrative authorities. Apart from negative obligations of state non-intervention, they are considered to create positive obligations of protection on the part of public authorities. Rights radiate in the legal system and affect the interpretation of abstract legal notions and sub-constitutional norms. They have a horizontal effect in private relationships. Departing from classical liberal distinctions between private and public law or between state and society, in proportionality theory, the constitution's reach constantly expands to cover not only the whole of public action, but also the whole of society. Kumm talks about the 'total constitution'.[6]

Democracy, Rights and Justification: What Proportionality Theorists Expect. Critics have argued that proportionality turns the constitution in a 'juridical genome' and that it leaves no discretion to Parliament or any place for reasonable disagreement on the relative importance of constitutional values.[7] Proportionality scholars, however,

[3] Möller (2007, p. 453) contests Alexy's rules/principles distinction but still accepts that the application of some important constitutional rights entails balancing.

[4] Alexy (2002), pp. 210 f.; Barak (2012), pp. 17 f., esp. pp. 42 f.; Klatt and Meister (2012a), pp. 45 f.

[5] Kumm (2004), p. 587.

[6] Kumm (2006b), p. 341.

[7] Forsthoff (1971); Böckenförde (1991), p. 185, cited by Alexy (2002), pp. 388 f.; Kahn (1987); Tsakyrakis (2008), pp. 6 f. also makes this observation. In the same vein, see

argue that legislative discretion remains unaffected, since the role of the judiciary is not to find the *correct* answer, but rather to 'police the boundaries of the reasonable'.[8] The judiciary assumes a mission of 'Socratic contestation', for which it is particularly well-suited given the procedural and institutional rules guaranteeing judicial independence and impartiality, as well as the obligation to justify judicial decisions.[9] Courts' analytical and reactive role in the policy-making process reduces necessities for access to fact and institutional expertise.[10] Hence, following Beatty, proportionality 'is able to reconcile both democracy and rights in a way that optimizes each'.[11]

The conceptualisation of rights as principles does not guarantee their priority over other values neither does it entail their absolute, categorical protection. The limitation of rights can be constitutionally valid, even when it consists of very serious restrictions, since the Alexyan proportionality theory does not recognise any categorically defined content to constitutional rights. In the end, the validity of rights limitations only depends on whether they respect the principle of proportionality.[12] Sceptics have criticised proportionality scholars' commitment to consequentialism, which in their view neglects the importance of rights as values and endangers the protection of minorities.[13] Proportionality enthusiasts retort, however, that giving strict precedence to rights over the public interest is not practicable. In their view, the proportionality structure can accommodate moral considerations based on liberal conceptions of rights. For example, the legitimate aim prong can serve to exclude paternalistic commands as to how individuals should conduct their lives from the notion of public interest. Further, rights can be assigned different weights in the balancing process, according to the substantive theory of justice that one adopts.[14] In this way,

Waldron (2005/6). For a more complete presentation of the debate, see Klatt and Meister (2012a), pp. 75 f.

8 Kumm (2009a), pp. 35 f.

9 Kumm (2010), p. 141. Other scholars submit to this idea: see, for example, Barak (2012), pp. 472 f.; Möller (2012), p. 108.

10 Kumm (2004), p. 595; Kumm (2009a), pp. 31 f.; Möller (2012), pp. 126 f.

11 Beatty (2004).

12 Kumm (2012), p. 201; Barak (2012), pp. 27 f., 493 f.; Klatt and Meister (2012a), pp. 17 f., 66 f.

13 Habermas (1996), p. 256; Tsakyrakis (2008), pp. 6 f. Webber (2017), p. 74. See also Webber (2009).

14 Kumm (2006a); Kumm (2007), pp. 141 f. For a more detailed analysis of this issue concerning the complex relation of balancing and human dignity, see Kumm and Walen (2014), p. 67. See also Schauer (1992); and, more recently, Schauer (2014), p. 173.

proportionality does not necessarily compromise rights protection, but it promotes a socially situated perception of rights and of the individual.[15]

Even though rights in the rational paradigm do not enjoy absolute protection, they can be 'formidable weapons', since they oblige public authorities to justify their infringement.[16] Proportionality allows structured argumentation based on the factual and legal possibilities of each case. Critics have contested the existence of rational criteria for arbitrating among competing values.[17] However, proportionality scholars do not consider balancing to be irrational but simply more open-ended than subsumption.[18] For Alexy, the constitution can provide a common point of reference that renders competing rights commensurable.[19] Furthermore, the concrete and fact-oriented character of the balancing process under proportionality makes it more transparent and rational than weighing constitutional principles such as freedom of speech and privacy at a high level of abstraction.[20] Proportionality responds both to equity considerations connected to the particularity of each case and to general requirements of objectivity and predictability imposed on judicial decisions.[21] Thus, it is believed to bring with it a whole institutional-political culture, in which every coercive act of the state results from a '*collective judgment of reason* about what justice and good policy requires'.[22] Kumm observes that:

> In institutional terms these features of human rights practice require a recharacterization of what courts do when they assess whether public authorities have violated rights. Courts are not simply engaged in applying rules or interpreting principles. They assess justifications. Call this *the turn from interpretation to justification.*[23]

Proportionality theorists contend that criticism as to the substantive outcomes of proportionality's application should not be addressed to the structural model per se, which does not predetermine the outcomes of judicial decisions. Everything depends on the substantive moral theory

15 Barak (2012), p. 165.
16 Kumm (2006a), p. 11.
17 On the objection of irrationality, see Habermas (1996), pp. 254 f. On the issue of commensurability, see Schauer (1994). See also Urbina (2017).
18 Alexy (2002), p. 401; Alexy (2003a), p. 139; Alexy (2003b), pp. 433–49.
19 Alexy (2003b), p. 442. Scholars have further developed this point by adducing insights from philosophy and practical reason. See Klatt and Meister (2012a), pp. 58 f.
20 Alexy (2002), pp. 105, 369 f.; Barak (2012), p. 357.
21 Perju (2012), p. 334.
22 Kumm (2009a), p. 21.
23 Kumm (2009a), p. 6.

that will complement the model and on its actual application by courts.[24] Proportionality, when correctly applied, simply renders this theory public and open to criticism. Thus, it leads to the 'rational optimization of the common good', no matter how different societies perceive it.[25] Proportionality and the rational human rights paradigm seem abstract enough to accommodate local visions of rights and democracy in constitutional democracies around the globe. They are promoted as a global model of rights-based adjudication. In Beatty's words: 'Applied impartially, proportionality is a formal principle that is capable of being used anywhere in the world. On a shrinking planet, it is appropriately multicultural.'[26] The occasional use of the transplant metaphor in the relevant literature does not imply defiance of the context that surrounds proportionality's use but rather a claim that it can and even should be accommodated and reframed within the proportionality structure.[27]

The German Origins of Proportionality. Still, the source of proportionality is local. Alexy's theory was initially purported to offer a reconstructive account of the case law of the GFCC. It is only since the 2000s that proportionality and the rational human rights paradigm acquired a universal range.[28] Even after the detachment of proportionality from Karlsruhe, scholarship has often used German constitutional case law as an example of the success of proportionality and of the rational human rights paradigm. The conditions for the felicity of proportionality theory should thus be sought in the particular discursive context in which proportionality emerged as a method of judicial review.

Cohen-Eliya and Porat observe that the success of proportionality is rooted in a communitarian conception of the state expressed in the German notion of *Rechtsstaat*.[29] In German post-war constitutionalism, the Basic Law, as Germans like to call their constitution, incorporates the core features of the political morality shared by society.[30] It establishes an 'objective order of values' (*objektive Wertordnung*) on which social

24 Kumm (2007), pp. 141 f. See also Kumm (2006a).

25 Rivers (2006), p. 181.

26 Beatty (2004), p. 168.

27 See Kumm (2017), pp. 30 f., on 'the problem of variance'. Perju (2017) accepts that the pronged framework might have to adapt itself to local needs. Thus, he proposes a fifth prong of proportionality for its successful transplant to the USA.

28 Kumm (2004), p. 575.

29 Cohen-Eliya and Porat (2013), chap. 3.

30 Ibid, pp. 46, 122 f.; Kommers (2012), pp. 356 f. See also, as an example, the value discourse in the *Abortion I* (1975), 39 BVerfGE 1, cited and translated by Kommers (2012), pp. 374 f.

integration is based.[31] In this sense, 'the Basic Law was designed not only to create a system of governance but also to foster a secured and preferred *way of life*.'[32] Bomhoff stresses that the GFCC jurisprudence expresses 'a faith in law of such fervour and ambition that nonbelievers may find difficult to take seriously'.[33] Faith in law is combined with faith in state organs and especially the GFCC itself, which was attributed the mission of substantiating the objective order of values that the Basic Law incorporates in individual cases.[34] As Bomhoff explains, while in the USA, judicial balancing has been connected to the illegitimate pursuance of political outcomes, in Germany, it is combined with a belief in juridical autonomy and purports to offer a refined method of legal reasoning that would lead to better *legal* outcomes. Proportionality balancing, in continuity with the movements of *Interessenjurisprudenz* and von Jhering's teleology, expresses a rational, scientific methodology for the entrenchment of the values expressed in the constitution in every case.[35] German lawyers' perception of legal knowledge as a rational and scientific enterprise, what Cohen-Eliyah and Porat call 'epistemological optimism',[36] is also manifest in formalist doctrines that accompany proportionality, like the 'theory of personal spheres' in the conflict between freedom of speech and right to privacy,[37] the 'gradation theory' (*Stufentheorie*) in cases concerning professional freedom[38] or the identification of 'scales of scrutiny' in cases of epistemic uncertainties.[39]

Proportionality Expressing Local Culture. Integration through law, institutional faith and epistemological optimism are cultural features that seem to favour the consistent application of proportionality. However,

[31] *Lüth* (1958), 7 BVerfGE 198.
[32] Kommers (2012), p. 47.
[33] Bomhoff (2013b), p. 8.
[34] Cohen-Eliya and Porat (2013), pp. 47 f. See also Kommers (2012), pp. 46 f.
[35] Bomhoff (2010), p. 108.
[36] Cohen-Eliya and Porat (2013), p. 90. See, generally, pp. 82 f.
[37] *Lebach* (1973), 35 BVerfGE 202, cited by Kommers (2012), p. 484.
[38] *Pharmacy* (1958), 7 BVerfGE 377, cited by Kommers (2012), pp. 666 f.
[39] *Codetermination* (1979), 50 BVerfGE 290. See also Grimm (2007), p. 391. On this point, see Bomhoff (2013b), p. 9. According to the author this belief is revealed by 'the tropes surrounding the vocabulary of balancing in Germany. There, a list of dominant terms would have to include words like *dialektisch* (dialectical), *prinzipiell* (principled), *durchtheoretisiert* (fully theorized), *Einheitsbildung* (fostering of unity), *logisch-teleologisch* (logicalteleological), *Optimierung* (optimization), and *Synthese* (synthesis).' The perception of proportionality as a rational reasoning method also informs the criticism of concrete GFCC's decisions, which often takes the form of a 'friendly advice' to the Court in the application of proportionality. See also Bomhoff (2013a), pp. 134 f.

they are not universal characteristics of legal culture. They can vary, even in liberal constitutional democracies, even in Europe. Divergence in the use of proportionality observed in Part I indicates that local cultural features affect the way proportionality is understood in different contexts. Divergence also points to local sources of resistance to the application of proportionality as a pronged fundamental rights structure.

Of course, proportionality itself can be a *source* of cultural change. Cohen-Eliya and Porat suggest that the spread of proportionality in different systems sets a global reference point for adjudication and could generate a 'race to the top' in the field of fundamental rights protection. This means that judges would tend to compete with one another as to which legal system protects fundamental rights better.[40] These authors also point out that the migration of a methodological tool such as proportionality can bring with it 'cultural baggage' from Germany.[41] Drawing on the example of Canadian and Israeli case law, they observe that the spread of proportionality can bring with it an organic perception of the state and openness of law to value-laden reasoning and to foreign ideas. Part I has described the way proportionality has been inserted to pre-existing discursive structures in the different contexts studied and the way it has affected these structures. It has shown that the influence of German constitutionalism and of fundamental rights language has certainly enhanced the spread of proportionality. That being said, proportionality has not always been connected to Germany and fundamental rights. What is more, even in cases where proportionality is used as a fundamental rights principle, it does not always lead judges to transparent value-laden reasoning. This indicates that things might be more complicated than the proportionality literature assumes.

In this part, my purpose is to make sense of the three stories on the spread of proportionality presented in Part I. I purport not only to observe the effects that proportionality has had on French, English and Greek legal cultures but also the way these cultures have affected proportionality. In all the contexts studied, proportionality has been perceived as a transfer from another context and has purported to change domestic law in a certain way. This shows that legal actors perceive their local discourse and the source context to be similar in a certain way. But expectations of proportionality considerably vary across space and

[40] Cohen-Eliya and Porat (2013), pp. 134 f., citing David Law.

[41] Ibid, pp. 134, 136 f.

time, according to the local stakes attached to legal argumentation. The goals of legal actors are set, and even thought of, within a certain culture, without which they would not even exist as such. The source context of proportionality is not always Karlsruhe or the rational human rights paradigm. Other influences, coming from other legal systems or even from other disciplines like economics, mathematics and philosophy, might be present and might affect the content of proportionality language according to local criteria for the evaluation of legal arguments. In the cultural study of law, metaphors such as migration or transplantation can only be a *starting point* for legal comparison. The meaning of proportionality and the goals that it is expected to accomplish largely depend on local imagination. Local meanings of proportionality enhance and constrain its use. They make sense of its evolution and of its success or failure in different settings.

The purpose of this part is to identify the particular domestic meaning of proportionality in France, England and Greece. I argue that objectivity and pretension to scientific exactness have been the major assets of proportionality language in France. Proportionality is used by French lawyers as a theory, part of a legal science that justifies the expansion of the reach of law and of judicial powers (Chapter 5). Quite differently, it is a function of myth-making that is attributed to proportionality in English public law. Proportionality is mobilised by common lawyers as a rationalist principle that, referring to substantive values, can establish coherence among sparse common law precedents (Chapter 6). The expectations of proportionality are greater in Greece. There, proportionality is perceived as a legal transplant and is expected to produce not only legal but also socio-political transformation (Chapter 7).

5

Searching for a Legal Science

In this chapter, I argue that rather than echoing a perception of fundamental rights as principles, and of law as practical reasoning, as the Alexyan theory would want it, the force of proportionality in French public law lies in its aura of value-proof objectivity and scientific correctness. The spread of proportionality thus expresses the mystery surrounding political moral choices in French legal thought. At the same time, it expresses domestic lawyers' search for a legal science, exempt from subjective moral or ideological evaluations, which could rationalise such choices. Proportionality in French public law has not served so much as a tool for legal change, as the transplant account of its spread would suggest, but rather as a conceptual tool in the hands of the *doctrine* for systematising and justifying evolutions in domestic judicial review.

The emergence and spread of proportionality in French public law did not unfold in a legal and cultural vacuum. Both the initial failure of proportionality and its recent proliferation should be read against the background of the evolution of French judicial review (Section 5.1). In this context, the main stakes of the transfer of proportionality have been the expansion of the reach of law and the extension of judicial powers (Section 5.2). Proportionality could bestow an appearance of objectivity on evaluations that were traditionally seen as subjective. Indeed, the genealogy of proportionality arguments shows that it represented both a moral-legal ideal imported from other jurisdictions and a mathematical equation imported from positive sciences (Section 5.3). In the public law literature, proportionality was developed as a theory of administrative science, implying the rational adaptation of the means of public action to its ends. In this sense, it found application in the famous *Entreprises de presse* decision (Section 5.4). While the function of proportionality as a positive law concept has been constrained by the traditional structures of judicial review, as a theoretical concept, proportionality has succeeded in justifying important changes in the domestic perception of the manifest error test (Section 5.5). The progressive assimilation of proportionality to the manifest error enhanced its diffusion as a fundamental rights principle. In this context, proportionality assumes a peculiar function of integration (Section 5.6).

5.1 Proportionality in French Public Law: Between Myth and Rationalisation

Proportionality and the Myths of French Public Law Thought. Proportionality in France is very different from the transplant described by the defenders of proportionality. While it emerged as a transfer from abroad, in the minds of domestic lawyers, it has represented a value of law-making, a general principle that pre-existed the emergence of the term in judicial decisions and that has persisted even in the absence of proportionality language in judicial practice. Although the German proportionality model has been mentioned in certain academic analyses, scholars have usually not argued for its adoption as such. Rather, this model has served the reconstruction of pre-existing domestic case law. Even the relatively recent reception of the pronged structure of proportionality has not been interpreted by French public lawyers as a radical change in already existing methods of judicial reasoning. This is why mainstream scholarship has accorded minor importance to the structural integrity of proportionality and is not much bothered by its inconsistent application. Few are those who have studied the analytical features of proportionality case law and even fewer those who pressure for the application of proportionality as an argumentative framework.[42] In particular in private law, the adoption of proportionality to the detriment of the traditional syllogistic model meets important resistance.[43]

The spread of proportionality in France has not been a question of rights optimisation, as the Alexyan theory envisages. Indeed, with some very rare exceptions, the promoters of proportionality have not combined it with a clearly articulated theory of fundamental rights as principles.[44] This is simply because subjective rights are difficult to conceive

[42] For some exceptions, see Bousta (2011); Jamin (2015).

[43] See the relevant discussion in *La semaine juridique*, Regards d'universitaires sur la réforme de la Cour de cassation– conférence débat 24 novembre 2015, supplément au no. 1–2 (2016).

[44] Such a perception of rights seems to be emerging in some private law analyses: see Jamin (2015); Zenati-Castaing (2016).

of in French public law.[45] The modern French legal tradition is dominated by the allegory of the social contract, mainly owing to the work of Rousseau and transcribed in the *DDHC*. According to this narration, men form societies and concede their freedom to the sovereign in order to preserve their natural and imprescriptible rights. These rights are defined by statutes, so that their exercise by every member of society can be assured. This means that, traditionally, rights cannot be conceived of in the absence of legal statutes. Typically, their exercise has been organised by law, such as the laws of 30 June 1881 and of 28 March 1907 concerning the freedom of assembly or the law of 9 December 1905 on the freedom of conscience and the free exercise of religion. For a long time, the constitution did not contain any catalogue of rights or freedoms. Neither the *DDHC* nor the Preambles of the 1946 and 1958 constitutions, proclaiming certain individual and social rights, initially possessed *valeur constitutionnelle*.

This makes sense of the fact that in the French context, proportionality long designated an administrative law principle and not a method for the judicial review of legislation. According to the French public law tradition, law is sacred and infallible; it cannot be put into question. It expresses the general will, *la volonté générale*. French public law is permeated by a voluntarist perception of the state and of legal norm production. Legislation is imagined as a sovereign will, emanating from a mythical entity, the Legislator, executed by the administration and pronounced by the judicial 'mouth', in the concrete and formal terms of judicial decisions.[46] One cannot help but notice the mythopoeic characteristics of French legal thought, which stand in stark contrast to the rational human rights paradigm underlying the theory of proportionality. The establishment of a republican regime, in which sovereignty belongs to the people, has entailed the supplementing of the myth of the general will with another, intermediary one: the myth of representation. Because the Parliament is composed of the elected representatives of the people, it expresses the sovereign will of the people through legal statutes.[47] In the foundations of the traditional

[45] Nevertheless, the idea of subjective public rights is not totally absent from administrative law in the nineteenth and twentieth centuries. See Foulquier (2003).

[46] This classical perception of the separation of powers, traditionally attributed to Montesquieu, has been contested by some prominent French public lawyers. See, for example, Eisenmann (1933), p. 165; Troper (1973).

[47] Brunet (2004); Brunet (2005b).

French *légicentrisme* then, lies a confusion between represented and representatives.[48]

Hence, in French public law, the public interest is not defined by the judge through a rational judicial process. In contrast to the institutional faith in the judiciary that permeates German constitutionalism, French legal tradition is characterised by distrust towards courts, inherited from the 1789 Revolution. The fear of a *gouvernement des juges* has been constantly present in French legal thought and has long constrained judges in a function of loyal application of the law.[49] It is the sovereign will, expressed in legal statutes, that evaluates social reality and, on this basis, decides policy goals as well as the measures to obtain them. It is the sovereign will that, from evaluating a certain situation in the *être*, will conclude to a certain *devoir être*. And, because law is infallible, the will expressed in legal statutes is external to judicial review. So are the goals of administrative action, whose function is traditionally limited to the execution of the legislative will.

French judicial review is thus characterised by a fusion of substance and form. Legal statutes incorporate substantive value choices that the judge 'discovers' and applies in concrete cases. Formalism in this context can be described as a species of 'dogmatism': judges affirm the value choices of Parliament as if they were positive facts. The judicial process resembles a ritual, by which judges seek for a transcendent truth. Garapon observes that: 'In France, law is assimilated to something transcendent whereas in the world of common law, it is best described as the rules of the game.'[50] Indeed, French lawyers often use the term '*consécration*' to designate the recognition of new legal rules or principles.

Judicial decision-making is perceived as a mechanical process of application of the law. It consists in a syllogism with a *majeure*, a *mineure* and a *conclusion*. Balancing of competing interests is excluded from this process. Initially, application of the law was purported to exclude even the process of interpretation itself.[51] Even today, the content of legal norms is presented as pre-established and untouchable in judicial

[48] Rousseau (1997). Gény (1919, p. 70) famously called this characteristic of French legal thought '*le fétichisme de la loi écrite*'.

[49] On this, Lasser (2004); Lasser (2009), pp. 35 f., 44 f. Lambert (1921) first used the expression '*gouvernement des juges*' to describe the US system of judicial review.

[50] Garapon (1995), p. 499.

[51] The *Décret du 16–24 août 1790, sur l'organisation judiciaire*, instituted a preliminary reference procedure by which courts were to refer questions of interpretation to the competent ministers. On this issue more generally, see Perelman (1990), esp. p. 623.

decisions. Dogmatism leaves no place for dissenting opinions or consideration of alternative lines of argumentation. The negotiations taking place in judicial deliberations are not accessible to the addressees of justice. The trust of the latter is not ensured through transparency, as the Alexyan theory would presuppose, or through procedural justice in its Rawlsian sense. Rather, it is precisely the insulation of the judges and councillors composing ordinary courts, their education in elite institutions and their affiliation in *corps*, which is deemed to endow them with expertise and independence from external interests. As Lasser observes: '[I]t is the state as a whole and unitary entity, complete with its representative institutions, that carries the imprimatur of republican legitimacy.'[52]

The Limited Potential for a Legal Science. The predominance of the norm-producing will undermines the potential for law as objective, scientific knowledge. While science is based on objective evaluations of fact and causation, facts are deemed external to the inquiry as to the content of legal norms. Hume's axiomatic separation between 'is' and 'ought' is fundamental in French public law. This makes sense of French lawyers' traditional suspicion towards historical, sociological, Marxist and other critical approaches to law, classically rejected as non-legal. It also makes sense of the distinction between *science* and *doctrine* that is a recurrent theme in this context. On the one hand, science in the sense of establishment of objective and exact knowledge is traditionally doomed never to participate in legal norm production, since it can only be established in situations of fact. On the other hand, *doctrine* in the sense of normative system-building is doomed to be non-scientific.[53] Hence, doctrinal systematisation is not solely the work of scholars, but also of practitioners. In particular in public law, the *commissaires du gouvernement* have assumed a role of *faiseurs de systèmes* through their published opinions preceding the Council of State decisions.[54] As we saw, it is in such opinions that proportionality emerged in French public law. Ever since, it has served the doctrinal systematisation of positive law, rather than the process of legal norm production itself.

The strict separation between facts and norms renders the function of proportionality as an ad hoc instance of balancing difficult to seize in this context. More generally, reference to ad hoc legal norm production is

[52] Lasser (2009), p. 53.
[53] See Chevallier (2002).
[54] Rivero (1951). On the relationship between private and public law *doctrine*, see Jamin and Melleray (2018).

very rare, almost inexistent in legal writings. French legal thought is distinctively formal, based on binary, all-or-nothing distinctions. This is neatly expressed in the traditional plan in *deux parties-deux sous-parties* that has been followed since the 1940s in theses and university writings.[55] The problem with applying the law according to the factual circumstances of each case is that it inevitably implies *subjective* – and thus potentially arbitrary – value judgments by the authorities of application, conditioned by considerations of morality, ideology or, even worse, interest. Domestic lawyers typically use the term 'abstract' as synonymous with 'objective' and the term 'concrete' as synonymous with 'subjective'. Contrary to what proportionality scholars assume, facts have a limited role to play in the appreciation of legality, which is traditionally perceived as the abstract confrontation of norms of different hierarchical statuses. The legally defined flaws that lead to the annulment of an administrative act (*cas d'ouverture*) traditionally concern competence, form, procedure and the misapplication of superior legal norms. Rare are the cases in which courts have sanctioned an abuse of power (*détournement de pouvoir*), that is, the pursuit of illegitimate goals by the reviewed authority.[56]

This is connected to the fact that French legal thought is pessimistic about the possibility of objective value judgments, and suspiciously levels the accusation of *jusnaturalisme* towards those who appeal to such judgments.[57] One of the most important attributes of French legal science is (pretension to) axiological neutrality.[58] It is indicative that *the* most important reference point in French legal thought during the last century has been Kelsen and his 'pure' theory of law. This feature has impeded the development of theories of inclusive positivism such as the ones developed in common law systems. Similarly, the Alexyan concept of law as including elements of morality is hardly conceivable within the fundamental assumptions of modern French legal thought.

Rationalisation Efforts. These traditional characteristics have been – just as traditionally – criticised in the French context. French public lawyers have always sought to impose constraints on the norm-making will of state authorities, either by appealing to the 'natural,

[55] See Audren and Halpérin (2013), pp. 223 f.

[56] On the *cas d'ouverture*, see Laferrière (1887), pp. 496 f.; for a recent presentation, see Plessix (2016), pp. 1390 f.

[57] On this tendency of French legal thought, see Jouanjan (2003), pp. 134 f.

[58] Champeil-Desplats (2016), pp. 107 f., 111 f.

imprescriptible and sacred rights' of the *DDHC*,[59] or by importing methods from the *sciences dures* and the *sciences sociales*.[60] Contestation of the traditional voluntarist common sense has not only been present in the writings of scholars, but also of some famous *commissaires du gouvernement*, who have called for judicial pragmatism in their opinions.[61] The Council of State has not been indifferent to these tendencies. It was the desire for rationalisation that led the administrative judges to increasingly monitor the facts grounding administrative action.[62] It was the will to impose equity constraints on legal norm production that, since the 1940s, inspired the creation of the normative category of general principles of law.[63] These developments prepared the ground for the emergence of proportionality in French public law. We saw that proportionality first appeared in the Council of State case law as a method for substantive judicial review, and that during the 1970s, scholars called for its recognition as a general principle.

Still, legal formality remained decisive in case law and preserved the mystery surrounding legal norm production. This is expressed in the persistence of the theory of the *loi écran*, which long impeded the application of proportionality in the review of legislation. According to this theory, whenever administrative action is confined to the implementation of clear and precise legislation, the judge must refuse her power to review its compatibility with the constitution.[64] Until the late 1980s, this applied to review on the basis of international law as well. More generally, legal formality has been expressed in a pervasive dogmatism in French judicial reasoning, in the sense of exclusion of legislative value choices from judicial review, which long constrained the dynamics of proportionality and impeded its announcement as a general principle in judicial practice. Dogmatism underlies the allegedly 'manifest' character of the

[59] Phrase taken from the preamble of the 1789 Declaration of the Rights of Man and of the Citizen. See, for example, the famous *Doyen* Hauriou (1930), pp. 306 f.

[60] Champeil-Desplats (2016), pp. 42 f., 145 f.

[61] See, especially, the *Commissaire du gouvernement* Chenot, criticising the '*faiseurs de systèmes*', in his opinion on CE 10 February 1950, *Sieur Gicquel*, Rec., p. 100, and the response by Rivero (1951).

[62] CE, 4 April 1914, *Gomel*, no. 55125, ECLI:FR:CEORD:1914:55125.19140404; 14 January 1916, *Camino*, no. 59619, ECLI:FR:CEORD:1916:59619.19160114. On this evolution, Goldenberg (1932).

[63] CE, 26 June 1959, *Syndicat général des ingénieurs conseils*, no. 92099, ECLI:FR:CESJS:1959:92099.19590626; 12 February 1960, *Société Eky*, nos. 46922 and 46923, ECLI:FR:CESJS:1960: 46922.19600212.

[64] CE, 6 November 1936, *Arrighi*, no. 41221, Rec. CE, p. 966.

factual errors sanctioned by the judge, the mystery surrounding the *détournement de pouvoir*, and even the fundamental distinction between *légalité* and *opportunité*, which has guided the evolution of French judicial review: in contrast to the impact-oriented notion of merits in UK public law, the taboo of *opportunité* excludes the scrutiny of the intent of the reviewed authorities.

Rationalisation and Constitutional Review. The rationalisation of Parliament was a major objective of the 1958 Constitution, which instituted for the first time the Constitutional Council. However, the introduction of constitutional review did not radically change the voluntarist perception of legal norm production. It is indicative that, for decades, no *a posteriori* review existed in this context and the Constitutional Council was not even perceived as a court, but as a political institution, whose main mission was to preserve and police the boundaries between *loi* and *règlement*.[65] The constitutional judges long refused to review the value choices of Parliament. The legislator was deemed to be sovereign in pursuit of the public interest, a notion that 'escaped constitutional mechanics and constitutional engineering'.[66] The application of proportionality as a judicial method for balancing constitutional rights was thus difficult to imagine for French lawyers.

The recognition of the normative value of the constitutional preamble did not bring about a radical change in this respect, even though this text – and especially the *DDHC* to which it refers – has served as a catalogue of substantive rights in judicial review.[67] Constitutional rights, or rather public freedoms (*libertés publiques*) are objective requirements of abstention in the French context. They do not impose optimisation requirements, as the Alexyan theory would want it; they do not constitute a separate normative category of fundamental rights. Rather, they belong to categories such as the general principles of law or the 'fundamental principles recognised by republican legislation' (what French lawyers call the *PFRLR*). Their function is to set objective limits on public action. Hence, their application consists in an abstract confrontation between the content of legal norms, following the syllogistic model. It traditionally acquires a distinctively formal or procedural style, even in the most significant Constitutional Council decisions. Among the requirements that public freedoms imply one most notably finds the preclusion of a

[65] On this, see Stone Sweet (1992), pp. 31–45.

[66] Saint Bonnet (2007), before fn. 5.

[67] See, most notably, Decision no. 71–44 DC, 16 July 1971, *Liberté d'association*, ECLI:FR:CC:1971:71.44.DC.

preliminary license requirement for the exercise of a right or the competence of the judiciary in cases involving individual freedom, announced in Article 66 of the constitution.[68]

Certainly, the 'juridicisation' of the Constitutional Council and the development of constitutional reasoning methods ended with the establishment of Parliament as a constituted institution and introduced a certain distance between the people and the law. The 'constitutional bases' [*bases constitutionnelles*] of different branches of law were affirmed, constraining Parliament in the exercise of its powers.[69] According to perhaps the most famous Constitutional Council formula, 'legislation [...] only expresses the general will insofar as it respects the Constitution'.[70] Law-making began to be represented as a process of reconciliation between competing constitutional values and the council started to censure manifest errors and manifest disproportionalities in its scrutiny of legislative bills. In this context, the constitutional status of proportionality was affirmed during the 1980s. Rather than a transplant then, the entrenchment of proportionality as a constitutional principle should be read as a systemic evolution of French public law. Proportionality, as one of the 'constitutional bases' of administrative law and of criminal law, was to become part of a 'unique conceptual system' that would serve in the analysis of the different branches of law.[71] This explains the differences between the French version of proportionality and the Alexyan model, observed in Chapter 2.

Still, idealisation of Parliament and the legislative process persisted in the constitutional case law. The legislator is constantly personified in judicial decisions. It is 'his' unitary will (invariably, Parliament is represented as a man) that is sought in the *travaux parlementaires*. Reconciliation of competing constitutional values is not (at least not explicitly) reviewed by the judge through judicial balancing or proportionality. Following a *considérant* that became consistent in the council's decisions: '[I]t is the competence of the legislator to proceed to the necessary reconciliation between the respect of freedoms and the preservation of public order, without which the exercise of freedoms cannot be safeguarded.'[72] It seems that reference to reconciliation corresponds to a

[68] Rousseau (2016), pp. 264 f.

[69] Vedel (1986).

[70] Decision no. 85-197 DC, 23 August 1985, *Loi sur l'évolution de la Nouvelle Calédonie*, ECLI:FR:CC:1985:85.197.DC, cons. 27.

[71] Vedel (1996).

[72] Decision no. 85-187 DC, 25 January 1985, *Loi relative à l'état d'urgence en Nouvelle-Calédonie et dépendances*, ECLI:FR:CC:1985:85.187.DC, cons.3.

ritual, which serves to reconstruct legislative intentions in a constitutionally legitimate way. Immunity of legislative goals still permeates the Constitutional Council's methods of reasoning. Thus, sanctioning an abuse of power is unthinkable in French constitutional law.[73] Instead, judges often use the technique of *réserve d'interprétation*, which allows them to 'speak' the words of the legislator according to a legislative will presumed to be legitimate. Rather than contesting the idealisation of Parliament, the affirmation of the constitutional status of proportionality enhanced it. We saw that it was in a *réserve d'interprétation* that the Constitutional Council first announced proportionality as a principle for the protection of public freedoms.[74]

Demystification and New Mythopoeia. At the same time, French public lawyers do not always believe in their myths and often even denounce them as such.[75] Since the mid-1990s, in the context of *crise de la loi* and under the increasing influence of European law in the domestic sphere, the French *doctrine* has appeared much more sceptical as to the possibility of determining the content of legal prescriptions. Traditional positivism is progressively abandoned to the advantage of hermeneutic or realist theories of law, or – more often – of an '*amorphe*' description and systematisation of case law.[76] The normative force of judicial decisions is increasingly affirmed. This has been combined with progressive openness of the legal system to influence from abroad, which was enhanced by the abandonment of the *théorie de la loi écran* in judicial review of convention compatibility.[77] Since the mid-1990s, comparative law became a key means of making sense of domestic constitutional case law. The once little valued Constitutional Council started to be compared to powerful European courts such as the Italian, the Spanish and the German constitutional courts.[78] Proportionality itself acquired a new meaning as a principle coming from Germany and Europe and its jurisprudential origin was increasingly affirmed.

Boas observed that 'mythological worlds seem to have been built up, only to be shattered again, and that new worlds were built from the

[73] Goesel-Le Bihan (2001), p. 67.

[74] Decision no. 94–352 DC, 18 January 1995, cons. 17.

[75] Already Carré de Malberg (1931, p. 222) talked about a 'fiction'; see also Brunet (2005b); Rousseau (1997).

[76] Jouanjan (2003), p. 142.

[77] Cass, 24 May 1975, *Société des cafés Jacques Vabre*, no. 73–13556, Bull. ch. mixte, no. 4, p. 6; CE (Pl.), 20 October 1989, *Nicolo*, no. 108243, ECLI:FR:CEASS:1989:108243.19891020.

[78] For some examples, see Xynopoulos (1995); Di Manno (1999); Pardini (2001).

fragments'.[79] Indeed, demystification of Parliament has been accompanied by an idealisation of the judiciary. Often personified in legal writings, the Judge fascinates French public lawyers. While critics present 'him' as a political institution with illegitimate or at least extra-legal motives,[80] mainstream scholars perceive 'him' as a protector of freedoms that are now called fundamental.[81] Mainstream *doctrine* often develops complex theoretical constructions to make sense of case law and to guide the judge in rights adjudication. Once a purely technical text, since the 2000s the constitution started to be described by some as a 'charter of rights and liberties of judicial inspiration'.[82] The new mission assigned to courts has been expressed in positive law as well, with the instauration of preliminary reference procedures explicitly reserved to the adjudication of freedoms, the *référé libertés* before the Council of State and the *QPC* before the Constitutional Council. This evolution has provided fertile ground for the recent proliferation of proportionality.

The spread of proportionality in French public law makes much more sense when it is read not as a transplant, but rather as part of a more general evolution of French judicial review. Still, this reading tells us little as to why, at a certain point, French public lawyers started reasoning in proportionality terms. It also tells us little as to why, even though proportionality is increasingly perceived as a transfer from Germany and Europe in this context, it preserves its proper characteristics that make domestic lawyers talk about a '*proportionnalité à la française*'. The stakes that French lawyers attach to the use of proportionality language become clearer when one examines the judicial methods that the *doctrine* categorises under this term.

5.2 French Lawyers' Expectations of Proportionality: An Extension of Judicial Powers

The Emergence of Necessity Review. According to the mainstream proportionality narrative in France, proportionality appeared during the 1930s in the case law of the Council of State. In 1930, Mr Benjamin, a writer well-known for his extreme right-wing ideas, was invited to a literature conference in Nevers. This provoked strong reactions from political opponents and a counter-protest was announced by

[79] Boas (1898), p. 18, cited by Lévi-Strauss (1966), p. 31.
[80] See, among others, Troper (1994); Meunier (1994).
[81] See Vedel (1988); Favoreu (2001), p. 143.
[82] Rousseau (2010), p. 449.

schoolteacher trade unions. The mayor of Nevers finally decided to prohibit the event for reasons of public peace. Mr Benjamin attacked the mayor's decision before the Council of State, which annulled it some years later as *ultra vires*.[83] The Council of State considered that, while the mayor had the power to take the appropriate measures in order to maintain public order, he should 'reconcile the exercise of his powers with the respect to the freedom of assembly', guaranteed by the law. However, the risks of a public order disturbance provoked by Mr Benjamin's conference were not serious enough to legally justify its prohibition.[84] Hence, the court imposed a strict necessity requirement on restrictions of the freedom of assembly. The prohibition of a conference is within the power of the mayor only when no alternative, less restrictive measures are available for maintaining public order.

Benjamin remained famous for establishing the axiom 'freedom is the rule, restriction is the exception' as an enforceable rule in French public law and never lost its place in the *GAJA*. However, Prélot points out that the substantive solution applied in *Benjamin* brings about nothing new compared to previous case law. As he observes, in terms of substance, the axiom 'freedom is the rule, restriction is the exception' comes 'directly from 1789' and was already enforced in French judicial review.[85] Further, the Council of State had already affirmed its power to review police measures in order to protect public freedoms, like the freedom to protest. What then, was so original about the *Benjamin* decision?

Necessity Review and the *Bilan* as Irritants. The novelty of the 1933 case lay in the establishment of the administrative *judge* as the protector of public freedoms, a role that until then belonged to Parliament. Indeed, at the time freedom of assembly was well organised by Third Republic legislation and no legal provision empowered the mayor to prohibit a literary conference for public order reasons, as he had done in the case at hand. However, the Council of State did not annul the mayor's decision for incompetence. This is because, according to the *Commissaire du gouvernement*, while the law did not provide for restrictions of the freedom of assembly for the protection of the public order, 'the legislator of 1881 […] certainly did not want to allow this freedom to generate serious [public order] troubles'.[86] Therefore, the council allowed the

[83] CE, 19 May 1933, *Benjamin*.

[84] Ibid.

[85] Prélot (2013), after fn. 3. The expression was originally used by the *Commissaire du gouvernement* Corneille in his opinion on CE, 10 August 1917, *Baldy*, Rec., p. 638.

[86] Michel, 'Conclusions sur CE, 19 May 1933, *Benjamin*', p. 6.

prohibition of an assembly for public order reasons by introducing an *exception* to the principle of legality. This unsettled Mestre, who pointed out a regressive interference with the principle of legality.[87]

In compensation, the administrative judges affirmed to themselves the power to protect public freedoms by exercising a necessity review of police restrictions. Until then, this kind of intensive review was only exercised in cases of 'bound' competence (*pouvoir lié*), where the conditions for the exercise of administrative powers are clearly defined by law. On the contrary, in the field of police measures law only defines the general objective of administrative intervention, which is the preservation of public order. The administration thus enjoyed discretion in the appreciation of the grounds of its action (*pouvoir discrétionnaire*).[88] And in cases of administrative discretion, the legal characterisation of facts was traditionally considered a matter of *opportunité*, for which courts can have no say. It seemed as if, by imposing a necessity requirement on police measures, the Council of State had transformed an instance of administrative discretion to an instance of bound competence.[89] *Benjamin* thus introduced a crack in the clear distinction between *légalité* and *opportunité* of administrative acts and in the strict distribution of competences between the judge and the administration.

A similar extension of judicial powers can be observed in the *bilan* case law. After the first wave of enthusiasm for what was perceived as a refinement of judicial methods, the question of the insertion of judicial balancing into the traditional distinctions of French public law arose. The promoters of judicial balancing had tried to play down the shift that this method brought about.[90] However, the *bilan* as a judicial technique irritated the traditional perception of the discretionary powers of public authorities as a clearly defined area of decision-making. It implied the review of the choice of administrative means, of the exercise of administrative discretion. Thus, it inevitably led to a review of the *opportunité* of administrative acts and involved an important extension of judicial powers.[91] Waline observed that the only way to such a review was to

[87] Mestre (1934).
[88] On the distinction between 'bound' competence and discretionary power, see Plessix (2016), pp. 1409–11.
[89] De Laubadère (1974), p. 535.
[90] Braibant, 'Conclusions sur CE Ass., 28 mai 1971, *Ville Nouvelle Est*'; Morisot, 'Conclusions sur CE Ass., 20 octobre 1972, *Société Sainte-Marie-de-l'Assomption*'.
[91] De Laubadère (1974), p. 531.

admit that the *opportunité* of expropriation was a legal requirement.[92] In French public law tradition this constituted a contradiction in terms.

Necessity Review and the *Bilan* as Instances of Proportionality. In a mysterious way, the use of proportionality language eased these doctrinal problems. According to its promoters, proportionality required a relationship of fair proportion between three elements: the factual situation; the administrative decision; and its goal.[93] In other words, it implied a legal requirement of adequacy of administrative action, which was to be appraised according to the particular factual circumstances, the *motifs de fait* on which the decision was grounded. Adequacy to the factual circumstances is very close to expediency. What proportionality discretely translated was a substantive legal requirement of *opportunité* of administrative decisions. Its entrenchment as a general principle was thus purported to provide the judge with a legal basis for expanding judicial review to cover the exercise of administrative discretion, at least in certain fields. The only instance where the Council of State monitored the exercise of discretionary powers was the necessity review of police measures, established in *Benjamin*. The similarity between the scrutiny exercised in *Ville Nouvelle Est* and the one exercised in *Benjamin* allowed designating both under the label of proportionality.

In spite of their similarities in terms of judicial review methods, however, a fundamental difference existed between the necessity and the *bilan*. In the 1933 decision, freedom remained central in judicial reasoning. The promoters of proportionality seemed to perceive individual rights' protection as a crucial moral-legal justification for entrenching the principle.[94] In the words of Braibant, the rule of proportionality requires that 'insofar as the Administration enjoys powers that allow it to impair citizens' rights and freedoms, it must not use them, except if it is necessary'.[95] Nonetheless, connection to public freedoms was not apparent in the *bilan* case law. Even more, in certain cases judicial balancing seemed to menace the liberal foundations of administrative law. Indeed, in some cases judicial balancing seemed to represent a new perception of the public interest as plural and polyvalent, no longer confronted with private interests, but, rather, including them in its scope.[96] This not only

[92] Waline (1974), p. 824.
[93] Dreyfus (1974), pp. 695–6; Braibant (1974), p. 298.
[94] Dreyfus (1974), p. 705.
[95] Braibant (1974), p. 298.
[96] See, for example, CE (Pl.), 20 October 1972, *Société civile Sainte-Marie-de-l'Assomption*; CE, 28 January 1976, no. 95507, ECLI:FR:CESSR:1993:95507.19930219.

undermined the objectivity of public interest assessments, but also blurred the liberal distinction between public and private altogether. Public utility would become a matter to be decided on a case by case basis. Judicial balancing was thus increasingly perceived as a danger for individual rights.[97]

The Quest for a Theory of Judicial Balancing. The irritation that the *bilan* provoked could be eased if a 'theory of balancing of interests' acted as 'a force of simplification and generalisation'.[98] In French public law, the deconstruction of legal categories and distinctions is often compensated for by the construction of theories. Even though concrete legal solutions are no longer determined by precise legal rules, theory still allows for the separation of the 'structure' from the 'event', for the separation of the legal necessity from the contingency of the subjective interests at stake.[99] Judicial techniques that involve the application of law according to the factual circumstances of the case are typically framed as parts of a more general theory: *théorie des circonstances exceptionnelles*, *théorie de l'erreur manifeste*, *théorie du changement de circonstances*. This explains French public lawyers' attention to the different methods of judicial reasoning, in contrast to common lawyers' attention to reasoning structures, patterns and heads of review.[100] Methods are ways of thinking, techniques of proceeding, according to an underlying theory or structure. Induced 'from the concrete to the abstract, passing from the multiple to one', methods provide French public law with material coherence.[101]

Judicial balancing did not escape the frenzy of theorisation and the term '*théorie du bilan*' is still often used to describe the method introduced in *Ville Nouvelle Est*. Still, most commentators at the time of the *Ville Nouvelle Est* case observed that there was no actual structure that could guide the comparison of advantages and disadvantages of an administrative operation by the judge.[102] Indeed, not only did balancing lack a general underlying theory, but it contested some of the most fundamental conceptual structures and distinctions of French administrative law. This restrained the potential of the *bilan* in French public law

97 On this point, Waline (1974), pp. 814, 828; Lemasurier (1974), p. 561.
98 De Laubadère (1974), p. 546.
99 The analysis here is inspired by Lévi-Strauss' comparison between science and '*bricolage*' (1966), pp. 25 f.
100 See, for example, Blanquer (2000); Gaudemet (2013); Champeil-Desplats (2016).
101 Rivero (1951), pp. 100–1.
102 De Laubadère (1974), pp. 546–7; Waline (1974), p. 818.

considerably. Many authors interpreted it as sanctioning only manifest errors or disproportionalities.[103] Even its promoters called for '*tact et mesure*' in its application.[104] In 1977, the *Commissaire du gouvernement* Kahn lamented: '[W]e could have spared the so-called "theory of balancing", where I see neither balancing nor theory.'[105]

The Stakes Attached to the Transfer of Proportionality. 'We have not developed a theory of the principle of proportionality – maybe because until relatively recently we did not need one.'[106] This is how Braibant, paraphrasing Lord Reid from the House of Lords, concluded his study on proportionality. Proportionality appeared in French *doctrine* as a response to the need to justify an advance of judicial review, without compromising the coherence and objectivity of French administrative law. In a magic way, proportionality encompassed the necessity, the manifest error and the *bilan* in its scope and was thus able to preserve the unity of judicial methods, while admitting their variable application according to the circumstances. Proportionality was a 'theory', a doctrinal construction that could constrain the subjectivity of pragmatist judicial solutions and that could bring about the 'simplification and generalisation' of administrative case law that French public lawyers sought.

The systematising function of proportionality has persisted in later writings. It is inherent in the perception of the *contrôle de proportionnalité* as a method used by public law judges. Besides, systematisation or reconstruction is also a major asset of the Alexyan proportionality theory, which is inspired by interpretative approaches to law. However, it is not clear how proportionality accomplished its systematising mission in the French context.

5.3 Searching for Objectivity: Proportionality Between Fact and Law

Objective but not Manifest. The early uses of proportionality language in French public law are characterised by 'epistemological optimism', that is, a belief in the possibility of objective factual evaluations.[107] Although not being manifest, proportionality preserved the objectivity of judicial review. Sometimes, this provoked confusion as to the intensity

103 Bockel (1978), p. 368; de Laubadère (1974), p. 547.
104 Braibant, 'Conclusions sur CE Ass., 28 mai 1971, *Ville Nouvelle Est*', p. 427.
105 Kahn (1978), p. 16; Guibal (1978), p. 486.
106 Braibant (1974), p. 306.
107 The analysis here is inspired by Cohen-Eliya and Porat (2013), chap. 5.

of review that it implied. Braibant for example, regarded both the *bilan* and the *erreur manifeste* as aspects of proportionality. However, at the same time he perceived the *bilan* as a method for more intensive scrutiny, through which the judge 'accurately weighs the proportions between the facts, the goal and the reviewed act'.[108] In the same vein, while Dreyfus proposed sanctioning *manifest* disproportionalities, she talked about a 'detailed examination' of the administrative file, which contradicted the manifest character of the review.[109]

The ambiguity was already latent in Braibant's famous opinion in the *Ville Nouvelle Est* case. The *Commissaire du gouvernement* had proposed the employment of the *bilan* only to censure administrative decisions that were 'arbitrary, unreasonable or poorly studied'.[110] Although the terms 'arbitrary' and 'unreasonable' imply a moral criticism of the intent of the primary decision-maker, the sanctioning of 'poorly studied' decisions is different. Such decisions need not necessarily contain *manifest* errors, and the state of mind of the primary decision-maker is in principle irrelevant in their scrutiny. Braibant's dicta appeared to contradict with his own observation more than a decade earlier that 'discretionary power implies the right to err'.[111] What, then, rendered administrative decisions so poorly studied or so erred that judicial intervention through balancing or proportionality was justified?

This question brings to the surface another paradox in the argumentation concerning the technique of the *bilan*. Despite Braibant's reference to the study and planning of administrative decisions, the application of the *bilan* was not a matter of *procedural* guarantees.[112] Indeed, in his observations in *Ville Nouvelle Est*, Braibant had argued against a strict application of the preliminary administrative procedure of expropriation. In his view, even though the procedure was simply and clearly defined in legal texts, it rendered expropriation too time-consuming and was often impracticable.[113] Thus, the application of the *bilan* did not have as an objective to ensure the consistency and completeness of the administrative file on which the contested decision was based. For Braibant, this

[108] Braibant (1974), p. 302.
[109] Dreyfus (1974), p. 698. See also Bockel (1978), p. 368.
[110] Braibant, 'Conclusions sur CE Ass., 28 mai 1971, *Ville Nouvelle Est*', p. 427.
[111] Braibant, 'Conclusions sur CE, 18 February 1958, *Société des éditions de la terre de feu*', Rec., p. 114.
[112] Waline (1974), pp. 819 f.
[113] Braibant, 'Conclusions sur CE Ass., 28 mai 1971, *Ville Nouvelle Est*', p. 423.

would require a legislative reform of the expropriation procedure, adapting it to the reality of administrative action.[114]

Therefore, the objective character of administrative errors that the *bilan* was to sanction did not result from the non-respect of legal forms and procedures. Rather, it resulted from the substantive judicial assessment of administrative action. This led Waline to the conclusion that the *Ville Nouvelle Est* case law was 'an act of faith in the omniscience of the administrative judge'.[115] Proportionality as well, as synonymous with adequacy, enhanced the shift of focus in judicial scrutiny from the procedure to the substance of administrative decisions. According to Braibant, proportionality assessments were a matter of common sense.[116] Clearly, however, as the reactions to the *bilan* case law express, the common-sensical knowledge to which Braibant appealed did not correspond to the *legal* common sense shared among French public lawyers. The objectivity of judicial review under proportionality balancing did not result from legal formality but rather from the opening of law to an extra-legal knowledge that was perceived as objective. What then, was the nature of the common sense that could allow for judicial balancing? In this respect, previous uses of proportionality language in French public law prove insightful.

The Financial Genes of Proportionality in French Public Law. Morisot's opinion was not the first time that the term 'proportion' was employed in judicial reasoning. As Braibant pointed out in his article, the term had been used before, especially in the field of public finances.[117] In this case law, proportion represented a purely factual or mathematical element, implying no legal evaluations. However, as Braibant stressed, the role of the judge is more important when proportion concerns the validity of an administrative act, rather than the correctness of a financial equation.[118] This is precisely what Morisot's opinion added to the use of proportionality terminology: for the first time, proportionality was connected to judicial balancing in French legal discourse. Although proportion was still used as a synonym for non-excess, it now required a *legal* – and not purely mathematical – evaluation of the factual situation before

114 Ibid, p. 424.

115 Waline (1974), p. 822.

116 Braibant (1974), p. 298.

117 Ibid, pp. 297 f., esp. p. 300. See CE, 16 November 1962, *Syndicat intercommunal d'électricité de la Nièvre et autres*, nos. 42202 and 44595, Rec., p. 612; 21 October 1988, nos. 72862, 72863, and 73062, ECLI:FR:CESSR:1988:72862.19881021.

118 Braibant (1974), p. 301.

the judge. Both Dreyfus and Braibant accentuated the moral-legal character of proportionality evaluations by referring to its morality and justice connotations, mostly coming from its uses in foreign jurisdictions. Still, as well as being a transfer from other legal systems, proportionality was a transfer from other disciplines. Hence, it claimed an accuracy and objectivity that one only finds in the *sciences exactes*.

A careful analysis of the *bilan* case law confirms the financial genes of proportionality. As we saw, the *Grassin* decision was the first use of proportionality as a judicial balancing standard. Interestingly, a reading of this case in the light of previous decisions reveals much about the nature of the review exercised by the judges when using this term. Since the 1960s, the term 'proportion' had been sporadically employed in the field of urban planning as a consequence of the applied legal norms. For example, the national regulation of town planning allowed for the refusal of an individual construction licence when, due to particular circumstances, the construction at stake imposed the realisation of public works, 'out of proportion' with the municipality's resources. Administrative courts had affirmed their power to evaluate whether the expenses required by the municipality were indeed disproportionate themselves – usually confirming the administrative refusal.[119] Moreover, in *Le Moulin Bellanger* the Council of State had imposed obligations to provide information where construction licences were refused for this reason.[120]

The *Néel* case had expanded this case law in the field of expropriation, even though no legal text referred to proportionality or proportion. In this case, the council had decided that the administrative file concerning the declaration of public utility should contain sufficient information as to the financial cost of the correlated expropriations. The *Commissaire du gouvernement* Baudouin had explicitly connected the check of the financial cost of an expropriation, in which the court typically used proportionality language, with the public utility appraisal. In his words, the administration's obligation to inform offered 'one of the most concrete and the most profound anchors for evaluating the character of public utility' of an expropriation.[121] One year later, when arguing for the first application of the *bilan*, Braibant also included the financial cost of an operation in the appreciation of public utility. While he did not use

119 Ibid, p. 301.

120 CE, 18 July 1973, no. 83745, ECLI:FR:CESSR:1973:83745.19730718; 23 June 1976, no. 96285, ECLI:FR:CESSR:1976:96285.19760623.

121 Baudouin, 'Conclusions sur CE Ass., 23 January 1970, *Epoux Néel*', Rec., p. 44, cited by Waline (1974), p. 819.

proportionality language, his *conclusions* contained many references to economics and finance, the most characteristic being the use of the term 'cost-benefit analysis' (*bilan coût-avantages*) to designate the review that he was proposing.

Therefore, by employing proportionality terminology in the evaluation of the public utility of the Peyratte airport, the judges of *Grassin* did nothing but draw out the consequences of previous case law. In the words of the council:

> [T]he cost of the operation at stake, which entails the fragmentation of many agricultural exploitations, is evaluated at 700 000 F, an amount out of proportion with the financial resources of the municipality, counting no more than 1 100 residents approximately. Further, it does not follow from the elements of the administrative file that the municipality benefitted from external financial aid.[122]

The proportionality reasoning of the court was not very far from a simple financial equation, like the one typically applied in the field of construction licences. Proportionality terminology was generally used in this way in the *bilan* case law, while in cases where no financial equation was at stake, the court did not necessarily employ proportionality language.[123]

Based on this evolution, the early French proportionality scholars described the whole process of judicial balancing in proportionality terms. In this way, they enhanced an important conceptual shift. While until then the proportionality of the financial cost of an expropriation to the resources of a municipality was only *part* of the evaluation of its public utility, proportionality came to designate *the whole* of this evaluation. This conceptual shift, which literary analysts would call a synecdoche, attributed the objective connotation of proportionality appreciations to the legal evaluation of public utility as a whole. This is what enabled proportionality language to preserve the objectivity of judicial review in the *bilan* case law. Commenting the application of the *bilan* during the 1970s, a public law professor often referred to as *Mademoiselle* Lemasurier observed that the Council of State 'tended to establish a rule that until then was implicit and diffused in its proper case law, but practiced explicitly and rationally by certain administrative

[122] CE, 26 October 1973, *Sieur Grassin*.

[123] See, for example, CE, 28 January 1976; 6 July 1977, no. 00267, ECLI:FR:CESSR:1977:00267.19770706. Contrast with CE (Pl.), 22 February 1974, *Adam*, nos. 91848 and 93520, ECLI:FR:CEASS:1974:91848.19740222.

authorities in the context of rationalisation of budgetary choices, as a general legal principle'.[124]

The Technique of the *Bilan* and the Alexyan Model of Proportionality. Objective but not manifest, common-sensical but escaping legal formality, the use of proportionality language reveals French public lawyers' general tendency to attribute the characteristics of economic rationality to moral-legal argumentation. Reference to cost-benefit analysis echoes Bentham's conception of utility, exempt from natural law considerations and based on an algebraic evaluation and calculation of advantages and disadvantages of legal decision-making. Jouanjan and Champeil-Desplats both point out that modern French legal thought has often borrowed models and methods from mathematics and the *sciences dures* in order to ground the scientificity of doctrinal legal constructions.[125] Besides, as we have seen, belief in the commensurability of values and the possibility of their rational comparative evaluation also characterises the Alexyan theory of proportionality. Indeed, the *bilan* is the closest one gets to the transnational proportionality theory in French public law at the level of judicial methods.

However, the epistemological optimism of French public lawyers remains very different from the one that animates proportionality scholars due to its focus on facts. In contrast to the Alexyan proportionality model, the *bilan* does not presuppose the attribution of an ad hoc normative power to the judge. Rather, it concerns the *in concreto* evaluation of the public utility of an administrative operation, that is, the process of the legal appreciation of facts. The *bilan* case law is not rights-oriented and thus leaves to the reviewed authorities the fundamental value choices that guide public action. This is also why this kind of reasoning did not spill over into other fields. Rather than implying a paradigmatic transformation of the legal order into a 'total constitution' of fundamental rights, proportionality, as it is employed in the *bilan* case law, simply embodies the '*hypertrophie du fait*' that more generally characterises the application of legal standards in French public law.[126] Rather than the myth of the judge as protector of fundamental rights, proportionality echoes the prosaic and technical rationality of legal decision-making.

[124] Lemasurier (1974), p. 554.
[125] Jouanjan (2003); Champeil-Desplats (2016), pp. 58 f.
[126] Rials (1980), p. 235.

Constrained in the Binding Arrangements of French Public Law. Of course, sceptics were not convinced by the double nature of proportionality, between fact and law, which contested the French positivist common sense.[127] For some time, the mythical ambiguity of the concept did not capture the imagination of French public law judges either. By their upbringing and experience, the members of the Council of State and of the Constitutional Council are immersed in the reality of public action and are disenchanted with the decision-making process that it implies. Hence, as we have seen, in case law proportionality long continued to designate a purely factual assessment, an arithmetic equation, and was deprived of concrete legal content. While part of a commonly accepted anti-formalist legal discourse, proportionality as a general principle did not itself become an official source of law, neither did it contest the traditional methods of official legal decision-making.

Lasser has neatly shown the shift between anti-formalist *doctrine* and formalist official discourse as a more general characteristic of French legal culture.[128] While the technical theories elaborated by the *faiseurs de systèmes* are certainly among the 'formants' of French legal knowledge, they are not always explicitly recognised in official legal texts. According to Lasser, this expresses a fundamental institutional compromise between judges and the political branches of government. In this sense then, the use of proportionality language followed more general tendencies in French public law and was contained within the binding arrangements of the discourse into which it was inserted.

Proportionality and the 'Double Discourse' of the Constitutional Council. The arithmetic connotations of proportionality have persisted, even after the affirmation of its constitutional status. When employed in the sense of *proportionnalité des peines et des sanctions*, proportionality designates a relation between two quantifiable elements, the imputed offence and the incurred penalty. As such, it concerns the *quantum* of the sanctions defined by law, most notably pecuniary ones. Its arithmetic nature was particularly present in the *Conseil supérieur de l'audiovisuel* case, where the principle was first explicitly announced.[129] In the area of sanctions then, proportionality represents a relation between two numbers and is not applied by reference to rights. It is a factual matter, to be appreciated by the administration or the first instance judge. The

[127] Bockel (1978), p. 370; Auby (1979), p. 238.
[128] Lasser (2004).
[129] See Decision no. 88–248 DC, 17 January 1989, esp. cons. 30.

comparison that it implies is dyadic and does not comprise the use of a right or a value as a yardstick.[130]

This is why, while the explicit recognition of proportionality in constitutional case law bolstered scholarly hopes for coherent fundamental rights adjudication, it did not lead to any radical change in practice. In fact, proportionality perfectly fitted what Vedel called the 'double discourse' grounding the legitimacy of the constitutional judge. On the one hand, addressed to the agents of the political game, proportionality designated a neutral mathematical relation that did not contest the value choices of the legislator and thus implied no radical redistribution of powers between the judiciary and Parliament. On the other hand, due to its function in the fundamental rights case law of other courts, proportionality acquired a particular value-laden content and participated in the mythopoeia surrounding the constitutional judge. Hence, addressed to the believers in 'the transcendence of fundamental rights', the use of proportionality language alluded to some natural values underpinning formalist judicial reasoning, whose protection the Constitutional Council had assumed.[131]

The ambiguity of proportionality, between an arithmetic assessment and a moral-legal requirement, between fact and law, is deeply rooted in French legal thought and has been reproduced in different contexts and throughout the various conceptual mutations of proportionality. We could even go further and say that it is the loss of precisely this pretension to neutrality that is at the source of scholarly scepticism and suspicion towards its diffusion as a fundamental rights principle. In any case, the scientific aesthetics of proportionality have allowed for its conceptual development independent of judicial practice and even for its application as a theory in French constitutional law.

5.4 Proportionality and the Administrativisation of Constitutional Law: Deconstructing *Entreprises de Presse*

Proportionality as a Technocratic Goal of Public Action. Proportionality not only attributes the scientific tone of economic rationality to legal reasoning; it also expresses a new view of administrative decision-making as rational and efficient, functional to the needs of modern society and functioning according to the objective rules of

130 On the dyadic and triadic structure of proportionality analysis, see Schlink (2012), pp. 719–20.

131 Vedel (1988).

science. In some cases, proportionality is presented as a goal of public action itself. This departs from the traditional vision of the administration as executing the policy goals set by Parliament.

Guibal's analysis on proportionality in 1978 illustrates this very well. According to this author 'the notion of proportionality is by itself simple, evident, permanent and … normal. […] one can think that it goes without saying'.[132] Applied in administrative decision-making, it constitutes an end of public action and corresponds to the adaptation of legal means to legal ends. For Guibal, proportionality considerations 'mingle the elements of legality and expediency, technique and law, numbers and will'.[133] While the author rejects a purely mathematical perception of proportionality, he contends that it can be rationally appreciated through comparative assessment of the costs and benefits of public action. Thus, he argues that proportionality is 'a key notion of administrative law and administrative science'[134] and that it can constitute 'the over-all justification of administrative action',[135] replacing previous ideas of public utility, public service or public power. There go the long debates between the *écoles* of Toulouse and Bordeaux on the fundament of administrative law.[136] There goes ideology in French public law.

In Guibal's analysis, the possibility for rational assessment of the relation between cost and benefit attributes to proportionality a critical function that it did not have in previous writings. The concept of proportionality transcends formal legal sources. In Guibal's words, it cannot be 'reduced to a stereotyped formula and even less to a simple element of judicial review'.[137] In this way, Guibal established the shift between the scholarly perception of proportionality and its application in practice. Proportionality designates an extra-legal value by reference to which legal scholarship should evaluate domestic case law, independently of whether courts actually used proportionality language or not. In Guibal's view, effective proportionality scrutiny involves the quest for a 'strict correspondence' between the costs and the advantages of an administrative decision. On this basis, Guibal described the review

[132] Guibal (1978), p. 477.
[133] Ibid, p. 480.
[134] Ibid, p. 477.
[135] Ibid, p. 479.
[136] I refer here to a major scholarly debate during the twentieth century: the *école* of Toulouse and its *doyen*, Hauriou, advanced the notion of *puissance publique* as the foundation of administrative law, while the *doyen* of Bordeaux, Duguit, provided a theory of the state and of administration based on the notion of *service public*.
[137] Guibal (1978), p. 478.

exercised by the Council of State as 'virtual and fictitious, at best embryonic'.[138] He called for the judges to set aside legal formalities that impeded the realisation of the ideal of proportionality. For this author, the refusal to exercise full proportionality review could have no valid justification.

While he admittedly failed to influence judicial practice, Guibal significantly influenced the content of proportionality in French public law. As we have seen, the detachment of the scholarly perception of proportionality from judicial practice was consolidated in the work of Philippe, where the concept of *contrôle de proportionnalité* was employed to describe the instances where the judge pursued proportionality in the sense of some kind of equilibrium. This author also accentuated the mathematical and philosophical origins of proportionality and seemed to believe in the possibility of objective proportionality appreciations. Thus, while proportionality was ascribed a major function in the adjudication of substantive rights, it simultaneously expressed an excision of moral choices from legal reasoning. In Philippe's words: '[I]f we want to avoid the most important risks of subjectivity [...] we should depart from a moral perception of proportionality that would be similar to reasonable, as close to just.'[139] Philippe's analysis was less radical than Guibal's: he did not seek in proportionality the fundament of administrative law. Still, by using proportionality language he too sought attenuation of legal formality in the name of law's simplicity and accessibility. In Philippe's work, proportionality is akin to a requirement of 'good legislation', similar to that of 'good administration' and implies the coherence, efficiency and rationality of public action.

Rejection of formalism; excision of ideology and of moral choices from legal reasoning; and efficiency and rationality as major aims of public action: more than attributing a scientific tone to moral-legal evaluations, the use of proportionality language revealed a technocratic shift in French public law *doctrine*. It revealed French public lawyers' growing belief in the determination of correct legal solutions by allegedly neutral or even scientific considerations of fact. This tendency transpires in Chevallier's and Lochak's interdisciplinary quest for an 'administrative science'[140] and meets more general theoretical movements, such as Tunc's idea of modernisation developed since the 1960s. Writing in

[138] Ibid, p. 485.
[139] Philippe (1990), p. 8.
[140] Chevallier and Lochak (1978).

1977, Atias and Linotte vigorously criticised what they perceived as a trend of legal determinism, which they called the 'myth of the adaptation of the law to fact'.[141] Interestingly, it is in this technocratic sense that the theory of proportionality found application in constitutional law, and in one of the most famous Constitutional Council decisions.

The Reasoning in *Entreprises de Presse*. *Entreprises de presse* is known for the unequivocal terms in which the Constitutional Council enforced the freedom of expression.[142] The bill brought before the council set maximum limits on the concentration of press enterprises at a national and local level. The measures particularly affected the interests of a major press group, owned by Hersant, who was politically opposed to the government. This is what motivated the *saisine* by the opposition MPs and gave much media attention to the case. After announcing the constitutional status of the freedom of expression and of press pluralism, the Constitutional Council examined the scope of the legislation in question.[143] The legislative restrictions affected the status of enterprises that until then had functioned under a more favourable regime. While the council affirmed, in principle, the power of Parliament to render legislation more restrictive, it imposed a strict necessity requirement in this respect. It declared that when legislative measures interfered with a legitimate status quo relating to the exercise of a public freedom, this interference should be 'really necessary for ensuring the realisation of the constitutional objective pursued'.[144] This requirement was not fulfilled in the case at hand. In the words of the council:

> [C]oncerning national newspapers, account taken of their number, the variety of their traits and tendencies, or the conditions of their diffusion, it cannot be validly argued that pluralism is actually so seriously impaired that its restoration necessitates challenging existing situations, especially through the transfer or the suppression of newspapers, sometimes against the will of their readers.[145]

Some scholars perceive the decision as implicitly sanctioning a legislative abuse of power.[146] Indeed, even though by referring to the necessity

[141] Atias and Linotte (1977).

[142] Decision no. 84–181 DC, 11 October 1984, *Loi visant à limiter la concentration et à assurer la transparence financière et le pluralisme des entreprises de presse*, ECLI:FR:CC:1984:84.181.DC.

[143] Ibid, cons. 35 f.

[144] Ibid, cons. 47.

[145] Ibid, cons. 49.

[146] On this, see Vedel (1996/1997), para. 40.

of the contested measures, the judges might appear to criticise the impact of legislation on constitutional rights, the legislative ends played an important role in the judicial reasoning. The council questioned the appreciation of the circumstances as constituting a real risk for press pluralism and stated that 'it [could not] be validly argued' that legislative intervention was necessary. In other words, it was the plausibility of the legislative justification that was challenged. The recently published deliberations of the Constitutional Council reveal that the judges indeed presumed that the contested legislation aimed to limit the influence of Hersant.[147] Still, criticism of legislative intent did pass through an evaluation of the impact of legislation, as the quite detailed consideration of this impact in the decision indicates.

Mainstream scholars saw in the council's dicta a whole 'general theory of constitutional freedoms', in which the freedom of press enjoyed a particular type of constitutional protection, called *effet cliquet*.[148] This would mean that in the field of press freedom, Parliament can affect legally established advantages only when this is necessary for the protection of a constitutional value. Otherwise, legislative intervention can only render more effective the protection of the freedom of press.[149] According to this purported fundamental rights 'architecture', other 'first range freedoms' would enjoy reinforced constitutional protection, for example, the freedom of association. Enforced guarantees would imply, most notably, the prohibition of a regime of preliminary licence for the exercise of these freedoms. However, once again scholarly expectations were frustrated by subsequent case law. The *effet cliquet* protection of constitutional freedoms has been very rarely used after the 1984 decision and the council has never referred to a theory of fundamental rights. What then, guided the council's reasoning in *Entreprises de presse*?

***Entreprises de Presse* as an Application of Proportionality.** Close attention to the judicial reasoning shows that the council criticised the whole means-ends relationship established by Parliament, that is, the adequacy of legislation to its objective. Presenting his report on the case during the deliberations, *Rapporteur* Vedel compared the review exercised by the Constitutional Council to that exercised by the Council of

[147] Philippe et al. (2011), after fn. 39. See the Deliberation, 10–11 October 1984, p. 12, available at www.conseil-constitutionnel.fr.

[148] Favoreu (1986); Philippe (1990), p. 185.

[149] Favoreu et al. (2018), no. 31.

State. In his view, 'in the field of public freedoms, the legislator is not more free than the administration'.[150] Vedel continued:

> By ensuring the adequacy of the means chosen by the legislative power to the ends pursued in the field of pubic freedoms, the Constitutional Council does nothing but fully exercising its competence and does not indulge itself to a scrutiny of expediency, as one could – mistakenly – think.[151]

Review of the legislative means-ends had the advantage of avoiding any judicial involvement with the legislative ends themselves that could be criticised as subjective or too audacious. As is typical in French public law, it was the application of a particular 'theory' that preserved the objectivity of judicial scrutiny in this respect. Indeed, Vedel admitted that his reasoning followed such a 'theory', even though this was not explicitly mentioned in the official justification of the decision.[152]

By referring to the Council of State methods, to the adequacy of the means to the pursued ends, to public freedoms and to the implicit application of a 'theory', Vedel certainly appealed to the perception of proportionality that was common at the time in French public law. This was confirmed by Vedel himself in subsequent analyses. In his words in another deliberation, 'the Council did not apply a theory of legitimately established rights in the field of public freedoms, but, more simply, a theory of proportionality of the employed means to the pursued ends'.[153] Contrary to scholarly readings of the case then, which saw an implicit application of the *détournement de pouvoir* or of the *effet cliquet*, it was another administrative law 'theory' that guided judicial reasoning in the decision. Proportionality, implying an objective appreciation of the legislative means-ends, had the advantage of allowing the court to stay away from a moral evaluation of the legislative goal. In spite of the intrusive review that it entailed, it still did not involve the risk of subjectivity that sanctioning an abuse of power involves.

Confirming the Immunity of Legislative Value Choices. *Entreprises de presse* thus confirmed the immunity of legislative goals from judicial review. The fact that the judges in this case characterised the legislative goal of pluralism as constitutional objective (*objectif de valeur*

[150] Deliberation, 10–11 October 1984, p. 10.
[151] Ibid.
[152] Ibid.
[153] Deliberation, 29 July 1986, p. 11, available at www.conseil-constitutionnel.fr. This reading is confirmed in Vedel (1996/1997), para. 40.

constitutionnelle) reinforces this conclusion.[154] The normative category of constitutional objectives had been first used in a 1982 decision, again concerning Article 11 *DDHC*, and had served to justify limitations on the freedom of communication, even though the relevant constitutional provisions did not provide for any such limitations.[155] At the level of appearances, the identification of constitutional objectives allows the court to intrude into the forbidden sphere of legislative intent. However, in practice, this normative category has mainly served to legitimise the legislative goals by translating them into constitutional terms.[156] In other words, the category of constitutional objectives, rather than entailing judicial review of the policy goals of Parliament, expresses the Constitutional Council's deference to legislative value choices.

The novelty of the *Entreprises de presse* decision lay in the searching scrutiny of facts to which the constitutional judges proceeded. It is by concretising and factualising the legislative intent in application of the theory of proportionality that the council arrived at the censure of the contested measures. The judicial reasoning in this case is thus comparable to the way that proportionality has been applied by Greek courts since its constitutional entrenchment: focus on facts, efficiency and rationalisation.[157] Hence, far from entrenching an underlying theory of constitutional rights or any other value-laden constitutional content, the application of proportionality in *Entreprises de presse* expressed what Vedel famously called the 'administrativisation' of constitutional law.[158] Indeed, as we have seen, the transposition of administrative law theories and methods into constitutional law was one of the major assets of Philippe's thesis on proportionality.

154 See Decision no. 84–181 DC, cons. 38.

155 Decision no. 82–141 DC, 27 July 1982, *Loi sur la communication audiovisuelle*, ECLI:FR:CC:1982:82.141.DC, cons. 5.

156 See, however, Decision no. 86–210 DC, 29 July 1986, *Loi portant réforme du régime juridique de la presse*, ECLI:FR:CC:1986:86.210.DC. Rousseau (2001, p. 110) raised the question whether the category of constitutional objectives could actually constitute a source of unconstitutionality. Interestingly, this question does not appear in later versions of this author's handbook. Among the rare cases where constitutional objectives have imposed constraints on legislative decision-making, the requirement of accessibility and intelligibility of the law figures prominently. However, the scrutiny that this requirement implies is all about formal, linguistic features of legislation and not about its substantive, value-laden content.

157 See Part I, Chapter 4.5.

158 Vedel (1996).

The Technocratic Connotations of Proportionality. The technocratic connotations of proportionality persist even after its establishment as a fundamental rights principle in constitutional case law. Concern with the simplification, efficiency and rationality of legislation characterises the use of proportionality language even today. It is expressed in the '*proportionnalité à la française*' applied by the Constitutional Council, which rarely questions the legitimacy of the legislative choices in principle. It transpires in the generally shared perception of the 'narrowly tailored' review exercised by French courts as an instance of proportionality. In the Warsmann report 'on the quality and simplification of legislation', proportionality is mentioned as a principle of good legislation.[159] According to this report, the legislator should 'proportionate' the measures enacted to impact studies and other factual information resulting from the procedure that precedes legislation. Similarly, scholars studying proportionality perceive it as a requirement of minimal effectiveness of legislation that is objectively appraised according to factual considerations. In their analyses, the role of the Constitutional Council is understood as similar to that of a mechanic: it checks the effectiveness of the legislative 'machine' in the cases that are brought before it and the adequacy of the law to obtain its objective.[160]

It is thus not surprising that, in spite of scholarly hopes for coherent fundamental rights case law, the spread of proportionality in constitutional law did not much change the taboo surrounding the value choices expressed in legislation. The exclusive competence of Parliament in the reconciliation of competing constitutional objectives has been repeatedly affirmed.[161] It is Parliament that defines the scope of constitutional values such as human dignity in the light of scientific and technical developments.[162] Similarly, the Constitutional Council is not willing to engage in 'moral, scientific, and, ultimately, political debates' on the existence of differences between homosexual and heterosexual couples that could

[159] Warsmann (2008).

[160] Duclerq (2015).

[161] See, for example, Decision no. 94–352 DC, cons. 3. This is also the typical reasoning followed in the state of emergency case law. See, for example, Decision no. 2016–536 QPC, 19 February 2016, cons. 5.

[162] Decision no. 94–343/344 DC, 27 July 1994, *Loi relative au respect du corps humain et loi relative au don et à l'utilisation des éléments et produits du corps humain, à l'assistance médicale à la procréation et au diagnostic prénatal*, ECLI:FR:CC:1994:94.343.DC, cons. 10.

justify their distinct treatment by law.[163] More generally, 'moral and social considerations' are within Parliament's power of appraisal, just like other '*questions de société*'.[164] Thus, while proportionality has undoubtedly increased judicial powers, its application has not established the judge as a fundamental rights protector in French public law.[165]

As a theory, proportionality has the asset of representing a new paradigm of public action as modern, efficient and rational, exempt from moral-legal considerations. At the same time, it establishes coherence between traditional methods of review. In a subtle way, proportionality rationalises French public law and demystifies traditional ghosts of judicial review. Along with these ghosts, the doctrinal distinctions that they used to sustain are deconstructed. In reality, the spread of proportionality language in French public law has enhanced important transformations in *other* judicial methods, long before the enunciation of proportionality itself as a constitutional principle. In order to understand the extent of the transformation that proportionality has enhanced, we must go back to *Ville Nouvelle Est* and its doctrinal impacts.

5.5 Forgotten Distinctions: Proportionality and Manifest Error

Displacing the Debate on the Scope of Application of the Manifest Error Test. Balancing the advantages and disadvantages of administrative decisions was not at all a given before *Ville Nouvelle Est*, not even in its manifest error version. Before the emergence of judicial balancing and proportionality, many scholars and *commissaires du gouvernement* had argued for an extension of the scope of the manifest error test, from the review of the grounds to the review of the content of discretionary administrative decisions. Braibant himself had proposed a manifest error review in his first opinion on *Ville Nouvelle Est* before the Council of State sub-sections.[166] However, the council had consistently refused this solution: the manifest error concerned solely the grounds of administrative decisions. Its application in the review of the content of public decisions would bring considerations of *opportunité* into the game

163 Decision no. 2010-39 QPC, 6 October 2010, *Isabelle D. et Isabelle B.*, ECLI:FR:CC:2010:2010.39.QPC. See the official comment on the decision, 'Commentaire de la Décision no 2010-39 QPC du 6 octobre 2010', *Cahiers du Conseil constitutionnel*, no. 30 (2010).

164 Conseil constitutionnel, 'Commentaire de la Décision no 2010-39 QPC du 6 octobre 2010', p. 10. See also Decision no. 2010-2 QPC, 11 June 2010, cons. 14.

165 Champeil-Desplats (2012); Goesel-Le Bihan (2012).

166 See Waline (1974), p. 823.

again. Indeed, review of the normative content of administrative decisions is traditionally abstract in French public law. It is represented as the confrontation of two norms with different ranks in the pyramid of hierarchy. On the contrary, the manifest error test involves concrete review, according to the circumstances of each case. Its extension in the area of exercise of administrative discretion would lead the judge to substitute her own assessments as to the adequacy of the reviewed decision for that of the administration and this was perceived as a prohibited trespassing of the limits of judicial competence.

Analyses contemporary to *Ville Nouvelle Est* maintained the strict conception of the manifest error review. In certain handbooks, the *bilan* was clearly distinguished from the manifest error: while the *bilan* implied a review of the content of administrative decisions, the manifest error concerned their factual grounds, that is, the appreciation by the administration of the facts that conditioned the exercise of its competence.[167] Nonetheless, *Ville Nouvelle Est* seemed to have totally displaced the debate. Since the judge had affirmed her power to balance the advantages and the disadvantages of administrative decisions, scholars progressively accepted *ad minus* the possibility for an objective scrutiny of the content of administrative decisions under a manifest error test. Some even argued that the only possible interpretation of judicial balancing that could preserve the 'logic' and the 'identity' of the French system of judicial review was to see it as an extension of the manifest error to the content of decisions.[168] In this way, focus on the justification of judicial balancing led the *doctrine* to neglect a major conceptual transformation of the manifest error test.

Blurring the Grounds/Content Distinction. The promotion of proportionality as a general principle further enhanced this evolution. Indeed, the early writings of proportionality described the manifest error as an application of the principle, which governs 'all aspects of discretionary power', independently of traditional doctrinal distinctions.[169] Interestingly, the promoters of proportionality nuanced the distinction between content and grounds of administrative decisions,

[167] See for example, Bockel (1978), p. 365. The author talks about 'case law that is not born yet'. See the decision CE, 15 February 1974, *Federation nationale des syndicats des fonctionnaires de l'agriculture et autres*, nos. 80772 and 80814, ECLI:FR:CESJS:1974:80772.19740215.

[168] De Laubadère (1974), pp. 547 and 549.

[169] Bockel (1978), p. 370.

which they perceived as 'fragile'.[170] They stressed that often substantive legality requirements imposed on the content of a decision could be seen as conditions for the exercise of administrative competence and vice versa. This was the case of the necessity review of police restrictions for example, where it was not clear whether necessity was part of the grounds of the restrictions or whether it was a substantive legal requirement imposed on the exercise of police powers. By imposing a legal requirement of adequacy of a public decision to its grounds and to the goal of administrative action, the recognition of a general principle of proportionality would put an end to what was perceived as an outdated distinction.[171]

Scholarly calls to abandon the distinction between grounds and content had found expression in judicial practice. In the famous *Lebon* case, the Council of State applied a manifest error test in the review of the content of disciplinary sanctions.[172] In doing so, the council abandoned its previous refusal to review the proportionality of these sanctions. Hence, even though the defenders of proportionality did not obtain the change that they called for in the form of an *official* enunciation of the general principle of proportionality, they did obtain some of the core advances in judicial review that proportionality was expected to bring about. The review of the content of discretionary public decisions was generalised. *Plus c'est la même chose, plus ça change.*[173] This is why public lawyers read the disciplinary sanctions case law as an application of proportionality, which followed the example of international courts.[174]

The justificatory force of proportionality soon concealed the transformation of the manifest error test. In the earlier editions of their handbook for example, Vedel and Delvolvé contested the possibility to exercise proportionality review through the manifest error.[175] However, in later analyses, the structural features that until the 1970s constrained the spread of the manifest error test seem to have been forgotten. Progressively, this test was understood as an aspect of the *contrôle de proportionnalité*. The transformation was further enhanced with the

[170] Dreyfus (1974), p. 703.

[171] Ibid, pp. 695, 700; Braibant (1974), p. 298.

[172] CE, 9 June 1978, *Sieur Lebon*, no. 05911, ECLI:FR:CESJS:1978:05911.19780609. See also CE (Pl.), 5 May 1976, *Bernette*, nos. 98647 and 98820, ECLI:FR:CEASS:1976:98647.19760505.

[173] Graziadei (2006, p. 462) observes this on legal transplants more generally.

[174] Auby (1979), pp. 237 f.

[175] Vedel and Delvolvé (1973), cited by Philippe (1990), p. 171, fn. 70.

transfer of the manifest error in constitutional law, where, due to the abstract character of constitutional requirements, the distinction grounds/content was more difficult to make. In *Sécurité et Liberté* for example, the Constitutional Council applied the manifest error as a method for the review of the necessity of penalties.[176]

A Distinction that Persisted in Constitutional Case Law. Still, at least for a while, proportionality and manifest error were distinguished in the Constitutional Council's reasoning. This can be illustrated by an analysis of *Loi sur l'évolution de la Nouvelle-Calédonie*, which concerned a bill organising the election of the New Caledonian legislative assembly. In this case, Parliament had delimited the circumscriptions on a geographic rather than a demographic basis and introduced important inequalities in the representation of the local population. In its scrutiny under the principle of voting equality, the council clearly distinguished the constitutional requirement for elections on a demographic basis from a strict requirement of proportionality between the populations of the various circumscriptions. The council affirmed that 'other general interest necessities' could compromise demographic representation. However, this was constitutionally acceptable 'only to a limited extent'.[177] The council found that this limit had been 'manifestly trespassed in the case at hand' and declared the reviewed provisions as unconstitutional.[178]

Although refusing to impose a strict proportionality rule on the legislator, the council did impose limits on the possibility of derogating from this rule in the name of demographic representation. And it sanctioned these limits by application of the manifest error test. A few days later, however, in the second New Caledonia case, the council seemed to have changed its mind.[179] While on 8 August, the judges concluded that one representative for 4,728 residents constituted a manifest error, on 23 August, it decided that one representative for 4,052 residents did not constitute such an error. French public lawyers have criticised what they have perceived to be a contradictory application of the manifest error test. In their view, the disproportion was equally flagrant in the second

[176] Decision no. 80–127 DC, 20 January 1981, *Loi renforçant la sécurité et protégeant la liberté des personnes*, ECLI:FR:CC:1981:80.127.DC.

[177] Decision no. 85–196 DC, 8 August 1985, *Loi sur l'évolution de la Nouvelle-Calédonie*, ECLI:FR:CC:1985:85.196.DC, cons. 16.

[178] Ibid.

[179] Decision no. 85–197 DC, 23 August 1985, *Loi sur l'évolution de la Nouvelle Calédonie*, ECLI:FR:CC:1985:85.197.DC, cons. 35.

decision, but the council still deferred to the legislative choice. Mainstream scholarship has thus contested the objectivity of the manifest error review or has, somewhat ironically, sought for a *particular* proportion, the trespassing of which would have led the judges to sanction the legislative measures.[180]

Criticism of the New Caledonia cases has neglected the difference in kind of the evaluations that proportionality and the manifest error implied. Indeed, scholars understood the manifest error to involve an objective factual test, generally valid and not depending on the context of legislative decision-making, just like calculations of proportionality. However, things were different in the council's reasoning: while proportionality (as a mathematical equation) was an *extra-legal quality* of legislative choices, the manifest error defined the *legal-constitutional limits*, the trespassing of which allowed for judicial intervention. In other words, the application of the manifest error preserved a moral-legal burden that proportionality lacked. While proportionality functioned as a criterion for the appraisal of legislative outcomes according to the rules of logic and science, the manifest error test concerned the concrete evaluation of the legislative grounds according to the constitution, the value-laden justification of legislative action. In practice, the manifest error functioned as a substitute for a legislative abuse of power. It was concerned with the state of mind of the primary decision-maker and its application depended on the particular context of each case.

The moral-legal evaluation that the manifest error test implied was difficult to grasp for French public lawyers, due to the taboo that surrounds the value-laden choices of Parliament in French legal thought. However, it is precisely the value-laden character of manifest error review that renders its seemingly contradictory application in the New Caledonia cases intelligible. Despite the approximation of the reviewed bills in terms of outcomes, a crucial difference separated the two. While in the first case, constitutional limits had been trespassed, in the second, the Parliament had taken into account the Constitutional Council's decision on the matter and had amended the unconstitutional provisions, in an effort to conform to the judicial precepts. Judicial intervention to sanction the parliamentary choices could thus be perceived as imposing an overly inflexible objective requirement of proportionality on the legislator, where the constitution provides for none. During the relevant deliberation, Vedel had pointed out that the council's methods did 'not

[180] Favoreu et al. (2018), no. 43.23.

present the "Pascalian" or "Euclidian" rigour'.[181] The manifest error only prohibited the legislator from doing '*n'importe quoi*'.[182]

In subsequent case law, the council used distinct standards to criticise the outcomes of legislation, on the one hand, and its justification, on the other. Concerning the election of the Marseille city council for example, it underscored that:

> [E]ven if the legislator did not consider it expedient, for the allocation of two among one hundred seats, to strictly apply the rule of proportionality [...], the disparity between the numbers of representatives of the [different city sectors] with regard to the respective importance of their populations [...] is not manifestly unjustifiable nor excessively disproportionate.[183]

The distinction between the 'manifestly unjustifiable' and 'excessively disproportionate' standards indicates that while the manifest error involved a value-laden evaluation of legislative grounds, the identification of excessive disproportionalities proceeded through a mere factual appreciation.

This is confirmed by the recently published judicial deliberation on the matter, which reveals that the use of one single standard of manifest disproportionality had been proposed by a member of the council. In response, the secretary general observed that such a formulation would exempt legislative value choices from judicial review. It would imply 'that the legislator is the only judge of the general interest grounds that he invokes', thus leaving open the risk of arbitrary legislation.[184] Vedel agreed and added:

> A baker can sell [a piece of] bread [claiming that it weighs] 450 grams, while it weighs less: this is measurable. On the contrary, to what extent can we say that there is venial or capital sin? This is not an error, but an appreciation of expediency. There should be a formulation of the manifest error that combines the *quantum* with the grounds of choice.[185]

A similar distinction between manifest error and proportionality language was typical of the Council of State's reasoning too. The

[181] Deliberation, 23 August 1985, available at www.conseil-constitutionnel.fr.
[182] Ibid, p. 24.
[183] Decision no. 87–227 DC, 7 July 1987, *Loi modifiant l'organisation administrative et le régime électoral de la ville de Marseille*, ECLI:FR:CC:1987:87.227.DC, cons. 6. Similarly, Decision no. 86–218 DC, 18 November 1986, *Loi relative à la délimitation des circonscriptions pour l'élection des députés*, ECLI:FR:CC:1986:86.218.DC, cons. 8.
[184] Deliberation, 7 July 1987, p. 43, available at www.conseil-constitutionnel.fr.
[185] Ibid.

administrative judges typically used expressions like '*disproportion marquée*', diligently avoiding the employment of a manifest disproportionality standard.[186] Still, the French *doctrine* perceived the manifest error as synonymous with manifest disproportionality and this synonymy was soon performed in judicial practice.

5.6 Reinventing Proportionality and Fundamental Rights: Social Integration as Assimilation

The Diffusion of Proportionality and the Idealisation of the Judiciary. Some months following the *Nouvelle-Calédonie* case law, in 1986, the Constitutional Council abandoned the meticulous distinction between proportionality language and manifest error.[187] This enhanced the transformation of the manifest error into an outcome-based test, concerned with the efficiency of legislative measures rather than with their moral-legal grounds. This is neatly exemplified in the emergence and spread of the 'manifest inappropriateness' standard in constitutional case law. This standard emerged in 1990, possibly under the influence of the ECJ case law.[188] It is commonly perceived as an instance of *contrôle de proportionnalité* and is used 'an objective substitute for the abuse of power review'.[189] Its spread expresses a more general tendency towards factualisation and rationalisation of moral-legal evaluations in the Constitutional Council's reasoning. In other words, the 'manifest inappropriateness' standard expresses the replacement of moral-legal constitutional limits with factual ones.

Inversely, the proximity between manifest error and manifest disproportion came at a cost for proportionality's arithmetic rigour. In *Loi portant amnistie* for example, the standard of manifest disproportionality was used as a '*belle marquise*'.[190] Addressed to trade unions, it expressed in simple and understandable terms that Parliament had reasonably

[186] See, for example, CE, 6 February 1981, no. 16660, ECLI:FR:CESSR:1981:16660.19810206. Only two examples of combination of manifest error and proportionality could be found in the Council of State case law until 1986: CE, 7 May 1982, no. 17713, ECLI:FR:CESSR:1982:17713.19820507, and 23 October 1986, no. 64900, ECLI:FR:CESSR:1985:64900.19851023. Still, in these cases proportionality represents an arithmetic relation.

[187] Decision no. 86–215 DC, 3 September 1986. On this case, see Part I, Chapter 2.3.

[188] Decision no. 90–280 DC, 6 December 1990, *Loi organisant la concomitance des renouvellements des conseils généraux et des conseils régionaux*, ECLI:FR:CC:1990:90.280.DC.

[189] Goesel-Le Bihan (1997), p. 237.

[190] Deliberation, 20 July 1988, pp. 24 f., esp. p. 28, available at www.conseil-constitutionnel.fr.

exercised its competence. The less rigorous perception of proportionality enhanced its diffusion in French law. Since the early 1990s, domestic courts increasingly employ proportionality in rights adjudication. Taking impulsion from the transnational proportionality and fundamental rights language, the disproportionate standard was transferred in constitutional case law too. Since 2008, proportionality proliferates in French law and has acquired a pervasive dynamic. The function of fundamental rights protection that proportionality assumes in this context seems akin to the one it has in the Alexyan model.

Undoubtedly, the diffusion of proportionality as a fundamental rights principle has contributed to the new mythopoeia surrounding the judiciary and its function as the protector of citizens' rights. It is not by chance that the study of proportionality increasingly excites judges themselves, and especially the presidents of the supreme courts.[191] In the new representation of the legal system as a fundamental rights order, legal reasoning is perceived as an instance of reconciliation of competing values and the judge as an institution that is well-qualified to perform it.[192] In the words of Philippe, for example, 'the *contrôle de proportionnalité* leads the judge to veritable Salomon judgments. In reality', the author continues, 'we can ask ourselves whether, by varying the intensity of review, the judge does not pertain to a general quest of coherence that proportionality allows him to obtain'.[193] Idealisation of the judiciary is a feature of German constitutionalism, and of mainstream proportionality scholarship too, where, as we saw, the judge is presented as Socrates and the judicial process as an instance of maieutic dialogue.

Idealisation of the judiciary is even more remarkable in French constitutional discourse, where proportionality has certainly benefitted from a quasi-religious belief shared by some domestic lawyers in 'the transcendence of human rights'.[194] The relevant studies, until recently rare – mainly produced by Goesel-Le Bihan – are characterised by an impressive faith in a court mainly composed by political personalities. Despite the lack of transparency in its use, optimistic scholars have perceived proportionality as a method for weighing constitutional rights. They have contended that its variable application reveals the pragmatism

191 Sauvé (2017); Louvel (2016).
192 Philippe (1990), pp. 421 f.
193 Ibid, p. 347.
194 Vedel (1988), p. 159, para. 20.

of the constitutional judge and have provided complex reconstructions of the constitutional case law under the proportionality prongs.[195] In their writings the Constitutional Council is often presented as a young apprentice.[196] Commenting on the proportionality case law of the council in 2007, Goesel-Le Bihan characterised it as 'a work of maturity', which proves the court's 'permeability to changing political contingencies'.[197] Even more optimistic judges have seen in the council's application of proportionality the 'beauty and harmony' that one finds in Chinese gardens, despite the 'disorder' that it provokes in French public lawyers' 'Cartesian spirits'.[198]

Proportionality as Republican Inculcation: The *Burqa* Affair. In German constitutionalism and in the Alexyan theory, proportionality as a fundamental rights principle expresses a belief in the possibility of rational resolution of axiological conflicts. Mainstream proportionality scholars thus believe that the consistent application of proportionality integrates minority values and worldviews into the public decision-making process. The same belief in the possibility of rational resolution of axiological conflicts also underlies certain French writings on proportionality.[199] However, in French practice, proportionality is inconsistently applied, usually leading to a self-evident affirmation of the legitimacy of fundamental rights restrictions. It is used interchangeably with other standards such as 'excessive interference' with the rights at stake. The absence of justification observed in the application of proportionality is a more general characteristic of French case law and is connected to the republican legitimation of public authorities, and especially of the judiciary. As Lasser observes, in French law '[t]he pedagogical process [is] one of proper republican *inculcation*, not one of mutual *explanation*'.[200]

This can be illustrated in the *Burqa* affair. The case arose in the context of a priori constitutional review and concerned the constitutionality of the legislative ban on fully covering one's face in public spaces.[201] The statute was voted through after extensive discussion of the subject in the

195 Goesel-Le Bihan (1997, 2007a).
196 Goesel-Le Bihan (2007b) even talks to the council.
197 Goesel-Le Bihan (2007a), p. 295.
198 Fraisse (2009), after fn. 2.
199 See, for example, Jamin (2015).
200 Lasser (2009), p. 141.
201 Decision no. 2010–613 DC, 7 October 2010, *Loi interdisant la dissimulation du visage dans l'espace public*, ECLI:FR:CC:2010:2010.613.DC. I will refer to this decision as the *Burqa* decision.

media and, in spite of its neutral formulation, had as a goal to prohibit the well-known religious and cultural practice of certain Muslim women to cover their face entirely when in public. During the parliamentary discussion of the statute, this practice was characterised as 'intolerable',[202] as a symbol of the position of women in the Islamic tradition that undermines fundamental republican values.[203] Prohibition of the *burqa* obtained strong consensus between the left and the right. Only one member in each chamber of Parliament voted against it. The bill was referred to the council by the presidents of the two chambers of Parliament – the first occurrence of such a referral since 1959 – without any arguments against its constitutionality. This '*saisine blanche*' could be seen as a plea for a 'certificate of constitutionality' that would impede future contestations of the statute via the *QPC* procedure.

In a surprisingly short decision, the council validated the reviewed legislation. The constitutional judges started by identifying the legislative goal. In spite of its neutral formulation, they considered that the bill was a response 'to practices, which until recently were of an exceptional nature, consisting in concealing the face in the public space'.[204] According to the council: 'Parliament has felt [sic] that such practices are dangerous for public safety and security and fail to comply with the minimum requirements of life in society.'[205] Having ascertained, or rather *certified*, the legitimacy of the legislative goal, the judges went on to exercise proportionality review on Parliament's reconciliation of the competing values at stake. In their words:

> In view of the purposes which it is sought to achieve and taking into account the penalty introduced for non-compliance with the rule laid down by law, Parliament has enacted provisions which ensure a conciliation which is not disproportionate between safeguarding public order and guaranteeing constitutionally protected rights.[206]

It seems that, in this case, proportionality concerned the reconciliation between public order and constitutional rights. Interestingly, however, the judgment does not mention which constitutional rights were in

[202] See the report of the National Assembly *Délégation aux droits des femmes et à l'égalité des chances entre les hommes et les femmes*, available at www.assemblee-nationale.fr.

[203] See the *résolution* voted by the National Assembly on 11 May 2010, on the commitment to the respect of republican values against the development of radical practices undermining it, available at www.assemblee-nationale.fr.

[204] *Burqa* decision (English translation), cons. 4.

[205] Ibid.

[206] Ibid, cons. 5.

question. Religious freedom was invoked, but only in a *réserve d'interprétation* that excluded the application of the contested measures in places of worship.[207] The explicit reference to the trivial character of the legislative sanctions indicates that it was rather the principle of proportionality of penalties that was applied by the council. However, proportionality of penalties is not really a constitutional right and, arguably, many such rights could have been invoked against the legislative provisions. Neither does proportionality concern the means-ends relationship of legislation. The judges do not specify with respect to *what* they evaluated the proportionality of the legislative provisions. Proportionality did not imply any scrutiny of the legislative value choices or of the effectiveness of the reviewed measures. It was used as an axiomatic affirmation that the legislative choices were reasonable and legitimate.

The Objectivisation of Proportionality and Fundamental Rights. Once again, the council left the definition of the value-laden content of the constitution to the political branches of government. However, the *Burqa* case is even more interesting because, in order to do so, the council followed a kind of reasoning that is quite rare in French constitutional case law. Apart from the reference to proportionality, the decision echoes fundamental rights language in its reference to freedom and equality. When discussing the legislative objective, the judges stressed that Parliament 'felt that those women who conceal their face, voluntarily or otherwise, are placed in a situation of exclusion and inferiority patently incompatible with constitutional principles of liberty and equality'.[208] The council took this feature into account when it validated the legislative reconciliation between public order and constitutional rights. Strikingly, however, freedom and equality were not qualified as rights themselves. They were mentioned as constitutional principles, and as such were part of the legislative objective of maintaining public order. Traditionally, the commonly shared perception of public order did not encompass the protection of political moral values.[209] Since the 1990s, however, it has progressively included the protection of fundamental rights.[210]

[207] Ibid.

[208] Ibid, cons. 4.

[209] See, however, CE, 18 December 1959, *Films Lutétia*, nos. 36385 and 36428, ECLI:FR:CESJS:1959:36385.19591218.

[210] CE (Pl.), 27 October 1995, *Commune de Morsang-sur-Orge*, no. 136727, ECLI:FR:CEASS:1995:136727.19951027.

Commentators impugned the reasoning in the *Burqa* decision as an 'abdication of constitutional review'.[211] The point of view of Muslim women was not considered at all by the judges. Their laconic affirmations, presented as self-evident and not subject to any institutional contestation, reveal the minimalist character of the adversarial procedure (if there can be said to be any such procedure) before the Constitutional Council. In fact, the *Burqa* case exemplifies the way French public law reinvents proportionality and its fundamental rights baggage according to local discursive needs and to local criteria for the evaluation of legal arguments. In this context, rights do not function as optimisation requirements, but rather represent objective values. Consent to their infringement is inoperative. The definition of their scope is exclusively left to the Parliament. In the republican French context, notions such as the general interest and, more recently, public order, are surrounded by a 'mythic halo' and are deemed to be the ultimate goal of public action.[212] They represent a 'reflex of republican union' that is not opposed to constitutional rights, since it presupposes and comprises their reconciliation.[213] Rights-based adjudication consists in an axiomatic affirmation that the only possible way for minorities to socially integrate is to conform to the majoritarian worldview. In this way, French public law is deemed to escape a 'fundamentalism of rights' or a '*conception jusqu'au-boutiste des droits subjectifs*'.[214]

In the current context of decline of fundamental rights, the inconsistent application of proportionality provokes scepticism. Even the scholars who were most faithful to proportionality and to the Constitutional Council seem to have lost faith in the principle's protective function.[215] Proportionality review is increasingly criticised for its subjectivity and for the confusion that it provokes in the traditional distribution of competences between the judge, the administration and the legislator.[216] The accusation of *jusnaturalisme* resurfaces and is readily addressed to proportionality and fundamental rights enthusiasts.[217] Besides, French public lawyers' short and sweet belief in the existence of objective value choices now seems to be fading away. The contemporary context is one

211 Fatin-Rouge Stéfanini and Philippe (2011), p. 549.
212 Merland (2007).
213 Mazeaud (2006).
214 Mazeaud (2008), p. 27.
215 Goesel-Le Bihan (2012).
216 Delvolvé (2016); Dutheillet de Lamothe and Odinet (2016).
217 De Béchillon (2016), p. 29.

of institutional suspicion, as the recent securitarian turn in French constitutional politics shows. In this respect, Delmas-Marty observes that the two-year long state of emergency and the extensive police powers provided for by normal legislation mark 'an anthropological rupture', the transition 'from a society of responsibility to a society of suspicion'.[218] The recent declaration of an *état d'urgence sanitaire* confirms this tendency.

***

Proportionality in French public law has provoked more significant changes as a theory than as a positive law concept. At least in its early uses in this context, proportionality was perceived as a transfer from other disciplines rather than a legal transplant from Germany. As such, it has expressed and enhanced domestic lawyers' belief in the possibility of objective determination of the content of legal and constitutional provisions. It has expressed and enhanced domestic lawyers' perception of legal decision-making as a rational enterprise following the rules of logic. In short, proportionality in French public law has expressed and enhanced domestic lawyers' belief in the possibility of law being a science exempt from considerations of morality or ideology. Only this kind of scientific knowledge could allow the judge to intrude into the norm-producing will of public authorities.

In a moment of fundamental rights optimism, and under the influence of the transnational fundamental rights rhetoric, proportionality traded off its scientific rigour for a value-laden content in French constitutional adjudication. However, far from involving the exchange of practical moral arguments and the mutual explanation of competing worldviews, the application of proportionality in this context resembles an instance of republican inculcation that state institutions impose on deviant minorities. Proportionality and its fundamental rights baggage have been reinvented by French public lawyers. Their dynamic has been contained within the structures of domestic public law. The decline of proportionality and fundamental rights is itself corollary to French public lawyers' disenchantment with the judiciary and loss of faith in the possibility for objective or scientific value choices.

More generally, the use of proportionality language has followed and furthered the long-existing quest for rationalisation that inspires the evolution of French public law. Proportionality echoes local lawyers'

[218] Delmas-Marty (2017).

view of the relationship between objective factual knowledge and legal technique. It expresses a belief in, and simultaneously a continuous effort to transcend, a distinction that is fundamental for French 'Cartesian spirits': the distinction between *science* and *doctrine*, between descriptive and prescriptive legal reasoning, between *être* and *devoir être*.

6

Searching for an English Public Law

Diametrically opposed to the French obsession with scientific legal knowledge, it is said that once a judge thanked God that the law of England was not a science.[1] We will see that the traditional English aversion to science has been a factor both for the initial rejection and for the subsequent success of proportionality in this context.

In this chapter, I argue that proportionality has represented a fusion of substance and form that is strange to the game-like nature of the common law. It has embodied a method of review, and a way of legal thinking more generally, situated in diametrical opposition to Diceyan analytical positivism. Precisely due to its anti-Diceyan meaning, proportionality has been promoted as a principle that could establish coherence in English public law through the recognition of minimum substantive values. By using proportionality language, English lawyers have sought a little bit of myth and ritual in judicial review. Hence, the spread of proportionality in English public law should be read against the background of the rise of common law constitutionalism. In this respect, the HRA officialised and enhanced more subtle and progressive cultural transformations. While it led to the proliferation of proportionality and to a fundamental rights shift in English public law, it also constrained these evolutions within Parliament's will and thus in a sense demystified them. The spill-over dynamic of proportionality expresses the continuing search for rationalism and myth in the ongoing construction of English public law. Here, as in France, rationalisation is a major stake in the spread of proportionality. However, rationalisation in this context has a very different meaning from the one it has on the opposite side of the English Channel.

In order to identify the stakes attached to the use of proportionality, its initial rejection is just as important as its later success. Initially,

[1] Cohen (1953), p. 115, cited by Atiyah (1987), p. 4, fn. 7.

proportionality failed in English public law as an objective unreasonableness test. Its application, echoing some kind of scientific theory *à la française*, was contrary to the fundamental assumptions of the common law tradition (Section 6.1). In spite of the conceptual fragmentation of proportionality in practice, scholars progressively understood it as a universal idea, a principle coming from continental law. The promotion of proportionality was connected to modernisation rhetoric and to a new kind of legal knowledge at the time emerging in English public law, similar to the French *doctrine* (Section 6.2). While proportionality was rejected as a domestic head of review, some instances of *Wednesbury* review were perceived as implicit applications of the principle. This indicates that, for English lawyers, at least some of the stakes attached to the use of proportionality had been accomplished (Section 6.3). The incorporation of convention rights in the domestic sphere engaged the rise of proportionality in English public law. Parliamentary sovereignty seems to be dying (Section 6.4). Institutional considerations and the quest for democratic government survive within the *doctrine*-made concept of deference. In this context, the intensity of substantive review is no longer a matter of legal forms, but a matter of choice left to courts (Section 6.5).

6.1 An Irritant: Proportionality in the Absence of Myth

Proportionality and the Ambiguity of the *Wednesbury* Standard. English law offers a well-known case of resistance to the spread of proportionality. The analytical tradition is the usual suspect, to which this and other instances of English exceptionalism are imputed. We saw that, in its first applications in judicial review, proportionality corresponded to a shade of *Wednesbury* unreasonableness. This test had been introduced in the famous *Wednesbury* case in 1947 as an objective, outcome-based test.[2] As such, it added an exception to the strict distribution of competences between the judiciary and the administration, which excludes any consideration of the merits of public action from judicial review.

Wednesbury unreasonableness was commonly defined as a distinct head from illegality, which encompasses bad faith and irrelevant

[2] *Associated Provincial Picture Houses Ltd* v. *Wednesbury Corporation* [1948] 1 KB 223 (CA, 7 November 1947), per Lord Greene. See Craig (1989), pp. 281 f., esp. p. 286.

considerations. Analytically, however, the distinction was not so easy to make. The ambiguity was already inherent in Lord Greene's dicta, according to which, judges intervene when a decision is 'so unreasonable that it might almost be described as being done in bad faith; and, in fact, all these things run into one another'.[3] Lord Greene famously used the example of a school teacher fired due to her having red hair, a case that can be classified under the irrelevant considerations head. English public lawyers have been content to affirm that irrationality and illegality 'overlap'.[4] Thus, under a commonly accepted account, *Wednesbury* unreasonableness has two senses: the first is the 'umbrella sense', which corresponds to a review of the intent of the primary decision-maker and regroups flaws that are sanctioned under other heads of review; the second is the 'substantive sense', which sanctions unacceptable outcomes.[5]

That being said, in his 1986 study on French substantive review, Bell observed that, contrary to what was the case in France, substantive review was almost never exercised by English courts, and that most of the examples cited by scholars in this respect were hypothetical. This made the author suspect that *Wednesbury* unreasonableness 'simply create[d] a presumption of unidentified error of law'.[6] Indeed, the extremeness of the substantive *Wednesbury* standard was abnormal, almost mythical, to the point that English lawyers doubted its actual existence. Lord Diplock in *GCHQ* said that the irrationality head only applied when 'a decision which is so outrageous in its defiance of logic or of accepted moral standards that no sensible person who had applied his mind to the question could have arrived at it'.[7] In his extra-legal writings, Laws LJ talked about 'a crude duty not to emulate brute beasts that have no understanding'.[8]

Proportionality language accentuated the focus of *Wednesbury* on outcomes, while it preserved an ambiguous criticism of the intents of the reviewed authorities. In *Hook*, having characterised the sanction imposed on the claimant as disproportionate, Lord Denning concluded:

[3] *Wednesbury*, p. 229. The ambiguity persists: see Craig (2016), para. 19–002.

[4] See, for instance, Taylor (1976), pp. 275–6.

[5] Craig (2016), para. 17–002.

[6] Bell (1986), esp. para. 118. Traditionally, errors of law are sanctioned under the head of illegality and concern the content and scope of the power or duty conferred upon the primary decision-maker.

[7] *GCHQ* (HL, 22 November 1984), p. 950.

[8] Laws (1992), p. 1392.

'[T]he Barnsley Corporation, *in all good faith but erroneously*, have taken away this man's licence to trade without justification and without having that due inquiry which the law requires.'[9] In *Assegai*, Woolf LJ considered the 'bias issue' separately from unreasonableness and proportionality, which only concerned the substance of the measures at stake, their 'width'.[10] Still, the judge stated that he would interfere under the unreasonableness standard, only if he found the measures to be 'capricious' or 'perverse'.[11]

Constrained by the Economy of the Common Law. The mystery surrounding the substantive standard of review is connected to a particular type of formalism that traditionally permeates the common law: analytical formalism. In contrast to French dogmatism, which is based on a fusion of substance and form, analytical formalism is based on the altogether exclusion of substantive values from legal reasoning. The common law long did not contain *principes généraux du droit* or other norms by reference to which public action could be evaluated in substance. Until quite recently, judges did not pronounce on matters of principle, but preferred reasoning by precedent and avoid far-reaching conclusions. They were imagined as 'political, economic, and social eunuchs', analytically applying the law to adversarial procedures.[12] Allison calls English courts' dislike for abstractions of principle the 'economy of the common law'.[13]

Hence, proportionality could not even be conceived of as a general principle. As a shade of unreasonableness, it was deprived of radical potential. Its function was quite similar to the manifest error in France. It sanctioned only manifest asymmetry and was concerned with the state of mind of the primary decision-maker: at most, it was an 'objective substitute for the abuse of power'.[14] No rights were involved in its application. Besides, the common law did not contain 'those declarations or definitions of rights so dear to foreign constitutionalists'.[15] Following the Whig narrative that dominated English legal analysis until the late nineteenth century, civil liberties are not the result of the constitution, but its very basis. To render them positive would be to affirm that

9 *Hook* (CA, Civil Division, 20 February 1976), p. 1058 (emphasis added).
10 *Assegai* (CA, Civil Division, 11 June 1987), per Woolf LJ.
11 Ibid.
12 Griffith (1981), p. 290.
13 Allison (2007), pp. 123 f.
14 Goesel-Le Bihan (1997), p. 237.
15 Dicey (1939), p. 197, cited by Atiyah (1987), p. 23, fn. 53.

Parliament has the power to take them away. Indeed, in this context, law is traditionally seen as a commandment and public action as an intervention in society, which provokes distrust. In this line of thought, the English constitution has guaranteed individual liberty better than any other through the checks and balances surrounding the parliamentary process.[16]

A Failed English Theory of the *Bilan* and Proportionality. Common law analytical formalism also impeded the development of a theory of proportionality that would be detached from the patterns of reasoning observed in judicial decisions. In the pragmatist common law tradition, lawyers share an aversion to theory.[17] The role of academics in the common law is very different from the normative system-building role assumed by the French *doctrine* and it mainly involves exposing, explaining and systematising law as it is. Legal categories are based on the practice of courts and lawyers do not search for underlying rationalising structures. Judges themselves do not draw on scientific objectivity and rationalisation to impose their own views on primary decision-makers. They are not searching for a transcendent or scientific truth.[18] Instead, they are compared to referees imposing the rules of a game. Lévi-Strauss explains that the difference between game and ritual lies precisely in the fusion of substance and form that the latter implies, which is traditionally absent from the game-like judicial process of the common law.

Hence, proportionality could not be thought of as a theory of judicial balancing *à la française*. It is indicative that, as an instance of domestic review similar to the French proportionality (in the sense of the *bilan*), Bell mentioned one of the most famous cases of judicial activism in English law, the *Bromley* case.[19] In this case, the Labour-led Greater London Council (GLC) had imposed a reduction on transport fares, the cost of which would be recovered through an extra tax imposed on physical and legal persons based in London. However, the GLC's decision was held to be *ultra vires* by the House of Lords. According to the judges, the 1969 Transport Act did not empower the GLC to promote social objectives through its fares policy. By doing so, the GLC had breached its fiduciary duty towards ratepayers. In order to reach this conclusion, Lord Diplock had followed a line of reasoning that is indeed similar to an

[16] Loughlin (2013), pp. 27 f., 87 f.; Atiyah (1987), p. 23.
[17] Atiyah (1987), pp. 3 f.
[18] Allison (1996), pp. 216 f. also makes this point.
[19] *Bromley London Borough Council* v. *Greater London Council* [1982] All ER 153 (HL, 17 December 1981). On this case, see Griffith (1981), pp. 123 f.

application of the *bilan*, involving calculation of the financial disadvantages of the decision and their allocation.

A whole theory of judicial balancing and proportionality could have emerged from *Bromley*, as it did from *Ville Nouvelle Est* in France. Indeed, Lord Diplock used the term 'proportion' several times in his opinion. Instead, the case is known as exceptional and contentious, even 'blatantly party political'.[20] English lawyers do not share the epistemological optimism of their continental colleagues and are not enchanted by allegedly objective factual evaluations, even when they have a financial or mathematical nature. Thus, they usually avoid reference to 'cost-benefit analysis'.[21] Mainstream public lawyers are aware of the fact that cost-benefit analysis 'has an enormous appetite for data that is disputable, unknown, and, sometimes, unknowable'.[22] The use of proportionality language has not concealed the subjectivity of factual evaluations in judicial opinions. For a long time, the only field in which the mathematical connotations of proportionality terminology persisted was that of administrative sanctions.[23]

Irritating the Fundamental Assumptions of the Analytical Tradition. English public lawyers' lack of epistemological optimism makes the taboo of merits review intelligible. As opposed to the French notion of *opportunité*, concerned with the state of mind of the primary decision-maker at the time the reviewed decision was taken, merits consist in the evaluation of the outcomes of administrative action at the time of judicial scrutiny. Hence, while the taboo of *opportunité* excludes a criticism of the intentions of public authorities, the merits taboo excludes judicial policy-making. In this context, the application of proportionality as a balancing test for assessing the outcomes of the reviewed decision long irritated the fundamental assumptions of the common law. Indeed, balancing was traditionally perceived as a type of reasoning characteristic of policy-making, liberated from a strict application of legal forms. Thus, it remained exceptional in judicial reasoning. In judicial review, in particular, balancing was applied only in the scope of application of European law or as an equity method.[24] This, according to Lord Lowry

[20] Griffith (2000), p. 172.

[21] Hickman (2010), pp. 190 f.

[22] Machaw (1985), p. 115, cited by Craig (2016), para. 12–020.

[23] *R* v. *Highbury Corner Magistrates' Court, ex parte Uchendu*, 158 JP 409 (HC, Queen's Bench Division, 12 January 1994). See also *R* v. *Eastbourne Magistrates' Court ex parte Hall* (HC, Queen's Bench) CO/2026/92.

[24] Craig (2016), paras. 12–001 f.

in *Brind*, was 'not a cause for regret', because courts did not enjoy the democratic legitimacy of the reviewed authorities and had limited access to facts.[25] As Lord Diplock noted in *GCHQ*, judges 'by their upbringing and experience are ill-qualified' to perform balancing exercises.[26]

Proportionality could not be presumed to be inherent in the intents of public authorities either. Constitutional orthodoxy held that courts implement and not supplement parliamentary intent. For a long time, there was no place for a technique similar to the continental *réserves d'interprétation*. This is connected to the fact that in English law, public authorities are not idealised as they are in continental traditions. Instead, they are treated similarly to private actors. The image of a game itself expresses the demystification that traditionally permeates the judicial process in this context. Hence, in contrast to French judicial decisions, where reference to reconciliation and balancing often has a symbolic function, the use of legal forms by English judges is instrumental. Common lawyers have always been aware of the important constitutional shift that the reception of proportionality entailed. In the analytical tradition, legal concepts and procedures serve specific purposes and lead to specific remedies. The choice of a particular legal form (concept, procedure or head of review) entails well-defined patterns of reasoning, what domestic lawyers call *analysis*. Thus, we talk of *rights analysis, duty analysis* etc. English public lawyers focus more on grounds than on methods of review, because the choice of this or the other ground determines the universe of different possibilities for legal argumentation in the game of the judicial process. Analytical rigour, clarity and transparency are major assets of judicial opinions, more important than consistency. They ensure the legitimacy of judges as impartial and fair referees.

Therefore, for a long time, the variable application of legal forms was completely strange to the English tradition of judicial review. This is perfectly illustrated in *Adams*. Gerry Adams, leader of Sinn Féin and occasionally member of the Westminster Parliament, was invited by an MP to express his views in the House of Commons. The secretary of state, when informed about the invitation, issued an exclusion order, under the Provision of Terrorism Act 1989, prohibiting Adams from entering Great Britain for three years. Adams challenged the exclusion. Among other arguments, he claimed that the order was disproportionate and thus

[25] *Brind* (HL, 7 February 1991), para. 20.
[26] *GCHQ*, p. 951, per Lord Diplock.

contrary to Article 8 of the Maastricht Treaty. Steyn J, at the time in the Queen's Bench Division, referred a question on proportionality to the Court of Justice. He submitted:

> [A]lthough the proportionality principle is part of our law through Community law, it seems to us that the explanations of the principle are not in harmony. [. . .] As English judges it seems to us that explanations of the principle span a spectrum of views from a narrow doctrine not essentially very different from *Wednesbury* unreasonableness to a de novo review of the administrative decision. On the other hand, there may be better explanations placing the principle between these extremes. Even in respect of proportionality there may be a margin of appreciation. And it is not self-evident that the principle of proportionality may not need to be adapted to the special circumstances of a case involving a tension between freedom of speech and national security.[27]

The reference would have led to interesting answers not only as to the nature of proportionality review but also as to the scope and actual meaning of Article 8 of the Maastricht Treaty at the time.[28] However, the European court did not have the occasion to respond, since the reference was withdrawn along with the withdrawal of the exclusion order in question. One thing is sure: for a long time, proportionality review was a 'peculiar technology' for English judges.[29] It irritated some of the most fundamental assumptions of the analytical tradition. It is thus not surprising that the promotion of proportionality as a transfer went hand in hand with the contestation of the Diceyan tradition's basic tenets.

6.2 A Transplant: Promoting Proportionality as an Anti-Diceyan Principle

Proportionality, Constitutional Modernisation and Substantive Rule of Law. Contrary to the unitary *Wednesbury* unreasonableness standard, a crucial characteristic of proportionality at its early stages of development in English law was its conceptual fragmentation. The irritating effect of proportionality made it so that, in judicial practice, there was a clear distinction between the EC law proportionality test and the

[27] *R* v. *Secretary of State for the Home Department, ex parte Adams* [1995] All ER (EC) 177 (HC, Queen's Bench Division, 26 July 1994).

[28] This was a case that was wholly internal to the United Kingdom. Adams lived and worked in Northern Ireland.

[29] Ward (1995), p. 24. The author refers to the deliberate indeterminacy of EU legal texts.

reasonableness-like standard applied in domestic cases.[30] Yet, from the first announcement of proportionality as an EC law head of review, it was also clear that the test was understood as part of a more universal idea. In *Goldstein*, Lord Diplock evoked the concept of proportionality, derived from German law, which he translated into the following phrase: 'You must not use a steam hammer to crack a nut, if a nutcracker would do.'[31] In *GCHQ*, the same judge referred to the principle of proportionality 'recognised in the administrative law of several of our fellow members of the European Economic Community'.[32] Other occurrences of proportionality in judicial opinions indicate that, paradoxically, the various facets of proportionality were perceived as manifestations of a more general idea, a principle that found its source in continental public law.[33]

Reference to a principle coming from abroad and being subject to variable application in the domestic sphere was quite new in the insular and formalist English legal discourse. Since the mid-1970s, however, the Diceyan orthodoxy was contested by an increasing quest for a separate and coherent system of public law and for the explicit, even codified, articulation of constitutional principles guiding and constraining public action.[34] Judicial review was progressively perceived as a general constitutional requirement, independent of the existence of statute.[35] An alternative justification for judicial review to the traditional *ultra vires* principle became dominant in English public law: the avoidance of the abuse of power by public bodies.[36] By the end of the 1980s, the need to hush 'the sound of silence' of the English constitution was becoming the new orthodoxy.[37] Loughlin talks about a general search for constitutional reform, which soon took the name of 'constitutional modernisation'.[38] The promotion of proportionality should thus be read in this context of discursive change. It is indicative that proportionality was referred to as a

[30] See, for example, *International Stock Exchange* (HC, Queen's Bench Division, 20 July 1992).
[31] *Goldstein* (HL, 20 January 1983), p. 155.
[32] *GCHQ*, p. 950.
[33] *R* v. *Waltham Forest London Borough, ex parte Waltham Borough Ratepayers Action Group* (HC, Queen's Bench, 29 July 1987), *The Times*, 31 July 1987; *Pegasus* (HC, Queen's Bench Division, 7 August 1987).
[34] Loughlin (2013), pp. 36 f., esp. p. 39.
[35] *Anisminic Ltd* v. *Foreign Compensation Commission* [1968] UKHL 6 (HL, 17 December 1968).
[36] See the influential lectures by Denning (1949).
[37] Sedley (2011). The paper was written in 1993. See also Allan (1988); Scarman (1990).
[38] Loughlin (2013), p. 3.

possible future evolution of domestic grounds of judicial review in *GCHQ*, a landmark case for the development of English judicial review.

Since the distinction public/private law was new, the modernisers turned to other systems to take examples. One observes a renaissance of comparative scholarship in the English context.[39] Most notably, English public lawyers have often looked at the French system of administrative law with a hidden sense of admiration.[40] The evolution of domestic judicial review was very often compared to French judicial achievements.[41] Judicial review concepts acquired special credit when they were claimed to have their origins in the French system, which was famous for the judicial construction of a coherent administrative law by 'this magnificent judicial instrument', the French Council of State.[42] It is thus not surprising that the early writings on proportionality also focused on the use of the principle in French administrative law.[43] The French accent of proportionality language was part of the concept's meaning as antithetical to the Diceyan tradition of domestic legal discourse. Indeed, Dicey's rejection of French-style administrative law remains famous to this day.

The rising influence of the convention bolstered the spread of proportionality. Condemning decisions by the Strasbourg Court put in question the Whig narrative on the common law and civil liberties.[44] The call for a rights-based approach was joined to the quest for modernisation and for limitation of government power. Democracy ceased to be perceived as lying exclusively in the supremacy of Parliament and started to comprise the protection of certain basic values.[45] The rule of law was progressively transformed, from a political aspiration left to the prudence of Parliament to a legal principle enforced by the judiciary.[46] The rise of fundamental rights language brought with it an idealisation of the judiciary similar to the one observed in France. Judges themselves significantly contributed to this through their increasing extra-judicial writings and speeches.[47] Griffith observed with irony that 'seldom, if ever, judges

[39] On this, see Allison (2007), pp. 186 f.
[40] Allison (1996). See also Woolf (1995).
[41] Wade and Forsyth (1982), p. 364; Bell (1986).
[42] Yardley (1970), p. 566.
[43] See Jowell and Lester (1988a), p. 858; Jowell and Lester (1988b); Boyron (1992).
[44] Allison (2007), pp. 186 f.
[45] Laws (1995).
[46] Loughlin (2013), pp. 31 f., 98. See also Craig (1997).
[47] Scarman (1990); Bingham (1992, 2000); Browne-Wilkinson (1992); Laws (1992, 1995); Sedley (1995); Woolf (1995).

admit the possibility of human frailty on the part of their brethren' and compared their writings to a 'pilgrimage'.[48]

With its connection to the convention, proportionality ceased to be a synonym of irrationality. It was progressively defined by opposition to the *Wednesbury* standard, as a standard going 'beyond it'.[49] Indeed, the assumptions that underpinned the promotion of proportionality as a continental principle were diametrically opposed to those underlying the traditional unreasonableness. While, in the Diceyan 'webs of significance', *Wednesbury* was the opposite of rights-based adjudication, proportionality was increasingly perceived by English lawyers as a useful tool for the judges in their new mission of rights protection.[50]

Hence, proportionality had all the characteristics of a transplant. It was seen as a feature of constitutional modernisation, as well as of openness to concepts and doctrines coming from abroad. It was a tool that would help the judges to accomplish the new constitutional role that the modernisers attributed to them. By adopting it, English judicial review would advance towards a developed system of public law, having nothing to envy from a system with a written constitution.

The Emergence of an English Public Law *Doctrine à la Française*. As is typical in transplant cases, certain personalities had a more prominent role in the promotion of proportionality than others. Notable barristers including Jowell, Lester and Pannick, have been ardent defenders of the principle and often based their argumentation on it, pushing judges to adopt it as a method of review. Certain judges, leaders of the modernisation movement such as Diplock, Laws and Sedley, have pressured for the adoption of proportionality in positive law through their decisions and their extra-judicial writings.[51] As the members of the French *doctrine*, the defenders of proportionality in the English context actively participated in the construction of a public law system, not only through their academic writings, but also through their role in legal practice. In this way, the study of the spread of proportionality sheds light on the emergence of a new kind of legal knowledge in English public law: doctrinal

[48] Griffith (2000), pp. 162, 163 resp.

[49] Jowell and Lester (1988a), p. 860.

[50] See Jowell and Lester (1988b), pp. 67 f.; Craig (1989), pp. 298 f.

[51] See Part I, Chapter 3. For some extra-judicial writings, see Laws (1992); Sedley (1995). Interestingly, as a QC, Laws had often argued against proportionality. See *R* v. *The Pharmaceutical Society of Great Britain, ex parte Association of Pharmaceutical Importers* [1987] 3 CMLR 951 (CA, Civil Division, 30 July 1987); *R* v. *Secretary of State for the Environment, ex parte National and Local Government Officers' Association* [1992] 5 AdminLR 785 (HC, Queen's Bench Division, 20 December 1991).

rationalisation. Judges ceased to be the sole 'oracles of the law'.[52] An English public law *doctrine* emerged as a legal formant in this context.

Since proportionality enjoyed no statutory basis in domestic judicial review, the way it could be transferred was also discussed by scholars and judges. Jowell and Lester proposed a presumption of statutory interpretation that unjustified infringement of fundamental rights was contrary to the will of Parliament.[53] In *GCHQ*, Lord Diplock envisaged a case-by-case evolution. Similarly, in a well-known article, Laws called for the reception of the principle of proportionality through the 'incremental decision-making' process of the common law.[54] The above debates are even more interesting if one considers that their existence itself was a considerable novelty for English public law at the time. Indeed, one of the characteristics of the newly formed English *doctrine* was its normative character, which contrasted with the traditionally descriptive, pragmatic and institution-oriented character of English public law scholarship. Under the influence of the modernisation movement, scholars became increasingly conscious of the importance of underpinning normative theories in the description and analysis of case law. In this context, the influential categorisations of 'green light' or 'red light' theories of judicial review appeared.[55]

The study of the early proportionality literature reveals another important feature of the new modernising English *doctrine*: its detachment from patterns of judicial reasoning. Although presenting it as a change at the level of heads of review, the defenders of proportionality sought continuity with existing common law concepts in their analyses – and continuity was easy to find at the level of judicial methods. Under the head of illegality English judges were already sanctioning public authorities' improper purposes or the taking into account of irrelevant considerations (similar to the suitability stage).[56] As for the necessity test, judges already performed it as an EC law ground of review. Cases involving balancing of competing interests were reread as examples of proportionality reasoning. Most notably, *Hook* was rediscovered as an application of the principle.[57] A whole proportionality mythology arose in English public law: domestic judges had been applying the principle, 'just as

52 Expression taken from Dawson (1978). On this point, see Atiyah (1987), pp. 165 f.
53 Jowell and Lester (1988a), p. 879.
54 Laws (1992).
55 Harlow (1984).
56 See Craig (1989), pp. 281 f.
57 See Jowell and Lester (1988b).

Moliere's Monsieur Jourdain had been speaking prose for more than 40 years without knowing it'.[58] The requirement of proportion seemed 'so characteristically English' that its explicit recognition was expected to increase the intellectual honesty of English law and the transparency of judicial reasoning.[59] Similarity with French writings on the matter is striking.

Focus on methods entailed the progressive abandonment of analytical formalism and rigour. Proportionality was deemed to encompass every kind of reasoning involving substantive evaluations. In fact, what was perceived to unify the various applications of the principle was a substantive requirement of equity, fairness or justice. The form of the scrutiny as an elimination of improper purposes, as a scrutiny of the means-ends relationship or as a balancing exercise was contingent. Although legal writings and opinions often referred to the three-pronged test applied by foreign courts, and especially the GFCC, the newly formed English *doctrine* did not care so much about structure. Surprisingly, the muddled application of proportionality in practice was even perceived as an asset of flexibility. The *Wednesbury* unreasonableness test started being perceived as 'monolithic', invariably applied as a self-evident standard of extreme irrationality. In contrast, proportionality was a general principle subject to variable application, according to the circumstances, following the example of Strasbourg case law.[60]

While anti-formalist, proportionality was anti-pragmatist too. Indeed, the defenders of proportionality thought they had found the theory that could build the fragmented 'bits and pieces' of the common law into a coherent and comprehensive system.[61] For once, it seemed that common lawyers' 'struggle for simplicity' proved fruitful.[62] In their writings, law, and proportionality as part of it, represented some kind of coherent knowledge that transcended the language actually used in judicial decisions. Hence, the insistent rejection of proportionality in judicial review until the 2000s did not impede domestic lawyers from interpreting some instances of judicial reasoning as applications of the principle.

58 Jowell and Lester (1988a), pp. 862–3. In their article, the authors refer to cases dating back from 1916. On the mythology of doctrines in intellectual history, see Skinner (2002), p. 60.
59 Jowell and Lester (1988a), p. 864.
60 Jowell and Lester (1988b), pp. 68–9; Laws (1992), pp. 1390, 1392.
61 Scarman (1990), p. 491.
62 Kirby (1998).

6.3 Proportionality 'In All but Name': The Rise of Common Law Constitutionalism

The Emergence of Anxious Scrutiny. The movement of modernisation and rationalisation found expression in judicial practice. By the end of the 1980s, the idea emerged that the more important the values at stake in the case before the judge, the more searching the judicial scrutiny should be. This was expressed in the concept of anxious scrutiny applied in fundamental rights cases, introduced by Lord Bridge in *Bugdaycay*. The case concerned the removal of a Ugandan refugee to Kenya. Mr Bugdaycay was facing fear of persecution and killing in Uganda and he had evidence that, if removed to Kenya, Kenyan authorities would send him there. Until then judges accepted that, when a country was signatory to the Geneva Convention, there was a presumption that removal to that country was safe. This practice was challenged in *Bugdaycay*. According to Lord Bridge, the refugee could not be removed to Kenya without violating the convention, if he provided evidence that he was facing a plausible fear of persecution after removal. In Lord Bridge's words:

> The most fundamental of all human rights is the individual's right to life and when an administrative decision under challenge is said to be one which may put the applicant's life at risk, the basis of the decision must surely call for the most anxious scrutiny.[63]

The introduction of the concept of anxious scrutiny marked an important step away from the formalist common law tradition. It implied that the use of a particular head of review did not lead invariably to identical methods of reasoning. Judicial scrutiny could be anxious or not, and this was a function of the substantive values at stake. Scholars noticed this fundamental change. They rediscovered cases where unreasonableness was not applied in such an extreme way as Lord Greene's words would suggest and described them as applications of the so-called 'relative *Wednesbury*'.[64] Also, cases where the threshold of perversity in order to quash a decision was set very high were described as applications of a 'super-*Wednesbury*' standard.[65] By the end of the 1990s, it was clear that irrationality was a 'variable standard', applied according to the

[63] *Bugdaycay*, p. 12.

[64] Craig (1999a), p. 96.

[65] See, most notably, *R* v. *Secretary of State for the Environment, ex parte London Borough of Hammersmith and Fulham* [1991] 1 AC 521 (HL, 4 October 1990).

importance of the values at stake.[66] In *Begbie*, Laws J described *Wednesbury* unreasonableness as a 'sliding scale of review'. In his words:

> Fairness and reasonableness (and their contraries) are objective concepts; otherwise there would be no public law, or if there were it would be palm tree justice. But each is a spectrum, not a single point, and they shade into one another. It is now well established that the *Wednesbury* principle itself constitutes a sliding scale of review, more or less intrusive according to the nature and gravity of what is at stake.[67]

Establishing Coherence Among Different Heads of Review. Reference to substantive extra-legal values in the application of legal concepts rendered more cogent the idea of unity among the various heads of review and reduced the difference between the European test of proportionality and the domestic standard of substantive review. Judges condensed the purpose and essence of judicial review into one idea: repudiation of abuse, rule of reason or fair administration. This is especially clear in Laws' opinions and extra-judicial writings. In *First City Trading*, the judge compared the EC law principle of proportionality to the domestic standard of review. In his view: '*Wednesbury* and European review are different models – one looser, one tighter – of the same juridical concept, which is the imposition of compulsory standards on decision-makers so as to secure the repudiation of arbitrary power.'[68] The quest for coherence among different heads of review led to the diffusion and dilution of proportionality in domestic standards and deprived it of its conceptual clarity in judicial practice. Besides, in many cases, the *Wednesbury* standard was reformulated in a way that echoed Strasbourg proportionality case law.[69]

Progressively, the variable intensity of review was itself perceived as an expression of fairness and proportionality. Scholars have described the searching application of the traditional standards of judicial review as proportionality 'in all but name'.[70] This seems to be the perception of certain judges as well. In *McQuillan*, for example, Sedley J cited with

[66] *Chesterfield Properties* (HC, Queen's Bench Division, 24 July 1997), p. 130.

[67] *R* v. *The Department of Education and Employment, ex parte Begbie* [2000] 1 WLR 1115 (CA, Civil Division, 20 August 1999), para. 78.

[68] *R* v. *Ministry of Agriculture, Fisheries and Food and Another, ex parte First City Trading* [1997] 1 CMLR 250 (HC, Queen's Bench Division, 29 November 1996), para. 69. Contra, *R* v. *Secretary of State for the Home Department, ex parte Arthur H Cox Ltd*, [1999] EuLR 677 (HC, Queen's Bench Division, 14 December 1998), where, in spite of the wide margin of appreciation, proportionality was not equated to irrationality.

[69] See, for example, *Brind*, analysed in Part I, Chapter 3.2.

[70] Hunt (1997), p. 216; Kavanagh (2009), p. 268; Craig (2016), pp. 624 f.

approval Laws' extra-judicial writings on the reception of the convention standards through the common law.[71] He argued that judicial supervision of public bodies' decisions should vary, according to whether the right affected was recognised by the law as fundamental or not. Sedley J concluded that:

> Once this point is reached, the standard of justification of infringements of rights and freedoms by executive decision must vary in proportion to the significance of the right which is at issue. Such an approach is indeed already enjoined by *Ex p Bugdaycay* in relation to a predominant value of the common law – the right to life – which, as it happens, the convention reflects. Whether this in itself is a doctrine of proportionality I do not now pause to ask; if it is, the House of Lords has long since contemplated its arrival with equanimity.[72]

Proportionality and Common Law Constitutionalism. The commonly shared perception of anxious scrutiny as an instance of proportionality reasoning should not surprise. In reality, anxious scrutiny brought about the major part of the changes that domestic public lawyers had expected of the adoption of proportionality. It entailed a rejection of traditional common law formalism and pragmatism. By referring to substantive values, it expressed the significant change in the role of judges that was taking place at the time: from impartial referees they became guarantors of fairness and justice. As a judicial method, anxious scrutiny established coherence among previously fragmented standards and heads. In this way, it manifested in an exemplary way the rationalisation process that English public law was undergoing. Once again, *plus c'est la même chose, plus ça change*. The rejection of proportionality as a head of judicial review did not impede the advent of the changes that domestic public lawyers had expected of it. The diffusion of proportionality in domestic concepts indicated that English lawyers had acquired their own system of public law, similar to the ones that continental lawyers had.

The subsequent evolution of proportionality in English public law should be read against the background of the rise of common law constitutionalism. The recognition of substantive values of fairness and justice imposed by courts was hardly reconcilable with the traditional perception of parliamentary sovereignty as the cornerstone of the English constitution. The Diceyan account was progressively perceived as ill-

[71] Laws (1992).

[72] *R* v. *Secretary of State for the Home Department, ex parte McQuillan* [1995] 4 All ER 400 (HC, Queen's Bench, 9 September 1994).

adapted to capture the practice of judicial review, as a 'misleadingly partial truth'.[73] Dicey himself became probably the most criticised author in English legal writings. Progressively, English lawyers became conscious of the fact that courts were supplementing and not simply implementing legislative intent.[74] The concept of sovereignty had to be reinvented to accommodate this newly acquired power of courts.[75] Talk of a 'bi-polar sovereignty' of Parliament and the judiciary, to which the government is accountable, became progressively recurrent in English legal discourse.[76] By the late 1990s, common law constitutionalism had become the dominant trend in English public law. Common law rights were progressively recognised as fundamental in case law.[77] Legality was transformed, from a formal quality to a principle requiring the protection of substantive values. The technique of presumptions of statutory interpretation, which resembles the French *réserves d'interprétation*, played an important role in this evolution.[78] In *Pierson*, the House of Lords announced that it would take into account fairness considerations when constructing the presumed will of Parliament.[79] In *Simms*, Lord Hoffmann proclaimed a general principle of legality, according to which 'general powers of decision-making conferred by statute were presumed to have been enacted as subject to fundamental civil liberties'.[80] This led to some intrusive applications of the common law standard of substantive review, which were indeed difficult to distinguish from European proportionality.[81]

The *Smith* Case. Still, anxious scrutiny and the operation of fairness standards did not always lead to optimal protection of fundamental

[73] Turpin (1999), p. 39. See also Sedley (1995); Hunt (1997); Craig (1999b).

[74] Craig (2016), para. 19–028.

[75] *X.* v. *Morgan-Grampian* [1991] 1 AC 1 (HL, 4 April 1990), per Lord Bridge, cited by Loughlin (2013), p. 99.

[76] Sedley (1995).

[77] *R* v. *Secretary of State for the Home Department, ex parte Leech* [1994] QB 198 (CA, Civil Division, 19 May 1993); See also *R* v. *Lord Chancellor, ex parte Witham* [1998] 2 WLR 849 (HC, Queen's Bench Division, 7 March 1997).

[78] Browne-Wilkinson (1992).

[79] *R* v. *Secretary of State for the Home Department, ex parte Pierson* [1998] AC 539 (HL, 24 July 1997).

[80] *R* v. *Secretary of State for the Home Department, ex parte Simms and O'Brien* [1999] 3 WLR 328 (HL, 8 July 1999).

[81] See, most notably, *Daly* (HL, 23 May 2001), paras. 17 f. Interestingly, no judge expressly engages proportionality analysis in this case. Lord Bingham reached his conclusions 'on an orthodox application of common law principles derived from the authorities and an orthodox domestic approach to judicial review' (para. 23).

rights. This became apparent in the famous *Smith* case.[82] The case concerned the policy of the UK army to discharge its homosexual members. This policy was applied to all members of the army who had admitted their homosexual orientation, without regard to their individual circumstances. It had often been reconsidered by Parliament but without change. The rule was justified by the need to preserve the morale and effectiveness of the military. It was claimed that the primary decision was not based on moral judgment but on the practical assessment of the consequences that the presence of homosexuals in the army had. Pannick QC, representing the applicants, called for a more intensive scrutiny than the irrationality standard would entail, due to the importance of the human rights at stake. The government in response argued that the *Wednesbury* threshold should be heightened due to the national security issues involved, which were traditionally considered non-justiciable in English law.

The Court of Appeal refused to depart from the traditional irrationality standard. However, this standard would not be mechanically applied:

> [W]here an administrative decision was made in the context of human rights the court would require proportionately greater justification before being satisfied that the decision was within the range of responses open to a reasonable decision-maker, according to the seriousness of the interference with those rights; that in applying the test of irrationality, which was sufficiently flexible to cover all situations, the court would show greater caution where the nature of the decision was esoteric, policy-laden or security-based.[83]

The court unanimously dismissed the appeals, even though two out of three judges expressed doubts as to the compatibility of the provision with the convention. Simon Brown LJ even expressed his 'hesitation and regret' in handing out the judgment and urged the government to re-examine the matter in light of the changing social circumstances.[84] However, the judges did not substitute their view for that of the reviewed authority. They considered that, until the convention was incorporated into domestic law, they were not 'entitled to ask whether the policy answer[ed] a pressing social need and whether the restriction on

[82] R v. *Admiralty Board of the Defence Council, ex parte Lustig-Prean*; R v. *Admiralty Board of the Defence Council, ex parte Beckett*; R v. *Secretary of State for Defence, ex parte Smith*; R v. *Ministry of Defence, ex parte Grady* [1996] QB 517 (CA, Civil Division, 3 November 1995).

[83] Ibid, p. 517.

[84] Ibid, p. 541.

human rights involved [could] be shown proportionate to its benefits'.[85] Rather, primary responsibility for these questions lay with Parliament, given that the belief in the existence of a practical risk for national security in this case was not deemed to be irrational or in defiance of accepted moral standards. Three years later, in its famous *Smith and Grady* decision, the ECtHR was called to judge on the same facts and found that the UK policy was contrary to both proportionality and the convention.[86]

Compromising the Fundamental Rights Function of Proportionality. Clearly, a difference between proportionality as a principle for the optimisation of fundamental rights and domestic review persisted. While proportionality sometimes prescribes an objective, rights-based evaluation of the outcomes of the reviewed decision, the standard of anxious or proportionate scrutiny could not concern these outcomes themselves. Instead, it concerned the conditions for permissible judicial interference with public authorities' decisions. In other words, the standard of anxious or proportionate scrutiny was a standard of review and not a standard of legality.[87] Indeed, the adjectives 'anxious' or 'proportionate', which were distinctive of this kind of scrutiny, characterised the judicial inquiry itself and not the impacts of the reviewed act. Anxious scrutiny did not imply an objective evaluation of the balancing made by the primary decision-maker and did not lead the court to impose its own view as to the importance of the public interest at stake. Judges were confined to ascertaining that the balancing actually took place, and that the individual right was taken into account.

Understood in this way, the English version of proportionality was akin to the way in which Greek courts applied the principle in administrative law: it implied a procedural requirement of equity and justice.[88] This was apparent in the writings of the most fervent defenders of proportionality, who described it as an extension of 'natural justice' requirements.[89] In their analyses, proportionality was connected to the normative priorities of the primary decision-maker. Its connection to fact-finding tests of necessity and cost-benefit balancing was only contingent. As Laws put it:

85 Ibid.
86 ECtHR, *Smith and Grady* v. *The UK*, 27 September 1999, nos. 33985/96 and 33986/96. On this case, see Part III, Chapter 8.2.
87 On this distinction, Hickman (2010), pp. 99 f.
88 See Part I, Chapter 4.3.
89 See Jowell and Lester (1988b), pp. 59 f.

> There is no room for [proportionality] at all in the fact-finding case; but if we are to entertain a form of review in which fundamental rights are to enjoy the court's distinct protection, the very exercise consists in an insistence that the decision-maker is not free to order his priorities as he chooses, confined only by a crude duty not to emulate the brute beasts that have no understanding [. . .]; an insistence that he accord the first priority to the right in question unless he can show a substantial, objective, public justification for overriding it.[90]

Proportionality was perceived and promoted as a standard of justification of the reviewed decision. It was connected to a duty, emerging at the time, of the administration to provide reasons.[91] At least at the time, its connection to fundamental rights was secondary. It is indicative that, in the 1995 edition of the de Smith handbook, the authors included a relatively extended analysis of proportionality in which fundamental or human rights were hardly mentioned.[92] This is what made Craig fear its dilution to a concept of fairness, equivalent to irrationality.[93]

English Public Lawyers' Expectations of Proportionality. Therefore, the English perception of proportionality is revealing as to the main stakes attached to its use in this context. This was not the optimisation of fundamental rights, since neither anxious scrutiny nor proportionality concerned the real impacts of public decisions on rights. Proportionality as a transplant was not so much about respecting the European human rights obligations of the country either, since English public lawyers classify as instances of proportionality cases in which domestic judicial review was found insufficient in Strasbourg, most notably *Smith*. Among the promoters of proportionality, Lord Diplock was known for not being favourable to the incorporation of the ECHR in the domestic sphere.[94] Similarly, in his 'Is the High Court the Protector of Fundamental Human Rights', Laws argued against the incorporation of the ECHR in the domestic sphere. In his words:

> [W]e may have regard to ECHR (and, for that matter, other international texts) but not think of incorporating it; we should apply differential standards in judicial review according to the subject-matter, and to do so deploy the tool of proportionality, not the bludgeon of *Wednesbury*;

[90] Laws (1992), p. 1392.
[91] See Craig (1989), pp. 221–2, 304–5. See also Birkinshaw (2003), p. 333. On the symbiotic relationship between administrative reason-giving and intensification of the standard of substantive review, see Daly (2020b).
[92] De Smith et al. (1995).
[93] Craig (1989), p. 299.
[94] Hickman (2010), p. 14.

> that a function of this is to recognise that decision-makers whose decisions affect fundamental rights must inevitably justify what they do by giving good reasons; [. . .] I think this is, in the end, a modest way forward, involving no sea-change in the law; but the growth of the common law has always been an incoming tide, not a storm of hurricane force; and it is better so; the tide leaves no wake of destruction when it ebbs.[95]

The assimilation of proportionality to anxious scrutiny demonstrates that what domestic lawyers expected of proportionality was a coherent system of judicial review, an English public law based on certain core substantive values. In this respect, proportionality and anxious scrutiny were similar. In the following years, efforts to construct an English public law were furthered by Parliament itself. Devolution, human rights and other issues of constitutional importance were codified in statutes. Constitutional reform, having been a constant preoccupation of English lawyers,[96] led for the first time to the adoption of acts explicitly using constitutional language in the Constitutional Reform Act of 2005.[97] In an oft-commented on book, Bogdanor has talked about the emergence of a 'new' constitution in a 'piecemeal' fashion.[98] Today, it is difficult to say that English law does not possess a written constitution. The reception of proportionality under the HRA in this context expressed pre-existing tendencies in English public law and embodied domestic lawyers' hopes and expectations. These expectations were quite different from the ones that Alexy and his followers attached to proportionality roughly at the same time. Understanding the local expectations of proportionality renders the current evolution of the concept in English public law less enigmatic.

6.4 A Successful Transplant: Proportionality and the Rationalisation of English Public Law

Substantive Values, Epistemological Optimism and Institutional Faith. The voting through of the HRA, part of the Labour programme of constitutional modernisation, introduced into the common law a catalogue of precisely those rights that are so dear to foreign constitutionalists. Thus, the barriers to the application of proportionality as a fundamental rights principle were superseded. Proportionality no longer

95 Laws (1992), pp. 1395–6.
96 Beatson, ed. (1998).
97 Loughlin (2013), pp. 112 f.
98 Bogdanor (2009), p. 5.

concerns the interference of the court in a domain of competence of public authorities. Instead, it is a requirement of fundamental rights protection addressed to public authorities themselves and concerned with the merits of their action. It requires the court to 'assess the balance' effectuated by the primary decision-maker and may also require 'attention to be directed to the relative weight accorded to interests and considerations'.[99] Contrary to the 'blunt' *Wednesbury* test,[100] which 'never completely lost its flavour of excessive deference',[101] it is widely accepted that proportionality leads to more exacting and precise justification of public decisions.[102]

The impact of public action on fundamental rights has become a central issue in judicial reasoning. Procedures have been institutionalised so that judges have access to the facts the initial decision-maker took into account.[103] Balancing is now a form of legal reasoning in the minds of English lawyers and is solemnly announced by judges as the fourth step of the proportionality test. According to Lord Mance in *Nicklinson*, it is 'a core feature of the court's role'.[104] In the writings of human rights enthusiasts, law and politics are no longer mutually exclusive but coexist in a relation of synthesis.[105] English public lawyers do not show the optimism of their continental colleagues as to the possibility of objective value-laden appreciations and do not talk about rights optimisation or of harmony. Still, most authors seem to believe in the potential of the proportionality framework to increase transparency in judicial reasoning and to ameliorate the results of judicial enquiry. The scientific terminology used by English lawyers gives a connotation of objectivity to proportionality evaluations: talk about the 'relative' or 'marginal' cost or benefit abounds in legal decisions and writings.[106] Some recent uses of proportionality language even acquire a connotation of mathematical exactness that brings them close to the way French public lawyers use the term.[107]

99 *Daly*. See Part I, Chapter 3.3.
100 Sedley (2005), p. 9.
101 Kavanagh (2009), p. 253.
102 Jowell (2000), p. 671; Hickman (2010), pp. 264 f.
103 Taggart (2003), pp. 325 f. See, for example, *Bank Mellat* (SC, 19 June 2013).
104 *Nicklinson* (SC, 25 June 2014), para. 171.
105 Kavanagh (2009), pp. 19 f., 185 f., 404 f. See also Hunt (1999), p. 93.
106 On this point, see Hickman (2010), pp. 190 f. See for example, *Lambert* (HL, 5 July 2001), per Lord Steyn. The judge analyses the relative merits of the chosen provision with respect to a less restrictive alternative.
107 See, for example, Neuberger (2012).

It seems that the HRA, and proportionality within it, implies an increase of institutional faith in the judiciary. Judges are considered more appropriate to adjudicate fundamental rights issues as against the will of parliamentary majorities and administrative authorities.[108] They are always deemed constitutionally competent to decide for themselves the question of the proportionality of the reviewed measures.[109] Hence, from impartial referees, courts become fundamental rights protectors.[110] They are no longer monitoring public authorities; they are participating in the policy-making process. Their new mission is one of system-building, concerned with justice and good governance.[111] This is very different from their 'mistake avoidance' role under the common law orthodoxy. Metaphors describing the relationship between Parliament and the judiciary as a form of 'partnership' or 'dialogue' express this.[112] Proportionality proves very useful to judges in their new fundamental rights mission. By accentuating notions of substantive justice and justification, it shifts the focus away from remedies to address the undergirding political moral reasons for public action.

Proportionality's Cultural Baggage. Proportionality carries with it rationalist baggage. Its reception is combined with the dominance of an expansive conception of rights, which departs from the traditional common law analytical rigour and resembles the rational human rights paradigm. Rights are generously defined and are accepted to have an 'indirect horizontal effect'.[113] Furthermore, the HRA provides for certain social rights and imposes positive obligations on public authorities.[114] English public law, from a model in which civil liberties are seen as negative, imposing public abstention, moves towards a model of rights as requirements of optimisation. More and more domains of public action are thus subject to judicial scrutiny and submitted to a requirement of rights-based justification. Scholars suggest the jettisoning of doctrinal barriers in judicial review and advocate the

[108] Kavanagh (2009), pp. 338 f.
[109] See *Begum* (HL, 22 March 2006), per Lord Bingham. Craig (2016), paras. 18–040 f.
[110] Jowell (2000), pp. 678 f.
[111] Nason (2016).
[112] Leckey (2015). For some examples, see Clayton (2004); Kavanagh (2009), p. 408. See also Hickman (2010), pp. 69 f., 81 f.
[113] Craig (2016), para. 18–026; *Campbell* v. *MGN Ltd* [2004] UKHL 22 (HL, 6 May 2004); *Douglas* v. *Hello! Ltd* [2005] EWCA Civ 595 (CA, Civil Division, 18 May 2005).
[114] *Kay* v. *Lambeth* [2006] UKHL 10 (HL, 8 March 2006). See, however, even before the HRA, Clapham (1993).

establishment of a general requirement of reason giving and of a culture of justification.[115]

In the words of Lord Neuberger, President of the Supreme Court at the time, after the adoption of the HRA, English law has entered the 'age of enlightenment'.[116] Under the HRA, statutory text and precedent cease to be decisive. Insofar as proportionality requires the identification of public goals, analysis yields to purposive interpretation. Statutory text is progressively perceived as a 'canvas' on which constitutional values are projected.[117] It is thus substantive principles and not linguistic structures that ensure law's continuity and coherence.[118] This does not pass without a certain idealisation of the legislative will. In *Countryside Alliance*, for example, Lord Bingham gave the following reasons for deferring to the choice of Parliament:

> There are of course many in England and Wales who do not consider that there is a pressing (or any) social need for the ban imposed by the Act. But after an intense debate a majority of the country's democratically elected representatives decided otherwise. It is of course true that the existence of duly enacted legislation does not conclude the issue. [...] Here we are dealing with a law which is very recent and must [...] be taken to reflect the conscience of a majority of the nation.[119]

The new human rights culture arising in the UK is communitarian rather than libertarian.[120] This represents a significant change in the ideological foundations of English public law. Domestic lawyers talk about the 'reinvention' of administrative law as a rights-based system.[121] Traditional liberal categories are replaced by a general quest for synthesis and harmony of conflicting social interests and values in each concrete case. Proportionality balancing proliferates in judicial review. It is an overarching head applied in all convention rights cases, even when they involve unqualified rights.[122] Its application is a matter of principle and

[115] Taggart (2003); Hunt (2003), p. 337; Allan (2006).

[116] Neuberger (2014), para. 5.

[117] Elliott (2015a), p. 549; Hain (2017).

[118] See, for example, *Ghaidan* v. *Mendoza* (HL, 21 June 2004), para. 30, per Lord Nicholls.

[119] *Countryside Alliance* (HL, 28 November 2007), para. 45. See also *R* v. *Secretary of State for Work and Pensions, ex parte SG and Others* [2015] UKSC 16 (SC, 18 March 2015), para. 95, per Lord Reed.

[120] Hunt (1999), pp. 88 f.

[121] Taggart (2003).

[122] See *Lambert*. Note, however, that Lord Steyn specifies that he applies proportionality at the stage of definition of the scope of the right and not at the stage of assessing the legality of its limitations.

neglects well-established categories and distinctions. As Lord Hope said in *Kebeline*:

> [I]n the hands of the national courts [. . .] the Convention should be seen as an expression of fundamental principles rather than as a set of mere rules. The questions which the courts will have to decide in the application of these principles will involve questions of balance between competing interests and issues of proportionality.[123]

Proportionality as a Continental Theory. Proportionality increasingly resembles a continental legal theory. It is no longer conceptually fragmented in academic writings. Either applied in the context of fundamental rights, EU economic freedoms or – more rarely – in English administrative law, it is perceived as a unique method of review with variable intensity.[124] Scholars are recurrently cited in its application. The defenders of proportionality share 'an evangelical belief' in its rationalising potential.[125] Due to its vagueness and indeterminacy, proportionality acquires a meaning similar to fairness, and is deemed to provide the principle that underpins every kind of judicial review. At the same time, it is perceived as an 'empty vessel' of structure and is deemed to offer a framework for all kinds of judicial decision-making.[126] Domestic lawyers talk about proportionality's 'chameleon-like appeal',[127] which serves in 'expressing both change and continuity in one and the same breath'.[128] Laws LJ's dictum in *Sinclair Collis* shows this with particular force:

> Though proportionality has its inspiration in the civilian systems, its alliance of firm principle (the standards) and varying application (the margin of appreciation) is highly characteristic of the common law's method. Principle and pragmatism are conformed by such alliances, and the law is more effective accordingly.[129]

Judicial review precedents cease to be 'a disorganised mass of single instances'.[130] They are rearranged as instances of proportionality review. Furthermore, they are articulated according to a rationale that much resembles the continental concept of administrative discretion.[131]

[123] *Kebeline* (HL, 28 October 1999), p. 380.
[124] Craig (2016), paras. 19–008 f. See also *Bank Mellat*, para. 68, per Lord Reed.
[125] Hickman (2010), p. 270. For an example, see Ramshaw (2019).
[126] Hickman (2010), p. 267.
[127] Leigh (2002), p. 279.
[128] Allison (2007), p. 232.
[129] *Sinclair Collis* (CA, Civil Division, 17 June 2011), para. 82.
[130] Bell (1986), p. 119.
[131] See, most notably, *Sinclair Collis*.

Section 6(2) HRA excludes the application of the illegality head against administrative action, in cases where the reviewed authority could not have acted differently. This echoes the theory of the *loi écran*, which excludes certain kinds of judicial review in France. Inversely, the Supreme Court refuses to declare the contested measures disproportionate per se in cases where the application authorities retain a residual discretion. This considerably compromises the effectiveness of proportionality review.[132] Indeed, as proportionality spreads, English judges, as do their French colleagues, seem increasingly concerned with the safeguards or guarantees defined by legislation rather than with the real impacts of the reviewed measures.[133]

Discretion also affects the intensity of judicial review. In this context, the flexibility of the proportionality framework proves to be an important asset. In *Miss Behavin'*, the refusal of a local authority to licence sex shops was impugned under Article 10 ECHR.[134] In view of the 'broad power of judgment' that local authorities enjoy in the domain of social control, the House of Lords accorded weight to the view of the primary decision-makers on the balance struck between the competing interests at stake.[135] In the words of Lord Hoffmann: 'If the local authority exercises that power rationally and in accordance with the purposes of the statute, it would require very unusual facts for it to amount to a disproportionate restriction on Convention rights.'[136] This is not far from the way French courts employ the manifest error test. Proportionality in English public law thus ceases to be synonymous to intensive scrutiny and encompasses minimum scrutiny as well.[137]

Continuity or Change? Proportionality is progressively perceived as an instance of rational decision-making and conquers increasingly more

[132] *R* v. *Secretary of State and Another, ex parte MM (Lebanon) and Others* [2017] UKSC 10 (SC, 22 February 2017).

[133] See, for example, *R* v. *Commissioner of Police of the Metropolis, ex parte Catt*; *R* v. *Commissioner of Police of the Metropolis, ex parte T* [2015] UKSC 9 (SC, 4 March 2015), paras. 27, 33 f., per Lord Sumption; paras. 50 f., per Lady Hale. The Supreme Court's decision was criticised by the ECtHR in *Catt* v. *The UK*, 24 January 2019, no. 43514/15.

[134] *Miss Behavin'* (HL, 25 April 2007).

[135] Ibid, para. 16.

[136] Ibid.

[137] See *Eastside Cheese Company* (CA, Civil Division, 1 July 1999), esp. paras. 41–9; *Sinclair Collis*, esp. paras. 126–34.

fields of legal reasoning in the rationalist post-HRA era.[138] In judicial review in particular, it becomes hegemonic and tends to absorb other reasoning methods. The story is well-known.[139] In cases such as *Daly*, *ABCIFER*, *Nadarajah*, *Paponette* and *Walker*, important judges have argued for the abandonment of traditional common law concepts and standards, most notably *Wednesbury*, and the adoption of proportionality as a general public law principle and head of review.[140] The persistence of traditional common law standards seems increasingly difficult to justify in institutional terms or in terms of transparency of judicial reasoning. Pressure for the adoption of proportionality as a general principle or head of review is also a recurrent theme in the literature.[141] However, courts have refused to perform *Wednesbury*'s 'burial rites'.[142]

Once again, the pervasive dynamic of proportionality deprives it of its conceptual neatness. Its defenders perceive it in continuity with domestic judicial review concepts, most notably *Wednesbury* unreasonableness. Hence, they contest the conceptual distinction between proportionality and irrationality established in *Daly*. This distinction is increasingly perceived as 'unnecessary and confusing'.[143] The difference between the two standards is argued to be 'one of degree rather than kind'.[144] However, it is often stressed that the assimilation of proportionality to *Wednesbury* undermines its intrusiveness and rigour.[145] It is argued that proportionality leads to more intensive scrutiny of public action than the traditional irrationality head, even in the cases of the most anxious scrutiny. Furthermore, it implies a structured approach and a shift in

138 See, for example, Constitution Committee, 'Fast-track Legislation: Constitutional Implications and Safeguards' (15th Report, Session 2008–9, HL Paper 116), para. 16. Concerning the recent response to the Covid-19 pandemic, see Daly (2020a).

139 Kavanagh (2009), pp. 253 f.; Craig (2016), paras. 19–009 f.

140 *Daly*, para. 32; *R* v. *Secretary of State for Defence, ex parte Association of British Civilian Internees: Far East Region (ABCIFER)* [2003] QB 1397 (CA, Civil Division, 3 April 2003), paras. 34–5; *Nadarajah, Abdi* v. *The Secretary of State for the Home Department* [2005] EWCA Civ 1363 (CA, Civil Division, 22 November 2005), paras. 67–8; *Francis Paponette and Others* v. *The Attorney General of Trinidad and Tobago* [2010] UKPC 32 (PC, 13 December 2010), para. 38; *R* v. *The Parole Board for England and Wales, ex parte Wells*; *R* v. *The Secretary of State for the Home Department, ex parte Walker* [2007] EWHC 1835 (HC, Queen's Bench Division, 31 July 2007), para. 38.

141 Kavanagh (2009), pp. 253 f.; Hunt (2009); Davies and Williams (2015); Craig (2016), paras. 19–026 f.; Nehushtan (2017).

142 *ABCIFER*, paras. 34–5.

143 *Alconbury* (HL, 9 May 2001), para. 55, per Lord Slynn.

144 Elliott (2001), p. 308; in the same vein, see Nehushtan (2017).

145 Hickman (2010, pp. 99 f.) proposes to preserve the conceptual clarity of proportionality. See also Srirangam (2016); Daly (2016).

the burden of proof in favour of the individual claimant. Why do human rights enthusiasts assimilate the two heads of review then?

Again, the answer is found in the particular stakes attached to the use of proportionality in English public law. As we saw, the promotion of proportionality as a transplant has not so much been about rights optimisation. Clearly, the spread of proportionality has not always led to an optimal protection of fundamental rights. Besides, for some defenders of proportionality, its application should not be restricted to fundamental rights cases. Bjorge and Williams, for instance, think of proportionality as a 'protean principle' that could apply in all judicial review cases.[146]

Rather, the promotion of proportionality as a transplant has been about the rationalisation and modernisation of English public law. Interestingly, while the HRA institutionalised proportionality and its fundamental rights baggage, it also constrained them within the scope of European law and thus within the 'Diceyan prison'.[147] It preserved the conceptual distinction between proportionality and *Wednesbury* in judicial practice and all that it represented: parliamentary sovereignty, dualism and analytical formalism. Hence, the defenders of the legal constitution complain that the principle of parliamentary sovereignty 'continues to blight contemporary public law and to prevent its evolution into a mature system regulating the legality of the exercise of power in a modern polity'.[148] On the contrary, the idea of continuity between proportionality and irrationality, even when it comes at a cost for fundamental rights optimisation, better satisfies domestic lawyers' expectations of proportionality. It is underpinned by the claim that the rationalisation of English administrative law is complete.

In this way, the debates on the spill-over of proportionality make sense: they reflect a more profound struggle for the fundamentals of the new English constitution. Will the constitution be based on the pragmatist precepts of the Diceyan legacy or on rationalist fundamental rights principles? Loughlin talks about a 'singular moment of imaginative constitutional self-reflection'.[149] During the last decades, the process of rationalisation has advanced well outside the scope of the HRA. Part I of the CRA 2005 explicitly confers constitutional status on the rule of law. Judges do not hesitate to proclaim their newly acquired constitutional

146 Bjorge and Williams (2016). See also Davies and Williams (2015).
147 Hunt (2003), p. 344.
148 Ibid, p. 339.
149 Loughlin (2013), p. 83.

powers.[150] The reign of reason replaces the reign of Parliament. For once, parliamentary sovereignty, or supremacy, as it is lately called, seems to yield before the legal constitution. This requires a rearrangement in the boundaries between politics and law, between the powers of Parliament and those of the judiciary.

6.5 Proportionality and Deference: Towards a Contextual Approach to Judicial Review

English Lawyers' Turn to Methods. While proportionality has not been officially established as an overarching head of review in English public law, it affects the application of traditional concepts as a judicial *method*. Indeed, the assimilation of proportionality to domestic concepts considerably enhanced the development of the common law standard of substantive review. As early as 2003, Lord Phillips had observed that, in common law cases as well, the courts had developed 'an issue-sensitive scale of intervention to enable them to perform their constitutional function in an increasingly complex polity'.[151] Scholarly systematisation has taken the lead in this evolution. English lawyers' complex doctrinal reconstructions of substantive review are reminiscent of the French classifications of the *cas d'ouverture*.[152] Following Craig's analysis, often quoted in judicial opinions:

> Both reasonableness review and proportionality involve considerations of weight and balance, with the intensity of the scrutiny and the weight to be given to any primary decision maker's view depending on the context. The advantage of the terminology of proportionality is that it introduces an element of structure into the exercise, by directing attention to factors such as suitability or appropriateness, necessity and the balance or imbalance of benefits and disadvantages.[153]

Proportionality and irrationality are increasingly perceived as similar methods of review with little or no difference in the practical outcome. In recent case law, the use of the head of proportionality or irrationality is reduced into a matter of terminology. In *Kennedy*, a freedom of

[150] See most notably, *R* v. *Attorney General, ex parte Jackson and Others* [2006] 1 AC 262 (HL, 13 October 2005), p. 302, per Lord Steyn; per Lord Hope. See also *R* v. *The Secretary of State for Transport and Another, ex parte HS2 Action Alliance Ltd* [2014] UKSC 3 (22 January 2014), para. 207.

[151] *R* v. *Secretary of State for the Home Department, ex parte Q* [2004] QB 36 (CA, Civil Division, 18 March 2003), para. 112.

[152] See Jowell (2015); de Smith et al. (2018), chap. 11.

[153] Craig (2013).

information case, the Supreme Court reproved the applicant for appealing directly to the convention, while common law statutes and instruments provide for equivalent protection of the competing rights and interests at stake.[154] Lord Mance said that he 'found it difficult to think that there would be any significant difference in the nature or outcome of a court's scrutiny' whether such scrutiny be based on common law principles or on the HRA. He added: 'The common law no longer insists on the uniform application of the rigid test of irrationality once thought applicable under the so-called *Wednesbury* principle. The nature of judicial review in every case depends upon the context.'[155]

Following scholarly suggestions to this direction, English judges progressively depart from the formalist focus on heads of review and turn to reasoning methods, employed according to the context that surrounds the case that they have to decide.[156] This tendency became even more explicit in *Pham*, concerning the home secretary's decision to deprive individuals of British citizenship.[157] In this case, the Supreme Court judges explicitly considered the application of proportionality as a domestic concept.[158] Lord Mance, citing *Kennedy*, Craig and German doctrine on the matter, referred to the availability of 'the tool of proportionality' in domestic cases concerning deprivation of citizenship.[159] In Lord Mance's view, proportionality can legitimately be used by judges in common law judicial review, since it implies no expansion of judicial powers. Lord Reed went further and cited *Hook*, *Leech* and *Daly* as cases in which proportionality review had already been applied in substance in the common law. In his words:

> One can infer from these cases that, where Parliament authorises significant interferences with important legal rights, the courts may interpret the legislation as requiring that any such interference should be no greater than is objectively established to be necessary to achieve the legitimate aim of the interference: in substance, a requirement of proportionality.[160]

154 *Kennedy* v. *The Charity Commission* [2014] UKSC 20 (SC, 26 March 2014).
155 Ibid, para. 51.
156 See Elliott (2014).
157 *Pham* v. *Secretary of State for the Home Department* [2015] UKSC 19 (SC, 25 March 2015).
158 For an analysis of the different opinions expressed by the Supreme Court judges on the matter, see Elliott (2015b).
159 *Pham*, para. 98.
160 Ibid, para. 119. See also *R* v. *Lord Chancellor, ex parte UNISON* [2017] UKSC 51 (SC, 26 July 2017), para. 89.

Lord Reed's dicta mark an important shift from the common law's analytical focus on clear-cut grounds of review to a new kind of judicial justification, based on methods of reasoning and underpinning principles. Lord Reed considered that proportionality had been applied 'in substance' in cases in which judges had explicitly declined to use the proportionality head of review. Indeed, legal methods are not necessarily explicit. They underpin legal reasoning just as the scientific method of physics underpins experiments of physicists. Hence, methods can also be presumed in public and judicial decisions. Proportionality as a method has been used to reinvent common law concepts and precedents in accordance with the precepts of the convention. In *Hesham Ali*, Lord Reed stated that proportionality 'has now become the established method of analysis' and should continue to be followed.[161]

The 'Afterlife' of Parliamentary Sovereignty.[162] Paradoxically, English judges' turn to methods allows them to avoid dealing with the crucial matter of the spill-over of proportionality as an overarching head of review. Hence, the principle of parliamentary supremacy is somehow preserved. *Keyu* is illustrative in this respect.[163] The case concerned the refusal by the executive to hold a public inquiry into the killing by the Scots Guards of twenty-four unarmed civilians in Batang Kali. Persons closely related to the victims challenged the refusal under the HRA and under the common law judicial review procedure. At the time of the killings (in 1948), Batang Kali was a British protectorate and today is part of the Malaysian territory. Thus, the question of the territorial application of the HRA arose. The majority of the Supreme Court judges agreed on the fact that the convention did not apply on the facts of the case. The appellants argued that proportionality should still be applied as a domestic standard. Lord Neuberger held the question to be of fundamental importance and considered it in detail. However, in his view, it was not necessary to provide an answer to this question to resolve the issue at stake, since both the proportionality and the *Wednesbury* claims of the appellants failed.[164]

Even without performing the burial rites of *Wednesbury*, however, English judges have certainly moved one step further away from

161 *Hesham Ali (Iraq)* v. *Secretary of State for the Home Department* [2016] UKSC 60 (SC, 16 November 2016), paras. 47–50.

162 Title inspired by Barber (2011).

163 *Keyu and Others* v. *Secretary of State for Foreign and Commonwealth Affairs and Another* [2015] UKSC 69 (SC, 25 November 2015).

164 Ibid, para. 136.

parliamentary sovereignty. This can be shown through a comparison of *Keyu* and *Brind*. What was at stake in both cases was the spread of proportionality as a domestic head of review. As we saw, in *Brind*, it was dualism and parliamentary sovereignty that impeded an expansion of the scope of proportionality. This was no longer the case in *Keyu*. What underlay Lord Neuberger's refusal were considerations of institutional order. In his words: 'It would not be appropriate for a five-Justice panel of this court to accept, or indeed to reject, [the proportionality] argument, which potentially has implications which are profound in constitutional terms and very wide in applicable scope.'[165] Hence, Lord Neuberger considered that, if the proportionality claim were to succeed in the case at hand, the case should be reargued before a nine-judge panel.

This kind of reasoning, familiar to continental lawyers, is quite strange to the common law tradition, where panel selection became an issue of discussion only since the 2000s, in the debates concerning the creation of the Supreme Court.[166] The contrast with the adoption of the irrationality standard, which for half a century dominated English substantive review, is striking. The 1947 *Wednesbury* case was decided by the Court of Appeal and it is Lord Greene's dicta that are typically cited as authority.

Considerations of institutional legitimacy and expertise are opposed to the traditional image of the judge as an impartial referee concerned with rules of form and procedure. However, they fitted well with the new policy-making function of courts under the HRA. Initially, relevant issues were considered in judicial analysis under the concept of 'margin of discretion' or 'discretionary area of judgment'.[167] This spatial metaphor emerged together with the application of proportionality and was a reaction to the shift of power that it implied. The margin of discretion purported to reinstate a category of cases where the supremacy of Parliament was still preserved, and proportionality did not apply.[168] However, the defenders of proportionality perceived the margin of discretion as a residue of Diceyan analytical formalism and promoted the jettisoning of categories in judicial reasoning.[169] The spatial approach has been superseded by a more contextual approach to the intensity of review. Judicial review is 'calibrated' by reference to underlying

[165] Ibid, para. 132.

[166] On this, see UK Supreme Court, 'Selecting the Panel and the Size of the Court [Updated]', *UKSCBlog*, 4 October 2009, ukscblog.com.

[167] See *Kebeline*, p. 380, per Lord Hope.

[168] Hunt (2003), pp. 344 f.

[169] Kavanagh (2009), pp. 257 f. Contra Leigh (2002).

normative and institutional considerations, which are taken into account within the proportionality framework.[170]

Once the margin of appreciation category falls apart, the idea of parliamentary sovereignty does not completely vanish. The quest for democratic government that it once embodied simply has to be reformulated in rationalist terms in order to be taken into account.[171] This is the function of the concept of 'deference'. With few exceptions,[172] proportionality enthusiasts talk about a duty of deference in the adjudication of HRA rights. According to Rivers, deference is 'practically required and constitutionally appropriate';[173] Kavanagh talks about a duty of 'minimal deference' to the democratically elected branches of government;[174] and Hunt emphasises that 'contemporary public law needs a concept of due deference'.[175] Deference is omnipresent, because it is part of the new binding arrangements between law and politics in the common law constitution. It ensures that the judicial and the political process remain distinct. It expresses the idea that fundamental rights remain, at least partially, a political project left to democratic decision-making. Rivers talks about a 'joint project' of Parliament and judiciary to render rights effective.[176] Interestingly, a major contribution of common law scholars to the transnational proportionality theory has been the construction of an institutionally sensitive theory of judicial deference.[177]

Replacing Legal Limits with Institutional Ones. The defenders of the legal constitution have reacted with enthusiasm to the contextual approach that becomes dominant in English judicial review. In the words of Elliott:

> Sensibly deployed, [the contextual] approach is capable of forming the foundation of a mature, nuanced and sophisticated body of substantive-review doctrine – one that is the servant of principle, rather than a Procrustean bed based on bald categorisation, and one that reflects the full complexity of this area of the law in normative, institutional and constitutional terms.[178]

170 Elliott (2013).
171 Analysis inspired by Balkin (1990a).
172 Jowell (2003a); Allan (2006).
173 Rivers (2006), p. 207.
174 Kavanagh (2009), pp. 181 f.
175 Hunt (2003).
176 Rivers (2006), p. 207.
177 See also Chapter 1.2 in this volume.
178 Elliott (2015b).

The author also identifies the risks that contextualism entails, namely judicial overreach and unprincipled – thus unpredictable – judicial reasoning. Indeed, under the new contextual approach underpinning judicial deference, judicial intervention ceases to be a matter of what legal forms impose and becomes a choice of the courts, according to certain factors. As Kavanagh observes: '[D]eference is not a matter of the legal limits on jurisdiction, but rather a matter of judicial restraint out of respect for, and sensitivity to, the appropriate constitutional boundaries between the branches of government.'[179] Legal limits are replaced by institutional ones and are defined by courts themselves. This made Lord Hoffmann criticise the deference metaphor for its 'overtones of servility, or perhaps gracious concession' in *ProLife Alliance*.[180]

The contextual approach considerably reduces the difference in the institutional functions of judiciary and legislature. *Nicklinson* is very illustrative in this respect. In this case, despite the large margin of appreciation left to national authorities under the convention concerning the ban on assisted suicide, the majority of the Supreme Court judges considered that the issue was one for domestic courts to decide and involved the balancing of the competing values at stake. According to Lord Neuberger, President of the Supreme Court at the time, sensitive political and moral issues should not necessarily be left to Parliament because judges may be better placed to decide on them.[181] In his view, although it is not for the Supreme Court to decide the correct legislative scheme and to define its details, it is the responsibility of judges to determine a number of feasible and proportionate schemes among which Parliament has to choose.[182] The majority of the judges held that the prohibition of assisted suicide was contrary to the right to private life. However, they refrained from issuing a declaration of incompatibility, since a bill on the matter was pending before Parliament. Lord Neuberger observed that 'it would be institutionally inappropriate at this juncture' to do otherwise.[183]

Nicklinson is a much-discussed decision that upsets the previous understanding of the distribution of competences, even under the HRA. Yet, it seems that, for the moment, it remains an exceptional

[179] Kavanagh (2009), p. 177.
[180] *R* v. *British Broadcasting Corporation, ex parte ProLife Alliance* [2003] UKHL 23 (HL, 15 May 2003), para. 75. See also Jowell (2003b).
[181] *Nicklinson*, para. 98.
[182] Ibid, para. 107.
[183] Ibid, para. 116.

case. Since its issuance, Parliament re-examined the legislation concerning assisted suicide and decided to maintain the prohibition, considering that it sufficiently served important, legitimate aims. In a recent affair on the issue, the High Court and the Supreme Court refused to re-examine the compatibility of English law with Article 8 ECHR.[184] In this way, the English judges avoided openly declaring an institutional war against Parliament. That being said, *Nicklinson* is an example of the potential conflict between the Supreme Court and the political branches of government. The Supreme Court increasingly resembles a constitutional court, and traditional common law doctrines seem incapable of ensuring institutional stability any longer. In this context, proportionality is progressively established as an overarching constitutional principle that guides the evolution of judicial review.[185]

***

Proportionality in English public law has been perceived as a transfer from continental Europe. Initially, it did not capture the English lawyerly imagination. As a scientific theory imported from France, it failed in justifying cases including *Bromley* and the extension of judicial powers that they entailed. Indeed, proportionality has expressed a way of thinking completely strange to the analytical formalism that since Dicey had dominated English legal thought. Its recognition as a principle has found its obstacle in the economy of the common law. Proportionality has expressed the belief in a substantive truth that transcends legal adjudication, a myth of law as science and of the judge as a conscientious scientist in search for a transcendent truth. Thus, it has been strange to the traditionally game-like nature of the judicial procedure, which remains impartial, no matter how fundamental the interests or principles at stake. Proportionality's spread was long perceived as antithetical to the

[184] R v. *Secretary of State for Justice, ex parte Conway* [2017] EWHC 2447 (HC, 5 October 2017); [2018] UKSC B1 (SC, 27 November 2018).

[185] See recent case law concerning access to justice: *UNISON* (SC, 26 July 2017); *R* v. *The Upper Tribunal, ex parte Cart*; *R* v. *The Upper Tribunal (Immigration and Asylum Chamber) and Secretary of State for the Home Department, ex parte MR (Pakistan)* [2011] UKSC 28 (SC, 22 June 2011); *R* v. *Investigatory Powers Tribunal and Others, ex parte Privacy International* [2019] UKSC 22 (SC, 15 May 2019), esp. paras. 85 f. See also Bell (2019).

The *Miller (No. 2)*, case has been interpreted by some as an application of the principle of proportionality, even though the Supreme Court did not use proportionality language in this case. See *R* v. *The Prime Minister, ex parte Miller*; *Cherry and Others* v. *Advocate General for Scotland* [2019] UKSC 41 (SC, 24 September 2019); Sendut (2019); McGaughey (2019).

formalism and pragmatism that has traditionally permeated English legal thought.

Precisely due to its antithetical relationship with the Diceyan tradition, proportionality has been promoted by certain judges and barristers in search of a domestic constitution that would gather together the bits and pieces of English administrative law. It soon ceased to designate a simple head of judicial review and became a judicial method or even an idea applied through domestic concepts and heads. In this way, proportionality expressed the reorientation of domestic legal discourse towards a more rationalist approach to legal reasoning, which focuses on substance and values rather than reasoning patterns and forms. Proportionality gave new meaning to common law concepts and institutions. It reflected the emergence of a new legacy of normative scholarship which participates in the production of coherent legal knowledge and is increasingly quoted in judicial decisions. English scholars are increasingly akin to the French *faiseurs de systèmes*.

The reception of proportionality under the HRA has furthered these evolutions, but at the same time it has contained them within the 'Diceyan prison'. For the moment, proportionality is applied as a head of review, only insofar as Parliament has wanted so. However, in this crucial constitutional moment, it is the abandonment of the analytical tradition and of the principle of parliamentary sovereignty itself that is at stake. Domestic lawyers have to choose between the legal and the political constitution. While proportionality and its fundamental rights baggage conquer English law, the Diceyan legacy and the faith in the political process that underpinned it resurface in doctrines of margin of discretion and deference. Rationalism and contextualism become dominant and legal limits seem unable to ensure the avoidance of institutional conflicts any longer. In this context, proportionality is progressively established as an overarching constitutional principle that guides the evolution of English judicial review.

7

Searching for a 'Species of Sympathetic Magic'

In contrast to the insular English tradition, proportionality never met resistance in Greek legal thought. However, its enthusiastic embracement by Greek lawyers has defied the actual practice of judicial review. While proportionality is venerated as a fundamental rights principle, it failed in establishing a new paradigm of rights and judicial review. In order to make sense of proportionality in this context, I propose to take its meaning as a transplant seriously. Nelken observes that, in many cases, legal transfers do not fit an existing social situation, but rather correspond to an imagined local future.[1] This is the case when their goal is social change, namely, when they are commonly perceived by legal actors as legal transplants. In this chapter, I argue that, like other legal transfers in Greek law, proportionality has enjoyed a value in itself, as part of an imported constitutional civilisation. As such, it has been expected to bring about legal and even social change. In other words, proportionality has expressed domestic lawyers' belief in the possibility of law to *act on* society, 'in what is almost a species of sympathetic magic'.[2]

The spread of proportionality in Greece fits well the transplant narrative, but this tells us little about the stakes that domestic lawyers have attached to proportionality's use (Section 7.1). While proportionality emerged in this context as a fundamental rights principle, it did not bring with it a new perception of those rights. Hence, its dynamic has been constrained in the binding arrangements of Greek public law (Section 7.2). The shift between the theory of proportionality and its use in judicial practice has been part of its local meaning as a transplant. Indeed, the long process of transplantation of proportionality has represented an equally long process of acculturation of the Greek polity to a European constitutional civilisation, finally accomplished with the 2001 reform. Ever since, proportionality is

[1] Nelken (2003), p. 457.
[2] Nelken (2007), p. 118.

hegemonic in Greek law (Section 7.3). As a kind of European science, proportionality replaces virtually every method of legal reasoning and transcends the limits of the constitution (Section 7.4). Its use purports to establish a whole new vision of the Greek polity as modern and European. However, this vision does not always correspond to local lawyers' worldview (Section 7.5).

7.1 Proportionality in Greek Public Law: A Transplant

The Success of Proportionality. At first glance, it seems that the spread of proportionality in Greece, as happened in England, follows Watson's legal transplant model. 'Success' would seem a proper term to characterising the trajectory of the principle in Greek law. Proportionality, first somewhat timidly recognised in certain judicial decisions and scholarly writings, was soon proclaimed as a constitutional principle in case law and was even explicitly entrenched as such in 2001. Domestic lawyers have perceived proportionality as a fundamental rights principle, as is the one applied in Karlsruhe. They think of it as a pronged structure for legal reasoning, they are enthusiastic about its entrenchment and they consider it as a correct method for adjudication. In their writings, they have never forgotten to point out proportionality's foreign roots and to refer to German theory and practice. Hence, the form and function of proportionality for Greek lawyers is very close to the theory developed by their German colleagues. The traditional structures of Greek public law discourse have not impeded the 'triumphant march' of proportionality in this context.

Of course, the Watsonian model must be adjusted to accommodate the influence of other European jurisdictions as well. Indeed, the transfer of proportionality in Greek law has not been a two-player phenomenon, simply involving the introduction of a German principle in Greece. Scholars have often mentioned European case law. The application of the principle in other countries, especially France, has also been important.[3] After all, we must bear in mind that 'no transplant is an island, and that complex modes of interaction color the process'.[4] Nevertheless, this does not discredit the fact that proportionality appeared in Greek law as a transplant and that its content in

[3] See, for example, Kapsali (2006).
[4] Cohn (2010), p. 584.

the minds of Greek lawyers has been defined by reference to its application in other jurisdictions.

Proportionality and Greek Law-Making Elites. Watson's approach also indicates some possible explanations for the success of proportionality in this content. Greek lawyers participate in the political or judicial classes with the power to produce legal change, and perfectly correspond to the law-making elites described by this author. Certain personalities have particularly promoted the spread of proportionality in domestic law. For instance, Pararas, constitutional law professor and prominent member of the Council of State, was one of the first to study proportionality as a constitutional principle.[5] He was *Rapporteur* in some milestone proportionality decisions.[6] Having completed part of his studies in Paris, Pararas was prolific in the subject of European human rights and, despite some initial hesitations, he was enthusiastic about the 2001 reform.[7] He has actively participated in the editing of *Δικαιώματα του Ανθρώπου* [*Human Rights*], an influential journal in which many studies on proportionality have been published. As a judge, he also participated ad hoc in *Tourkiki Enosi Xanthis*, a case in which the Strasbourg court famously concluded that Greece had violated the principle of proportionality.[8] Pararas is one among numerous influential personalities who promoted proportionality in the domestic context, others being Skouris, Contiades and Venizelos, who was the main inspirer of the 2001 constitutional amendment.

The image of an elite law-producing group is reinforced by the seclusion of legal discourse from society, which Alivizatos has called the 'Greek misfortune'.[9] This feature makes legal transplants 'socially easy' in this context.[10] It has long been apparent, even in the language in which lawyers expressed themselves. Until the 1980s, legal writings employed an artificial idiom called *katharevousa* (*καθαρεύουσα*, meaning 'purifying').[11] This language, resembling Ancient Greek more than the modern-day language used in everyday life, was deemed to 'purify' cultural practices from oriental relics of the Ottoman occupation. Its use in legal writings and official state documents reproduced and amplified

5 Pararas (1976), p. 350.
6 StE (Pl.) 2112/1984 and StE 3682/1986.
7 Pararas (2001, 2003, 2011, 2012b).
8 ECtHR, *Tourkiki Enosi Xanthis* v. *Greece*, 27 March 2008, no. 26698/05.
9 Alivizatos (2001a), p. 96.
10 Watson (1974), p. 95.
11 Drossos (1996), p. 116.

the chasm between social practices and the image of the society that lawyers and state officials held. While *katharevousa* ceased to be the official language of the Greek state in 1982, it continued to be used in judicial decisions and other legal texts for some years. But even the progressive abandonment of this idiom did not bring about the appropriation of law by society. Greek legal discourse has a particularly technical, scientific tone, which is also apparent in the writings on proportionality.

Comparative Law as a Legal Formant. Greek law-making elites have often studied abroad, and are well aware of foreign academic debates, which they subsequently teach in universities and reproduce in Parliament, in judicial deliberations or on media panels. Transplantation is a common method of legal change in this context, in contrast to the English case. Since the beginnings of its existence, the modern Greek state has been constructed in the light of foreign models. The Greek Constitution of 1832 followed its Belgian and French counterparts at the time[12] and the Greek Council of State was instituted under the French model of the *Conseil d'Etat.*[13] Foreign influence is also easy to detect in judicial decisions. Domestic courts often follow the reasoning structures or substantive solutions adopted by prestigious foreign courts. Lately, Greek judges do not hesitate to explicitly consider foreign legal solutions,[14] cite foreign decisions[15] and even employ foreign legal terms.[16] In this context, comparative law is a 'formant' of legal scientific knowledge; it constitutes what local legal actors perceive as correct law. Transplants are thought of as an evolution of legal science.[17]

Proportionality certainly benefitted from the openness of Greek legal discourse abroad. It has also been perceived as some kind of correct law, as recurrent reference to reasoning 'errors', 'successful' interpretations or 'fatal' judicial mistakes in relevant analyses reveals.[18] The reception of proportionality was not perceived as a 'spectacular innovation', but rather as 'a natural and necessary evolution, maturation and perfecting'

[12] Manessis (1959).
[13] Gaudemet (1998).
[14] StE 2110/2003, para. 6
[15] StE (Pl.) 460/2013 *ΕΔΔΔ* 2013, pp. 121, 445, paras. 12, 14.
[16] For example, in decision StE (Pl.) 668/2012, p. 384, some members of the Council of State refer to the German concept of '*Existenzminimum*' (para. 36).
[17] On such tendencies observed in constitutional transfers during the nineteenth century, see Drossos (1996), pp. 39 f.
[18] See, for example, Pararas (1976), p. 350; Kassimatis (1977), pp. 627–8.

of the Council of State's scrutiny.[19] Strikingly, in contrast to their French and English colleagues, Greek public lawyers did not at all object to the deconstruction of traditional judicial review distinctions that proportionality potentially implied. More generally, the rise in power of the judiciary that proportionality enhanced was perceived as 'an irreversible historical tendency of the post-industrial society'. Hence, discussion on whether it was wanted or not was dismissed as 'unnecessary'.[20]

The Insufficiency of the Transplant Metaphor. While the transplant metaphor accounts well for the spread of proportionality in Greece, it only makes sense of a small part of the use of proportionality language in this context. Indeed, the analysis in Chapter 4 has shown that even though proportionality has generally been thought of as a pronged framework for the adjudication of fundamental rights, similar to the one applied in Germany, this structure and function are typically forgotten when it comes to the application of the principle by courts. The transplant account proves incapable of explaining this shift between theory and practice and the fragmented and inconsistent application of proportionality by domestic courts. One can doubt the utility of an approach which only makes sense of certain instances of legal reasoning, the rest being rejected as irrational practices related to obscure socio-cultural characteristics. How to make sense of proportionality in Greek public law? What are the expectations attached to it in this context? Has its transfer achieved those expectations? And if not, why is proportionality so important to Greek public lawyers? In order to identify the stakes of proportionality in Greek law, we must return to its 'birth' during the 1980s.

7.2 A Fundamental Rights Principle Without Fundamental Rights: Constrained by the Binding Arrangements of Greek Public Law

The 'Birth' of Proportionality. While proportionality had already emerged during the 1970s, and had even been applied by the Council of State, the 2112/1984 decision brought about something new in its use. Domestic lawyers talked about the 'birth' of proportionality in constitutional law.[21] In an article dedicated to the matter, Skouris, subsequently president of the ECJ, argued that the decision 'opened the way' to the

19 Kontogiorga (1989b), p. 923.
20 Manitakis (1990a), p. 21.
21 Kontogiorga (1989a), p. 9; Orfanoudakis (2003), p. 79.

introduction of the principle in Greek public law.[22] Previous uses of the term were simply forgotten. The change was expressed in the new terminology employed by the Council itself. Instead of referring to 'relativity' or 'proportion', as it had done in previous cases, the judges used the term 'proportionality', which, before the 1970s, was absent not only from domestic legal discourse, but from the Greek language altogether. This is quite impressive for a court that used to write in *katharevousa*. Where did the novelty of the 2112/1984 decision lie?

While the Council of State did not cite the neglected cases of the 1970s, it did refer to previous case law in its application of proportionality. It cited decision 4036/1979, in which, surprisingly, it had not used proportionality terminology at all.[23] Instead, what was relevant in this decision was that the council had affirmed the constitutional rank of professional freedom and had attached its protection to Article 5(1) of the constitution.[24] Since the enactment of the 1975 Constitution, scholars had been reticent in attributing direct normative effect to this provision due to its vagueness and indeterminacy.[25] In the 1979 decision, professional freedom had been generously defined by the council, as encompassing both the choice and the exercise a certain profession. As far as liberal professions were concerned, the judges had stated that Article 5 also protected the freedom to choose the location where the exercise of the profession would take place.

Still, Article 5(1) not only allowed for a broad definition of the scope of the rights protected therein. It empowered equally broad legislative limitations on these rights, in pursuit of other constitutional values, the protection of the rights of others or good morals. If this article was to place concrete constraints on Parliament, a denser normative framework was needed. In decision 4036/1979, the council held that restrictions on professional freedom should be 'defined in a general and objective way' and 'justified by important reasons of general public or social interest'; they 'should not lead to a substantial weakening of the constitutionally protected right' and 'should constitute an exception' to the principle of professional freedom.[26] It is this last point that decision 2112/1984 replaced with an application of the principle of proportionality.

[22] Skouris (1987), p. 773.

[23] StE (Pl.) 4036/1979 *APM* 1980, p. 327.

[24] Ibid; StE 630/1979 *ToΣ* 1980, p. 153. See also Skouris (1987), pp. 776 f.

[25] Manessis (1978), pp. 114 f.; Manessis (2007), pp. 529 f.

[26] StE (Pl.) 4036/1979.

Proportionality then was closely intertwined with the judicial enforcement of a concrete normative content for constitutional rights. Its application implied an impact-based evaluation of legislation by reference to rights. Scholars immediately perceived proportionality as a guarantee of the essence of rights or of their effective exercise.[27] Its function was to ensure the exceptional character of rights' restrictions.[28] In this sense, proportionality was very akin to what German scholars call *Schranke-Schranke*, a phrase translated and often used by Greek proportionality scholars (*περιορισμός των περιορισμών*) meaning 'limitation on limitations' on constitutional rights.[29] The novelty of the 1984 decision thus did not lie in the application of proportionality or in the entrenchment of constitutional rights. It lay in the concrete connection that the Council of State effected between the two.

Greek Lawyers' Expectations of Proportionality. Concrete connection to constitutional rights was a major feature of the new conceptual content of proportionality. This is what differentiated this new version from the vague requirement of equity that proportionality had represented before. Kontogiorga observed that the 1984 decision 'promoted and elevated proportionality from an empirical to a legal principle'.[30] For the first time in this decision, proportionality acquired a concrete form and function in Greek public law. Its constitutional status, affirmed already in the early applications of the principle during the 1970s, produced concrete legal effect and actually led to the disapplication of legislation. For the first time, proportionality was articulated and applied as a requirement concerning the outcomes of legislation. The 'birth' of proportionality meant its emergence as a legal transplant, namely as a concrete, imported judicial tool that was purported to serve rights adjudication.

Hence, with decision 2112/1984, proportionality also acquired a user: the judge. The institutional implications of its explicit recognition were immediately noticed by scholars commenting on the 1984 decision. The power of the judge as against the political branches was affirmed.[31] Scholars pointed out that proportionality allowed for creative judicial interpretation (*διάπλαση*) and implied a change of paradigm in Greek judicial methods, which were henceforth to be guided by the values

[27] Gerontas (1983). In the same vein, see Dagtoglou (2004), p. 135.
[28] Tsatsos (1988), p. 245; see also Dalakouras (1993), p. 24.
[29] Orfanoudakis (2003), pp. 16 f., and literature cited.
[30] Kontogiorga (1989b), p. 906.
[31] Skouris (1987), p. 778.

undergirding the legal order.[32] Proportionality, by imposing 'relevance', in the sense of reasonableness, between legislative means and constitutionally acceptable ends, was expected to establish the constitution as a central point of reference in legal practice.[33] It was expected to bring about a shift of the attention, from the interpretation of constitutional rules, to the realisation of constitutional values.[34]

Therefore, the spread of proportionality in Greek public law should be read in the background of the timid interpretative turn in Greek legal literature during the 1990s. This theoretical tendency was mainly expressed in the writings of Manitakis, an influential public law professor. In a book published in 1994, Manitakis defended an interpretative approach close to that of Dworkin and Zagrebelsky. His goal was to 'reconnect Law to Morality and social values', thus to incorporate into legal technique empirical and normative features that, according to the positivist orthodoxy, were external to it.[35] In his work, the ideal of a state ruled by law, apart from a procedural and formal function, also assumes a substantive one, protecting minorities from the abuses of the majority and mandating public intervention in order to protect the most vulnerable. The judge, from a 'servant of the law' becomes 'a guarantor of constitutional rights and a mediator of [social] conflicts',[36] a 'central figure' of the contemporary constitutional state.[37]

The Infelicity of Proportionality. Still, theoretical remarks on proportionality and the role of the judiciary were not combined with a coherent theory of fundamental rights. Domestic public lawyers did not pay much attention to the structural implications of proportionality. In his comment on the 1984 decision, Skouris mentioned that in Germany the principle of proportionality was related to the 'theory of stages of protection' (*Stufentheorie*).[38] However, he observed that the Council of State's reasoning did not follow this theory. One of the rare scholars who provided us with a theory of rights at the time of the emergence of proportionality is Dagtoglou, an influential public and European lawyer

[32] Voutsakis (1990), p. 205.
[33] Manitakis (1999), pp. 186 f.
[34] See also Voutsakis (1990); Manitakis (1990b), pp. 5–6.
[35] Manitakis (1994), Introduction.
[36] Manitakis (1999).
[37] Ibid, p. 184.
[38] Skouris (1987).

with German academic roots.[39] However, this author adopted an ultra-liberal view of the state as a threat to the individual, in which proportionality and balancing have a limited role.[40] Greek public lawyers' lack of attention to the structure of constitutional rights was noticed by Dimitropoulos in his study on the spread and implications of another German theory, the *Drittwirkung*, in Greek public law.[41]

Proportionality was 'born' as a fundamental rights principle without a fundamental rights background. While it contributed to the multiplication of constitutional rights claims and the diffusion of the constitution in everyday life, it did not lead to systematisation of judicial review methods under a coherent rights theory. Its spread did not lead to the establishment of a 'total' constitutional order, but to the constitution's vulgarisation. It only increased the 'dust of its numerous trivial and fragmented invocations'.[42] Hence, proportionality frustrated the expectations that domestic lawyers attached to it. Some years after the enunciation of proportionality as a constitutional principle, its function was limited to that of a manifest error test in decision 1149/1988 on medical centres.[43] This conceptual mutation of proportionality was underpinned by a perception of constitutional rights that was completely different from the one underpinning decision 2112/1984. While in 1984, the Council of State had introduced a concrete connection between rights and proportionality, in 1988 proportionality was applied as a free-standing standard. Its application was disconnected from the scope of Article 5, which was categorically defined.[44]

Categorical reasoning is pervasive in judicial review. Greek jurisprudence traditionally lacks the generosity professed by proportionality enthusiasts and observed in Karlsruhe case law.[45] This is because rights are not imagined as optimisation requirements, but as freedoms, as

[39] On this author's work, see Drossos (1996), pp. 555 f. Dagtoglou was also among the first systematically to analyse proportionality as a constitutional principle and as a general principle of European law.

[40] Dagtoglou (2005), pp. 138 f.

[41] Dimitropoulos (1981). In the absence of Greek literature on the matter, this scholar cited German scholars.

[42] Drossos (1996, p. 498) makes this remark for the spread of constitutional rights language.

[43] See Part I, Chapter 4.2.

[44] StE 1149/1988.

[45] For example, for a long time, the Greek supreme courts refused to include pecuniary rights to the protective scope of the right to property. See the famous decision ES 28/1994 *ΔEN* 1994, p. 439. This case law was abandoned after ECtHR criticism, in AP (Pl.) 40/1998 *APM* 1999, p. 46.

negative requirements of abstention. As Yannakopoulos neatly observes, the 1975 Constitution has functioned as a 'constitution of limits' on the exercise of public power.[46] This means that constitutional values are not thought of as goals of the constitutional order, which require realisation by public authorities, but as limits imposed on the competence of public actors. This has ensured that judges do not intrude into the setting of public policy goals. Judicial review only sanctions 'the transgression of the extreme rational limits' of public authorities' discretion.[47]

This was expressed in the application of proportionality. Indeed, what long impeded its use as an impact-based test was the perception of the judges as to the limits of their own competence and, most importantly, the distinction between expediency and legality. In decision 1149/1988, the court stated that 'the question of whether more expedient, namely less restrictive, measures' are available is a question of expediency and not of legality that exceeds the competence of 'the judge of legality'.[48] Proportionality, rather than imposing concrete substantive outcomes on legislative action, concerned the distribution of competences between the judiciary and the political branches of government. The function of proportionality as a manifest error test resembled that of the *Wednesbury* unreasonableness standard in English law. Proportionality corresponded to a standard of review and not to a standard of constitutional legality.[49] In subsequent case law, it was applied even when no constitutional rights were invoked by the claimants.[50]

Therefore, proportionality was long deprived of radical potential. Its spread did not bring about the rise in power of the judiciary. Contrary to the dominant narrative, domestic courts have rarely used proportionality language in their activist decisions. In spite of its commonly shared content among Greek public lawyers, until the late 1990s, proportionality conserved the institutional status quo and expressed the binding arrangements between local legal discourse and its political context. Far from indicating the advent of the rational human rights paradigm and of a culture of justification, the spread of proportionality in Greece expresses the myths that underlie local legal thought.

[46] Yannakopoulos (2008).

[47] AP 1094/1987 *ΔΕΝ* 1988, p. 412.

[48] StE 1149/1988 *ΤοΣ* 1988, p. 324.

[49] On the distinction between standards of review and standards of legality, see Hickman (2010), pp. 99 f.

[50] StE 268/1993 *ΑΡΜ* 1993, p. 180.

Constrained by Modern Greek Myths. In Greek legal thought, as in France and in Germany, law is deemed to preserve certain core substantive values. Thus, one observes a fusion between substantive values and legal form in this context. However, the justification of Greek judicial decisions cannot be compared to the transparent reasoning that one finds in Karlsruhe and hardly resembles an instance of Socratic contestation. Rather similarly to the French context, Greek judicial practice is characterised by an excision of value-laden argumentation from judicial reasoning. The definition of the substantive content of the law and the constitution in judicial decisions follows the methods of an alleged legal science and is akin to a syllogism composed of long phrases. In this sense, judicial reasoning in Greece is characterised by the dogmatism that has also been observed in the French context. Judges affirm the value choices embodied in legislation as if they were positive facts. Dogmatism is apparent in the Greek version of proportionality. Indeed, be it as a standard of justification, a standard of equity or a manifest error standard, proportionality does not contest in principle the value-laden choices of the primary decision-maker. Instead, by adding a particularly formal-technical tone to rights-based reasoning, proportionality expresses and enhances a tendency towards the administrativisation of constitutional law.[51]

Proportionality does not involve balancing of competing constitutional values. As in English law, balancing has traditionally been perceived as a method for setting policy objectives and not for judicial decision-making. In judicial decisions, balancing has usually served the reconstruction of the policy-making reasoning of Parliament in a constitutionally legitimate way, and not the explication of the judicial reasoning itself. Hence, rather than a judicial method balancing has been a ritual and has invariably led to the approval of legislative intentions. This was noticed by Pavlopoulos, who criticised the deferent attitude of the Council of State. This author (later president of the republic) pointed out that balancing served the legitimation of legislative value choices, by presenting them as an instance of reconciliation between competing constitutional values. Pavlopoulos concluded that balancing finally led the court to interpret the constitution in the light of legal statutes, and not the inverse.[52]

[51] Perju (2012) identifies this effect of proportionality (which he calls ‘administratization’).
[52] Pavlopoulos (1988).

Since balancing only has an exceptional character in case law, the rare instances in which judges have engaged themselves in balancing are noted as instances of judicial activism. This is most notably the case with the Council of State's environmental case law during the 1990s.[53] In application of the principle of 'sustainable growth' (*βιώσιμη ανάπτυξη*), judges sometimes took to an impact-based balancing of the protection of the environment with other constitutional values and substituted their own view for that of public authorities on the matter. However, judicial balancing in this context was not combined with the formulation of the relevant questions in proportionality and fundamental rights terms. Instead, stringent application of the principle of sustainable growth was based on a more general theoretical construction on the 'sustainable state', mainly developed by the judges themselves.[54] Written in a scientific tone and replete with analogies to biology and *les sciences exactes*, this theory echoes corporatist accounts of the state developed in Germany and France almost a century before.[55] In this sense, it is very different from the Alexyan view of law as an instance of practical reasoning.

Interestingly, since the 2001 constitutional reform, the manifest disproportionality standard replaced the principle of sustainable growth. Ever since, whenever manifest disproportionality has been used to contest the balancing effectuated by public authorities in this field, it has provoked suspicion among domestic lawyers.[56] Ensuring judicial restraint on the matter was indeed one of the objectives of the 2001 reform, which explicitly qualified the assessments in the field of environmental protection as 'technical' and governed by 'the rules of science'.[57]

Following its French model, Greek judicial review is dominated by a voluntarist perception of legal decision-making. Parliament's policy choices are deemed to be untouchable. As Stratilatis put it, 'the aim of the legislator is perceived as a given, as a non-contestable constitutional

[53] StE 53/1993 *ΤΝΠΔΣΑ*; StE (Pl.) 2537/1996 *ΤΝΠΔΣΑ*; AP (Pl.) 13/1999 *ΕλλΔνη* 1999, p. 753. This case law is the only known instance of consistent judicial policy in opposition to the will of the political branches of government. Scholars consider the environmental jurisprudence of the Council of State as an instance of judicial 'activism', even when they affirm its 'strict methodological rigour'. See, for example, Alivizatos (2001a), p. 52.

[54] Dekleris (1996); Karamanof (2011).

[55] Champeil-Desplats (2016), pp. 71 f.

[56] Most notably, StE (Pl.) 613/2002 *NoB* 2002, p. 1972, para. 7. The decision was criticised by Gerapetritis (2006), pp. 272 f.

[57] Article 24 of the 1975/1986/2001 Constitution.

"end in itself".[58] The 1975 Constitution has traditionally been thought of as a text that is 'open' to the realisation of any political ideology parliamentary majorities adopt.[59] Hence, it has sometimes sufficed to Parliament to invoke a 'more general public interest' in order to justify the circumvention of the most precise constitutional requirements.[60] Typically, controversy in judicial opinions or in lawyerly argumentation does not so much concern values, as the Alexyan model of proportionality would want it, but rather the construction of the public interest aim of legislation. The major criterion for assessing the validity of legal solutions in Greece is the possibility for them to be presented as the result of the presumed legislative will.[61] It is indicative that, like in the French context, the application of proportionality is often analysed into a *réserve d'interprétation* of the impugned legislation.[62]

Voluntarism expresses Greek lawyers' tendency to idealise public authorities, and especially Parliament. Manitakis observes that the state:

> [A]s a Subject possesses its own reason and its own will and does not decide in its real capacity as a public power, but in another capacity, as a father or a god, a protector or a tyrant.[63]

Hence, even though judicial review is a secular practice in this context, the Greek system of judicial review is considerably weak.[64] Courts have shown restraint when it comes to important policy decisions. Idealisation is manifest in the constant personification of the political branches of government in legal writings (the Administration and the Legislator are among the protagonists of Greek legal mythopoeia). In the absence of *commissaires du gouvernement* before the Council of State, it is the authority party in the proceedings that represents the public interest. This considerably undermines the fair character of the judicial process and brings it close to a ritual. As Lévi-Strauss, explains, a ritual is like a 'favoured instance of a game': while it is 'played' according to specific rules, its

[58] Stratilatis (2001), p. 532.
[59] Drossos (1996), p. 356.
[60] StE 400/1986 *APM* 1987, p. 430. See Dagtoglou (1986).
[61] For an illustrative example, see decision AED 36/1990 *Δ/NH* 1993, p. 552 (Supreme Special Court), which concerned the proportionality of electoral representation. What was contested in this case was not the 'mathematical' rule that proportionality implied, but whether Parliament had wanted to strictly respect this rule.
[62] See, for example, StE 4050–1/1990.
[63] Manitakis (1994), pp. 116–17, cited by Yannakopoulos (2013), pp. 139–40.
[64] Kaidatzis (2013), p. 29. See also Kaidatzis (2010, 2011).

specificity lies in the fact that it 'results in a particular type of equilibrium between the two sides'.[65]

A fundamental rights principle without a fundamental rights background, a strong judicial weapon without a strong judiciary: how to make sense of the gap between the triumph of proportionality in legal theory and its application in practice? Why is proportionality still revered by Greek public lawyers while its application has frustrated their expectations?

7.3 Taking the Transplant Meaning Seriously: Proportionality as Part of an Imported Constitutional Civilisation

Proportionality in a Heaven of Legal Transplants. In order to understand the articulation of the different uses of proportionality by Greek public lawyers, it is necessary to take its meaning as a transplant seriously. Indeed, infelicity is not particular to proportionality but seems to be a more general characteristic of public law theories imported from abroad. Once imported, transplants are confined to the 'heaven' of concepts[66] used in Greek legal scholarship, which local lawyers like to call legal theory or legal science (*νομική θεωρία, νομική επιστήμη*). Legal practice is much more nuanced than the ideal scientific concepts described in the literature. It is simply perceived as their 'imperfect and deformed' application.[67] In contrast to their French colleagues, Greek public lawyers are not much interested in systematisation of domestic judicial *methods*. In contrast to English lawyers too, they are generally indifferent to the *patterns* of domestic judicial reasoning, even though some important authors have been supreme judges.

Greek legal science does not owe its authority to any kind of connection to practice. Neither does it owe this authority to its internal coherence, as does the conceptual heaven described by von Jhering. Rather, what is important is the connection to foreign debates and theories. Greek scholars have often been taken by over-detailed translations of foreign academic analyses that have no echo or relevance in the domestic context.[68] The reduction of academic work to a process of translation

[65] Lévi-Strauss (1966), p. 30. The author gives the example of the Gahuku-Gama, who played football (a game), but who played as many matches as necessary for the opposite teams to reach the same score (they played it as a rite).

[66] Von Jhering (1985).

[67] Ibid, p. 802.

[68] Drossos (1996), p. 175.

marks Greek public law discourse since the beginnings of the modern Greek state. In the words of Kalligas, a prominent legal scholar and politician of the mid-nineteenth century:

> [W]hatever was translated was immediately considered Greek too, even though only the translator and his colleagues understood it. [Greek constitutional scholars] translated [foreign] constitutions and regimes and could not understand why they were not applied in practice, when no error existed in grammar or syntax.[69]

Translation has been a major feature of the domestic theory of proportionality too. Proportionality scholars have often exclusively cited foreign academic analyses and debates and referred to the foreign terms that designate the legal concepts that they use.[70]

Hence, the use of proportionality language in Greece makes much more sense as a reference to *foreign* theoretical developments. Proportionality was applied in urban planning, expropriation and labour law during the 1970s because it is in *these* domains that it had found application in other European systems. It was perceived as a general constitutional principle even before its explicit entrenchment because *this* is the status that German constitutional lawyers attributed to it. It was perceived as a three-pronged balancing test because *this* was its structure in the jurisprudence of the GFCC. It was venerated as a guarantee of the protection of constitutional rights because *this* had been its function in other jurisdictions. Its application as a manifest error test was not problematic because *this* was the way proportionality was applied in the French and the European legal orders. It reflected a post-industrial state and society because *this* was the representation that other European societies had of themselves.

Reference to foreign theories has attributed conceptual unity to proportionality, despite the plurality of forms and functions in which it has vested in the domestic sphere. Decisions 2112/1984 and 1149/1988 have often been cited by domestic courts simultaneously, no matter the version of proportionality applied in the judicial reasoning that followed. In scholarship too, the conception of proportionality was unitary. Like a mythical figure, proportionality was able to mean different things and take various forms. From a substantive point of view, it has corresponded to a universal value of equity or reasonableness, which was 'as old as the notion of humanism'.[71] In this sense,

69 Kalligas (1842), p. 29, cited by Drossos (1996), pp. 175–6.

70 See, for example, Kassimatis (1977); for a more recent study, see Anthopoulos (2001).

71 Kontogiorga (1989b), p. 893.

proportionality was rediscovered in the writings of legendary authorities like Aristotle.[72] Proportionality was even attributed a name in the *katharevousa*: *ήττον επαχθές μέτρο*, meaning 'less onerous means'. At the level of constitutional technique, however, proportionality's correct content was defined by reference to its application in jurisdictions perceived as more advanced. This content was transplanted as such in the domestic context. Its inconsistent application by domestic courts was perceived as a deviant Greek particularity.

In other words, the shift between the theory of proportionality and its application in practice was *part of the domestic meaning of proportionality as a transplant*. It expressed the perception of other European legal orders as models for the Greek legal order and as representations of its locally imagined future. While proportionality did not bring about the expected results, it had a value in itself for Greek public lawyers. Even more than offering a method for the correct application of constitutional provisions, reference to foreign constitutional systems attributed a particular prestige to domestic constitutional law and its agents. Proportionality was part of 'a style that highlights, magnifies, overflows'.[73]

Importing a European Constitutional Civilisation. Proportionality was not an isolated transplant. As the importation of the *Drittwirkung* or Skouris' reference to the *Dreistufentheorie* show, a heteroclite *bricolage* of foreign theories, usually of German origin, was being fashioned since the enactment of the 1975 Constitution, and especially during the 1980s.[74] The constitution itself was a fruit of the influence of the post-war European rights discourse. Declaring the rejection of the nationalist *junta*, it 'reconnected Greece to the European constitutional tradition'.[75] Alivizatos observes that 'for the Greek constitutional scholars, 1974 was what 1945 had been for their European colleagues'.[76] A whole legal science was thus imported from more experienced courts to guide domestic judges and other public authorities in the application of the new constitutional text in conformity with the European constitutionalist paradigm.

72 See, for example, Kontogiorga (1989b), p. 891; Gerapetritis (2006), p. 187; Beis (1999), pp. 469 f.

73 Saripolos (1851), p. 47, cited by Drossos (1996), p. 129.

74 This tendency is not only a Greek particularity, but has been observed in other contexts as well. See Geertz (1983), pp. 218 f.

75 Alivizatos (2001a), p. 174.

76 Ibid, p. 23.

The development of supranational rights orders, and of the ECHR in particular, established European fundamental rights as part of a 'constitutional civilisation' (*συνταγματικός πολιτισμός*) that was seen as a model for Greek constitutional law.[77] The use of the term 'civilisation' is indicative of the perception of this spirit as higher and progressive compared to the domestic reality.[78] Tsatsos argued that European rights constituted 'a pre-hermeneutic theory', that is, a theory that pre-existed the drafting of the constitution, had bound this drafting and thus was binding in constitutional interpretation.[79] Manitakis talked about the 'real' constitution, that is, the core of constitutional principles that is commonly accepted as valid by legal actors and orients the interpretation of constitutional provisions.[80] The transfer of proportionality should be read in this particular context, as part of a more general process of acculturation.

The constitutional amendment of 2001 accomplished the process of constitutional acculturation that proportionality was purported to have brought about. Scholars celebrated the 'renewal' of the formal constitution in order to meet the 'real' one.[81] The relevant literature is animated by the same faith in law and the judge that animate German constitutionalist writings, often cited in Greek analyses.[82] Paralleled with the adoption of the EU Fundamental Rights Charter, the amendment institutionalised the 'European constitutional perception of fundamental rights'.[83] By explicitly entrenching proportionality as a limitation imposed on the legislative limitations of rights, the Greek Constitution was said to have achieved the 'progress' that the ECHR had already been achieving since the 1950s.[84] Hence, proportionality transcends political cleavages and quiets the critiques of the 2001 reform.[85] As a social justice principle, it is part of 'a minimum core

77 Chryssogonos (2001a), pp. 192 f. and 540; Pararas (2001); Dagtoglou (2005), p. 24.

78 On the many possible uses of 'legal culture', see Nelken (2012), pp. 5 f.

79 Tsatsos (1994).

80 Manitakis (1994), p. 310.

81 Anthopoulos (2001); Venizelos (2002), p. 468.

82 See, for example, Contiades (2002), who, citing mainly German authors, proposes a new paradigm of rights very similar to the rational human rights paradigm for Greek constitutionalism.

83 Gerontas (2006), p. 467; Venizelos (2000); Anthopoulos (2001), p. 171. In the same vein, see Chryssogonos (2000), esp. p. 541.

84 Venizelos (2002), p. 141.

85 In the words of Venizelos (2004a): '[T]he new article 25 by itself would suffice to give right to the constitutional reform, as it lays down the principles for the interpretation and application of all constitutional rights.'

of overlapping consensus'.[86] The only reason for criticising its constitutional entrenchment has been the fact that such entrenchment is absent from other European constitutional texts.[87]

In 2001, the European constitutional civilisation was appropriated by domestic lawyers as an *acquis* of Greek constitutional civilisation. Proportionality, as part of this civilisation, started being perceived as ubiquitous in domestic case law. Manifestations of balancing have been discovered in the most historic Greek constitutional decisions, even in the oral arguments of the public prosecutor Tzivanopoulos in the nineteenth century, who first called for *Areios Pagos* to review the constitutionality of legislation.[88] Similarly to their French colleagues, Greek public lawyers have reread Council of State case law dating from the 1930s as an instance of proportionality reasoning.[89] In one of the most extensive and comprehensive studies on the matter, Orfanoudakis only scarcely referred to the application of the principle abroad.[90] Appropriation of the European civilisation of rights has been expressed in judicial practice as well. Since the 2000s, Greek courts have indiscriminately applied constitutional and European rights, and proportionality, as if they derived from the same text.[91] Chryssogonos talks about the 'interpretative osmosis' of the domestic and the European legal orders.[92] This has sometimes attributed to proportionality a quasi-scientific function.

7.4 Proportionality as a European Science: Transcending Constitutional Limits

The Realisation of the 'Greek-as-European' Metaphor. Lévi-Strauss observed that 'the transformation of a metaphor is achieved in a

86 Katrougkalos (2001), pp. 470–1. It is characteristic that during parliamentary discussions on the reform, a few Communist MPs objected the entrenchment of proportionality. Based on the Greek case law, they observed that proportionality had served as a tool for limiting collective labour rights, especially for prohibiting strikes as abusive. To this suspicious remark, constitutional scholars retorted that according to their expertise, proportionality tended to increase constitutional rights' protection and that this was the function that it had in other European legal orders (pp. 469–70).

87 See, for example, Chryssogonos (2001b).

88 Orfanoudakis (2003), pp. 13 f.; Renesi (2005), pp. 1401 f.

89 See, most notably, StE (Pl.) 300/1936 *ΤΝΠΔΣΑ*. Voutsakis (1990), pp. 216 f.; Beis (1999), p. 468; Orfanoudakis (2003), pp. 72 f.

90 Orfanoudakis (2003).

91 See, for example, decision StE 1065/2002 *ΕλλΔνη* 2003, p. 1073; AP (Pl.) 26/2003 *ΕλλΔνη* 2003, p. 1263.

92 Chryssogonos (2001a), pp. 192 f.; Gerontas (2006), p. 491.

metonymy'.[93] The metaphor 'Greek-as-European' did not escape this rule. With the accomplishment of the process of constitutional acculturation, the 'Greek-as-European' metaphor was to become literal, the Greek polity was to become European, and this was to be accomplished first at the level of law. Supranational norms began to be interpreted as imposing specific legal methods. Proportionality became the correct method for legal reasoning and acquired a hegemonic place in Greek law. As a method for teleological interpretation, it has served the reinvention of domestic concepts, institutions and procedures in the light of the precepts of the European constitutional civilisation.[94]

In the minds of Greek public lawyers, proportionality represents something more than law, even more than constitutional law. Its validity is axiomatic and uncontested. Its application relativises the scope of the most concrete and detailed provisions.[95] Proportionality is presumed to be inherent in the indeterminate concepts of Greek legal codes and can lead to the censuring of legislative omissions. It is a common framework used by the legislator and the administration.[96] It tends to replace virtually every method of legal reasoning.[97] As a structure, a framework of argumentation, proportionality serves the interpreter of the constitution, 'like the microscope the biologist or the telescope the astrologist', in her search for the correct constitutional solution.[98] Domestic scholars perceive it as 'an indispensable methodological tool for contemporary legal science'.[99] Proportionality is part of a total constitutional theory that transcends the separation between private and public, the various branches of law and even the written constitution itself.

The *Michaniki Affair*. The famous *Michaniki* affair, commonly called the 'major shareholder affair' (*υπόθεση του βασικού μετόχου*), offers an illustrative example. This affair concerned the reconciliation of the amended constitution with EC competition law. The relevant litigation lasted almost ten years and was at the source of three Council of State decisions and one ECJ preliminary ruling. The story starts with Article 14(9) of the constitution, which after the 2001 amendment declares:

93 Lévi-Strauss (1966), p. 106.

94 Mitsopoulos (2002). See also Vellis (1999). In case law, AP 1597/2000; 254/2000.

95 See also AP (Pl.) 20/2000 *ΤΝΠΔΣΑ*.

96 APD 147/2001 *ΠΟΙΝΔ/ΝΗ* 2002, p. 37 (Data Protection Authority); EPA 193/2001 *ΔΕΕ* 2001, p. 995 (Competition Commission); NSK 357/2001 *NOMOS* (opinion by the Legal Council of the State).

97 Matthias (2006); Vassilakakis (2008).

98 Orfanoudakis (2003), pp. 58–9.

99 Beis (1999), p. 498.

> The capacity of owner, partner, major shareholder or managing director of an information media enterprise, is incompatible with the capacity of owner, partner, major shareholder or managing director of an enterprise that undertakes towards the Public Administration or towards a legal entity of the wider public sector to perform works or to supply goods or services.

The incompatibility was also extended to 'all types of intermediary persons, such as spouses, relatives, financially dependent persons or companies'. According to the constitution, legislation can provide for sanctions in case of infringement of the above provisions. These sanctions can comprise licence withdrawal for a radio or television station and prohibition of the conclusion or annulment of the public contract in question. By including the above provisions in Article 14(9), the reformers conferred constitutional status on a statute that had already stipulated them.[100]

The goal of the new provisions met with broad consensus in Parliament and in public opinion. It consisted in the prevention of illegitimate media influence on the award of public contracts and on politics more generally.[101] Otherwise, the constitutional text delegated the regulation of the matter to Parliament. However, the statute implementing Article 14(9) of the constitution, dating from 2002, stood in stark contrast to the 'very rigid, even draconian' constitutional regime.[102] According to the law, the sole proof of the spouses' and relatives' economic independence, sufficed for the presumption of Article 14(9) that they act as 'intermediaries' not to apply.[103]

In application of the law, the National Radio-Television Council (ESR) issued an act in 2002, certifying that the incompatibility established by Article 14(9) did not concern the company Sarantopoulos (later called Pantechniki), even if one of its major shareholders and vice-chairman of its board of directors was the father of G. Sarantopoulos, a member of the board of directors of two companies that were active in the field of the media. The ESR considered that, since father and son were financially independent, the presumption that they acted as intermediaries did not apply and the company was free to conclude the public contract in question. Michaniki, a concurrent of Pantechniki, attacked the ESR

100 Article 11 para. 1, Law no. 2328/95.

101 See Manitakis (2014), before fn. 7. See StE 3242/2004 *NoB* 2005, p. 1878, para. 14, referring to the relevant parliamentary debates.

102 Venizelos (2000).

103 Law no. 3021/2002.

certificate in annulment, claiming that the 2002 statute had rendered the constitutional presumptions reversible and had thus reduced the scope of Article 14(9) of the constitution.

The Council of State Section Decision. In the first decision on the matter in 2004, the Fourth Section of the Council of State gave support to Michaniki's arguments. The judges started by specifying that Article 14(9) did not only aim at the '*ex post* retribution' of concrete acts of illegitimate influence of the media on the award of public contracts. In their view, such influence 'in any case [was] difficult to establish with certainty, and thus difficult to prevent by threatening with sanctions only in the cases where it would be ascertained'.[104] Instead, the council considered that the constitutional provision 'primarily aim[ed] to prevent the creation of conditions that could generate a risk of such illegitimate influence, which is particularly detrimental to the public interest'.[105] The preventive function of the constitutional measures was understood as maximal, taking place at a very early stage. The judges also held that the presumption that spouses and relatives act as 'intermediaries' was irrefutable. In their view, only this interpretation could ensure the effective application of the constitutional rules in question. Hence, the Fourth Section concluded as to the unconstitutionality of the implementing statute and referred the case to the Council of State Plenum.[106]

In the meantime, the 2002 statute was already rigid enough to provoke the reaction of European institutions, which considered it to be incompatible with EC competition law. Article 24 of the Directive 93/37/EEC defined certain reasons for the exclusion of enterprises from public contract contests but did not stipulate incompatibilities such as the ones defined in Article 14(9). The Fourth Section of the Council of State had refused to examine the compatibility of the constitution with the directive. For the judges, a preliminary reference to the ECJ to ascertain whether an imperative provision of the Greek constitution is compatible with a provision of community law was 'in any case inconceivable'.[107] Moreover, in the majority's view, the domestic legislation on the matter did not enter the scope of Article 24 of the directive, which aimed only for the partial harmonisation of national regimes. Thus,

[104] See StE 3242/2004, para. 14.
[105] Ibid.
[106] The amendment Article 100(5) of the constitution imposed the obligation to refer supreme courts' section decisions declaring the unconstitutionality of legal statutes to the plenum.
[107] StE 3242/2004, para. 19.

coherence between domestic and European law was preserved through the delimitation of their respective scope.

The Preliminary Reference to the ECJ. Two years later, the Council of State Plenum also adopted a rigid stance as far as the incompatibilities of Article 14(9) were concerned. In the council's view, the constitution established an absolute prohibition on media companies from concluding public contracts. The goal of this provision was preventive. Thus, the constitution imposed an obligation on Parliament to 'institute sanctions that [would] be sufficiently deterrent' in case of breach of article 14(9).[108] Therefore, in the judges' view, an interpretation of article 14(9) in the light of the principle of proportionality would 'void [the constitutional provision] of its content or would reverse its clear formulation and its equally clear goals'.[109] As for the 'intermediaries', the court accepted the possibility of reversing the presumption established for spouses, relatives and economically dependent persons, but only if these persons could prove that in the concrete case at hand they acted independently and for their own sake.[110] Hence, the council still held the implementing legislation to be too lenient and inefficient in pursuing the goals set by the constitution.

However, contrary to the section judges, the plenum decided that the conformity of Article 14(9) provisions with European law should be examined by the ECJ.[111] In its preliminary reference to the ECJ, the council asked, among others questions, whether the domestic constitutional provision pursued legitimate goals under the directive and whether the domestic measures were compatible with proportionality as applied in EC law.[112] According to the view that prevailed, in case of incompatibility, the domestic regime as a whole should not be applied, despite its constitutional basis.[113] In the council's decision then, proportionality transcended the domestic constitution, which was to be applied only 'in the proportion' that it was compatible with European law. The constitution was deprived of its function as 'an act of separation and definition of the limits' between the domestic and the European legal spheres.[114] This function was ascribed to proportionality instead.

108 StE (Pl.) 3670/2006 *ΕΔΔΔ* 2009, p. 461, para. 14.
109 Ibid, para. 14.
110 Ibid, para. 15.
111 Ibid, paras. 28 f.
112 Ibid.
113 Ibid, para. 20.
114 Drossos (1996), p. 647.

The ECJ's response came in the well-known *Michaniki* decision.[115] The Luxembourg judges declared Article 14(9) contrary to the principle of proportionality. The domestic provisions, excluding a whole category of media enterprises from the public contract sector without affording them any possibility to prove that no risk of illegitimate influence exists in concrete cases, went beyond what was necessary to eliminate the risk of corruption.[116] The fact that, in the 2006 decision, the Council of State had held that the presumption concerning spouses, relatives and economically dependent persons was refutable, was not enough to reconcile the provision with EC law. The European court criticised the *formulation* of the domestic constitutional text itself. In its view, the breadth of the concepts 'major shareholder' and 'intermediary' contributed to the disproportionate character of the domestic provisions.[117]

The Final Michaniki Decision and the 'True Meaning' of the Greek Constitution. In the final 'major shareholder' case in 2011, the Council of State Plenum implemented the ECJ decision. By doing so, it unanimously reversed the interpretation of Article 14(9) that it had adopted in previous cases. Instead of a 'preventive incompatibility', which was general, abstract and absolute, Article 14(9) was now taken to establish an ad hoc 'incompatibility of actions'.[118] This means that, every businessman active in the field of the media is allowed to conclude a public contract, unless 'it is established with certainty that the individual committed an illegal or illegitimate act in the process of award'.[119]

The requirement of proof and certainty stands opposed to the preventive approach that the court had adopted in its previous decisions. In total contrast to these decisions, the council declared the 2002 statute as unconstitutional, not because it was too lenient, but due to the general and absolute character of the incompatibilities and presumptions that it contained. The supreme judges unanimously concluded that the law was 'contrary to the true meaning' of Article 14(9).[120] What in 2006 had been deemed to 'void' Article 14(9) of its content and to 'reverse its clear formulation and its equally clear goals', was now declared to be its 'true meaning'. The constitutional text was interpreted according to the 'real' constitution, the one that is in conformity with

[115] ECJ, C-213/07, 16 December 2008, *Michaniki*, ECLI:EU:C:2008:731.
[116] Ibid, paras. 62–3.
[117] Ibid, para. 83.
[118] See Anthopoulos (2006).
[119] StE (Pl.) 3470–1/2011 *ΕΔΔΔ* 2012, p. 199.
[120] Ibid, para. 14.

European law.[121] What allowed for this striking change was not the supremacy of European law over the domestic constitution – this question was not raised in the Council of State's reasoning. Rather, it was the interpretation of the constitutional provisions according to the principle of proportionality, 'a principle both of the Greek legal order [. . .] and of Community law'.[122]

Decision 3471/2011 is one of the most applauded applications of proportionality in the Greek context. Prominent Greek scholars had also defended this interpretation of Article 14(9).[123] The rupture in the Council of State case law that it introduced does not seem to bother Greek public lawyers. The coherence of the domestic constitution with the EU legal order, be it at the level of aesthetics, seems to be more important to local legal actors than the internal coherence of domestic constitutional discourse itself. Thus, *Michaniki* was perceived as a fair compromise that did not undermine the authority of the national constitution. Proportionality functioned as an 'intermediary' between EU and domestic law and rendered escapable the conflict between the two.[124]

Constitutional change through supranational law is not new in the Greek context. The determination of the content of domestic constitutional values and requirements by supranational law is provided for in Article 28 of the constitution, which allows for the transfer of constitutional competences to international organisations and for limitations on the exercise of national sovereignty insofar as they are dictated by an important national interest. Drossos has pointed out that, by separating the holder of national sovereignty from the holder of the national interest, this provision blurs the constitutional limits between Greece and the supranational organisations of which it is a member.[125] Mainstream scholarship generally agreed on the 'tacit constitutional reform' function of this provision in the context of European integration.[126] In *Michaniki*, this function was assumed by proportionality, which transcended the limits of the domestic constitution as a principle shared between domestic and EU law. Even more, 'in what is almost a species of sympathetic magic', by establishing aesthetic coherence between domestic and

121 Manitakis (2007).
122 StE (Pl.) 3470/2011, para. 9; 3471/2011, para. 13.
123 See, among others, Contiades (2002), pp. 305–6; Anthopoulos (2006). Venizelos (2005) also proposed such an interpretation of Article 14(9).
124 Nikiforos (2012). See also Manitakis (2015b).
125 Drossos (1996), pp. 649 f.
126 On this matter, see Papadopoulou (2003), p. 176, citing Julia Iliopoulou-Stragga.

European law, the application of proportionality in *Michaniki* represented the Greek society as modern and European.

7.5 Displacing Local Knowledge: Proportionality and the Aesthetics of Modernisation

Proportionality and Modernisation.[127] Drossos neatly observes that Greek constitutional discourse has generally contributed to the construction of the '*katharevousa politeia*' (*καθαρεύουσα πολιτεία*, meaning 'purifying polity'), a polity full of rituals, the function of which has mainly been metaphorical: it has represented the Greek society as its foreign models.[128] This author explains with irony that 'Greece, in its constitutional mirror does not see itself but ... England.'[129] In the context of proportionality language, the desired constitutional idol is Germany or, more generally, Europe. The *Michaniki* affair is particularly illustrative in this respect.

Indeed, behind the different interpretations of Article 14(9) in the 'major shareholder' cases are different views of the Greek socio-political reality altogether. In the 2004 and 2006 decisions, the media were distrusted as a priori suspects of corruption.[130] In the words of the court, 'in view of the – well-known to everyone – huge influence [of the media] on public opinion in contemporary societies', illegitimate media influence could 'even lead to a distortion of popular sovereignty [...], which is the foundation of the polity'.[131] This dictum stands in total contrast to the council's dicta in 2011. According to the latest decision, Article 14(9) 'certainly does not aim at the prevention of any influence of the media on the exercise of political power in general, which, moreover, is inherent in the role of the media in contemporary modern societies'.[132] Surprisingly, in 2011, democracy and popular sovereignty were no longer at danger due to opaque media practices but due to restrictive state interference with their political role. The media were trusted as normal political actors in modern societies. In fact, the 'draconian' interpretation of Article 14(9) was abandoned because it depicted the Greek

[127] The analysis in this section was inspired by a discussion with Jacco Bomhoff, whom I thank.

[128] Drossos (1996), pp. 116 f., 129.

[129] Ibid, pp. 39, 148, observing similar patterns in constitutional transfers during the nineteenth century.

[130] Anthopoulos (2006), pp. 320–1; Nikiforos (2012), p. 7.

[131] StE 3242/2004, para. 14.

[132] StE (Pl.) 3471/2011, para. 13.

constitutional-political reality in a way that did not correspond to a 'contemporary modern society'.

As in the English case, the application of proportionality in Greece has been to a large extent about modernisation. Modernisation was a much-praised rationale of the 2001 reform, which entrenched proportionality. Writing at the time of the relevant public debates, Papatolias observed that it was 'almost impossible to track down even one argument concerning the reform which [did] not refer to the epode of modernisation'.[133] The quest for modernisation was expressed in neologisms included in the constitutional text, like 'genetic identity' or 'Society of Information'.[134] These new terms and formulas were purported to symbolise the adaptation of the constitution to the evolving social, economic, technological, and other circumstances and its possibility to act upon them. Proportionality, itself a 'neoteric' element, was purported to express this rationale.[135] In *Michaniki*, the application of proportionality by the Council of State *performed* the image of the Greek society as a modern 'Society of Information', in which the media are a legitimate source of power.

Modernisation in the English context has proceeded through the quest for substantive values, myth and ritual to unify the bits and pieces of the common law. In contrast, in Greece modernisation has implied efficiency, rationalisation and the excision of values from legal reasoning. Most importantly, what the reformers claimed to convey in 2001 was an outcome-based legitimation of state authorities, adapted to the post-modern 'risk society'.[136] As Pararas observed, in 2001 the constitution 'abandoned its ideal sacredness for the sake of its functionality'.[137] The reformers' concern with efficiency was expressed in the technocratic spirit permeating the constitutional text, which provided for a number of specialised and independent administrative authorities. This made Sotirelis lament that the 2001 reform substituted 'a sterile technocratic-legal conception [. . .] to lively constitutional politics'.[138] The scientific connotations of proportionality express this spirit of technocracy too. In judicial review in particular, proportionality functions as an efficiency and rationalisation test. As

[133] Papatolias (1999), p. 33.
[134] Articles 5 and 5A of the Constitution, resp.
[135] Venizelos (2002), p. 92.
[136] Mantzoufas (2004). See, more generally, Contiades (2002).
[137] Pararas (2012a). See also Alivizatos (2001b), p. 446.
[138] Sotirelis (2000), pp. 53–4.

such, it articulates an instrumental perception of legal rules, since it can justify only efficient legal solutions.

Paradoxically, however, the application of proportionality as a European scientific tool does not seem to fit local legal imagination. While proportionality flourishes in a context of epistemological optimism and institutional faith, in Greece there seems to be a climate of suspicion among constitutional actors. Constitutional interpretation represents an act of political power.[139] Accusations of 'hermeneutic relativism' are unleashed against the Council of State when applying proportionality.[140] Greek public lawyers have not been convinced by the modernisation rhetoric of the 2001 reform.[141] Neither are they optimistic as to the effectiveness of the new interpretation of Article 14(9) in preventing corruption. Manitakis, for instance, expresses his serious doubt in this respect and criticises the reform of Article 14(9) as 'inoperative and deceitful'.[142] In this context of constitutional pessimism and institutional distrust, proportionality is deprived of its purpose. A scientific tool without a science, it displaces 'local knowledge', which sustained the credibility of the domestic constitution until then.[143]

Proportionality v. Local Knowledge. This can be observed in the *Michaniki* case. A close look at the last 'major shareholder' decision shows that the re-interpretation of Article 14(9) that proportionality produced obliged the council to reformulate the goal of the constitutional provision as a whole. It rendered this goal much more concrete and far less preventive. It transformed it to an *objective*, a 'projected reality'.[144] According to the 2011 decision, the constitutional restrictions aimed 'only to prevent [...] the concrete illegitimate influence that can be exercised on the procedure of public contracts, with an intention to obtain the award of the contract'.[145] It is this concrete case of deliberate influence that was held to be the target of the constitutional restrictions

139 Drossos (1996), pp. 593 f., esp. p. 599.

140 Venizelos (2008); Nikiforos (2012).

141 Alivizatos (2001a).

142 See Manitakis (2014), section Ib.

143 See Geertz (1983), p. 215. The author observes that: '[Law] comes to describing a particular course of events and an overall conception of life in such a way that the credibility of each reinforces the credibility of the other. Any legal system that hopes to be viable must contrive to connect the if-then structure of existence, as locally imagined, and the as-therefore course of experience, as locally perceived, so that they seem but depth and surface versions of the same thing.'

144 Marzal Yetano (2013), no. 235.

145 StE (Pl.) 3471/2011, para. 13.

and not generally the 'creation of conditions that could generate a risk' of corruption, as the court had stated in previous decisions.

The reformulation of the constitutional goal allowed the court to limit the scope of the constitutional provisions to *concrete* and *ascertained* attempts at corruption, in conformity with proportionality. Under the new interpretation of Article 14(9), prevention takes place at a much later stage. This is at odds with a belief expressed by the administrative judges in previous decisions, that the institution of ex post sanctions would be ineffective and would even void the constitutional provision of its content. Not only did the European principle of proportionality impose a new interpretation of constitutional provisions and of their goal, but also a *particular vision* of what was an effective sanction in fighting corruption.

Indeed, the belief in the effectiveness of ex post sanctions that proportionality bore resulted from a whole new faith in the possibility of fact determination in the field of corruption. In previous cases, the Council of State judges had described the particular image of illegitimate media influence that they had in mind. In their words, such influence 'is normally opaque, and is combined with the line generally followed by the media and with the position that they adopt on political matters'.[146] As for the 'intermediaries' presumption, in 2004, the council had justified its irrefutable character by invoking the particular conditions concerning family relations in Greece:

> [A]ccording to empirical data on the social conditions that are dominant particularly in Greece, special relations of dependence are created among relatives. [These relations] do not only have an economic character, but are based on various social, even psychological factors, and therefore take the form of informal influence relations, which are extremely difficult to establish.[147]

The judges expressed some kind of local superstition, according to which, media influence on politics is often illegitimate and family relations always produce informal influence. This superstition was based on generally mentioned 'empirical data' and on the 'opaque' and 'difficult to establish' character of the relevant influence relations. It concerned 'the social conditions that are dominant particularly in Greece' and not those generally dominant in constitutional democracies. On the contrary, in the 2011 decision, judicial suspicion towards the media was rationalised.

[146] StE 3242/2004, para. 14.

[147] Ibid; StE (Pl.) 3670/2006, para. 15, minority opinion.

The fear of corruption was concretised and demystified. Only 'the concrete illegitimate influence that can be exercised on the procedure of public contracts, with an intention to obtain the award of the contract' was considered detrimental to democracy. By limiting the scope of the constitutional provision in this way, the Council of State expressed its belief that attempts to achieve illegitimate influence *can* be 'established with certainty'.[148] It also expressed a faith in the ability and eagerness of fact-finding authorities to ascertain and prove such illegitimate acts.[149]

This was not the first time that proportionality as a European science displaced local superstitions. In 1997, the government had subjected the compensation of medical expenses incurred by Greek nationals abroad to approval by social security organisations. Approval was obligatory whenever medical treatment by domestic health services would have been insufficient. In 2001, the Athens Administrative Court of First Instance, following the ECJ case law on the matter, examined the compatibility of this provision with the freedom to provide services under EC law. After establishing that the measure constituted an obstacle to trade, the court stressed that it should be justified by public interest reasons and conform to the principle of proportionality, understood as a strict necessity requirement. The court went on to state that:

> The assessment of the possibility of medical treatment [. . .] is not solely based on medical approaches dominant in this country, but on the data of international medical science, taking every treatment that has been tried and internationally recognised into account.[150]

Thus, it was for the judiciary to assess the possibility of medical treatment in Greece, substituting its view on the issue for that of the social security organisation or for medical experts. This solution was subsequently adopted by other courts.[151] In this series of cases, proportionality not only ensured the effective application of EU legal rules, but also the dominance of an internationally recognised medical science in the domestic sphere. Its function was to censure peculiarly local medical 'approaches' that do not conform to international scientific 'data'.

By transforming law into science, proportionality increasingly postulates its hegemony over other types of scientific discourse.[152] Its mission

[148] StE (Pl.) 3471/2011, para. 14.
[149] Analysis inspired by Geertz (1983), p. 171.
[150] DPrAth 7287/2001.
[151] On the relevant case law, see Katrougkalos (2006), p. 150.
[152] Analysis inspired by Teubner (1997).

is to expand the reach of law to 'conquer' and 'civilise' formerly extra-legal spaces and fields.[153] However, in the Greek context, the science that proportionality conveys is not a *domestic* constitutional science. Instead, the content of proportionality is defined outside the borders of domestic constitutional discourse, in Europe. What has preserved the normativity of the domestic Constitution has been its aesthetic coherence with European law and the corollary representation of the Greek polity as modern and European. The '*katharevousa politeia*' instituted with the 2001 reform rejects 'indigenous needs' when they do not correspond to its modern European image.[154]

***

In Greece, as in France, proportionality has been part of a legal theory that claims scientific correctness. Thus, its development as a legal concept has been detached from its application in case law, from the structures of judicial review and from formal legal sources more generally. Still, contrary to what is observed in the French context, the use of proportionality language has not expressed a particularly local image as to how law is determined by its surrounding factual context. Instead, the legal theory of which proportionality was part expressed an imagined local *future* that never arrived. Greek public lawyers aspired to transform the Greek polity to a European and modern polity, to transform the Greek society itself to a European and modern society. They pursued this locally imagined future through importation of legal rules and methods from abroad. Since its emergence then, proportionality has had the meaning of a legal transplant from Europe. It has been part of an imported constitutional civilisation. Its transfer then, has been part of a more general process of constitutional acculturation. In this respect proportionality language followed long existing tendencies in Greek legal culture and long existing paths of cultural change.

The process of constitutional acculturation was finally accomplished with the 2001 reform and the institutionalisation of the European human rights paradigm in the Greek constitution. Ever since, proportionality has been appropriated by Greek public lawyers as an *acquis* of domestic constitutional civilisation. It has expressed their view as to how law *acts on* its surrounding factual context. Its application has been disconnected from Greek social reality and from local perceptions of causality and effectiveness. Proportionality as a European science has been hegemonic.

153 Manitakis (1990b), p. 20.

154 Drossos (1996), pp. 116 f.; esp. pp. 174–5.

It has replaced other methods of legal reasoning and has blurred constitutional limits. Its main function has been to establish coherence between the domestic constitution and European law, a coherence that is so precious for Greek lawyers. The use of proportionality language in this context represents the Greek Constitution as a 'purifying polity' and symbolically connects Greece to its European models, while it rejects local needs and particularities. This symbolic or even aesthetic function has been a more general feature of domestic constitutional discourse until the recent economic crisis.

Conclusion of Part II

The Expressive Function of Proportionality. The study of difference in the use of proportionality unveils certain core characteristics of the legal cultures that embrace it. As proportionality spreads in different jurisdictions its meaning changes to adapt to local criteria for evaluating legal arguments and to local actors' expectations of its use. It assumes a function that is sometimes very different from the one it has in the global model or in German constitutionalism. Proportionality becomes a French legal theory claiming scientific exactness, a tool for the construction of an English public law or a transplant for the Europeanisation of the Greek polity. The different meanings of proportionality in different contexts make sense, at least in part, of differences in its form and evolution observed in Part I. Indeed, even though German and European influence is present in the conceptual development of proportionality in all contexts, it is not decisive for the content that proportionality will assume each time. In spite of using elements of a transnational idiom, local actors serve their own goals, which are conceived of and set within a particular culture. Hence, proportionality, precisely due to its transnational character, acquires an expressive function. The way its meaning, form and function vary across jurisdictions despite the commonality of the terminology used, reveals the peculiar logic of local legal discourses. It reveals local ways of thinking, taboos and myths, expectations and ambitions. It also reveals local patterns of legal change.

Proportionality and Legal Formalism. In all the jurisdictions studied, proportionality has been inserted into a context of autonomy of law from other discursive systems. The study of law as it *is* is perceived as different from the study of law as it *ought to be*. This feature, an instance of legal formalism, renders law in these contexts quite different from its Alexyan perception as an instance of practical reasoning. Formal legal sources play a much more decisive role in legal argumentation and reasoning than the defenders of proportionality maintain.

Initially, proportionality was not even thought of as a fundamental rights transfer in France and was rejected as such in England. In Greece, too, even though proportionality was received with enthusiasm as a fundamental rights principle, its use did not bring about the changes that domestic lawyers expected.

Thus, while the use of proportionality language in France, England and Greece did express a common European constitutional civilisation, this civilisation was one of liberal formalism rather than fundamental rights. Indeed, for a long time, convergence between French, English and Greek judicial review has lain in the unitary perception of democracy that underpins their fundamental concepts and distinctions. Democratic decision-making, institutional structures and procedural rules are traditionally deemed sufficient for legitimately defining the public interest. In substance, this definition is perceived as external to legal technique and judicial review. Practical reasoning is external to legal reasoning, even when it concerns values entrenched in the constitution. In this context, law does not assume a function of social integration, like in German constitutionalism. Social integration and the reconciliation of conflicting social values is the mission of parliamentary decision-making and of administrative action. Proportionality, when it is not rejected in judicial review, it serves as an instance of 'republican inculcation', that is, as a self-evident affirmation of the legitimacy of majoritarian value choices.

Expressing Local Myths and Representations. Legal formalism has been preserved and justified in different ways across systems. It has been underpinned by narratives that are commonly shared among local legal actors. Like myths, these narratives are stories that make sense of the present, the past and the future of law, society and the state. They usually represent an idealistic image of the respective local polities and of the community of legal actors.[155] Locally shared narratives result in specifically local legal structures, distinctions, rituals, taboos and representations that affect the use of proportionality language.

English analytical formalism postulates the economy of the common law in matters of substance and principle. Following the account of Whig historians, the parliamentary process and the common law have long succeeded in protecting civil liberties and democracy in the UK, without needing substantive constitutional rights and ideals or, indeed, even any constitution whatsoever. The adoption of the principle of

[155] Analysis inspired by Lévi-Strauss (1955) and Kennedy (1995).

proportionality was thus perceived as contrary to the Diceyan orthodoxy. In this context, myth is external to law and lies in the idealisation of the political process itself. Law is typically seen as a patchwork of commandments equally imposed on private and public action. Judicial review is seen as imposing the rules of a game on individual players. The judge is represented as an impartial referee concerned with rules of procedure and form, as opposed to substance. Hence, the application of proportionality as a head of judicial review found its obstacle in the taboo of merits review. Against the will of Parliament, proportionality would blur a distinction that is fundamental in the common law: that between review and appeal.

Quite differently, in French and Greek legal thought, legal form incorporates substantive value choices. Law is a kind of objective, commonly shared knowledge, part of a common sense or civilisation on which social life is based. Proportionality itself is part of this civilisation. The term designates a value or an ideal of public decision-making akin to reasonableness or equity. As such, proportionality is considered a natural quality of legislation and even a general principle of law. Structural features, like the pronged structure or the use of proportionality language, are not perceived as decisive by local legal actors in its application. Proportionality does not lead to a rational justification process and it has a marginal function in the judicial review of Parliament. Instead of a concrete legal rule or method, proportionality is a political moral *end* of public action and rights are *means* of submitting its advancement to a minimal judicial scrutiny.

The fusion between substantive values and legal form observed in the continental systems confers a quasi-sacred status to law. Adjudication resembles a ritual for the 'consecration' of concrete legal solutions. In this ritual, the judge is a modest and conscientious public official. She seeks a true and transcendent meaning for the principle of legality and its manifestation in the concrete circumstances of each case. Judicial review dissolves private interests into a quest for the general interest. Proportionality and balancing are part of the ritual of judicial review and serve the reconstruction of legislative intentions in a constitutionally legitimate way. In constitutional case law, proportionality is typically applied through the technique of *réserves d'interprétation*, which allows the judge to 'speak' the words of Parliament according to a will presumed to be legitimate.

Interestingly, Bomhoff observes the same tendency to synthesise substance and form in the context of German constitutionalism.[156]

[156] Bomhoff (2013a), pp. 217 f.

Nonetheless, while in Germany fusion of substance and form leads to the inclusion of considerations of political morality into constitutional reasoning and adjudication, in French and Greek legal thought it is traditionally expressed in dogmatism. Dogmatism reflects the dominant voluntarist perception of legal norm production and the idealisation of the legislator and the state. Law is deemed to represent the general will and by definition serves the public interest. Hence, substantive value choices embodied in legislation are traditionally immune from judicial scrutiny, they are affirmed as if they were positive facts. Traditional distinctions like the distinction between conditions and content of public action when it comes to facts-based review; between the 'whether' and the 'how' of public competence; or between *légalité* and *opportunité* express this dogmatism. Proportionality in this context is typically characterised by focus on the means-ends and does not involve balancing competing rights and interests.

This is related to the fact that, in contrast to the communitarian German constitutional culture, French and Greek cultures are animated by institutional suspicion. Constitutional rights are imagined as freedoms and not as goals imposed on public action or optimisation requirements, as the Alexyan theory professes. Rights correspond to objective rules of competence. They require abstention on the part of public authorities from interfering with their scope and not state intervention for their realisation. The limit-like nature of constitutional rights ensures that the judiciary is constrained in its institutional mission and eliminates risks for a *gouvernement des juges*. It is part of the binding arrangements between local legal discourses and politics. In this context, proportionality corresponds to an objective legal principle of 'good administration', inspired by the liberal suspicion towards the executive. It is applied as a threshold requirement of relevance, necessity, reasonableness or equity and is disconnected from the content of rights. The function of proportionality review is to eliminate arbitrary decisions, and thus it exceptionally leads to the censure of the reviewed act. Judicial intervention is usually limited to cases of manifest disproportionality.

A Deviant Application? By excluding legislative value choices from judicial review, the 'dogmatic' version of proportionality described above is very different from the Alexyan theory, in which the public interest results from a structured balancing of rights as principles. In this version, proportionality fails in its function of justification and rational optimisation of the common good. Indeed, it changes little traditional methods of reasoning and the substantive outcomes of judicial review in the contexts where it spreads. It seems that a perception of rights akin to the rational human rights paradigm is indeed a condition for the success of proportionality. Therefore, Möller is right when he observes that: '[P]roportionality is not just an isolated standard of review but part and parcel of a conception of rights that must be adopted or rejected as a whole.'[157]

Still, it would be inaccurate to characterise the French and Greek versions of proportionality as deviant or imperfect applications of the concept, since they are very close to the original version of the principle in Prussian administrative law. Indeed, as Cohen-Eliya and Porat observe, proportionality in its historical origins was opposed to balancing.[158] It was a requirement of reasonableness, advanced by legal formalists and purporting to exclude administrative arbitrariness. As such, it was solely addressed to the state and focused on the means of public action. The formalist meaning of proportionality persisted when the principle was first mentioned in the case law of the GFCC. Indeed, as Bomhoff observes, in its first uses in German constitutional law balancing was not necessarily connected to proportionality.[159] In the well-known *Mephisto* case, the GFCC even invoked proportionality as a public law principle in contrast to balancing of interests in private law.[160] Therefore, the traditional version of proportionality in French and Greek public law is not deviant or wrong, but simply *one of the possible ways* of using it. Legal actors in France and Greece chose *this* version because it best advanced their purposes in their local culture.

Proportionality, Rationalisation and Modernisation. The autonomy of law from other systems is constantly negotiated by local participants.[161] The transfer of proportionality itself is part of the process of negotiation of legal autonomy to the profit of considerations of substantive justice. Proportionality carries its own semantic baggage, connected to the sources of inspiration of the personalities that promote its use. In the various domestic contexts, it is mobilised by alternative narratives to orthodox legal formalism. Thus, it acquires its proper dynamic, which is more or less radical, depending on the context. Proportionality's success

157 Möller (2017), p. 131.

158 On this point, see Cohen-Eliya and Porat (2013), pp. 24 f.

159 See, for example, *Lüth Case* (1958) 7 BVerfGE 198 (B.II.4), as cited by Kommers (2012), p. 447. On this point, see Bomhoff (2013a), pp. 87 f. See also GFCC (1954) 3 BVerfGE, 383. In this case, the court seems to perceive proportionality as akin to a requirement of necessity of rights' limitations. See Grimm (2007), p. 385, fn. 10. See also Kennedy (2011).

160 *Mephisto Case* (1971) 30 BVerfGE 173, IV. 2, cited and translated by Kommers (2012), pp. 358 f.

161 On this point, see Bomhoff (2012b), pp. 87 f.

or failure depends on the local criteria for the evaluation of legal arguments. Proportionality's meaning is shaped by what are locally perceived as 'formants' of legal knowledge. Since alternative discourses are constructed in opposition to the dominant narrative each time, they vary considerably between them and they variably shape the content of proportionality. What they have in common is the idealisation of the judiciary that underpins them, a feature that also underpins the proportionality theory and its depiction of the judge as Socrates. In the various domestic contexts studied, the spread of proportionality expresses and enhances the belief that judges are well-qualified for policy decisions. Hence, proportionality entails the progressive affirmation of the competence of the judiciary to define and realise the general interest.

In France, proportionality finds its dynamic within domestic lawyers' efforts to rationalise the legislative will. The concept acquired an increasingly important role in the writings of the French *doctrine*, which often draws on developments in other disciplines and in the *sciences exactes* in order to expand the reach of law and judicial review. As a scientific theory, proportionality was inserted into the myth of the adaptation of law to fact and it enhanced local lawyers' belief in the possibility of law as science. In the name of common sense and reason proportionality assumes a function of rationalisation of value choices, similar to the one it should have in a culture of justification. Indeed, as the analysis of *Entreprises de presse* shows, proportionality, albeit being an objective test, is not result-oriented but is concerned with the justification of public decisions. Its objectivity lies in its fact-oriented, allegedly scientific application. Thus, the spread of proportionality in this context is closely intertwined with French public lawyers' epistemological optimism, a characteristic that, as we saw in the introduction of this part, they share with their German colleagues.

Still, while German lawyers entrust the GFCC with the mission of substantiation of the constitutional order of values, French lawyers do not share the same faith in the capacity of judges to optimally realise social values. In French public law, the spread of proportionality is not connected to the perception of law as rational value-laden reasoning, as the Alexyan theory wishes. The connection of proportionality to fundamental rights language provokes scholarly suspicion and criticism. Instead, in this context proportionality expresses and enhances a technocratic vision of policy-making, characterised by 'ever-greater reliance on expertise and an aseptic formalization of legal reasons'.[162] The use of

[162] Perju (2012), p. 367.

proportionality thus illustrates what Geertz has identified as a more general tendency of Western legal systems: the 'rising expectations as to the possibilities of fact determination and its power to settle intractable issues'.[163] Perju calls this effect of proportionality the 'administratization' of constitutional law, a tendency that in his view should be resisted.[164] Built on allegedly objective factual assessments, legal doctrine expands to cover issues previously considered inaccessible to legal knowledge. This tendency is also present in the writings of some proportionality scholars. Beatty, for example, suggests that '[t]here is an objectivity and neutrality about facts that words rarely if ever match'.[165]

Quite differently, in England negotiation of legal autonomy has been expressed through a quest for modernisation and through efforts to construct an English public law, following the model of continental systems. Proportionality was initially mobilised by this modernisation rhetoric as a transplant that could bring about rationalisation. As opposed to what is observed in France, here rationalisation does not entail demystification. On the contrary, it consists in a quest for myth and ritual around the bits and pieces of the common law. In the writings of English lawyers during the 1980s and the 1990s, proportionality included the consideration of certain core substantive values into legal reasoning. It progressively detached itself from judicial reasoning patterns to become a *method* of review. Albeit without being named, proportionality underpinned judicial decisions and it allowed for the reconstruction of the fragmented common law precedents into a coherent whole. Proportionality became a tool in the hands of a new type of legal knowledge, which sacrificed the traditional precepts of analytical formalism for the pursuit of political moral values. Thus, the spread of proportionality in English public law should be read against the rise of common law constitutionalism, which since the 1970s contests the fundamental assumptions of the common law tradition.

In this respect, the HRA 1998 and the reception of proportionality in the field of the convention expressed and enhanced already existing tendencies of cultural change. In the post-HRA era, proportionality generates spectacular constitutional transformation and is a core issue of debate among public lawyers. It carries with it continental cultural baggage and participates in a mythopoeia that establishes itself as a new

163 Geertz (1983), p. 171.
164 Perju (2012).
165 Beatty (2004), pp. 72–3.

truth. In the 'brave new world' of the HRA, the rule of law has a substantive content for the preserving of core societal values. Judges, in their mission as fundamental rights protectors, acquire important policy-making powers. Proportionality becomes an overarching method (and not head) of review that tends to replace other kinds of judicial reasoning. Traditional judicial review concepts are reorganised around a rational basis and concepts like 'variable intensity', 'manifest error' and 'discretionary power' are developed in English public law. The common law, with its renovated rationalist outfitting, seems to supersede parliamentary sovereignty. The quest for democratic governance that this principle has long embodied must itself be reformulated in the rationalist terms of deference in order to be taken seriously by local legal actors. Interestingly, the construction of an institutionally sensitive doctrine of deference is a major contribution of common lawyers to the transnational proportionality theory.

Modernisation under European influence has been a major stake of the spread of proportionality in Greece as well, albeit in a more 'magical' way. Despite the dogmatic and inconsistent application of proportionality in practice, Greek lawyers have conceived of it as a transplant. Their obsession with the content of proportionality in foreign and supranational jurisdictions has led them to largely neglect structural evolutions in domestic judicial reasoning. In Greek legal theory, proportionality frameworks developed in Europe have been uncontestably accepted as scientific in the domestic sphere and have evolved in a 'heaven' of legal transplants. This is because, in Greece, the kind of knowledge, science or civilisation that law represents is not home-bred but imported. Comparative law, in the sense of translation of foreign legal concepts and doctrines, is a 'legal formant', it constitutes local legal knowledge.

In this context, the importation of proportionality from abroad acquired a value in itself as part of a more general process of acculturation that was expected to bring about the modernisation of the Greek polity. This makes sense of the explicit entrenchment of proportionality and of the European rights paradigm with the 2001 constitutional reform. Ever since, proportionality has become hegemonic, a scientific theory that transcends the limits set by the constitution. It displaces local reasoning patterns and the local knowledge that until recently preserved the normativity of the Greek constitutional order. By establishing aesthetic coherence between the domestic constitution and the European treaties, proportionality acquires a symbolic power: its application represents the Greek polity as a modern European one. Hence, proportionality is part of a '*katharevousa politeia*', which rejects indigenous needs when they do not correspond to its modern European image.

Proporitonality, Convergence and Divergence. Proportionality, but also peripheral notions of formalism, modernisation and rationalisation, have very different meanings in local contexts, according to the particularly local criteria for the evaluation of legal arguments. These criteria are, in turn, related to particularly local perceptions of democracy, rights and law, as well as to particularly local aspirations for the future. This does not exclude the possibility of legal convergence. Proportionality, charged with its transnational semantic baggage, brings closer the discourses into which it is inserted. For instance, by attracting legal actors' attention to the structure of legal arguments, proportionality introduces a kind of legal *analysis* in continental jurisdictions. In a quite inverse trajectory, due to its abstract and value-laden character, proportionality enhances prescriptive legal discourse in England. The English tradition of analytical formalism and the continental *doctrine* thus resemble one another more.

Still, describing proportionality as a successful transplant that will eventually lead to the adoption of a global fundamental rights grammar is too simplistic. New 'dissonances' arise from the convergence that proportionality provokes at the level of legal terms.[166] The application of proportionality across time expresses pre-existing arrangements and tendencies in its host legal culture. It reveals the way lawyers see the law, rights, the state and society. Whenever the use of proportionality has evolved away from local cultural features, this was not so much connected to proportionality's inherent qualities and nature, but was rather the result of European influence. It is to this aspect of the evolution of proportionality that we will now turn our attention.

[166] Teubner (1998), p. 20.

PART III

European Integrations

Proportionality and Integration Through Law in Europe. While the idea of integration through law might not have entirely captured the imaginations of legal actors in France, England and Greece, it has certainly captured the imaginations of European lawyers and judges. It is well-known that the building of European regional organisations has followed institutional models found within the nation-state. European courts themselves have engaged different processes of European integration, inspired by the 'constitutional traditions common to the member states'.[1] In the development of European rules and institutions, comparative law has assumed a 'scientific' function.[2] Comparison is the daily work of the research and documentation services of supranational institutions. It serves to identify similarities and possible paths of convergence between national legal systems.

The most well-known examples of communication between domestic and European law are the general principles of law, mainly elaborated in the ECJ jurisprudence. These principles find their source in domestic, mainly public law and govern the organisation of the state and its relations with individuals. However, once appropriated by the ECJ they acquire an autonomous EU law content and serve the promotion of supranational goals. Tridimas observes that general principles 'are children of national law but, as brought up by the Court, they become *enfants terribles*: they are extended, narrowed, restated, transformed by a creative and eclectic judicial process'.[3] General principles of law exemplify the creative role of the ECJ in the making of the EU a 'constitutional order of states'.[4] Most importantly, they were used by this court in the

[1] C-11/70, 17 December 1970, *Internationale Handelsgesellschaft*, ECLI:EU:C:1970:114, para. 2.

[2] Sacco (1991), pp. 3 f.

[3] Tridimas (1999), p. 4.

[4] Dashwood (1996), p. 113, cited by Tridimas (1999), p. 4.

incorporation of a bill of rights in the European legal order, which did not exist before.[5] Indeed, among the general principles of community law the ECJ was very early in proclaiming the protection of fundamental rights and proportionality.[6]

Empowering individuals was a major step in the advancement of European integration. Proportionality and rights provided national legal actors with a concrete interest in invoking EU law before domestic courts. The supremacy and the direct effect doctrines had already provided domestic courts with the technical means for enforcing EU law against national policies. Soon, proportionality acquired a pervasive dynamic in the field of market freedoms and became the major criterion for identifying indirect discriminations. In other fields, however, the ECJ long applied a formalist version of proportionality, which resembled its application in Greek constitutional case law at the time. Indeed, in the 1990 *Fedesa* case, the ECJ established a manifest inappropriateness standard in the scrutiny of EU policy interventions.[7] In the field of penalties and charges imposed on individuals for the advancement of EU policy objectives, proportionality took the form of *nécessité des peines* and no specific right was mentioned in its application.[8] Thus, for some time, in the ECJ case law, proportionality was solely an aspect of the rule of law and expressed the constitutional civilisation of liberal formalism.[9] As a requirement of moderation imposed on the exercise of public power, it functioned as a 'substitute for fundamental rights'.[10]

It was under the impulsion of the ECtHR that proportionality obtained the appeal of a European fundamental rights principle. According to a typical restriction clause in the convention, rights such as the freedom of expression or the freedom of religion can be subject to restrictions in accordance with the law if the restrictions pursue a legitimate aim and are 'necessary in a democratic society'.[11] In the 1976 *Handyside* case, the ECtHR interpreted this last formula as implying a requirement of

[5] De Witte (1999).

[6] *Internationale Handelsgesellschaft*, para. 4. See also the opinion by Advocate General Dutheillet de Lamothe, delivered on 2 December 1970, ECLI: ECLI:EU:C:1970:100, p. 1146.

[7] ECJ, C-331/88, 13 November 1990, *Fedesa*, ECLI:EU:C:1990:391.

[8] See already *Internationale Handelsgesellschaft*, para. 2. See also C-114/76, 5 July 1977, *Bela-Mühle*, ECLI:EU:C:1977:116. Tridimas (1999, pp. 100 f.) compares the function of proportionality in this field to *Wednesbury* unreasonableness.

[9] On the formal conception of the rule of law in the EU, see Weiler (2012), pp. 149 f.

[10] Schwarze (1992), p. 719.

[11] See the second paragraph of articles 8–11 ECHR.

proportionality imposed on rights limitations.[12] Proportionality has enhanced the dynamic interpretation of the convention and has significantly increased the powers of judges, especially lower courts, in its enforcement.[13] In the meantime, the language of rights became increasingly important in EU law, where it has assumed a legitimising and integrationist function.[14] Strasbourg case law has been a source of inspiration for the ECJ.[15] The status of proportionality as a fundamental rights principle is now consolidated in EU law. Article 52 of the EU Fundamental Rights Charter establishes proportionality as a principle that governs rights limitations. Moreover, Article 5(3) entrenches proportionality as a principle that governs the competence of EU institutions.[16]

European Integration from the Point of View of the Proportionality Literature. Mainstream proportionality literature accords particular importance to the application of proportionality by European supranational courts. Scholars often use ECtHR decisions to illustrate the application of the Alexyan proportionality model.[17] European case law and the margin of appreciation doctrine have also served the further refinement of the model to accommodate complex institutional problems faced by international courts.[18] Most importantly, European courts have a special place in the narrative of the global spread of proportionality. Luxembourg and Strasbourg have exercised formal pressure on domestic judges to consistently apply proportionality and have certainly enhanced the diffusion of proportionality language in domestic case law. Due to this, proportionality scholars tend to assume that European supranational courts have *actually obtained* uniform application of proportionality in the scope of European law. Hence, the adoption of proportionality by the ECJ and the ECtHR are seen as 'critical milestones' in the migration of the global proportionality

[12] *Handyside* v. *The UK*, 7 December 1976.

[13] On this point, Keller and Stone Sweet (2008).

[14] See generally de Búrca (1995).

[15] C-4/73, *Nold*, 11 January 1977, ECLI:EU:C:1975:114, para. 13.

[16] See the recent disagreement between the ECJ and the GFCC on the application of proportionality in the assessment of the *ultra vires* character of the ECB's Public Sector Purchase Programme: ECJ, C-493/17, *Weiss and Others*, 11 December 2018, ECLI:EU:C:2018:1000; GFCC, *Weiss* (2020), available in English at www.bundesverfassungsgericht.de.

[17] See, for instance, Rivers (2006), pp. 182 f.; Kumm (2006a), pp. 18 f.; Tsakyrakis (2008); Kumm (2009a), pp. 10 f.

[18] See, for example, Pirker (2013).

model.[19] Stone Sweet and Mathews observe that the ECJ and the ECtHR, by mandating that national courts apply proportionality and by supervising national practice in this respect, have engaged a process of 'coercive isomorphism'.[20] In the view of these authors, this, in turn, has established normative consensus among legal experts on proportionality as 'the emerging best-practice standard' and has produced mimetic tendencies in other jurisdictions.[21]

In the relevant analyses, structural differences between European and domestic proportionality reasoning are typically neglected.[22] Again, the use of proportionality *language* is assimilated into the use of proportionality as a *reasoning process*. However, legal concepts, and language altogether, escape the intentions of their author. Simply because the ECJ and the ECtHR impose proportionality as a legal obligation on domestic courts does not mean these actually apply proportionality as European judges would. What is more, even when domestic judges refer to the principle of proportionality in European case law they do not necessarily apply it as such. The classification of the reception of proportionality in this context as a case of 'forced adaptation'[23] is certainly useful if one seeks to causally explain the spread of proportionality language. Yet it gives little information about the *meaning* of this language in different settings. Domestic legal actors can always misinterpret and mistranslate the obligations that European law imposes on them, obeying local reasoning patterns and rules instead. The indeterminacy of European legal terms and the possibility for divergence and change that they leave is at the core of European integration itself.[24] In fact, supranational courts' case law has not led to a uniform understanding of proportionality across the states subjected to their jurisdiction, not even in the scope of European law. The practice of proportionality in this field reveals itself to be an instance of 'systematically distorted communication' between European and domestic legal actors.[25]

19 Cohen-Eliya and Porat (2013), p. 11. In the same vein, see Barak (2012), pp. 181 f.

20 Stone Sweet and Mathews (2008), pp. 161 f., citing Powell and DiMaggio.

21 Stone Sweet and Mathews (2008), p. 162.

22 For instance, in their country-specific analyses on the reception of the ECHR in domestic spheres, Keller and Stone Sweet typically refer to the application of 'the proportionality test', regardless of whether domestic courts apply it as a pronged structure or a unitary standard and of the kind of reasoning that proportionality implies. See Keller and Stone Sweet, eds. (2008).

23 See, for instance, Lambert Abdelgawad and Weber (2008).

24 Ward (1995), p. 26.

25 Teubner (1991/1992), p. 1455.

European Integration and Legal Culture. European integration and the idea of convergence between legal systems in Europe has been challenged by comparative law scholars who consider cultural diversity to be valuable in its own right. The most radical critic, Legrand, argues that 'European legal systems are not converging' and that 'the ambition of a European *concordantia* is (and must be) a chimera'.[26] Taking the example of reasonableness and proportionality, Legrand argues that there is an irreducible difference between common law and civil law representations of judicial review. For Legrand, appeal to culture is a way to resist the rhetoric of harmonisation and the 'totalitarian rationality' that underpins it,[27] which in his view is 'dictated by the ethos of capital and technology'.[28] Thus, this author does not use the term culture in the case of the EU. Quite differently, Harlow admits that the EU has its own legal culture and 'mindset'.[29] Still, she argues against Europeanisation, which, in her view, takes place in a political vacuum. Harlow reproves European integrationist tendencies for perverting the national democratic process by transferring decision-making powers from parliaments to the judiciary and to supranational institutions.

More moderate scholars have criticised the radical scepticism towards European integration. De Búrca recalls that it is too simplistic to see the EU as an elite-driven liberal trade regime and the nation-state as a site of pluralist democracy. She stresses that the EU evolves to promote its own distinctive human rights policy, which might have a desirable impact in national democratic decision-making.[30] In a similar vein, Walker rejects convergence and divergence fundamentalism and points to the desirability of contingent or selective convergence, which can accommodate pluralism in Europe.[31] European integration has not only been about the construction of a common market but also of a '*communauté de culture constitutionnelle*' between European states.[32]

The debate focuses on the EU, due to the specific legitimacy concerns that its market-centred approach raises. Insofar as the ECHR is concerned, the debate joins a more general discussion in international law,

[26] Legrand (1996), p. 81.
[27] Legrand (2002), p. 256.
[28] Legrand (2003), p. 294.
[29] Harlow (2002), p. 177.
[30] De Búrca (2002).
[31] Walker (2002), p. 257.
[32] AG Cruz Villalón, opinion on C-62/14, *Peter Gauweiler and Others* v. *Deutscher Bundestag*, delivered on 14 January 2015, ECLI:EU:C:2015:7, para. 61 (citation omitted).

conducted in terms of statist democracy v. global or cosmopolitan constitutionalism.[33] Critics of global constitutional law typically stress the ineffectiveness and inconsistent practice of international law. They lament the internationalisation of public law principles for the harm this provokes to democratic self-government by excessively empowering the judiciary and neglecting local cultural particularity. The defenders of global constitutionalism, however, argue that the use of a constitutionalist framework in the context of international law better makes sense of the way this law is perceived and practiced, as well as of the complex institutional architecture of certain international organisations. They contend that constitutionalism beyond the nation-state could strengthen human rights culture and empower minorities that are excluded from the national political process. Following this line of argument, international human rights treaties establish 'a common point of reference' for the discussion of human rights, which could 'create awareness for cognitive limitations connected to national parochialism'.[34]

Regardless of its desirability, supranational integration is a fact, especially in Europe. Cultures overlap geographically and the nation-state is no longer the privileged site of formation for a collective identity. National cultures are themselves highly heterogeneous, while transnational or supranational movements raise alternative claims to cultural recognition.[35] Muir-Watt identifies the move from nation-states to epistemic communities and the creation of a transnational public space as the methodological challenge of contemporary comparative law. Globalisation language is performative and leads to the spread of ideas and ways of thinking about the law. It creates network effects such as exchanges among judges or NGOs.[36] To ignore these evolutions and to deny any possibility of communication between national legal systems would be to ignore an important aspect of legal culture and meaning itself. How does Europeanisation colour the use of proportionality? How does proportionality as a European law principle deploy its integration dynamics in domestic legal spheres?

Expressing Local Visions of European Integration. The purpose of this part is to inquire into the way proportionality transforms local legal culture and is itself transformed by this culture, in the particular context of European integration. This is a valuable inquiry, not only because it

33 On this debate, see, among others, Muir-Watt and Tusseau (2016), pp. 215 f.

34 Kumm (2009b), p. 307. See also Peters (2009).

35 Walker (2002), pp. 264 f. See also Nelken (2012), p. 1.

36 Muir-Watt (2006), pp. 583 f.

enriches our understanding of the local meanings of proportionality, but also because, more importantly, it gives valuable information about local visions of Europe and Europeanisation. These visions are central to our understanding of European integration itself. The acknowledgment of legal diversity in Europe is not inspired by a priori opposition to Europeanisation. Instead, it is inspired by the idea that preserving diversity is *the only* possible way to further European integration. Following Ward: 'Integration can only be identified by the plurality of disintegration. It is the ambition to do away with difference which is both dangerous and inherently flawed.'[37] Divergence and diversity are within Europe itself, since integration presumes difference. Resisting the 'modernist ambition of a "totalized" and teleologically determinable political "union"', we can accept that 'integration and disintegration are not, finally, mutually exclusive'.[38]

The analysis should be distinguished both from arguments about the ideology underpinning European case law and from realist or critical studies of European integration. What I am focused on here are not the particular economic, political or other interests that national and European legal actors promote when applying or invoking European law. Neither is it my purpose to classify different uses of proportionality as activist or hostile towards European integration. More modestly, it is to identify the European integration dynamics ascribed to proportionality in different settings. Contrary to what the mainstream proportionality literature seems to assume, the European baggage of proportionality does not coincide with its German constitutional baggage. Moreover, once inserted into the domestic legal discourses, the European integration dynamics of proportionality are constrained by pre-existing understandings of the relationship between domestic and international law, such as monism or dualism and by particularly local characteristics of legal thought, such as pragmatism or rationalism. Hence, in the field of European integration, proportionality is an example of 'intertextuality', in the sense of the mutual invasion between texts that compromises semantic integrity and defeats any search for an autonomous structure of meaning.[39]

[37] Ward (1995), p. 28.

[38] Ibid.

[39] On the use of Derrida's concept of intertextuality in debates on intellectual history, see Brett (2002), p. 122. On this point, I benefitted from a discussion with Mirko Caricato, whom I sincerely thank.

Put differently, the goal of this part is to enhance our understanding of local expectations of European integration, by advancing our understanding of the different ways in which local legal actors have received proportionality as a European principle. I schematically distinguish between three phases of European integration, which produce three different readings of proportionality and inscribe their particular logics into its use. The ECtHR has as a mission to integrate the contracting parties to the convention into a European legal order of rights. In this court's case law, proportionality has assumed the function of promoting a European culture of rights (Chapter 8). Quite differently, EU integration has largely proceeded through the construction of a common market. In this context, proportionality has primarily functioned as a principle of economic integration (Chapter 9). Recent socio-political shocks upset traditional patterns of Europeanisation. The use of proportionality in domestic law expresses a tendency towards disintegration, which, paradoxically, is transnational (Chapter 10). The different phases of European integration do not occur simultaneously or in an orderly manner, either at a European or at a domestic level. They are not linked by any relation of evolutionary progress or moral hierarchy. Neither do the different versions of proportionality deploy their dynamics in a uniform way in domestic legal spheres. Proportionality, as a European principle, has been understood differently by domestic actors, according to local narratives about law, rights and Europe and to local paths of cultural change.

8

A Common European Culture of Rights

Proportionality as a Principle of Acculturation. The idea of integration through law underpins the convention. Its preamble declares that: '[T]he aim of the Council of Europe is the achievement of greater unity between its Members and one of the methods by which the aim is to be pursued is the maintenance and further realisation of Human Rights and Fundamental Freedoms.' Proportionality is a crucial feature of Strasbourg jurisprudence and a major tool in the hands of the ECtHR for accomplishing this aim. In this context, however, institutional constraints impede the optimal realisation of fundamental rights as the Alexyan theory professes. National authorities enjoy a margin of appreciation in the application of the 'necessary in a democratic society' standard and the ECtHR often contents itself with ensuring that national measures are justified in principle. Proportionality sanctions particular mentalities of domestic public authorities and imposes the taking of rights into account, both in the process of norm production and in the application of the law.[40]

Rather than a function of fundamental rights optimisation then, in Strasbourg, case law proportionality assumes a function of integration into a common European culture of rights. While consensus among the contracting states is central in the dynamic interpretation of the convention, the Strasbourg case law does not postulate a uniform understanding of fundamental rights and proportionality. Proportionality deploys differently its integration dynamics in different settings. This chapter proceeds through a comparative analysis of the application of proportionality in the field of convention rights in France and England, both known for their insular legal traditions and for the crucial influences that they have exercised in the process of European integration. But

[40] On the application of proportionality in this context, see, among others, McBride (1999); Van Drooghenbroeck (2001); Arai-Takahashi (2002); Christoffersen (2009); Pirker (2013), pp. 202 f.

insularity, like formalism, can have very different meanings in different settings. This leads to different reactions to proportionality as a European principle and to different patterns of Europeanisation.

In this chapter, I argue that the local paths of reception of proportionality by French and English lawyers in the field of the convention are shaped by local narratives concerning human rights protection and by local patterns of cultural change. In France, *la patrie des droits de l'Homme*, proportionality was received as a principle already inherent in domestic judicial review concepts and methods. Its reception in this context has followed the patterns of the monist French public law tradition and has expressed the rationalism that characterises French legal thought (Section 8.1). On the contrary, dualism and analytical formalism did not allow for an unthinking assimilation of domestic and ECHR concepts in the common law. Until the incorporation of the convention in domestic law, fundamental or human rights had no legal status and their protection was deemed to be ensured through the checks and balances of the political process. The application of proportionality as a human rights principle was thus long perceived as contrary to parliamentary sovereignty and to the authority of Parliament's commandments (Section 8.2).

Differences in domestic lawyers' reactions to proportionality as a European human rights principle affect the ways in which proportionality deploys its acculturation dynamic in the field of convention rights. In France, the institutional/procedural aspect of proportionality has generally been neglected by domestic lawyers, who have instead focused on the substantive requirements of the Strasbourg case law in concrete cases. The employment of proportionality as a European standard in judicial reasoning is residual and accomplishes a rather symbolic function (Section 8.3). In England, on the contrary, since its reception under the HRA proportionality has served the fulfilment of the UK's international obligations. English lawyers take its acculturation function seriously and proportionality as a European principle generates an important cultural shift in English public law (Section 8.4).

8.1 The Reception of Proportionality in French Public Law: An Inaccurate Translation

The Emergence of Proportionality in Convention-Compatibility Review. The analysis in Chapter 2 shows that until the 1990s, proportionality had no specific legal content in French judicial review. This was the case within the scope of European law as well. *La loi, expression de la volonté générale*, escaped judicial scrutiny on the basis of international treaties. Further, the theory of the *loi écran* impeded contestation of the convention-compatibility of important administrative acts, when their content was dictated by legislation. The convention was not directly applied by courts neither was it much invoked by claimants, since its abstract precepts were not deemed to impose specific constraints on domestic public authorities. Besides, Strasbourg case law long remained unknown to French public lawyers, who adopted a literal interpretation of the convention.[41] It is only with the enforcement of the supremacy of international treaties against legislation that proportionality was received in the *contrôle de conventionnalité*. This evolution began in the field of the ECHR.

The first time that the Council of State annulled an administrative measure on the basis of Article 8 ECHR was in 1991, in the *Belgacem* and *Babas* cases, decided the same day.[42] After the conviction of Mr Belgacem for petty crimes, the immigration police ordered his expulsion. Mr Belgacem contested the compatibility of this measure with the convention claiming that even though he was of Algerian nationality, he was born in France and had no family elsewhere. Indeed, all his brothers and sisters lived in France and so did his father, whose charge Mr Belgacem had partially assumed. Following the observations of the *Commissaire du gouvernement* Abraham, the Council of State abandoned its previous deferent stance towards immigration police authorities and concretely examined the situation of the applicant. It held that:

> [T]he measure of expulsion against Mr Belgacem has exceeded what was necessary for the preservation of public order, given his behaviour after the inflicted condemnations [...], and taking into account the seriousness of the interference with his family life.[43]

In a similar way, the council applied the convention in the case of Mme Babas, albeit without annulling the reviewed decision. The judges concluded that Mme Babas' deportation while she was pregnant 'did not disproportionately restrict [her] right for the respect of her family life'.[44]

[41] Girard (2015), p. 25.

[42] CE (Pl.), 19 April 1991, *M. Belgacem*, no. 107470, ECLI:FR:CEASS:1991:107470.19910419; *Mme Babas*, no. 117680, ECLI:FR:CEASS:1991:117680.19910419.

[43] *Belgacem*.

[44] *Babas*.

Ever since, the council has applied the disproportionality standard in its reasoning under Article 8. This has produced an ever-increasing source of litigation, the *contentieux des étrangers*. The supreme administrative court expanded this kind of review to other rights guaranteed by the convention, including the freedom of expression.[45] During the 1990s, the *Cour de cassation* also adopted proportionality terminology in criminal law, and in rights-based adjudication.[46] By the late 1990s, proportionality had acquired a new content in French public law: that of a European principle and method of review.[47]

Proportionality as *Contrôle de Proportionnalité*. *Belgacem* and *Babas* are generally thought of as the first applications of proportionality in its version of a European fundamental rights principle.[48] However, one will notice that it is only in *Babas* that proportionality terminology was actually used. Instead, in *Belgacem*, the application of Article 8 ECHR only implied an extension of the necessity review already applied in police measures. In other words, the standard of necessity used in *Belgacem* and the standard of disproportionality used in *Babas* are understood as synonymous. This indicates that despite the fact that proportionality acquired a new content as a European principle and technique, its application did not bring about any radical change when compared with pre-existing judicial methods. Its reception in French public law proceeded through its translation to domestic concepts and methods of review. Proportionality was understood as another instance of the *contrôle de proportionnalité* exercised by domestic judges. Because of their shared *nom propre*, European proportionality and domestic *proportionnalité* have been taken to share the same content.[49] They have been understood as having the same meaning, structure and function in legal reasoning. This idea was also expressed in certain studies contemporaneous with *Belgacem* and *Babas*.[50]

[45] Cassia and Saulnier (1997).

[46] Cass. comm., 1 October 1996, no. 94–18845, unreported; Cass. civ. 3, 19 June 1996, no. 94–70323, unreported; Cass. comm., 8 December 1992, nos. 90–20258, 90–20271, 90–20273, 90–20282, 90–20286, 90–20287, 90–20306, 90–20314, 90–20350, 90–20351, and 90–20352, Bull. 1992, no. 404, p. 283.

[47] See Cassia and Saulnier (1997); Markus (1999).

[48] Sauvé (2017).

[49] Analysis inspired by Teubner (1991/1992), p. 1458.

[50] See Fromont (1995). In the same vein, see Markus (1999), who seems to perceive the *contrôle de proportionnalité* and the *contrôle de conventionnalité* as being in continuity with traditional Council of State methods. Ziller (1996) is more sensitive to difference, but he still rejects the idea of a French exceptionalism and affirms that French courts apply

Assimilation of European and domestic proportionality scrutiny was more obvious in cases where a disproportionality standard was already employed by domestic courts. In the field of administrative sanctions, for instance, whenever the convention was invoked by the claimants, the Council of State applied its traditional manifest disproportionality test. Often it did so without referring to the convention in the body of its judgment, although it did mention it in the *visas* of the decision.[51] The invocation of the ECHR in such cases sometimes led the Council of State to abandon its traditional manifest disproportionality scrutiny and to exercise a full proportionality review.[52] Apart from an intensification of the pre-existing *contrôle de proportionnalité*, the operation of the convention in the domestic sphere produced a spill-over of proportionality terminology into purely domestic cases involving individual rights.[53] Proportionality as a European principle was diffused in domestic judicial review.

Assimilation, Monism and Rationalism. Assimilation of the concepts of international treaties to corresponding domestic concepts is not a particularity of proportionality neither is it limited to the application of the ECHR. It is deeply rooted in the monist French public law tradition and is a corollary of the dogmatism that is peculiar to French legal thought. As the famous technique of the *acte clair* exemplifies, the interpretation of international treaties in conformity with domestic law has been a common way of managing the conflicts between domestic and international law.[54] This practice has preserved the consistency of the law applicable by domestic judges, which is so dear to French lawyers. It is indicative that, until 1990, the Council of State referred questions on the interpretation of international treaties to the minister of foreign affairs. Hence, in spite of the fact that the constitution conferred treaties with a

proportionality. He does not see the different proportionality methods as leading to different substantive outcomes.

[51] See, for example, CE, 28 July 1999, nos. 202606, 203438, 203487, 203541, and 203589, ECLI:FR:CESSR:1999:202606.19990728.

[52] CE, 12 March 1999, nos. 181976, 182549, 182572, and 182624, ECLI:FR:CESSR:1999:181976.19990312.

[53] See, for example, CE, 12 July 1993, no. 121337, ECLI:FR:CESSR:1993:121337.19930712 on the right to property; 6 December 1993, no. 124984, ECLI:FR:CESSR:1993:124984.1993120 on individual freedom.

[54] See CE, 19 June 1964, *Société des pétroles Shell-Berre*, no. 47007, Rec., p. 344; Cass. civ. 1, 19 December 1995, *Banque africaine de développement*, no. 93–20424, Bull. 1995, no. 470, p. 326. On proportionality in EU law in particular, see the analysis by Sirinelli and Bertrand (2010), p. 628.

supra-legislative status, in case of doubt, the content of their provisions was to be defined by the French government. International treaties' terms could have no other content than the one that domestic authorities gave to them. Even though, in the 1990 *GISTI* case, the council affirmed to itself the power to interpret international conventions, it did so by reference to the 'pieces of the [administrative] file'.[55]

In particular, insofar as the ECHR is concerned, assimilation of domestic and European concepts is also underpinned by another feature: French public lawyers' shared belief in a common European civilisation of rights, of which France is the motherland. Indeed, European human rights standards have been received in France, *la patrie des droits de l'Homme,* as already part of domestic law.[56] The assimilation of ECHR concepts to domestic ones can be understood as an instance of the rationalism that characterises French legal thought. It fits with the perception of law as a system, a coherent whole, imbued with rational moral-legal principles. These principles were acquired with the French Revolution and have been entrenched in republican legislation ever since. We saw that proportionality, even before its connection to the *bilan*, was connected to the *DDHC*, especially in its version of *necessité des peines*. During the 1980s, despite the absence of explicit recognition of proportionality as a principle in domestic case law, the French *doctrine* considered it part of the *bloc de légalité*, that is, the norms of reference used by the administrative judge.[57]

For French public lawyers then, ECtHR jurisprudence added nothing to already existing theories on judicial review. Simply, by including proportionality in the *bloc de conventionnalité*, the ECHR has expanded its scope of application, and most importantly, has opened the way for its application by ordinary courts against Parliament.[58] During the 1990s, proportionality was perceived as a unitary principle or ideal, in spite of its variable application by domestic, foreign and European courts. It corresponded to an objective liberal principle prescribing the moderation of public power and connected to a common European perception of individual rights. Thus, the *Cour de cassation* sometimes referred to the general principle of proportionality 'guaranteed by the European Convention for the protection of Human Rights and Fundamental

[55] CE (Pl.), 29 June 1990, *GISTI*, no. 78519, ECLI:FR:CEASS:1990:78519.19900629.
[56] Girard (2015), p. 276.
[57] See Part I, Chapter 2.2.
[58] On the *bloc de conventionnalité*, see Markus (1999).

Freedoms, the Treaty of Rome and the Declaration of the Rights of Man and of the Citizen'.[59]

8.2 The Rejection of Proportionality in the Common Law: Constrained by Analytical Formalism

Dualism, Pragmatism and the Fragmentation of Proportionality. The common law analytical tradition did not allow for an unthinking assimilation of English and ECHR concepts in the name of law's consistency. While EC law rights and proportionality were applied through the 'gateway' of the ECA, Convention rights for long were not incorporated in domestic law. Hence, they did not constitute standards of legality for the breach of which administrative action could be impugned.[60] Proportionality as a convention head of review was perceived as distinct from domestic standards of judicial review. In the dualist English system, applying proportionality would be as if judges incorporated the convention into the domestic sphere 'by the back door'.[61] It was the principle of parliamentary sovereignty that was at stake. And, following the Whig account of history, parliamentary sovereignty and the rule of law have long succeeded in protecting civil liberties and democracy in the UK, without needing substantive constitutional rights and ideals, or even any constitution whatsoever.

Outside the scope of judicial review, proportionality was applied only insofar as convention rights were at play. For instance, courts made recourse to the ECHR to clarify ambiguities in the common law. On the contrary, the application of proportionality was rejected when the applicable common law principles needed no clarification. This was the case even when the reasonableness standard applied. As we saw, reasonableness exceeded the confines of public law. The promoters of proportionality thus encouraged proportionality's spread in private law cases.[62] However, judges emphatically rejected horizontal application of proportionality balancing. They refused to impose a proportionality requirement in cases that included no clear asymmetry between the parties of the

[59] Cass. civ. 1, 13 February 1996, no. 93-12750, Bull. 1996, no. 73, p. 47.

[60] Loughlin (2013), pp. 36 f. See *Malone* v. *Commissioner of Police of the Metropolis (No. 2)* [1979] 1 Ch 344 (HC, Chancery Division, 28 February 1979); ECtHR, *Malone* v. *The UK*, 2 August 1984, no. 8691/79.

[61] *Brind* (HL, 7 February 1991), p. 762, per Lord Ackner. See Part I, Chapter 3.2.

[62] Jowell and Lester (1988b), p. 66; Laws (1992), p. 1388.

dispute.[63] In *Allied Dunbar*, Millett J declared that the concept of proportionality in contract law 'is novel and dangerous and requires the court to perform an impossible balancing act'.[64] The judge considered that contractual restrictions should be left to negotiation between the parties. In his words, 'the price is the best means of adjusting the otherwise disproportionate advantages and disadvantages of the other terms of the contract'.[65] In Millet J's view, the application of proportionality in this field would entail the 'revival of an obsolete and discredited doctrine'.[66]

For a long time, English lawyers easily coped with the fragmented application of proportionality and human rights standards in case law. Contrary to what is observed in rationalist French legal thought, a plurality of formal and conceptual frameworks is not necessarily a problem in the pragmatist common law tradition. Rather, it demonstrates 'the traditional English preference for "muddling through"'.[67] In English legal thought, legal form is not a uniform whole imposed by some kind of rational and objective reality. Instead, it is understood as a tool, chosen by decision-makers (including judges) for the regulation of various activities in order to achieve the distinctive purposes of each. In this context, law is seen as a commandment, and its autonomy and authority are crucial. Contextual accounts of law, embedding it in evolutions of the surrounding circumstances, are traditionally rejected, both in theory and practice.[68] This was illustrated in the *Spycatcher* litigation, where proportionality found its first application as an ECHR principle.

The Application of Proportionality in *Spycatcher*. In this famous series of cases, the *Guardian* and the *Observer* wanted to publish information contained in *Spycatcher*, a book written by a former agent of the British security service. This information involved details about the penetration of the service by foreign agents. The attorney general, who had sought to restrain the publication of the book in Australia, was also seeking interim injunctions against the British newspapers. Lester QC and Pannick, representing the newspapers, built a defence against the

[63] *Express Newspapers Ltd* v. *MacShane and Another* [1980] 1 All ER 65 (HL, 13 December 1979), pp. 72 f.

[64] *Allied Dunbar (Frank Weisinger) Ltd* v. *Frank Weisinger* [1988] IRLR 60 (HC, Queen's Bench Division, 1 January 1988).

[65] Ibid.

[66] Ibid.

[67] Atiyah (1987), p. 4.

[68] Dicey famously criticised the historical method in legal analysis. On this point, see Walters (2012), p. 22.

restrictions on the fundamental right to freedom of press and expression protected by Article 10 ECHR.[69]

In the first decision on the case in 1987, Millett J granted the injunctions after weighing the relevant conflicting public interests: the freedom of the press to inform the public, especially when unlawful conduct by civil servants was suspected; and the need for an effective and leak-proof secret service in the interests of national security.[70] The judge stated that 'the restrictions imposed by the court should not go beyond the strict requirements of the interest which it is sought to safeguard'.[71] Thus, he exempted from the injunction information disclosed in open court in Australia. On appeal, Sir Donaldson MoR confirmed Millett J's decision expressly referring to the principle of proportionality. In his words:

> Where there is confidentiality, the public interest in its maintenance has to be overborne by a countervailing public interest, if publication is not to be restrained. In some cases the weight of the public interest in the maintenance of the confidentiality will be small and the weight of the public interest in publication will be great. But in weighing these countervailing public interests or, perhaps more accurately, those countervailing aspects of a single public interest, both the nature and circumstances of the confidentiality and the nature and circumstances of the proposed publication have to be examined with considerable care. This is what is sometimes referred to as the principle of proportionality – is the restraint or lack of restraint proportionate to the overall assessment of the public interest.[72]

The use of proportionality language shows that already since the mid-1980s, ECHR influence introduced fundamental rights considerations into common law techniques and precedents. Here, proportionality was explicitly used as a guiding principle for the 'balance of convenience', that is, the judicial assessment of the pros and contras for granting an injunction according to the normative and factual circumstances of the case. Its function was akin to the one that it assumes in Strasbourg case law. However, taking into account the convention did not necessarily presuppose that the rights entrenched therein enjoyed legal status in the

[69] I refer here only to the interim injunctions series of cases. The *Spycatcher* litigation is much more complex and also involved main proceedings on breach of confidentiality, as well as proceedings for contempt of court against certain newspapers.

[70] *Attorney General* v. *Guardian Newspapers Ltd and Others; Attorney General* v. *The Observer Ltd. and Others* [1989] 2 FSR 3 (interlocutory injunction, HC, Chancery Division, 11 July 1986 – CA, 25 July 1986).

[71] Ibid, p. 14.

[72] Ibid, p. 22.

domestic sphere. Interestingly, in Sir Donaldson's dicta proportionality designated a kind of judicial reasoning that involved the balancing of 'countervailing public interests or, perhaps more accurately, those countervailing aspects of a single public interest'. The only right recognised in this decision was the common law right to confidentiality. Convention rights were taken into account among the various *circumstances* of the case. Thus, their realisation was trumped in the presence of clear legal rules, even when these rules were no longer adapted to social reality or constituted a violation of the international obligations of the UK. This became apparent in the sequel to the *Spycatcher* affair.

Irritating Law's Authority. In July 1987, *Spycatcher* was published in the USA and individual copies were obtainable in the UK. At the same time, the *Sunday Times* published extracts from the book. The *Guardian* and the *Observer* applied to have their injunctions discharged because of the new circumstances. Meanwhile, the attorney general started proceedings against the *Sunday Times* for contempt of court. The causes were examined together by Sir Browne-Wilkinson V-C. Referring to Sir Donaldson's application of proportionality in the previous *Spycatcher* case, Sir Browne-Wilkinson observed that the harm to the national security that the attorney general was seeking to prevent had already been produced, because the book was accessible to anyone who was interested in buying it. In his words: 'The purpose ha[d] been destroyed'.[73] He held:

> I think the public interest requires that we have a legal system and courts which command public respect. It is frequently said that the law is an ass. I, of course, do not agree. But there is a limit to what can be achieved by orders of the court. If the courts were to make orders manifestly incapable of achieving their avowed purpose, such as to prevent the dissemination of information which is already disseminated, the law would to my mind indeed be an ass.[74]

The attorney general also claimed that further dissemination of the book in the UK would encourage others who wanted to follow the example of the author of the *Spycatcher*. Still, the judge found this public interest too trivial with respect to the importance of the freedom of the press. In Sir Browne-Wilkinson's decision then, the application of

[73] *Attorney General* v. *Guardian Newspapers Ltd and Others; and Related Appeals* [1987] 1 WLR 1248 (interlocutory injunction, CA, Civil Division, 24 July 1987; HL, 13 August 1987), p. 1269.

[74] Ibid.

proportionality as an instance of consequentialist balancing introduced an exception to a clearly defined legal rule, namely, the prohibition from disseminating information obtained through breach of duty by a public official.

However, Sir Browne-Wilkinson's decision was reversed by the Court of Appeal. The appellate judges held that since the attorney general had an arguable cause in the main trial, his rights should be preserved. Thus, they granted the injunction and even deleted Millett J's exemption concerning the Australian proceedings. In the Court of Appeal decision law's formality and authority excluded proportionality balancing or any other type of reasoning according to the circumstances of the case. In the words of Russell LJ:

> The 'purpose' of the proceedings cannot be the preservation of secrecy in the British security service: that has been irretrievably lost. Nor can it be, save to a very limited extent, the restoration of confidence amongst other organisations. But, in my judgment, the law and the courts must still continue to strive, and must give all the appearances of continuing to strive, to deter the commercial dissemination of the contents of *Spycatcher* when every word written in the book is prima facie in breach of duty.[75]

When the case arrived before the House of Lords, Lester QC and Pannick finished their address on behalf of the *Sunday Times* with the following words: 'This case cries out for a sense of proportion.'[76] With a 3:2 majority, however, the Lords of Appeal confirmed the appellate judges' decision. Lord Brandon and Lord Ackner again referred to the fact that the attorney general had an arguable cause and thus his interests should be preserved until the case was tried. Lord Templeman went even further and, citing ECHR case law, declared that the restrictions were necessary in a democratic society in the interests of national security. In his view, the allegations included in the *Spycatcher* might not be true and the honest members of the security service would not be able to defend themselves without breaching their duty of confidentiality.[77]

Before the House of Lords, law's authority trumped any countervailing substantive considerations. Proportionality, as a fundamental rights principle imposing the adaptation of the law to the changing circumstances, irritated the particular version of formalism that traditionally permeates in English legal thought. This is neatly expressed in Lord

[75] Ibid, p. 1281.
[76] Ibid, p. 1300.
[77] Ibid, p. 1297.

Ackner's dicta, who responded to the proportionality argument of the newspapers by citing another judge sixty years before him:

> 'Amid the shifting sands and cross-currents of public life the law is like a great rock on which men may set their feet and be safe.'
>
> For the word 'rock' the appellants would have your Lordships now read 'jellyfish'![78]

Lord Bridge, dissenting, had foreseen that: 'If the government are determined to fight to maintain the ban to the end, they will face inevitable condemnation and humiliation by the European Court of Human Rights in Strasbourg.'[79] Indeed, condemnation and humiliation were not long in coming. In its 1991 decision on the issue, the ECHR applied a proportionality test and declared that the restrictions on publication imposed by the English authorities after July 1987 were unjustified.[80] The fact that the Lords of Appeal had taken the convention into account did not save their decision. In the end, the *Spycatcher* litigation is not remembered as a landmark for the application of the convention in English law. However, it did bring about an important contribution in this respect: it was in this case that the link between the ECHR and proportionality was for the first time authoritatively established.

The Persisting Difference Between Anxious Scrutiny and European Proportionality Review. In subsequent case law, Strasbourg influence became increasingly explicit in judicial decisions, to the point that domestic lawyers started talking about the application of proportionality 'in all but name'.[81] However, in judicial practice, an important difference between the European proportionality review and domestic standards persisted. While, when the circumstances warranted it, the ECtHR could impose its own view as to the justification or the proportionality of the reviewed measures, the English courts could never become appellate jurisdictions in judicial review cases. Merits review was excluded, no matter the importance of the right at stake or the intensity of interference with it. In other words, there was always a zone of immunity in the substantive review of administrative action.[82] In *Smith and Grady*, the

[78] Ibid, p. 1306, citing John Sankey.
[79] Ibid, p. 1286.
[80] ECtHR, *Observer and Guardian* v. *The UK*, 26 November 1991, no. 13585/88.
[81] See Part II, Chapter 6.3.
[82] See also the analysis by Elliott (2001).

Strasbourg court identified the difference in the kind of review exercised under the irrationality and proportionality tests.[83]

The difference between domestic and European standards reveals a deeper normative conflict between English public law and the convention, which persisted before the voting through of the HRA. Even though fundamental rights were widely accepted as important values in case law, they remained the 'background' of the application of legal forms, or at best, a 'relevant consideration'.[84] Their definition and protection was still mainly remitted to the political branches of government. They did not impose particular outcomes on public action. Besides, Whig historians' idea that the common law and parliamentary sovereignty sufficiently protected fundamental rights persisted. In this respect, Lord Goff's dictum in *Spycatcher* is illustrative:

> I wish to observe that I can see no inconsistency between English law on this subject and article 10 of the European Convention on Human Rights. This is scarcely surprising, since we may pride ourselves on the fact that freedom of speech has existed in this country perhaps as long as, if not longer than, it has existed in any other country in the world.[85]

Hence, different narratives about law and rights have differently shaped the process of reception of proportionality as a European human rights principle in French and English law. Local legal actors' reactions to proportionality have constrained proportionality's acculturation dynamic in different ways and have led to local patterns of Europeanisation in the context of the convention. While in France proportionality as a European human rights principle is residually applied and accomplishes a rather symbolic function, since its reception in England, proportionality as an HRA head of review assumes a function of cultural transformation.

8.3 Lost in Translation: The Institutional Dimension of Proportionality in French Public Law

Neglecting Structural Differences Between European and Domestic Proportionality Review. Since proportionality and convention rights standards were deemed as already existing in French public law, the

83 *Smith and Grady* v. *The UK*, 27 September 1999, para. 138.

84 See Hunt (1997), pp. 221 f.

85 *Attorney General* v. *Guardian Newspapers Ltd (No. 2); Attorney General* v. *The Observer Ltd and Others* [1990] 1 AC 109 (HL, 13 October 1988), per Lord Goff. See also *Derbyshire* (CA, Civil Division, 19 February 1992).

acculturation process into which the ECtHR invited domestic authorities has not been perceived as necessary in the French context. The institutional aspects of proportionality have been lost in the process of translation of the convention principle to domestic methods. Indeed, the merging of domestic and European proportionality review apparently came at a cost for the European test's structure and rigour. In the Council of State case law, proportionality did not correspond to a pronged test similar to the one applied by European courts. Full-fledged proportionality analysis was incompatible with the laconic and formal style in which French courts traditionally expressed themselves. Structural differences between European and domestic proportionality review were neglected in the *doctrine* as well. In the most elliptic of the Council of State's formulations, scholars saw instances of a 'full proportionality review', involving the balancing of competing values.[86]

Proportionality as an ECHR concept has been deemed to prescribe substantive norms and solutions rather than a particular process of reasoning. Its application thus implied a threshold review, based on the particular factual circumstances of the case. In family life cases, the field of application of proportionality par excellence, the council typically took into account the duration and the importance of the family relations invoked by the claimant, her attachment to her country of origin and the risk that her remaining in France caused to public order. In *Babas*, for example, in order to reach its decision on the proportionality of the measure, the court considered 'all the circumstances of the case, and especially the time and the conditions of Mme Babas' stay in France', as well as 'the effects of the measure of deportation'.[87] The judges had access to these factual elements indirectly, through the file compiled by the administration in the procedure preceding the contested act. Proportionality remained a factual matter primarily considered by the administration.

The Limited Role of Proportionality in the Accommodation of the Convention in French Public Law. Hence, proportionality has had a limited role in the adaptation of French public law to the ECHR. In this context, compliance with the convention has not acquired the form of a concrete remedy or head of judicial review. Instead, it has proceeded through the accommodation of convention standards within the French public law tradition, sometimes without even referring to the convention

[86] Markus (1999), before fn. 129.
[87] *Babas*.

at all. Judges and law-makers have often cooperated in this process. For example, long before the direct application of Article 8 by the Council of State, a governmental decree had instituted family reunification for foreign country nationals.[88] Based on this and on the Preamble of the 1946 Constitution, the council had recognised the status of the right to family life as a general principle of law.[89] Furthermore, legislation dating from 1979 had set the conditions and guarantees applicable to the procedure of expulsion, thus leading the judge to scrutinise, albeit with restraint, some of the relevant administrative acts.[90] The status of foreigners was further ameliorated by legislation at the end of the 1980s, and certain categories of foreigners were excluded from expulsion. In the definition of these categories, the personal and family situation of the affected persons was taken into account. The Council of State interpreted the relevant provisions broadly and applied a manifest error test in assessing whether immigration authorities respected them.[91] With the emergence of the disproportionality standard in *Babas* and *Belgacem*, the manifest error review lost its utility in such cases and was progressively abandoned.[92] Still, one cannot help but notice the continuity in administrative case law, which nuances the importance of the introduction of the disproportionality standard itself.

During the 1980s and the 1990s, the whole of the French institutional apparatus has strived to abide by the substantive requirements of Strasbourg case law, without radically challenging traditional reasoning methods and the distribution of competences in judicial review. Indeed, in 1986 the Constitutional Council delegated the fulfilment of supranational rights obligations to 'the various State authorities [...] in the context of their respective competences'.[93] The Constitutional Council itself has actively participated in the process of adaptation of the domestic constitutional order to the convention. It did so by proclaiming the constitutional status of fundamental rights and principles, among them

[88] Decree of 29 April 1976.

[89] CE (Pl.), 8 December 1978, *GISTI, CFDT et CGT*, nos. 10097, 10677, and 10679, ECLI:FR:CEASS:1978:10097.19781208.

[90] Law of 11 July 1979. On this point, see Long et al. (2019) no. 83.10.

[91] See CE (Pl.), 29 June 1990, no. 115971, ECLI:FR:CEASS:1990:115971.19900629.

[92] See, however, CE, 11 October 1991, no. 125101, ECLI:FR:CEORD:1991:125101.19911011, where manifest error and proportionality are applied cumulatively.

[93] Decision no. 86–216 DC, 3 September 1986, *Loi relative aux conditions d'entrée et de séjour des étrangers en France*, ECLI:FR:CC:1986:86.216.DC, cons. 6.

proportionality.[94] Indeed, in a quite paradoxical way, while being a systemic evolution of French public law, the recognition of the constitutional basis of proportionality at the same time connected this law to European fundamental rights. Hence, while proportionality and its fundamental rights baggage have been reinvented by French constitutional judges as objective, republican principles, their application has echoed the ECtHR case law.

Proportionality as a Corrective 'Patch' in Ordinary Courts' Case Law. The European principle of proportionality being perceived as equally domestic, the direct application of proportionality as a convention standard in ordinary courts' case law has had a corrective function. It has only served to clear French law of 'flaws, rust and incongruities that it accumulated with time'.[95] In other words, proportionality as a convention principle has assumed the function of a 'patch'. In certain cases, domestic courts have used it as such to ensure the convention compatibility of legislation. For example, the town planning code imposed duties on the owners of certain properties to the benefit of neighbouring properties, while it excluded the owners' compensation for the damages that they suffered in result. An aggrieved individual contested the compatibility of this provision with Article 1 of the First Additional Protocol to the ECHR before the Council of State. The council decided that the legislation in question should be interpreted, contrary to its plain reading, as not always impeding the owner from obtaining compensation. Compensation was still due 'in the exceptional cases where it results from all the conditions and circumstances [...] that the property owner suffers an unusual and excessive charge, out of proportion with the general interest pursued' by the law.[96] The exception of disproportionality added by the Council of State was sufficient to render domestic legislation compatible with the convention.

In French administrative law, disproportionality has functioned as an exception, a condition for defeating domestic general rules in particular circumstances. The corrective function of proportionality is expressed in the residual use of proportionality terminology in case law, which contrasts with the perception of proportionality as a general principle in the

94 On the protection of human dignity for example, see Decision no. 94–343/344 DC, 27 July 1994; on the right to private and family life, see Decision no. 93–325 DC, 13 August 1993, cons. 104; on the principle of proportionality, Decision no. 94–352 DC, 18 January 1995. See Part I, Chapter 2.3.

95 Cassia and Saulnier (1997), fn. 45, citing Yves Madiot.

96 CE, 3 July 1998, no. 158592, ECLI:FR:CESJS:1998:158592.19980703.

minds of French public lawyers. Indeed, in judicial review, the Council of State has employed the disproportionality standard mainly in ECHR cases, and especially in the *contentieux des étrangers*. Among the approximately 10,500 Council of State decisions that mention the term 'disproportionate', more than 8,600 concern the right to family life under Article 8 ECHR.[97] Otherwise, the use of proportionality by the supreme administrative court has been inconsistent. In margin of appreciation cases, judges have typically declared domestic measures compatible with the convention without using proportionality at all. The corrective function of proportionality as an ECHR standard is confirmed by a reading of the *Commissaire du gouvernement* Abraham's opinion in *Belgacem* and *Babas*. Indeed, what pushed the judge, and subsequently the Council of State, to exercise a proportionality review of immigration police measures was the fear that if domestic courts did not do so, it would be Strasbourg that would rule in this field.[98]

The residual application of proportionality has led to a paradox. While proportionality is understood as a fundamental rights principle, its invocation as such has mainly served foreigners. And at a closer look, it has not much served them either. As a corrective standard, proportionality operates when traditional concepts and methods of review are insufficient to fulfil convention requirements. In the *patrie des droits de l'Homme*, this happens only exceptionally. Hence, in most cases, deportation orders against immigrants have been found to be justified in a democratic society. As a negative standard, disproportionality only rarely led to the annulment of the impugned decision. After a survey of Article 8 case law, Cassia and Saulnier described the council as being convinced that, 'by nature, immigration police measures did not infringe the family life of the foreigner, since no one prohibits her family from leaving the [French] territory after her'.[99] Dogmatism, judicial restraint and lack of justification also characterise the proportionality case law of the *Cour de cassation*.[100] Due to its factual nature, proportionality is primarily considered by inferior

[97] Based on a research of terms in the Council of State database *ArianeWeb*, www.conseil-etat.fr, on 23 January 2018. More than 9,100 decisions concern the right to family life more generally, provided for by other international texts or by domestic legislation.

[98] Abraham, 'Conclusions sur CE Ass., 19 avril 1991, *Belgacem* et *Babas*', *RFDA*, 1991, p. 502; on this point, see Andriantsimbazovina (1998), p. 437.

[99] Cassia and Saulnier (1997), fn. 71, citing Martine Denis-Linton.

[100] See, for example, Cass. crim., 19 March 1996, no. 94–81420, Bull. crim., 1996, no. 117, p. 340.

judges. This long limited the possibilities for its invocation before the cassation judge considerably.[101]

The Symbolic Function of Proportionality in French Judicial Review. Mainly serving the compliance with the convention, the disproportionality standard has not contested the procedural and institutional features that generally characterise the application of convention requirements.[102] For a long time, the preservation of traditional concepts and methods also preserved traditional taboos, representations and myths. Most importantly, the role of the legislator as the protector of public freedoms, even of those enshrined in the convention, was not questioned. Indeed, domestic courts typically refused to declare legislation incompatible with the ECHR. Violations of the convention were presented not as the result of legislation itself but of its application.[103] They were perceived as a distortion of the legislative will, an *effet pervers* connected to the concrete circumstances of the case.[104]

The dogmatic application of the convention has been criticised repeatedly by the ECtHR since the end of the 1990s. This has sometimes led domestic courts to adopt more pragmatic methods of adjudication, although without always referring to the convention ('each one has his dignity', in the words of Olivier Dutheillet de Lamothe, member of the Constitutional Council at the time).[105] In *Association Ekin* in 2001, the Strasbourg court censured the practice of French judges of avoiding declarations of incompatibility of domestic legislation.[106] After this decision, the Council of State started to abandon its deferent stance and to apply proportionality against Parliament too.[107] This opened the way for

[101] Cass. crim., 10 March 1993, no. 91-86197, Bull. crim., 1993, no. 108, p. 261.

[102] On such features, see Markus (1999), section 'Le déclenchement du contrôle'.

[103] For instance, CE, 2 June 1999, *Meyet*, no. 207752, ECLI:FR:CESJS:1999:207752.19990602.

[104] In the same vein, see Girard (2015), p. 25.

[105] Dutheillet de Lamothe (2008), p. 301. The author refers to the requirement for a 'sufficient general interest' conditioning the constitutionality of retroactive validations of administrative acts by legislation.

[106] ECtHR, *Association Ekin* v. *France*, 17 October 2001, no. 39288/98.

[107] CE (Pl.), 30 November 2001, *Diop*, no. 212179, ECLI:FR:CEASS:2001:212179.20011130; CE, 24 February 2006, no. 250704, ECLI:FR:CESSR:2006:250704.20060224, concerning the *loi 'anti-Perruche'*. The Council of State's decision followed a Strasbourg decision that had found violation of the legitimate expectations of the victims under article 1 FAP ECHR (*Maurice* v. *France*, 6 October 2005, no. 11810/03). On the application of proportionality in the judicial review of legislation, see Markus (1999), section 'Les manifestations d'un contrôle de proportionnalité'.

lower courts to disapply domestic legal provisions that they found disproportionate.

Still, until recently the Council of State hesitated to review the convention-compatibility of domestic legislation in the *référé libertés* procedure, under which the administrative judges sanction 'serious and manifestly illegal' interferences with the plaintiffs' fundamental rights.[108] Confusion as to the intensity of review that proportionality implied also impeded its application against the administration in this context. Anxious of exceeding their competence, the interim judges initially required that public measures be manifestly disproportionate in order to suspend their application.[109] The difference as compared with the normal application of the disproportionate standard, already exceptional, was difficult to discern. The council thus ended by generally avoiding the use of proportionality terminology in interim measures case law.[110] In recent case law, the three prongs of proportionality are announced as a requirement imposed on rights restrictions but not applied in the reasoning that follows.[111]

The application of proportionality by French courts in the context of the convention has not radically changed domestic judicial review structures, underlying myths and substantive outcomes. As a European fundamental rights principle, proportionality has had a more significant impact in the development and expansion of pre-existing methods of review. Whenever it has been explicitly applied in the form of the disproportionate standard, its function has mainly been symbolic in the effort of domestic courts to affirm the conformity of French law to European rights precepts and their proper role as fundamental rights protectors. Indeed, in French case law in the field of the convention proportionality's function has been one of 'signalisation'.[112] Addressed

[108] CE, 30 December 2002, *Carminati*, no. 240430, ECLI:FR:CESSR:2002:240430.20021230. On this point, see Dutheillet de Lamothe and Odinet (2016). The *Gonzalez-Gomez* case brought about significant change in this respect and is extensively debated in French *doctrine* during the last years. The case will be discussed in Part III, Chapter 10.1, due to its exceptional nature, which attributes a particular expressive function to it.

[109] CE ord., 30 October 2001, no. 238211, ECLI:FR:CESJS:2001:238211.20011030.

[110] See CE ord., 9 November 2005, no. 286321, ECLI:FR:CEORD:2005:286321.20051109.

[111] See CE ord., 9 January 2014, *Ministre de l'intérieur c. Société Les Productions de la Plume et M. Dieudonné M'Bala M'Bala*, no. 374508, ECLI:FR:CEORD:2014:374508.20140109, cons. 5 f.; CE, 9 November 2015, Le *Mur (Dieudonné)*; CE ord., 27 January 2016, *Ligue des droits de l'homme et autres*, no. 396220, ECLI:FR:CEORD:2016:396220.20160127; CE ord., 26 August 2016, *Ligue des droits de l'homme et autres – association de défense des droits de l'homme collectif contre l'islamophobie en France*, nos. 402742 and 402777, ECLI:FR:CEORD:2016:402742.20160826.

[112] Cohn (2010), p. 588, citing Assaf Likhovski.

to domestic public lawyers and to Strasbourg judges, proportionality has expressed the domestic courts' attempt to persuade as to the compliance of domestic law with ECHR requirements. Most often, the self-evident affirmation of the legitimacy of domestic measures has not even proceeded through the use of proportionality language.[113]

8.4 A Tool for Complying with Convention Rights: Taking Proportionality Seriously in the Common Law

The Instrumental Perception of Proportionality in the Common Law. In contrast to the symbolic use of proportionality in French case law, the employment of proportionality by English judges under the HRA is instrumental: proportionality is a head of review for the adjudication of human rights. Its application involves a clear, pronged structure of reasoning. Instrumentalism is already apparent in the fragmented application of proportionality, which has persisted even after the incorporation of the convention. While the rationalist approach that underpins proportionality spreads in judicial review, proportionality itself as a head of review is constrained within the scope of human rights cases. Outside this scope, traditional judicial review categories and doctrines still operate. Even the most prominent defenders of proportionality's spill-over admit that proportionality is not appropriate for certain kinds of judicial decision-making.[114] Furthermore, courts typically distinguish the proportionality head applied under the HRA from the one applied in EU law cases.[115]

What the fragmentation of proportionality reveals is that the 'righting' of English public law is not yet complete.[116] Human rights are not deemed to be a framework sufficient to frame the whole of public action. Indeed, sceptics criticise the discourse on the reign of human rights and proportionality as typical of lawyers obsessed with courts and judicial review. In their view, 'modern-day arch-simplifiers' neglect that in the

[113] See, for example, the decision by the *Cour de cassation* in the *SAS* case, later brought before the ECtHR: Cass. crim., 5 March 2013, no. 12–80891, Bull. crim., 2013, no. 54. See however, CE (Pl.), 12 June 2020, *Archives du président Mitterrand sur le Rwanda*, nos. 422327 and 431026, ECLI: FR:CEASS:2020:422327.20200612, where proportionality is applied as an ad hoc reasoning method that is clearly distinct from the manifest error test and involves value-laden balancing in view of the concrete circumstances of the case.

[114] Craig (2016), para. 19–027.

[115] *Countryside Alliance* (HL, 28 November 2007). More recently, *R* v. *Legal Services Board, ex parte Lumsdon and Others* [2015] UKSC 41 (SC, 24 June 2015).

[116] Taggart (2003), pp. 323 f.

instrumental English legal culture forms exist because they *serve* various purposes in the various contexts in which they are employed.[117] Fragmentation and complexity in English administrative law serve the fragmented and complex functioning of public administration, which is its main object. Poole talks about 'a polyglot patchwork of decision-making institutions and players' in public administration.[118]

Serving the UK's Compliance with the Convention. Interestingly, the critics of proportionality's reign share a belief in the possibility of categorising the various administrative law fields according to the substantive values that underpin them. Taggart, for example, talked about the 'bifurcation' of administrative law cases into those involving rights and those involving 'public wrongs'.[119] In this author's view, proportionality is an appropriate form only for the first type of cases. Similarly, Hickman and King argue for the application of proportionality only where it is justified by the importance of the value at stake. They identify categories of substantive values, with fundamental rights being the central one.[120]

Categorisation is mainly achieved through the definition of human rights values by reference to the ECHR and to Strasbourg case law. English legal writings typically employ the term 'convention rights' to designate rights standards. This is also expressed in positive law. When applying the HRA, courts do not perceive their role as one of enforcement of a domestic fundamental rights bill. Instead, they claim that in their capacity as public authorities under Section 6 HRA, they act in conformity with the UK's international obligations.[121] In *Al-Skeini*, the House of Lords held that 'the central purpose of the 1998 Act was to provide a remedial structure in domestic law for the rights guaranteed by the Convention'.[122] That is why the right to an effective domestic remedy is not incorporated by the HRA: the act itself is deemed to accomplish the purpose of Article 13 ECHR. More than a fundamental rights principle then, proportionality is *one among the remedies* provided by the 1998 Act for the violation of the convention. As such, it serves to achieve the UK's compliance with its international obligations. This has the result that, in contrast to what is observed in French public law, it is the formal-

[117] Hickman (2010), p. 270.
[118] Poole (2009), pp. 153 f.
[119] Taggart (2008).
[120] Hickman (2010); King (2010).
[121] *Wilson* (HL, 10 July 2003).
[122] *R* v. *Secretary of State for Defence, ex parte Al-Skeini* [2008] 1 AC 153 (HL, 13 June 2007), p. 154.

procedural rather than the substantive aspects of proportionality that are accentuated in English judicial review.

This is especially true in relation to the scope of the application of proportionality as a HRA head of review. Just like convention rights, only 'victims' of fundamental rights violations have the right to bring proceedings under the HRA and to contest public measures as disproportionate. This results in a narrower *locus standi* than in ordinary judicial review cases.[123] The scope of the applicability of rights and proportionality is limited by the scope of the convention, which often differs from the scope of the HRA itself.[124] Moreover, proportionality is applied with the variations that one finds in the ECHR case law. In *Daly*, Lord Steyn specified that his observations on the distinct nature of proportionality review as compared to the traditional *Wednesbury* standard apply 'making due allowance for important structural differences between various convention rights'.[125] In some cases concerning matters of social policy, proportionality corresponds to a unitary standard, following the ECtHR approach to positive obligations imposed on national authorities.[126] Similarly, in cases involving the right to property, domestic courts do not impose a strict necessity requirement on public authorities.[127]

The 'Mirror Principle'. Chapter 6 has shown that the spread of rationalism that underpins proportionality contributes to the construction of a public law that operates in the domestic sphere. However, this public law is not yet exactly *English* (or it was not, at least until quite recently). It is the reflection of the convention in English law. Section 2 HRA imposes on domestic courts the obligation to 'take into account' Strasbourg case law and is thus perceived as constraining domestic courts' interpretation of the convention. Following the opinion that prevailed in judicial practice, in the cases in which Strasbourg has had the occasion to deal with the subject matter at hand, domestic jurisprudence should reflect Strasbourg case law in the same way a mirror reflects the view. Departure from Strasbourg solutions should be exceptional. In the words of Lord Rodger's illustrative dictum, '*Argentoratum locutum, iudicium finitum* – Strasbourg has spoken, the case is closed'.[128] As a

[123] Elliott (2001); Craig (2016), chap. 24.
[124] *Lambert* (HL, 5 July 2001); *In re McCaughey* [2011] UKSC 20 (SC, 18 May 2011).
[125] *Daly* (HL, 23 May 2001), para. 27.
[126] *ProLife Alliance* (HL, 15 May 2003).
[127] *Countryside Alliance*, para. 75, per Lord Hope.
[128] *Secretary of State for the Home Department* v. *AF, AN and AE* (No.3) [2009] UKHL 28 (HL, 10 June 2009), para. 98.

consequence, domestic judges have presumed an obligation not to 'outpace' ECtHR case law. That is, they have often refused to accord more extensive protection to convention rights than the Strasbourg court. In *Ullah*, Lord Bingham clearly stated this:

> It is indeed unlawful under section 6 of the 1998 Act for a public authority, including a court, to act in a way which is incompatible with a Convention right. It is of course open to member states to provide for rights more generous than those guaranteed by the Convention, but such provision should not be the product of interpretation of the Convention by national courts, since the meaning of the Convention should be uniform throughout the states party to it. The duty of national courts is to keep pace with the Strasbourg jurisprudence as it evolves over time: no more, but certainly no less.[129]

In the same vein, in *Ambrose* v. *Harris*, Lord Hope stated:

> Lord Bingham's point, [...] with which I respectfully agree, was that Parliament never intended to give the courts of this country the power to give a more generous scope to those rights than that which was to be found in the jurisprudence of the Strasbourg court. To do so would have the effect of changing them from Convention rights, based on the treaty obligation, into free-standing rights of the court's own creation.[130]

Neither convention rights nor the head of review of proportionality acquire a free-standing status in English judicial review. They are applied only through the 'gateway' of the HRA. If English judges want to develop fundamental rights case law, they must do it through the common law. The head of review of proportionality would have no place in such an evolution, although synonym, and even homonym, *methods of reasoning* might be used.[131] Indeed, at least until recently, proportionality in case law is mainly perceived and defined as a European head of review.[132]

The lack of free-standing status for convention rights in the domestic sphere becomes problematic in margin of appreciation cases. In such cases, reference to the ECtHR case law leads to further reference by

[129] *R* v. *Special Adjudicator, ex parte Ullah* [2004] UKHR 26 (HL, 17 June 2004), para. 20.
[130] *Ambrose* v. *Harris* [2011] UKSC 43 (SC, 6 October 2011), para. 19.
[131] Poole (2009, p. 2) argues that in the area of common law rights, proportionality's rationalising function could be assumed by the principle of legality. In *Pham*, Lord Reed considered the application of proportionality as a common law method of review ensuring the protection of fundamental rights. See Part II, Chapter 6.5.
[132] This idea was initially accepted even by certain fundamental rights enthusiasts. See, for example, Kavanagh (2009), pp. 153 f. However, it is increasingly criticised by the defenders of proportionality. See Klug and Wildbore (2010). On this debate, see Fenwick (2012).

Strasbourg to domestic authorities. If convention rights had no domestic legal status at all, the whole process would be a nonsense and would necessarily lead to the validation of domestic legislation. This, as we have seen, is the way the margin of appreciation has typically been understood by French courts, which presume that legislation has considered convention rights and thus neglect the acculturation function of the ECHR. In contrast, English public lawyers understand the HRA as establishing convention rights as domestic legal standards, imposed on the decision-making process of public authorities within the scope of the convention. In this sense, in *re P*, Lord Hoffmann stated that 'Convention rights are domestic and not international rights.'[133]

The case concerned the bar set by Northern Irish legislation to adoption by unmarried couples. In a decision on the matter, the ECtHR had left the question to the margin of appreciation of national authorities. In Lord Hoffmann's view, this meant that domestic courts should apply 'the division between the decision-making powers of courts and Parliament in the way which appears appropriate for the United Kingdom'.[134] Thus, the court applied traditional constitutional principles in this case. The Northern Irish Adoption Order was found to be irrational – proportionality was not at play. In recent case law, English judges apply proportionality reasoning despite the margin of appreciation left to national authorities by the ECtHR. In this case law, however, proportionality is not applied as a European head of review but as a domestic method or reasoning tool.[135]

Proportionality and the Human Rights Culture in England. Despite the instrumental perception of proportionality, or precisely due to this perception, English lawyers and judges have taken its function seriously in the cases where it operates. Contrary to what is observed in the French *contrôle de conventionnalité*, proportionality as a head of review provokes fundamental constitutional change under the HRA. It upsets the traditional distribution of competences between courts and the political branches of government in the common law. Thus, it assumes the

[133] *In re P (Adoption: Unmarried Couple)* [2009] 1 AC 173 (HL, 18 June 2008), para. 33, per Lord Hoffmann.

[134] Ibid, para. 37.

[135] *Nicklinson* (SC, 25 June 2014), per Lord Mance; *MM (Lebanon)* (SC, 22 February 2017). Therefore, rather than indicating the transformation of local patterns of Europeanisation, this case law is indicative of the process of rationalisation that English public law is undergoing, which does not necessarily further European integration. On this issue, see Part III, Chapter 10.2.

function of acculturation that the Strasbourg court has ascribed to it. Since the passing of the HRA, English lawyers have perceived the act as establishing a 'human rights culture' or a 'culture of justification'.[136] Proportionality plays a crucial role in the cultural shift produced by the HRA, since it places the burden of justifying and adducing evidence as to the legitimacy of rights restrictions on public authorities. Contrary to the patchwork-like role it assumes in France, in English public law proportionality applies as a matter of principle in human rights cases. Exceptions to its application are framed as such and justified by domestic courts.[137] Hence, far from only exceptionally serving foreigners, as in the French case, proportionality transforms the whole of English public law and has become a core issue of debate in this context.

The culture that the HRA establishes is not solely moral-legal but also institutional.[138] As an instance of indifference review, proportionality leads courts to reframe the policy objectives of Parliament in terms that are acceptable to the convention.[139] Proportionality, due to the variable intensity of review that it entails, encourages Parliament to internalise human rights standards in its decision-making process. Besides, Section 19 of the HRA mandates the competent minister to make a statement concerning the compatibility of government bills with convention rights. Internalisation of rights standards in the parliamentary process was furthered with the institution of the Joint Committee on Human Rights, which considers the compatibility of legislation with fundamental rights principles.[140] Hence, Parliament and government ministers often reason in proportionality terms. The proportionality of domestic legislation, just like the protection of human rights, becomes a 'joint project', in which the legislature and the judiciary cooperate.[141]

Judges become partners of policy-making authorities in the protection of human rights. Following a common practice of continental courts, they reconstruct the reasoning of the primary decision-makers in

[136] Hunt (1999); Kavanagh (2009), pp. 241 f.; Hickman (2010), pp. 236 f. Poole (2009) talks about an 'administrative culture of rights-conscious justification'. See also Mead (2012); Taggart (2003), pp. 332 f.

[137] See, for example, *Kay* v. *Lambeth* (HL, 8 March 2006), paras. 53 f.; *Doherty and Others* v. *Birmingham City Council* [2008] UKHL 57 (HL, 30 July 2008); *Pinnock* (SC, 3 November 2010).

[138] Hickman (2010), pp. 236 f.

[139] *Wilson*, para. 61, per Lord Nicholls.

[140] Hiebert (2006). See, for example, the debates on the Counter-Terrorism and Security Act 2015, 13 January 2015, available at www.publications.parliament.uk.

[141] Rivers (2006), p. 207.

conformity with the convention. In this process, weighing and balancing increasingly resemble a ritual similar to the one performed by continental courts. In *Kennedy*, for example, Lord Sumption reconstructed the reasoning of the reviewed authority in the following way:

> In its letter of 4 July 2007, the Commission showed that it was well aware of the 'public interest ... for transparency of the decisions and reasons for them, so as to promote public confidence in charities'. But it considered at that time that its dependence on the co-operation of third parties in carrying out its inquiry meant that that particular public interest was outweighed by the competing public interest in its being able to discover the relevant facts.[142]

English courts also impose proportionality as a reasoning framework on tribunals when deciding on public authorities' decisions on appeal.[143] The idea thus emerges that proportionality should be employed in the decision-making process of public bodies too.[144] Certain scholars and judges have assumed a positive requirement to explicitly use the proportionality framework by policy-makers. This was criticised by Poole and other scholars as leading to some kind of 'new formalism'.[145] The House of Lords emphatically rejected it in *Begum*: public bodies 'cannot be expected to make such decisions with textbooks on human rights law at their elbows'.[146] Nevertheless, courts have made clear that they will give weight to the considered opinions of the reviewed authorities and that they will find it difficult to interfere when these authorities have explicitly attempted to strike a balance between the competing rights and interests at stake.[147] Far from being symbolic then, the function of proportionality in English law is one of profound cultural and constitutional transformation that tends to affect the whole of public action.

***

Proportionality in the Strasbourg case law pushes towards the establishment of a human rights culture. However, domestic lawyers have perceived the integration function of proportionality in the field of the

[142] *Kennedy* (SC, 26 March 2014), para. 159, per Lord Sumption.

[143] See *Huang* (HL, 21 March 2007).

[144] See, for example, *R* v. *Governors of Denbigh High School, ex parte Begum* [2005] 1 WLR 3372 (CA, Civil Division, 2 March 2005), per Brooke LJ. On this point, Hickman (2010), pp. 245 f.; Mead (2012); Kavanagh (2014).

[145] Poole (2005); Poole (2009), pp. 691 f.

[146] *Begum* (HL, 22 March 2006), para. 68, per Lord Hoffmann. See also para. 31.

[147] *Kebeline* (HL, 28 October 1999), per Lord Hope; *Miss Behavin'* (HL, 25 April 2007), para. 37, per Baroness Hale. See also Craig (2016), para. 19–018.

convention differently, according to local narratives on rights, to local paths of reception of supranational law and to local paths of cultural change.

In France, *la patrie des droits de l'Homme*, the ECHR has represented a European rights civilisation that already permeated domestic law. Accommodation of convention standards has not proceeded through transformation of the structures and theories of judicial review. Neither has it taken the form of a specific remedy for convention violations. In French *doctrine*, proportionality has not been perceived as a head of review limited within the scope of the convention but as an objective general principle that already existed in the *bloc de légalité* and inspired judicial review. It has been translated and assimilated to already existing concepts and methods. Hence, its reception has followed the patterns of the monist French public law tradition and has expressed the rationalism that characterises French legal thought.

In this context, compliance with the convention and with proportionality did not contest the traditional distribution of competences between domestic authorities. A partnership was established between the Parliament, the administration and the judiciary, so as to ensure the application of domestic law in accordance with Strasbourg case law. Violations of the convention and of the principle of proportionality guaranteed therein, have been perceived as exceptional, resulting from the circumstances of concrete cases rather than from a shift between the French and the European constitutional civilisations. Thus, in contrast to its perception as a general principle in the *doctrine*, in practice, proportionality has been residually applied as a 'patch', mainly in the scope of the ECHR. Its function has mostly been to 'signal' France's commitment to convention rights.

By way of contrast, English analytical formalism did not allow for an unthinking assimilation of domestic and ECHR concepts in the name of law's consistency. Following the traditional patterns of dualism, proportionality has been perceived as distinct from domestic concepts and standards of review and its application as a European human rights principle has been rejected in judicial review before the incorporation of the convention. In the pragmatist common law tradition, law's autonomy and authority are crucial. Indeed, according to the Whig historians' account, rights in the UK have not been protected through law but through the enforcement of the principle of parliamentary sovereignty. Legal forms, such as concepts, procedures and heads of review, are seen as tools, ensuring institutional balance and effective decision-making according to the will of Parliament. They are not perceived as a coherent whole but as a 'polyglot patchwork'.

The HRA added proportionality to the toolbox of common law judges. As a head of review, proportionality serves the adjudication of convention rights and thus ensures the UK's compliance with its international obligations. This is why it is constrained within the scope of the convention. It is not a domestic head of review, just as the HRA is not a domestic bill of rights. It is applied by reference to Strasbourg case law and does not outpace it. Albeit fragmented and instrumentalised, proportionality plainly assumes its acculturation function. In contrast to France, where its use in judicial reasoning is exceptional and circumstantial, in England, the application of proportionality in the ever-expanding scope of human rights is a matter of principle. The rationalism that proportionality conveys provokes an important constitutional and cultural change in English judicial review.

The analysis presented in this chapter thus allows nuancing the importance of traditional doctrines of monism and dualism in shaping the relationship between domestic and international law. Indeed, after many decades of resistance to the effective application of the convention in the domestic sphere, the dualist common law system proves much more open to the integration dynamics of proportionality than the monist French public law doctrine.

9

A Common Market

Proportionality as a Principle of Economic Integration. The function of proportionality in the context of EU law is again a function of integration. Yet, whereas in the case of the ECHR integration has been value-oriented, consisting in the establishment of rights as decision-making standards, in the EU law context, it has been focused mainly on facts and 'concrete achievements'.[1] Indeed, it is well-known that EC treaties were initially instrumental to the establishment of a common market, as a first step on the road to an 'ever-closer union among the peoples of Europe'.[2] In the field of EU market freedoms, proportionality functions as a principle of economic integration.[3] First, it reframes domestic policy goals as legitimate objectives from the point of view of the common market project. Then, it entails an objective evaluation of the appropriateness and necessity of domestic measures for obtaining those goals.[4] Proportionality thus eliminates unnecessary or inefficient restrictions to EU market freedoms and guarantees the *effet utile* of EU law. Due to its focus on concrete cases, its effective application, like the effective application of EU law more generally, continually relies on national authorities' cooperation and especially on the cooperation of national judges. The Luxembourg court asks domestic courts to be the '*juges communautaires de droit commun*'.[5]

Of course, European integration has not only been about the common market. Overshooting the expectations of those who inspired its creation, today the EU promotes vaster and more far-reaching goals and values. Most notably, EU institutions have affirmed their role as crucial actors in

[1] Robert Schuman, 'Declaration of the French Government for the Creation of the European Coal and Steel Community', Paris, 9 May 1950.

[2] Preamble of the Treaty of Rome, 25 March 1957.

[3] Marzal Yetano (2013).

[4] On the absence of balancing from the ECJ market freedoms case law, see Davies (2016).

[5] TPI, T-51/89, 10 July 1990, *Tetra Pak Rausing SA*, ECLI:EU:T:1990:41, para. 42.

the field of fundamental rights protection in Europe.[6] In spite of the interest that these developments present, for the sake of simplicity, the application of proportionality in the field of EU fundamental rights will not be studied here. Indeed, this chapter does not purport to be exhaustive or to make general conclusions about proportionality in EU law. More modestly, through the selective study of some examples, it seeks to shed light on the different ways in which proportionality, and the peculiar dynamic of EU integration that it conveys, operate in domestic contexts. The choice of the field of economic freedoms is justified by the fact that the construction of the common market has been the major engine of European integration and constitutes its originality even today.

The chapter consists in a comparative study of the application of proportionality by English and Greek judges in the field of EC market freedoms. The Greek legal culture, rationalist and eclectic, is almost as different as one can get from the English common law. Nonetheless, this difference is not so much reflected in the use of the EC law concept of proportionality by domestic courts. Indeed, both English and Greek judges have assumed their mission of *juges communautaires de droit commun*. In spite of this appearance of convergence, I argue, the reception of proportionality follows local patterns of cultural change and local knowledge practices.

In the common law, proportionality has been received as an EC law head of review. It has been clearly distinguished from domestic concepts and applied by reference to the ECJ case law. Its effect has been contained within the scope of the treaties. The reception of proportionality in this context thus follows the patterns of dualism and analytical formalism (Section 9.1). Like their English colleagues, Greek judges have followed closely the ECJ case law on proportionality. However, contrary to what is observed in the common law, in the monist Greek system the EC law concept of proportionality has not been distinguished from domestic concepts of judicial review. Instead, proportionality, like other legal transfers in this context, has been applied by means of translation of the ECJ case law. Domestic lawyers have perceived its application by the ECJ as scientifically correct, and have followed it even outside the scope of the treaties (Section 9.2).

[6] See de Búrca (1993a), p. 283; Alston, ed. (1999); de Búrca, De Witte, and Ogertschnig (2005); de Búrca (2013). For an overview of the application of proportionality in the ECJ case law more generally, see Schwarze (1992), p. 726; de Búrca (1993b); Tridimas (1999), pp. 215 f. More recently, see Craig (2018), pp. 669 f.

Legal culture affects local lawyers' possibilities to resist to the process of European integration, as well as their capacity shape this process. Common law pragmatism has allowed English courts to frame normative conflicts between domestic and EC law. When proportionality and the *effet utile* of EC market freedoms entered into conflict with fundamental constitutional principles of the common law, English judges have occasionally objected to their application. The analysis of the Sunday trading litigation sheds light on an instance of transnational communication between English and Luxembourg judges, at the issue of which the ECJ was forced to acknowledge normative pluralism in the EU (Section 9.3). On the contrary, the perception of law as science has not allowed Greek lawyers to frame normative conflicts between domestic and EC law. Proportionality as a European science has engineered important constitutional change and has considerably compromised the normativity of the Greek Constitution (Section 9.4).

9.1 Ensuring the *Effet Utile* of EC Market Freedoms: The Application of Proportionality by Reference to the ECJ Case Law in England

The First Application of Proportionality as an EC Law Principle. The ECA 1972 incorporated the European treaties into UK law and opened the way to the transfer of proportionality as a test for the protection of community law rights and freedoms. While proportionality had already appeared in the argumentation of the parties, the first time that it was applied by a domestic court as an EC law principle was only ten years later, in *Goldstein.*[7] An act dating from 1968 prohibited the importation of radios emitting a certain frequency. The ban was justified by public interest reasons, since the use of the particular wave band would affect devices used by airports, hospitals, the police and other public services. Mr Goldstein was accused of fraudulently importing such apparatus. In the first instance, he claimed that the prohibition was contrary to Article 30 TEC (now Article 36 TFEU). The court accepted that the measures constituted a quantitative restriction in the terms of that article and went on to examine the question of their proportionality. It was convinced that the restriction was justified and held Mr Goldstein guilty of the fraudulent evasion of the prohibition.

[7] *Goldstein* (CA, Criminal Division, 2 April 1982; HL, 20 January 1983).

On appeal, Mr Goldstein argued that the first instance judge failed properly to consider whether the measures were necessary or whether alternative, less detrimental measures could have been employed to achieve the statutory purpose. Examining his allegations, the Court of Appeal deduced from the treaties a necessity requirement. When the case arrived before the House of Lords, Lord Diplock found the occasion to announce for the first time in English law the three stages of the principle of proportionality:

> [I]n order to enable a state to avail itself of the derogation from article 30 [...], it is necessary to adduce factual evidence (1) to identify the various mischiefs which the challenged restrictive measures were intended to prevent, (2) to show that those mischiefs could not have equally effectively been cured by other measures less restrictive of trade, and (3) to show that the measures were not disproportionately severe having regard to the gravity of the mischiefs against which they were directed. This last mentioned consideration involves the concept in Community law (derived principally from German law) called 'proportionality'. In plain English it means 'You must not use a steam hammer to crack a nut, if a nutcracker would do.'[8]

An EC Law Head of Review. In spite of its formulation in Lord Diplock's dicta, in subsequent case law the test of Article 30 TEC did not always imply a three-pronged proportionality analysis. One year later, in *Bell Line*, for example, proportionality was applied as a strict necessity test.[9] In *Pharmaceutical Society*, proportionality was only mentioned as excluding blanket prohibitions, when alternative less restrictive measures are available.[10] The equation of proportionality to necessity review is not surprising, if one considers that this is how the ECJ applied the test when European economic freedoms were at stake. Indeed, section 3 of the ECA disposes that English courts should interpret any point of European law in accordance ECJ case law. Hence, the content of proportionality in English law was mainly determined by reference to the ECJ case law. Proportionality was invested the form that the ECJ gave to it each time, as a function of the subject matter: penalties, non-discrimination, discretionary

[8] *Goldstein* (HL), pp. 154–5.

[9] *Bell Line* (HC, Queen's Bench Division, 9 April 1984). See also *Roberts* (HC, Queen's Bench Division, 11 November 1990).

[10] *R* v. *The Pharmaceutical Society of Great Britain, ex parte Association of Pharmaceutical Importers* [1987] 3 CMLR 951 (CA, Civil Division, 30 July 1987).

policy decisions, economic freedoms etc.[11] Parallelism was bolstered by the recurrent citations and thorough consideration of ECJ decisions in English judicial opinions, as well as by the repeated references to the ECJ on the issue.[12]

The application of proportionality by reference to the ECJ was normal, since proportionality was itself an EC law head of review: it was applied through the 'gateway' of the ECA 1972 and only in EC law cases. It emerged and developed under the exhortation and influence of big companies' barristers, who sought to exempt their clients from restrictions to trade or relative sanctions and penalties.[13] It was a test for assessing the validity of national measures in the scope of EC law. In the dualist English system, proportionality was clearly distinguished from domestic concepts and involved more intensive scrutiny than the traditional *Wednesbury* standard.[14] It involved merits review of domestic public acts, and even of legislation, from the point of view of their appropriateness and necessity. Just as in convention cases, the English perception of proportionality as an EC law principle was instrumental. By applying it, English judges ensured the UK's compliance with its European obligations and the realisation of the *effet utile* of EC market freedoms, sometimes to the detriment of the traditional distribution of competences in the common law. Hence, they assumed the function of *juges communautaires de droit commun* that the ECA assigned to them.

The Irritating Operation of Proportionality. The ambiguous nature of proportionality evaluations, between fact and law, sometimes troubled English judges. The question was raised already in *Goldstein*. When the issue of proportionality arose, the first instance judge heard evidence adduced by the Crown as to the existence and the importance of the

[11] See, for example, *R* v. *Secretary of State for Education, ex parte Schaffter* [1987] IRLR 53 (HC, Queen's Bench Division, 1 January 1987); *Rainey* v. *Greater Glasgow Health Board* [1987] IRLR 26 (HL, 27 November 1986).

[12] See *Customs and Excise Commissioners* v. *ApS Samex (Hanil Synthetic Fiber Industrial Co Ltd, third party)* [1983] 1 All ER 1042 (HC, Queen's Bench Division, 14 December 1982). For only some of the numerous preliminary references, see *R.* v. *Intervention Board for Agricultural Produce, ex parte ED & F Man (Sugar) Ltd* [1984] 3 CMLR 633 (HC, Queen's Bench Division, 18 June 1984); *Fedesa* (HC, Queen's Bench Division, 19 February 1988); *Pharmaceutical Society*; *Rochdale Borough Council* v. *Anders* [1988] 3 All ER 490 (HC, Queen's Bench Division, 23 May 1988).

[13] Most prominently, Vaughan QC repeatedly used proportionality in his argumentation during the first years of the principle's evolution in EC law. See, for example, *Bell Line*; *Pharmaceutical Society*; and the Sunday trading litigation, on which see below, Section 9.3.

[14] See Part I, Chapter 3.1.

public interest served by the statute, considering that it was a legal question for the judge alone and not for the jury. Mr Goldstein complained that the proportionality question was a mixed question of law and fact and thus one for the jury to decide. Both the Court of Appeal and the House of Lords rejected his contention. Section 3(1) of the ECA 1972 declares:

> For the purposes of all legal proceedings any question as to the meaning or effect of any of the Treaties, or as to the validity, meaning or effect of any Community instrument, shall be treated as a question of law (and, if not referred to the European Court, be for determination as such in accordance with the principles laid down by and any relevant decision of the European Court).

The situation was complicated because the ECJ itself required that the competent authority – the Crown in this case – must adduce substantial evidence to prove that a certain measure was proportional and justified. Lord Diplock resolved this apparent contradiction, by observing that proportionality is 'a question as to the meaning and effect of one of the Treaties. It thus falls fairly and squarely within section 3 (1) of the European Communities Act 1972'.[15]

Furthermore, the intensity of review that proportionality implied necessarily entailed fact-finding. This was incompatible with the traditional perception of the role of courts in judicial review. Indeed, the adversarial English system was perceived as ill-adapted to resolving the polycentric and complex fact-finding issues that certain public law disputes involve.[16] In *Bell Line*, Forbes J rejected that the court, by virtue of EC law, had become 'a fact-finding tribunal or anything of that kind'. Still, he stressed that the Court of Justice had declared that the justifiability of national restrictions is for the national court to decide and that he would find it 'very remarkable [...] if there were no court in this country which was able to take up the invitation of the European Court'.[17] Forbes J went on to say:

> It is plain that this court is, some may think unfortunately but nevertheless ineluctably, being drawn into the business of fact-finding. Indeed, there are pronouncements in the House of Lords which make it clear that the provisions for cross-examination of deponents on affidavits and so on and so forth mean that in certain cases this court can be required to find facts

15 *Goldstein* (HL), p. 156.
16 See Allison (1996), pp. 183 f.
17 *Bell Line*, para. 20.

> at least if it is necessary to find certain facts in order to define its jurisdiction. I do not believe that this country should be left in a situation where, if it were plain that a decision of a Minister was one which was contrary to Community law, or that part of Community law which becomes part of this country's domestic law, those persons with rights arising under Community law should be denied any means of enforcing them.[18]

Still, the factual or legal nature of proportionality continued to confuse English lawyers. In subsequent cases, the problem of the competence of the ECJ in the preliminary reference procedure arose. According to consistent case law, the facts of the case should be decided before the domestic court introduced a preliminary reference to the ECJ.[19] However, the fact-finding issues raised by proportionality led the Court of Appeal to introduce an exception to this rule in *Pharmaceutical Society*. This case concerned a guidance note issued by the Pharmaceutical Society of Great Britain, requiring that chemists meticulously follow the doctor's prescription and not substitute drugs imported from EC member states to therapeutically identical drugs prescribed in the UK. Determining the facts of the case thus implied complicated considerations as to the impacts of the notice on trade and the equivalent effect of the drugs in question. The court held that, exceptionally, a preliminary reference to the ECJ could be made without consideration of the merits.[20]

The Containment of Proportionality within the Scope of EC Law. Proportionality was an irritant and its application was carefully contained within the scope of European law, in spite of certain judges' efforts to the contrary. The reception of proportionality as an EC law principle thus followed the patterns of analytical formalism. In *Hamble Fisheries*, Sedley J argued that the domestic law of legitimate expectations should align itself with the community legal order, when applied in the UK's implementation of the common agricultural policy.[21] According to the judge:

> [L]egitimacy is itself a relative concept, to be gauged proportionately to the legal and policy implications of the expectation. This, no doubt, is why

[18] Ibid, para. 21. In this case, Forbes J found necessary to reformulate the *Wednesbury* rule in order to make it fit the standard applied. See para. 27.

[19] *Bulmer (HP) Ltd* v. *Bollinger SA* [1974] 2 All ER 1226 (CA, Civil Division, 22 May 1974), per Lord Denning MoR.

[20] Concerning the competence of the ECJ, see *Pharmaceutical Society*, paras. 28–30.

[21] *R* v. *Ministry of Agriculture, Fisheries and Food, ex parte Hamble Fisheries* [1995] 1 CMLR 533 (HC, Queen's Bench Division, 3 November 1994).

> it has proved easier to establish a legitimate expectation that an applicant will be listened to than that a particular outcome will be arrived at by the decision maker. But the same principle of fairness in my judgment governs both situations.[22]

In this way, Sedley J attempted to introduce a new proportionality test in the assessment of the legitimacy of citizens' substantive expectations towards public authorities. This would render proportionality a criterion and a reason for the spill-over of EC law rights in domestic law. However, Sedley J's decision was characterised as 'heresy' and was overruled by the Court of Appeal in *Hargreaves*.[23] In the words of Hirst LJ: 'On matters of substance (as contrasted with procedure) *Wednesbury* provides the correct test'.[24] The judges emphatically denied the extension of available remedies by relying on fairness considerations, on law's internal logic and consistency. *Wednesbury* and the economy of principle that it implied was the only standard that fitted the pragmatic approach of the common law.[25]

Until the late 1980s, the meaning of proportionality as an EC law head of review was dominant among English public lawyers and was mentioned as such in legal dictionaries.[26] In spite of the complex issues that its application raised, proportionality did not attract much scholarly attention. This is because, as an EC law principle, it was not likely to spill over the rest of English law. The application of the EC law concept of proportionality by reference to the ECJ case law has persisted until today.[27] It has attributed integrity to the concept and certainty as to its scope of application.

9.2 Ensuring the *Effet Utile* of EC Market Freedoms: The Application of Proportionality by Means of Translation of the ECJ Case Law in Greece

The First Preliminary References to the ECJ on Proportionality. In the monist Greek system, the reception of proportionality in the field of EC law did not require a special 'gateway'. Greek handbooks started

[22] Ibid, pp. 544–5.

[23] *R* v. *Secretary of State for the Home Department and Another, ex parte Hargreaves* [1997] 1 WLR 906 (CA, Civil Division, 20 November 1996).

[24] Ibid, p. 917.

[25] Allison (1996), pp. 109 f.

[26] See 'Proportionality', *Halsbury's Laws of England*.

[27] *Lumsdon* (SC, 24 June 2015). *Contra Sinclair Collis* (CA, Civil Division, 17 June 2011).

mentioning proportionality as an EC law principle by the mid-1980s already.[28] By the end of the decade, the EC law aspect of proportionality began to be invoked in courtrooms too. Yet until the mid-1990s proportionality was mainly understood and applied as a principle of domestic law imported from Germany. Its application was not perceived as a supranational obligation, since EC law was understood as imposing substantive legal requirements rather than any particular scrutiny method. One has to wait until the mid-1990s for the first judicial applications of proportionality in the field of European law. The movement started in lower administrative courts.[29]

Among the supreme courts, it was *Areios Pagos* that first sent a preliminary reference to the ECJ on proportionality in 1996. A statute dating from 1987 instituted expulsion from Greek territory as an additional penalty for foreigners in possession of illegal drugs, except in cases where important reasons, especially connected to family life, justified their remaining in the country. Expulsion was imposed for life, while the minister of justice had the power to reconsider the decision three years after the conviction. In the case at hand, Italian citizens invoked EC law to contest their conviction for illegal drug use in cassation, insofar as it obligated them to leave the country.[30] After extensive consideration of the treaties and Luxembourg case law, *Areios Pagos* observed that the freedom of movement was a fundamental EC law principle, derogations from which should be interpreted strictly. In cases in which restrictions had been imposed as a criminal penalty, the ECJ required that they not be disproportionate to the nature of the committed offence. *Areios Pagos* understood this as a requirement 'that the (general) principle of proportionality not be violated'.[31]

The judges referred to the *Rutili* case to underscore that the ECJ individual freedoms case law had been inspired by the ECHR. They understood the ECHR 'necessary in a democratic society' requirement to be equivalent to the principle of proportionality in EC law. In the case at hand, they decided that a preliminary reference to the ECJ was necessary in order to assess the compatibility of the domestic measures with proportionality. Hence, proportionality was established as the criterion for the compatibility of Greek legislation with EC freedoms in the scope

[28] Most prominently Dagtoglou (1985), pp. 160 f.

[29] See, for instance, DPrThess 921/1995 *ΔΔΙΚΗ* 1995, p. 730 (Thessaloniki Administrative Court of First Instance).

[30] AP 1067/1996 *NOB* 1997, p. 480.

[31] Ibid.

of the treaties. The appraisal of proportionality was left to the ECJ, even though the principle was understood as synonymous with the domestic general principle of proportionality and with the ECHR requirement of necessity in a democratic society.

Translating the ECJ Case Law on Proportionality. During the same period, in decision 5116/1996, proportionality was applied as an EC law principle by the Council of State Plenum as well. The case concerned a council regulation in the field of tobacco. The regulation had brought about important changes in the regime of subsidies for tobacco producers, with the goal of adjusting production to market conditions.[32] More precisely, replacing the previous collective responsibility regime, the regulation had defined individual production quotas for a four-year period and had limited community subsidies only to the amount of tobacco that did not exceed these quotas. The quotas were to be allocated according to tobacco production during the years preceding the enactment of the regulation. A ministerial decision had implemented the community regulation and had individually defined the quotas for tobacco producers. The plaintiffs, newly established tobacco producers, were excluded from subsidies under this new system and impugned the regulation, together with the implementing administrative act, for violation of their legitimate expectations and of the principle of proportionality. They alleged that community policy on the matter had encouraged them to invest important sums in tobacco production. However, they contended, the policy changes introduced with the regulation made it impossible for them to obtain a satisfactory income.

Examining the proportionality of the measures, the Council of State followed the ECJ case law on community policy measures closely. In the council's view, European case law was sufficiently clear and rendered a preliminary reference to Luxembourg unnecessary. The judges held that:

> [A]ccording to the consistent case law of the Court of the European Communities, the principle of proportionality is among the general principles of European Community law, and accordingly, the measures chosen for obtaining the objectives of a regulation must be suitable and necessary. Every time that it is possible to choose among various appropriate measures, the less onerous measure must be chosen, while the impacts of the measure must not be disproportionate to the objective pursued. However, in view of the large discretion of the Community legislator in the domain of common agricultural policy, judicial review [...] is limited to the examination of whether the measure is manifestly

[32] Council Regulation (EEC) 2075/92.

> inappropriate for obtaining the objective pursued (cf. the above-mentioned decisions *CEC Crispoltoni II*, case C-133, 300, 362/93, and *Germany v. Council*, case C-280/93).[33]

The Council of State found that, in the case at hand, it could not be said that the establishment of individual quotas was manifestly inappropriate for the stabilisation of the tobacco market, given that the previous system of collective responsibility in the allocation of quotas had been unsuccessful in this respect. The judges thus employed proportionality in the same way that Luxembourg judges do. Just like the ECJ, they announced proportionality as a general principle of EC law. Following Luxembourg case law, they attributed a large margin of appreciation to the community legislator. Thus, while proportionality was announced as a three-pronged requirement imposed on public interference with market freedoms, it was only the manifest inappropriateness of the community measures that was subsequently investigated. Greek judges acted as translators of ECJ case law.

The application of proportionality by means of translation was subsequently extended to other fields. In 1999, the Council of State stated that in intra-communitarian trade cases, proportionality as an EC law principle conditions the validity of domestic legislation even in areas not subject to EC law harmonisation, like customs law. This was the case, 'independently of the matter of discrimination' that traditionally triggered the application of EC law.[34]

Defying Traditional Distinctions. In some cases, the application of proportionality by means of translation of the ECJ case law defied traditional structures and distinctions of judicial review. In decision 1918/1998, domestic legislation had set quotas that limited women's access to special training in order to become member of the police forces. Examining the compatibility of this rule with EC law, the Council of State followed the ECJ case law on sex equality in the field of access to profession and professional education. The judges stressed that exceptions to the principle of sex equality are legitimate only as far as they are provided for by a specific law. The wording of the law or the relevant debates in Parliament should indicate the 'concrete and appropriate criteria', according to which such exceptions are introduced. This will allow 'the affected citizens and the courts to check, in every concrete case, if the exception [...] is justified by

33 StE (Pl.) 5116/1996 *ΔΔΙΚΗ* 1998, p. 252, para. 14.
34 StE 2245/1999 *ΔΔΙΚΗ* 2000, p. 458.

sufficient reasons and is necessary and appropriate for obtaining its purpose'.[35]

In the case at hand, derogation from sex equality was not justified by the mission of the Hellenic Police, since this mission is very general and comprises duties for the exercise of which the gender factor is irrelevant.[36] Proportionality thus allowed the scrutiny of the criteria set by the law, not only in order to ascertain the sincerity of the legislator, but also the real necessity of the contested measures. It implied judicial interference with the 'how' of the exercise of Parliament's discretion. In this way, the Council of State, *juge communautaire de droit commun*, ensured the effective application of the EC law principle of sex equality in the field of professional freedom. This came at a cost for the traditional distribution of competences between Parliament and the judiciary. Indeed, the question of 'how' discretionary power has been exercised traditionally is a question of expediency (*σκοπιμότητα*) that exceeds the competence of the judge of legality (*νομιμότητα*).[37] Clearly, proportionality as an EC law principle had a radical potential in Greek public law.

By the end of the 1990s the meaning of proportionality as an EC law principle and method of review had been consolidated in Greek public law. The domestic judiciary remained loyal to the application of proportionality by the ECJ in its various domains of case law, despite its complexity.[38] Proportionality of the restrictive measures acquired the content of an exception, 'interpreted restrictively', thus always engaging judicial scrutiny and ensuring that EC principles remain the rule.[39] Domestic courts, especially the lower ones, assumed the mission of ensuring the effective application of EC law in the Greek legal order, through domestic procedures and heads of review. Cast with this new EC law content, proportionality was extensively studied by various scholars and practitioners.[40]

The Spread of the EC Law Concept of Proportionality in Domestic Law. Quite paradoxically, very different legal cultures lead to similar patterns of Europeanisation. Indeed, Greek judges, like their English colleagues,

[35] StE (Pl.) 1918/1998 *NOMOS*, para. 5.
[36] Ibid, para. 8.
[37] See Part I, Chapter 4.2.
[38] StE 2245/1999 *ΔΔΙΚΗ* 2000, p. 458; DPrAth 7287/2001 *ΔΔΙΚΗ* 2002, p. 736 (Athens Administrative Court of First Instance); DPrHer 367/1999 *ΔΕΕ* 2000, p. 217 (Herakleion Administrative Court of First Instance).
[39] NSK 385/2001 *NOMOS* (opinion by the Legal Council of the State).
[40] Prevedourou (1997); Kroustallakis (1999).

have generally assumed the mission of *juges communautaires de droit commun* that the ECJ assigned to them and have followed the ECJ case law in the application of proportionality. Under the surface of convergence however, new dissonances arise. While the application of proportionality by reference to the ECJ case law reflects common lawyers' instrumental perception of proportionality as an EC law head of review, in the monist Greek system the EC law concept of proportionality has been perceived as equally domestic. In other words, Greek lawyers, like their French colleagues in the context of the convention, have assimilated the domestic principle of proportionality with the version applied by the European court. In the Greek case, however, this has led to an EC law-conforming interpretation of domestic law rather than the inverse.[41]

This is related to the fact that in Greece, translation has not been a specific feature of the proportionality literature neither has it been limited to the scope of European law; it has been a major characteristic of local legal knowledge more generally.[42] Legal transfers are thought of as an evolution of legal science. Hence, Greek lawyers did not react to the important constitutional changes that EC law proportionality brought about. Since the 2000s, mainstream scholarship has even perceived the ECJ version of proportionality as scientifically correct and has criticised its deviant application in domestic judicial practice. Gerapetritis, for instance, has argued for a more consistent application of the principle according to the ECJ precepts, appealing to 'a common scientific understanding of its conceptual content'.[43] Even in cases that did not fall within the scope of EC law, scholars assumed a self-evident obligation of domestic courts to apply proportionality according to the ECJ case law.[44] Greek public law scholarship delegated the definition of the conceptual content of proportionality as a scientific tool to the ECJ.

As a European science, proportionality spread in domestic case law. Decision 990/2004 concerned the strict pecuniary sanctions defined by the Greek customs code for customs law offences.[45] Mr Mamidakis, a well-known businessman, received a fine eight times the amount of the duties that his businesses had evaded. He argued that the fines imposed by the law constituted a flagrant violation of the principle of

[41] Yannakopoulos (2008) shows that the determination of domestic concepts by EU law is a more general characteristic of domestic legal thought and of domestic judicial practice.

[42] See Part II, Chapter 7.

[43] Gerapetritis (2006), p. 278.

[44] Papadopoulou (2006), p. 298.

[45] StE (Pl.) 990/2004, *ΕΔΚΑ* 2004, p. 585.

proportionality. Even though the case at hand did not concern intra-community trade, the Plenum of the Council of State announced that:

> [T]he principle of proportionality, resulting from the ideal and the guarantees of a State ruled by Law, is explicitly entrenched in the Constitution (article 25 § 1) and according to the consistent case law of the Court of the European Communities, is among the general principles of Community law.

In this particular case, the council rejected Mr Mamidakis' arguments. Nonetheless, some prominent councillors, among them Pararas, argued for the application of proportionality in conformity with EC law, that is, as a strict necessity test. As such, proportionality would have led to the annulment of the strict sanctions inflicted on Mr Mamidakis.

Therefore, while English and Greek patterns of Europeanisation might seem quite similar at first glance, they reflect local knowledge practices and patterns of cultural change. Both English and Greek courts generally follow the ECJ case law and ensure the *effet utile* of EC market freedoms in the domestic sphere. Yet, whereas English judges refer to the application of proportionality by the ECJ, Greek judges simply translate it. This difference might seem trivial, but it has affected domestic courts' capacity to shape the process of EU integration in crucial constitutional moments. English judges have not hesitated to oppose domestic cultural particularities to the application of the ECJ decisions. On the contrary, Greek judges have ensured the effective application of EC market freedoms, even at the cost of the effective realisation of domestic constitutional goals.

9.3 *Ce Truc Machin Culturel:* The Objection of English Courts to the EC Law Principle of Proportionality

The Sunday Trading Litigation. Even contained within the scope of EC law, proportionality required important constitutional changes that common law courts were not ready to assume. This became apparent in the Sunday trading litigation.[46] The Shops Act 1950 prohibited the selling of most products on Sunday. The violation of this act by many private companies raised a substantial amount of litigation before English courts. B&Q, a nationwide chain of do-it-yourself shops, had repeatedly transgressed this prohibition. From the early 1980s, the City Council of the Stoke-on-Trent had brought civil proceedings against the company to

[46] See the interesting history of the Sunday trading litigation in Micklitz (2005), pp. 43 f.

enforce the prohibition, since criminal fines had proved ineffective.[47] From 1988, Arthur Hugh Vaughan QC, B&Q's barrister, invoked EC law in support of his clients. In many cases, he argued that the prohibition of Sunday trading was an unjustified restriction of trade, since some of B&Q's products were coming from other EC member states. The Sunday traders sought a preliminary reference to the ECJ, which, regardless of its substantive outcome, served their short-term interests by delaying the granting of interlocutory injunctions. They obtained such a preliminary reference in the proceedings before the Cwmbran Magistrates' Court.

Until then, the case did not much concern proportionality. The main issue was whether the prohibition of Sunday trading constituted a restriction of trade that triggered the application of Article 30 TEC (now Article 36 TFEU). In the well-known *Torfaen* case, the Court of Justice declared that rules such as the one contained in the main proceedings constituted an indirect restriction of trade and fell within the scope of Article 30 TEC.[48] However, in the court's view, such restrictions could be justified since they 'reflect[ed] certain political and economic choices in so far as their purpose [was] to ensure that working and non-working hours [were] so arranged as to accord with national or regional socio-cultural characteristics'.[49] The court left this matter to the member states to decide.

Placing Limits on Proportionality's Integration Dynamic. Meanwhile, new proceedings had been brought before the High Court by the City Councils of Stoke-on-Trent and Norwich, where B&Q had raised the defence based on Article 30.[50] Hoffmann J, in the High Court, started his opinion by asking: 'Who is to decide whether shops should be allowed to open on Sundays? Is it to be Parliament or this court?'[51] The judge acknowledged that the EEC treaty had the status of supreme law in the UK. By entering into the community, the Parliament had proceeded to 'a high act of social and economic policy, by which the partial surrender of sovereignty was seen as more than compensated by the advantages of membership'.[52] In this way, the judge accepted that by virtue of the ECA 1972, in the scope of application of the EC treaties, policy objectives were

[47] *Stoke-On-Trent City Council* v. *B&Q (Retail) Ltd* [1984] 1 AC 754 (HL, 17 May 1984).
[48] ECJ, C-145/88, 23 November 1989, *Torfaen Borough Council* v. *B&Q Plc.* [1990] 2 QB 19.
[49] Ibid, para. 14.
[50] *Stoke-on-Trent and Norwich* [1991] Ch. 48 (HC, Chancery Division, 18 July 1990).
[51] Ibid, p. 55.
[52] Ibid, p. 56.

to be defined by EC law, even when sensitive social or cultural matters were at stake.

Hoffmann J stressed that: 'It is the function of the European Court of Justice in Luxembourg to interpret the Treaty and for the national court to apply it'.[53] He further acknowledged that in its interpretation of EC treaties, the ECJ had tried 'to tread a careful line which permits both boldness in advancing the objects of the community and sensitivity to the domestic interests of member states'.[54] Contrary to the rationalism and the search for substantive coherence that was observed in the opinions of continental lawyers and judges, Hoffmann J made a clear distinction between the objectives of the community and member states' domestic interests, and seemed well aware of the conflict that sometimes exists between them. Still, on the particular issue of Sunday trading, Hoffmann J objected to the application of the ECJ precepts. In his words:

> In applying the Treaty as interpreted by the European Court, the national court has to be aware of another division of powers: not between European and national jurisdiction, but between legislature and judiciary. The fact that the European Court has said that a particular question is one for decision by the national court does not endow that court with quasi-legislative powers. It must confine itself within the area of judicial intervention required by the Treaty and not trespass on questions which are for democratic decision in Parliament.[55]

The European integration mission that Parliament had ascribed to judges through the ECA 1972 now entered into conflict with Parliament's own sovereignty in setting policy goals.

Opposing the English Legal Culture to Proportionality. Examining the justification of the prohibition of Sunday trading, Hoffmann J first considered its aim. He stated that although the immediate purpose of legislation was not universally shared by the members of Parliament, its general aim was 'to maintain what they regarded as the traditional English Sunday'.[56] Concerning the other proportionality prongs, Sunday traders argued that less damaging, alternative solutions were available, such as exempting do-it-yourself companies from the prohibition. They also adduced evidence that the measures were

[53] Ibid.
[54] Ibid.
[55] Ibid.
[56] Ibid, p. 66.

disproportionate, since their cost was very important with respect to the minimal benefits that they entailed.[57]

The company claimed that, according to ECJ case law, the burden of proof for the justification of the obstacles to trade fell on the local authorities. Indeed, in the words of the ECJ in *Torfaen*, domestic courts should examine whether 'the restrictive effect of such measures on the free movement of goods exceed[ed] the effects intrinsic to trade rules'.[58] The Luxembourg judges, in a dictum that became famous in English law, declared that this question was 'a question of fact to be determined by the national court'.[59] The local authorities, by way of contrast, claimed that the necessity of the restrictions was not a question of fact.[60] Thus, they did not adduce any factual evidence. If Hoffmann J were to follow the ECJ in its application of proportionality, the local authorities' case was bound to fail. What is more, Sunday traders advocated a high standard of proof, equivalent to that required in criminal proceedings (since the matter was a criminal one in the first place).[61]

Hoffmann J regretted the 'troupe of experts [who had] toured the country', giving their views on the effects of the measures and leading to contradictory judicial decisions.[62] In his view, the requirement of factual evidence should be reduced to one of judicial notice, that is, to facts that are so well-known that their establishment does not require evidence; their knowledge is a matter of common sense. Judicial notice, he claimed, would lead to uniform answers as to factual questions and could be settled by way of precedent. Legal certainty, a quality so precious to the common law, would thus prevail.[63]

Ultimately, proportionality required the judge to proceed to the balancing of competing interests. Hoffmann J considered that this was not the function of the High Court, especially in a matter as socially sensitive as Sunday trading. This and similar matters are political issues, for which Parliament should take decisions through the democratic process.[64] With the famous following dicta, Hoffmann J refused to apply the ECJ decision and discharged local authorities of the burden of proof:

[57] Ibid, p. 55.
[58] *Torfaen*, para. 15.
[59] Ibid, para. 16.
[60] *Stoke-on-Trent and Norwich*, p. 64.
[61] Ibid, pp. 53–4.
[62] Ibid, pp. 65–6.
[63] Ibid.
[64] Ibid, pp. 59 f.

> By far the most important question in this case concerns the function of the court in applying the proportionality tests. (…) The question is one on which strong and differing views may be held and which has been the subject of frequent parliamentary debate. Is the court to apply its own opinion of the importance of ensuring that shop workers do not have to work on Sundays and weigh that against its opinion of the importance of selling more Dutch bulbs or Italian furniture? If the legislature has declined to adopt any modification of the existing exceptions, is the court to say that modifications should nevertheless be introduced because in its opinion they would not detract from the legislative object and would mean that the Act was less of a hindrance to community trade?
>
> In my judgment it is not my function to carry out the balancing exercise or to form my own view on whether the legislative objective could be achieved by other means. These questions involve compromises between competing interests which in a democratic society must be resolved by the legislature. The duty of the court is only to inquire whether the compromise adopted by the United Kingdom Parliament, so far as it affects community trade, is one which a reasonable legislature could have reached. The function of the court is to review the acts of the legislature but not to substitute its own policies or values.
>
> This is not an abdication of judicial responsibility. The primacy of the democratic process is far more important than the question of whether our Sunday trading laws could or could not be improved.[65]

Instead of applying *Torfaen*, the judge referred to similar cases from Commonwealth countries, where the courts are familiar with judicial review of legislation, like Canada, the USA and Australia. Following their example, he applied a 'rational basis' test.[66] Contrary to the impact-based test applied by the ECJ, examination of the rational basis of legislation focuses on the state of mind of the primary decision-maker, the reasonableness or the plausibility of her assessments as to the appropriateness or the necessity of the contested measures. In this respect, the company suggested that broad exceptions to the Sunday trading prohibition rendered the legislation incoherent and betrayed a discriminatory purpose.

Hoffmann J rejected these claims. He held that exceptions to Sunday trading provided for by the law were not furthering illegitimate legislative purposes but were necessary concessions, given that the public interest aim of the relevant legislation was impossible to fully achieve in practice: some stores had to be open on Sunday.[67] In Hoffmann J's words:

65 Ibid, p. 69.
66 Ibid, pp. 69–71.
67 Ibid, pp. 66–8.

> [T]he history of the Sunday trading law shows that the existing exceptions are regarded by Parliament as the limits of what is necessary to achieve the legislative object. Of course there are illogicalities in Schedule 5 and opinions may differ about whether it draws the line in the right place. On the other hand, illogical compromise tends to be a British 'socio-cultural characteristic', to adopt the language of the European Court of Justice. That may also explain why Sunday trading is permitted in Scotland but not in England and Wales. In my judgment Parliament was entitled to decide that the present restrictions were necessary to attain the objects of the Act and that different restrictions would be inadequate, even though they might have less effect on Community trade.[68]

Engaging in Transnational Communication with the ECJ. Was Hoffmann J's decision part of a dialogue or a proper threat, pronounced by a judge 'well known for his lively decisions and willingness to break with convention'?[69] In any case, the message was well-heard in Luxembourg. Hoffmann J's decision was appealed. In the meantime, the Court of Justice had issued two important decisions in similar French cases, *Conforama* and *Marchandise*.[70] The Luxembourg court had changed its position from the *Torfaen* case and had itself assessed the issue of proportionality, finding in favour of the national authorities. This had caused uncertainty as to the application of proportionality in this field.[71] The parties disagreed on the interpretation of the European case law before the House of Lords.

The Lords of Appeal referred the relevant questions to the ECJ, which replied in the famous *Stoke-on-Trent* decision.[72] The European court stated that, in the *Conforama* and *Marchandise* cases, it considered that it had all necessary information in order to assess the proportionality of such measures itself, and to help national courts to reach uniform decisions. The judges observed that 'such an assessment [could not] be allowed to vary according to the findings of fact made by individual courts in particular cases'.[73] Thus, they declared that Sunday trading

[68] Ibid, p. 72.

[69] 'Lennie Hoffmann, Baron Hoffmann', in *Wikipedia, The Free Encyclopedia*, available at en.wikipedia.org.

[70] ECJ, C-312/89, 28 February 1991, *Union Départementale des Syndicats C.G.T. de l'Aisne* v. *SIDEF Conforama*, ECLI:EU:C:1991:93; C-332/89, 28 February 1991, *André Marchandise, Jean-Marie Chapuis and SA Trafitex*, ECLI:EU:C:1991:94.

[71] See *Kirklees Borough Council* v. *Wickes Building Supplies Ltd; Mendip District Council* v. *B&Q plc* [1991] 4 All ER 240 (CA, Civil Division, 30 April 1991).

[72] ECJ, C-169/91, 16 December 1992, *Council of the City of Stoke-on-Trent and Norwich City Council* v. *B&Q plc*, ECLI:EU:C:1992:519.

[73] Ibid, para. 14.

restrictions were not prohibited by Article 30. The House of Lords subsequently applied the judgment.[74]

The response from Luxembourg resolved the situation on Sunday trading, but it still left questions about the application of proportionality unanswered. The issue provoked contradictory decisions and confusion in national case law. The European court was aware of this and tried to give some guidance as to the application of the principle in EC market freedoms. Interestingly, this provided us with one of the rare occasions where the ECJ employed a language of weighing and balancing in this field of case law. For once, in the 1992 *Stoke-on-Trent* case, national value scales were authoritatively recognised. In the words of the court: 'Appraising the proportionality of national rules which pursue a legitimate aim under Community law involves weighing the national interest in attaining that aim against the Community interest in ensuring the free movement of goods.'[75]

Therefore, it is not the application of proportionality that allowed English courts to enter into a dialogue with their European counterparts. Rather, it is English courts' *reasoned refusal* to follow EC proportionality case law that led the ECJ to explicitly acknowledge normative pluralism in the EU. In her account on the making of the European rule of law, Alter also observes that what has allowed domestic courts to influence the process of European integration has been their willingness to oppose domestic law to the effective application of European law.[76]

9.4 Engineering Constitutional Change: Proportionality and Greek Constitutional Goals

The Impossibility of Framing Domestic Constitutional Particularities. Common law dualism and pragmatism has allowed English judges to frame normative conflicts between EC law and the domestic constitution and to depart from the case law of supranational courts whenever it is incompatible with fundamental features of the domestic legal culture. Indeed, English courts decide by reference to European case law and not by means of its translation in the domestic sphere. Quite to the contrary, the scientific aesthetics of law in Greece have deprived domestic courts of the possibility of framing normative conflicts

[74] See *Stoke-on-Trent and Norwich (No. 2)* [1993] 2 WLR 730 (HL, 31 March 1993).
[75] See the ECJ *Stoke-on-Trent and Norwich* decision, C-169/91, para. 15.
[76] Alter (2002), pp. 60–3.

between domestic and EU law and of resisting the integration dynamic of the EC law principle of proportionality.

In *Michaniki*, the perception of proportionality as a kind of European science even led the Council of State to raise the question of the proportionality of certain constitutional provisions before the ECJ. Following the ECJ's response, the Greek court overruled its settled case law as to the meaning of Article 14(9) of the constitution. In this way, the Greek supreme judges deferred to the ECJ's determination of the 'true meaning' of the domestic constitution and established coherence between domestic and European law, albeit at a cost for the consistency of the domestic constitutional discourse.[77] By establishing coherence between the domestic constitution and the treaties at the level of aesthetics, proportionality represented the domestic society as a modern European one. Hence, rather than a corollary of rationalist tendencies, assimilation of the domestic and the European concepts of proportionality was the result of the classicist tastes of Greek public lawyers.

The importance of aesthetics in the Greek context makes it so that constitutional identity is a concept that is difficult to invoke in Greek legal discourse. Yannakopoulos explains that in Greece: '[I]t is generally impossible – if not explicitly denied – to identify national particularities in order to solidly take them into account in the process of determination and implementation of specific state policies.'[78] Besides, an eventual conflict between European and domestic constitutional values has traditionally been difficult to conceive of in Greek legal thought. Article 28(3) states that concessions of national sovereignty should respect human rights and democratic government. However, in the minds of Greek lawyers, fundamental rights and democracy are values that international organisations are deemed to respect *by definition*.[79] Concerning the EU, this feature is explicit in the interpretative clause added to Article 28 in 2001, which specifies that this provision 'constitutes the foundation for the participation of the Country in the European integration process'. As Venizelos put it in 2006, 'in any case [the Greeks] politically equate the European Union to democracy, the State ruled by Law, the feeling of growth'.[80]

Normative Conflict in *Michaniki*. Normative conflicts between domestic and European law are thus typically neglected by Greek legal

[77] See Part II, Chapter 7.4.
[78] Yannakopoulos (2013), p. 375.
[79] Drossos (1996), p. 652.
[80] Venizelos (2006).

actors. This is exemplified in the application of proportionality in *Michaniki*. Focusing on questions of fact and evidence in each concrete case, proportionality distracted attention from possible conflicts that underpinned its application. Neglect of normative issues, both by national and by EU institutions, was evident in the fact that the constitutional basis of the domestic provisions had no impact on the Council of State's preliminary reference or the ECJ judgment. Nonetheless, a careful reading of the Council of State's preliminary reference to the ECJ shows that there *was* a normative conflict in *Michaniki*. The Greek court called on the European judges to deviate from an unsparing application of proportionality. The council made it clear that, in its view, if the ECJ found that the domestic measures were not proportionate, the directive would be incompatible with general European law principles, such as democratic government, media pluralism, transparency and free competition. This is because Article 14(9) was enacted in order to protect those principles, 'in view of the situation configured in Greek reality'.[81]

The question of the discretion left to the domestic authorities (the Constituent Assembly in this case) for the pursuit of constitutional goals was at the core of the conflict between domestic and European legal orders. Yannakopoulos observes that the 2001 reform had instituted transparency as a primary goal of the domestic constitution. Exceptionally, the constitution had functioned in domestic judicial reasoning as a 'constitution of goals', justifying and even imposing restrictions on constitutional freedoms, among them market freedoms, for its effective realisation.[82] In its preliminary reference the council stated that prevention of corruption entailed an obligation for Parliament to 'institute sanctions that will be sufficiently deterrent' in case of breach of the Article 14(9) prohibitions.[83] In the judges' view then, an unsparing application of proportionality in this case 'would void [Article 14(9)] of its content or would reverse its clear formulation and its equally clear goals'.[84]

What is more, the Greek court perceived domestic constitutional goals as goals of the European legal order, too. Due to their shared *nom propre*, the domestic and European concepts of democratic government, media pluralism, transparency and free competition were understood to share the same structure and function in judicial reasoning. The resonance

81 StE (Pl.) 3670/2006, para. 31.
82 Yannakopoulos (2008), p. 737.
83 StE (Pl.) 3670/2006, para. 14.
84 Ibid.

between EU and domestic legal orders did not allow for the matter to be analysed as a normative difference. Therefore, the council considered that the ECJ should not set limits on the pursuit of these goals through the application of proportionality as an efficiency principle. The judges argued that in case of incompatibility of the domestic constitutional provision with the directive, the directive might violate the principle of subsidiarity. According to the Council of State, this principle applies in the areas which are not subject to the exclusive competence of EU law, and mandates the community 'not to impede member-states from pursuing goals that are simultaneously goals of the Community legal order, and in cases where due to local conditions this is appropriate, to provide them with the discretion to act in principle first'.[85]

Reframing Domestic Policy Goals According to the Common Market Rationale. The ECJ refused to depart from its case law and pronounced on the limits that EC law sets on the pursuit of domestic policy goals, even when they are decided at a constitutional level. The court observed that the objectives of equal treatment and transparency pursued by the measures were legitimate and constituted the basis of community directives on the matter.[86] It further admitted that 'each Member State is best placed to identify, in the light of historical, legal, economic or social considerations specific to it [...], situations propitious to conduct' which is liable to undermine these objectives.[87] The ECJ stressed that 'Community law does not seek to call into question the assessment of a Member State, in the light of the specific context of that Member State', as to the existence of a risk of corruption and the need to confront it.[88] Put briefly, domestic choices as to the level of protection of domestic constitutional values could be accommodated by EC law. Still, in the court's view this did not exclude the application of proportionality. The ECJ declared Article 14(9) to be contrary to EC law. In its view, by excluding a whole category of enterprises from the public contract sector, the domestic provisions went beyond what was necessary to eliminate the risk of corruption.[89]

85 Ibid.

86 ECJ, C-213/07, 16 December 2008, *Michaniki*, para. 55.

87 Ibid, para. 56.

88 Ibid, para. 57.

89 Ibid, paras. 62–3. Interestingly, in margin of appreciation cases, the court requires from domestic authorities to *justify* exceptions to the application of the domestic measures. This kind of reasoning is the inverse from the one observed here, where the court sanctioned the too broad application of legislation. On this issue, see Réveillère (2017), pp. 425 f.

In the ECJ case law, the acknowledgment of value-laden differences between domestic and European legal orders engages the application of the margin of appreciation doctrine. In this context, the courts' scrutiny is intent-based, concerned with the coherence of domestic measures with respect to their goal.[90] However, this reasoning was not followed in *Michaniki*, where proportionality functioned as an efficiency principle. This is because the 'specific context' invoked by the Greek authorities did not imply any value-laden difference between the domestic and the European legal orders. Only the acknowledgment of such a difference would allow domestic authorities to implement legislation according to their own value scale. Instead, in the ECJ ruling the normative conflict between domestic and EU law was silenced. The implementation of domestic policies was inserted into the proportionality framework and was reframed as an obstacle to free trade and competition. Thus, the pursuit of public interest goals, no matter how important in the particular circumstances, did not escape the dynamic of economic integration.

The 'Self-Denying Transformation' of the Greek Constitution. The Council of State applied the ECJ decision through an impressive overruling of its previous interpretation of the domestic constitution. While the aesthetic coherence between constitutional and European provisions was established through the application of the principle of proportionality, 'a principle both of the Greek legal order […] and of Community law',[91] the internal coherence of the domestic constitution was damaged. As we saw, in order to produce its impressive *revirement*, the council had to reformulate the goals pursued by the domestic constitution so as to minimise their restrictive effect. In the last 'major shareholder' decision, the constitutional goal of transparency that Article 14(9) pursued was reformulated to a concrete objective: in the court's words, the provision aimed 'only to prevent […] the concrete illegitimate influence that can be exercised on the procedure of public contracts, with an intention to obtain the award of the contract'.[92] The application of proportionality thus led to a 'self-denying transformation' of the domestic constitution to the profit of European integration.[93]

In *Michaniki*, not only did proportionality displace local knowledge and local representations of the Greek polity; at a normative level, it

[90] C-42/07, 8 September 2009, *Liga Portuguesa*, ECLI:EU:C:2009:519, paras. 57–9. On this point, see De Witte (2013), who talks about a 'procedural' standard of proportionality.

[91] StE (Pl.) 3470/2011, para. 9; 3741/2011, para. 13.

[92] StE (Pl.) 3471/2011, para. 13.

[93] Cotterrell (2007), p. 136.

weakened the effective realisation of domestic constitutional goals. In other words, proportionality undermined the *effet utile* of the domestic constitution, to the profit of EU market freedoms. Yannakopoulos shows that Greek courts have often opted for a liberal interpretation of the constitution, to the detriment of domestic constitutional goals. In some cases, the enforcement of individual, and especially economic, freedoms has limited the discretion of public authorities considerably.[94] It is thus not surprising that proportionality has not fulfilled the expectations that Greek scholars attached to it for the realisation of the social state.[95] The failure of proportionality in this respect became even more evident in the context of the economic crisis.

The *First MoU* Decision. In decision 668/2012, for the first time the council was confronted with austerity measures adopted in application of the economic adjustment programme that Greece had agreed with its institutional creditors.[96] The measures were concretely agreed at a staff level, between the representatives of the Greek government, the ECB, the IMF and the European Commission. They were specified in an English-language document, the so-called memorandum of understanding (MoU), which was annexed to law 3845/2010.[97] Domestic legislation implementing austerity policies imposed severe cuts on wages and allowances in the public sector, as well as on pensions. The constitutionality of the cuts was contested by several trade unions and professional associations in a case that attracted media attention. Among the main arguments of the claimants was the violation of the principle of proportionality.

The plaintiffs contested the narrowly tailored character of the measures and their efficacy in facing the crisis. In contrast to *Michaniki* however, proportionality in this case did not function as an objective efficiency test concerned with evidence and data. The proportionality review was restricted to a check of the coherence of the domestic measures, which were viewed as part of a broader legislative policy. As to the impact of the legislative restrictions, the Council of State contented itself with the observation that the domestic authorities had struck a balance between the public interest and individual rights.[98] While from the point

94 Yannakopoulos (2008). For an example, see the litigation concerning pharmacy licences, analysed in Part I, Chapter 4.5.

95 Katrougkalos (2006), p. 141.

96 StE (Pl.) 668/2012 *NoB* 2012, p. 384. On this case, see, among others, Antoniou (2012).

97 Law no. 3845/2010 of 6 May 2010, Government Gazette A 65.

98 StE (Pl.) 668/2012. For a more detailed description of the Council of State's reasoning, see Marketou and Dekastros (2015).

of view of judicial politics, restraint in the context of crisis might seem reasonable, how can we make sense of the application of proportionality from a domestic constitutional viewpoint?

The wording of the decision shows that what led the court to defer to legislative assessments was the importance it accorded to the legislative aim. The Council of State dedicated a long part of its reasoning to the economic and political developments that had led to the activation of the support mechanism for the Greek economy.[99] Even though, at the stage of the identification of the aim, the court did not explicitly use the term emergency, it talked about an 'acute financial crisis' and the need for its 'immediate' confrontation, a 'long period of economic depression' or even a 'crucial financial situation'.[100] Later in its reasoning, the court actually referred to the existence of a financial emergency.[101]

Nonetheless, it was not only the emergency that justified the application of proportionality as a manifest error test. Interestingly, for once, EU law pointed in the direction of judicial restraint as well. While the rights invoked by the claimants were not among EU market freedoms, the objective pursued by the domestic legislator was perceived as an EU goal. According to the council, facing the crisis and consolidating public finances:

> [A]re generally compelling public interest reasons and at the same time goals that are commonly shared among Eurozone member states and entrenched in European Union legislation, in view of the obligation of fiscal discipline and of ensuring the stability of the Eurozone as a whole.[102]

Thus, in the judicial assessment of the public interest pursued by Parliament, the Council of State took into account the common interest of Eurozone member states. Once again, EU law played an important role in the determination of domestic constitutional goals and policies. The coincidence between domestic and EU goals made the council adopt a holistic view of legislation and simply check the coherence of the domestic measures. Indeed, the type of review that proportionality entailed resembled the test that the ECJ performs in margin of appreciation cases.

This reading is reinforced by the council's reasoning concerning the nature of the MoU itself. The claimants argued that this document was an international convention that had been introduced into the domestic

[99] StE (Pl.) 668/2012, paras. 19–24.
[100] Ibid, para. 35.
[101] Ibid.
[102] Ibid.

legal sphere in an irregular manner. The council, on the contrary, considered the MoU to contain the political programme of the Greek government and not an international agreement, 'despite the fact that it [was] a product of cooperation between Greek authorities, the European Commission, the European Central Bank and the International Monetary Fund' and 'despite the obligations that Greece assumed vis-à-vis the rest of the Eurozone member states with the subsequent Loan Facility Agreement'.[103] This excluded the judicial review of the MoU, both by domestic and by supranational courts.

Replacing Constitutional Limits with Factual Ones. Thus, under the circumstances of economic crisis, Greek lawyers' tendency to search for the value-laden content of the domestic constitution abroad acquired a new dynamic. Before, under the influence of EU law, the effective application of constitutional limits, most notably negative freedoms of an economic nature, absorbed constitutional goals like transparency or social rights. This led courts to review public interventions more intrusively, to the benefit of market integration. Proportionality functioned as a strict necessity test. In the context of economic adjustment, in contrast, European goals have reinforced domestic financial goals. Domestic constitutional limits have thus been considerably weakened. In the *First MoU* decision, the council repeatedly stressed that its proportionality scrutiny was only 'marginal'.[104] The court was only concerned with the plausibility of public authorities' assessments.

In the context of an economic emergency, the improvement of the economic situation of the country has been sought at all costs. Domestic constitutional values and European human rights have been reduced to a minimum requirement for decent living. In their application, there is no place left for proportionality as an instance of value-laden balancing. Indeed, the Council of State rejected the claimants' allegations concerning the violation of their constitutional and convention rights, since they had not specifically claimed that their 'decent way of life' was at stake.[105] The Strasbourg court rewarded this solution. It affirmed that appeal to the convention in such cases was 'manifestly ill-founded', insofar as the measures did not place the affected individuals 'at risk of having insufficient means to live'.[106]

[103] Ibid, para. 28.
[104] Ibid, paras. 34, 35, 38.
[105] Ibid, para. 35.
[106] ECtHR, *Koufaki and ADEDY* v. *Greece*, 7 May 2013, nos. 57665/12 and 57657/12, para. 46. Some proportionality scholars profess this kind of protection to social rights. See Alexy (2002), pp. 288 f., 349 f.; Kumm (2004), pp. 582 f.; Contiades and Fotiadou (2012a).

Something that long preserved the normativity of the domestic constitution was its apparent coherence with European law and the underlying representation of the Greek polity as modern and European. In a species of sympathetic magic, by translating European legal rules in the domestic sphere, Greek lawyers purported to modernise Greek society. The Eurozone crisis abruptly exposed this representation as illusionary. Since then, modernisation of the Greek society and the corollary compliance with EU law precepts has required a species of constitutional magic that is not so sympathetic. In fact, it has questioned the normativity of the domestic constitution as a whole. In the implementation of the economic adjustment programmes, defiance of constitutional limits became more apparent in the circumvention of precise and unconditional constitutional rules and procedures.[107]

In this context, the Council of State assumes a function of justifying constitutional deviance. In its reasoning then, proportionality reflects a peculiar 'turn to justification'. In the *First MoU* decision, while proportionality was pronounced as a manifest error test, it led to a kind of reasoning that was very different from its traditional application as a self-evident standard. Indeed, it entailed extensive justification of the austerity measures introduced with law 3845/2010. The court, as a partner of policy-making authorities, felt the need to reply to the plaintiffs' unconstitutionality arguments one by one. It forced domestic policies into constitutional categories, changing well-established interpretations of domestic constitutional concepts like the public interest.[108] Partnership between the government and the Council of State in the implementation of economic adjustment was also manifested at an institutional level, with the appointment of the president of the council as interim prime minister in 2012.

Domestic scholars have grappled with this new constitutional situation, when they have not simply denounced it. However, in their accounts too, there is little space left for constitutional limits. In a comment on the 668/2012 decision, Contiades and Fotiadou argued:

> In order for a theory of social rights to be convincing, it must prove applicable independently of the changing economic and political circumstances. If the approaches that defend that social rights incorporate a stable and untouchable core of protection [...] prove inapplicable in

[107] Marketou (2015).
[108] Mathioudakis (2011), p. 478.

practice, this is not due to the changing reality but to these approaches themselves.[109]

In this new kind of constitutionalism then, the constitution is normative only in so far as it is applicable in practice. Instead of being interpreted, the constitution is observed.[110] Due to its pragmatic and consequentialist connotations, proportionality becomes *the only* possible theoretical structure through which to make sense of domestic constitutional practice.[111] Its promoters argue that it is the only way for adjudicating fundamental rights.[112] Rather than the establishment of fundamental rights as principles, the recent hegemony of proportionality in Greek constitutional discourse expresses the intrusion of considerations from other disciplines (most notably economics and finance) in the definition of domestic constitutional values.

***

In the ECJ market freedoms case law, proportionality acquires a function of economic integration. Its application ensures the *effet utile* of EC law and is imposed as an obligation on domestic courts in this field. However, the economic integration function of proportionality is nuanced once the test is inserted into local discursive contexts. The success or failure of proportionality in its integration mission is connected to the cultural particularities of domestic judicial review systems and to local lawyers' perception of EC law and of the project of EU integration. In this chapter, I have argued that the similarities in the ways English and Greek courts apply proportionality reflect similar local patterns of Europeanisation. Indeed, both English and Greek judges have assumed the mission of *juges communautaires de droit commun* that the ECJ assigned to them and have followed the ECJ case law in the application of proportionality. Under the surface of convergence however, new dissonances arise. While proportionality is applied by *reference* to the ECJ case law in England, it is applied it by means of *translation* of this case law in Greece.

The difference lies in local legal actors' possibility of framing normative conflicts between domestic and European law. English dualism has allowed for the framing of such conflicts, which have usually been avoided through the strict containment of EC legal concepts within the scope of EC law. Quite differently, in Greece domestic lawyers and judges

[109] Contiades and Fotiadou (2012b), p. 29.

[110] See, in this sense, Yannakopoulos (2015).

[111] See Contiades and Fotiadou (2012b), p. 29.

[112] See Part I, Chapter 4.4.

have perceived the application of proportionality by the ECJ as scientifically correct. Normative conflicts have thus been concealed behind the EC law-conform interpretation of domestic law. Hence the local use of proportionality as an EC law principle reflects more general knowledge practices that are characteristic of local legal thought: English analytical formalism and Greek lawyers' tendency to search for the content of domestic legal concepts in Europe.

Local patterns of Europeanisation are themselves connected to local visions of Europe. They affect differently legal actors' capacity to shape the process of European integration in crucial constitutional moments. As the reach of EC law expanded, the accomplishment by common law courts of their European integration mission has sometimes entered into conflict with the sovereignty of Parliament in setting policy goals. This led English and European judges to engage in transnational communication in the Sunday trading litigation and to explicitly acknowledge normative pluralism within the EC. Thus, the common law constitution, albeit unwritten, has proved much more solid than the formal Greek one. Indeed, the economic integration dynamic of proportionality has not met major constitutional obstacles in Greece. Since the end of the 1990s, proportionality in the field of EC law has functioned as a mechanism that serves the redefinition of domestic constitutional goals as parts of the common market project. Its application has led to a 'self-denying transformation' of the Greek Constitution to the profit of European integration. In the context of economic crisis in particular, the hegemony of proportionality reflects the displacement of domestic constitutional limits in the pursuit of financial goals, as required both by government's economic policy and by EU law.

10

Disintegration

Proportionality and the Rupture in the Traditional Local Patterns of Europeanisation. European integration is in crisis. Paradoxically, disintegration seems to be a transnational tendency. In the domestic legal sphere, it is manifested in derogations from the application of European treaties and of the convention, as well as in talks about Frexit, Brexit and Grexit, which, especially in the English case, have led to the adoption of concrete legal instruments.[1] Challenges and constraints connected to the rise of Euroscepticism are sometimes apparent in the practice of European institutions themselves, in the context of both the EU and the convention. However, this is not the focus of this chapter. What will be analysed instead is the way disintegration tendencies are expressed in the use of proportionality language by courts in France, England and Greece.

While one cannot say that proportionality bears the dynamics of disintegration itself, relevant tendencies affect its form and function in different settings. This chapter offers a particular reading of proportionality cases that have provoked much discussion among domestic legal actors. I argue that what is new about these cases is not so much the application of proportionality itself, which follows already existing local patterns characterising the reception and the evolution of proportionality. Rather, it is the particular context of disintegration in which proportionality operates. Indeed, what is observed in these much debated uses of proportionality is a rupture in the traditional local patterns of Europeanisation.

Disintegration obliges French lawyers to acknowledge pluralism in Europe and the parochialism of their republican perception of rights. This attributes a radical function to proportionality as a convention principle (Section 10.1). Disintegration in English law is expressed in

[1] European Union (Withdrawal) Act 2018 and European Union (Withdrawal Agreement) Act 2020.

the spread of proportionality and of the rationalist methodology that it entails. English judges reinvent proportionality as a common law concept. By doing so, they affirm to themselves the powers that Parliament had conceded to European supranational courts (Section 10.2). In Greece, as in France, disintegration is manifested in the acknowledgement of normative conflicts between domestic and European law. This introduces a new kind of dualism in Greek legal thought. Greek supreme courts increasingly affirm the autonomy of domestic constitutional values and assume the role of guarantors of the constitution. For once, proportionality might prove a 'formidable weapon' in this new judicial mission (Section 10.3).

10.1 European Human Rights v. Republican Legislation: Proportionality Bounding the Normativity of French Law

French Exceptionalism in the Field of Fundamental Rights. We saw that, in France, integration into a European rights order has proceeded through a process of inaccurate translation of European concepts into existing domestic ones. European rights have been perceived as part of a common civilisation of rights, of which France is thought to be the motherland. Proportionality and its European rights baggage have been accommodated in the already existing structures of judicial review and have been reinvented as objective, republican values. Their institutional aspect has been neglected, so has their integration dynamic. In this context, disintegration has been expressed in the progressive acknowledgment of normative conflict between the European rights civilisation and French legislation. Indeed, the European human rights case law increasingly forces French lawyers to abandon their belief in the commonly shared character of republican values.

Called to judge on the *burqa* ban in *SAS* v. *France*, the ECtHR criticised the French objectivised understanding of fundamental rights. The Strasbourg judges were 'not convinced' by the arguments based on the principle of equality.[2] Rights' holders cannot be protected from the exercise of their own rights. Neither did the human dignity argument work out. Although the judges observed that 'the clothing in question is perceived as strange by many of those who observe it', it pointed out, 'however, that it is the expression of a cultural identity which contributes

[2] ECtHR, *SAS* v. *France* 1 July 2014, no. 43835/11, para. 118.

to the pluralism that is inherent in democracy'.[3] The European court finally accepted the legitimacy of the domestic measures by appealing to the respect for the minimum requirements of life in society.[4] In other words, it considered the only plausible justification for the *burqa* ban to be a majoritarian perception of social interaction. The judges underscored that the public interest aim invoked by the French authorities did 'not expressly correspond to any of the legitimate aims' provided for by the convention.[5] Still, they were 'able to accept that the barrier raised against others by a veil concealing the face is perceived by the respondent State as breaching the right of others to live in a space of socialisation which makes living together easier'.[6]

That being said, the court did not readily accept the French republican perception of life in society as compatible with the European conception of fundamental rights. It underscored that:

> Although individual interests must on occasion be subordinated to those of a group, democracy does not simply mean that the views of a majority must always prevail: a balance must be achieved which ensures the fair treatment of people from minorities and avoids any abuse of a dominant position.[7]

In a series of long paragraphs, the judges carefully monitored the necessity of the impugned legislation. They proceeded to a thorough impact-based examination of the blanket ban on the *burqa* in public spaces. They stressed that even though a very small proportion of the French population is affected by the ban, the impacts on the women in question are very significant. The ban has the effect of 'isolating them and restricting their autonomy, as well as impairing the exercise of their freedom to manifest their beliefs and their right to respect for their private life'.[8] Even more, the judges pointed out that it was 'understandable that the women concerned may perceive the ban as a threat to their identity'.[9] The intrusive scrutiny exercised by the ECtHR and the extensive consideration of the point of view of Muslim women stand in stark contrast with the *Burqa* decision by the Constitutional Council.

[3] Ibid, para. 120.
[4] Ibid, para. 117.
[5] Ibid, para. 121.
[6] Ibid, paras. 121–2.
[7] Ibid, para. 128.
[8] Ibid, para. 146.
[9] Ibid, para. 145.

In the absence of common ground among convention parties on the issue, the Strasbourg court finally deferred to what it considered as 'a choice of society'[10] and held that the *burqa* ban 'can be regarded' as proportionate and necessary in a democratic society.[11] The judges did not affirm the proportionality of the measures per se, but only the plausibility of domestic authorities' claims as to the justification of the ban of the *burqa*. The *burqa* ban was accommodated by the convention as an instance of French exceptionalism. In this respect, the court underscored that 'a large number of actors, both international and national, in the field of fundamental rights protection have found a blanket ban to be disproportionate'.[12] Further, it claimed to be 'very concerned' by certain Islamophobic remarks that marked the debate on the adoption of the law on the *burqa*.[13] In the court's view:

> A State which enters into a legislative process of this kind takes the risk of contributing to the consolidation of the stereotypes which affect certain categories of the population and of encouraging the expression of intolerance, when it has a duty, on the contrary, to promote tolerance.[14]

No doubt the European court could not be more hostile to the domestic legislation in an era of terrorism and disintegration. The *SAS* decision made clear that the French republican understanding of fundamental rights would not always be found compatible with the convention. A future condemnation of the French attitude on the matter looked very probable. The 'stateless' court based in Strasbourg (according to the former vice-president of the French Council of State and member of the Constitutional Council) would not prove any more sensible to domestic republican values, no matter how fundamental they are considered by French officials.[15]

European human rights law forces French public lawyers to become aware of normative pluralism in Europe and of 'cognitive limitations connected to national parochialism' in the field of human rights.[16] This upsets traditional legal categories and distinctions and contests the most

[10] Ibid, para. 153.
[11] Ibid, para. 157.
[12] Ibid, para. 147.
[13] Ibid, para. 149.
[14] Ibid.
[15] '*Cette cour apatride*': this phrase was pronounced by Denoix de Saint-Marc, member of the Constitutional Council and formerly vice-president of the Council of State, in a speech delivered in May 2010 during a student visit at the Council of State.
[16] Kumm (2009b), p. 307.

fundamental assumptions of rationalist French legal thought. As French lawyers become conscious of the possibility of normative conflict between objective republican values and European rights, proportionality acquires a radical dynamic.

The *Gonzalez-Gomez* Case. Recently, it appears that domestic courts have proceeded to a revolutionary application of the convention and especially of proportionality. In the field of public law, this is exemplified by the *Gonzalez-Gomez* case, decided by the Council of State Plenum in 2016.[17] Ms Gonzalez-Gomez wished to export to Spain the gametes of her deceased husband, in order to perform posthumous insemination. The French hospital refused. Contrary to what is the case in Spain, French legislation prohibits posthumous insemination, as well as the exportation of gametes stored in France for a use that would be incompatible with the bioethics principles entrenched in French law.

The claimant challenged the refusal and applied to the administrative courts for an interlocutory injunction under the *référé libertés* procedure. She claimed that the refusal to export her deceased husband's gametes constituted a violation of her right to private and family life under the ECHR. Her application being rejected in first instance, Ms Gonzalez-Gomez appealed before the Council of State. Until then, the council had hesitated to proceed to a convention-compatibility review of legislation in the *référé libertés* procedure, since its view was that an ultimate incompatibility could not be manifest and thus could not ground interim relief. In *Gonzalez-Gomez*, however, the judges agreed to scrutinise the manifest incompatibility of domestic law with the convention.[18]

The council explicitly divided its analysis in two steps. First, it examined *in abstracto* the compatibility of the law with the convention as a whole. In its view, regarding bioethical matters, states enjoy a wide margin of appreciation and the domestic law, both concerning posthumous insemination and the exportation of gametes for this purpose, fell within this margin. Therefore, viewed abstractly, French legislation was

[17] CE (Pl.) ord., 31 May 2016, *Gonzalez-Gomez*, no. 396848, ECLI:FR:CEASS:2016:396848.20160531. Concerning recent *Cour de cassation* case law that has provoked relevant debates, see Cass. civ. 1, 4 December 2013, no. 12-26066, Bull. 2013, no. 234. On this issue, see Dutheillet de Lamothe and Odinet (2016), esp. 'Le contrôle in concreto avant la décision *Gonzalez Gomez*'. Note that in most of the cases mentioned by the authors, the *Cour de cassation* does not use proportionality language. See however, Cass. civ. 3, 17 December 2015, no. 14-22095, Bull. 2016, no. 841, where the court annuls a Court of Appeal decision for not having reviewed *in concreto* the proportionality of legislation that interferes with the claimants' rights under Article 8 ECHR.

[18] Dutheillet de Lamothe and Odinet (2016).

not considered disproportionate by itself. Still, the judges did not content themselves with the in-principle affirmation of legitimacy; they went on to examine *in concreto* whether, 'in certain specific circumstances, the application of legislative provisions [...] constitute[d] a disproportionate interference [with] the rights guaranteed' by the convention.[19]

Contrary to the traditional formalist assumptions of French legal thought then, the application of legislation in concrete circumstances was perceived as a question that could affect the law's compatibility with the convention.[20] This was so even though the legislation in question did not allow for administrative discretion. What is more, in the concrete case of Ms Gonzalez-Gomez, judicial review led to the disapplication of the French law. The council decided that, 'having regard to all the circumstances of this case', the application of the French law to Ms Gonzalez-Gomez 'is manifestly excessive and infringes her right to respect for private and family life'.[21] The council thus held that the refusal to export Mr Gomez' gametes resulted in a 'serious and manifestly illegal infringement of a fundamental freedom' and enjoined the French hospital to ensure the transfer of the gametes to a Spanish hospital.[22]

A Revolutionary Application of Proportionality? The decision is perceived as a revolutionary application of proportionality, an instance of 'subjectivisation' of the law, or even a change of paradigm in French judicial review.[23] Proportionality, appreciated on a case-by-case basis, allows the judges to substitute their own view as to which solution would be just in the circumstances of each case, for that of the legislator. Public lawyers and judges do not know how to interpret the Council of State's attitude.[24] Scholars usually explain the decision as inspired by the council's indulgence of a sentiment of equity or by an implicit will to conform to the European freedom of movement. In any case, the solution adopted by the *juge des référés* was certainly not manifest, as the code of administrative justice requires for granting interim injunctions.

Proportionality seems to acquire a radical function in French public law, to the detriment of this law's most fundamental formal features, such

[19] *Gonzalez-Gomez*, Council of State official translation available at www.conseil-etat.fr/en/judging, para. 9.
[20] Contrast with CE, 2 June 1999, *Meyet*.
[21] *Gonzalez-Gomez* official translation, para. 11.
[22] Ibid.
[23] Delvolvé (2016).
[24] See Crépey, 'Conclusions sur CE, 28 décembre 2017, *M. Molenat*', ECLI:FR:CECHR:2017:396571.20171228. The *Rapporteur public* admits that he is unable to understand the reasoning underlying *Gonzalez-Gomez*.

as equality or the separation of powers. The transcendence of traditional formalities is expressed in the direct style of the *Gonzalez-Gomez* decision, which departs from the council's long-established habit of reasoning in one phrase composed by *considérants*.[25] *Gonzalez-Gomez* gave the chance to the council to participate in the ongoing transnational dialogue on proportionality between prestigious courts. A press release of the decision in English is available on the official *Conseil d'Etat* website.[26]

However, close attention to judicial reasoning shows that the function of proportionality in the *Gomez-Gonzalez* case is not new.[27] As is typically the case in the Council of State's reasoning, the European principle of proportionality was applied as an exception to the in principle conventionality of legislation. As such, it operated according to the concrete circumstances of the case. Neither the proportionality of the law nor the republican value choices that it embodied were contested in principle. It is in the concrete review of conventionality that proportionality entered into play. It simply eliminated the *effets pervers* of a law that was considered too general. The *Rapporteur public* Bretonneau referred to 'an absolute prohibition', which is 'deprived of nuances'.[28]

In other words, proportionality's function was once again corrective of the 'Cartesian paradigm, which relies on the belief in the legislator's capacity to anticipate all situations'.[29] *Gonzalez-Gomez* is not the first time that proportionality as a convention principle introduced a condition for defeating domestic legislation.[30] But it *is* the first time that this has been made so explicit. Besides, despite its direct style, the council's decision remains laconic and is still very far from the 'European style of decision-*dissertation*'.[31] If it was not a radical application of proportionality, what led the administrative judges to the revolutionary *Gomez-Gonzalez* decision?

Proportionality and the Limits of Republican Inculcation. Judicial activism in this case proceeded through the judicial construction of the legislative purpose. Even though it was formulated in abstract terms, the Council of State held that the prohibition on the export of gametes sought

25 Deumier (2016).
26 See www.conseil-etat.fr/en/press-releases.
27 Crépey, 'Conclusions sur CE, 28 décembre 2017, *M. Molenat*'.
28 Bretonneau, 'Conclusions sur CE Ass., 31 mai 2016, *Gonzalez-Gomez*', *RFDA*, 2016, p. 740.
29 Deumier (2016).
30 See Chapter 8.3.
31 Deumier (2016).

to impede any circumvention of the law on the prohibition of post mortem insemination.[32] This allowed for Ms Gonzalez-Gomez to be exempted from the prohibition. Indeed, the judges underscored 'the absence of any fraudulent intent by the applicant'.[33] By excluding Ms Gonzalez-Gomez from the scope of the prohibition, proportionality functioned as a method of teleological interpretation. It excluded from the scope of legislation a case that was not covered by its purpose, as this purpose was judicially constructed so as to be compatible with the convention. Bretonneau explained that the judges could have arrived at the same solution by using the classical technique of *réserve d'interprétation*.[34]

Still, what is not clear is why the particular case of Ms Gonzalez-Gomez was not covered by the goal of French legislation. Clearly, she wished to export the gametes to Spain in order to perform a posthumous insemination, a process that, just as clearly, is precluded by French law. French scholars observe that, paradoxically, the Council of State treated French law as if it were not French. It put aside its application and applied Spanish law to Ms Gonzalez-Gomez, while she was still in France. Moreover, it did so in contravention of the notion of public order, as it is commonly understood in private international law.[35]

What rendered the application of French legislation in Ms Gonzalez-Gomez' case disproportionate were the particular circumstances of the case: the applicant's Spanish nationality, the fact that she joined her family in Spain and the fact that she had carefully planned with her husband a posthumous insemination in this country. Put briefly, what was decisive for the judges was the fact that Ms Gonzalez-Gomez 'came back to Spain to live there'.[36] This impeded the application of proportionality as an instance of republican inculcation. Imposing republican value choices on Ms Gonzalez-Gomez was not justified since she simply did not wish to integrate into French society. Republican legislation was defeated; it was put aside and Spanish law applied. Interestingly, this particularity deprives the *Gonzalez-Gomez* decision of its normativity in

[32] *Gonzalez-Gomez*, para. 8.

[33] Ibid, para. 11.

[34] Bretonneau, 'Conclusions sur CE Ass., 31 mai 2016, *Gonzalez-Gomez*'.

[35] Delvolvé (2016).

[36] See the press release in English. See also CE ord., 24 January 2020, no 437328, ECLI:FR:CEORD:2020:437328.20200124. In this case, the council rejected an application for the transfer of embryos in Spain, on the basis that the applicant was French and was not related to Spain otherwise.

the French context. Indeed, for the first time the Council of State underscored the *in concreto* character of its review. Arguably, this limits the possibilities for applying the *Gonzalez-Gomez* case law in future circumstances.[37]

Gonzalez-Gomez is indeed a revolutionary case. Until this, the formalism and rationalism that are pervasive in French legal thought had made it difficult to accommodate the existence of alternative worldviews and moral choices. Proportionality resembled an instance of republican inculcation, a self-evident affirmation of legitimacy against which no counter-arguments were possible. It expressed a particularly French perception of social integration as assimilation.[38] The ECHR, however, progressively necessitates that French lawyers become aware of the particularity of their republican perception of rights, that they become aware of the pluralism in the perception and prioritisation of fundamental rights in Europe. French judges' effort to accommodate normative pluralism contests the rationalist foundations of French public law.

In *Gonzalez-Gomez*, the Council of State recognised the existence of alternative choices in the field of post mortem insemination, which are equally acceptable to the convention and the European paradigm of rights. However, to do so the court was obliged to introduce an exception to French republican legality. It excluded a case from the scope of French law even though it occurred within the French territory and was judged by French courts. What defined the legitimate limits of the normativity of republican legislation were not the rules of private international law or any legal rules whatsoever. Instead, it was proportionality as a European fundamental rights principle, which, in a context of normative pluralism, also allows for social *dis*integration.

10.2 English Public Law v. European Integration: Reinventing Proportionality as a Common Law Method

Proportionality, Rationalism and Disintegration in English Public Law. While the recognition of normative pluralism runs contrary to the most fundamental assumptions of French republican legality, it traditionally underpins English dualism and analytical formalism. Quite paradoxically, in England, disintegration is expressed in the spread of rationalism. Domestic lawyers increasingly deny the existence of

[37] Delvolvé (2016), nos. 8 and 14.

[38] See Part II, Chapter 5.6.

substantive conflict between the domestic and the European legal orders. Indeed, during the last decade distinguished members of the newly formed English public law *doctrine* claim that if the government were to repeal the HRA, the common law constitution would not change much.[39] This view tends to become dominant in case law, too.[40] English scholars are rather enthusiastic about the development of common law towards the establishment of a rationalist public law system. However, what has largely been neglected in the relevant debates is the fact that, in the context of disintegration from Europe, the rationalisation of English public law often comes at a cost for the effective application of European law in the domestic sphere. This is very well illustrated in the recent case law on proportionality and contextual judicial review.

In cases such as *Nicklinson*, *Kennedy* and *Pham*, proportionality was applied as a common law method, even when the doctrine of the margin of appreciation was at stake or even outside the 'gateway' of the statutes incorporating European law. These cases show that, as the rationalisation of English public law advances, European and domestic review will rarely lead to different intensities of review and to different outcomes.[41] Still, the development of the irrationality standard, even when it is in proportionality terms, is often preceded by English judges declining to use proportionality *as a European head of review* and thus to apply European law. Therefore, while the spread of proportionality in the common law exemplifies the maturity and sophistication of the newly constructed English public law, it also exemplifies English judges' scepticism towards European case law. It illustrates disintegration tendencies more generally observed in the English context. In an extra-judicial speech, Lady Hale pointed to the possibility that the development of common law methods is a response to the 'rising tide of anti-European sentiment'.[42]

Neglecting the Dynamic Interpretation of the Convention. In *Kennedy*, a journalist at *The Times* asked for disclosure of information under the Freedom of Information Act (FOIA). The information in question concerned 'the Mariam Appeal', a political campaign conducted by a British MP for the treatment of Iraqi children with leukaemia. Mr Kennedy thought that the relevant reports by the Charity Commission

[39] Allan (2013), p. 324; Neuberger (2014).
[40] *Osborn* v. *The Parole Board* [2013] UKSC 61 (SC, 9 October 2013).
[41] See however, *Elgizouli* v. *Secretary of State for the Home Department* [2020] UKSC 10 (25 March 2020).
[42] Hale (2014).

did not sufficiently address issues relating to the campaign, especially those resulting from Mr Kennedy's own findings as to the use of campaign monies. The Charity Commission refused disclosure, claiming that the information that it held was exempt from disclosure under section 32 of the FOIA. This section provides for an absolute exemption, when information is held by a public authority for the purposes of an inquiry or arbitration. Mr Kennedy appealed the refusal, claiming that section 32 ceases to apply after the end of the inquiry in question. Alternatively, he advanced that section 32 should be read down in conformity with Article 10 ECHR or be declared incompatible with the convention.

The majority of the Supreme Court judges refused to apply the convention in Mr Kennedy's case. As we saw, one of the reasons was that it did not put the applicant in a more favourable situation than common law statutes, which he had not invoked and which, according to the judges, applied to his case. Another reason was given by Lord Mance in a long obiter: according to the judge, Article 10 ECHR did not encompass a right to access to information in cases like the one Mr Kennedy was bringing.[43] Concerning the interpretation of the convention on this point, the Charity Commission invoked the original meaning of Article 10 as encompassing the freedom, and not the obligation, to express and receive information. Mr Kennedy, by way of contrast, contended that Strasbourg case law had evolved towards the recognition of a positive obligation to disclose information. In his words: 'Strasbourg case law has taken a direction of travel, towards a destination which should now be regarded as reached.'[44]

After a thorough consideration of Strasbourg case law on the matter, Lord Mance rejected Mr Kennedy's argument. In this respect, he accorded weight to a previous Supreme Court case where relevant Strasbourg case law had been considered.[45] While, in early Grand Chamber cases, the European court had denied a right to access information under the convention, in a series of later section cases it had conferred such a right, especially where disclosure of information was requested by social watchdogs such as the press or NGOs. Due to the contradictory statements in Strasbourg decisions, Lord Mance finally concluded that the present state of Strasbourg case law was

[43] *Kennedy* (SC, 26 March 2014), paras. 57 f.
[44] Ibid, para. 58.
[45] *Sugar* v. *BBC* [2012] 1 WLR 439 (SC, 15 February 2012).

'unsatisfactory' and thus insufficient to establish a positive obligation for the Charity Commission to disclose information.[46]

In passing, Lord Mance did not miss the opportunity to criticise the ambiguity of Strasbourg jurisprudence. He pointed out that:

> The Strasbourg jurisprudence is neither clear nor easy to reconcile [...]. In the present case, Strasbourg has spoken on a number of occasions to apparently different effects. Further, a number of these occasions are Grand Chamber decisions, which do contain apparently clear-cut statements of principle. But they are surrounded by individual section decisions, which appear to suggest that at least some members of the Court disagree with and wish to move on from the Grand Chamber statements of principle. If that is a correct reading, then it may be unfortunate that the relevant sections did not prefer to release the matter before them to a Grand Chamber. It is not helpful for national courts seeking to take into account the jurisprudence of the European Court of Human Rights to have different section decisions pointing in directions inconsistent with Grand Chamber authority without clear explanation.[47]

Lord Mance clearly found that Strasbourg judges had much to learn from their common law colleagues. This was also obvious in the revival of the Whig narrative in his dicta:

> The Convention rights represent a threshold protection; and, especially in view of the contribution which common lawyers made to the Convention's inception, they may be expected, at least generally even if not always, to reflect and to find their homologue in the common or domestic statute law. [...] Greater focus in domestic litigation on the domestic legal position might also have the incidental benefit that less time was taken in domestic courts seeking to interpret and reconcile different judgments (often only given by individual sections of the European Court of Human Rights) in a way which that Court itself, not being bound by any doctrine of precedent, would not itself undertake.[48]

However, as Clayton QC (lawyering for the applicants in *Kennedy*) pointed out, Lord Mance's criticism of Strasbourg case law seems to neglect the methods of this court and especially the rules governing the distribution of cases among its chambers.[49] Most importantly, it seems to neglect one of the major features of Strasbourg jurisprudence itself, which has been at the source of its integration function: dynamic

[46] *Kennedy*, para. 94.
[47] Ibid, para. 59.
[48] Ibid, para. 46.
[49] Clayton (2014).

interpretation.[50] Indeed, Strasbourg reasoning techniques are very different from the common law techniques of precedent, distinguishing and overruling. This was pointed out by Lord Wilson in his dissenting opinion. In this judge's view, 'the wider approach' lately adopted by the ECtHR as to the scope of Article 10 is not in conflict with the 'basic' approach adopted in early decisions; 'it is a dynamic extension of it'.[51]

Lord Mance's negligence of this particularity of Strasbourg reasoning echoes traditional and stereotypical common law criticisms of continental judicial decision-making.[52] His inaccurate translation of Strasbourg methods and techniques in common law terms can be compared to the French practice of domestic law-conform interpretation of European law, which long deprived the convention of its effectiveness in the French sphere. In a Grand Chamber decision, the Strasbourg court responded to Lord Mance's remarks. It pointed out that while legal certainty is important in the interpretation of international conventions, in the application of human rights standards the evolving practice of domestic authorities and international bodies will also be relevant. Concerning the right to have access to information, such evolutions pointed in the direction of 'a clarification' of early Strasbourg case law, so as to encompass such a right for social watchdogs.[53]

Affirming Parliamentary Sovereignty Against the ECJ. In *Kennedy*, while Lord Mance criticised Strasbourg case law, he still held that English judges 'have to do [their] best to understand the underlying principles' of Strasbourg decisions and to follow them.[54] This was not the case in *Pham*, where the Supreme Court judges entered in direct conflict with ECJ case law in the field of EU citizenship.[55] Mr Pham, born in Vietnam, had acquired British citizenship while keeping his Vietnamese nationality. In 2011, he was accused of having participated in terrorist activities in Yemen. The home secretary thus decided to strip him of his British citizenship and to deport him to Vietnam. Mr Pham contested this decision. Among other arguments, he claimed that the home secretary's

50 For a more recent example in which Lord Mance explicitly criticises Strasbourg's dynamic extension of the scope of convention rights, see *Commissioner of Police of the Metropolis* v. *DSD and Another* [2018] UKSC 11 (SC, 21 February 2018), para. 142.

51 *Kennedy*, para. 188.

52 For this criticism and alternative methods of reasoning with previous decisions, see Komárek (2013).

53 ECtHR, *Magyar Helsinki Bizottság* v. *Hungary*, 8 November 2016, no. 18030/11, esp. paras. 150 f.

54 *Kennedy*, para. 60.

55 *Pham* (SC, 25 March 2015).

decision deprived him of his European citizenship and did not pass the proportionality test.

The Supreme Court judges expressed doubts as to whether EU law applied in this case. Examining Mr Pham's EU law argument, Lord Carnwath observed that no cross-border element triggered the application of the treaties. Counsel for the applicant relied on the ECJ decision in *Rottmann*, which required no such element even though the advocate general had referred to cross-border movement in his opinion.[56] In response, Lord Carnwath considered the *G1* case, which was decided by the Court of Appeal in 2012 and dealt with a situation similar to the case at hand.[57] In his leading judgment in *G1*, Laws LJ had found difficulties with the European court's reasoning in *Rottmann*. He had objected that there was no basis for mandating English courts to take EU law into account in purely domestic citizenship cases. Laws LJ considered EU citizenship to be 'wholly parasitic' on national citizenship.[58] In his view, a 'generalised aspiration to the enjoyment of a "fundamental status" [could] surely carry the matter no further'.[59]

Lord Carnwath and the rest of the Supreme Court Justices agreed with Laws LJ's observations in *G1*. The Supreme Court held that the difficulties to which the Court of Appeal judge had referred to had not been sufficiently addressed by the European court. In a similar vein, Lord Carnwath rejected the applicants' arguments based on the ECJ *Zambrano* decision, pointing out that 'the scope of *Zambrano* remains a matter of controversy in domestic case-law'.[60] Hence, in *Pham*, English judges once again required the conceptual clarity of a common law analytical approach from a supranational court. They explicitly expressed their disenchantment with the aspirations that underpinned the expansive and dynamic interpretative techniques of the ECJ.

However, contestation of ECJ case law in this case went further. In his judgment in *G1*, Laws LJ had also framed the matter in terms of EU law competences. In his words:

> If it appeared that the Court of Justice had sought to be the judge of any procedural conditions governing [national citizenship] matters, so that its

[56] ECJ, C-135/08, 2 March 2010, *Rottmann*, ECLI:EU:C:2010:104. See also the opinion by AG Poiares Maduro, delivered on 30 September 2009, ECLI:EU:C:2009:588.

[57] *G1* v. *Secretary of State for the Home Department* [2012] EWCA Civ 867 (CA, Civil Division, 4 July 2012).

[58] *G1*, paras. 37 f., esp. para. 39, cited by Lord Carnwath in *Pham*, paras. 50 f.

[59] *G1*, para. 39.

[60] *Pham*, para. 55. See ECJ, C-34/09, 8 March 2011, *Ruiz Zambrano*, ECLI:EU:C:2011:124.

> ruling was to apply in a case with no cross-border element, then in my judgment a question would arise whether the European Communities Act 1972 or any successor statute had conferred any authority on the Court of Justice to exercise such a jurisdiction.[61]

In *Pham*, Lord Carnwath cited Laws LJ's dicta with approval and considered this to be 'an issue which would need to be considered, in the Court of Appeal or this court, before it would become appropriate to consider a reference to the European court'.[62] Lord Mance also cited Laws LJ and recalled that the UK applied a dualist approach to international obligations. He stressed that despite the spectacular evolution of EU law, Parliament remained sovereign in the UK. Domestic constitutional arrangements resulted in certain 'jurisdictional limits' for the ECJ that were set at the level of European treaties.[63] English judges, contrary to their Greek colleagues in *Michaniki*, refused to delegate the definition of domestic constitutional limits to the ECJ. They stressed that the will of Parliament calibrates the scope of European law in the domestic sphere. They opposed the purposive interpretation of the ECA 1972 and of posterior statutes, based on the original intent of the legislator, to the ECJ's teleological reasoning.

A Rationalist (or Nationalist?) Reformulation of English Judges' Objections to the Full Effect of European Law. Paradoxically however, parliamentary sovereignty was voided of substantive content in this case. Indeed, English judges did not consider it necessary to resolve the problem of the limits between EU law and the domestic constitution as far as the case of Mr Pham was concerned. In their view, when a status as fundamental as national citizenship is at stake, proportionality and domestic standards of substantive review lead to similar methods of reasoning and substantive outcomes. Rationalism expands in English public law and increasingly constrains democratic decision-making. Nothing is less sure than the reinstatement of parliamentary sovereignty once Brexit is definite or if the HRA is ever repealed. Indeed, while English judges will no longer be bound by European decisions, the rationalist principles of public law are by now well established in domestic jurisprudence and will continue to constrain domestic authorities, the British Parliament included, whether the UK is part of the EU and the convention or not.[64]

[61] *G1*, para. 43, cited in *Pham*, para. 54.
[62] *Pham*, para. 58.
[63] Ibid, para. 80.
[64] In the same vein, see Gearty (2014).

In fact, since the common law and EU law lead to the same kind of judicial review and to the same substantive outcomes, delimiting the jurisdiction of the ECJ becomes a matter of identity and nationalism. In *Pham*, Lord Mance held that no EU treaty provision provided the ECJ with the competence to review the withdrawal of national citizenship. To support this argument, he cited Laws LJ's dicta in *G1* with approval: 'The conditions on which national citizenship is conferred, withheld or revoked are integral to the identity of the nation State. They touch the constitution; for they identify the constitution's participants.'[65] In passing, Lord Mance also noted that: 'Europe has not yet reached a situation where it is axiomatic that there is constitutional identity between the Union and its Members.'[66]

It seems that disintegration in the UK is not so much about democratic government but about national identity. Hence, by appealing to parliamentary sovereignty, English judges actually affirm *their own* power to co-define the limits set on Parliament by the legal constitution. This became clear in the famous *HS2* case, where the Supreme Court stated:

> It is, putting the point at its lowest, certainly arguable (and it is for United Kingdom law and courts to determine) that there may be fundamental principles, whether contained in other constitutional instruments or recognised at common law, of which Parliament when it enacted the European Communities Act 1972 did not either contemplate or authorise the abrogation.[67]

In this context, proportionality and contextual review are reinvented by English lawyers. In their new garb as common law methods they are progressively *opposed* to European integration, together with other methods, like originalist interpretation and precedent. This is exemplified in *Poshteh*, which concerned housing authorities' duty to provide suitable housing to persons in need.[68] Previously, in *Ali* v. *Birmingham City Council*, the Supreme Court had held that Article 6 had no application insofar as such duties were concerned.[69] This restrictive interpretation of Article 6 was criticised by Strasbourg judges in *Ali* v. *the UK*, on which Ms Poshteh relied.[70] What was at stake then, was whether the Supreme Court should depart from its previous case law in the light of the

[65] *G1*, para. 43, cited in *Pham*, para. 54.
[66] *Pham*, para. 77.
[67] *HS2* (SC, 22 January 2014), para. 207.
[68] *Poshteh* v. *Royal Borough of Kensington and Chelsea* [2017] UKSC 36 (SC, 10 May 2017).
[69] *Tomlinson and Others* v. *Birmingham City Council* [2010] UKSC 8 (SC, 17 February 2010).
[70] *Ali* v. *the UK*, 20 October 2015, no. 40378/10.

Strasbourg decision. Lord Carnwath, followed by his colleagues in the Supreme Court, stated:

> The unanimous judgment of this court in *Ali* was intended to settle the issue at domestic level, after a full review of all the relevant Strasbourg authorities. Against this background it is necessary to consider whether the reasoning in the recent Chamber decision makes it necessary or appropriate for us to depart from that decision.[71]

This gave the opportunity to the Supreme Court to address another tutorial on common law methods to their colleagues in Strasbourg. The judges finally refused to apply the Strasbourg decision on the basis that it was a chamber judgment and that the ECtHR had not engaged with the issues relied on by the Supreme Court in its case law. While the application of proportionality was not at stake in *Poshteh*, Lord Carnwath's dicta, reminiscent of proportionality terminology, open up the way for the future use of proportionality as a test conditioning the application of European case law. The promotion of proportionality as a transplant in the common law was never mainly about European integration in the first place. Rather, it was about the construction of an English public law. Thus, it is not surprising that, while proportionality as a method is appropriated by English lawyers, its European integration dynamic is progressively marginalised.

10.3 Greek Constitutional Values v. European Law: New Possibilities for Proportionality

Normative Conflict, Dualism and the Fragmentation of Proportionality. While in England, proportionality language until recently remained external to common law structures, in Greece, it has always been part of a constitutional civilisation that domestic lawyers take as a model. The 2001 reform even established the European perception of proportionality as some kind of science that transcends the formality of domestic legal discourse and displaces domestic constitutional limits. Greek public lawyers, like their French colleagues, have found it difficult to conceive the possibility of normative conflict between domestic and European law. However, in the case of Greece, this has led to a European law-conform interpretation of the domestic constitutional order and not the inverse. In this context, disintegration has proceeded through the affirmation of the autonomy of domestic concepts against

71 *Poshteh*, para. 32.

EU law, in what seems to be a new kind of dualism in Greek legal thought. This has produced the conceptual fragmentation of proportionality.

Since the mid-2000s, Greek scholars started to affirm the shift between domestic and European versions of proportionality and to justify domestic divergence by appealing to different or even opposing goals of the constitution and the European Community. Orfanoudakis and Kokota, for example, have argued that in the domestic constitutional context, proportionality serves the protection of fundamental rights and thus 'maintains and accentuates its substantive aspect, which consists in striking a proportion between conflicting constitutional rights'.[72] In contrast, according to these authors, in the context of European law, proportionality is applied in various domains as a principle of efficiency for the establishment of the common market. Therefore, in EU law cases it functions 'instrumentally – procedurally', as a principle for the division of competences between national and community law-making authorities.[73] Kaidatzis also pointed out the divergence between Greek courts and the ECJ in the application of proportionality in the field of professional freedom and attributed it to the different goals pursued by the EU and the domestic constitutional orders.[74]

The study of domestic judicial practice and its systematisation according to domestic constitutional values is quite new in Greek scholarship, traditionally suspicious towards domestic judges and obsessed with foreign doctrinal and jurisprudential developments. A new type of legal knowledge, more attentive to judicial reasoning structures and to the normative context that surrounds them, seems to be emerging in Greek public law. The consciousness of normative conflict between domestic and European law has also been expressed in judicial practice and during the last decade it has led the Council of State to explicitly refuse to apply European courts' decisions.[75] Disintegration increasingly forces Greek judges to enter into a process of transnational communication with their European colleagues, even though it would be 'eulogistic' to apply the metaphor of dialogue to such instances of explicit disagreement.[76]

[72] Orfanoudakis and Kokota (2007), pp. 719–20.

[73] Ibid.

[74] Kaidatzis (2006).

[75] Concerning the ECJ, see StE (Pl.) 3031/2008 *ΕΔΔΔ* 2009, p. 71; ECJ, C-81/09, 21 October 2010, *Idrima Tipou AE*, ECLI:EU:C:2010:622, esp. paras. 65 f.; StE (Pl.) 1617/2012 *ΕΔΔΔ* 2012, p. 632. Concerning the ECtHR, see StE 2067/2011, *NoB* 2011, p. 1952; ECtHR, *Kapetanios and Others* v. *Greece*, 30 April 2015, nos. 3453/12, 42941/12, and 9028/13; StE (Pl.) 1741/2015, *NoB* 2015, p. 1065.

[76] Muir-Watt and Tusseau (2016), p. 198.

The '*Special Payrolls*' Case and the Affirmation of Social Rights. The Council of State's willingness to affirm the autonomy of domestic constitutional discourse was firmly expressed in decisions related to the Euro crisis. In 2012, an austerity package imposed important cuts on the salaries and pensions of members of the army, the police and the security services in application of the second MoU and the medium term budgetary objective. The aggrieved individuals were subject to 'special payrolls' (*ειδικά μισθολόγια*), that is, special remuneration statuses reserved for certain public officials whose services are deemed important for the functioning of the state. The cuts were retroactively imposed for a period of three months; the amounts already paid were to be automatically deduced from future salaries and pensions. Trade unions of the military and security forces questioned the constitutionality of the measures, claiming their constitutional rights had been violated.

The case was examined by the Council of State Plenum. The judges started by referring to the constitutional status of the police, security and army forces. In a reasoning which is quite rare in Greek constitutional law, they solemnly pronounced the 'principle of special remuneration' of the members of the armed forces as an implicit constitutional obligation, an 'institutional guarantee', which 'ensures the effective accomplishment of [these forces'] mission'.[77] The council did not content itself with the entrenchment of special remuneration as a positive obligation of Parliament, but went on to proclaim the 'right of the military personnel' to such remuneration.[78] Significantly, for the first time the Council of State accorded concrete normative content to a social right.

Following a reasoning that is familiar to the specialists of the ECtHR jurisprudence, the judges specified that the right to special remuneration does not guarantee *a certain amount* of remuneration. Parliament can impose cuts on the revenues of armed and military forces personnel in the context of economic policy, insofar as this is necessary. However, contrary to the *First MoU* decision, the constitutional rights of the claimants in the *'special payrolls'* case did not solely require the minimum standard of a decent way of life. Instead they required special assessments and planning for legislative policy-making.[79] The judges described in the following words the reasoning to which the legislator should proceed:

77 StE (Pl.) 2192/2014 *ΤΝΠΔΣΑ*, paras. 7 f., esp. para. 12.

78 Ibid.

79 In this respect, the council's reasoning is akin to the one followed in environmental protection cases during the 1990s. Yannakopoulos observes that in this case law, the council imposed rational planning and fact-finding obligations on the political branches

> A cut on the military personnel's income of such a nature or extent so as to entail a reversal of the payment status valid until then, cannot be imposed without preliminary appraisal of its fiscal benefit in relation to the negative impact that it may have on the operation of the armed forces. [Also, it cannot be imposed without preliminary appraisal of] whether the cut is necessary or could be replaced by less restrictive measures with an equivalent effect.[80]

In an obiter dictum, the council acknowledged that the obligation to proceed to an appraisal of the costs and benefits of legislation 'applies, in principle, for every important reduction on the income of a certain category of public servants or officials'.[81] In this way, the court explicitly attributed constitutional status to the social *acquis* of a large category of public employees.

The reasoning described by the council is akin to proportionality analysis: a strict necessity test consisting of a calculation of the costs and benefits of the contested measures. Nonetheless, proportionality was not pronounced or applied at this stage. The council went on to stress that the revenues of the members of the armed forces 'must be sufficient for their decent way of life and commensurate to the importance of their mission'.[82] The judges enumerated a number of concrete criteria that Parliament should consider, such as the grade of the concerned official or the special responsibilities resulting from her duties. In the end of this long set of normative considerations, the council pronounced that its scrutiny of the legislative measures would be 'marginal', limited to the question whether Parliament took into account the above criteria and 'no other, manifestly inappropriate ones'.[83]

The Application of Proportionality in the '*Special Payrolls*' Case. Reference to the manifest inappropriateness standard echoes the traditional version of proportionality in Greek constitutional law. So does the judicial concern with the criteria of legislation. However, as in the *First MoU* decision, proportionality entailed a very extensive judicial reasoning that had nothing to do with its traditional application as a self-evident standard. The Council of State analysed the goal of the contested measures in a series of long paragraphs. It stressed that the cuts on the

of government. See Yannakopoulos (2004), pp. 448 f.; Yannakopoulos (2008), pp. 736 f.; Yannakopoulos (2015), fn. 5.

80 StE (Pl.) 2192/2014.

81 Ibid, para. 12.

82 Ibid.

83 Ibid.

revenues of employees subject to the 'special payrolls' were in principle justified by the need to face the prolonged economic and financial crisis.[84] The particular economic conjuncture surrounding the council's decision affected judicial reasoning. The judges underscored that in times of prolonged economic depression, Parliament may enact legislation that burdens specific social groups in pursuance of the fiscal interests of the state. However, when doing so it should respect domestic constitutional principles. Most notably, the constitutional duty of solidarity requires the even allocation of public burdens, so as to avoid a manifestly disproportionate burdening of a particular social group.[85]

The Council of State's reasoning was akin to the *First MoU* decision, to which the court repeatedly referred. However, proportionality review in this case was much more intensive. The judges examined the concrete criteria that Parliament took into account, as they appeared in the preliminary works of the relevant legislation. In their words:

> Even though each one of the 'special' payrolls concerned a different category of officials and servants, with clearly distinguished duties and mission, the legislator treated them collectively as a unitary economic number, which should be calculated cumulatively and reduced by 10 percent in the context of the policy of reducing the financial deficit and the public debt. [...] Furthermore, the legislator, [...] when determining the amount of the cuts imposed on each payroll and on each grade within this payroll, took exclusively the revenues accorded until then into account and calculated them in numbers.[86]

Contrary to the *First MoU* decision, the scrutiny that proportionality entailed not only concerned the legislative intents, but also the impact of the measures in question. The court calculated the cumulative effect of austerity policies implemented since 2010 on the net income of the plaintiffs in detail.[87] The council concluded unanimously that the legislative measures failed even the minimal review that entered within its competence. The effects of austerity policies on the specific social group represented by the claimants rendered the cuts 'profoundly disproportionate and unequal'.[88] This is even more so due to the fact that the state had been unable to promote other structural and tax reforms and that

[84] Ibid, paras. 13–14.
[85] Ibid, para. 19.
[86] Ibid.
[87] Ibid, paras. 15–16, 20.
[88] Ibid, para. 21.

this was one of the factors that had led to the adoption of new austerity measures.

What the council mainly criticised was Parliament's indifference towards domestic constitutional values. The court carefully considered the wording of the law and the relevant preliminary documents to conclude that the lawmakers had 'relied exclusively upon a purely mathematical, thus profoundly inappropriate, criterion, namely the average reduction of public spending on payments', without taking into account the special status of the armed forces officers and the importance of their mission.[89] The judges also criticised the absence of 'special assessments' as to the impact of the cuts on the functioning of the armed forces or as to the efficiency of the measures.[90] Indeed, they did not accept a study adduced by the administration in this respect, since it had not been effected in view of the concrete financial strategy examined in the case at hand. Finally, the council condemned the absence of concrete examination of 'whether the income of the armed forces and security personnel is sufficient for facing the cost of a decent way of living and commensurate to their mission'.[91]

Preserving the Normativity of the Domestic Constitution. In the *'special payrolls'* case, contrary to what had been the case in the *First MoU* decision, the council did not hesitate to affirm domestic constitutional goals and obligations against the public interest invoked by the Parliament. Even though the legislator still referred to exceptional economic circumstances, in the court's view, 'the fiscal interest of the state was no longer peremptory'.[92] Appealing to the constitution, the judges thus affirmed their own power to participate in the setting of policy-making goals. This is what led to the application of proportionality as a searching test that sanctioned Parliament's indifference towards these goals.

Interestingly, the judicial affirmation of constitutional goals proceeded through the excision of EU law from the domestic constitutional order. The contested measures in the *'special payrolls'* case, as the measures in the *First MoU* decision, were characterised by an ambiguity as to their origin. While austerity was imposed as a domestic policy in the implementation of the medium term budgetary objective, it clearly resulted from the second MoU and thus from an agreement between Greek

89 Ibid.
90 Ibid.
91 Ibid.
92 Ibid, para. 21.

governmental officials and the troika. What is more, the measures were also in line with an EU Council decision, which in the context of budgetary discipline procedures, had reiterated the MoU obligations and had required important cuts on the wages of military and armed forces.[93]

Following the *First MoU* decision on this point, the council stressed that the measures 'were enacted by the Greek Parliament in sovereignty' and thus excluded the relevance of Article 28 of the Constitution concerning the ratification of international treaties and the concession of national sovereignty.[94] This time however, the judges clearly distinguished EU law requirements from the compelling public interest of the state and from domestic constitutional values. In their words, 'in the exercise of financial policy in the context of the international obligations of the Country, the national legislator is not exempted from compliance with […] constitutional rules and principles'.[95] In the *First MoU* decision, the Council of State had defined domestic constitutional goals by referring to the common interest of Eurozone member states. In contrast, in the *'special payrolls'* case domestic constitutional rules and principles were clearly separated from EU requirements of fiscal discipline, which were even characterised as 'international' obligations.

This kind of reasoning was followed in subsequent decisions concerning the 'special payroll' of the public university personnel and private employees' pensions.[96] Adopting the council's line of reasoning, the Court of Audit also declared as unconstitutional the cuts imposed on the wages of judges.[97] In recent case law concerning economic adjustment measures, domestic courts have required 'a special, thorough and well-documented study', which will allow them to scrutinise the appropriateness and necessity of the measures and to censure any 'prohibited violation of the core of the constitutional right to social security'.[98] In this way, they have preserved the autonomy of domestic constitutional law vis-à-vis both the economic rationality of the executive and EU institutions.

Claiming the relevance of constitutional law in economic policy decisions has led domestic courts to also claim an important role as

[93] Cf. Decision 2011/734/EU, 12 July 2011, OJ L 296, 15.11.2011, p. 38, and its amendments.
[94] StE (Pl.) 2192/2014, para. 17.
[95] Ibid, para. 21.
[96] See StE (Pl.) 4741/2014 *ΕΔΔΔ* 2015, p. 170 and 2287/2015 *ΑΡΜ* 2015, p. 1371 resp.
[97] ES (Pl.) 4327/2014 *ΑΡΜ* 2015, p. 1194.
[98] StE (Pl.) 2287/2015, esp. para. 24.

constitutional political actors. Decisions annulling austerity measures have been touted in domestic and international media. In domestic scholarship, there is increasing talk about 'hard' or 'great' cases in constitutional adjudication.[99] The fiscal impacts of the Council of State's decisions were even explicitly mentioned in the Euro Summit Statement of 12 July 2015, where the Council of State itself was referred to as a 'Constitutional Court'.[100] The courts increasingly adapt their reasoning to their new role. In decision 4741/2014, the Court of Audit Plenum proceeded to 'a balancing between the public interest relating to the acute financial crisis and the commonly known cash difficulty of the Greek state' and for the first time affirmed its power to report the effects of its decision over time.[101] Consequentialist balancing is certainly new in Greek judicial review and offers new possibilities for the evolution of proportionality in this context.

***

Recent applications of proportionality in France, England and Greece express disintegration tendencies that are apparent in other fields of legal and political discourse. Once again, however, the transformations of proportionality in this context of disintegration are not uniform. They follow particular local patterns and largely depend on the local meanings of proportionality, on the local perceptions of European integration and on the local patterns of Europeanisation.

In the rationalist French context, the affirmation of republican values has long been perceived as by definition compatible with European rights. The ECtHR case law however, exposed this perception as wrong. In *SAS*, while the Strasbourg court accepted French majoritarian value choices, it underscored that they operated at the margin of the European rights paradigm. It thus reluctantly declared that French exceptionalism could be regarded as proportionate, but only insofar as it was perceived as necessary for preserving the minimum requirements of life in society. Under the influence of European case law, French lawyers and judges are becoming increasingly aware of the normative pluralism in the field of European rights and of the particularity of their republican reinvention of those rights. In this context, European law and proportionality acquire a radical dynamic. Conformity with the convention and accommodation

99 Mantzoufas and Pavlopoulos (2017).
100 See the Euro Summit Statement 12 July 2015 (SN 4070/15), available at www.consilium.europa.eu.
101 ES (Pl.) 4347/2014.

of normative pluralism proceeds through the contestation of the traditional assumptions of republican legality. In convention cases, proportionality becomes a new condition for the normativity of French legislation, replacing the traditional criteria of legality and equality.

In the English context, while proportionality spreads in English public law as a *method*, disintegration proceeds through the abandonment of proportionality as a *head of review*. By developing common law concepts and standards in light of rationalist human rights principles, English judges are preparing themselves for the 'ebb' of European rights in the domestic sphere. Following a practice well-known to their continental colleagues, they deny normative conflicts between European and domestic law and affirm their own role as fundamental rights protectors. Nothing is less sure than the reinstatement of parliamentary sovereignty after Brexit or the repeal of the HRA. However, what is already sure is that English judges oppose national constitutional identity to the effective application of European law. In what resembles the English counterpart of the French *acte clair* doctrine, they require from supranational courts the analytical rigour and techniques of common law courts. In this way, they deprive European case law of one of the most important factors of its integrationist dynamic: teleology. In this context, proportionality is reinvented as a common law method and it is increasingly opposed to European integration.

In Greece, the application of proportionality as a European principle has been perceived as an achievement of domestic constitutional civilisation. For a long time, the constitution was normative insofar as it was compatible with European law and proportionality, albeit only at the level of aesthetics. However, disintegration has forced Greek lawyers to acknowledge normative conflicts between domestic and European law. In this context, the content of the domestic constitutional order ceases to be determined by European case law. In what resembles a new species of dualism in Greek legal thought, scholars and judges distinguish domestic from European concepts. In the intersection between the domestic and the EU legal order, Greek courts acquire a new role. They are no longer partners of the government in the realisation of legislative aims. They now acquire a mission as guarantors of the constitution and affirm their power to co-define policy goals and criteria. This opens up new possibilities for the application of proportionality as a structure for consequentialist balancing. Indeed, paradoxically, it is in a context of disintegration that one gets the closest to the application of the Alexyan proportionality model in Greece.

The analysis in this chapter makes no pretension to either exhaustiveness or to scientific correctness. The cases studied have been chosen due to the fact that local legal actors perceive them as important, sometimes even revolutionary. However, the particular reading of these cases presented here is only one among various possible readings. Other cases might express different, even exactly opposing tendencies that coexist in domestic contexts. This should not be seen as a weakness of the analysis in this chapter, but rather as an illustration of the contested and malleable content of law, legal culture and proportionality itself, which allows integration and disintegration to coexist in different settings.[102]

[102] Ward (1995).

Conclusion of Part III

Proportionality Expressing Local Visions of European Integration. European integration has relied on the idea of integration through law. Using domestic constitutional traditions as sources of inspiration, European courts have engaged different processes of integration according to the particular goals of supranational legal orders. Proportionality and the language of rights have played a major role in these processes. In Strasbourg case law, proportionality has been used as a principle of acculturation, which obliges national authorities to integrate common European constitutional values into domestic policy-making processes. In contrast, the kind of integration triggered by Luxembourg case law has traditionally focused on facts. It has consisted in the construction of a common market through the effective enforcement of EU market freedoms, sometimes to the detriment of other domestic values. European integration projects in turn have been perceived differently by domestic lawyers according to the particularly local understanding of proportionality, to local narratives about law and rights and to well-established local perceptions of legal knowledge itself. Uncovering standard features in the way the integration dynamics of proportionality operate in domestic legal orders allows us to discern more general patterns in the way local actors perceive the different projects of European integration. It also sheds light on local tendencies of disintegration and closure towards Europe.

Rationalism and the Denial of Normative Conflicts. In the rationalist French and Greek public law tradition, law represents a kind of objective, even scientific knowledge that is obtained through the use of legal methods. The values that law conveys are perceived as part of a civilisation that claims objectivity and universal application. The use the term 'civilisation' instead of 'culture' in this context is indicative of this idealist perception of legal knowledge. Legal rules are drawn from universal principles and form a legal order. Supranational legal orders are perceived as ensuring the same values as domestic law by definition. Hence, European rights and proportionality are typically perceived as equally domestic. Their reception has not proceeded through formal incorporation or institutional change but through translation of European concepts to corresponding domestic ones. Thus, it has not even been noticed by domestic lawyers. In France, the European rights civilisation is deemed to have been achieved since the French Revolution and expressed in the rights of the *DDHC*. In Greece, in contrast, the European rights civilisation is perceived as the *telos* of the Greek legal order, what it should ideally be.

In this context, condemnations by supranational jurisdictions, rather than resulting from a value-laden difference between domestic and European law are claimed to result from different substantive solutions in *concrete cases*. Establishing substantive coherence between domestic and European law is a stake attached to the application of the law and especially to judicial review. Typically, the institutional-procedural aspects of proportionality are neglected by domestic lawyers, who have also found it difficult to grasp the function of the margin of appreciation. Indeed, the normative pluralism that underpins this concept is difficult to understand and to frame for continental lawyers. So too are domestic constitutional particularities. Proportionality is not perceived as a remedy institutionalised for the violation of European rights but as an objective liberal principle that is naturally presumed in legislative intentions. Its adjudication consists in a means-ends test, ensuring the realisation of the 'true meaning' of domestic law. Thus, proportionality is inconsistently used in judicial practice and its integration dynamic is constrained.

The deployment of proportionality's dynamic is mainly a matter of aesthetics and depends on the possibility of presenting domestic constitutional values as equally European. In this respect, local narratives concerning the protection of rights are important. In France, the motherland of human rights, the application of proportionality and European rights often takes the form of republican inculcation. It does not contest legislative value choices in principle but only affirms their legitimacy as if it were self-evident. The use of proportionality language does not change much judicial reasoning and mainly has a function of 'signalisation'. In Greece, on the contrary, domestic constitutional values and goals have been traditionally defined in Europe. Therefore, as a teleological method, proportionality engineers important legal and constitutional change. It produces the interpretation of the domestic legal order in the light of

European law. In *Michaniki*, proportionality even provoked a 'self-denying transformation' of the Greek constitution.

Pragmatism and the Accommodation of Normative Pluralism. In contrast to what is observed in France and in Greece, the rationalism that underpins proportionality and the European integration projects has been difficult to accommodate in the context of English law. The analysis of this difficulty has been one of the major objectives of this book. Here only a few remarks concerning European integration are appropriate. In the pragmatist common law tradition, European rights and proportionality have been incorporated into the domestic legal sphere as remedies, serving the UK's compliance with its international obligations. Paradoxically, this has made English judges take their integration function seriously. English courts have generally decided by reference to European case law. They have assumed their function as *juges de droit commun du droit européen* and they have imposed convention rights on domestic authorities as part of a culture. Proportionality as a head for substantive review has irritated certain fundamental assumptions of the common law. When European courts have insufficiently taken domestic constitutional particularities into account, English judges have proceeded to a reasoned refusal to apply their decisions and have thus initiated a fruitful transnational judicial dialogue. In other words, what gave English courts the possibility to communicate with their European counterparts and to influence European integration was not so much the application of proportionality, but the *explicit and reasoned disagreement* with European precepts.

Hence, legal culture provides legal actors with more or less effective tools for influencing the construction of Europe. In contrast to their rationalist continental colleagues, English lawyers are aware of the possibility of conflict between domestic and European values. Traditionally, such conflicts have been managed through dualism and analytical formalism. English judges have long constrained the integration function of proportionality and of substantive rights within the scope of the European law. They have perceived the rationality that underlies these texts as particular and have insistently objected to its pretensions to universality. Common law pragmatism, the 'illogical compromise' that characterises it, or the particularly English 'muddling through', has allowed domestic judges to legally frame normative conflicts between domestic and European law, thus recalling to their continental colleagues the imperfect character of European integration.

However, as the rationalist baggage of proportionality spills over into English public law, the framing of normative conflicts becomes increasingly difficult. In recent cases, English judges deny the substantive differences between common law and European rights protection. The application of proportionality as a head of review is progressively abandoned for that of common law principles and heads of review perceived as equivalent, like the principle of legality and the *Wednesbury* standard. The main stake attached to the proportionality transplant has been the construction of an *English* public law. Thus, its accomplishment does not necessarily proceed through the application of proportionality as a *European* head of review. As the common law progressively acquires a rationalist public law system, the quest for parliamentary sovereignty is slowly transformed into a quest for national identity, which is to be safeguarded by judges and the legal constitution. English judges oppose common law methods, such as originalist interpretation and reasoning by precedent, to supranational courts' dynamic and teleological reasoning. This undermines the European integration dynamics of proportionality, which is reinvented as a common law concept itself.

In an inverse trajectory, continental lawyers' increasing awareness of the possibility of normative conflict between domestic and European law has introduced elements of pragmatism in their rationalist legal cultures. Pragmatism gives the possibility to continental courts to legally frame normative conflicts and to enter the 'global community of judges' who communicate through their judicial decisions. Thus, French judges have ceased to axiomatically affirm the coincidence between supranational and domestic values. As *Gonzalez-Gomez* illustrates, the ECtHR forces French lawyers to recognise the exceptional character of their republican perception of fundamental rights and to acknowledge normative pluralism in Europe. French judges' effort to accommodate alternative worldviews progressively deconstructs the binary distinctions of domestic law and renders proportionality the ultimate criterion of the normativity of republican legislation.

In Greece, the Euro crisis has exposed the modernisation aesthetics of the domestic constitution as illusionary. The collapse of the aesthetic coherence between the domestic polity and Europe provokes a constitutional crisis with existential dimensions. The normativity of domestic constitutional limits is minimised before the pursuit of common European and domestic financial goals. Faced with this situation, judges abandon their previously deferent stance and affirm the autonomy of domestic constitutional concepts and their own power to define domestic constitutional goals. In doing so, they enter in direct and explicit conflict with Parliament and with supranational courts. The affirmation of the dualism of Greek and European law is connected to the emergence of a new type of legal knowledge, which is more attentive to domestic judicial reasoning structures, and to the newly affirmed role of judges as important constitutional political actors. Quite paradoxically, the detachment of proportionality from European integration in the minds of Greek legal actors opens the way to its actual transfer as a structure for consequentialist balancing in Greek law.

The Radical Dynamic of Proportionality in the Context of European Integration. It is difficult to infer causal explanations linking the local understanding of proportionality as a European principle and its cultural context. Law's binding arrangements are not real but symbolic, and leave possibilities for many interpretations. One thing is sure: proportionality is not a purely internal construction of each domestic legal discourse. It carries European baggage and creates convergence among local legal practices in various ways. In all the systems studied, proportionality and European integration have ultimately acquired a radical dynamic and have significantly transformed local legal culture. However, this development is related to different phases of European integration every time. While in England, the radicalism of proportionality lies in its rationalising function in the context of European human rights, in Greece, it is entwined with its modernising connotations in the context of the common market. Quite paradoxically, in France, proportionality becomes radical in a context of disintegration, which forces domestic lawyers to an awareness of the parochialism of their traditional republican perception of rights and society.

Conclusion

Local Versions of Proportionality. The study of difference in the use of proportionality is crucial to understanding its spread and its effects. Throughout this work, I have attempted to render the differences in the use of proportionality in France, England and Greece less enigmatic by placing them within their own context. To do so, I have approached law and proportionality as instances of language that make sense within a particular legal culture. My purpose has been to identify and interpret the local versions of proportionality, and the way they have evolved over time. Hence, I have attempted to construct a coherent discourse around the emergence and evolution of proportionality in different contexts that makes sense of its peculiar characteristics. Put briefly, I have attempted to unravel the local meanings of proportionality by reconstructing the expectations that legal actors have attached to it each time. Local meanings of proportionality unveil local paths of cultural change under pressure from external influence. Hence, their examination proves insightful as to the possibility of convergence between legal systems and as to the past and future of European integration.

Attention to French, English and Greek judicial practice reveals that, even when received in different contexts, proportionality is not always used as a pronged framework for balancing constitutional rights neither does it necessarily have a standardising effect on legal cultures, as the mainstream literature on the matter seems to assume. In its early version as the *bilan* in the French Council of State case law, proportionality was not directly connected to rights. In its version as the *contrôle de proportionnalité*, it is a theory that serves the systematisation of judicial practice, but is not explicitly used by judges as such. In England, proportionality has long corresponded to a European head of review, which served the adjudication of substantive European standards rather than of domestic constitutional rights. Divergence is observed even when there is explicit appeal to the Alexyan model. In Greece, although legal actors have always perceived proportionality as a three-pronged principle coming from Germany, in judicial practice, proportionality has led to a review of legislation for manifest errors.

Therefore, attention to the use of proportionality in different settings exposes the dominant rhetoric of convergence as too simplistic. This is not to say that external influence is not present in the local construction and evolution of proportionality. It is already apparent in the use of the transnational idiom of proportionality itself, which, before the 1970s, did not exist as a legal language in the contexts studied. Indeed, contrary to the belief of certain proportionality theorists and of local legal actors themselves, proportionality is neither natural nor inherent in legal argumentation. In Greece, proportionality even corresponds to an entirely new term in Greek language, *αναλογικότητα*, which distinguishes it from the almost homonymous language of analogy used since Aristotle. As a new idiom, proportionality provokes discursive and cultural change. In all the contexts studied, it emerged as a transfer and was promoted by certain personalities with the purpose of provoking precisely such change. Further, in different settings proportionality has occasionally taken the form of a pronged framework for rights-based adjudication.

This notwithstanding, the evolution or migration of legal concepts does not only depend on the motivations of individual actors or on the influences that they are subject to. The way proportionality will affect legal culture escapes proportionality theorists themselves, as well as the legal actors who introduce it into their local discursive context. Local concepts, distinctions and taboos affect the version of proportionality that legal actors will adopt. Hence, proportionality is understood as a method of review in France, as a head of review in England and as an overarching principle in Greece. It is constrained by the taboo of *opportunité* in France and of *σκοπιμότητα* in Greece, while its spread was long hindered by the taboo of merits review in England. New dissonances appear in the use of the common idiom of proportionality, and express the particular logic of the discourses in which it operates.

Local Versions of Formalism. The peculiar discursive structures that affect proportionality are themselves related to peculiar ways in which law is locally conceived of and practiced. Thus, local versions of proportionality unveil the local visions of law that underpin them and the different ways in which legal actors preserve law's autonomy from moral, political, economic or other theories and ideologies. In other words, proportionality expresses local versions of formalism. In

England, analytical formalism excludes the consideration of substantive values in judicial review. In this way, the common law avoids judicial policy-making and safeguards parliamentary sovereignty. Quite differently, formalism takes the form of dogmatism in the continental systems studied. Judges defer to the substantive value choices embodied in legislation and content themselves with affirming these choices as if they were scientific truths. While in England judges as referees impose rules of manner and form on a priori equal parties, in France and Greece, judges as scientists seek the general will expressed in legislation. In England, myth is external to judicial review, which rather resembles a game. In contrast, judicial review in continental systems is closer to a ritual, in which the interests of the parties are diluted in the pursuit of the general interest. This is expressed in the role of balancing itself. While balancing is traditionally absent in English judicial review, in the continental systems studied, it is a ritual that serves the reconstruction of legislative intentions in a constitutionally legitimate way.

Cultural features lead to different kinds of resistance to the Alexyan model. Proportionality was long explicitly rejected as a common law head of review, while in France and Greece, it has long been appropriated and reinvented by legal actors as a formalist, or rather dogmatic, judicial method that does not contest the intentions of public authorities. Difference in the practice of proportionality reveals new types of exceptionalism in the global model of constitutional rights, which does not necessarily involve explicit refusal to apply proportionality. Moreover, the study of the way French, English and Greek lawyers resist the application of the global model of proportionality shows that the success of this model does not have much to do with its merits at a moral or philosophical level. Rather, it has to do with local reasoning patterns and habits, local perceptions of law and courts and local binding arrangements between law and other discourses. Rights cannot be optimisation requirements in France and Greece because the judge only imposes *limits* on the exercise of public power. Similarly, for a long time, proportionality as a judicial method could not involve balancing in England because 'by their upbringing and experience' judges were deemed 'ill-qualified' to perform it.

Interestingly, resistance to the global model reminds us that until some decades ago, constitutional democracies around the world were converging towards another model of constitutional adjudication, one of liberal formalism rather than one of fundamental rights as principles. Indeed, the dogmatic version of proportionality that one finds in continental legal systems is akin to the way it was originally conceived of in Prussian administrative law and to the way it was initially applied in post-war German constitutional law.

Proportionality and Local Knowledge. Different versions of proportionality are not simply deviant or deficient applications of an ideal model. They express local imagination, myths, rituals and representations. Their examination unravels the different ways in which legal actors view the world from within the law. For instance, the English economy on substantive principles and on far-reaching legal theories is related to the Whig historians' account of the evolution of the common law and the idealisation of the political process that underpins it. In contrast, the rationalism that permeates continental legal thought is inherited from the nationalist revolutions of previous centuries and from the rupture with past authoritarian regimes.

Different local narratives determine the ways in which legal knowledge is locally produced. They shape local 'legal formants' and set local criteria for evaluating legal arguments, according to which different versions of proportionality will succeed or fail to capture local legal imagination. For instance, proportionality as an arithmetic equation succeeded in providing a French theory of judicial balancing but initially failed to do so in England. This is because, in contrast to their optimistic civil law colleagues, common lawyers are doubtful as to the possibility of resolving moral-legal issues on the basis of facts and numbers. While in France, law is perceived as a kind of rational and scientific knowledge, in England, law represents an ensemble of fragmented commandments. In the common law, coherent legal knowledge is not obtained through theoretical constructions, but by reference to Parliament's will. As for Greek lawyers, they have their own original way for establishing coherence among legal fragments: through the translation of foreign theories and debates.

In this work, my purpose has been to connect comparative law to developments in intellectual history and cultural anthropology and to stress that the evolution and spread of legal concepts such as proportionality is not the product of the evolution of a universal legal science. Legal knowledge and meaning are locally constructed. In the different settings studied, legal actors have attached different expectations to the spread of proportionality and have accentuated different aspects in its use. The local genealogies of proportionality reveal its peculiar semantic baggage. In France, proportionality emerged as a requirement of financial prudence. It has corresponded to a scientific legal theory coming from other disciplines and has been expected to rationalise policy choices. In

England, proportionality has corresponded to a continental theory. As such, initially it was rejected by judges but promoted by anti-Diceyan scholars and lawyers, who aspired to rationalise the bits and pieces of the common law around standards of substantive justice. Finally, Greek legal theory has always conceived of proportionality as a transplant. Its transfer from Germany and Europe has been expected to modernise the Greek polity.

Proportionality expresses local paths of cultural change, local ways of expanding the reach of law and negotiating its autonomy with regard to other discourses. The reasons for its spread differ across jurisdictions. It has not always been about the optimisation of fundamental rights or about social integration of minorities. Proportionality enhanced the 'administrativisation' of constitutional law in France; the rise of common law constitutionalism in England; and the Europeanisation of Greek public law. While the themes of modernisation, rationalisation and Europeanisation have offered a common background to the evolution of proportionality, these terms themselves are understood very differently in different settings. The cultural study of law seeks difference in meaning that can hide behind the similarity of legal terms and rules.

The Effects of Proportionality. Albeit not universal, meaning and culture are public. They are found in the particularities that local legal actors perceive as common-sensical. The spread of proportionality has not only been about promoting the interests of a particular class or establishing 'juristocracy'.[1] Individual motives of legal actors when promoting proportionality are neutralised by the publicity of the language and culture in which these actors express themselves. Hence, the effects of proportionality should be sought in the cultural change that it provokes.

In all the contexts studied, proportionality expresses a belief in the possibility of law as a kind of rational knowledge, whose reach transcends the interpretation of formal legal texts. Proportionality tends to rationalise policy-making through appeal to community values, most notably, human rights. It idealises the judge as an institution that is able to decide in the general interest and requires important institutional changes in the systems where it spreads. Hence, at the level of legal discourse, the 'doctrinal imperialism' of proportionality contributes to the deconstruction of pre-existing formalist distinctions that have traditionally served to delimit judicial competence: *contenu* v. *motifs* of administrative acts in

[1] Hirschl (2004).

France, *review v. appeal* in England, *whether v. how* of public discretion in Greece.

Proportionality certainly provokes convergence among legal systems. As judges increasingly become policy-makers, they are inclined to use the proportionality framework for its standardising and pedagogic characteristics. Thus the first signs of legal *analysis* emerge in continental systems. In the common law proportionality has even acquired a radical force. By connecting law to policy-making, it leads to the development of normative legal scholarship. While in France and Greece, normative scholarship has traditionally been the work of the French *doctrine* or the Greek *legal theory*, in England, the new kind of rational legal knowledge that proportionality conveys has represented a rupture with the Diceyan orthodoxy. In this context, proportionality has been a revolutionary tool in the hands of common lawyers, who have used it to build a system of public law based on human rights values, in the model of continental systems. During the last two decades, proportionality has borne a culture of fundamental rights and justification in English judicial review. Its spread and evolution in this context is an exemplary case of cultural transformation.

That being said, proportionality has not always been accompanied by its fundamental rights baggage. Neither has its spread always produced a 'race to the top' in the field of fundamental rights protection. In France and Greece, in particular, while proportionality has been promoted as a fundamental rights principle, its application in practice has not involved value-laden justifications. In this context, proportionality has rather assumed a symbolic or even aesthetic function: it has represented law and adjudication as a rational, scientific enterprise. Thus, it has enhanced a pre-existing tendency towards 'administrativisation' of law. Its spread as a modern, rational method of legal reasoning expresses continental lawyers' increasing reliance on facts and expertise when dealing with contentious socio-political matters.

The effects of proportionality provoke varying reactions among legal actors. The failure of proportionality to bring about modernisation and to ensure fundamental rights protection in Greece was not noticed by Greek lawyers. In this context, the meaning of proportionality as part of a desired European civilisation was, until recently, hegemonic. The use of proportionality language in official legal texts has enjoyed a value in itself, since it has represented the Greek society as modern and European. However, in different settings, the use of proportionality is not always uniform and uncontested. Asymmetries and debates among legal actors reveal tensions among different legal ideologies within the same culture and provide insights as to the potential evolution of proportionality. For instance, while the use of proportionality in French case law excites judges themselves, it provokes increasing suspicion among scholars. That is because the current context of terrorism, polarisation and state of emergency has rendered French lawyers less optimistic about the possibility of objective, scientific solutions to fundamental rights conflicts. In England, the debate about the spill-over of proportionality on domestic public law reflects a struggle about the fundamentals of the English constitution. This debate expresses a long-existing tension in this context, between substantive justice and parliamentary sovereignty. As the rationalism that underpins proportionality expands in the common law, the quest for democratic decision-making that parliamentary sovereignty has long embodied is reformulated in terms of deference.

Proportionality and European Integration. The use and evolution of proportionality makes sense within its particular cultural context. However, this context is neither unchangeable nor immune to external influence. Unravelling the local meanings of proportionality is impossible without taking European integration into account. The idea of integration through law is at the core of the European enterprise. The ECJ and the ECtHR have inscribed into proportionality the peculiar logic of European legal orders. In their case law, the language of proportionality and rights has acquired a particular dynamic, different from the one it has in German constitutionalism and connected to the supranational goals that these courts promote. When received in domestic spheres, proportionality carries with it European cultural baggage.

Still, the way proportionality deploys its integration dynamics varies across jurisdictions and across time. Although its application is a legal obligation for domestic courts, judicial practice in the field is not uniform. Even in the scope of European law, proportionality is affected by local discursive patterns and structures. French lawyers and judges have assimilated proportionality to pre-existing methods of review and have deprived it of its radical potential. In diametrical opposition, proportionality in England has corresponded to a special remedy for the violation of substantive European rights. English judges have taken its integration dynamic seriously, while they have tried to contain it within the scope of European law. In Greek legal theory, proportionality has been understood as a scientific method that transcends legal texts and even the constitution. As is typical in this context, domestic lawyers have sought the correct conceptual content of proportionality in Europe.

The practice on proportionality in the field of European law thus reveals itself as an instance of 'systematically distorted communication'. Differences in this practice express more general patterns of cultural change under pressure from external influence: French insularity, English dualism and Greek eclecticism. They also express local ways of responding to the pressure for European integration. The rationalism that permeates continental legal systems has necessitated that judges establish substantive coherence in the law that they apply. Hence, courts have typically denied the existence of normative conflicts between domestic and European law. The application of European case law and of proportionality in particular has proceeded through the translation of European legal concepts into pre-existing domestic ones. In contrast, pragmatism and instrumentalism has allowed common lawyers to explicitly articulate the differences between the English and European legal systems and their underlying values. Proportionality has served the UK's compliance with its international obligations. When these obligations have entered into conflict with fundamental assumptions of the common law, English judges have proceeded to a reasoned refusal to apply proportionality. As the Sunday trading litigation shows, it is pragmatism (and not proportionality) that has given English courts access to 'the global community of judges' engaging in transnational communication.

Convergence, Divergence and Disintegration. Once again, in the context of European integration proportionality provokes cultural change and convergence among legal systems. This is more obvious in the English case. Proportionality rationalises English judicial review and brings with it continental doctrinal baggage. New terms such as 'discretion', 'manifest error' and 'variable intensity of review' emerge, expressing a new tendency towards myth and idealisation in English legal thought. In the rationalist continental systems, the transformative effect of proportionality has been rather superficial. As a matter of aesthetics, it has ultimately depended on local narratives of European integration. In France, the motherland of human rights, proportionality is applied as a corrective 'patch', it effects minor adjustments to domestic judicial review to keep up with the evolution of European rights. When used in judicial decisions, proportionality mainly assumes a function of 'signalisation'. Quite differently, in Greece proportionality has functioned as a method of teleological interpretation and has sometimes led to a 'self-denying transformation' of the domestic constitution. That is because Greek lawyers see Europe as a model and its system of rights protection as a constitutional civilisation to which they aspire. Hence, in this context convergence has taken the form of 'interpretive osmosis' between the domestic and the European constitutions.

Under the surface of convergence, however, dissonances reappear. As rationalism expands in English public law, common law judges deny normative conflicts between domestic and European law and abandon the application of proportionality as a European head of review. While this expresses the evolution of common law judicial review, at the same time, it reveals local tendencies towards disintegration from Europe. English judges increasingly juxtapose common law methods, like originalist interpretation and precedent, against the dynamic and teleological reasoning of supranational courts. By doing so, they affirm to themselves the powers that Parliament had conceded to European institutions. The quest for parliamentary sovereignty is slowly transformed into a quest for national identity under the legal constitution. In this process, proportionality itself is progressively reinvented as a common law method, which is now *opposed* to European integration.

In Greece, dissonances are the result of the shock of the Euro crisis, which has exposed the aesthetic coherence between the domestic and the European constitution as illusionary. Greek lawyers progressively acknowledge the existence of value-laden conflicts between domestic and European law. Consciousness of normative conflict is translated into a new form of dualism in domestic legal thought. Courts increasingly deny the relevance of European law in domestic constitutional adjudication and turn to the traditional version of proportionality as a manifest error test. Scholars increasingly distinguish between the domestic and the European application of the principle. Contrary to the traditional obsession with foreign doctrinal developments, they justify the deviant domestic judicial practice by appealing to domestic constitutional values. Thus, the traditionally unitary concept of proportionality is fragmented in Greek legal thought.

It seems that disintegration pushes continental lawyers to abandon their previous commitment to rationalism and modernisation and to search for pragmatic solutions, which are more sensitive to context. This is even more apparent in the French case. Pragmatism and normative conflict challenge the traditional French republican perception of rights and contest certain fundamental assumptions of French legal thought. As courts strive to accommodate normative pluralism, the application of proportionality in concrete cases goes so far as to contest the normativity of republican legislation. Paradoxically, for the first time in France,

European integration acquires a radical dynamic in a context of disintegration.

As a discourse, the cultural interpretation of law 'can only be more or less persuasive and can never be "true"'.[2] Its findings 'will always be provisional, partial and contested'.[3] Still, cultural comparative law is a worthy enterprise. By enhancing the understanding of other cultures, it can point to new ways of providing legal solutions that are more responsive to cultural sensibilities. Most importantly, by unravelling seemingly remote worldviews and mentalities, cultural comparative law gives lawyers the opportunity to reflect on their own and to reweave them in a way that respects alterity and tolerates difference.

[2] Legrand (2002), p. 245.
[3] Cotterrell (2007), p. 149.

BIBLIOGRAPHY

Christina Akrivopoulou (2012), Ο πολιτικός δικαστής αντιμέτωπος με την αναλογικότητα κατά τον αναιρετικό έλεγχο της εύλογης χρηματικής αποζημίωσης [Civil Law Courts Faced with Proportionality in the Review of the Legality of Reasonable Compensation], in Τομος τιμητικος Πετρου Ι. Παραρα 29 (Athens: Αντ. Ν. Σάκκουλας)

Alexander Aleinikoff (1987), Constitutional Law in the Age of Balancing, 96 Yale Law Journal 943

Robert Alexy (1985), Theorie der Grundrechte (Baden-Baden: Nomos)

Robert Alexy (2002), A Theory of Constitutional Rights (Translated and with an Introduction by Julian Rivers) (Oxford; New York: Oxford University Press)

Robert Alexy (2003a), Constitutional Rights, Balancing and Rationality, 16 Ratio Juris 131

Robert Alexy (2003b), On Balancing and Subsumption. A Structural Comparison, 16 Ratio Juris 433

Robert Alexy (2005), Balancing, Constitutional Review, and Representation, 3 International Journal of Constitutional Law 572

Robert Alexy (2008), On the Concept and the Nature of Law, 21 Ratio Juris 281

Robert Alexy (2010), A Theory of Legal Argumentation: The Theory of Rational Discourse as Theory of Legal Justification (Ruth Adler and Neil McCormick, trans.) (Oxford; New York: Clarendon Press; Oxford University Press)

Nicos Alivizatos (2001a), Ο αβεβαιος εκσυγχρονισμος και η θολη συνταγματικη αναθεωρηση [Uncertain Modernization and Vague Constitutional Reform] (Athens: Πόλις)

Nicos Alivizatos (2001b), Συνολική αποτίμηση του αναθεωρητικού εγχειρήματος [Overall Evaluation of the Reform], in Το Νεο Συνταγμα 437 (Dimitrios Tsatsos, Evaggelos Venizelos and Xenophon Contiades, eds.) (Athens; Komotini: Αντ. Ν. Σάκκουλας)

Trevor Allan (1988), Pragmatism and Theory in Public Law, 104 Law Quarterly Review 422

Trevor Allan (2006), Human Rights and Judicial Review: A Critique of 'Due Deference', 65 Cambridge Law Journal 671

Trevor Allan (2013), The Sovereignty of Law: Freedom, Constitution, and Common Law (Oxford: Oxford University Press)

John Allison (1996), A Continental Distinction in the Common Law: A Historical and Comparative Perspective on English Public Law (Oxford; New York: Oxford University Press)

John Allison (2007), The English Historical Constitution: Continuity, Change and European Effects (Cambridge: Cambridge University Press)

Philip Alston, ed. (1999), The EU and Human Rights (Oxford: Oxford University Press)

Karen Alter (2002), Establishing the Supremacy of European Law: The Making of an International Rule of Law in Europe (Oxford; New York: Oxford University Press)

Joël Andriantsimbazovina (1998), L'autorité des décisions de justice constitutionnelles et européennes sur le juge administratif franÇais (Paris: LGDJ)

Nikolaos Androulakis (1972), Θεμελιωδεις εννοιαι της ποινικης δικης [Fundamental Concepts of the Criminal Process] (Athens: Σάκκουλα)

Nikolaos Androulakis (1975), Τα όρια της ανακριτικής δράσεως και η 'αρχή της αναγκαιότητας' [The Limits of Inquisitory Action and the 'Principle of Necessity'], Ποινικα Χρονικα 1

Nikolaos Androulakis (1985), Το 'κράτος των δικαστών' – ένα ανύπαρκτο σκιάχτρο; [The 'government of judges' – an inexistent scarecrow?], 33 Νομικο Βημα 1505

Charalampos Anthopoulos (2001), Όψεις της συνταγματικής δημοκρατίας στο παράδειγμα του άρθρου 25 παρ. 1 του Συντάγματος [Aspects of Constitutional Democracy in the Example of Article 25 par. 1 of the Constitution], in Το νΕο ΣΥνταγμα 153 (Dimitrios Tsatsos, Evaggelos Venizelos and Xenophon Contiades, eds.) (Athens; Komotini: Αντ. Ν. Σάκκουλας)

Charalampos Anthopoulos (2006), Το ασυμβίβαστο των ιδιοκτητών μέσων ενημέρωσης πριν και μετά το νέο άρθρο 14 παρ. 9 του Συντάγματος [The Incompatibility Concerning Media Owners before and after the New Article 14 par. 9 of the Constitution], in Πεντε χρονια μετα τη συνταγματικη αναθεωρηση του 2001 313 (Xenophon Contiades, ed.) (Athens; Komotini: Αντ. Ν. Σάκκουλας)

Theodora Antoniou (2012), Η απόφαση της Ολομελείας του Συμβουλίου της Επικρατείας για το Μνημόνιο – Μια ευρωπαϊκή υπόθεση χωρίς ευρωπαϊκή προσέγγιση [The Council of State Plenum Decision on the Memorandum – A European Affair Lacking a European Approach], Το ΣΥνταγμα 197

Yutaka Arai-Takahashi (2002), The Margin of Appreciation Doctrine and the Principle of Proportionality in the Jurisprudence of the ECHR (Antwerp; Oxford: Intersentia)

Christian Atias and Didier Linotte (1977), Le mythe de l'adaptation du droit au fait, Recueil Dalloz 251

Patrick Atiyah (1987), Pragmatism and Theory in English Law (London: Sweet & Maxwell)

Jean-Marie Auby (1979), Le contrôle juridictionnel du degré de gravité d'une sanction disciplinaire, note sous CE, 9 juin 1978, *Lebon*, Revue du Droit Public 227

Frédéric Audren and Jean-Louis Halpérin (2013), La culture juridique française: Entre mythes et réalités: XIXe-XXe siècles (Paris: CNRS)

John Austin (1975), How to Do Things with Words (Oxford: Clarendon Press)

Jack Balkin (1986), The Crystalline Structure of Legal Thought, 39 Rutgers Law Review 1

Jack Balkin (1990a), Nested Oppositions, 99 Yale Law Journal 1669

Jack Balkin (1990b), The Hohfeldian Approach to Law and Semiotics, 44 University of Miami Law Review 1119

Jack Balkin (1991), The Promise of Legal Semiotics, 69 Texas Law Review 1831

Aharon Barak (2012), Proportionality: Constitutional Rights and Their Limitations (New York: Cambridge University Press)

Nick Barber (2011), The Afterlife of Parliamentary Sovereignty, 9 International Journal of Constitutional Law 144

Jack Beatson, ed. (1998), Constitutional Reform in the United Kingdom: Practice and Principles (Oxford: Hart)

David Beatty (2004), The Ultimate Rule of Law (Oxford; New York: Oxford University Press)

Kostas Beis (1998), Το ελληνικο ελλειμμα κρατουσ δικαιου [The Greek Rule Of Law Deficit] (Athens: Eunomia)

Kostas Beis (1999), Η αρχή της αναλογικότητας [The Principle of Proportionality] 30 Δικη 467

Johanna Bell (2019), Rethinking the Story of *Cart v Upper Tribunal* and Its Implications for Administrative Law, 39 Oxford Journal of Legal Studies 74

John Bell (1986), The Expansion of Judicial Review over Discretionary Powers in France, Public Law 99

Carlos Bernal Pulido (2007), El principio de proporcionalidad y los derechos fundamentales (Madrid: Centro de Estudios Políticos y Constitucionales)

Jean-Jacques Bienvenu (1979), L'interprétation juridictionnelle des actes administratifs et des lois: Sa nature et sa fonction dans l'élaboration du droit administratif (Paris II: unpublished PhD thesis)

Jean-Jacques Bienvenu (1985), Note sous décision n° 85–192 DC, Actualité Juridique Droit Administratif 485

Tom Bingham (1992), 'There Is a World Elsewhere': The Changing Perspectives of English Law, 41 International and Comparative Law Quarterly 513

Tom Bingham (2000), The European Convention on Human Rights: Time to Incorporate, in The Business of Judging. Selected Essays and Speeches 131 (Oxford: Oxford University Press)

Patrick Birkinshaw (2003), European Public Law (London: Butterworths)

Eirik Bjorge and Jack Williams (2016), The Protean Principle of Proportionality: How Different Is Proportionality in EU Contexts?, 75 Cambridge Law Journal 186

Jean-Michel Blanquer (2000), Les méthodes du juge constitutionnel (Paris: LGDJ)

Franz Boas (1898), Introduction, in James Alexander Teit, Traditions of the Thompson River Indians of British Columbia (Boston, MA; New York: Houghton, Mifflin & Company)

Alain Bockel (1978), Contribution à l'étude du pouvoir discrétionnaire de l'administration, Actualité Juridique Droit Administratif 355

Ernst Wolfgang Böckenförde (1991), Grundrechte als Grundsatznormen. Zur Gegenwärtigen Lage der Grundrechtsdogmatik, in Staat, Verfassung, Demokratie: Studien zur Verfassungstheorie und zum Verfassungsrecht 185 (Frankfurt am Main: Suhrkamp)

Jacco Bomhoff (2010), Genealogies of Balancing as Discourse, 4 Law & Ethics of Human Rights 108

Jacco Bomhoff (2012a), Perfectionism in European Law, in 14 Cambridge Yearbook of European Legal Studies 75 (Catherine Barnard, Markus Gehring and Iyiola Solanke eds.) (Oxford: Hart)

Jacco Bomhoff (2012b), Comparing Legal Argument, in 74 Practice and Theory in Comparative Law (Maurice Adams and Jacco Bomhoff eds.) (Cambridge; New York: Cambridge University Press)

Jacco Bomhoff (2013a), Balancing Constitutional Rights. The Origins and Meanings of Postwar Legal Discourse (Cambridge: Cambridge University Press)

Jacco Bomhoff (2013b), Balancing Constitutional Rights: Introduction, 22 LSE Legal Studies Working Paper, available at: papers.ssrn.com/sol3/papers.cfm?abstract_id=2343536

Jacco Bomhoff (2017), Beyond Proportionality: Thinking Comparatively about Constitutional Review and Punitiveness, in Proportionality: New Frontiers, New Challenges 148 (Vicki Jackson and Mark Tushnet, eds.) (Cambridge; New York: Cambridge University Press)

Rhita Bousta (2007), La spécificité du contrôle constitutionnel français de proportionnalité, Revue Internationale de Droit Comparé 859

Rhita Bousta (2011), Contrôle constitutionnel de proportionnalité: La 'spécificité française' à l'épreuve des évolutions récentes, REVUE FRANÇAISE DE DROIT CONSTITUTIONNEL 913

Sophie Boyron (1992), Proportionality in English Administrative Law: A Faulty Translation?, 12 OXFORD JOURNAL OF LEGAL STUDIES 237

Vernon Bogdanor (2009), THE NEW BRITISH CONSTITUTION (Oxford: Hart)

Alan Brady (2012), PROPORTIONALITY AND DEFERENCE UNDER THE UK HUMAN RIGHTS ACT: AN INSTITUTIONALLY SENSITIVE APPROACH (Cambridge: Cambridge University Press)

Guy Braibant (1974), Le principe de proportionnalité, in MÉLANGES OFFERTS À MARCEL WALINE: LE JUGE ET LE DROIT PUBLIC 297 (Paris: LGDJ)

Annabel Brett (2002), What Is Intellectual History Now?, in WHAT IS HISTORY NOW? 113 (David Cannadine, ed.) (New York: Palgrave Macmillan)

Stephen Breyer (2010), MAKING OUR DEMOCRACY WORK: A JUDGE'S VIEW (New York: Knopf)

Neville Brown (1978), General Principles of Law and the English Legal System, in NEW PERSPECTIVES FOR A COMMON LAW OF EUROPE [NOUVELLES PERSPECTIVES D'UN DROIT COMMUN DE L'EUROPE] 177 (Mauro Cappelletti and Neville Brown, eds.) (Publications of the European University Institute. Leiden; London: Sijthoff)

Nick Browne-Wilkinson (1992), The Infiltration of a Bill of Rights, PUBLIC LAW 397

Pierre Brunet (2004), VOULOIR POUR LA NATION: LE CONCEPT DE REPRÉSENTATION DANS LA THÉORIE DE L'ÉTAT (Rouen: Publications de l'Université de Rouen)

Pierre Brunet (2005a), Le juge constitutionnel est-il un juge comme les autres? Réflexions méthodologiques sur la justice constitutionnelle, in LA NOTION DE 'JUSTICE CONSTITUTIONNELLE' (Institut de recherches Carré de Malberg) (Paris: Dalloz)

Pierre Brunet (2005b), Que reste-t-il de la volonté générale? Sur les nouvelles fictions du droit constitutionnel français, 114 POUVOIRS 5

Loïc Cadiet (2016), Introduction, LA SEMAINE JURIDIQUE, NUMÉRO SPÉCIAL: REGARDS D'UNIVERSITAIRES SUR LA RÉFORME DE LA COUR DE CASSATION (CONFÉRENCE-DÉBAT 24 NOVEMBRE 2015) 10

Raymond Carré de Malberg (1931), LA LOI, EXPRESSION DE LA VOLONTÉ GÉNÉRALE: ÉTUDE SUR LE CONCEPT DE LA LOI DANS LA CONSTITUTION DE 1875 (Paris: Sirey)

Paul Cassia and Emmanuelle Saulnier (1997), Le Conseil d'État et la Convention européenne des droits de l'Homme, ACTUALITÉ JURIDIQUE DROIT ADMINISTRATIF 411

René Cassin, Marcel Waline, Prosper Weil, Long Marceau and Guy Braibant (1956), LES GRANDS ARRÊTS DE LA JURISPRUDENCE ADMINISTRATIVE (1st ed.) (Paris: Sirey)

Véronique Champeil-Desplats (2012), Le Conseil constitutionnel a-t-il une conception des libertés publiques?, 7 JUS POLITICUM, available at: juspoliticum

.com/article/Le-Conseil-constitutionnel-a-t-il-une-conception-des-libertes-publiques-402.html

Véronique Champeil-Desplats (2016), Méthodologies du droit et des sciences du droit (Paris: Dalloz)

Jacques Chevallier (2002), Doctrine juridique et science juridique, 50 Droit et Société 103

Jacques Chevallier and Danièle Lochak (1978), Science administrative (Paris: LGDJ)

Sujit Choudhry, ed. (2006), The Migration of Constitutional Ideas (Cambridge: Cambridge University Press)

Jonas Christoffersen (2009), Fair Balance: Proportionality, Subsidiarity and Primarity in the European Convention on Human Rights (Leiden; Boston, MA: Martinus Nijhoff Publishers)

Kostas Chryssogonos (2000), Μια βεβαιωτικη αναθεΩρηση. Η αναθεΩρηση των διαταξεων του Συνταγματος για τα ατομικα και κοινωνικα δικαιωματα [A Confirmatory Amendment. The Amendment of the Constitutional Provisions on Individual and Social Rights] (Athens: Αντ. Ν. Σάκκουλας)

Kostas Chryssogonos (2001a), Η ενσωματωση της Ευρωπαϊκης Συμβασης των Δικαιωματων του Ανθρωπου στην εθνικη εννομη ταξη [The Incorporation of the European Convention on Human Rights into the National Legal Order] (Athens; Komotini: Αντ. Ν. Σάκκουλας)

Kostas Chryssogonos (2001b), Η προστασία των θεμελιωδών δικαιωμάτων στην Ελλάδα πριν και μετά την αναθεώρηση του 2001 [The Protection of Fundamental Rights in Greece before and after the 2001 Reform], 10 Δικαιωματα του Ανθρωπου 529

Andrew Clapham (1993), Human Rights in the Private Sphere (Oxford; New York: Clarendon Press; Oxford University Press)

Richard Clayton (2002), Proportionality and the HRA 1998: Implications for Substantive Review, Judicial Review 124

Richard Clayton (2004), Judicial Deference and Democratic Dialogue: The Legitimacy of Judicial Intervention under the Human Rights Act 1998, Public Law 33

Richard Clayton (2014), The Curious Case of *Kennedy v Charity Commission*, UK Constitutional Law Association Blog (18 April 2014), available at: ukconstitutionallaw.org

Morris Cohen (1953), Law and Scientific Method, in Jurisprudence in Action: A Pleader's Anthology (London: Sweet & Maxwell)

Moshe Cohen-Eliya and Iddo Porat (2010), American Balancing and German Proportionality: The Historical Origins, 8 International Journal of Constitutional Law 263

Moshe Cohen-Eliya and Iddo Porat (2013), Proportionality and Constitutional Culture (Cambridge: Cambridge University Press)

Moshe Cohen-Eliya and Iddo Porat (2017), The Administrative Origins of Constitutional Rights and Global Constitutionalism, in PROPORTIONALITY: NEW FRONTIERS, NEW CHALLENGES 75 (Vicki Jackson and Mark Tushnet, eds.) (Cambridge; New York: Cambridge University Press)

Margit Cohn (2010), Legal Transplant Chronicles: The Evolution of Unreasonableness and Proportionality Review of the Administration in the United Kingdom, 58 AMERICAN JOURNAL OF COMPARATIVE LAW 583

Xenophon Contiades (2002), Ο ΝΕΟΣ ΣΥΝΤΑΓΜΑΤΙΣΜΟΣ ΚΑΙ ΤΑ ΘΕΜΕΛΙΩΔΗ ΔΙΚΑΙΩΜΑΤΑ ΜΕΤΑ ΤΗΝ ΑΝΑΘΕΩΡΗΣΗ ΤΟΥ 2001 [THE NEW CONSTITUTIONALISM AND FUNDAMENTAL RIGHTS AFTER THE 2001 REFORM] (Athens; Komotini: Αντ. Ν. Σάκκουλας)

Xenophon Contiades and Alkmene Fotiadou (2012a), Social Rights in the Age of Proportionality: Global Economic Crisis and Constitutional Litigation, 10 INTERNATIONAL JOURNAL OF CONSTITUTIONAL LAW 660

Xenophon Contiades and Alkmene Fotiadou (2012b), Κοινωνικά δικαιώματα, αναλογικότητα και δημοσιονομική κρίση, θεωρητικές επισημάνσεις επ' ευκαιρία της ΟλΣΕ 668/2012 [Social Rights, Proportionality and Financial Crisis: Theoretical Remarks on the Occasion of StE (Pl.) 668/2012], 53 ΔΙΚΑΙΩΜΑΤΑ ΤΟΥ ΑΝΘΡΩΠΟΥ 27

Jean-Paul Costa (1988), Le principe de proportionnalité dans la jurisprudence du Conseil d'État, ACTUALITÉ JURIDIQUE DROIT ADMINISTRATIF 434

Roger Cotterrell (2006), Comparative Law and Legal Culture, in THE OXFORD HANDBOOK OF COMPARATIVE LAW 710 (Mathias Reimann and Reinhard Zimmermann, eds.) (Oxford; New York: Oxford University Press)

Roger Cotterrell (2007), Is It so Bad to Be Different? Comparative Law and the Appreciation of Diversity, in COMPARATIVE LAW: A HANDBOOK 133 (Esin Örücü and David Nelken, eds.) (Oxford; Portland, OR: Hart)

Paul Craig (1989), ADMINISTRATIVE LAW (2nd ed.) (London: Sweet & Maxwell)

Paul Craig (1994), ADMINISTRATIVE LAW (3rd ed.) (London: Sweet & Maxwell)

Paul Craig (1997), Formal and Substantive Conceptions of the Rule of Law: An Analytical Framework, PUBLIC LAW 467

Paul Craig (1999a), Unreasonableness and Proportionality in UK Law, in THE PRINCIPLE OF PROPORTIONALITY IN THE LAWS OF EUROPE 107 (Evelyn Elllis, ed.) (London: Bloomsbury Publishing)

Paul Craig (1999b), Competing Models of Judicial Review, PUBLIC LAW 428

Paul Craig (2013), The Nature of Reasonableness Review, 66 CURRENT LEGAL PROBLEMS 131

Paul Craig (2016), ADMINISTRATIVE LAW (8th ed.) (London: Sweet & Maxwell)

Paul Craig (2017), Proportionality and Judicial Review: A UK Historical Perspective, in GENERAL PRINCIPLES OF LAW, EUROPEAN AND COMPARATIVE

Perspectives (Stephan Vogenauer and Stephen Weatherill, eds.) (Oxford: Hart)

Paul Craig (2018), EU Administrative Law (3rd ed.) (Oxford; New York: Oxford University Press)

Prodromos Dagtoglou (1985), Ευρωπαϊκο Κοινοτικο Δικαιο [European Community Law] (2nd ed.) (Athens: Αντ. Σάκκουλας)

Prodromos Dagtoglou (1986), Δημόσιο συμφέρον και Σύνταγμα [Public Interest and the Constitution], Το Συνταγμα 425

Prodromos Dagtoglou (1991), Συνταγματικο Δικαιο. Ατομικα Δικαιωματα [Constitutional Law. Individual Rights] (1st ed.) (Athens; Komotini: Αντ. Ν. Σάκκουλας)

Prodromos Dagtoglou (2004), Γενικο Διοικητικο Δικαιο [General Administrative Law] (4th ed.) (Athens; Komotini: Αντ. Σάκκουλας)

Prodromos Dagtoglou (2005), Συνταγματικο Δικαιο. Ατομικα Δικαιωματα [Constitutional Law. Individual Rights] (2nd rev. ed.) (Athens; Komotini: Αντ. Ν. Σάκκουλας)

Prodromos Dagtoglou (2015), Συνταγματικο Δικαιο. Ατομικα Δικαιωματα [Constitutional Law. Individual Rights] (7th ed.) (Athens; Komotini: Αντ. Ν. Σάκκουλας)

Theocharis Dalakouras (1993), Η αρχη της αναλογικότητας και τα μετρα δικονομικου καταναγκασμου [The Principle of Proportionality and Coercive Measures in Criminal Proceedings] (Thessaloniki: Σάκκουλα)

Paul Daly (2016), Proportionality and Rationality: The Debate Goes On, Administrative Law Matters Blog (17 February 2016), available at: www.administrativelawmatters.com

Paul Daly (2020a), The Covid-19 Pandemic and Proportionality: A Framework, Administrative Law Matters Blog (31 March 2020), available at: www.administrativelawmatters.com

Paul Daly (2020b), The Culture of Justification in Administrative Law, UK Constitutional Law Association Blog (6 July 2020), available at: ukconstitutionallaw.org

Alan Dashwood (1996), The Limits of European Community Powers, 21 European Law Review 113

Anne Davies and Jack Williams (2015), Proportionality in English Law, in The Judge and the Proportionate Use of Discretion: A Comparative Study 73 (Sofia Ranchordás and Boudewijn Willem Nicolaas de Waard, eds.) (New York: Routledge)

Gareth Davies (2012), Constitutional Disagreement in Europe and the Search for Pluralism, in Constitutional Pluralism in the European Union and beyond 269 (Jan Komárek and Matej Avbelj, eds.) (Oxford: Hart)

Gareth Davies (2016), Free Movement, the Quality of Life, and the Myth That the Court Balances Interests, in EXCEPTIONS FROM EU FREE MOVEMENT LAW. DEROGATION, JUSTIFICATION AND PROPORTIONALITY 218 (Oxford: Hart)

John Philip Dawson (1978), THE ORACLES OF THE LAW (Westport, CO: Greenwood Press)

Denys de Béchillon (2016), Observations sur le contrôle de proportionnalité, LA SEMAINE JURIDIQUE, NUMÉRO SPÉCIAL: REGARDS D'UNIVERSITAIRES SUR LA RÉFORME DE LA COUR DE CASSATION (CONFÉRENCE-DÉBAT 24 NOVEMBRE 2015) 27

Gráinne de Búrca (1993a), Fundamental Human Rights and the Reach of EC Law, 13 OXFORD JOURNAL OF LEGAL STUDIES 283

Gráinne de Búrca (1993b), The Principle of Proportionality and Its Application in EC Law, 13 YEARBOOK OF EUROPEAN LAW 105

Gráinne de Búrca (1995), The Language of Rights and European Integration, in NEW LEGAL DYNAMICS OF EUROPEAN UNION 29 (Jo Shaw and Gillian More, eds.) (New York: Clarendon Press)

Gráinne de Búrca (2002), Convergence and Divergence in European Public Law: The Case of Human Rights, in CONVERGENCE AND DIVERGENCE IN EUROPEAN PUBLIC LAW 131 (Paul Beaumont, Carole Lyons and Neil Walker, eds.) (Oxford; Portland, OR: Hart)

Gráinne de Búrca (2013), After the EU Charter of Fundamental Rights: The Court of Justice as a Human Rights Adjudicator?, 20 MAASTRICHT JOURNAL OF EUROPEAN AND COMPARATIVE LAW 168

Gráinne de Búrca, Bruno De Witte and Larissa Ogertschnig (2005), SOCIAL RIGHTS IN EUROPE (New York: Oxford University Press)

André de Laubadère (1974), Le contrôle juridictionnel du pouvoir discrétionnaire dans la jurisprudence récente du Conseil d'État français, in MÉLANGES OFFERTS À MARCEL WALINE: LE JUGE ET LE DROIT PUBLIC 531 (Paris: LGDJ)

Stanley Alexander de Smith (1959), JUDICIAL REVIEW OF ADMINISTRATIVE ACTION (New York: Oceana Publications)

Stanley Alexander de Smith (1971), CONSTITUTIONAL AND ADMINISTRATIVE LAW (London: Penguin Books)

Stanley Alexander de Smith, Harry Woolf, Jeffrey Jowell and Andrew Le Sueur (1995), JUDICIAL REVIEW OF ADMINISTRATIVE ACTION (5th ed.) (London: Sweet & Maxwell)

Stanley Alexander de Smith, Harry Woolf, Jeffrey Jowell and Andrew Le Sueur (2018), JUDICIAL REVIEW OF ADMINISTRATIVE ACTION (8th ed.) (London: Sweet & Maxwell)

Bruno De Witte (1999), The Past and Future Role of the European Court of Justice in the Protection of Human Rights, in THE EU AND HUMAN RIGHTS 859 (Philip Alston, ed.) (Oxford; New York: Oxford University Press)

Floris De Witte (2013), Sex, Drugs & EU Law: The Recognition of Ethical and Moral Diversity in Europe, 50 Common Market Law Review 1545

Michail Dekleris (1996), Ο δωδεκαδελτος του περιβαλλοντος. Εγκολπιο βιωσιμου αναπτυξεως [The Twelve Tables of the Environment. A Handbook of Sustainable Growth] (Athens; Komotini: Αντ. Ν. Σάκκουλας)

Mireille Delmas-Marty (2017), De l'état d'urgence au despotisme doux, Libération, 16 July 2017

Pierre Delvolvé (2016), Droits subjectifs contre interdit législatif, Revue Française de Droit Administratif 754

Alfred Denning (1949), Freedom under the Law (London: Stevens & Sons)

Pascale Deumier (2016), Contrôle concret de conventionnalité: L'esprit et la méthode, Revue Trimestrielle de Droit Civil 578

Thierry Di Manno (1999), Le juge constitutionnel et la technique des décisions 'interprétatives' en France et en Italie (Paris: Economica)

Albert Venn Dicey (1939), Introduction to the Study of the Law of the Constitution (9th ed.) (London: Macmillan & Co.)

Andreas Dimitropoulos (1981), Τα αμυντικα δικαιωματα του ανθρωπου και η μεταβολη της εννομης ταξης [Negative Human Rights and the Transformation of the Legal Order] (Athens; Komotini: Αντ. Ν. Σάκκουλας)

Filippos Doris (2004), Η αρχή της αναλογικότητας στο πεδίο ρύθμισης των ιδιωτικού δικαίου σχέσεων και ιδιαίτερα στο αστικό δίκαιο [The Principle of Proportionality in the Field of Private Law Relations and Especially in Civil Law], in Τομος τιμητικος του Συμβουλιου της Επικρατειας – 75 χρονια 229 (Thessaloniki: Σάκκουλα)

Guillaume Drago (1991), La conciliation entre principes constitutionnels, Recueil Dalloz 265

Françoise Dreyfus (1974), Les limitations du pouvoir discrétionnaire par l'application du principe de proportionnalité: À propos de trois jugements du tribunal administratif de l'OIT, Revue du Droit Public 691

Yannis Drossos (1996), Δοκιμιο ελληνικης συνταγματικης θεωριας [Essay on Greek Constitutional Theory] (Athens; Komotini: Αντ. Ν. Σάκκουλας)

Louis Dubouis (1962), La théorie de l'abus de droit et la jurisprudence administrative (Paris: LGDJ)

Jean-Baptiste Duclerq (2015), Les mutations du contrôle de proportionnalité dans la jurisprudence du Conseil constitutionnel (Paris: LGDJ)

Olivier Dutheillet de Lamothe (2008), La Convention européenne et le Conseil constitutionnel, Revue Internationale de Droit Comparé 293

Louis Dutheillet de Lamothe and Guillaume Odinet (2016), Contrôle de conventionnalité: *In concreto veritas*?, Actualité Juridique Droit Administratif 1398

Ronald Dworkin (1967), The Model of Rules, 35 University of Chicago Law Review 14

Ronald Dworkin (1978), Taking Rights Seriously (new impression, with a reply to critics) (London: Duckworth)

Ronald Dworkin (1986), Law's Empire (London: Fontana)

David Dyzenhaus, Murray Hunt and Michael Taggart (2001), The Principle of Legality in Administrative Law: Internationalisation as Constitutionalisation, Oxford University Commonwealth Law Journal 5

Charles Eisenmann (1933), L'esprit des lois et la séparation des pouvoirs, in Mélanges Raymond Carré de Malberg 165 (Paris: Duchemin)

Mark Elliott (2001), The Human Rights Act 1998 and the Standard of Substantive Review, 60 Cambridge Law Journal 301

Mark Elliott (2013), Justification, Calibration and Substantive Judicial Review: Putting Doctrine in Its Place, UK Constitutional Law Association Blog (17 September 2013), available at: ukconstitutionallaw.org

Mark Elliott (2014), Common-Law Constitutionalism and Proportionality in the Supreme Court: *Kennedy v The Charity Commission*, Public Law for Everyone Blog (31 March 2014), available at: publiclawforeveryone.com

Mark Elliott (2015a), A Tangled Constitutional Web: The Black-Spider Memos and the British Constitution's Relational Architecture, Public Law 539

Mark Elliott (2015b), Proportionality and Contextualism in Common-Law Review: The Supreme Court's Judgment in *Pham*, Public Law for Everyone Blog (17 April 2015), available at: publiclawforeveryone.com

Samuel Etoa (2011), La terminologie des 'droits fondamentaux' dans la jurisprudence du Conseil constitutionnel, 9 Cahiers de la Recherche sur les Droits Fondamentaux 23

Marthe Fatin-Rouge Stéfanini and Xavier Philippe (2011), Jurisprudence du Conseil constitutionnel octobre 2010–mars 2011, Revue Française de Droit Constitutionnel 547

Louis Favoreu (1985), Note sous décision no. 84–181 DC, Revue du Droit Public 395

Louis Favoreu (2001), Droit des libertés fondamentales (2nd ed.) (Paris: Dalloz)

Louis Favoreu and Loïc Philip (1975), Les grandes décisions du Conseil constitutionnel (1st ed.) (Paris: Dalloz-Sirey)

Louis Favoreu, Loïc Philip, Patrick Gaïa, Richard Ghevontian and André Roux (2018), Les grandes décisions du Conseil constitutionnel (19th ed.) (Paris: Dalloz)

Helen Fenwick (2012), What's Wrong with s.2 of the Human Rights Act?, UK Constitutional Law Association Blog (9 October 2012), available at: ukconstitutionallaw.org

Spyridon Flogaitis (1986), ADMINISTRATIVE LAW ET DROIT ADMINISTRATIF (Paris: Pichon et Durand-Auzias)

Michael Fordham and Thomas de la Mare (2001), Identifying the Principles of Proportionality, in UNDERSTANDING HUMAN RIGHTS PRINCIPLES 27 (Jeffrey Jowell and Jonathan Cooper, eds.) (Oxford; Portland, OR: Hart)

Ernst Forsthoff (1971), DER STAAT DER INDUSTRIEGESELLSCHAFT: DARGESTELLT AM BEISPIEL DER BUNDESREPUBLIK DEUTSCHLAND (München: Beck)

Michel Foucault (1969), L'ARCHÉOLOGIE DU SAVOIR (Paris: Gallimard)

Norbert Foulquier (2003), LES DROITS PUBLICS SUBJECTIFS DES ADMINISTRÉS: ÉMERGENCE D'UN CONCEPT EN DROIT ADMINISTRATIF FRANÇAIS DU XIXE AU XXE SIÈCLE (Paris: Dalloz)

Régis Fraisse (2009), Le Conseil constitutionnel exerce un contrôle conditionné, diversifié et modulé de la proportionnalité, 46 LES PETITES AFFICHES, NUMÉRO SPÉCIAL 74

Bastien François (1990), Une revendication de juridiction. Compétence et justice dans le droit constitutionnel de la Ve République, 3 POLITIX 92

Lawrence Friedman and Gunther Teubner (1986), Legal Education and Legal Integration: European Hopes and American Experience, in INTEGRATION THROUGH LAW: FORCES AND POTENTIAL FOR A EUROPEAN IDENTITY 345 (Mauro Cappelletti, Monica Seccombe and Joseph Weiler, eds.) (Berlin: de Gruyter)

Michel Fromont (1995), Le principe de proportionnalité, ACTUALITÉ JURIDIQUE DROIT ADMINISTRATIF, NUMÉRO SPÉCIAL 156

Antoine Garapon (1995), French Legal Culture and the Shock of 'Globalization', 4 SOCIAL AND LEGAL STUDIES, SPECIAL ISSUE ON LEGAL CULTURE, DIVERSITY AND GLOBALIZATION 493

Stephen Gardbaum (2017), Positive and Horizontal Rights: Proportionality's Next Frontier or a Bridge Too Far?, in PROPORTIONALITY: NEW FRONTIERS, NEW CHALLENGES 221 (Vicki Jackson and Mark Tushnet, eds.) (Cambridge; New York: Cambridge University Press)

Yves Gaudemet (1998), Les nouvelles méthodes du juge administratif français, in ÉTAT-LOI-ADMINISTRATION. MÉLANGES EN L'HONNEUR DE EPAMINONDAS SPILIOTOPOULOS 147 (Petros Pararas, ed.) (Athens; Brussels: Αντ. Ν. Σάκκουλας; Bruylant)

Yves Gaudemet (2013), LES MÉTHODES DU JUGE ADMINISTRATIF (Paris: LGDJ)

Conor Gearty (2007), CIVIL LIBERTIES (Oxford; New York: Oxford University Press)

Conor Gearty (2014), The Tories' Proposal for a British Bill of Rights Is Incoherent, but They Don't Care, THE GUARDIAN, 3 October 2014

Clifford Geertz (1983), LOCAL KNOWLEDGE: FURTHER ESSAYS IN INTERPRETIVE ANTHROPOLOGY (New York: Basic Books)

Clifford Geertz (2000), The Interpretation of Cultures: Selected Essays (New York: Basic Books)

Bruno Genevois (1988), L'application du principe de proportionnalité aux amendes fiscales (à propos de la décision du Conseil constitutionnel no. 87–237 DC du 30 décembre 1987), Revue Française de Droit Administratif 350

Bruno Genevois (1989), Le Conseil constitutionnel et la définition des pouvoirs du Conseil supérieur de l'audiovisuel, Revue Française de Droit Administratif 215

François Gény (1919), Méthodes d'interprétation et sources en droit privé positif (Paris: LGDJ)

George Gerapetritis (1997), Proportionality in Administrative Law: Judicial Review in France, Greece, England and in the European Community (Athens: Σάκκουλα)

George Gerapetritis (2005), Στο δρόμο για την θεσμικά ισόρροπη παρέμβαση του δικαστή [Towards an Institutionally Balanced Judicial Intervention], 25 Δικαιωματα του Ανθρωπου 187

George Gerapetritis (2006), Πρόσωπα και προσωπεία του ελέγχου της αναλογικότητας [Faces and Guises of Proportionality Review], IV Δικαιωματα του Ανθρωπου 269

George Gerapetritis (2012), Συνταγμα και Βουλη. Αυτονομια και ανελεγκτο των εσωτερικων του σωματος [Constitution and Parliament. Autonomy and the Exemption of the Interna Corporis Affairs from Judicial Review] (Athens: Νομική Βιβλιοθήκη)

Apostolos Gerontas (1983), Η αρχή της αναλογικότητας στο γερμανικό δημόσιο δίκαιο [The Principle of Proportionality in German Public Law], Το Συνταγμα 20

Apostolos Gerontas (2006), Η αρχή της αναλογικότητας και η τριτενέργεια των θεμελιωδών δικαιωμάτων μετά την αναθεώρηση του 2001 [The Principle of Proportionality and the Third-Party Effect of Fundamental Rights after the 2001 Reform], in Πεντε χρονια μετα τη συνταγματικη αναθεωρηση του 2001 462 (Xenophon Contiades, ed.) (Athens; Komotini: Αντ. Ν. Σάκκουλας)

Dionysis Giakoumis (2005), Οι αόριστες έννοιες, η διακριτική ευχέρεια του δικαστή ως αόριστη νομική έννοια, η εξειδίκευσή της και η δυνατότητα αναιρετικού ελέγχου υπό το πρίσμα της αρχής της αναλογικότητας [Indeterminate Notions, Judicial Discretion as an Indeterminate Legal Notion, Its Concretisation, and the Possibility of Cassation under the Framework of the Principle of Proportionality], 36 Δικη 48

Didier Girard (2015), La France devant la Cour européenne des droits de l'Homme: Contribution à l'analyse du comportement étatique devant une juridiction internationale (Paris: L'Harmattan)

Patrick Glenn (2004), Legal Cultures and Legal Traditions, in EPISTEMOLOGY AND METHODOLOGY OF COMPARATIVE LAW: EPISTEMOLOGY AND METHODOLOGY OF COMPARATIVE LAW 7 (Mark Van Hoecke, ed.) (London: Bloomsbury Publishing)

Valérie Goesel-Le Bihan (1997), Réflexion iconoclaste sur le contrôle de proportionnalité exercé par le conseil constitutionnel, REVUE FRANÇAISE DE DROIT CONSTITUTIONNEL 227

Valérie Goesel-Le Bihan (2001), Le contrôle exercé par le Conseil constitutionnel: Défense et illustration d'une théorie générale, REVUE FRANÇAISE DE DROIT CONSTITUTIONNEL 67

Valérie Goesel-Le Bihan (2007a), Le contrôle de proportionnalité dans la jurisprudence du Conseil constitutionnel: Figures récentes, REVUE FRANÇAISE DE DROIT CONSTITUTIONNEL 269

Valérie Goesel-Le Bihan (2007b), Le contrôle de proportionnalité exercé par le Conseil constitutionnel, 22 CAHIERS DU CONSEIL CONSTITUTIONNEL, DOSSIER: LE RÉALISME EN DROIT CONSTITUTIONNEL, available at: www.conseil-constitutionnel.fr/nouveaux-cahiers-du-conseil-constitutionnel/le-controle-de-proportionnalite-exerce-par-le-conseil-constitutionnel

Valérie Goesel-Le Bihan (2012), Le contrôle de proportionnalité exercé par le Conseil constitutionnel, technique de protection des libertés publiques ?, 7 JUS POLITICUM, available at: juspoliticum.com/article/Le-controle-de-proportionnalite-exerce-par-le-Conseil-constitutionnel-technique-de-protection-des-libertes-publiques-456.html

Konstantinos Gogos (2005), Πτυχές του ελέγχου αναλογικότητας στη νομολογία του Συμβουλίου της Επικρατείας [Aspects of Proportionality Review in the Case Law of the Council of State], III ΔΙΚΑΙΩΜΑΤΑ ΤΟΥ ΑΝΘΡΩΠΟΥ 299

Léo Goldenberg (1932), LE CONSEIL D'ÉTAT, JUGE DU FAIT (Paris: Dalloz)

Michele Graziadei (2003), The Functionalist Heritage, in COMPARATIVE LEGAL STUDIES: TRADITIONS AND TRANSITIONS 100 (Pierre Legrand and Roderick Munday, eds.) (Cambridge; New York: Cambridge University Press)

Michele Graziadei (2006), Comparative Law as the Study of Transplants and Receptions, in OXFORD HANDBOOK OF COMPARATIVE LAW 441 (Mathias Reimann and Reinhard Zimmermann, eds.) (Oxford: Oxford University Press)

Nicholas Green (1999), Proportionality and the Supremacy of Parliament in the UK, in THE PRINCIPLE OF PROPORTIONALITY IN THE LAWS OF EUROPE 145 (Evelyn Elllis, ed.) (London: Bloomsbury Publishing)

John Griffith (1981), THE POLITICS OF THE JUDICIARY (London: Fontana)

John Griffith (2000), The Brave New World of Sir John Laws, 63 MODERN LAW REVIEW 159

Dieter Grimm (2007), Proportionality in Canadian and German Constitutional Jurisprudence, 57 UNIVERSITY OF TORONTO LAW JOURNAL 383

Michel Guibal (1978), De la proportionnalité, ACTUALITÉ JURIDIQUE DROIT ADMINISTRATIF 477

Jürgen Habermas (1996), BETWEEN FACTS AND NORMS: CONTRIBUTIONS TO A DISCOURSE THEORY OF LAW AND DEMOCRACY (Cambridge, MA: MIT Press)

Michael Hain (2017), Guardians of the Constitution – the Constitutional Implications of a Substantive Rule of Law, UK CONSTITUTIONAL LAW ASSOCIATION BLOG (12 September 2017), available at: ukconstitutionallaw.org

Brenda Hale (2014), UK Court Rulings Show Move Away from European to Common Law, THE GUARDIAN, 15 August 2014

Jefferi Hamzah Sendut (2019), The Prorogation Case: Proportionality in All but Name?, UK CONSTITUTIONAL LAW ASSOCIATION BLOG (8 October 2019), available at: ukconstitutionallaw.org

Carol Harlow (1984), LAW AND ADMINISTRATION (London: Weidenfeld & Nicolson)

Carol Harlow (2002), Voices of Difference in a Plural Community, in CONVERGENCE AND DIVERGENCE IN EUROPEAN PUBLIC LAW 177 (Paul Beaumont, Carole Lyons and Neil Walker, eds.) (Oxford; Portland, OR: Hart)

Herbert Hart (1961), THE CONCEPT OF LAW (Oxford: Oxford University Press)

Herbert Hart (1983), ESSAYS IN JURISPRUDENCE AND PHILOSOPHY (Oxford; New York: Clarendon Press; Oxford University Press)

Maurice Hauriou (1930), PRÉCIS ÉLÉMENTAIRE DE DROIT CONSTITUTIONNEL (Paris: Sirey)

Tom Hickman (2010), PUBLIC LAW AFTER THE HUMAN RIGHTS ACT (Oxford: Hart)

Janet Hiebert (2006), Parliament and the Human Rights Act: Can the JCHR Help Facilitate a Culture of Rights?, 4 INTERNATIONAL JOURNAL OF CONSTITUTIONAL LAW 1

Ran Hirschl (2004), TOWARDS JURISTOCRACY: THE ORIGINS AND CONSEQUENCES OF THE NEW CONSTITUTIONALISM (Cambridge, MA; London: Harvard University Press)

Ran Hirschl (2005), The Question of Case Selection in Comparative Constitutional Law, 53 AMERICAN JOURNAL OF COMPARATIVE LAW 125

Leonard Hoffmann (1999), The Influence of the European Principle of Proportionality upon UK Law, in THE PRINCIPLE OF PROPORTIONALITY IN THE LAWS OF EUROPE 85 (Evelyn Elllis, ed.) (London: Bloomsbury Publishing)

Quintin Hogg, ed. (1989), HALSBURY'S LAWS OF ENGLAND (London: Butterworths)

Murray Hunt (1997), USING HUMAN RIGHTS LAW IN ENGLISH COURTS (Oxford: Hart)

Murray Hunt (1999), The Human Rights Act and Legal Culture: The Judiciary and the Legal Profession, 26 JOURNAL OF LAW AND SOCIETY 86

Murray Hunt (2003), Sovereignty's Blight: Why Contemporary Public Law Needs the Concept of 'Due Deference', in PUBLIC LAW IN A MULTI-LAYERED

Constitution 337 (Nicholas Bamforth and Peter Leyland, eds.) (Oxford; Portland, OR: Hart)

Murray Hunt (2009), Against Bifurcation, in A Simple Common Lawyer: Essays in Honour of Michael Taggart 108 (David Dyzenhaus, Murray Hunt and Grant Huscroft, eds.) (Oxford; Portland, OR: Hart)

Grant Huscroft, Bradley Miller and Grégoire Webber, eds. (2014), Proportionality and the Rule of Law: Rights, Justification, Reasoning (New York: Cambridge University Press)

Michael Ignatieff (2005), American Exceptionalism and Human Rights (Princeton, NJ: Princeton University Press)

Julia Iliopoulou-Stragga (1996), Ελληνικο Συνταγματικο Δικαιο και Ευρωπαϊκη Ενοποιηση [Greek Constitutional Law and European Integration] (Athens; Komotini: Αντ. Ν. Σάκκουλας)

Vicki Jackson (2015), Constitutional Law in an Age of Proportionality, 124 Yale Law Journal 3094

Vicki Jackson (2017), Proportionality and Equality, in Proportionality: New Frontiers, New Challenges 148 (Vicki Jackson and Mark Tushnet, eds.) (Cambridge; New York: Cambridge University Press)

Christophe Jamin (2015), Juger et motiver. Introduction comparative à la question du contrôle de proportionnalité en matière de droits fondamentaux, historique des travaux de la commission de réflexion sur la réforme de la cour de cassation, available at: www.courdecassation.fr/cour_cassation_1/reforme_cour_7109/introduction_comparative_31563.html

Christophe Jamin and Fabrice Melleray (2018), Droit civil et droit administratif. Dialogues sur un modèle doctrinal (Paris: Dalloz)

Emmanuel Jeuland (2016), Réforme de la Cour de cassation. Une approche non utilitariste du contrôle de proportionnalité, La Semaine Juridique, Numéro Spécial: Regards d'universitaires sur la réforme de la Cour de cassation (conférence-débat 24 novembre 2015) 20

Rudolf von Jhering (1985), In the Heaven for Legal Concepts: A Fantasy (Charlotte Levy, trans.), 58 Temple Law Quarterly 799

Olivier Jouanjan (2003), De la vocation de notre temps pour la science du droit: Modèles scientifiques et preuve de la validité des énoncés juridiques, XLI-128 Revue européenne des sciences sociales 129

Jeffrey Jowell (2000), Beyond the Rule of Law: Towards Constitutional Judicial Review, Public Law 671

Jeffrey Jowell (2003a), Judicial Deference and Human Rights: A Question of Competence, in Law and Administration in Europe: Essays in Honour of Carol Harlow 67 (Paul Craig and Richard Rawlings, eds.) (Oxford; New York: Oxford University Press)

Jeffrey Jowell (2003b), Judicial Deference: Servility, Civility or Institutional Capacity?, Public Law 592

Jeffrey Jowell (2015), Proportionality and Unreasonableness: Neither Merger nor Takeover, in The Scope and Intensity of Substantive Review 41 (Hanna Wilberg and Mark Elliott, eds.) (Oxford: Hart)

Jeffrey Jowell (2018), Proportionality in the United Kingdom, (Speech at the conférence-débat du Centre de Droit Public Comparé sur Le principe de proportionnalité, Centre Panthéon, 8 février 2018) Revue Générale du Droit, available at: www.revuegeneraledudroit.eu/?p=29678

Jeffrey Jowell and Anthony Lester (1988a), Beyond Wednesbury: Substantive Principles of Administrative Law, 14 Commonwealth Law Bulletin 858

Jeffrey Jowell and Anthony Lester (1988b), Proportionality: Neither Novel nor Dangerous, in New Directions in Judicial Review 51 (Jeffrey Jowell and Dawn Oliver, eds.) (London: Stevens)

Jean Kahn (1973), Note sous CE Ass., 26 October 1973, *Grassin*, Actualité Juridique Droit Administratif 586

Jean Kahn (1978), Le pouvoir discrétionnaire du juge administratif, in Le pouvoir discrétionnaire et le juge administratif 9 (Institut Français des Sciences Administratives, ed.) (Paris: Cujas)

Paul Kahn (1978), The Court, the Community and the Judicial Balance: The Jurisprudence of Justice Powell, 97 Yale Law Journal 9

Paul Kahn (2004), Comparative Constitutionalism in a New Key, 101 Michigan Law Review 2677

Otto Kahn-Freund (1974), On Uses and Misuses of Comparative Law, 37 Modern Law Review 1

Akritas Kaidatzis (2006), Παρατηρήσεις σχετικά με τις ΣτΕ (Ολ.) 1991/2005 και ΔΕΚ C-140/2003, 21.4.2005 *Επιτροπή Κατά Ελλάδας* [Comment on StE (Pl.) 1991/2005 and ECJ C-140/03, 21 April 2005, *Commission v Greece*], Το Συνταγμα 181

Akritas Kaidatzis (2010), Δικαστικός έλεγχος των μέτρων οικονομικής πολιτικής. Νομολογιακές τάσεις και προσαρμογές στο μεταβαλλόμενο οικονομικο-πολιτικό περιβάλλον [Judicial Review of Economic Policy Measures. Jurisprudential Tendencies and Adaptation to the Changing Economic-Political Context], Constitutionalism.gr Blog (10 June 2010), available at: www.constitutionalism.gr

Akritas Kaidatzis (2011), 'Μεγάλη πολιτική' και ασθενής δικαστικός έλεγχος. Ένα σχόλιο για τις στρατηγικές τήρησης του Συντάγματος στην εποχή του 'Μνημονίου' ['Big Policy' and Weak Judicial Review. A Comment on the Strategies for Observing the Constitution in the Age of the 'Memorandum'], Constitutionalism.gr Blog (21 March 2011), available at: www.constitutionalism.gr

Akritas Kaidatzis (2013), Ο έλεγχος της συνταγματικότητας των νόμων στην Ελλάδα, ενόψει της διάκρισης σε συστήματα ισχυρού και ασθενούς τύπου [Judicial Review of the Constitutionality of Legislation in Greece, in View of the Distinction between Strong and Weak Systems], CONSTITUTIONALISM.GR BLOG (9 April 2013), available at: www.constitutionalism.gr

Grégory Kalflèche (2009), Le contrôle de proportionnalité exercé par les juridictions administratives, 46 LES PETITES AFFICHES, NUMÉRO SPÉCIAL 46

Pavlos Kalligas (1842), Η ΕΞΑΝΤΛΗΣΙΣ ΤΩΝ ΚΟΜΜΑΤΩΝ, ΗΤΟΙ ΗΘΙΚΑ ΓΕΓΟΝΟΤΑ ΤΗΣ ΚΟΙΝΩΝΙΑΣ ΜΑΣ [THE EFFETENESS OF POLITICAL PARTIES, NAMELY MORAL ISSUES OF OUR SOCIETY] (Athens: Μελαχούρης – Καραμπίνης)

Ifigeneia Kamtsidou (2001), Η ΕΠΙΦΥΛΑΞΗ ΥΠΕΡ ΤΟΥ ΝΟΜΟΥ [THE CLAUSE OF LEGISLATIVE COMPETENCE] (Athens; Thessaloniki: Σάκκουλα)

Vassiliki Kapsali (2006), Η αρχή της αναλογικότητας στο γαλλικό δημόσιο δίκαιο [The Principle of Proportionality in French Public Law], IV ΔΙΚΑΙΩΜΑΤΑ ΤΟΥ ΑΝΘΡΩΠΟΥ 309

Maria Karamanof (2011), ΒΙΩΣΙΜΟ ΚΡΑΤΟΣ ΚΑΙ ΔΗΜΟΣΙΑ ΚΤΗΣΗ. ΤΑ ΟΡΙΑ ΤΩΝ ΙΔΙΩΤΙΚΟΠΟΙΗΣΕΩΝ [SUSTAINABLE STATE AND PUBLIC PROPERTY. THE LIMITS OF PRIVATIZATION] (Athens: Κυριακίδης Π.)

Alphonse Karr (1871), PLUS ÇA CHANGE ET PLUS C'EST LA MÊME CHOSE: NOTES DE VOYAGE (Nice: A. Gilletta)

Giorgos Kassimatis (1977), Παρατηρήσεις στην ΣτΕ (Ολ.) 58/1977 [Comment on StE (Pl.) 58/1977], ΤΟ ΣΥΝΤΑΓΜΑ 625

Giorgos Katrougkalos (2001), Νομική και πολιτική σημασία της αναθεώρησης του άρθρου 25 του Συντάγματος [Legal and Political Significance of the Amendment of Article 25 of the Constitution], 10 ΔΙΚΑΙΩΜΑΤΑ ΤΟΥ ΑΝΘΡΩΠΟΥ 457

Giorgos Katrougkalos (2006), Αρχή της αναλογικότητας και κοινωνικά δικαιώματα [The Principle of Proportionality and Social Rights], IV ΔΙΚΑΙΩΜΑΤΑ ΤΟΥ ΑΝΘΡΩΠΟΥ 141

Aileen Kavanagh (2009), CONSTITUTIONAL REVIEW UNDER THE UK HUMAN RIGHTS ACT (Cambridge: Cambridge University Press)

Aileen Kavanagh (2014), Proportionality and Parliamentary Debates: Exploring Some Forbidden Territory, 34 OXFORD JOURNAL OF LEGAL STUDIES 443

Helen Keller and Alec Stone Sweet (2008), Assessing the Impact of the ECHR on National Legal Orders, in A EUROPE OF RIGHTS: THE IMPACT OF THE ECHR ON NATIONAL LEGAL SYSTEMS 675 (Helen Keller and Alec Stone Sweet, eds.) (Oxford: Oxford University Press)

Helen Keller and Alec Stone Sweet, eds. (2008), A EUROPE OF RIGHTS: THE IMPACT OF THE ECHR ON NATIONAL LEGAL SYSTEMS (Oxford: Oxford University Press)

Duncan Kennedy (1995), American Constitutionalism as Civil Religion: Notes of an Atheist, 19 NOVA LAW REVIEW 908

Duncan Kennedy (2011), A Transnational Genealogy of Proportionality in Private Law, in THE FOUNDATIONS OF EUROPEAN PRIVATE LAW 185 (Roger Brownsword, Hans Micklitz, Leone Niglia and Stephen Weatherill, eds.) (Oxford; Portland, OR: Hart)

Madhav Khosla (2010), Proportionality: An Assault on Human Rights?: A Reply, 8 International Journal of Constitutional Law 298

Jeff King (2010), Proportionality: A Halfway House, New Zealand Law Review 327

Michael Kirby (1998), The Struggle for Simplicity: Lord Cooke and Fundamental Rights, 24 Commonwealth Law Bulletin 496

Matthias Klatt and Moritz Meister (2012a), The Constitutional Structure of Proportionality (Oxford: Oxford University Press)

Matthias Klatt and Moritz Meister (2012b), Proportionality – A Benefit to Human Rights? Remarks on the I·CON Controversy, 10 International Journal of Constitutional Law 687

Francesca Klug and Helen Wildbore (2010), Follow or Lead?: The Human Rights Act and the European Court of Human Rights, 6 European Human Rights Law Review 621

Jan Komárek (2013), Reasoning with Previous Decisions: Beyond the Doctrine of Precedence, 61 American Journal of Comparative Law 149

Donald Kommers (2012), The Constitutional Jurisprudence of the Federal Republic of Germany (Durham, NC: Duke University Press)

Dimitra Kontogiorga-Theocharopoulou (1989a), Η ΑΡΧΗ ΤΗΣ ΑΝΑΛΟΓΙΚΟΤΗΤΑΣ ΣΤΟ ΕΣΩΤΕΡΙΚΟ ΔΗΜΟΣΙΟ ΔΙΚΑΙΟ [The Principle of Proportionality in Domestic Public Law] (Thessaloniki: Σάκκουλα)

Dimitra Kontogiorga-Theocharopoulou (1989b), Σημεία εργασίας επί της αρχής της αναλογικότητος [Elements of Study on the Principle of Proportionality], in Συμμεικτα προσ τιμην Γεωργιου Μ. Παπαχατζη 889 (Athens: Σάκκουλα)

Christina Koumpli (2010), Un essai sur la clarification de l'inférence: État de droit – principe de proportionnalité, unpublished conference paper (Mexico, 8 December 2010)

Mordechai Kremnitzer, Talya Steiner and Andrej Lang, eds. (2020), Proportionality in Action: Comparative and Empirical Perspectives on the Judicial Practice (Cambridge: Cambridge University Press, 2020)

Evaggelos Kroustallakis (1999), Ελληνική πολιτική δικονομία και κοινοτικό δίκαιο: άμεσες και έμμεσες επιδράσεις [Greek Civil Procedure and Community Law: Direct and Indirect Influences], Δικαιοσυνη 1457

Martin Krygier (1986), Law as Tradition, 5 *Law and Philosophy* 237

Mattias Kumm (2004), Constitutional Rights as Principles: On the Structure and Domain of Constitutional Justice. A Review Essay on *A Theory of Constitutional Rights*, 2 International Journal of Constitutional Law 574

Mattias Kumm (2006a), What Do You Have in Virtue of Having a Constitutional Right? On the Place and Limits of the Proportionality Requirement, 46 New York University Public Law and Legal Theory Working Papers, available at: papers.ssrn.com/sol3/papers.cfm?abstract_id=952034

Mattias Kumm (2006b), Who Is Afraid of the Total Constitution? Constitutional Rights as Principles and the Constitutionalization of Private Law, 7 German Law Journal 341

Mattias Kumm (2007), Political Liberalism and the Structure of Rights: On the Place and Limits of the Proportionality Requirement, in Law, Rights and Discourse: The Legal Philosophy of Robert Alexy 131 (George Pavlakos, ed.) (Oxford: Hart)

Mattias Kumm (2009a), Democracy Is Not Enough: Rights, Proportionality and the Point of Judicial Review, 9–10 NYU School of Law, Public Law Research Paper, available at: papers.ssrn.com/abstract =1356793

Mattias Kumm (2009b), The Cosmopolitan Turn in Constitutionalism: On the Relationship between Constitutionalism in and beyond the State, in Ruling the World?: Constitutionalism, International Law, and Global Governance 258 (Jeffrey Dunoff and Joel Trachtman, eds.) (Cambridge; New York: Cambridge University Press)

Mattias Kumm (2010), The Idea of Socratic Contestation and the Right to Justification: The Point of Rights-Based Proportionality Review, 41 Law and Ethics of Human Rights 141

Mattias Kumm (2012), Alexy's Theory of Constitutional Rights and the Problem of Judicial Review, in Institutionalized Reason: The Jurisprudence of Robert Alexy 201 (Matthias Klatt, ed.) (Oxford; New York: Oxford University Press)

Mattias Kumm (2017), Is the Structure of Human Rights Practice Defensible? Three Puzzles and Their Resolution, in Proportionality: New Frontiers, New Challenges 30 (Vicki Jackson and Mark Tushnet, eds.) (Cambridge; New York: Cambridge University Press)

Mattias Kumm and Alec Walen (2014), Human Dignity and Proportionality: Deontic Pluralism in Balancing, in Proportionality and the Rule of Law: Rights, Justification, Reasoning 67 (Grant Huscroft, Bradley Miller and Grégoire Webber, eds.) (New York: Cambridge University Press)

Édouard Laferrière (1887), Traité de la juridiction administrative et des recours contentieux (Paris: Berger-Levrault et Cie)

Édouard Lambert (1921), Le gouvernement des juges et la lutte contre la législation sociale aux États-Unis: L'expérience américaine du contrôle judiciaire de la constitutionnalité des lois (Paris: Giard)

Elisabeth Lambert Abdelgawad and Anne Weber (2008), The Reception Process in France and Germany, in A Europe of Rights: The Impact of the ECHR on National Legal Systems 107 (Helen Keller and Alec Stone Sweet, eds.) (Oxford: Oxford University Press)

Mitchel Lasser (2004), Judicial Deliberations: A Comparative Analysis of Judicial Transparency and Legitimacy (Oxford; New York: Oxford University Press)

Mitchel Lasser (2009), Judicial Transformations: The Rights Revolution in the Courts of Europe (Oxford; New York: Oxford University Press)

Bruno Latour (2002), La fabrique du droit: Une ethnographie du Conseil d'État (Paris: La Découverte)

John Laws (1992), Is the High Court the Guardian of Fundamental Constitutional Rights?, 18 Commonwealth Law Bulletin 1385

John Laws (1995), Law and Democracy, Public Law 72

John Laws (1998), The Limitations of Human Rights, Public Law 254

Robert Leckey (2015), Bills of Rights in the Common Law (Cambridge: Cambridge University Press)

Pierre Legrand (1996), European Legal Systems Are Not Converging, 45 International and Comparative Law Quarterly 52

Pierre Legrand (1997), The Impossibility of Legal Transplants, 4 Maastricht Journal of European and Comparative Law 111

Pierre Legrand (2002), Public Law, Europeanisation and Convergence, in Convergence and Divergence in European Public Law 225 (Paul Beaumont, Carole Lyons and Neil Walker, eds.) (Oxford; Portland, OR: Hart)

Pierre Legrand (2003), The Same and the Different, in Comparative Legal Studies: Traditions and Transitions 240 (Pierre Legrand and Roderick Munday, eds.) (Cambridge; New York: Cambridge University Press)

Ian Leigh (2002), Taking Rights Proportionately: Judicial Review, the Human Rights Act and Strasbourg, Public Law 265

Jeanne Lemasurier (1974), Vers un nouveau principe général du droit? Le principe 'bilan-coût-avantages', in Mélanges offerts à Marcel Waline: Le juge et le droit public 551 (Paris: LGDJ)

Claude Lévi-Strauss (1955), The Structural Study of Myth, 68 Journal of American Folklore 428

Claude Lévi-Strauss (1966), The Savage Mind (Chicago, IL: University of Chicago Press)

Marceau Long, Prosper Weil, Guy Braibant, Pierre Delvolvé and Bruno Genevois (2019), Les grands arrêts de la jurisprudence administrative (22nd ed.) (Paris: Dalloz)

Martin Loughlin (2003), Constitutional Law: The Third Order of the Political, in Public Law in a Multi-Layered Constitution 27 (Nicholas Bamforth and Peter Leyland, eds.) (Oxford: Hart)

Martin Loughlin (2013), The British Constitution: A Very Short Introduction (Oxford: Oxford University Press)

Bertrand Louvel (2016), Réflexions à la Cour de cassation: Contribution à la refondation de la justice, La Semaine Juridique, Numéro Spécial: Regards d'universitaires sur la réforme de la Cour de cassation (conférence-débat 24 novembre 2015) 1

Jerry Machaw (1985), DUE PROCESS IN THE ADMINISTRATIVE STATE (New Haven, CO: Yale University Press)

Aristovoulos Manessis (1959), DEUX ÉTATS NÉS EN 1830: RESSEMBLANCES ET DISSEMBLANCES CONSTITUTIONNELLES ENTRE LA BELGIQUE ET LA GRÈCE (Brussels: Maison Ferdinand Larcier)

Aristovoulos Manessis (1978), ΣΥΝΤΑΓΜΑΤΙΚΑ ΔΙΚΑΙΩΜΑΤΑ [CONSTITUTIONAL RIGHTS] (Thessaloniki: Σάκκουλα)

Aristovoulos Manessis (1982), ΣΥΝΤΑΓΜΑΤΙΚΑ ΔΙΚΑΙΩΜΑΤΑ [CONSTITUTIONAL RIGHTS] (2nd ed.) (Thessaloniki: Σάκκουλα)

Aristovoulos Manessis (2007), Οι κύριες συνιστώσες του συστήματος θεμελιωδών δικαιωμάτων του Συντάγματος του 1975 [The Main Components of the Fundamental Rights System in the Constitution of 1975], in ΣΥΝΤΑΓΜΑΤΙΚΗ ΘΕΩΡΙΑ ΚΑΙ ΠΡΑΞΗ 529 (Athens: Σάκκουλα)

Antonis Manitakis (1988), Fondement et légitimité du contrôle juridictionnel des lois en Grèce, 40 REVUE INTERNATIONALE DE DROIT COMPARÉ 39

Antonis Manitakis (1990a), Η πολυσήμαντη επιστροφή του Κράτους Δικαίου [The Multifaceted Return of the Ideal of a State Ruled by Law], in ΌΨΕΙΣ ΤΟΥ ΚΡΑΤΟΥΣ ΔΙΚΑΙΟΥ 27 (Konstantinos Stamatis and Antonis Manitakis, eds.) (Thessaloniki: Σάκκουλα)

Antonis Manitakis (1990b), Πρόλογος [Preface], in ΌΨΕΙΣ ΤΟΥ ΚΡΑΤΟΥΣ ΔΙΚΑΙΟΥ 5 (Konstantinos Stamatis and Antonis Manitakis, eds.) (Thessaloniki: Σάκκουλα)

Antonis Manitakis (1994), ΚΡΑΤΟΣ ΔΙΚΑΙΟΥ ΚΑΙ ΔΙΚΑΣΤΙΚΟΣ ΕΛΕΓΧΟΣ ΤΗΣ ΣΥΝΤΑΓΜΑΤΙΚΟΤΗΤΑΣ [THE IDEAL OF A STATE RULED BY LAW AND JUDICIAL REVIEW OF CONSTITUTIONALITY] (Thessaloniki: Σάκκουλα)

Antonis Manitakis (1999), Ο δικαστής υπηρέτης του νόμου ή εγγυητής των συνταγματικών δικαιωμάτων και μεσολαβητής διαφορών [The Judge, Servant of the Law or Guarantor of Constitutional Rights and Mediator in Legal Disputes], 47 ΝΟΜΙΚΟ ΒΗΜΑ 177

Antonis Manitakis (2003), Ιστορικά γνωρίσματα και λογικά προαπαιτούμενα του δικαστικού ελέγχου της συνταγματικότητας των νόμων στην Ελλάδα [Historical Traits and Logical Assumptions of Judicial Review of the Constitutionality of Legislation in Greece], in ΤΙΜΗΤΙΚΟΣ ΤΟΜΟΣ ΤΟΥ Κ. ΜΠΕΗ 3121 (Athens: Αντ. Σάκκουλας)

Antonis Manitakis (2004), ΕΛΛΗΝΙΚΟ ΣΥΝΤΑΓΜΑΤΙΚΟ ΔΙΚΑΙΟ [GREEK CONSTITUTIONAL LAW] (Thessaloniki: Σάκκουλα)

Antonis Manitakis (2006), Οι (αυτο)δεσμεύσεις του δικαστή από τον παρεμπίπτοντα έλεγχο της (αντι)συνταγματικότητας των νόμων [Judicial (Self-)Restraint Resulting from the Incidental System of Judicial Review of the (Un)constitutionality of Legislation], ΤΟ ΣΥΝΤΑΓΜΑ 403

Antonis Manitakis (2007), Η αναγκαιότητα της αναθεώρησης μεταξύ πλειοψηφικού κοινοβουλευτισμού και αναθεωρητικής συναίνεσης [The Need for the Constitutional Reform, between Majoritarian Parliamentarism and Consensus], Το Σύνταγμα 3

Antonis Manitakis (2015a), Οι θεσμικές παρενέργειες της υπόθεσης του 'βασικού μετόχου' [The Institutional Side-Effects of the 'Major Shareholder Affair'], Το Σύνταγμα 783

Antonis Manitakis (2015b), Η προτεραιότητα εφαρμογής του κοινοτικού δικαίου έναντι του Συντάγματος, η εναρμονισμένη με το κοινοτικό δίκαιο ερμηνεία του Συντάγματος και η τεχνική της αναλογικότητας [The Primacy of Community Law over the Constitution, the Interpretation of the Constitution in Conformity with Community Law and the Technique of Proportionality], Εφημερίδα Δημοσίου Δικαίου 317

Kassiani Manolakoglou (2011), Η αρχή της αναλογικότητας ως τεχνική του δικαστικού ελέγχου πράξεων διακριτικής ευχέρειας της διοίκησης [The Principle of Proportionality as a Technique for the Judicial Scrutiny of Discretionary Administrative Acts], Constitutionalism.gr Blog (22 April 2011), available at: www.constitutionalism.gr

Panagiotis Mantzoufas (2004), Ασφάλεια και πρόληψη στην εποχή της διακινδύνευσης [Security and Prevention in the Age of Risk], in Τόμος τιμητικός του Συμβουλίου της Επικρατείας – 75 χρόνια 55 (Thessaloniki: Σάκκουλα)

Panagiotis Mantzoufas and Anastasios Pavlopoulos (2017), Η μεγάλη απόφαση για τις τηλεοπτικές άδειες και η μεγαλύτερη δοκιμασία της ερμηνείας του Συντάγματος [The Great Case on TV Licences and the Greater Challenge of Constitutional Interpretation], Συνήγορος 22

Afroditi Ioanna Marketou (2015), Economic Energy and the Loss of Faith in the Greek Constitution: How Does a Constitution Function When It Is Dying?, Cambridge Journal of International and Comparative Law 289

Afroditi Ioanna Marketou and Michail Dekastros (2015), Report on Greece, EUI Constitutional Change Through Euro-Crisis Law project Country report, available at: eurocrisislaw.eui.eu

Jean-Paul Markus (1999), Le contrôle de conventionnalité des lois par le Conseil d'État, Actualité Juridique Droit Administratif 99

Paul Martens (1992), L'irrésistible ascension du principe de proportionnalité, in Présence du droit Public et des droits de l'Homme: Mélanges offerts à Jacques Velu 49 (Brussels: Bruylant)

Antonio Marzal Yetano (2013), La dynamique du principe de proportionnalité: Essai dans le contexte des libertés de circulation du droit de l'union européenne (Clermont-Ferrand: Institut universitaire Varenne)

Jud Mathews and Alec Stone Sweet (2011), All Things in Proportion? American Rights Doctrine and the Problem of Balancing, 60 Emory Law Journal 799

Iakovos Mathioudakis (2011), Μετασχηματισμοί του ταμειακού συμφέροντος του δημοσίου σε περίοδο έντονης οικονομικής κρίσης [Transformations of the Cash

Interest of the State in a Period of Intense Economic Crisis], ΕΦΗΜΕΡΙΔΑ ΔΗΜΟΣΙΟΥ ΔΙΚΑΙΟΥ 478

Stefanos Matthias (2006), Το πεδίο λειτουργίας της αρχής της αναλογικότητας [The Scope of the Principle of Proportionality], 47 ΕΛΛΗΝΙΚΗ ΔΙΚΑΙΟΣΥΝΗ 1

Pierre Mazeaud (2006), Voeux du Président du Conseil constitutionnel au Président de la République (Speech at Palais de l'Elysée, 3 January 2006), 20 CAHIERS DU CONSEIL CONSTITUTIONNEL, available at: www.conseil-constitutionnel.fr/nouveaux-cahiers-du-conseil-constitutionnel/voeux-du-president-du-conseil-constitutionnel-m-pierre-mazeaud-au-president-de-la-republique

Pierre Mazeaud (2008), 2, rue de Montpensier: Un bilan, 25 CAHIERS DU CONSEIL CONSTITUTIONNEL, DOSSIER: 50ÈME ANNIVERSAIRE, available at: www.conseil-constitutionnel.fr/nouveaux-cahiers-du-conseil-constitutionnel/2-rue-de-montpensier-un-bilan

Jeremy McBride (1999), Proportionality and the European Convention on Human Rights, in THE PRINCIPLE OF PROPORTIONALITY IN THE LAWS OF EUROPE 23 (Evelyn Ellis, ed.) (Oxford; Portland, OR: Hart)

Ewan McGaughey (2019), Is There a 'Legal Measure' to Judge Parliament's Prorogation?, UK CONSTITUTIONAL LAW ASSOCIATION BLOG, available at: ukconstitutionallaw.org

David Mead (2012), Outcomes Aren't All: Defending Process-Based Review of Public Authority Decisions under the Human Rights Act, PUBLIC LAW 63

Guillaume Merland (2007), L'intérêt général dans la jurisprudence du Conseil constitutionnel, in L'INTÉRÊT GÉNÉRAL, NORME CONSTITUTIONNELLE (Bertrand Mathieu and Michel Verpeaux, eds.) (Paris: Dalloz), available at: www.conseil-constitutionnel.fr/sites/default/files/as/root/bank_mm/pdf/Conseil/merland.pdf

Achille Mestre (1934), Note sous CE, 19 mai 1933, *Benjamin*, RECUEIL SIREY 1

Jacques Meunier (1994), LES POUVOIRS DU CONSEIL CONSTITUTIONNEL. ESSAI D'ANALYSE STRATÉGIQUE (Paris; Brussels: LGDJ; Bruylant)

Frank Michelman (2017), Proportionality Outside the Courts with Special Reference to Popular and Political Constitutionalism, in PROPORTIONALITY: NEW FRONTIERS, NEW CHALLENGES 13 (Vicki Jackson and Mark Tushnet, eds.) (Cambridge; New York: Cambridge University Press)

Hans Micklitz (2005), THE POLITICS OF JUDICIAL CO-OPERATION IN THE EU: SUNDAY TRADING, EQUAL TREATMENT AND GOOD FAITH (Cambridge: Cambridge University Press)

Georgios Mitsopoulos (2002), 'Τριτενέργεια' και 'αναλογικότητα' ως διατάξεις του αναθεωρηθέντος Συντάγματος ['Third-Party Effect' and 'Proportionality' as Provisions of the Amended Constitution], 15 ΔΙΚΑΙΩΜΑΤΑ ΤΟΥ ΑΝΘΡΩΠΟΥ 641

Kai Möller (2007), Balancing and the Structure of Constitutional Rights, 5 INTERNATIONAL JOURNAL OF CONSTITUTIONAL LAW 453

Kai Möller (2012), The Global Model of Constitutional Rights (Oxford: Oxford University Press)

Kai Möller (2017), US Constitutional Law, Proportionality, and the Global Model, Proportionality: New Frontiers, New Challenges 103 (Vicki Jackson and Mark Tushnet, eds.) (Cambridge; New York: Cambridge University Press)

Montesquieu (1979), De l'esprit des lois (Paris: Flammarion)

Horatia Muir-Watt (2000), La fonction subversive du droit comparé, 52 Revue Internationale de Droit Comparé 503

Horatia Muir-Watt (2006), Globalization and Comparative Law, in The Oxford Handbook of Comparative Law 579 (Mathias Reimann and Reinhard Zimmermann, eds.) (Oxford: Oxford University Press)

Horatia Muir-Watt and Guillaume Tusseau (2016), Repenser le dévoilement de l'idéologie juridique: Une approche fictionnelle de la gouvernance globale, in Traité des rapports entre ordres juridiques 169 (Baptiste Bonnet, ed.) (Paris: LGDJ)

Petr Muzny (2008), Proportionnalité, in Dictionnaire des droits de l'Homme (Joël Andriantsimbazovina, Hélène Gaudin and Jean-Pierre Marguénaud, eds.) (Paris: Presses Universitaires de France)

Sarah Nason (2016), Reconstructing Judicial Review (Oxford Portland, OR: Hart)

Yossi Nehushtan (2017), The Non-Identical Twins in UK Public Law: Reasonableness and Proportionality, 50 Israel Law Review 69

David Nelken (1995), Disclosing/Invoking Legal Culture: An Introduction, Social and Legal Studies, Special issue on Legal culture, Diversity and Globalization 435

David Nelken (2003), Comparatists and Transferability, in Comparative Legal Studies: Traditions and Transitions 437 (Pierre Legrand and Roderick Munday, eds.) (Cambridge; New York: Cambridge University Press)

David Nelken (2007), Defining and Using the Concept of Legal Culture, in Comparative Law: A Handbook 109 (Esin Örücü and David Nelken, eds.) (Oxford; Portland, OR: Hart)

David Nelken (2012), Using Legal Culture: Purposes and Problems, in Using Legal Culture 1 (David Nelken, ed.) (London: Wildy, Simmonds & Hill)

David Neuberger (2012), Proportionate Costs (Fifteenth Lecture in the Implementation Programme, Law Society, 29 May 2012), available at: www.judiciary.uk/wp-content/uploads/JCO/Documents/Speeches/proportionate-costs-fifteenth-lecture-30052012.pdf

David Neuberger (2014), The Role of Judges in Human Rights Jurisprudence: A Comparison of the Australian and UK Experience (Speech at the Supreme Court of Victoria, Melbourne, 8 August 2014), available at: www.supremecourt.uk/docs/speech-140808.pdf

Dimitris Nikiforos (2012), Η αναλογικότητα ως διάμεσος της εθνικής και της ενωσιακής έννομης τάξης [Proportionality as an Intermediary between the Domestic and the EU Legal Order], CONSTITUTIONALISM.GR BLOG (17 September 2012), available at: www.constitutionalism.gr

Sarantis Orfanoudakis (2003), Η ΑΡΧΗ ΤΗΣ ΑΝΑΛΟΓΙΚΟΤΗΤΑΣ ΣΤΗΝ ΕΛΛΗΝΙΚΗ ΕΝΝΟΜΗ ΤΑΞΗ: ΑΠΟ ΤΗ ΝΟΜΟΛΟΓΙΑΚΗ ΕΦΑΡΜΟΓΗ ΤΗΣ ΣΤΗ ΣΥΝΤΑΓΜΑΤΙΚΗ ΤΗΣ ΚΑΘΙΕΡΩΣΗ [THE PRINCIPLE OF PROPORTIONALITY IN THE GREEK LEGAL ORDER: FROM ITS JUDICIAL APPLICATION TO ITS CONSTITUTIONAL CONSECRATION] (Thessaloniki: Σάκκουλα)

Sarantis Orfanoudakis and Vassiliki Kokota (2007), Η εφαρμογή της αρχής της αναλογικότητας στην ελληνική και την κοινοτική έννομη τάξη: συγκλίσεις και αποκλίσεις [The Application of the Principle of Proportionality in the Greek and the Community Legal Order: Convergences and Divergences], ΕΛΛΗΝΙΚΗ ΕΠΙΘΕΩΡΗΣΗ ΕΥΡΩΠΑΪΚΟΥ ΔΙΚΑΙΟΥ 691

David Pannick (1998), Principles of Interpretation of Convention Rights under the Human Rights Act and the Discretionary Area of Judgment, PUBLIC LAW 545

Lina Papadopoulou (2003), Η συνταγματική οικοδόμηση της Ευρώπης από τη σκοπιά του ελληνικού Συντάγματος [The Constitutional Construction of Europe from the Point of View of the Greek Constitution], in Η ΠΡΟΟΠΤΙΚΗ ΕΝΟΣ ΣΥΝΤΑΓΜΑΤΟΣ ΓΙΑ ΤΗΝ ΕΥΡΩΠΗ 147 (Lina Papadopoulou and Antonis Manitakis, eds.) (Athens: Σάκκουλα)

Manouela Papadopoulou (2006), Η κοινοτική αρχή της αναλογικότητας ενώπιον του εθνικού δικαστή [The EC Principle of Proportionality before National Judges], IV ΔΙΚΑΙΩΜΑΤΑ ΤΟΥ ΑΝΘΡΩΠΟΥ 279

Apostolos Papatolias (1999), ΣΥΝΤΑΓΜΑΤΙΚΕΣ ΕΠΙΧΕΙΡΗΜΑΤΟΛΟΓΙΕΣ ΓΙΑ ΤΗΝ ΣΥΝΤΑΓΜΑΤΙΚΗ ΑΝΑΘΕΩΡΗΣΗ [CONSTITUTIONAL ARGUMENTATION ON THE CONSTITUTIONAL REFORM] (Athens: Αντ. Ν. Σάκκουλας)

Petros Pararas (1976), Παρατηρήσεις υπο την ΣτΕ (Ολ.) 2952/1975 [Comment on StE (Pl.) 2952/1975], ΤΟ ΣΥΝΤΑΓΜΑ 347

Petros Pararas (2001), ΤΟ ΚΕΚΤΗΜΕΝΟ ΤΟΥ ΕΥΡΩΠΑΪΚΟΥ ΣΥΝΤΑΓΜΑΤΙΚΟΥ ΠΟΛΙΤΙΣΜΟΥ [THE ACQUIS OF THE EUROPEAN CONSTITUTIONAL CIVILISATION] (Athens: Αντ. Ν. Σάκκουλας)

Petros Pararas (2003), Το νέο Σύνταγμα [The New Constitution], ΤΟ ΒΗΜΑ, 19 January 2003

Petros Pararas (2011), ΣΥΝΤΑΓΜΑΤΙΚΟΣ ΠΟΛΙΤΙΣΜΟΣ ΚΑΙ ΔΙΚΑΙΩΜΑΤΑ ΤΟΥ ΑΝΘΡΩΠΟΥ [CONSTITUTIONAL CIVILISATION AND HUMAN RIGHTS] (Athens; Komotini: Αντ. Ν. Σάκκουλας)

Petros Pararas (2012a), Κριτικό σημείωμα – Recension X. Contiades (Ed.), Engineering Constitutional Change. A Comparative Perspective on Europe, Canada and the USA, 55 ΔΙΚΑΙΩΜΑΤΑ ΤΟΥ ΑΝΘΡΩΠΟΥ 895

Petros Pararas (2012b), Το Ευρωπαϊκό Δίκαιο των Δικαιωμάτων του Ανθρώπου [European Human Rights Law], 86 Δικαιωματα του Ανθρωπου 1131

Jean-Jacques Pardini (2001), Le juge constitutionnel et le 'fait' en Italie et en France (Aix-en-Provence: Presses Universitaires d'Aix-Marseille)

Prokopis Pavlopoulos (1988), Δικαστικός έλεγχος της συνταγματικότητας των νόμων ή δικαστικός έλεγχος της νομιμότητας του Συντάγματος; [Judicial Review of the Constitutionality of Legislation or Judicial Review of the Legality of the Constitution?], 36 Νομικο Βημα 13

Chaïm Perelman (1990), Droit, logique et épistémologie, in Éthique et Droit 619 (Brussels: Éditions de l'Université de Bruxelles)

Vlad Perju (2012), Proportionality and Freedom – An Essay on Method in Constitutional Law, 1 Global Constitutionalism 334

Vlad Perju (2017), Proportionality and Stare Decisis: Proposal for a New Structure, in Proportionality: New Frontiers, New Challenges 175 (Vicki Jackson and Mark Tushnet, eds.) (Cambridge; New York: Cambridge University Press)

Anne Peters (2009), The Merits of Global Constitutionalism, XVI Indiana Journal of Global Legal Studies 397

Niels Petersen (2017), Proportionality and Judicial Activism: Fundamental Rights Adjudication in Canada, Germany and South Africa (Cambridge; New York: Cambridge University Press)

Xavier Philippe (1990), Le contrôle de proportionnalité dans les jurisprudences constitutionnelle et administrative françaises (Paris: Économica)

Xavier Philippe, Ariane Vidal-Naquet, Aurélie Duffy-Meunier and Olivier Le Bot (2011), Les délibérations du Conseil constitutionnel – Année 1984, 32 Cahiers du Conseil constitutionnel, available at: www.conseil-constitutionnel.fr/nouveaux-cahiers-du-conseil-constitutionnel/les-deliberations-du-conseil-constitutionnel-annee-1984

Benedikt Pirker (2013), Proportionality Analysis and Models of Judicial Review: A Theoretical and Comparative Study (Groningen: Europa Law Pub)

Benoît Plessix (2016), Droit administratif général (Paris: LexisNexis)

Thomas Poole (2005), Of Headscarves and Heresies: The Denbigh High School Case and Public Authority Decision Making under the Human Rights Act, Public Law 685

Thomas Poole (2009), The Reformation of English Administrative Law, 68 Cambridge Law Journal 142

Thomas Poole and Sangeeta Shah (2009), The Impact of the Human Rights Act on the House of Lords, Public Law 347

Alain Pottage (2014), Law after Anthropology: Object and Technique in Roman Law, 31 Theory, Culture & Society 147

Walter Powell and Paul DiMaggio (1991), The Iron Cage Revisited: Institutional Isomorphism and Collective Rationality in Organizational Fields, in The New Institutionalism in Organizational Analysis 63 (Walter Powell and Paul DiMaggio, ed.) (Chicago, IL: University of Chicago Press)

Pierre-Henri Prélot (2013), L'actualité de l'arrêt *Benjamin*, Revue Française de Droit Administratif 1020

Evaggelia Prevedourou (1997), Η αρχή της αναλογικότητας στη νομολογία του ΔΕΚ [The Principle of Proportionality in the ECJ Case Law], Ελληνική Επιθεώρηση Ευρωπαϊκού Δικαίου 1, 297

Hilary Putnam (2002), The Collapse of the Fact/Value Dichotomy and Other Essays (Cambridge, MA; London: Harvard University Press)

Mads Qvortrup, ed. (2013), The British Constitution: Continuity and Change: A Festschrift for Vernon Bogdanor (Oxford: Hart)

Athanasios Raikos (1983), Παραδόσεις Συνταγματικού Δικαίου: Θεμελιώδη Δικαιώματα [Lectures in Constitutional Law: Fundamental Rights] (Athens: Σάκκουλα)

Athanasios Raikos (2008), Συνταγματικό Δίκαιο: Θεμελιώδη Δικαιώματα [Constitutional Law: Fundamental Rights] (3rd ed.) (Athens: Αντ. Ν. Σάκκουλας)

Adam Ramshaw (2019), The Case for Replicable Structured Full Proportionality Analysis in All Cases Concerning Fundamental Rights, 39 Legal Studies 120

Sofia Ranchordás and Boudewijn Willem Nicolaas de Waard, eds. (2015), The Judge and the Proportionate Use of Discretion: A Comparative Study (New York: Routledge)

Nikoleta Renesi (2005), Η αρχή της αναλογικότητας στη νομολογία του Ελεγκτικού Συνεδρίου [The Principle of Proportionality in the Case Law of the Court of Audit], 17 Διοικητική Δίκη 1401

Vincent Réveillère (2017), Le juge et le travail des concepts juridiques: Le cas de la citoyenneté de l'Union européenne (Clermont-Ferrand: Institut universitaire Varenne)

Stéphane Rials (1980), Le juge administratif français et la technique du standard (essai sur le traitement juridictionnel de l'idée de normalité) (Paris: LGDJ)

Annelise Riles (2005), A New Agenda for the Cultural Study of Law: Taking on the Technicalities, 53 Buffalo Law Review 973

Jean Rivero (1951), Apologie pour les 'faiseurs de systèmes', Recueil Dalloz 99

Jean Rivero (1981), Note sous décision no. 80–127 DC, Actualité Juridique Droit Administratif 275

Julian Rivers (2006), Proportionality and Variable Intensity of Review, 65 Cambridge Law Journal 174

Julian Rivers (2007), Proportionality, Discretion and the Second Law of Balancing, in LAW, RIGHTS AND DISCOURSE: THE LEGAL PHILOSOPHY OF ROBERT ALEXY 167 (George Pavlakos, ed.) (Oxford: Hart)

Julian Rivers (2014), The Presumption of Proportionality, 77 MODERN LAW REVIEW 409

Dominique Rousseau (1997), La démocratie continue, 96 LE DÉBAT 73

Dominique Rousseau (2001), DROIT DU CONTENTIEUX CONSTITUTIONNEL (6th ed.) (Paris: Montchrestien)

Dominique Rousseau (2010), DROIT DU CONTENTIEUX CONSTITUTIONNEL (9th ed.) (Paris: Montchrestien)

Dominique Rousseau (2016), DROIT DU CONTENTIEUX CONSTITUTIONNEL (11th ed.) (Paris: Montchrestien)

Rodolfo Sacco (1991), Legal Formants: A Dynamic Approach to Comparative Law, 39 AMERICAN JOURNAL OF COMPARATIVE LAW 1, 343

François Saint Bonnet (2007), L'intérêt général dans l'ancien droit constitutionnel, in L'INTÉRÊT GÉNÉRAL, NORME CONSTITUTIONNELLE (Bertrand Mathieu and Michel Verpeaux, eds.) (Paris: LGDJ), available at: www.conseil-constitutionnel.fr/sites/default/files/as/root/bank_mm/pdf/Conseil/saintbonnet.pdf

Nikolaos I. Saripolos (1851), ΠΡΑΓΜΑΤΕΙΑ ΤΟΥ ΣΥΝΤΑΓΜΑΤΙΚΟΥ ΔΙΚΑΙΟΥ [TREATISE OF CONSTITUTIONAL LAW] (Athens)

Jean-Marc Sauvé (2016), Le juge administratif, protecteur des libertés (Speech at the Colloque organisé pour les dix ans de l'Association française pour la recherche en droit administratif, Université d'Auvergne, 16 June 2016), available at: www.conseil-etat.fr/actualites/discours-et-interventions/le-juge-administratif-protecteur-des-libertes

Jean-Marc Sauvé (2017), Le principe de proportionnalité, protecteur des libertés (Speech at the Institut Portalis, Aix-en-Provence, 17 March 2017), available at: www.conseil-etat.fr/actualites/discours-et-interventions/le-principe-de-proportionnalite-protecteur-des-libertes

Leslie Scarman (1990), The Development of Administrative Law: Obstacles and Opportunities, PUBLIC LAW 490

Frederick Schauer (1992), A Comment on the Structure of Rights, 27 GEORGIA LAW REVIEW 415

Frederick Schauer (1994), Commensurability and Its Constitutional Consequences, 45 HASTINGS LAW JOURNAL 785

Frederick Schauer (2014), Proportionality and the Question of Weight, in PROPORTIONALITY AND THE RULE OF LAW: RIGHTS, JUSTIFICATION, REASONING 173 (Grant Huscroft, Bradley Miller and Grégoire Webber, eds.) (New York: Cambridge University Press)

Pierre Schlag (2002), The Aesthetics of American Law, 115 HARVARD LAW REVIEW 1047

Bernhard Schlink (2012), Proportionality, in The Oxford Handbook of Comparative Constitutional Law 718 (Michel Rosenfeld and András Sajó, eds.) (Oxford: Oxford University Press)

David Schneiderman (2015), Proportionality and Constitutional Culture, 13 International Journal of Constitutional Law 769

Jürgen Schwarze (1992), European Administrative Law (Luxembourg; London: Office for Official Publications of the European Communities; Sweet & Maxwell)

Stephen Sedley (1995), Human Rights: A Twenty-First Century Agenda, Public Law 386

Stephen Sedley (2005), The Rocks or the Open Sea: Where Is the Human Rights Act Heading?, 32 Journal of Law and Society 3

Stephen Sedley (2011), The Sound of Silence, in Ashes and Sparks 64 (Cambridge: Cambridge University Press)

Jean-Baptiste Seube (2009), Le contrôle de proportionnalité exercé par le juge judiciaire: Présentation générale, 46 Les Petites Affiches, Numéro Spécial 86

Konstantinos Simantiras (1990), Γενικεσ αρχεσ αστικου δικαιου [General Principles of Civil Law] (4th ed.) (Athens: Αντ. Σάκκουλας)

Jean Sirinelli and Brunessen Bertrand (2010), La proportionnalité, in L'influence du droit européen sur les catégories du droit public 623 (Jean-Bernard Auby, ed.) (Paris: Dalloz)

Quentin Skinner (2002), Visions of Politics (Cambridge: Cambridge University Press)

Vassilios Skouris (1987), Η συνταγματική αρχή της αναλογικότητας και οι νομοθετικοί περιορισμοί της επαγγελματικής ελευθερίας [The Constitutional Principle of Proportionality and Legislative Restrictions on Professional Freedom], 28 Ελληνικη Δικαιοσυνη 773

Vassilios Skouris (2001), Συνολική αποτίμηση του αναθεωρητικού εγχειρήματος [Overall Evaluation of the Reform], in Το νεο Συνταγμα 457 (Dimitrios Tsatsos, Evaggelos Venizelos and Xenophon Contiades, eds.) (Athens; Komotini: Αντ. Ν. Σάκκουλας)

Giorgos Sotirelis (2000), Συνταγμα και δημοκρατια στην εποχη της παγκοσμιοποιησησ [Constitution and Democracy in the Age of Globalization] (Athens: Αντ. Ν. Σάκκουλας)

Epaminondas Spiliotopoulos (2004), Droit administratif hellénique (2nd ed.) (Athens; Brussels: Sakkoula; Bruylant)

Veena Srirangam (2016), A Difference in Kind – Proportionality and Wednesbury, 4 Institute of Advanced Legal Studies Student Law Review 46

Michail Stassinopoulos (1951), Δικαιον των διοικητικων πραξεων [Law of Administrative Acts] (unpublished monograph)

Alec Stone Sweet (1992), The Birth of Judicial Politics in France: The Constitutional Council in Comparative Perspective (New York: Oxford University Press)

Alec Stone Sweet and Jud Mathews (2008), Proportionality Balancing and Global Constitutionalism, 47 Columbia Journal of Transnational Law 73

Kostas Stratilatis (2001), Η συγκεκριμένη στάθμιση των συνταγματικών αξιών κατά τη δικαστική ερμηνεία του συντάγματος [The Concrete Balancing of Constitutional Values in the Judicial Interpretation of the Constitution], To Συνταγμα 495

Frédéric Sudre (2015), La Convention européenne des droits de l'Homme (10th ed.) (Paris: Presses Universitaires de France)

Frédéric Sudre (2019), Droit européen et international des droits de l'Homme (14th ed.) (Paris: Presses Universitaires de France)

Thomas Sullivan and Richard Frase (2009), Proportionality Principles in American Law: Controlling Excessive Government Actions (Oxford; New York: Oxford University Press)

Anastasios Tachos (1984), Παρατηρήσεις στην ΣτΕ 2112/1984 [Comment on StE 2112/1984], Αρμενοπουλος 907

Michael Taggart (2003), Reinventing Administrative Law, in Public Law in a Multi-Layered Constitution 251 (Nicholas Bamforth and Peter Leyland, eds.) (Oxford; Portland, OR: Hart)

Michael Taggart (2008), Proportionality, Deference, Wednesbury, New Zealand Law Review 423

Ioannis Tassopoulos (2001), Η συνταγματική θέση της δικαιοσύνης στο πολιτικό μας σύστημα [The Constitutional Role of Justice in Our Political System], in To νεο Συνταγμα 357 (Dimitrios Tsatsos, Evaggelos Venizelos and Xenophon Contiades, eds.) (Athens; Komotini: Αντ. Ν. Σάκκουλας)

Graham Taylor (1976), Judicial Review of Improper Purposes and Irrelevant Considerations, 35 Cambridge Law Journal 272

Francis Teitgen (1985), Le principe de proportionnalité en droit français, in Der Grundsatz der Verhältnismäßigkeit in europäischen Rechtsordnungen 53 (Hans Kutscher, Georg Ress and Francis Teitgen, eds.) (Heidelberg: Müller)

Gunther Teubner (1991/1992), The Two Faces of Janus: Rethinking Legal Pluralism, 13 Cardozo Law Review 1443

Gunther Teubner (1997), *Altera Pars Audiatur*: Law in the Collision of Discourses, in Law, Society and Economy 149 (Richard Rawlings, ed.) (Oxford; New York: Oxford University Press)

Gunther Teubner (1998), Legal Irritants: Good Faith in British Law or How Unifying Law Ends Up in New Differences, 61 Modern Law Review 11

Yan Thomas (1973), La langue du droit romain. Problèmes et méthodes, 18 Archives de Philosophie du Droit 103

Giorgos Triantafyllou (1990), Η αρχή της αναλογικότητας στην ποινική δίκη [The Principle of Proportionality in the Criminal Process], 31 Ελληνικη Δικαιοσυνη 301

Takis Tridimas (1999), The General Principles of EC Law (Oxford; New York: Oxford University Press)

Michel Troper (1973), La séparation des pouvoirs et l'histoire constitutionnelle française (Paris: LGDJ)

Michel Troper (1994), Pour une théorie juridique de l'État (Paris: Presses Universitaires de France)

Stavros Tsakyrakis (2008), Proportionality: An Assault on Human Rights?, 9 New York School Jean Monnet Working Paper Series, available at: jeanmonnetprogram.org/paper/proportionality-an-assault-on-human-rights-2/

Dimitrios Tsatsos (1988), Συνταγματικο Δικαιο: Θεμελιωδη Δικαιωματα [Constitutional Law: Fundamental Rights] (2nd ed.) (Athens: Αντ. Ν. Σάκκουλας)

Dimitrios Tsatsos (1994), Συνταγματικο Δικαιο: Θεωρητικο Θεμελιο [Constitutional Law: Fundamental Rights: Theoretical Underpinnings] (4th ed.) (Athens: Αντ. Ν. Σάκκουλας)

Colin Turpin (1999), British Government and the Constitution: Text, Cases and Material (4th ed.) (Cambridge: Cambridge University Press)

Dominique Turpin (1985), Le traitement des antinomies des droits de l'Homme par le Conseil constitutionnel, Droits 85

Mark Tushnet, Making Easy Cases Harder, in Proportionality: New Frontiers, New Challenges 303 (Vicki Jackson and Mark Tushnet, eds.) (Cambridge; New York: Cambridge University Press)

Guillaume Tusseau (2013), A Plea for a Hint of Empiricism in Constitutional Theory: A Comment on Cesare Pinelli's Constitutional Reasoning and Political Deliberation, 14 German Law Journal 1183

Francisco Javier Urbina Molfino (2017), A Critique of Proportionality and Balancing (Cambridge; New York: Cambridge University Press)

Pieter Van Dijk and Yutaka Arai (2006), Theory and Practice of the European Convention on Human Rights (4th ed.) (Antwerp: Intersentia)

Sébastien Van Drooghenbroeck (2001), La proportionnalité dans le droit de la Convention européenne des droits de l'Homme: Prendre l'idée simple au sérieux (Brussels: Publications Fac St Louis)

Mark Van Hoecke (2004), Deep Level Comparative Law, in Epistemology and Methodology of Comparative Law 165 (Mark van Hoecke, ed.) (Oxford: Hart)

Giorgos Vassilakakis (2008), Η αρχή της αναλογικότητας. Ο αναιρετικός έλεγχος της εφαρμογής της από τον Άρειο Πάγο επί χρηματικής ικανοποιήσεως λόγω ηθικής βλάβης [The Principle of Proportionality. The Review of Its Application in Cassation by Areios Pagos in the Field of Compensation for Moral Damages], 50 Νομικα Χρονικα, available at: www.nomikaxronika.gr/article.aspx?issue=50

Georges Vedel (1960), Note sous CE, 12 février 1960, *Société Eky*, II Juris-Classeur périodique 11629

Georges Vedel (1986), Les bases constitutionnelles du droit administratif (Paris: Economica)

Georges Vedel (1988), Le Conseil constitutionnel, gardien du droit positif ou défenseur de la transcendance des droits de l'homme? 45 Pouvoirs 149

Georges Vedel (1992), Réflexions sur quelques apports de la jurisprudence du Conseil d'État à la jurisprudence du Conseil constitutionnel, in Mélanges René Chapus 647 (Paris: LGDJ; Lextenso)

Georges Vedel (1995), Réflexions sur les singularités de la procédure devant le Conseil constitutionnel, in Nouveaux juges, nouveaux pouvoirs?: Mélanges en l'honneur de Roger Perrot 537 (Paris: Dalloz)

Georges Vedel (1996), Introduction, in L'unité du droit: Mélanges en hommage à Roland Drago 1 (Paris: Economica)

Georges Vedel (1996/1997), Excès de pouvoir législatif et excès de pouvoir administratif, 1–2 Cahiers du Conseil constitutionnel, available at: www.conseil-constitutionnel.fr/nouveaux-cahiers-du-conseil-constitutionnel/exces-de-pouvoir-legislatif-et-exces-de-pouvoir-administratif

Georges Vedel and Pierre Delvolvé (1973), Droit administratif (5th ed.) (Paris: Presses Universitaires de France)

Phédon Vegleris (1967), La Constitution, la loi et les tribunaux en Grèce, in Annales de la faculté de droit de Liège 437 (Liège: Faculté de droit)

Phédon Vegleris (1977), Η Συμβαση των Δικαιωματων του Ανθρωπου και το Συνταγμα [The European Convention on Human Rights and the Constitution] (Athens: Σάκκουλας)

Phédon Vegleris (1981), Τα όρια του ελέγχου της συνταγματικότητας [The Limits of Constitutional Review], Το Συνταγμα 455

Giorgos Vellis (1999), Η προσωπική κράτηση μετά το Ν. 2462/1997 [Personal Detention after Law no. 2462/1997], 40 ΕλληνικΗ ΔικαιοσΥνη 9

Evaggelos Venizelos (1983), Η θέση του ΣτΕ στο σύστημα δικαστικού ελέγχου της συνταγματικότητας των νόμων [The Role of the Council of State in the System of Judicial Review of the Constitutionality of Legislation], 6 Δικαιο και Πολιτικη 9

Evaggelos Venizelos (1990), Το γενικο συμφερον και οι περιορισμοι των συνταγματικων δικαιωματων [The General Interest and Limitations on Constitutional Rights] (Thessaloniki: Παρατηρητής)

Evaggelos Venizelos (2000), Το σχεδιο της αναθεωρησης του Συνταγματος [The Draft of the Constitutional Amendment] (Athens: Αντ. Ν. Σάκκουλας)

Evaggelos Venizelos (2002), Το αναθεωρητικο κεκτημενο. Το συνταγματικο φαινομενο στον 21° αιωνα και η εισφορα της αναθεωρησης του 2001 [The Acquis of the Constitutional Amendment. The Constitutional Phenomenon in the 21st Century and the Contribution of the 2001 Amendment] (Athens: Αντ. Ν. Σάκκουλας)

Evaggelos Venizelos (2004a), Η νομικοπολιτική σημασία της αναθεώρησης του Συντάγματος [The Legal-Political Significance of the Constitutional Reform]

(Speech during the last session of the 7th Constitutional Amendment Parliament, Hellenic Parliament, 6 April 2004), available at: www.evenizelos.gr/parliament/constitutionalreview2001/694-2009-04-18-18-39-52.html

Evaggelos Venizelos (2004b), Οι εγγυήσεις πολυφωνίας και διαφάνειας στα ΜΜΕ κατά το άρθρο 14 παρ. 9. Οι κανόνες ερμηνείας του Συντάγματος και οι σχέσεις Συντάγματος – Κοινοτικού Δικαίου [The Guarantees of Media Pluralism and Transparency according to Article 14 par. 9. The Rules for Constitutional Interpretation and the Relations between the Constitution and Community Law], 53 Νομικο Βημα 425

Evaggelos Venizelos (2006), Η σχέση Συντάγματος και Ευρωπαϊκής Ολοκλήρωσης [The Relationship between the Constitution and European Integration] (Speech before the Committee for the Constitutional Amendment presented at the Discussion on the amendment of article 28 of the Constitution, Hellenic Parliament, 25 October 2006), available at: www.evenizelos.gr/parliament/constitutionalreview2008/220-2009-03-25-21-53-15.html

Evaggelos Venizelos (2008), Ερμηνευτικός σχετικισμός, δικονομικοί καταναγκασμοί, δογματικές αντιφάσεις και πολιτικά διλήμματα στη νομολογία του Συμβουλίου της Επικρατείας για τις σχέσεις εθνικού Συντάγματος και Ευρωπαϊκού Κοινοτικού δικαίου [Hermeneutic Relativism, Procedural Constraints, Doctrinal Inconsistencies and Political Dilemmas in the Council of State Case Law on the Relationship between the National Constitution and European Community Law], Εφημεριδα Δημοσιου Δικαιου 85

Vincent Vigneau (2017), Libres propos d'un juge sur le contrôle de proportionnalité, Recueil Dalloz 123

Vassilios Voutsakis (1990), Η αρχή της αναλογικότητας: από την ερμηνεία στη διάπλαση του δικαίου [The Principle of Proportionality: From Legal Interpretation to Legal Formation], in Όψεις του Κρατους Δικαιου 205 (Konstantinos Stamatis and Antonis Manitakis, eds.) (Thessaloniki: Σάκκουλα)

Vassilios Voutsakis (2002), Η αρχή του Κράτους Δικαίου και οι νέες διατάξεις περί ατομικών και κοινωνικών δικαιωμάτων [The Principle of a State Ruled by Law and the New Provisions on Individual and Social Rights], 50 Νομικο Βημα 7

Michail Vrontakis (2011), Ο δικαστής ως κριτής σταθμίσεων, αξιών και επιλογών του νομοθέτη κατά την πρόκριση των προς θέσπιση ρυθμίσεων [The Judge as a Reviewer of Legislative Weighing, Values and Choices in Legal Norm-Production] (Speech at the Aristoteleio University of Thessaloniki, 28 February 2011), available at: www.constitutionalism.gr/2099-o-dikastis-ws-kritis-statmisewn-axiwn-kai-epilogwn/

Patrick Wachsmann (2007), Des chameaux et des moustiques. Réflexions critiques sur le Conseil constitutionnel, in Billet d'humeur en l'honneur de Danièle Lochak 279 (Véronique Champeil-Desplats and Nathalie Ferré, eds.) (Paris: LGDJ)

William Wade (1955), The Basis of Legal Sovereignty, 13 CAMBRIDGE LAW JOURNAL 172

William Wade (1966), Sovereignty - Revolution or Evolution?, 112 LAW QUARTERLY REVIEW 568

William Wade and Christopher Forsyth (1961), ADMINISTRATIVE LAW (1st ed.) (Oxford; New York: Clarendon Press; Oxford University Press)

William Wade and Christopher Forsyth (1982), ADMINISTRATIVE LAW (5th ed.) (Oxford; New York: Clarendon Press; Oxford University Press)

William Wade and Christopher Forsyth (1988), ADMINISTRATIVE LAW (6th ed.) (Oxford; New York: Clarendon Press; Oxford University Press)

William Wade and Christopher Forsyth (2004), ADMINISTRATIVE LAW (9th ed.) (Oxford; New York: Clarendon Press; Oxford University Press)

Jeremy Waldron (1994), Fake Incommensurability. A Response to Professor Schauer, 45 HASTINGS LAW JOURNAL 813

Jeremy Waldron (2005/2006), The Core of the Case against Judicial Review, 115 YALE LAW JOURNAL 1346

Marcel Waline (1972), Note sous CE Ass., 28 mai 1971, *Ville Nouvelle Est*, REVUE DU DROIT PUBLIC 454

Jean Waline (1974), Le rôle du juge administratif dans la détermination de l'utilité publique justifiant l'expropriation, in MÉLANGES OFFERTS À MARCEL WALINE: LE JUGE ET LE DROIT PUBLIC 811 (Paris: LGDJ)

Neil Walker (2002), Culture, Democracy and the Convergence of Public Law: Some Scepticisms about Scepticism, in CONVERGENCE AND DIVERGENCE IN EUROPEAN PUBLIC LAW 257 (Paul Beaumont, Carole Lyons and Neil Walker, eds.) (Oxford; Portland, OR: Hart)

Mark Walters (2012), Dicey on Writing the Law of the Constitution, 32 OXFORD JOURNAL OF LEGAL STUDIES 21

Ian Ward (1995), Identity and Difference: The European Union and Postmodernism, in NEW LEGAL DYNAMICS OF EUROPEAN UNION 15 (Jo Shaw and Gillian More, eds.) (New York: Clarendon Press)

Jean-Luc Warsmann (2008), La qualité et la simplification du droit. Report to the president of the republic, December 2008, available at: www.marche-public.fr/contrats-publics/Rapport-warsmann-simplification-PME.pdf

Alan Watson (1974), LEGAL TRANSPLANTS: AN APPROACH TO COMPARATIVE LAW (2nd ed.) (Athens, GA: University of Georgia Press)

Grégoire Webber (2009), THE NEGOTIABLE CONSTITUTION: ON THE LIMITATION OF RIGHTS (Cambridge; New York: Cambridge University Press)

Grégoire Webber (2017), Proportionality and Absolute Rights, in PROPORTIONALITY: NEW FRONTIERS, NEW CHALLENGES 51 (Vicki Jackson and Mark Tushnet, eds.) (Cambridge; New York: Cambridge University Press)

Joseph Weiler (2012), Deciphering the Political and Legal DNA of European Integration, in PHILOSOPHICAL FOUNDATIONS OF EUROPEAN UNION LAW 137 (Julie Dickson and Pavlos Eleftheriadis, eds.) (Oxford: Oxford University Press)

James Whitman (2003), The Neo-Romantic Turn, in COMPARATIVE LEGAL STUDIES: TRADITIONS AND TRANSITIONS 312 (Pierre Legrand and Roderick Munday, eds.) (Cambridge; New York: Cambridge University Press)

Garreth Wong (2000), Towards the Nutcracker Principle, Reconsidering the Objections to Proportionality, PUBLIC LAW 92

Harry Woolf (1995), Droit Public – English Style, PUBLIC LAW 57

Georges Xynopoulos (1993), LE CONTRÔLE DE PROPORTIONNALITÉ DANS LE CONTENTIEUX DE LA CONSTITUTIONNALITÉ ET DE LA LÉGALITÉ EN FRANCE, EN ALLEMAGNE ET EN ANGLETERRE (Paris: LGDJ)

Georges Xynopoulos (1998), Réflexions sur le contrôle de proportionnalité en Europe continentale et en Grèce, in ÉTAT-LOI-ADMINISTRATION. MÉLANGES EN L'HONNEUR DE EPAMINONDAS SPILIOTOPOULOS 461 (Petros Pararas, ed.) (Athens; Brussels: Ant. N. Sakkoulas; Bruylant)

Constantinos Yannakopoulos (2002), Ο αυτεπάγγελτος έλεγχος (αντι) συνταγματικότητας των νόμων [The Ex Officio Judicial Review of the (Un) constitutionality of Legislation], 16 ΔΙΚΑΙΩΜΑΤΑ ΤΟΥ ΑΝΘΡΩΠΟΥ 1175

Constantinos Yannakopoulos (2004), Τα δικαιώματα στη νομολογία του Συμβουλίου της Επικρατείας [Rights in the Council of State Case Law], in ΤΑ ΔΙΚΑΙΩΜΑΤΑ ΣΤΗΝ ΕΛΛΑΔΑ 1953–2003 439 (Michalis Tsapogas and Dimitris Christopoulos, eds.) (Athens: Καστανιώτης)

Constantinos Yannakopoulos (2008), Μεταξύ συνταγματικών σκοπών και συνταγματικών ορίων: η διαλεκτική εξέλιξη της συνταγματικής πραγματικότητας στην εθνική και στην κοινοτική έννομη τάξη [Between Constitutional Goals and Constitutional Limits: The Dialectical Evolution of Constitutional Reality in the National and the Community Legal Orders], ΕΦΗΜΕΡΙΔΑ ΔΗΜΟΣΙΟΥ ΔΙΚΑΙΟΥ 733

Constantinos Yannakopoulos (2011), Μεταξύ εθνικής και ενωσιακής έννομης τάξης: το 'Μνημόνιο' ως αναπαραγωγή της κρίσης του κράτους δικαίου [Between National and EU Legal Order: The 'Memorandum' Reverberating the Crisis in the Ideal of a State Ruled by Law], CONSTITUTIONALISM.GR BLOG (30 January 2011), available at: www.constitutionalism.gr

Constantinos Yannakopoulos (2012), Η μετάλλαξη του υποκειμένου των συνταγματικών δικαιωμάτων [The Transformation of the Subject of Constitutional Rights], ΕΦΗΜΕΡΙΔΑ ΔΗΜΟΣΙΟΥ ΔΙΚΑΙΟΥ 146

Constantinos Yannakopoulos (2013), Η ΕΠΙΔΡΑΣΗ ΤΟΥ ΔΙΚΑΙΟΥ ΤΗΣ ΕΥΡΩΠΑΪΚΗΣ ΕΝΩΣΗΣ ΣΤΟΝ ΔΙΚΑΣΤΙΚΟ ΕΛΕΓΧΟ ΤΗΣ ΣΥΝΤΑΓΜΑΤΙΚΟΤΗΤΑΣ ΤΩΝ ΝΟΜΩΝ [THE INFLUENCE OF EU LAW ON JUDICIAL REVIEW OF THE CONSTITUTIONALITY OF LEGISLATION] (Athens; Thessaloniki: Σάκκουλα)

Constantinos Yannakopoulos (2015), Το ελληνικό Σύνταγμα και η επιφύλαξη του εφικτού της προστασίας των κοινωνικών δικαιωμάτων [The Greek Constitution and the Feasibility Clause of Social Rights Protection], ΕΦΗΜΕΡΙΔΑ ΔΗΜΟΣΙΟΥ ΔΙΚΑΙΟΥ 417

David Yardley (1970), The Abuse of Powers and Its Control in English Administrative Law, 18 AMERICAN JOURNAL OF COMPARATIVE LAW 565

Frédéric Zenati-Castaing (2016), La juridictionnalisation de la Cour de cassation, REVUE TRIMESTRIELLE DE DROIT CIVIL 511

Jacques Ziller (1996), Le principe de proportionnalité, ACTUALITÉ JURIDIQUE DROIT ADMINISTRATIF, NUMÉRO SPÉCIAL 185

Konrad Zweigert and Hein Kötz (1977), AN INTRODUCTION TO COMPARATIVE LAW (Amsterdam; New York: North-Holland Publishing)

INDEX

acculturation, 223, 239, 241, 252, 261, 271–2, 283, 284, 294, 295, 298, 355
administrativisation or administratization,165–73, 233, 260, 364, 365
aesthetics, 165, 246, 253, 318, 319, 353, 356, 358, 365, 367
Alexy, Robert, 1, 3, 4, 6, 9, 17, 37, 40, 77, 97, 134, 207
analytical tradition
  analytical formalism, 190, 191, 199, 214, 218, 221, 255, 260, 262, 272, 277–83, 297, 300, 305, 328, 337, 357, 362
  analytical rigour, 193, 209, 353
  economy of the common law, 190, 221, 255
  instrumentalism, 104, 193, 290, 294, 303, 367
  law's authority, 280–2
  pragmatism, 104, 149, 181, 191, 198, 202, 211, 222, 269, 297, 301, 306, 318, 357–9, 367, 368
  ultra vires, 80, 84, 154, 191, 195
anthropology, 2, 30, 32, 363
anxious scrutiny, 86, 91, 200–1, 202, 203, 205, 206, 207, 213, 282–3
assisted suicide, 97, 220, 221

Babas (French Council of State), 273, 274, 284, 285, 287
balance of convenience, 279
balancing
  as a ritual, 152, 233, 256, 296, 362
  as policy-making, 24, 192, 233
  as reconciliation, 49, 55, 68, 70, 109, 115, 151, 233, 255
  definitional v. *ad hoc*, 40
  pervasiveness of, 12
  the Law of, 39
Bank Mellat (UK Supreme Court), 96
Belgacem (French Council of State), 273, 274, 285, 287
Benjamin (French Council of State), 46, 154, 155, 156
bilan coût-avantages, 47, 48, 54, 61, 71, 154–163, 174, 191, 192, 276, 360
binding arrangements, 22, 23, 164, 219, 223, 227–36, 257, 359, 362
Braibant, Guy, 47, 49, 50, 133, 156, 158, 159, 160, 161, 173
Brind (UK House of Lords), 82, 85, 87, 193, 218
Bromley (UK House of Lords), 191, 192, 221
Bugdaycay (UK House of Lords), 86, 200, 202
Burqa affair, 181–185, 290, 330–333

Canada, 3, 5, 11, 25, 316
categorical reasoning, 6, 7, 11, 18, 40, 62, 96, 102, 134, 231
coherence
  aesthetic, 246, 252, 261, 322, 358, 368
  consistency, 53, 72, 74, 157, 193, 275, 277, 297, 306, 319
  continuity, 210
common law. *See* analytical tradition
  v. civil law, 20, 23, 267
common law constitutionalism. *See* constitutionalisation
Commonwealth, 87–9, 316

comparative law, 1, 2, 5, 10, 13, 16, 19, 21, 23, 28, 32, 42, 61, 152, 261, 263, 267, 268, 363, 369
as a formant, 226
Conseil supérieur de l'audiovisuel (French Constitutional Council), 58, 59, 164
consequentialism, 134, 327
consequentialist legal reasoning, 281, 352, 353, 359
constitutionalisation, 2
bases constitutionnelles, 151
diffusion of the Constitution, 231
rise of common law constitutionalism, 187, 200–1, 202, 260, 364
contextualism, 215, 218, 219, 220, 222, 344
Contiades, Xenophon, 124, 125, 225, 326
continental public law, 195
contrôle v. *principe de proportionnalité*, 54
Costa, Jean-Paul, 52
criminal law, 57, 58, 59, 68, 107, 121, 124, 151, 274
cultural baggage, 134, 209–11, 260, 366
cultural change, local patterns of
administrativisation of constitutional law (France), 165–73
constitutionalisation of the common law (England), 364
importation of a constitutional civilisation (Greece), 223, 236–40
culture. *See* legal culture

Dagtoglou, Prodromos, 230
Daly (UK House of Lords), 89, 90, 91, 101, 213, 216, 292
DDHC, 56, 57, 58, 59, 62, 145, 149, 150, 171, 276, 356
de Freitas (Privy Council), 87, 89, 90, 95
deference, 8, 11, 69, 77, 101, 102, 171, 188, 208, 215–22, 261, 366
definitional generosity, 38, 134, 209, 231
Dicey, Albert Venn, 196, 203, 221
Diceyan orthodoxy, 80, 195, 256, 365
Diplock, William John Kenneth, 82, 133, 189, 191, 192, 193, 195, 197, 198, 206, 302, 304
discretion
administrative discretion, 50, 53, 60, 78, 111, 155, 156, 174, 211, 334
legislative discretion, 134
doctrinal imperialism, 41, 132, 364
Dreyfus, Françoise, 49, 50, 133, 159, 161
dualism. *See* influence, local patterns of

economic crisis, 125, 126, 253, 323, 325, 328
economic freedom, 81, 116, 129, 211, 300, 302, 303, 323
economy of the common law. *See* analytical tradition
efficiency, 53, 54, 107, 126, 127, 129, 131, 167, 171, 172, 179, 248, 321, 322, 323, 346, 350
English legal culture. *See* analytical tradition
enterprise, freedom of, 62, 63, 64
Entreprises de presse (French Constitutional Council), 143, 165–73, 259
epistemological optimism, 134, 158, 163, 192, 249, 259
equality, 52, 64, 65, 110, 176, 183, 330, 335, 353
sex equality, 309, 310
equity, 49, 73, 107, 118, 121, 122, 126, 130, 134, 149, 192, 199, 205, 229, 233, 237, 256, 257, 334
ethnography, 14, 29, 30
Europe, visions of
as an idealised version of domestic polity, 247, 358
as international law, international obligations, 291, 351, 357, 367
as part of domestic civilisation, 240, 276
European Communities Act, 80, 85, 87, 277, 301, 302, 303, 304, 313, 314, 343, 344

European culture of rights, European fundamental rights, 239, 240, 252, 264, 271, 274, 276, 286, 289, 337
European integration
  acculturation, 355
  disintegration, 269, 329, 337, 355, 367, 369
  economic integration, 328
Europeanisation, local patterns of
  acknowledgment of normative conflict, 301, 314, 318, 327, 330, 333, 346, 353, 358, 368
  self-denying transformation, 322–5, 328, 357, 367
  signalisation, 289, 356, 367
exceptionalism
  English, 188
  French, 330–4, 352
  United States, 3, 13, 25
expertise, 55, 102, 134, 147, 218, 259, 365
expressive function of law, 14
expropriation, 46, 47, 51, 106, 107, 108, 109, 156, 159, 160, 161, 162, 237

fact-finding, 129, 205, 251, 304, 305
factualisation, 179
family life, 89, 273, 284, 285, 287, 307, 333, 334
First MoU (Greek Council of State), 323–5, 326, 347, 348, 349, 350, 351
formalism
  analytical formalism. *See* analytical tradition
  dogmatism. *See* French legal culture
  seclusion from social practices. *See* Greek legal culture, the Greek misfortune
French legal culture
  doctrine, 47, 48, 52, 74, 104, 147, 152, 153, 164, 188, 191, 197, 262, 365
  dogmatism, 146, 149, 190, 233, 257, 275, 362
  republican inculcation, 181, 185, 255, 335, 336, 337, 356
  republican legitimacy, 147
  voluntarism, 145, 149, 150, 234, 235, 257
fundamental rights
  as civil liberties, 190, 209, 255
  as limits, requirements of abstention, 18, 150, 232, 257
  as objective values, 184
  as optimisation requirements, 6, 17, 63, 134, 150, 184
  as principles, 6, 124, 134
  as public freedoms, 150
  common law rights as, 203
  global human rights paradigm. *See* rational human rights paradigm

GCHQ (UK House of Lords), 82, 189
general principles of law, 149, 150, 190, 263
Gerapetritis, Konstantinos, 105, 118, 311
Germany, 2, 18, 24, 26, 50, 61, 65, 106, 112, 113, 115, 123, 130, 133, 152, 153, 180, 181, 195, 216, 224, 227, 229, 230, 231, 233, 234, 237, 238, 239, 247, 256, 257, 258, 259, 302
Gerontas, Apostolos, 112, 113, 133
global constitutionalism, 3, 24, 33, 268
global model of proportionality, 14, 35, 37–40, 46, 362
globalisation, 20, 21, 268
glocalisation, 20
Goesel-Le Bihan, Valérie, 61, 180, 181
Goldstein (UK House of Lords), 195, 301, 303
Gonzalez-Gomez (French Council of State), 333–4, 335, 336, 337, 358
good administration, 55, 120, 167, 257
good legislation, 55, 167, 172
gouvernement des juges, 146, 257
Grassin (French Council of State), 49, 161, 162
Greek legal culture
  classicism, 319
  Greek misfortune, the, 225
  katharevousa, 225, 226, 228, 238
  legal theory or legal science, 236, 365
Guibal, Michel, 166, 167

Hagiographers case (Greek Council of State), 112–15

Handyside (European Court of Human rights), 264
head of review, 29, 31, 77, 78–87, 91, 103, 104, 132, 188, 195, 198, 200, 213, 215, 217, 218, 222, 277, 283, 290, 292, 293, 294, 297, 298, 300, 302–3, 306, 311, 358, 360, 361, 362, 368
Hook (Court of Appeal of England and Wales), 78, 79, 189, 198, 216
horizontal effect, 134
Huang (UK House of Lords), 95, 96
Human Rights Act, 77, 89–103, 187, 207–221, 260, 261, 290–296, 298, 338, 343, 353

idealisation
  of Parliament, 151, 152, 210, 235, 257
  of the judiciary, 153, 179–83, 196, 259, 364
  of the political process, 219, 256, 363
immigration, 89, 90, 94, 273, 285, 287
imprisonment for debt, 120, 124, 127
individual freedom, 60, 65, 114, 151, 307
influence, local patterns of
  dualism, 22, 27, 84, 214, 218, 269, 272, 277, 297, 298, 300, 303, 318, 327, 330, 337, 343, 345, 346, 353, 357, 359, 367, 368
  eclecticism, 26, 105, 300, 367
  insularity, 9, 26, 195, 223, 271, 272, 367
  monism, 22, 27, 269, 272, 275, 297, 298, 300, 306, 311
institutional competence, 8, 118–22
institutional faith, 134, 146, 180, 207–9, 249, 259
integration
  economic, 270, 299–301, 322, 327, 328
  European, 18–23, 246, 263–358, 360, 366–9
  social, 134, 179–86, 255, 337, 364
  through law, 21, 134, 263–5, 271, 355, 366
intellectual history, 2, 28, 29, 363
Israel, 3, 5

Jowell, Jeffrey, 81, 133, 197, 198
judge
  as a partner of the political branches, 164, 209, 221, 295, 297, 326
  as a referee, 80, 191, 193, 202, 209, 218, 256, 362
  as a scientist, 221, 362
  as *bouche de la loi*, 144–6
  as fundamental rights protector, 61, 62, 153, 154, 163, 173, 180, 209, 261, 289, 353
  as Salomon, 180
  as Socrates, 180, 259
judicial review
  as a game, 146, 191, 193, 221, 256, 362
  as a ritual, 146, 191, 235, 256, 362
  indifference, 63, 100, 114, 295, 350
  intent-based, 38, 81, 83, 118, 150, 159, 169, 171, 189, 203, 322, 343, 349
  marginal, 117, 126
  minimal, 63, 117, 120, 255, 349
  outcome-based, 67, 99, 115, 127, 188, 189, 229, 232, 234, 316, 331
  variable intensity of, 201, 211, 261, 295, 367
jusnaturalisme, 148, 184
justification
  culture of. *See* legal culture.
  reason giving, 97, 210
  relevant circumstances, 119
  turn to, 326

Kassimatis, Georgios, 110, 112
Kennedy (UK Supreme Court), 76, 215, 216, 296, 338, 341, 342
Keyu (UK Supreme Court), 217, 218
Kontogiorga, Dimitra, 229

labour law, 121, 237
Laws, John, 86, 89, 102, 189, 197, 201, 202, 205, 206, 211, 342, 343, 344
Lebon (French Council of State), 175
Leech (Court of Appeal of England and Wales), 216

legal culture
civilisation, 239, 355
English. *See* analytical tradition
European, 21, 27, 267–8, 357, 358, 359
French. *See* French legal culture
German, 134, 254
Greek. *See* Greek legal culture
of authority, 17, 18
of justification, 17, 19, 28, 40, 45, 70, 210, 232, 259, 295
legal formants, 31, 198, 261, 363
legal irritant, 23, 154, 155, 157, 188–94, 280, 281, 303, 305, 357
legal knowledge, 9, 19, 20, 31, 74, 134, 160, 164, 187, 188, 197, 222, 259, 260, 261, 311, 346, 355, 359, 363, 365
as scientific, 134, 147, 163, 185, 226, 233, 251, 318, 355, 363, 365
legal knowledge practices
analysis, 193, 210, 262, 365
theorisation, 157, 362
translation, 237, 261, 311, 363
legal reasoning
ad hoc, 40, 96, 147, 163
categorical *See* categorical reasoning.
consequentialist, 359
in concreto, 163
legal transfer, 15–18, 19, 22, 23, 24, 25, 28, 32, 223, 300, 311
legal transplant, 1, 2, 5, 15, 16, 18, 19, 20, 23, 25, 27, 28, 34, 35, 134, 143, 144, 151, 153, 185, 194–9, 206, 214, 223, 224–7, 229, 236–40, 252, 254, 260, 261, 262, 345, 358
legality, principle of, 56, 107, 155, 256, 358
legality of penalties, 56
less onerous means, 112, 119, 238
Lester, Anthony, 81, 83, 197, 198, 278, 281
life, right to, 200, 202
linguistics, 28, 29, 46
metaphor, 1, 9, 12, 16, 18, 19, 20, 23, 24, 107, 134, 209, 218, 220, 227, 240, 241, 247, 346
metonymy, 241
synecdoche, 162
local knowledge, 17, 247–62, 300, 322, 363
distrust or suspicion, 17, 126, 146, 147, 165, 185, 191, 234, 247, 249, 250, 256, 259, 365
local paths of reception
appropriation, 240
reinvention, 179, 286, 330, 337, 344, 352, 353
rejection, 82, 277
Loi d'orientation et de programmation relative à la sécurité (French Constitutional Council), 59
Loi interdisant la dissimulation du visage dans l'espace public (French Constitutional Council), 181
Loi sur l'évolution de la Nouvelle-Cal édonie (French Constitutional Council), 176
Lüth (German Federal Constitutional Court), 140, 258

Mance, Jonathan, 97, 208, 216, 339, 340, 341, 342, 343, 344
Manessis, Aristovoulos, 112, 113
manifest disproportionality, 57, 58, 83, 111, 178, 179, 234, 257, 275
manifest error test, 50, 51, 52, 53, 54, 57, 61, 106, 116, 117, 118, 120, 126, 130, 144, 151, 158, 159, 173–9, 190, 212, 231, 232, 233, 237, 261, 285, 324, 326, 361, 367, 368
manifestly inappropriate, 63, 309
Manitakis, Antonis, 230, 235, 239, 249
margin of appreciation, 81, 84, 87, 93, 101, 194, 219, 220, 265, 271, 287, 293, 294, 309, 322, 324, 333, 338, 356
marginal, 325, 348
media pluralism, 63, 320
Medical Centres (Greek Council of State), 116, 231
Mephisto (German Federal Constitutional Court), 258
merits review, 84, 99, 188, 208
methods of reasoning, 157, 199, 215, 216, 217
Michaniki affair, 241–3, 247

Miss Behavin' (UK House of Lords), 212
modernisation, 31, 35, 167, 188, 196, 197, 198, 200, 207, 214, 247–62, 326, 358, 364, 365, 368
monism. *See* influence, local patterns of
Morisot, Michel, 48, 49, 160
movement, freedom of, 307, 334
myths
  katharevousa politeia, 247, 252, 262
  la France, la patrie des droits de l'homme, 272, 276, 297, 330, 356, 367
  la loi, expression de la volonté générale, 145, 151, 257, 273, 362
  Whig history, 190, 196, 255, 277, 283, 297, 340, 363

narrowly tailored test, 39, 60, 67, 68, 99, 172, 323
necessity of penalties, 56–8, 176
necessity review, 38, 50, 51, 53, 54, 61, 67, 90, 93, 95, 114, 153–7, 168, 175, 198, 251, 274, 302, 310, 312, 325, 348
Neuberger, David, 97, 210, 217, 218, 220
New Zealand, 3, 25
Nicklinson (UK Supreme Court), 97, 208, 220, 221, 338

objectifs de valeur constitutionnelle, 171
objectivisation, 183–5
objectivity, 4, 134, 143, 157, 158–65, 170, 177, 191, 208, 259, 260, 355
optimisation, 17, 31, 34, 35, 63, 100, 134, 144, 150, 184, 205, 206, 208, 209, 214, 231, 257, 271, 362, 364
Orfanoudakis, Sarantis, 240, 346

Pannick, David, 83, 84, 197, 204, 278, 281
Pararas, Petros, 108, 111, 112, 113, 133, 225, 248, 312
parliamentary sovereignty, 83–5, 98, 103, 188, 202, 214, 215, 217–19, 222, 261, 272, 277, 283, 297, 341–3, 344, 353, 358, 362, 366, 368
performativity, 134, 268
Pham (UK Supreme Court), 76, 216, 338, 341, 342, 343, 344
pharmacies, 127, 128, 129
Philippe, Xavier, 52, 53–5, 167, 171, 180
practical moral reasoning, 3, 39, 40, 123, 143, 234, 254, 255
precedent, 12, 15, 17, 22, 40, 134, 190, 210, 211, 217, 260, 279, 315, 340, 341, 344, 358, 368
presumption of constitutionality, 117
presumption of statutory interpretation, 198
prisoners, rights of, 90
private law, 9, 16, 66, 72, 73, 76, 77, 78, 81, 85, 110, 121, 130, 144, 196, 258, 277
professional freedom, 106, 112, 113, 114, 115, 127, 129, 134, 228, 310, 346
property, right to, 63, 108, 109, 292
proportion, 1, 49, 63, 76, 79, 83, 106, 107, 110, 111, 122–6, 156, 159, 160, 161, 177, 192, 199, 228, 244, 331, 346
proportionability, 76
proportionality
  as a general principle, 49, 51, 115, 125, 144, 149, 156, 164, 174, 175, 190, 199, 256, 297
  as a head of review, 85, 222, 290, 293, 294, 298, 338, 353, 358, 360, 361, 368
  as a mathematic equation, 51, 52, 76, 143, 160, 165, 177, 208
  as a method of interpretation, 217, 241, 336, 367
  as a theory, 134, 143, 158, 173, 185, 188, 191, 211
  as a threshold requirement, 63, 79, 112, 257, 284
  as a value, an ideal, 45, 53, 75, 105, 118, 144, 256
  as an analytical structure, an argumentation framework, 2, 16, 18, 34, 37, 64, 92, 112, 125, 133, 134, 211, 224, 227, 241, 290, 296, 353
  as an objective test, 99, 259
  as language, 2, 46, 76, 106

as science, 134, 143, 161, 208, 240, 241, 249, 251, 252, 261, 311, 319, 345, 363, 366
failure of, 10, 51, 191, 230, 257, 323, 365
genealogy of, 143, 160
hegemony of, 26, 41, 43, 107, 124–6, 132, 213, 224, 241, 252, 261, 327, 328, 365
spread of, 1–3
success of, 2–7, 15, 19, 37–43, 134, 187, 224–5, 258
proportionnalité à la française, 153, 172
proportionnalité de l'impôt, 51
proportionnalité des peines et des sanctions, 59, 79, 164
punishment. *See* sanctions

question prioritaire de constitutionnalité (QPC), 65
questions de société, 173

rational basis test, 38, 316
rational human rights paradigm, 134, 145, 209, 232, 258
rationalisation, 31, 35, 107, 128, 144–53, 163, 171, 179, 185, 187, 191, 198, 200, 202, 207–15, 248, 258, 259, 260, 262, 338, 364
of budgetary choices, 163
of English public law, 207–15, 338
of Parliament, 150
of public action, 128, 165, 167
rationalism, 187, 222, 269, 272, 275–7, 292, 297, 298, 314, 337–8, 343, 355–9, 363, 366, 367, 368
reasonableness, 17, 23, 32, 42, 77, 78–82, 83, 85, 86, 90, 115, 118, 122, 126, 215, 230, 237, 256, 257, 258, 267, 277, 316
reception, local paths of
assimilation, 207, 272, 275
reinvention, 330
référé libertés, 153, 289, 333
representation, 52, 176, 235, 238, 255–7, 267, 288, 322, 363
réserves d'interprétation, 70, 193, 203, 256
Rétention de sûreté (French Constitutional Council), 64, 66, 67, 68, 71
ritual, 31, 146, 152, 187, 191, 235, 247, 248, 255, 256, 260, 296, 362, 363
Roth (Court of Appeal of England and Wales), 102

sanctions (penalties and sanctions), 50, 56, 58, 59, 60, 71, 78, 79, 81, 95, 100, 102, 117, 160, 164, 175, 177, 183, 192, 232, 242, 243, 244, 250, 271, 275, 289, 303, 311, 312, 320
SAS v. *France* (European Court of Human Rights), 330
science, 1, 18, 32, 53, 134, 143–86, 187, 221, 224, 226, 233, 234, 236, 238, 240–7, 249, 251, 252, 259, 261, 301, 311, 363
law as. *See* legal knowledge, as scientific.
Sedley, Stephen, 79, 197, 201, 202, 305, 306
Simms (UK House of Lords), 203
Skouris, Vassilios, 225, 227, 230, 238
Smith (UK House of Lords), 203–5, 206
Smith and Grady (European Court of Human Rights), 205, 282
social rights
'*special payrolls*' (Greek Council of State), 347–50
proportionality and, 6, 126
social security, 251, 351
Société civile Sainte-Marie-de-l' Assomption (French Council of State), 49
Spycatcher affair, 278, 280, 281, 282, 283
standardization, 365
state of emergency, 26, 66–74, 110, 185, 366
Stoke-on-Trent affair, 312, 313, 317, 318
strike, right to, 68, 110, 111, 121
substantive review, 53, 54, 119, 120, 188, 189, 201, 203, 215, 218, 282, 343, 357
substantive rule of law, 194–7
Sunday trading, 301, 312–13, 314, 315, 316, 317, 318, 328, 367

sustainable growth, 234
syllogism, 68, 146, 233

taboos
  détournement de pouvoir, 148, 150, 170
  whether v. how, 115, 310, 365
  merits review, 85, 192, 256, 361
  opportunité v. légalité, 47, 150, 155, 156, 173, 192, 257, 361
  review v. appeal, 84, 99, 255, 364
  σκοπιμότητα v. νομιμότητα, 115, 309–10
tax law, 51–2, 71, 191–2
Teitgen, Francis, 52
terrorism, 93, 102, 332, 366
théorie de la loi écran, 149, 152, 212, 273
Torfaen (European Court of Justice), 313, 315, 316, 317
total constitution, 134, 163
transparency, 4, 9, 12, 15, 73, 147, 180, 193, 199, 208, 213, 296, 320, 321, 322, 325
transplant. *See* legal transplant

United States, 5, 9, 12, 15, 17, 19, 24, 25, 26, 134, 280, 316

values, value-laden reasoning, 46, 68, 71, 73, 103, 127, 133, 134, 165, 171, 177, 178, 183, 185, 208, 233, 259, 262, 322, 325, 356, 365, 368
Vedel, Georges, 52, 56, 57, 165, 169, 170, 171, 175, 177, 178
Venizelos, Evaggelos, 225, 319
Ville Nouvelle Est (French Council of State), 47, 49, 50, 156, 157, 159, 160, 173, 174, 192
Voutsakis, Vassilios, 115, 123

Wednesbury (Court of Appeal of England and Wales), 188, 218
Wednesbury unreasonableness, 11, 29, 42, 75, 76, 77, 79, 80, 81, 82, 83, 84, 86, 87, 89, 90, 103, 117, 120, 188, 189, 194, 197, 199, 200, 201, 204, 206, 208, 213, 214, 216, 217, 232, 292, 303, 306, 358

Xynopoulos, Georgios, 61, 122

Zante (Greek Council of State), 119

αναλογία, 28, 106

www.ingramcontent.com/pod-product-compliance
Lightning Source LLC
LaVergne TN
LVHW011700200926
848484LV00004B/1005
9781108834483